A STUDY OF HISTORY

Arnold Toynbee writes:

IN the first volume of *A Study of History,* I start by searching for a unit of historical study that is relatively self-contained and is therefore more or less intelligible in isolation from the rest of history. I was led into this quest by finding myself dissatisfied with the present-day habit of studying history in terms of national states. These seemed, and still seem, to me to be fragments of something larger, and I found this larger and more satisfying unit of study in a civilization. The history of the United States, for instance, or the history of Britain, is, as I see it, a fragment of the history of Western Christendom or the Western Christian World, and I believe I can put my finger on a number of other societies, living or extinct, that are of the same species. Examples of other living civilizations besides the Western Civilization are the Islamic and the Civilization of Eastern Asia, centring on China. Examples of extinct civilizations are the Greco-Roman and the Ancient Egyptian. This practice of dealing in civilizations instead of nations is taken for granted by orientalists, ancient-historians, archaeologists, and anthropologists. The carving-up of a civilization into pieces labelled 'nations' is, I believe, something peculiar to students of modern Western history, and, with them too, this present practice of theirs is only recent. Down to the beginning of the eighteenth century, the classic works of Western historians took for their field the whole history of Western Christendom or even the whole history of the World from the Creation to the Last Judgement.

Having rounded up my horses, I set myself to put them through their paces. See how civilizations come into existence: that is the subject of the rest of Volume 1. Here I am asking myself what it is that brings a civilization to birth. I first try Race and then try Environment, and I find both these explanations unsatisfying, because they assume that living beings are subject to inexorable laws of nature, like dead matter. So I look for an explanation in terms of life, which in human affairs means in terms of free-will, and I find this in the Old Testament. Here we see human beings responding, or failing to respond, to challenges from God. In Volume 2, I try to discover the limits within which the interplay of challenge and response is effectively creative. I explore this by examining a number of test cases. In Volume 3, I go on to study the growth of a civilization that has succeeded in coming to birth. After growth there comes breakdown and disintegration, but these are the subjects of the second group of volumes, which will follow these first three in the present paperback edition.

'Work . . . while it is day . . .'

JOHN IX. 4

'Nox ruit, Aenea . . .'

AENEID VI. 539

'Thought shall be the harder,
Heart the keener,
Mood shall be the more,
As our might lessens.'

THE LAY OF THE BATTLE OF MALDON

A STUDY OF HISTORY

1

Introduction

The Geneses of Civilizations, Part One

ARNOLD J. TOYNBEE

A Galaxy Book

New York   OXFORD UNIVERSITY PRESS   1962

A Study of History was first issued under the auspices of the Royal Institute of International Affairs, of which Arnold J. Toynbee was then Director of Studies.

First Edition, 1934
Second Edition, 1935
First published as a Galaxy Book, 1962

The illustration on the cover of this volume is a rendering by Charles Gottlieb of The Sumerian Goddess of Vegetation, *c.* 3000 B.C. [Berlin Museum].

PRINTED IN THE UNITED STATES OF AMERICA

PREFACE TO THE PAPERBACK EDITION

THIS is the first instalment of a paperback edition of the complete text of this work. It differs from the original hardbound edition in only one respect: owing to length, Volume 7 has been divided into two paperback volumes, 7A and 7B, but pagination has been left unchanged so that all references apply equally to hardbound and paperback editions. In this new format, the volumes will be brought out in successive instalments, and it is hoped that, in this way, would-be readers of the work will be able to possess it without too severe a tax on their purse, or even on their time.

The publication of the complete work in the present form will not diminish the value of the existing abridgement. Mr. Somervell has been remarkably successful in reproducing the structure and argument of the book in relatively small compass. But abridgement is another name for reduction; and one of the ways in which Mr. Somervell has succeeded in drastically reducing the bulk of the full text has been to epitomize, or omit altogether, a number of the historical examples that I have cited, in the original version of this work, to illustrate my theses. This habit of citing examples is partly responsible for the length to which the full text runs. At the same time, it is a characteristic feature of the work. The present edition of the full text will, it is hoped, give a wider circle of readers the opportunity to judge for themselves whether or not, besides being characteristic, this method of exposition is also illuminating.

The length of the full text is not due solely to this extensive use of illustrations. It is also due, in part, to the size of the field that the work attempts to cover. The history here studied is, in the first place, the history of the civilizations that have made their appearance within the last 5000 years of mankind's history; and, even within these limits, the field is formidably large. Yet these last 5000 years are only a small fraction of the time during which the human race has been in existence to date; and the human race is one of the youngest forms of life on the face of this planet. If we are to try to see the Age of the Civilizations in its true historical perspective, we have to look at it against the background of these vastly longer historical vistas. Above all, we have to pay serious attention to the latest, at any rate, of the pre-civilizational stages of human history. In fact, the farther we pursue our study, the wider its field becomes, and the growth of the field cannot be confined to the dimensions of time and space. Other dimensions unfold themselves and demand exploration. The religious, psychological, and epistemological dimensions are three of these.

The size of the work's field has determined its length, and its un-avoidable length has made it take a long time to write. The general plan of the work was put on paper in 1921; Volume 12 was published in 1961. The intervening forty years brought with them a number of changes, and these have left their mark on the text as this has been gradually written and published.

Presumably the events of these forty years have not been able to change retro-actively the previous events that, by the year 1921, were already what is called 'accomplished facts.' This is, however, rather a hazardous proposition, and the word 'presumably' is therefore of the essence of it. It is hazardous because the existence of so-called 'facts' cannot be vouched for by human minds independently of these minds' apprehension of what they observe, and we therefore cannot tell how much of these ostensibly objective facts may or may not have been our minds' own subjective contribution to the construction of them. Whatever the answer to this epistemological question may be, it is unquestionable that the past, short of undergoing changes, receives increments through the passage of time, since this is perpetually relegating to the past some part of what, at each successive moment of elapsing time, has hitherto still lain in the womb of the future. The additions to past history that were made during the eventful forty years 1921-1961 are appreciable in their quantity, and significant in their effect, even when viewed in the perspective of the preceding 5000 years of human history. They make the retrospective picture of these last 5000 years look perceptibly different, as seen from the standpoint of the year 1961, from the picture as seen from the standpoint of the year 1921.

This transfer of the events of forty more years from the future into the past was not, however, the only change, occurring during those same forty years, that altered the picture of the past as that picture presented itself to my mind. There had been some epoch-making addi-tions to the archaeologists' knowledge of the past, and some perhaps even more revolutionary changes in their interpretation of their knowl-edge, new and old. Simultaneously, I myself had been acquiring addi-tions to my own knowledge that were more modest, and had been experiencing changes in my own outlook that were perhaps not less revolutionary. It would, indeed, have been surprising if forty years of adult life, between the ages of 32 and 72, had not worked changes in my mind and had not impressed the marks of these changes on a work that I was engaged in writing during the course of that forty years' period.

I myself was already aware of these changes before some of the critics of my work began to draw attention to them. I had published

Volumes 4-6 forty-one days before the outbreak of the Second World War. I was engaged on war-work for the next seven years, and Volumes 7-10 were not published till 1954. In this latter batch of volumes I found opportunities for taking account of new knowledge, and new interpretations of old knowledge, in the field of scholarship, and also for reconsidering part of my former picture of the configuration of history in the light of changes in my own point of view. In the field of scholarship, for instance, I revised, in these volumes, my former views about the Orphic religion and about the dating of the First Dynasty of Babylon. In the field of my own picture of history, I revised my former views about the nature of the historical relations between the civilizations and the higher religions. I followed up these parenthetical revisions of earlier views by publishing, in 1961, a whole volume of 'reconsiderations' of some of the views that I had put forward in the first ten volumes of the book.

Reconsiderations of forty years' work could hardly fail to be considerable. As far as I myself can judge, my own reconsiderations have not been so far-reaching as to undermine the unity and continuity of the work. At the same time, they have been considerable enough to have made it impracticable to incorporate them in the first ten volumes by making corresponding changes in the text of these. A number of particular errors had already been corrected in the latest impression that is now being reproduced in the present paperback edition of the whole work. To have tried to go farther than that would have required a virtual re-writing of a number of passages in the earlier volumes, and, even then, the result might have been a patchwork in which the sutures would have been obvious. Keeping the reconsiderations separate from the earlier passages to which they refer has left me free to present them in the form and on the scale that have seemed most appropriate for them.

There was, however, a more important reason than mere literary convenience for leaving the earlier volumes as they originally stood, apart from relatively minor corrections. Suppose that they had been re-written, and that the re-writing had been more or less successful: the result would have been, not to clarify the exposition, but to obscure it. Like every other human activity, thought is a form of action, and, as such, it develops itself progressively, in process of time. No particular stage of thought ever attains finality. The most successful thought is never more than an approximation towards a knowledge and an understanding that it never achieves completely. In consequence, no particular stage of thought is ever completely devalued or superseded. Every stage retains its place in a series in which one stage may be in advance of another but in which none is, or ever could be, definitive.

This is true of the successive stages in even the shortest train of thought. It must surely be true, all the more, of a train that has been drawn out over a span of forty years. A reader would be misunderstanding the nature of thinking in general, as well as the nature of my line of thought in particular, if he were to expect to find, in the twelve volumes of this study, a completely homogeneous body of definitive information and ideas. This work, like all other products of the human mind, ought to be taken as being a series of successive interim reports made by a particular human mind in response to its experience at various stages of life. As the serial instalments of the present paperback edition are published, the student who is seriously concerned to acquaint himself with my ideas would do well to persevere in reading each batch of volumes without stopping short of Volume 12—the volume that bears the sub-title 'Reconsiderations.' But, even if the reader has had the staying-power to reach this volume, and the curiosity to review the previous volumes in the light of it, I cannot hold out to him, as his reward, an assurance that he will then find himself at the end of his labours. The one thing certain about the process of thought is that it will continue to develop as long as there are human minds alive and at work. I cannot guarantee that my own mind will not live long enough to be impelled, by further thinking, to add a thirteenth volume to the present twelve. On the other hand, I can guarantee, and this with assurance, that, long after I myself am dead, other minds will be continuing my work. They will be continuing it by going beyond it; and they will go beyond it in so far as they confirm it, as well as in so far as they contradict it.

The most that any thinker can hope to achieve is to add a thimbleful to the volume of the stream of thought that flows on from generation to generation. If he achieves that much, he will have been well re-paid for the work of a lifetime.

23 *June* 1961   ARNOLD J. TOYNBEE

NOTE

IN this, as in the fifth, impression of Volumes I–VI, the opportunity has been taken for bringing a few statements up-to-date and for correcting misprints and mistakes on points of fact that have been noticed by the author or have been pointed out to him by readers who have been so kind as to do him this very valuable service. The number of misprints so far detected has been small, thanks to the excellence of the original printing.

These corrections have all been within limits that have not required any considerable re-setting of the type. In addition to these, however, the writer has notes of a number of passages in which he will have eventually to make additions, deletions, or other changes in the light either of new discoveries—especially in the field of archaeological research—or of improvements in his own acquaintance with facts that were already known and accessible at the time when these six volumes were being written.

The most striking of the archaeological discoveries made between A.D. 1939 and A.D. 1950 were those which showed that, even on the shortest of the reckonings worked out on the basis of the previous information at the disposal of chronologists, the events of Sumeric history, down to and including the sack of Babylon by the Hittites, had been ante-dated by something between 150 and 200 years. Another archaeological achievement, of comparable importance, was the confirmation, by archaeological evidence, of the Sinic tradition that the Chóu culture had not been the first civilization to establish itself in the Yellow River Basin, but had been preceded there by an antecedent Shang culture.

The writer hopes to be able to make the more extensive alterations that this new knowledge demands in a future edition of the first six volumes of the book. The publication of Volumes VII–X on the 14th October, 1954, makes it possible for him to begin to reconsider Volumes I–VI with an eye to an eventual revision of the whole work.

29 *July*, 1954   ARNOLD TOYNBEE

PREFACE TO THE SECOND EDITION

DURING the six months that have passed since the publication of the first edition of these first three volumes of the book, a number of readers have been so kind as to draw the writer's attention to certain printer's errors and author's mistakes, besides com-

municating to him their observations and criticisms on general questions of presentation, proportion, and principle. The definite errors
and mistakes of which the writer has been made aware in this way
have been corrected in this second edition (though, no doubt, there
are others which have remained undetected by the writer and his
friends). As for the general criticisms, the writer has not attempted
to deal with these in this new edition of Volumes I–III, partly
because that would have meant virtually rewriting certain passages,
and partly because the writer feels that he can probably do greater
justice to the suggestions which his critics have made by taking
account of them in later parts of the book which are still in process
of being written, than by recasting those parts that have already set
hard in print.

For the rest, the writer wishes to renew the expression of his
thanks to the persons and institutions whose names are mentioned
in the first edition, and to add to these the name of the Leverhulme
Research Fellowship Fund, which has greatly assisted him in the
work of producing Parts IV–VIII, on which he is at present engaged, by generously making it possible for him to release a larger
proportion of his time and energy than before.

This preface to the second edition of Parts I–III has been written
on the day on which the manuscript of Part IV has been completed.

ARNOLD J. TOYNBEE

LONDON,
New Year's Day, 1935.

PREFACE TO THE FIRST EDITION

THESE three volumes contain Parts I–III of the thirteen parts
which are set out in the plan of the book on page v above. The
writer hopes to publish the rest in two more batches: Parts IV–
VIII in one batch and Parts IX–XIII in the other.

The index to the volumes now published has been made by the
writer's colleague, Miss V. M. Boulter. In a book like this, which
is an attempt to expound and illustrate a system of ideas, the index
is a particularly important and a particularly difficult part of the
work; and the writer has been fortunate in having this index made
for him by Miss Boulter. But his debt to her is much greater than
that. It is her collaboration with him in his other work—a collaboration on which he has always known that he can absolutely
rely—that has given him, in his margin of leisure, the freedom of
mind which the writing of the present work has required.

Both the writer and the printer have been fortunate in the fact
that the whole of a long and rather intricate manuscript has been

typed out by Miss Reddin, from whose accuracy and patience they have also both benefited annually—till they have perhaps too easily come to take these virtues for granted—in the production and publication of another work.

The writer is also deeply indebted to a number of other friends of his—all of them very busy people—who, in their kindness, have found time to read parts of these volumes in the typescript and to give him their comments. The writer is very conscious of the use which he has been able to make of these observations in diminishing a number of weaknesses in his original draft, though of course this does not involve any of his kind critics in any sort of responsibility for the final product. The friends in question, to whom the writer wishes to express his most sincere gratitude, are Professor Gilbert Murray, Dr. G. P. Gooch, Professor H. J. Paton, Professor N. H. Baynes, Professor H. A. R. Gibb, Mr. and Mrs. J. L. Hammond, Professor A. E. Zimmern, Sir Arnold Wilson, Professor C. K. Webster, Mr. David Davies, Dr. Chaim Weizmann, and Mr. G. F. Hudson.

The writer also takes this opportunity of expressing his gratitude to several learned institutions. The Stevenson Research Professorship in International History which he has the honour to hold in one of the constituent bodies of the University of London—the London School of Economics and Political Science—has made an inestimably valuable addition to the amount of leisure which has been at his disposal while he has been writing these volumes, through releasing time and energy which otherwise he would have had to spend on 'pot-boiling'. He is equally grateful to the Council of the Royal Institute of International Affairs for their action in making, out of a grant which they have received from the Rockefeller Fund for research in the field of international studies, an allocation for the purpose of releasing the writer's time and energy further by giving him additional assistance in his work as a member of the staff of Chatham House.

Finally, the writer cannot lay down his pen without mentioning one earliest debt of all, which has been in his mind throughout; and this is the debt which he owes to his Mother, who first turned his thoughts towards History by being a historian herself.

LONDON   ARNOLD J. TOYNBEE
16th May, 1933.

The sum and substance of a considerable part of the first three volumes of this book was presented orally, before publication, in two different courses of lectures which were delivered on the invitation of two foundations in the United States: the Lowell Institute at Boston, Mass., and the Norman Wait Harris Foundation at Northwestern University, Evanston, Ill. The course of Lowell Lectures, delivered in October, 1933, covered the ground of Parts I. A, I. B, II. C II (a), II. C II (b), III. A, III. B, III. C I, III. C II (a). The course of Norman Wait Harris Lectures, delivered in November, 1933, covered the ground of Parts I. A and B, II. C II, III. B, III. C I, III. C II (a), III. C II (b). The author is glad to take this opportunity to express his appreciation of these invitations from the Norman Wait Harris Foundation and the Lowell Institute, and his gratitude for the courtesy and hospitality with which he was received in Evanston and in Boston while the lectures were being given.

ΣΥΓΓΡΑΦΕΩΣ ΒΙΟΣ

ΚΗΡΕΣ ὅσαι θανάτοιο πιέζετέ μ', οὐ γὰρ ἔτ' ὕμμιν
    εἶξας ὀφλήσω αὐτὸς ἑκὼν κακίην,
οὔ, μὰ θεοῦ μέγαν ὅρκον, ὃς ὤμοσε μή με ματαίως
    οἰχήσεσθαι, ἅπαξ καλὸν ἰδόντα φάος
ἠελίου, ῥέξαντα δ' ἐν ἀνθρώποισιν ἀέθλους·
    τῷ πίσυνος κείναις οὐκέτι δοῦλος ἐγώ.
'Αλλ' ἔρξω, καιρὸς γάρ· ἀλάστορες ὦ σκιόεντες,
    ἔρρετε· σωτείρας ηὗρον· ὑποτρέσατε.

Μοῦσαι μειλιχίαι ἐλεήμονες, ἤλθετε κἀμοί,
    χειμερίῳ 'ν πόντῳ νηΐ τινασσομένῃ
πένθεος ἐν χειμῶνι· καὶ αἰνῶς μ' ἐστυφέλιξεν
    ἲς ἀνέμων, κοὐδὲν τέρμ' ἐπέφαντο κακοῦ,
αἰανὴς δ' ἔπι μόχθος, ἐφίκετο δ' ὅσσον ὀπωπὴ
    ἀήρ τ' ἄξενά τ' ἦν κύματα παλλόμενα.
τῶν μ' ἄπο, σώτειραι, τότ' ἐλύσατε, καὶ πάλιν ὀρθῇ
    στείρῃ λευγαλέης ποντοπορῶ δι' ἁλός.
Μούσας ὑμνήσω νόος ἔμπεδος εἰς ὅ κ' ἔπηται,
    Μούσαις λατρεύσω παντὶ χερὸς σθένεϊ,
Μούσας ἂν δὲ προδῶ, τῷ γ' ἤματι κἀμὲ προδοίης,
    φιλτάτη ὠκυμόρων—μηδ' ἐλεοῖς με—βροτῶν.

'Αλλ' ἔραμαι· Μοῦσαι δὲ καλοῦσί με. τηλόθι, Μοῦσαι,
    στρωφᾶσθ' ἀνθρώπων, τήλ', 'Ελικωνιάδες.
πίδακες ὕμμιν ἐκεῖ καὶ τέμπεα δενδρήεντα,
    τρηχὺς ὁ δ' οἶμος ἐὼν ζῆλον ἐνῆκε ποδί,
τέρμα δ' ὁδοῦ προὔστηκε μέγα ῥίον αἰθερίη τε
    στίλβουσ' εὐαγὴς—εἴθε θίγοιμι—νιφάς.
οὐκέτ' Ἔρως ἔταρος δέ· τὰ μείλιχα ἔργ' ἀνθρώπων
    κεῖνος δὴ νέμεται· τὸν δ' ἄρα θελγόμενος
καλλείπω στρεφθεὶς πρὸς τὤρεα· ἀλλ' ἔραμαί σου.
    ἴσχε, φίλη, μ', ὤμοις χεῖρα βαλοῦσα πέρι.

Ἔσχες ἀδημονέοντά μ', ὑπέστρεψεν δ', ἀπιών περ,
    σῇ χερὶ θελγόμενος, κοὐκ ἄρα φροῦδος, Ἔρως·
ἀλλ' ἔπεται τρίτος αὐτὸς ὁδοιπόρος—οὐ τρίτος οἶος,
    Μουσῶν γὰρ θιάσου κεῖνος ἅμ' ἡγέεται.
χαίρετέ μοι, στίλβουσαν ἕδρην 'Ελικῶνα λιποῦσαι
    πότνιαι· ἡ δὲ γελῶσ' ἵλαα Καλλιόπη
"Τέκνω," ἔφη, "στείχωμεν ὁμὴν ὁδόν, ἧς ῥα πέφανται
    τέρμ' οὐ δῆθ' 'Ελίκων, οὐ ῥίον οὐδὲ νιφάς·

ΣΥΓΓΡΑΦΕΩΣ ΒΙΟΣ

τῆλε γὰρ οὐ στρωφώμεθ'—ἔπος φύγεν ἔρκος ὀδόντων
κεῖνό σοι εἰκαῖον—κοινὸς ὁδηγὸς ὅδε."

Ἐρχόμενον γὰρ ὁρῶ σε, τελεσφόρε παυσιμέριμνε
πασὶ βροτοῖς, κἀμοὶ καίριε νῦν, Θάνατε—
χαῖρέ μοι οὔ ῥα μάτην βεβιωκότι, ὦ Ῥοσαλίνδη
σύζυγος, ὀργεῶνες Μοῦσαι, ὁδηγὸς Ἔρως.

CONTENTS OF VOLUMES I–III

VOLUME I

CONTENTS xix

VOLUME II

CONTENTS

VOLUME III

ERRATA AND ADDENDA

While the second edition was in the press, the following valuable comments on volume i reached the author too late to allow of the appropriate changes being made in the text:

Page 23, footnote 2: To call administrative efficiency a new Italian 'invention' perhaps does less than justice to the native administrative efficiency which was displayed in England, at any rate, if not in other Transalpine kingdoms, in the Middle Ages. 'New Italian methods' would be a truer description of the Transalpine effects of Italian influence in the administrative sphere.

Page 28, lines 18–19: The statement in the text is too sweeping; for there was, of course, a fitful co-operation between France and the Ottoman Empire against the Hapsburg Power from the generation of Francis I and Suleymān the Magnificent onwards, while in the eighteenth century Sweden and Poland were drawn towards the Ottoman Empire by their common concern over the rising power of Russia.

Page 212: An apologist for the English Protestant colonists in North America might perhaps be inclined to suggest that the difference between their way and the Spanish Catholics' way of treating the 'Native' peoples of the New World was due not so much to a difference between the respective moral standards of these two sets of European intruders as to a difference between the respective social conditions of the two sets of American 'Natives' upon whom they happened respectively to stumble. The 'Red Indians' whom the English Protestants exterminated were a handful of incorrigibly militant savages, whereas the subjects of the Aztecs and the Incas, whom the Spanish Catholics spared, were a numerous and peaceful peasantry whose native level of culture was relatively high. This apologia would be plausible if the English Protestants' colonization of North America and the Spanish Catholics' colonization of Central and South America had been the only two European colonizing enterprises in the New World. When, however, we see the French Catholics colonizing North America side by side with the English Protestants and there fraternizing with those 'incorrigibly militant savages' whom the English Protestants were exterminating, we are confirmed in our view that the difference in the respective outcomes of these Protestant and Catholic colonizing activities in the New World is accounted for by some moral difference between the two sets of colonizers rather than by any social differences between the several sets of 'Natives' whom they respectively encountered. On the other hand, in the matter of the Negro slave-trade, it should have been mentioned that the Genoese and Portuguese Catholics (as well as the Dutch Protestants) had had a share in it before the monopoly of it was acquired by the English Protestants in A.D. 1713.

Page 232, last line of text: While the Black Race perhaps cannot be credited for certain with having made any active contribution to any civilization, there is some indication of a Negroid strain in certain of the occupants of the Lower Nile Valley during the twilight before the dawn of the Egyptiac Civilization (see page 241).

Page 245, footnote 1: An acceptance of Monsieur Demolins' exposure of the racial fallacy does not, of course, involve us in capitulating of this scholar's own environmental thesis.

THE PLAN OF THE BOOK

I

INTRODUCTION

A. THE RELATIVITY OF HISTORICAL THOUGHT

'The Aethiopians say that their Gods are snub-nosed and black-skinned, and the Thracians that theirs are blue-eyed and red-haired. If only oxen and horses had hands and wanted to draw with their hands or to make the works of art that men make, then horses would draw the figures of their Gods like horses, and oxen like oxen, and would make their bodies on the model of their own.'[1]   XENOPHANES.

IN any age of any society the study of history, like other social activities, is governed by the dominant tendencies of the time and the place. The Western World in our age has been living under the dominion of two institutions: the Industrial System of economy and a hardly less complicated system of politics which we call 'Democracy' as a short title for responsible parliamentary representative government in a sovereign independent national state. These two institutions, the one economic and the other political, attained a general supremacy in the Western World at the close of the age preceding our own[2] because they offered provisional solutions for the chief problems with which that age had been confronted. Their enthronement signified the completion of the age which had sought and found salvation in them; their survival bears witness to the creative power of our predecessors; and we, who

---

[1]   Αἰθίοπές τε θεοὺς σφετέρους σιμοὺς μέλανάς τε
        Θρῆκές τε γλαυκοὺς καὶ πυρρούς φασι πέλεσθαι.
        ἀλλ' εἰ χεῖρας ἔχον γε βόες θ' ἵπποι τ', ἠὲ λέοντες
        ἢ γράψαι χείρεσσιν ἢ ἔργα τελεῖν ἅπερ ἄνδρες,
        ἵπποι μέν θ' ἵπποισι, βόες δέ τε βουσὶν ὁμοίας
        καί κε θεῶν ἰδέας ἔγραφον καὶ σώματ' ἐποίουν
        τοιαῦθ', οἷόν περ καὐτοὶ δέμας εἶχον ἕκαστοι.

(Text as in Diehl, E.: *Anthologia Lyrica,* i (Leipzig 1922, Teubner), pp. 58-9.)

[2] For the Western World as a whole the close of this preceding age may be equated approximately with the end of the third quarter of the nineteenth century of our era. The idea that the 'sixties and 'seventies of the nineteenth century were a time of transition from one age of our common civilization to another is familiar to Continental Europeans and to Americans (both in the United States and in Canada). It is less familiar to people brought up in Great Britain, who usually think of these decades not as the close but as the zenith of an age—the Victorian Age—which began earlier and ended later than this. From the standpoint of Great Britain, that is perhaps the natural view; but it will be suggested below (in I. C (iii) (*b*), pp. 171-1, and III. C (ii) (*b*), vol. iii, pp. 350-63) that the position of Great Britain in the Western World at that time was exceptional. In the invention of Industrialism and 'Democracy' the people of Great Britain had been pioneers; and the process by which the supremacy of these two institutions was established was already past history in Great Britain at the time when it was attaining or approaching completion in other parts of the Western World. Hence the people of Great Britain were conscious of relative continuity at a time when the peoples of most other countries in the Western World were conscious of a transition from one age to another. The sense of the majority must be taken as the standard when we are considering the Western World as a whole.

did not create them, have grown up under their shadow. In the Industrial System and the Parliamentary National State we still live and move and have our being; and the power of these two inherited institutions over our lives is reflected in the hold which they possess over our imaginations. Their prestige is apparent at almost every point in the work of our historians.

The Industrial System has a human aspect in the Division of Labour and a non-human aspect in the application of modern Western scientific thought to the physical environment of human life. Its method of operation is to maintain, up to the maximum of its productive capacity, an incessant output of such articles as can be manufactured from raw materials by the mechanically co-ordinated work of a number of human beings. These features of the Industrial System have been reproduced in the theory and even in the practice of Western thought during the past half-century.

When I was a child I used to stay from time to time in the house of a distinguished professor of one of the physical sciences. There was a study lined with book-shelves, and I remember how, between one visit and another, the books used to change. When first I knew the room, many shelves were filled with general literature, with general scientific works, and with general works on that branch of science in which my host was an expert. As the years passed, these shelves were invaded, one after another, by the relentless advance of half a dozen specialized periodicals—gaunt volumes in grim bindings, each containing many monographs by different hands. These volumes were not books in the literary sense of the word, for there was no unity in their contents and indeed no relation whatever between one monograph and another beyond the very feeble link of their all having something to do with the branch of science in question. The books retreated as the periodicals advanced. I afterwards rediscovered them in the attics, where the *Poems* of Shelley and *The Origin of Species*, thrown together in a common exile, shared shelves of a rougher workmanship with microbes kept on gelatine in glass bottles. Each time I found the study a less agreeable room to look at and to live in than before.

Those periodicals were the Industrial System 'in book form', with its Division of Labour and its sustained maximum output of articles manufactured from raw materials mechanically. In my dislike of those rows of volumes I used to regard them as the abomination of desolation standing in the place where it ought not,[1] but I am now ready to believe that they may not have been out of place in a physical scientist's work-room in the early years of the twentieth century of our era. Since the Industrial System, in its

[1] Matt. xxiv. 15; Dan. ix. 27.

non-human aspect, is based on Physical Science, there may well be some kind of 'pre-established harmony' between the two; and so it is possible that no violence is done to the nature of scientific thought through its being conducted on industrial lines.[1] At any rate, this may well be the right way of handling any branch of Physical Science in its early stages—and all our modern Western Science is still very young, even compared with the age of our Western Society—since discursive thought of any kind needs an initial supply of 'data' on which to work. The same method, however, has latterly been applied in many realms of thought beyond the bounds of Physical Science—to thought which is concerned with Life and not with Inanimate Nature, and even to thought which is concerned with human activities.[2] Historical thought is among these foreign realms in which the prestige of the Industrial System has asserted itself; and here—in a mental domain which has had a far longer history than our Western Society and which is concerned not with things but with people—there is no assurance that the modern Western Industrial System is the best régime under which to live and to labour.[3]

The subjugation of this ancient kingdom of historical thought by the modern Industrialism of Western life is illustrated in the career of Theodor Mommsen. In his younger days Mommsen wrote a great book, which certainly will always be reckoned among the masterpieces of Western historical literature. This book was *The History of the Roman Republic*, published in 1854-6; but Mommsen had hardly written it before he became almost ashamed of it and turned his magnificent energy and ability into other channels. Mommsen made it his life work to organize the exhaustive publication of Latin inscriptions and the encyclopaedic

[1] Physical Science and Industrialism may be conceived as a pair of dancers, both of whom know their steps and have an ear for the rhythm of the music. If the partner who has been leading chooses to change parts and to follow instead, there is perhaps no reason to expect that he will dance less correctly than before.

[2] On this point, see Dilthey, W.: *Gesammelte Schriften*, vol. vii (Leipzig and Berlin 1927, Teubner). The Geisteswissenschaften tend to borrow the methods of the Naturwissenschaften, owing to the seniority of these latter disciplines, notwithstanding the fact that their respective Verfahrungsweisen differ *ab initio* (p. 130). 'Die realen Kategorien sind . . . in den Geisteswissenschaften nirgends dieselben als in den Naturwissenschaften' (p. 195).

[3] It is noteworthy that while many of our historians still acquiesce in this régime, and even hug their chains, the leading minds in the field of contemporary Physical Science have already passed the stage of study in which the Industrial System seems to be a fruitful and adequate method of research. The organized Division of Labour for the extraction and 'working up' of raw 'data' has now ceased to be the guiding principle of their work. In the work of Einstein, for instance, the layman—however far he may fall short of understanding the great man's thought—can at least perceive that he is thinking about the Physical Universe as a whole and not just about this or that slice of physical reality. Perhaps the layman may even venture further and conjecture that this broad attitude of mind—this comprehensive way of thinking—has been an essential condition of Einstein's achievement. 'I have not found so great faith, no not in Israel' (Matt. viii. 10). Let our historians take heed. For when the Gentiles are flocking into the Kingdom of God, it is assuredly time for the children of the Covenant to move (Acts iii. 25).

presentation of Roman Constitutional Law. *Das Römische Staats-recht* and the *Corpus Inscriptionum Latinarum* were the monuments by which, in later life, he would have preferred to be remembered; and the volumes of his collected works—a congeries of unrelated monographs and articles—are like so many volumes of a learned periodical which happens to have had only one contributor. In all this, Mommsen was representative of the Western historians of his generation—a generation in which the prestige of the Industrial System imposed itself upon the 'intellectual workers' of the Western World. Since the days of Mommsen and Ranke, his-torians have given their best energies to the 'assemblage' of raw materials—inscriptions, documents, and the like—in 'corpus'es and periodicals; and, when they have attempted to 'work' these materials 'up' into 'manufactured' or 'semi-manufactured' articles, they have had recourse, once again, to the Division of Labour and have produced synthetic histories like the several series of volumes now in course of publication by the Cambridge University Press. Such series are monuments of the laboriousness, the 'factual' knowledge, the mechanical skill, and the organizing power of our society. They will take their rank with our stupendous tunnels and bridges and dams and liners and battleships and skyscrapers, and their editors will be remembered among the famous Western engineers. In invading the realm of historical thought, the Industrial System has given scope to great strategists and has set up marvellous trophies of victory. Yet, in a detached onlooker's mind, the doubt arises whether this conquest may not, after all, be a *tour de force* and the confidence of victory the delusion of a false analogy.

Some historical teachers of our day deliberately describe their 'seminars' as 'laboratories' and, perhaps less consciously but no less decidedly, restrict the term 'original work' to denote the discovery or verification of some fact or facts not previously established.[1] At the furthest, the term is extended to cover the interim reports upon such work which are contributed to learned journals or to synthetic histories. There is a strong tendency to depreciate works of historical literature which are created by single minds, and the depreciation becomes the more emphatic the nearer such works approximate to being 'Universal Histories'. For example, Mr. H. G. Wells's *The Outline of History* was received with unmis-takable hostility by a number of historical specialists. They criticized severely the errors which they discovered at the points where the writer, in his long journey through Time and Space, happened to traverse their tiny allotments. They seemed not to

---

[1] 'Established', that is, in the subjective meaning of the French verb *constater*.

realize that, in re-living the entire life of Mankind as a single imaginative experience, Mr. Wells was achieving something which they themselves would hardly have dared to attempt—something, perhaps, of which they had never conceived the possibility. In fact, the purpose and value of Mr. Wells's book seem to have been better appreciated by the general public than by the professional historians of the day.

The industrialization of historical thought has proceeded so far that it has even reproduced the pathological exaggerations of the industrial spirit. It is well known that individuals or communities whose energies are concentrated upon turning raw materials into light, heat, locomotion, or manufactured articles are inclined to feel that the discovery and exploitation of natural resources is a valuable activity in itself, apart from the value for Mankind of any results produced by the process. They are even tempted to feel it reprehensible in other people when they neglect to develop all the natural resources at their disposal; and they themselves readily become slaves to their fetish if they happen to live in a region where natural resources, and opportunities for developing them, abound. This state of mind appears to European observers to be characteristic of a certain type of American business man; but this type is simply an extreme product of a tendency which is characteristic of our Western World as a whole; and our contemporary European historians sometimes ignore the fact that in our time the same morbidity, resulting in the same loss of proportion, is also discernible in their own frame of mind.

The point may be brought home by an illustration. After Alexander the Great had broken up the Achaemenian Empire, the Dynasty of the Ptolemies built some of the fragments into a Great Power based on Egypt, while the Seleucids built up another Great Power out of the former provinces of the Empire in Asia. No one who studies these two Great Powers in their historical perspective can doubt which of them is the more interesting and important. The Seleucid Monarchy was the bridal chamber in which the Hellenic and Syriac civilizations were married, and their union there produced titanic offspring: to begin with, a divine kingship as a principle of association between city-states which was the prototype of the Roman Empire,[1] and then a whole series of syncretistic religions: Mithraism, Christianity, Manichaeism, and Islam. For nearly two centuries the Seleucid Monarchy was the greatest field of creative human activity that existed in the World; and long after it had fallen the movements generated during its comparatively brief span of existence continued to mould the

[1] For this institution, see further Parts V and VI below.

destinies of Mankind. Compared with this, the marriage of Hellenism with the Egyptiac Civilization in the Ptolemaic Empire was unfruitful. The introduction into the Roman Empire of the worship of Isis and of certain forms of economic and social organization is really all that can be placed to its account. Owing, however, to a climatic accident, the amount of raw information regarding these two monarchies which happens to be accessible to us is in inverse ratio to their intrinsic importance in history. The dry-as-dust soil of Upper Egypt yields the scientific Western excavator a wealth of papyri, beyond the dreams of the scholars of the Renaissance, and these papyri afford minute information regarding local methods of agriculture, manufacture, trade, and public administration, whereas the history of the Seleucid Monarchy has to be pieced together from scattered coins and inscriptions and from fragments of literary records. The significant point is that the Ptolemaic papyri have attracted almost all the spare energies of Western scholarship in the field of Ancient History, and that the comparatively large number of scholars who have been devoting themselves, with admirable skill and patience, to elucidating the minutiae of papyrus texts have tended to measure the historical importance of the Ptolemaic Monarchy by the amount of raw material accessible for the reconstruction of its history and by the intensity of the labour which they themselves have devoted to this reconstructive work.

An outside observer is tempted to regret that part of this energy was not reserved for equally intensive work upon the meagre and hardly increasing quantity of materials that is at our disposal for the reconstruction of Seleucid history. One additional gleam of light thrown upon the darkness of this page might add more to our understanding of the History of Mankind than floods of light thrown upon the social and economic organization of Ptolemaic Egypt. And, beyond this, the observer is moved to a psychological reflection. He suspects that the scholar who has become a Ptolemaic papyrologist has seldom asked himself the prior question: 'Is Ptolemaic Egypt the most interesting and important phenomenon to study in the particular age of the particular society to which it belonged?' More probably he has asked himself instead: 'What is the richest mine of unworked raw material in this field?' And, finding that the answer is 'Ptolemaic papyri', he has become a papyrologist for the rest of his working life without thinking twice about it. Thus in modern Western historical research, as in modern Western industry, the quantity and location of raw materials threaten to govern the activities and the lives of human beings. Yet there is little doubt that our imaginary papyrologist has made a wrong choice by all humane standards. Intrinsically, the Seleucid Monarchy and not the Ptolemaic Monarchy is the field in which the pearl of great price awaits the historical explorer. For this judgement it is sufficient to quote the authority of Professor Eduard Meyer[1]—a scholar who has been not without honour in his own generation, though he has used his mastery of modern scientific equipment and technique in order to write 'Universal History' in the great tradition of *Essai sur les Mœurs* or *The History of the Decline and Fall of the Roman Empire*, like some son of Anak born out of due time.

This tendency for the potter to become the slave of his clay is so evident an aberration that a corrective may be found for it without abandoning the fashionable analogy between the processes of historical thought and the processes of industry. In industry, after all, to be hypnotized by the raw material does not pay. The successful industrialist is the man who first perceives that there is a strong economic demand for some particular commodity or service, and then lays hands upon just those raw materials and that 'man power' with which, at a profit to himself, he can manufacture that object or perform that service efficiently. Raw materials and 'man power' which do not happen to serve the purpose have no interest for him. In other words, he is a master of natural resources, and not their slave, and so he becomes a captain of industry and makes his fortune.

This, however, is a digression from the course of our argument, which has been leading us up to the point of calling in question the analogy between historical thought and industrial production altogether. In the world of action, we know that it is disastrous to treat animals or human beings as though they were stocks and stones. Why should we suppose this treatment to be any less mistaken in the world of ideas? Why should we suppose that the scientific method of thought—a method which has been devised for thinking about Inanimate Nature—should be applicable to historical thought, which is a study of living creatures and indeed of human beings? When a professor of history calls his 'seminar' a 'laboratory', is he not wilfully expatriating himself from his natural environment? Both names are metaphors, and either metaphor is apt in its own sphere. The historian's *seminarium* is a

---

[1] See Meyer, Eduard: 'Der Gang der alten Geschichte' in *Kleine Schriften* (Halle 1910, Niemeyer); and *Blüte und Niedergang des Hellenismus in Asien* (Berlin 1925, Curtius). In another place, Meyer points out that the historian's access to historical evidence is always and everywhere at the mercy of Chance, so that there is no rational correspondence between the intrinsic importance and interest of any given historical event and the quantity and credibility of the historical evidence that is at our disposal for the study of it (*Geschichte des Alte tums*, vol. i (i), 4th edition (Stuttgart and Berlin 1921, Cotta), pp. 211–12).

nursery-garden in which living ideas about living creatures are taught to shoot. The physical scientist's *laboratorium* is—or was till the other day[1]—a workshop in which manufactured or semi-manufactured articles are produced mechanically out of inanimate raw materials. No practical man, however, would think of conducting a nursery garden on the principles of a factory or a factory on the principles of a nursery garden; and, in the world of ideas, the corresponding misapplications of method ought to be avoided by scholars. We are sufficiently on our guard against the so-called 'Pathetic Fallacy' of imaginatively endowing inanimate objects with life. We now fall victims to the inverse 'Apathetic Fallacy' of treating living creatures as though they were inanimate.

If the Industrial System had been the sole dominant institution in contemporary Western life, the influence of its prestige over Western historical thought might have broken down under its own weight; for the Industrial System can only be applied to historical thought by a very drastic Division of Labour. In industry, the Division of Labour is readily (perhaps too readily) accepted by Mankind as a price which has to be paid for material well-being; and there appears—or appeared till recently—to be little repugnance to it in that realm of thought which is concerned with the Physical Universe. It is conceivable that, as Bergson suggests, the mechanism of our intellect is specifically constructed so as to isolate our apprehension of Physical Nature in a form which enables us to take action upon it.[2] Yet even if this is the original structure of the human mind, and if other methods of thinking are in some sense unnatural, there yet exists a human faculty, as Bergson goes on to point out, which insists, not upon looking at Inanimate Nature, but upon feeling Life and feeling it as a whole.[3] This deep impulse to envisage and comprehend the whole of Life is certainly immanent in the mind of the historian; and such violence is done to it by the Division of Labour which the analogy of the Industrial System imposes on historical thought, that our historians would almost certainly have revolted against this tyranny if there had not been a second dominant institution in contemporary Western life which has appeared to make unity of vision still compatible with the industrialization of historical

---

[1] The pioneers of to-day in the field of Physical Science would probably admit this description as being true of the *laboratorium* of their 'classical' predecessors, but would indignantly—and perhaps justly—deny that their own work was being conducted on 'classical' principles or under the shadow of 'classical' traditions.

[2] See Bergson's inquiry into the 'Fonction Primordiale de l'Intelligence' in *L'Évolution Creatrice*, 24th edition (Paris 1921, Alcan), pp. 164–79. In this suggestion, Bergson has been anticipated by Turgot. See the 'Plan de Deux Discours sur l'Histoire Universelle' in *Œuvres de Turgot*, nouvelle édition (Paris 1844, Guillaumin, 2 vols.), vol. ii, p. 654.

[3] See Bergson, Henri: op. cit., especially chapter iii.

thought. This second institution, which has peacefully divided with the Industrial System the allegiance of modern Western historians, is the Sovereign State, which is inspired in our 'democratic' age by the spirit of Nationality.

Here, again, an institution dominating a particular age of a particular society has influenced the outlook and activity of historians who happen to have been brought up under its shadow. The spirit of Nationality is a sour ferment of the new wine of Democracy in the old bottles of Tribalism. The ideal of our modern Western Democracy has been to apply in practical politics the Christian intuition of the fraternity of all Mankind;[1] but the practical politics which this new democratic ideal found in operation in the Western World were not oecumenical and humanitarian but were tribal and militant.[2] The modern Western democratic ideal is thus an attempt to reconcile two spirits and to resolve two forces which are in almost diametrical opposition; the spirit of Nationality is the psychic product of this political *tour de force*; and the spirit of Nationality may be defined (negatively but not inaccurately) as a spirit which makes people feel and act and think about a part of any given society as though it were the whole of that society.[3] This strange compromise between Democracy and Tribalism has been far more potent in the practical politics of our modern Western World than Democracy itself. Industrialism and Nationalism, rather than Industrialism and Democracy, are the two forces which have exercised dominion *de facto* over our Western Society in our age; and, during the century that ended about A.D. 1875, the Industrial Revolution and the contemporary emergence of Nationalism in the Western World were working together to build up 'Great Powers', each of which claimed to be a universe in itself.

Of course this claim was false. The simple fact that there were more Great Powers than one proved that no single one of them was coextensive with the sum total of that society which embraced them all. Every Great Power, however, did succeed in exerting a continual effect upon the general life of Society, so that in some

---

[1] 'La démocratie est d'essence évangélique, et . . . elle a pour moteur l'amour'—Bergson, Henri: *Les Deux Sources de la Morale et de la Religion* (Paris 1932, Alcan), pp. 304–5.

[2] In exhibiting these characteristics, our modern Western politics are not peculiar. Monsieur Bergson has pointed out that parochialism is a normal feature of human social groups, from the most primitive to the least imperfectly civilized; and the philosopher goes on to suggest that this parochialism, and the militancy between different parochial groups which is its corollary, is not only normal but is even in a certain sense 'natural'. (See Bergson, op. cit., especially pp. 25–8, 249–50, and 306–9.)

[3] A political counterpart to the sin which is denounced in the Qur'ān as شِرْك (For the bearing of this political aberration upon the prospects of our Western Civilization, see further Part XII below.)

sense it could regard itself as a pivot round which the whole of Society revolved; and every Great Power also aspired to be a substitute for Society in the sense of being self-contained and self-sufficient, not only in politics and economics but even in spiritual culture. The state of mind thus engendered among the people of communities which constituted Great Powers spread to communities of lesser calibre. In that age in the history of our Western Society, all national states, from the greatest down to the least, put forward the same claim to be enduring entities, each sufficient unto itself and independent of the rest of the World. The claim was so insistently advanced and so widely accepted that the true duration and true unity of the Western Society itself were temporarily obscured; and the deep human impulse to feel Life as a whole, which is perpetually seeking to find satisfaction in the changing circumstances of Life as it passes, attached itself to particular nations rather than to the larger society of which those nations were members. Such fixations of social emotion upon national groups became almost universal, and historians have been no more immune from them than other people. Indeed, the spirit of Nationality has appealed to historians with special force, because it has offered them some prospect of reconciling the common human desire for unity of vision with the Division of Labour imposed upon them by the application of the Industrial System to their work. To grapple with 'Universal History' on industrial principles is so evidently beyond the compass even of the most gifted and the most vigorous individual that, for a scientific historian, the admission that unity could not be found in anything short of 'Universal History' would be tantamount to renouncing unity of vision altogether—a renunciation which would take the light out of any historian's landscape. If, however, he could seize upon a unit of historical thought which was of more manageable proportions yet was still in some sense a universe too, the psychological problem of reconciling his intellect with his emotions might be solved; and such a solution appeared to be offered by the Principle of Nationality.

On this account the national standpoint has proved specially attractive to modern Western historians, and it has been commended to their minds through more than one channel. They have been led to it not only because it has been prevalent in the communities in which they have grown up, but also because their raw material has presented itself to a large extent in the form of separate national deposits. The richest mines which they have worked have been the public archives of Western Governments. Indeed, the abundance of this particular natural resource is what chiefly accounts for their astonishing success in increasing their volume of production. Thus our historians have been drawn partly by professional experience, partly by a psychological conflict, and partly by the general spirit of their age in one and the same direction.

The lengths to which this tendency may go can be observed in the work of a distinguished historian belonging to one of the greatest nations of the modern Western World. Monsieur Camille Jullian is perhaps the foremost living authority upon the 'pre-history' of that portion of Continental Europe which at the present time constitutes the territory of 'France', and in 1922 he published a book called *De la Gaule à la France: Nos Origines Historiques*.[1] This book is a first-rate piece of historical writing; yet, in reading it, it is difficult to keep the attention fixed upon the matters with which Monsieur Jullian intends to deal, because the reader is continually being made aware that the writer is not only a historian but a Frenchman, and a Frenchman who has lived through the General War of 1914–18. The sub-title—*Nos Origines Historiques* —gives the key. All the time Monsieur Jullian is projecting back into the past his own burning consciousness of France as she exists for him to-day—a spiritual France which furnishes him with the experience of human life so exhaustively that, if the rest of the World were to be annihilated and France left solitary but intact, Monsieur Jullian would perhaps hardly be sensible of any spiritual impoverishment; and a material France with clear-cut frontiers which have been constantly overrun by invaders and constantly re-established by the patriotism of the French nation. The self-sufficiency of France and her separateness from the rest of the World are ideas which dominate Monsieur Jullian's imagination even when he is dealing with the history of this piece of territory at dates hundreds or thousands of years before such a conception as 'France' existed. Into however distant a past he travels back, he carries France with him—contented if he can do so with ease, embarrassed if he cannot do so without difficulty, but ever incapable of leaving France behind him. For example, he is gravely embarrassed when he has to deal with the incorporation of the several dozen independent states of Gaul into the Roman Empire, and he does his best to make credible the thesis that, even during the five centuries that intervened between the generation of Julius Caesar and the generation of Sidonius Apollinaris, the local individuality of Gaul was a more important fact in the life of its inhabitants than their membership in an Empire which embraced the whole *orbis terrarum* of the Mediterranean Basin. On the other

[1] Paris 1922, Hachette.

hand, Monsieur Jullian cannot contain his delight when he discerns the lineaments of France upon the face of Europe in the
Neolithic Age. Here is a passage[1] which occurs at the end of a
brilliant reconstruction of certain aspects of Neolithic life through
an examination of the trails along which the Neolithic people did
their travelling:

'L'on peut parler maintenant de ces routes vitales, par lesquelles,
pour une si grande part, se fera la France. Aussi bien, ce trafic ne sort
pas des limites qui seront plus tard celles de la Gaule, comme si l'entente
humaine reconnaît déjà la valeur de ces limites.'

Here, in the twinkling of an eye, the scientific Western historian
of the Neolithic Age has been transfigured into the French patriot
of A.D. 1918, crying: 'Ils ne passeront pas!'

This is perhaps an extreme case of the emotional and intellectual
substitution of a nation for Mankind. At the same time, when the
nation thus magnified happens to be France, the degree in which
history is thrown out of perspective is the least possible in the
circumstances. After all, some entity corresponding to the name
'France' actually has maintained its individuality within the universe of our Western Society for nearly a millennium;[2] and though
a thousand years is not a long time in the history of Mankind, it
covers almost the whole lifetime of our own Western Society,
which only began to emerge from the ruins of the Roman Empire
about 250 years before France herself began to emerge as a distinct
element in this new Western World.[3] Moreover, France, since her
emergence, has continuously played a central and a leading part in
Western history; and thus, while Monsieur Jullian's attempt to
present the Roman Empire or the Neolithic Age in terms of France
is a palpable *tour de force*, the distortion is not so apparent to the
eye when modern Western history is focused from the French
standpoint, with France in the centre and everything else on the
periphery. France perhaps approaches nearer than any other
national state to being co-central and co-extensive with the whole
of our Western Society If, however, instead of France, we were to
take Norway or Portugal, or even Holland or Switzerland, and
attempt to write the history of the Western Society round any one
of these countries, we can see at once that the attempt would break
down. As a *reductio ad absurdum*, let us try to imagine ourselves

[1] Op. cit., p 62, chapter ii: 'L'Époque des Agricolteurs (Temps Néolithiques).'
[2] Nearly a millennium, but certainly not longer than this; for 'Vor einem Jahrtausend,
zur Zeit der Zersetzung der Karolingischen Monarchie, kaum ein einziges der Völker
des gegenwärtigen Europas existiert hat, nicht nur seinem äusseren Bestande, sondern
seinem inneren Wesen nach' (Meyer, E.: *Geschichte des Altertums*, vol. i (i), 4th edition
(Stuttgart and Berlin 1921, Cotta), p. 78.)
[3] For the emergence of France, in the present meaning of the name, see further
II. D (v), vol. ii, pp. 197–201, below.

writing the history of the Western Society round one of those national states which have only attained their statehood since the termination of the General War of 1914–18. That would involve writing the history of a society which has been in existence for more than twelve centuries round a nation whose existence is not yet securely established. Whether a Czechoslovak or a Jugoslav national consciousness yet exists has hardly ceased to be a debatable question. Certainly such consciousnesses were non-existent as recently as fifty years ago; and even if we attempted to present the history of the West in terms of the constituent parts of these nascent nationalities—in terms, that is, of Czechs or Slovaks or Croats or Serbs, whose history as distinct groups goes back further —the absurdity, while less great in terms of relative age, would be greater in terms of relative population and territorial extension. Western history cannot be conceived in terms of nationalities of this calibre. Indeed, short of writing a Slovako-centric or a Croato-centric history of the West, we should find it impossible to write even a Slovako-centric history of Slovakia or a Croato-centric history of Croatia. In contrast to France, Slovakia and Croatia fall so far short of constituting historical universes in themselves that, when isolated, they cease to be intelligible. It would be impossible to write intelligible histories of Slovakia or Croatia in which those territories, or their peoples, were given the role of protagonists, even in their own small corners of the broad Western stage. It would be impossible, in their case, to distinguish from their external relations an internal history which was something specifically their own. It would be found that every experience which they underwent and every activity into which they entered had been shared by them with other communities whose share had been greater than theirs, and in attempting to make their history intelligible we should find ourselves extending our field of vision to include one after another of these other peoples. Possibly we should have to extend it until we had included the whole of our Western Society. In any case, the intelligible field, when we found it, would certainly prove to be some field of which Slovakia or Croatia itself was a small and comparatively unimportant fraction.[1]

The emergence of new national states like Czechoslovakia and Jugoslavia which have no history at all, and whose component parts have no history that is intelligible in isolation, signifies the

---

[1] Dr. H. W. V. Temperley's masterly *History of Serbia* (London 1917, Bell) illustrates the difficulties with which a historian has to contend in attempting to write a history of a nation of this calibre. In order to make Serbian history intelligible and consecutive, he has to present it within the successive frameworks of Byzantine and Ottoman History and finally in relation to the 'Eastern Question': that is to say, as a function of the modern European Balance of Power. There are few chapters in which he succeeds in disengaging Serbian history from its context and treating it in isolation.

arrival of a new age and indicates what its character is to be. The general conditions of our Western Society have already become profoundly different from those which were in the ascendant during the century ending about A.D. 1875 and which have stamped the minds of Western historians with an impress which they still retain. Down to about 1875, the two dominant institutions of Industrialism and Nationalism were working together to build up Great Powers. After 1875 they began to work in opposite directions—Industrialism increasing the scale of its operations beyond the compass of the greatest of the Great Powers and feeling its way towards a world-wide range, while Nationalism, percolating downwards, began to implant a separate consciousness in peoples of so small a calibre that they were incapable not only of forming Great Powers but even of forming minor states possessed of full political, economic, and cultural independence in the established sense of those terms.

The General War of 1914–18 brought to the surface a tendency which had been at work for nearly half a century before its outbreak. By the end of the year 1918, one out of the eight Great Powers which existed in 1914 had completely disappeared, two others had been mutilated and laid prostrate, and one of those which had survived more or less intact was undergoing rapid structural transformations in the direction of 'Dominion Self-Government'. The general upshot of these partly revolutionary and partly evolutionary changes is the same. The stage has ceased to be dominated by the Great Powers with their pretension to be universes in themselves, and the characteristic communities of the new age are states whose independence is limited on one or other plane. Some of these (for example the Dominions of the British Commonwealth) are not completely separate political entities; others (for example Czechoslovakia, Austria, and Hungary) possess no seaboard; and others, again, no distinctive or satisfying national culture. In this new world, moreover, even the surviving Great Powers are dwarfed in the economic sphere by the world-wide scale on which Industrialism has now come to conduct its operations. All states alike are feeling less and less able to stand by themselves economically and are either kicking violently against the pricks by pursuing militant monetary and tariff and quota and migration policies or else are turning for assistance to the technical organizations of an international scope which are being built up round the Secretariat of the League of Nations and the International Labour Office at Geneva. Finally, all but the strongest or the most recalcitrant states are also beginning to feel the same lack of self-sufficiency on the political plane and are displaying a readiness (which would have been inconceivable in 1914) to accommodate their sovereign independence to the international procedure of the League of Nations Council and Assembly or to some other form of international limitation and control such as is implied in the Pact of Paris for the Renunciation of War as an instrument of national policy.[1]

These multiple tendencies can be summed up in a single formula: In the new age, the dominant note in the corporate consciousness of communities is a sense of being parts of some larger universe, whereas, in the age which is now over, the dominant note in their consciousness was an aspiration to be universes in themselves. This change of note indicates an unmistakable turn in a tide which, when it reached high-water mark about the year 1875, had been flowing steadily in one direction for four centuries. It may portend a return, in this respect, to the conditions of the preceding phase (the so-called 'medieval' phase) of Western history, when the consciousness of the Western Society was dominated by institutions like the Papacy and the Holy Roman Empire which incorporated some aspect of its life as a whole, while kingdoms and city-states and fiefs and other local institutions were felt to be something parochial and subordinate. At any rate, that is the direction in which the tide seems to be flowing now—as far as it is possible to discern its direction so short a time after it has turned.

If this observation is correct, and if it is also true that historians cannot abstract their thoughts and feelings from the influence of the environment in which they live, then we may expect to witness in the near future a change in the outlook and activities of Western historians corresponding to the recent change in the general conditions of the Western Society. Just as, at the close of the age which we have left behind, the historians' work was brought into conformity with the Industrial System and their vision was caught and bounded by the idea of Nationality, so, in the new age upon which we have entered, they will probably find their intelligible field of study in some landscape where the horizon is not restricted to the boundaries of a single nationality, and will adapt their present method of work to mental operations on a larger scale.

This raises two questions, one of immediate interest: 'What is the intelligible field of study which Western historians will discover for themselves in this new age?'—and another of permanent importance: 'Is there some intelligible field of historical study

[1] The play and interplay of Industrialism and Nationalism, the two dominant forces in the life of our Western Society in our age, are examined more closely in Parts IV and XII below. For the contrast between the coincidence in the direction of the two forces during the century ending about A.D. 1875 and the divergence since about 1875, see further Toynbee, A. J.: *The World after the Peace Conference* (London 1925, Milford), pp. 13-25, and the present work, IV. C (iii) (*b*) 3, vol. iv, pp. 167-85, below.

which is absolute and not merely relative to the particular social environment of particular historians?' So far, our inquiry seems to have brought out the fact that historical thought takes a deep impress from the dominant institutions of the transient social environment in which the thinker happens to live. If this impress proved to be so profound and so pervasive as actually to constitute the *a priori* categories in the historian's mind, that conclusion would bring our inquiry to an end. It would mean that the relativity of historical thought to the social environment was absolute; and in that case it would be useless to gaze any longer at the moving film of historical literature in the hope of discerning in it the lineaments of some abiding form. The historian would have to admit that, while it might be possible for him to work out a morphology of his own mind by analysing the influences exerted upon it by the particular society in which he lived, it was not possible for him to discover the structure of that society itself, or of the other societies in which other historians and other human beings had lived in different times and places. That conclusion, however, does not yet confront us. So far, we have simply found that in the foreground of historical thought there is a shimmer of relativity, and it is not impossible that the ascertainment of this fact may prove to be the first step towards ascertaining the presence of some constant and absolute object of historical thought in the background. Our next step, therefore, is to take up the search for an intelligible field of historical study independent of the local and temporary standpoints and activities of historians upon which we have focused our attention hitherto.

B. THE FIELD OF HISTORICAL STUDY

I. THE TEST CASE OF GREAT BRITAIN

In setting out to look for some objective 'intelligible field of historical study', it seems best to start with what is the usual field of vision of contemporary Western historians, that is, with some national state. Let us pick out, from among the national states of the West, whichever one seems most likely, at first sight, to correspond to our contemporary historians' ideal of what their field should be, and then let us test their outlook in this instance in the light of the 'historical facts' (taking 'historical facts' in the popularly accepted sense and begging provisionally the prior philosophical question as to the meaning of the word 'fact' in this term).

Great Britain seems as good a choice as any. She is not merely a national state but a Great Power. Her principal constituent, England, who incorporated herself into Great Britain two centuries ago without any breach of continuity or change of identity, is as old a figure in Western history as France, and on the whole as important a figure, though she has performed quite a different historical function.[1] Her peculiar merit for our purpose is that, to an exceptional degree, she has been kept in isolation—first by certain permanent features of physical geography, and secondly by a certain policy on the part of her statesmen in the age during which she has been most creative and most powerful. As regards her geographical isolation, the shores of an island provide frontiers which are incomparably more clear-cut than the land-frontiers of France, however precise and eternal Monsieur Jullian may feel those land-frontiers to be. For instance, we should not smile at Monsieur Jullian if he made the discovery that the Neolithic trails in Britain broke off along the same line at which the roads and railways of Britain break off to-day, or if he quoted *et penitus toto divisos orbe Britannos*[2] in describing the position of Britain in the Roman Empire. As regards her political isolation, Britain has been something of an *alter orbis*[3] throughout Western history—though less so in the Middle Ages than since England lost her last territorial foothold on the continental side of the Channel in A.D. 1558. Of course it is easy to exaggerate the degree of this 'splendid isolation'. Great Britain has never been able to disinterest herself from continental negotiations or wars in which the European

---

[1] For the function of England in modern Western history as a 'creative minority', see III. C (ii) (*b*), vol. iii, pp. 350–63, below.
[2] Vergil: *Eclogue I*, l. 66.
[3] See Freeman, E. A.: *Historical Essays: Fourth Series*, ix: 'Alter Orbis' (London 1892, Macmillan).

Balance of Power has been at stake; and, even when successfully maintained, the isolation has been deliberately one-sided. The *alter orbis* which Great Britain has aspired to be is not simply a world apart from continental Europe but a world embracing non-European continents and islands overseas. Like her daughter, the United States, she has only detached herself from the old world which lies near to her in order to liberate her energies for the creative task of calling into existence a new world far away. Yet, when all is said, her relative isolation is perhaps the most important single distinctive fact about her. At any rate, we shall not easily discover a Western nation which is more isolated than she is and which yet has played so prominent a part over so long a span of Western history. In fact, if Great Britain (as the heir and assign of England) is not found to constitute in herself an 'intelligible field of historical study', we may confidently infer that no other modern Western national state will pass muster.

Is English history, then, intelligible when taken by itself? Can we abstract an internal history of England from her external relations? If we can, shall we find that these residual external relations are of secondary importance? And in analysing these, again, shall we find that the foreign influences upon England are slight in comparison with the English influences upon other parts of the World? If all these questions receive affirmative answers, we may be justified in concluding that while it may not be possible to understand other histories without reference to England, it is possible, more or less, to understand English history without reference to other parts of the World. The best way to approach these questions is to direct our thought backwards over the course of English history and recall the principal chapters.

In this inverse order, we may take those chapters to be:

(*a*) The establishment of the Industrial System of economy (since the last quarter of the eighteenth century of our era);

(*b*) the establishment of Responsible Parliamentary Government (since the last quarter of the seventeenth century);

(*c*) the expansion overseas (beginning in the third quarter of the sixteenth century with piracy and developing gradually into a world-wide foreign trade, the acquisition of tropical dependencies and the foundation of new English-speaking communities in overseas countries with temperate climates);

(*d*) the Reformation (since the second quarter of the sixteenth century);

(*e*) the Renaissance, including the political and economic as well as the artistic and intellectual aspects of this movement (since the last quarter of the fifteenth century);

(f) the establishment of the Feudal System (since the eleventh century);

(g) the conversion of the English from the religion of the so-called 'Heroic Age'[1] to Western Christianity (since the last years of the sixth century).

This summary glance backwards from the present date over the general course of English history would appear to show that the further back we look the less evidence do we find of self-sufficiency or isolation. The conversion, which was really the beginning of all things in English history, was the direct antithesis of that: it was an act which merged half a dozen isolated communities of barbarians in the common weal of a nascent Western Society. As for the Feudal System, Vinogradoff has brilliantly demonstrated[2] that the seeds of it had already sprouted on English soil before the Norman Conquest. Yet, even so, the sprouting was stimulated by an external factor, the Danish invasions;[3] these invasions were part of the Scandinavian *Völkerwanderung* which was stimulating simultaneously a similar growth in France; and the Norman Conquest of England, though it may not have sown the seed, undoubtedly brought the harvest to a rapid maturity. Thus it may fairly be said that any account of the establishment of the Feudal System in England would not be intelligible unless France and Scandinavia, at least, were brought into the picture. As for the Renaissance, in both its cultural and its political aspects it is universally admitted to have been a breath of life from Northern Italy. If, in Northern Italy, Humanism, Absolutism, and the Balance of Power had not been cultivated in miniature, like seedlings in a sheltered nursery garden, during two centuries that fall approximately between A.D. 1275 and A.D. 1475,[4] they could never have been bedded out north of the Alps from about 1475 onwards. The Reformation, again, was not a specifically English phenomenon, but a general movement in the Promethean North of Western Europe (where the Baltic, the North Sea, and the Atlantic all beckoned towards new worlds) for emancipation from the Epimethean South (where the Western Mediterranean held the eye fixed upon worlds that were dead and gone).[5] In the Reformation, England did not take the initiative, nor did she take it even in the competition between the European nations of the Atlantic

---

[1] See Part VIII below.

[2] Vinogradoff, Paul: *English Society in the Eleventh Century* (Oxford 1908, Clarendon Press).

[3] On this point, see further II. D (v), vol. ii, pp. 196–201, below.

[4] For the role of the medieval Italian city-states as a 'creative minority' in Western history, see further III. C (ii) (b), vol. iii, pp. 341–50, below.

[5] For the role of such 'ghosts from the past' in the histories of civilizations, see further Part X, below.

sea-board for the prize of the new worlds overseas. She won that prize as a comparatively late comer, in a series of struggles, which lasted for several centuries, with Powers which were before her in the field. In order to understand the history of English expansion over-seas, it is necessary to appreciate the consequences of all the general European wars, and indeed to take into account all the vicissitudes of the European Balance of Power, from about the last quarter of the fifteenth century onwards—in fact, to extend the field of vision across the whole horizon of modern Western history.

It remains to consider the two latest chapters: the geneses of the Parliamentary System and of the Industrial System—institutions which are commonly regarded as having been first evolved locally on English soil and afterwards propagated from England into other parts of the World. For our purpose, these are the crucial chapters in English history, and an inquirer who is an amateur in this field will be wise to fall back here upon quoting recognized authorities. For the Parliamentary System, the following passage from Lord Acton's lecture on Henry IV and Richelieu[1] will serve:

'General History naturally depends on the action of forces which are not national, but proceed from wider causes. The rise of modern king-ship in France is part of a similar movement in England. Bourbons and Stuarts obeyed the same law, though with a different result.'

In other words, the Parliamentary System, which was the local result in England, was the product of a force which was not peculiar to England but was operative in England and in France simultaneously.[2]

As regards the Industrial Revolution in England, its genesis is thus summed up by two of the foremost living English students of the subject, Mr. and Mrs. Hammond:

'Why did this revolution come to England in the eighteenth century?

'For the new commerce the Atlantic was as important as the Mediter-ranean had been for the old. The most active trading peoples, after the discoveries of Columbus, were those who looked out on the Atlantic. Of these peoples the English were in a specially favourable position, in the middle of the eighteenth century, as a result of their geographical situation, their climate, and their history. The Spaniards used their control of the New World for politics, and the wealth they drew from the American mines was spent, in the main, in ways that discouraged industrial expansion. The English colonists in America, on the other hand, settled where there was little gold and silver, and they grew into communities which needed British goods for their own consumption, and sent home products that were useful for industry.

'Events in Europe also favoured the more rapid expansion of English

---

[1] Lord Acton: *Lectures on Modern History* (London 1906, Macmillan).
[2] On this point, see further III. C (ii) (*b*), vol. iii, pp. 359–63, below.

industry, for the European wars of the seventeenth and eighteenth centuries did more harm to industry on the Continent than in England, and the religious and political strife of the seventeenth century left England with a constitution and a government more favourable to commercial development than those of France. Among other advantages which a comparison of the state of England with that of France discloses are the supremacy of the common law, internal free trade, an aristocracy interested in commerce, a mistrust of State regulation, fostered by memories of the Stuarts, and toleration in religion. The stagnation of politics, religion, and local life in the eighteenth century encouraged the concentration on industry, and this concentration drew to mechanical invention all the ardour and imagination that had been fired by the revival of mathematics and the discoveries of physical science. For these reasons England was the most likely theatre for the Industrial Revolution.'[1]

This authoritative judgement regarding a chapter in English history which is commonly regarded as national *par excellence* is particularly significant. While, in the latter part of the last paragraph here quoted, the writers certainly mention several factors which might be classified as internal to England and even as peculiar to her, it is clear that, in their view, the factor which goes furthest towards accounting for the genesis of the Industrial Revolution in England is England's general position in the world of the day—her geographical position in respect of the Atlantic and her political position in respect of the European Balance of Power. Evidently they would pronounce that, if these general factors were ignored, an intelligible account of the rise of modern industry in England could not be given. It seems, then, that Great Britain is not an 'intelligible field of study' in itself even in this most recent and most British chapter of all; and the advocate of the national field of study cannot take refuge in conjectures regarding the future, for the Industrial Revolution itself, with its conquest of distance, its thoroughgoing internationalization of trade even in bulky staple commodities, and its latest inventions, the submarine and the aeroplane, has unmistakably laid the foundations for an unprecedented solidarity—for good or for evil—between Great Britain and other parts of the World. Thus British national history is not, never has been, and almost certainly never will be an 'intelligible field of study' in isolation; and if that is true of Great Britain, it must surely be true *a fortiori* of any other national state. Therefore, if we are to pursue our quest, it is clear that we must take some larger entity than the nation as our field.

'Ce n'est . . . pas la forme politiquement agrégative qui donne la vie

[1] Hammond, J. L. and Barbara: *The Rise of Modern Industry*, Preface, pp. viii–ix (London 1925, Methuen).

intellectuelle à des multitudes, qui leur fait une volonté, qui leur inspire
une manière d'être. Elles ont tout cela sans posséder de frontières
propres. Ces dons résultent d'une impulsion suprême qu'elles reçoivent
d'un domaine plus haut qu'elles-mêmes. Ici s'ouvrent ces régions
inexplorées où l'horizon élargi dans une mesure incomparable ne livre
plus seulement aux regards le territoire borné de tel royaume ou de telles
républiques, ni les fluctuations étroites des populations qui les habitent,
mais étale toutes les perspectives de la société qui les contient, avec
les grands rouages et les puissants mobiles de la civilisation qui les
anime. . . . Avant d'écrire l'histoire d'un pays distinct et de prétendre
expliquer les problèmes dont une pareille tâche est semée, il est indispensable de sonder, de scruter, de bien connaître les sources et la
nature de la société dont ce pays n'est qu'une fraction.'[1]

II. THE FIELD OF WHICH GREAT BRITAIN IS A PART

Our brief examination of English history, though its direct
result has been negative, has given us a clue. The chapters which
caught our eye in our glance backwards over the course of English
history were real chapters in some story or other, but that story
was the history of some society of which Great Britain was only a
part, and the experiences were experiences in which other nations
besides the English were participants. The 'intelligible field of
study', in fact, appears to be a society containing a number of
communities of the species represented by Great Britain—not only
Great Britain herself but France, Spain, Portugal, the Netherlands,
the Scandinavian countries, and so on—and the passage quoted
from Lord Acton indicates the historical relation between these
parts and this whole.

The forces in action are not national but proceed from wider
causes, which operate upon all the parts simultaneously and which
are not intelligible in their partial operation unless a comprehensive view is taken of their operation throughout the society.
At the same time, different parts are differently affected by an
identical general cause, because they each react, and each contribute, in a different way to the forces which that same cause sets in
motion. In this analysis, Lord Acton has employed the scientific
metaphors of his generation, while we, who are learning to be on
our guard against the 'Apathetic Fallacy', might find it more
natural to describe the experience of History in human terms. A
society, we should say, is confronted in the course of its life by a

[1] De Gobineau, J. A.: *Essai sur l'Inégalité des Races Humaines* (Paris 1853–5, Firmin-
Didot, 4 vols.), vol. iv, pp. 327–8 and 333. For an authoritative, as well as emphatic,
rejection of the idea that any mere national histories can be 'intelligible fields of study',
see Meyer, E.: 'Zur Theorie und Methodik der Geschichte' in the writer's collected
Kleine Schriften (Halle 1910, Niemeyer), p. 41; and his *Geschichte des Altertums*, vol. i (i),
4th edition (Stuttgart and Berlin 1921, Cotta), pp. 198–9.

succession of problems, which every member has to solve for himself as best as he may. The presentation of each problem is a challenge to undergo an ordeal, and through this series of ordeals the members of the society progressively differentiate themselves from one another.[1] On each occasion some fail, while others succeed in finding a solution; and, again, some of the solutions found are imperfect or commonplace or inimical to success in solving subsequent problems, while others are exact or original or fertile in possibilities of further progress. As ordeal follows ordeal, some members of the society at some moment fail altogether to adjust themselves, and fall by the way; others struggle on, strained or warped or stunted; others grow in wisdom and stature, and in making their own way discover new avenues for a general advance of the society to which they belong.[2] Throughout, it is impossible to grasp the significance of a particular member's behaviour under a particular ordeal without taking some account of the similar or dissimilar behaviour of his fellows and without viewing the successive ordeals as a series of events in the life of the whole society.

Thus English history does not become intelligible until we view it as the history of a wider society of which Great Britain is a member in company with other national states, each of which reacts, though each in its own way, to the common experiences of the society as a whole. Similarly, Venetian history has to be viewed as the history of a temporary sub-society including Milan, Genoa, Florence, and the other 'medieval' city-states in Northern Italy;[3] Athenian history as the history of a society including Thebes, Corinth, Sparta, and the other 'ancient' city-states in Greece. In each case we have to think in terms of the whole and not of the parts; to see the chapters of the story as events in the life of the society and not of some particular member; and to follow the fortunes of the members, not separately but concurrently, as variations on a single theme or as contributions to an orchestra which are significant as a harmony but have no meaning as so many separate series of notes. In so far as we succeed in studying history from this point of view, we find that order arises out of chaos in our minds and that we begin to understand what was not intelligible before.

This method of interpreting 'historical facts' will perhaps be

---

[1] For the nature and extent of the differentiation that arises out of successive responses to successive challenges, see further III. C (iii), vol. iii, below.

[2] This last kind of response is exemplified in the historic English response to the ordeal of adapting Transalpine political constitutions to suit the new Italian invention of administrative efficiency—an ordeal to which all the Transalpine countries of Western Christendom were subjected from the close of the fifteenth century onwards. The differentiating effect of this particular ordeal upon the constitutional histories of the several communities that were exposed to it—e.g. England, France, and the Iberian kingdoms—is very striking. (See further III. C (ii) (b), vol. iii, pp. 359–63, below.)

[3] See III. C (ii) (b), vol. iii, pp. 341–50, below.

made clearer by a concrete example, which may be taken from the history of the city-states of ancient Greece during the four centuries falling approximately between 725 and 325 B.C.

Soon after the beginning of that age, the society of which these numerous states were all members was confronted with the problem of the pressure of population upon the means of subsistence—means which the Hellenic peoples at that time were apparently obtaining almost entirely by raising a varied agricultural produce in their home territories for home consumption. When the crisis came, different states contended with it in different ways. Some, like Corinth and Chalcis,[1] disposed of their surplus population by seizing and colonizing agricultural territories overseas—in Sicily, Southern Italy, Thrace, and elsewhere—where the native population was either too sparse or too incompetent to resist invasion. The Greek colonies thus founded simply extended the geographical area of the Hellenic Society without altering its character. The agriculture which they practised and the institutions under which they lived were substantially reproductions of the conditions which they had left behind them in their home countries.

On the other hand, certain states sought solutions which entailed a variation in their way of life. Sparta,[2] for instance, satisfied the land-hunger of her citizens not by colonizing overseas territories outside the previous geographical limits of the Hellenic World[3] but by attacking and conquering her nearest Greek neighbours in Messene. The consequences were that Sparta only obtained her necessary additional lands at the cost of obstinate and repeated wars with neighbouring peoples of her own calibre; that, even when the conquest was completed, the retention of the conquered territories required a permanent military effort; and that this permanent strain bore upon Sparta herself and not upon some independent daughter-state overseas who would have been responsible for her own security. In order to meet this situation, Spartan statesmen were compelled to militarize Spartan life from top to bottom—which they did by reinvigorating and adapting certain primitive social institutions, common to a number of Greek communities, at a moment when, in Sparta as elsewhere, these institutions were on the point of disappearance.[4]

Athens reacted to the population problem in a different way again.[5] At first she neglected it—neither planting colonies over-

---

[1] For Chalcis, see further II. D (ii), vol. ii, pp. 42–35, below.
[2] For Sparta, see further III. A, vol. iii, pp. 50–79, below.
[3] The only Spartan overseas colony was Tarentum, and the foundation of Tarentum appears to have been an exceptional measure.
[4] See Nilsson, M. P.: 'Die Grundlagen des spartanischen Lebens', in Klio, xii (1912).
[5] For a fuller discussion of the part played by Athens in this crisis of Hellenic history see II. D (ii), vol. ii, pp. 39–42, and III. B, vol. iii, p. 122, below.

seas nor conquering the territory of her Greek neighbours—until the pressure threatened to find vent in a social revolution. At that point, when the solutions sought by other states were no longer open to her, she discovered an original solution of her own by specializing her agricultural production for export, starting manufactures also for export, and then developing her political institutions so as to give a fair share of political power to the new classes which had been called into being by these economic innovations. In other words, Athenian statesmen averted a social revolution by successfully carrying through an economic and a political revolution; and, discovering this solution for the common problem as far as it affected themselves, they incidentally opened up a new avenue of advance for the whole of the Hellenic Society. This was what Pericles meant when, in the crisis of his country's material fortunes, he claimed that she was 'the education of Hellas'.[1] In so far as she lived unto herself, as a city-state, Athens came to grief before that age of Hellenic history had reached its close. In so far as she lived for Hellas, Pericles' claim was justified by the event; for in the next age of Hellenic history, which began about 325 B.C., the new ideas and institutions which had been worked out by Athens in order to discover a particular solution for the general problem of the preceding age, were adopted by the rest of the Hellenic Society (which by that time had expanded far beyond the narrow domain of the Greek-speaking peoples) as their common social heritage. This phase of Hellenic history is commonly called 'the Hellenistic Age', but 'the Atticistic Age' is the proper name for it.

From this angle of vision, which takes not Athens or Sparta or Corinth or Chalcis but the whole of the Hellenic Society as its field, we are able to understand both the significance of the histories of these several communities during the period 725–325 B.C. and the significance of the transition from this period to that which followed. Questions are answered to which no answer could be found so long as we looked for an intelligible field of study in Chalcidian history or Corinthian history or Spartan history or Athenian history examined in isolation. From this point of view it was merely possible to observe that Chalcidian or Corinthian history was in some sense normal, whereas Spartan and Athenian history departed from the norm in different directions. It was not possible to explain the way in which this departure took place; and historians were reduced to suggesting that the Spartans and Athenians were already differentiated from other Greeks by the possession of special innate qualities at the dawn of Hellenic

[1] Thucydides, Book II, chap. 41.

history. This was equivalent to explaining Spartan and Athenian development by postulating that there had been no development at all,[1] and that these two particular Greek peoples were as peculiar at the beginning of the story as at the end of it. That hypothesis, however, is in contradiction with established historical facts. In regard to Sparta, for example, the excavations conducted by the British Archaeological School at Athens have produced striking evidence that, down to about the middle of the sixth century B.C., Spartan life was not abnormal in the ways which thereafter were to differentiate it so sharply from life in other Hellenic communities. After the middle of that century there was a revolutionary change which has to be explained, and an explanation can only be found through looking at Spartan history in this period as a special local response to an ordeal which confronted the whole of the Hellenic Society.[2] The special characteristics of Athens, which she communicated to the whole Hellenic World in the so-called 'Hellenistic' Age (in contrast to Sparta, whose peculiar turning proved to be a blind alley), were likewise acquired characteristics, the genesis of which can only be apprehended from a general standpoint. It is the same with the differentiation between Venice, Milan, Genoa, Florence, and the other city-states in Northern Italy in the so-called 'Middle Ages' of our Western history, and with the differentiation between France, Spain, the Netherlands, Great Britain, and the other national states of the West in more recent times. In order to understand the parts, we must first focus our attention upon the whole, because this whole is the field of study which is intelligible in itself.

III. THE EXTENSION OF OUR FIELD IN SPACE

It is of little practical use, however, to come to the conclusion that an intelligible field of study exists, of which the conventional fields are parts, so long as we have only defined this field negatively as the whole to which the parts belong. The parts which we know may not be intelligible in themselves, but at least they are palpable. Great Britain, for example, has an ascertained geographical situation and spatial extension; the English nation, as a nation, has an ascertained age. We cannot be content until we have defined the whole society of which Great Britain is a member in similarly positive and concrete terms. Let us explore its extension first in Space and then in Time.

[1] For this fatal weakness of all the 'racial' explanations of history, see further II. C (ii) (a) 1, below. Bagehot points out that neither race nor climate will explain the historic contrast between Sparta and Athens. (*Physics and Politics*, 10th edition (London 1894, Kegan Paul), pp. 84–6.)

[2] See Wade-Gery, H. T.: 'The Growth of the Dorian States' in *The Cambridge Ancient History*, vol. iii (Cambridge 1925, University Press).

In exploring the spatial extension of the society which includes Great Britain, it seems best to start by reviewing those chapters which caught our eye when we first glanced backwards over the course of English history. In our first examination of them, we found that they were events in the life of a society of which Great Britain and her sister countries were only parts, and we thus established the fact that the 'intelligible field of historical study' in this instance was something larger than any single national state. Let us now re-examine these same chapters with a view to discovering where the outer spatial limits of this 'intelligible field of study' lie. Is the society to which these chapters belong coextensive with Mankind? Or, as we extend our horizon from Great Britain outwards, do we reach, sooner or later, a line at which the intelligibility of history, expressed in terms of these chapters, is at its maximum? And beyond that line, if we do reach it, do we find that these chapters cease to correspond to the order of the facts which there confront us—in other words, do we find that there are other societies, existing simultaneously with ours and side by side with it, whose history falls into quite different chapters and is not intelligible in terms of ours?

If we start with our latest chapter—the establishment of the Industrial System—we find that the geographical extension of the 'intelligible field of study' which it presupposes is world-wide. In order to explain the Industrial Revolution in England, we have to take account of economic conditions not only in other West-European countries but in Tropical Africa, America, Russia, the Levant, India, and the Far East. When, however, we go back to the establishment of the Parliamentary System, and pass, in so doing, from the economic to the political plane, our horizon contracts. 'The law' which 'Bourbons and Stuarts obeyed' in France and England was not in force for Romanovs in Russia or for 'Osmanlis in Turkey or for Timurids in Hindustan or for Manchus in China or for the contemporary Shoguns in Japan. The political histories of these other countries under these other dynasties cannot be explained in the same terms. If we examine them, we find that the chapters into which they fall, and the 'intelligible fields of study' which those chapters presuppose, are quite different. The laws which can be observed at work in the political history of England and France do not apply to them, and, conversely, the laws which can be observed at work in their political history throw no direct light upon contemporary political phenomena in England or France. We lay our finger here upon a frontier which is a sharper and a deeper line of division than Monsieur Jullian's emotional frontiers of France—sharper and deeper even than our own physical frontiers of Great Britain. The operation of 'the law' which 'Bourbons and Stuarts obeyed' in France and England extended to the other countries of Western Europe and to the new communities planted overseas by West-European colonists. On the European Continent, however, the domain of this law stopped short at the western frontiers of Turkey and Russia. Eastward of that line, other political laws were being obeyed at the time with other consequences.[1]

Again, the expansion overseas in which England began to participate in the third quarter of the sixteenth century was confined not merely to Western Europe but almost entirely to West-European countries with sea-boards on the Atlantic and the North Sea. The overseas activities of Denmark and Sweden and Courland were feeble, while the states of Germany and Italy hardly participated at all. Even when we consider this expansion, as we must, in relation to a wider balance of power, we find that for several centuries this particular balance did not transcend the limits of Western and Central Europe. For example, no Islamic countries entered into it until the General War of 1792–1815, and no Far Eastern countries until the conclusion of the Anglo-Japanese Alliance a dozen years before the outbreak of the General War of 1914–18.

As for the Reformation, while it is impossible to understand it without extending our horizon from England and Scotland to the whole of Western Christendom, this understanding would be confused and not clarified if we attempted to extend the horizon still further. In studying the Reformation, we may ignore the history of the Orthodox Church since the schism of the eleventh century after Christ, and the history of the Monophysite and Nestorian Churches since the schisms of the fifth century after Christ. Conversely, no light is thrown upon the histories of these churches in the sixteenth century after Christ by the phenomena of the West-Christian Reformation of that time.

The Renaissance, again, was produced by a bedding-out of North-Italian ideas and institutions not merely in England but in the other Transalpine countries of Western Europe and in their new colonies overseas; but those were the limits of the area brought under this form of Italian cultivation. At the very time when Englishmen, Frenchmen, Spaniards, Germans, and Poles were falling

---

[1] Compare the following passage in E. A. Freeman's lecture on 'The Unity of History' which is published in his *Comparative Politics* (London 1873 Macmillan): 'European history forms one whole in the strictest sense, but between European and Asiatic history the connexion is only occasional and incidental. The fortunes of the Roman Empire had no effect on the internal revolutions of the Saracenic Caliphate, still less effect had they on the momentary dominion of the House of Jenghiz or on the Mogul Empire in India.' (*Op. cit.*, p. 333.)

under the spell of Italian culture, the Greeks were declaring 'the turban of the Prophet' preferable to the 'tiara of the Pope'[1] and were becoming converted in greater numbers to Islam than to Humanism. Nor did the spell of Italian culture produce any appreciable effect upon the Turks, though they were in close and continuous contact with the Venetians and Genoese in the activities of trade, diplomacy, and war.[2] The only prominent trace of Italian cultural influence upon Turkish life is to be found in the architecture of certain eighteenth-century mosques in Constantinople. In Muslim India, the Italian influence (through a Portuguese medium) upon the art and architecture of the Mughal Court, during and after the reign of Akbar, was exotic and transitory. As for the Hindus or the peoples of the Far East, they were probably unaware, at the time, that Western Europe was experiencing a renaissance and *a fortiori* unaware of the Italian source from which the stimulus came.

The establishment of the Feudal System, again, as it came about in England, was a specifically West-European development. It is true that there were feudal phenomena in the contemporary Byzantine and Islamic worlds, but it is not proven that these phenomena were derived from the same origins as those in the West, and many superficial resemblances are found on closer inspection to be false analogies. The feudal systems of Western Europe, of the Byzantine Empire, and of Islamic Egypt, Turkey, and Hindustan, not to speak of feudalism in Japan, have to be studied as distinct and separate institutions.

Finally, the conversion of the English to Western Christianity since the last years of the sixth century has admitted us to membership in one society at the cost of excluding us from the possibility of membership in others. Down to the Synod of Whitby in A.D. 664, the English were potential converts to the 'Far Western' Christianity of the 'Celtic Fringe';[3] and had Augustine's mission eventually proved a failure the English might have joined the Welsh and Irish in founding a new Christian church out of communion with Rome—as veritable an *alter orbis* as the world of the Nestorians on the Far Eastern fringe of Christendom.[4] Later on, when the Muslim Arabs appeared on the Atlantic seaboard, these 'Far Western' Christians of the British Isles might have lost touch as completely as the Christians of Abyssinia or Central Asia with their co-religionists on the European Continent. They might even conceivably have become converts to Islam, as so many

---

[1] Gibbon, Edward: *The History of the Decline and Fall of the Roman Empire*, chapter lxviii.   [2] Italian was actually the official language of the Ottoman navy.
[3] See further II. D (vii), vol. ii, pp. 334–6, below.
[4] See further II. D (vii), vol. ii, pp. 369–84, below.

Monophysites and Nestorians actually did when the Middle East came under Arab rule. These suggested alternatives may be dismissed as fantastic. Possibly they are not so fantastic as they appear at first sight.[1] At any rate, the contemplation of them serves to remind us that while the conversion of A.D. 597 has made us one with Western Christendom it has not made us one with all Mankind, but has simultaneously drawn a sharp line of division between ourselves as Western Christians and the members of other religious communions (not only the now extinct Far Western Christians but the Orthodox Christians,[2] Monophysites, Nestorians, Muslims, Buddhists, and so on)—a line by which we were not circumscribed in the days of our indeterminate paganism, when we were potential converts to any would-be 'universal church' which might choose to compete for our allegiance.

This second review of our chapters of history has given us the means for taking spatial cross-sections, at several different dates, of that society which includes Great Britain and which is the 'intelligible field of historical study' as far as Great Britain is concerned. In taking these cross-sections we shall have to distinguish between certain different planes of social life—the economic, the political, and the cultural[3]—because it is already evident, from the foregoing analysis, that the spatial extension of this society differs perceptibly according to the plane on which we focus our attention. For example, if we take our first cross-section at the present day, we find that on the economic plane at this moment the society which includes Great Britain is undoubtedly coextensive with the whole habitable and navigable surface of the planet. There is hardly any habitable portion of the Earth's surface with which Great Britain herself does not at present exchange goods and services.[4] On the political plane, again, the world-wide character of this society at the present day is almost equally apparent. The United Kingdom is now linked with 60 out of 66 other states in the World (including the self-governing Dominions of the British Crown and the Kingdom of Egypt) by the Pact of Paris for the Renunciation of War as

[1] See Gibbon's reflections upon what might have happened in Western Europe if the Arabs had won the Battle of Tours in A.D. 732 (*The History of the Decline and Fall of the Roman Empire*, chapter lii). These speculations are taken up again in II. D (vii), Annex IV, vol. ii, pp. 427–33, below.

[2] Since the Protestant Reformation in the West, there have been overtures on at least two occasions—once in the early seventeeth century, when the Oecumenical Patriarchate at Constantinople was occupied by Cyril Loukaris (A.D. 1621–37), and again in our own day—for a re-establishment of communion between the Anglican fragment of the Western Church and Orthodox Christendom.

[3] For an examination of this refraction of social life into three distinct 'planes', see Parts VIII and IX, below, as well as Part II. A, vol. i, p. 187, Part III. C (i) (a), vol. iii, pp. 151 3, and V. C (i) (c) 3, vol. v, pp. 196–203.

[4] The World Economic Conference that met in London on the 12th June, 1933, was attended by representatives of no less than sixty-six states—the sole absentee being Panama.

an instrument of National Policy,[1] and with 56 of these by the further and more positive bond of common membership in a formal association of states, the League of Nations, which has a constitution, a budget, and a regular programme of activities. Moreover, of the nine states which have so far remained non-members of the League (the U.S., the U.S.S.R., Egypt, Afghanistan, the Najd-Hijaz, the Yaman, Iceland, Danzig, and Ecuador)[1] and the two ex-members which have withdrawn (Brazil and Costa Rica),[2] all except the three which lie in Latin America are of intimate concern to Great Britain politically, apart from the special importance of at least three of them in the international relations of Great Britain on the economic plane. A more detailed political survey of the World from a British standpoint would probably show that Latin America and Eastern Europe were the only regions in which Great Britain's political interests[3] could conceivably be written off as negligible quantities, and even that would only be by contrast with her absorbing political interests elsewhere. Negatively, Latin America, which is the field of the Monroe Doctrine, and Eastern Europe, which is the crux of the 'post-war' problem of European security, both affect Great Britain, even on the political plane, profoundly.

When, however, we pass to the cultural plane, the present geographical extension of the society to which Great Britain belongs appears to be very much smaller. Substantially, it is confined to the countries occupied by Catholic and Protestant peoples in Western Europe and America and the South Seas; and when we examine the culture of even these peoples more closely we detect the influence of cultural elements of other origin, such as Russian literature, Far Eastern painting, and Indian religion. In the Catholic and Protestant countries, however, these influences, though magnified by the genius of some of the minds by which they have been conveyed, are really exotic and superficial. In spite of them, and in spite of the much stronger cultural influences of the modern West upon living non-Western societies, the members of such societies—for example, the Orthodox and other Oriental Christians, the Muslims, the Hindus, and the peoples of the Far East—are still living, with few exceptions, beyond the pale of that cultural world to which England and Scotland belong.

[1] These are the figures as they stood in the June of the year 1933. The states which were still not parties to the Pact at that date were Argentina, Bolivia, Brazil, Salvador, Uruguay, Yaman.

[2] This is the list as it stood in the June of the year 1933. At this date 57 out of 68 states in the World were League members. Out of these 57, however, 2—namely Japan and Mexico—had given notice of intention to withdraw.

[3] The *economic* interests of Great Britain in Latin America were, of course, enormous at this time; and, beyond a point, it is hardly possible to divorce economic and political interests from one another.

As we take further cross-sections at earlier dates, we find that, on all three planes, the geographical limits of the society which we are examining contract progressively. In a cross-section taken about A.D. 1675, while the contraction is not perhaps very great on the economic plane (at least if we take into account the mere extension of international trade and ignore its matter and volume), the boundaries on the political plane shrink until in Europe they coincide approximately with those on the cultural plane at the present day, while overseas they only include the fringes of America. In a cross-section taken about A.D. 1475, the overseas portions of the area disappear on all three planes alike, and even on the economic plane the boundaries contract until they too coincide approximately with those on the cultural plane—now confined to Western and Central Europe—except for a fast dissolving chain of commercial outposts round the eastern shores of the Mediterranean. In this cross-section, the boundaries of the society on all three planes are more or less coincident with those of the area in which the ecclesiastical primacy of the Pope was at that time effectively asserted. In a primitive cross-section, taken about A.D. 775, the boundaries shrink still further on all three planes, while becoming still more closely coincident as between one plane and another. At this date, the area of our society is almost restricted to what were then the dominions of Charlemagne on the West-European Continent and to the English 'successor-states' of the Roman Empire in Britain. It consists substantially of what the Romans had known as Gaul, with no foothold yet south-west of the Pyrenees and with only a narrow foothold north-east of the Rhine, but with lateral extensions into the northern parts of Italy beyond the Alps and into the southern parts of Britain beyond the Channel.[1] These limits are thrown into relief by the presence of recognizably alien societies on the further side of them. The Iberian Peninsula (apart from one enclave in Asturia) at this date belongs to the domain of a Muslim Arab Caliphate, Northern and North-Eastern Europe is in the hands of unconverted barbarians, the north-western fringes of the British Isles are held by 'Far Western' Christians who are unwilling to accept the pretensions of the Papacy, and South-Eastern Italy is under the ascendency of the Byzantines.

A closer examination of this earliest cross-section enables us to give the cradle of our society a local name. As the ecclesiastical

---

[1] The late Sir J. W. Headlam-Morley defines the geographical nucleus of the Western World as the triangle Paris–Rome–Barcelona, and the furthest limits of its [eastward] expansion as Budapest–Prague–Cracow–Warsaw–Riga–Reval ("The Cultural Unity of Western Europe', in *The New Past*, ed. by Carter, E. H. (Oxford 1925, Blackwell), pp. 84–5). 'All outside [the] original homeland is foreign conquest; and other races, though apparently assimilated, still remain alien.' (Op. cit., p. 87.)

domain of the Pope it may be called Western Christendom;[1] as the political domain of Charlemagne, whose home territory was the Frankish State of Austrasia, it may be called the World of the Franks—a name which survives in the Oriental Christian word 'Frangià' and in the Muslim word 'Feringhistan'.[2]

This 'Frankish' name is not altogether apt, for even in Charlemagne's time, when the geographical extension of our society was smaller than it has ever been since, while Charlemagne's dominions covered a larger portion of Western Europe than has ever subsequently been united under a single government, the Kingdom of the Franks and the area of our society did not exactly coincide. The English, for example, had become members of the society by that time without ever having come under Frankish rule, and there were other prominent members, like the Lombards, over whom the Frankish dominion was only transitory. Moreover, the name has been obsolete among the 'Franks' themselves since the close of the so-called 'Middle Ages'. At the same time, this name, as applied to us collectively by members of other societies, is the only common name which exists to-day for the whole of our society, and the fact that we have ceased to apply any common name to ourselves is historically significant. It means that we are no longer conscious of the presence in the World of other societies of equal standing; and that we now regard our society as being identical with 'civilized' Mankind and the peoples outside its pale as being mere 'Natives' of territories which they inhabit on sufferance, but which are morally as well as practically at our disposal, by the higher right of our assumed monopoly of civilization, whenever we choose to take possession.[3] Conversely, we regard the internal divisions of our society—the national parts into which this society has come to be articulated—as the grand divisions of Mankind, and classify the members of the Human Race as Frenchmen, Englishmen, Germans, and so on, without remembering that these are merely subdivisions of a single group within the human family.

It is no accident that our common name for ourselves became extinct, and our separate names for our various national allegiances became prominent, towards the beginning of the so-called 'modern' period of our history, when our society began to establish what

---

[1] Not, of course, 'Christendom' without qualification, since the Christians of the Far West, the Near East, and the Middle East had at least an equal claim to the name, though Western Christendom (like these other Christendoms) did in practice call itself and think of itself as Christendom *par excellence* until the close of the so-called 'Middle Ages', when it ceased to have any common name for itself at all.

[2] 'All the Franks appear to have an uniform character to the Eastern nations.'— Hume, David: *Of National Characters.* Compare La Rue Franque, which was the principal commercial street in Smyrna before the great fire of 1922; Firank Zahmeti, the Turkish name for syphilis; and the term *lingua franca.*

[3] What is the converse of 'Natives'? 'Lords of Creation'? For the connotation of the word 'Natives', see further I. C (iii) (*b*), below.

seemed until lately to be a secure and permanent ascendency over the other living societies of the same class.[1] The historical fact, however, which is implicit in this oblivion of our common name is chiefly a feature of our own microcosm. It is not a fact which has an objective existence in the field of study which we are seeking to explore. The other societies have not ceased to exist simply because we have ceased to be aware of their existence; and we can hardly advance further in our search for an 'intelligible field of study' without reviving or inventing some name to denote our society as a whole and to distinguish it from other representatives of the species. Since the word 'Franks' has always been inaccurate and has now become exotic, it seems preferable to revive the name 'Western Christendom'. The objection to this is that, since the Reformation, religious allegiance has not only ceased to be the principal expression of the unity of our society, but has actually become one of the principal factors in its internal differentiation. It is therefore perhaps more accurate, as well as more concise, to omit the word 'Christendom' and to speak simply of 'the West' or 'the Western Society' or 'the Western World'—a geographical title which combines the logical merits of being without prejudice and without ambiguity with the practical merit of being equally applicable to a cross-section taken in Charlemagne's time and to a cross-section taken to-day, when this society has spread westward across the Atlantic Ocean and the American Continent until it now confronts the Far Eastern World, on the opposite shores of the Pacific, from the Philippines and Australia.

As soon as we bring our mental image of our own society into focus by finding a name for it, the images and the names of its counterparts in the contemporary world come into focus side by side with it, especially if we keep our attention fixed upon the cultural plane. On this plane, we can distinguish unmistakably the presence, in the world of to-day, of at least four other living societies of the same species as ours:

first, an 'Orthodox Christian' or Byzantine Society—whichever title we prefer[2]—in South-Eastern Europe and Russia[3];

[1] From the time of the Renaissance and the Reformation, 'expansion abroad and dissolution at home' became the key-notes of our Western history. (Headlam-Morley, op. cit., p. 86.)

[2] The title 'Orthodox Christian' is not inappropriate, since in this society (unlike our Western Society) religious allegiance has remained the principal expression of social unity. The alternative title 'Byzantine' has the merits of a geographical term. The geographical title which it would be most natural for a Western observer of the Byzantine World to employ, from his standpoint, is 'Near Eastern'. This, however, is inconvenient, because, in the modern Near East, the Byzantine Society is not the only inhabitant. An Islamic Society is also established there; and for this reason the title 'Near Eastern' is inconveniently ambiguous.

[3] Notwithstanding the Communist régime which has been attempting, since A.D. 1917, to transform the complexion of society in Russia out of all recognition.

second, an 'Islamic' Society[1] with its focus in the arid zone
which stretches diagonally across North Africa and the Middle
East from the Atlantic to the outer face of the Great Wall of
China;

third, a 'Hindu' Society[2] in the tropical sub-continent of India,
south-east of the arid zone;

fourth, a 'Far Eastern' Society in the sub-tropical and temperate
regions between the arid zone and the Pacific.

On a closer inspection, we can also discern two sets of what
appear to be fossilized relics of similar societies now extinct,
namely:

one set including the Monophysite Christians of Armenia,
Mesopotamia, Egypt, and Abyssinia and the Nestorian
Christians of Kurdistan and Malabar,[3] as well as the Jews and
the Parsees;

a second set including the Lamaistic Mahayanian Buddhists of
Tibet and Mongolia and the Hinayanian Buddhists of Ceylon,
Burma, and Siam, as well as the Jains in India.

It is interesting to notice that, when we turn back to the cross-
section at A.D. 775, we find that the number and the identity of the
societies on the world-map are nearly the same as at the present
time. Substantially, the world-map of societies of this species has
remained constant since the first emergence of our Western
Society. In the struggle for existence, the West has driven its
contemporaries to the wall and has entangled them in the meshes of
its economic and political ascendancy, but it has not yet disarmed
them of their distinctive cultures.[4] Hard pressed though they are,
they can still call their souls their own, and this means that the
mental strife has not yet reached a decision.[5] In the gladiatorial
arena, the Secutor, even when the Retiarius's net was about his

---

[1] This title is not inappropriate, for the same reason that the title 'Orthodox Christian'
is not inappropriate for the Byzantine Society; and there is no simple geographical label
ready to hand.

[2] Not 'Indian', since this society extends beyond the geographical boundaries of
Continental India—e.g. into the Indonesian Archipelago (Bali)—while in Continental
India it is not the only inhabitant, the Islamic Society being established there also, as in
the Near East.

[3] The Nestorian community in Malabar, after half a century of union with the Roman
Church, transferred its allegiance to the Monophysite Patriarch of Antioch in the
third quarter of the seventeenth century after Christ.

[4] 'In the valley of the Rhine, throughout the whole of France and the Latin countries,
one can never be far away from the consciousness of the Roman period, which is the
matrix from which all later stages have sprung. In Cologne or Trèves, that which is of
the tenth or eleventh century already begins to wear the air of modernity; in Danzig or in
Cracow, anything before the fourteenth century is remote antiquity. And, as you go
still farther east, new, strange and foreign elements intrude themselves upon you—the
cupolas and minarets of Russia and the Moslem—but nowhere do we find anything
comparable to the succession of the Gothic and the Renaissance. Here we find that our
familiar formulas no longer serve us.' (Headlam-Morley, in op. cit., p. 83.)

[5] This phenomenon of 'collisions' between societies of this species ('Contact in Space')
is examined in Part IX, below.

shoulders, had no cause to despair so long as he had not let the sword fall from his hand.[1]

This reflection concludes our inquiry into the geographical situation and spatial extension of that 'intelligible field of historical study' which first attracted our attention as the unknown whole of which English history proved to be a part. We have succeeded in giving this 'intelligible field of study' a name—'the Western Society'—and we have reached the positive conclusion that while even the original nucleus of this Western Society had a much wider geographical extension than any one of the nations into which it has become articulated, and while this extension has increased as the Western Society has grown older, the West has never become coextensive with the World on all planes of social life, and other societies of the same species have never ceased to exist in the World side by side with it.[2]

This conclusion on matters of historical fact carries with it a corollary regarding methods of historical study. It is evident that we must draw a sharp distinction between relations of two kinds: those between communities within the same society and those of different societies with one another. In the technical language of contemporary Western historians, who have perhaps over-emphasized the individuality of national communities and unduly ignored the individuality of the societies of which the nations are parts, these two kinds of relation are at present confounded under the ambiguous title 'international'; and hitherto much more attention has been paid to international relations in the literal sense of the term than to the other kind. For the advancement of historical knowledge, it seems desirable that our historians should distinguish the parochial relations between states within societies from the oecumenical relations between the societies themselves, and should devote a larger share of their energy and acumen to the study of these.

IV. THE EXTENSION OF OUR FIELD IN TIME

Having explored the extension of our Western Society in Space, we have next to examine its extension in Time. We are at once con-

---

[1] The representatives of the non-Western societies might find relief for their feelings in addressing us in the language in which Job replies to his comforters:

'No doubt but ye are the people, and wisdom shall die with you.

'But I have understanding as well as you; I am not inferior to you: yea who knoweth not such things as these?' (Job xii. 2–3.)

[2] 'We cannot write a history of Western Europe and of China in the same work. We can indeed write two separate histories and bind them in one volume, and include in it tracts on the history of India and that of the Bantu races, of the South American Indians and the Dyaks of New Guinea; but none the less we shall have no history here in any reasonable sense which we may give to the word, because throughout the greater part of their existence these different tribes and peoples lived their own life, completely independent of one another.' (Headlam-Morley in op. cit., p. 98.)

fronted with the difficulty that we cannot see into the future—a limitation which greatly restricts the amount of light that the contemporary historical study of this Western Society can throw upon the nature of the species to which the Western Society belongs. *Ex hypothesi*, we cannot survey the whole life of a society of which we ourselves are members, and which therefore will still be living its life as long as we remain alive to observe it. Western history will only become visible at full length and in true perspective after the Western Society has become extinct; and this spectacle—if it is ever to be beheld by human eyes—is necessarily reserved for future historians living in a different social environment from ours and taking their historical observations from a different angle of vision. For our part, we must inevitably be content to explore the time extension of the Western Society in the direction of its origins only, and must resign ourselves to ignorance of its latter end.[1]

Let us try to analyse the geographical nucleus which was revealed by our earliest spatial cross-section, taken about A.D. 775; and let us begin by examining the analysis of this nucleus which our Western predecessors of that age made for themselves.

When Charlemagne's dominions were partitioned between his three grandsons by the Treaty of Verdun in A.D. 843, Lothaire as the eldest established his claim to possess his grandfather's two capitals of Aachen and Rome; and, in order that these might be connected by a continuous belt of territory, Lothaire was assigned a portion which straggled across the face of Western Europe from the mouths of the Tiber and the Po to the mouth of the Rhine, ignoring the barrier of the Alps and uniting Northern Italy under a single sovereignty with the Rhineland and the Netherlands. Lothaire's portion is commonly regarded as one of the curiosities of historical geography, chiefly because it finds no place on the political map of modern Europe as it is now articulated into national states. Nevertheless, the three Carolingian brothers were right in believing that Lothaire's portion was a zone of peculiar importance in our Western World. If we produce this zone northwestwards (ignoring the Channel as the treaty of A.D. 843 ignored the Alps) by adding to Lothaire's continental dominions the domain in Britain over which King Ecgberht of Wessex had established his hegemony before his death in A.D. 839, we shall find that we have plotted out the locus of a line which twice over has constituted one of the structural axes in the human geography of Western Europe.

If we go back to our spatial cross-section of the Western Society

[1] On this point see further Part V. C (ii) (*b*), vol. vi, p. 313, as well as Part XII, below.

at A.D. 775, and then watch it grow until it becomes the cross-section of the present day, we observe that a straight line running roughly south-east and north-west and drawn from Rome to the Roman Wall is, so to speak, the transverse axis of our geometrical figure. Its mid-point falls near Metz in Lorraine (Lotharingia)—once the capital of the Austrasian State which was the nucleus of Charlemagne's Empire, and now the principal fortress on the frontier between France and Germany. If, through Metz, we proceed to draw another line, at right angles to the first and therefore running roughly south-west and north-east, we obtain the main axis along which the Western Society has increased its geographical extension overland in both directions. South-westwards, this main axis was carried across the Pyrenees by Charlemagne himself in A.D. 778, extended to the mouth of the Guadalquivir by the Castilian conquests in the thirteenth century after Christ, and eventually produced across the Southern Atlantic into what is now Latin America. North-eastwards the same line was carried forward from the Rhine bridge-heads to the Elbe by Charlemagne between A.D. 772 and 804; to the Baltic, the Vistula, and the Carpathians within two centuries of Charlemagne's death, when Scandinavia, Poland, and Hungary were admitted to membership in Western Christendom; and to the Pacific at the close of the seventeenth century, when the Muscovite Empire, which had expanded to the Pacific rather more than half a century earlier, was received into the Western Society as a proselyte.

The West has also increased its extension by producing first one end of the transverse axis and then the other across the sea. In 'the Middle Ages', the North Italian arm was produced first into Southern Italy and Sicily and then over the Mediterranean into its eastern hinterlands, in the movement of political and economic expansion which is conveniently though inadequately described as 'the Crusades'.[1] In its day, this south-eastward expansion went very far. The thrust, at its strongest, carried Venetian trade to India across the Isthmus of Suez and the Venetian traveller Marco Polo to Peking across the Eurasian Steppe in the hinterland of the Black Sea. Ultimately, the movement was a failure, and nearly all the ground gained in four centuries had been lost by A.D. 1475.[2] The production of the transverse axis from its north-western extremity in England, which followed in the succeeding age of Western history, has achieved results which are to all appearance of a more enduring character. It has filled North America with an English-speaking population from the Rio Grande to the Arctic

---

[1] For the character of this movement, see further V. C (i) (c) 3, vol. v, pp. 242-4, as well as Parts IX and X, below.

[2] For the nature of the failure, see further Parts IX and X, below.

Circle, and, radiating from the North Atlantic into all the other seas of the World, it has planted new communities of English origin and Western culture round the southern rim of the Pacific to share the possession of that ocean with the peoples of India and the Far East. This was the bearing of the line embedded in Lotharingia upon the subsequent geographical expansion of the Western Society; but Lothaire and his brothers were no more able to look into the future than we are; and, if they divined that this line was important, that was because they in their generation were living under the shadow of a past in which the geographical significance of the line had also been great, though in relation to a different geometrical figure.

Both Lothaire and his grandfather ruled from Aachen to Rome under the title of Roman Emperor; the Imperial title was also occasionally assumed by the English Kings of Wessex, who in the Carolingian Age exercised a miniature hegemony of their own in the *alter orbis* of Britain; and the line stretching from Rome across the Alps to Aachen and from Aachen across the Channel to the Roman Wall had once been one of the principal bulwarks of the then extinct Roman Empire. By running a line of communications north-westwards from Rome across the Alps, establishing a military frontier along the left bank of the Rhine, and covering the left flank of that frontier by the annexation of Southern Britain, the Romans had cut off the western extremity of Transalpine Continental Europe and annexed it to an empire which, except in this quarter, was substantially confined to the periphery of the Mediterranean Basin. Thus the line embedded in Lotharingia entered into the geographical structure of the Roman Empire before Lothaire's time as well as into that of the Western World after it; but the geometrical figures of the Roman Empire and the Western World were not the same, and the function of this particular line in their respective geographical structures was utterly different. In the Roman Empire it was the latest outer frontier of a society, at the limit where its expansion in one direction had come to an end; in the Western World it has been the original base-line from which a society has expanded in all directions. During the deep sleep of the interregnum (*circa* A.D. 375–675) which intervened between the break-up of the Roman Empire and the gradual emergence of our Western World out of the chaos, a rib was taken from the side of the older society and was fashioned into the backbone of a new creature of the same species.

This geographical analysis has been pursued at some length because it offers us a clue for following the Time-extension of our Western Society further back towards its ultimate origins. It indicates two things: first, that in tracing the life of the Western Society back behind our earliest spatial cross-section at A.D. 775, we begin to find it presented to us in terms of something other than itself—in terms of the Roman Empire and of the society to which the Roman Empire belonged—and, second, that any elements which we can trace back from Western history into the history of that other society may have quite different functions and different degrees of importance in these two different associations.

Lothaire's portion became the base-line of the Western World because 'the Church', pushing up towards the Roman frontier from the rear, here encountered 'the Barbarians' pressing down upon the frontier from the 'no-man's-land' outside, and eventually here gave birth to a new society. Accordingly, the historian of the Western Society, in tracing its roots down into the past from this point, will concentrate his attention at lower levels (that is to say, at earlier dates) upon the histories of 'the Church' on the one hand and of 'the Barbarians' on the other; and he will find it possible to follow both these histories downwards (that is to say, backwards in time) as far as the economic and social and political revolutions of the last two centuries B.C. into which 'the Graeco-Roman World' was thrown by the vast shock of the Hannibalic War. Why did Rome stretch out a long arm towards the north-west and gather into her Empire the western corner of Transalpine Europe? Because she was drawn in that direction by her life-and-death struggle with Carthage. Why, having once crossed the Alps, did she stop at the Rhine and not push on to the better physical frontier of the Baltic, the Vistula, and the Dniestr? Because in the Augustan Age her vitality gave out after two centuries of exhausting wars and revolutions. Why did 'the Barbarians' ultimately break through? Because, when a frontier between a more highly and a less highly civilized society ceases to advance at the more backward society's expense, the balance does not settle down into a stable equilibrium but inclines, with the passage of time, in the more backward society's favour.[1] Why, when 'the Barbarians' broke through the Roman frontier, did they encounter 'the Church' on the other side? Materially, because the economic and social revolutions following the Hannibalic War had brought multitudes of slaves from the Oriental World to work in the devastated areas of the West, and this forced migration of Oriental labour had been followed by the peaceful propagation of Oriental religions through 'the Graeco-Roman World'.[2] Spiritually, because these religions, with their promise of an 'other-worldly' personal salvation, found

[1] For an examination of this phenomenon see Part VIII, below.
[2] For this, see further II. D (vi), vol. ii, pp. 213–6, below.

fallow fields to cultivate in the devastated souls of a 'dominant minority' which had failed, in this world, to save the fortunes of the 'Graeco-Roman' Society.[1]

At this point the student of Western history will be inclined to stop. He will have traced the roots of his Western Society down as far as it seems possible to distinguish them. It is noticeable, however, that although by the time he reaches this level he is forced to think almost entirely in 'Graeco-Roman' and not in Western terms, the elements in 'Graeco-Roman' history which are engaging his attention are not those which would appear to be of capital importance to a historian who was studying 'Graeco-Roman' or 'Hellenic'[2] history in the same age for its own sake.

To the student of Hellenic history, both the Christians and the Barbarians would present themselves as creatures of an alien underworld—the 'internal' and the 'external' proletariat,[3] as he might call them, of the Hellenic Society in its last phase.[4] He would point out that the great masters of Hellenic culture, down to and including Marcus Aurelius, almost ignore their existence, and that in fact they did not begin to come into existence until after the Hannibalic War. He would diagnose both the Christian Church and the Barbarian war-bands as morbid affections which only appeared in the body of the Hellenic Society after its physique

---

[1] For this spiritual movement, see further V. C (i) (c) 2, vol. v, pp. 80–2, below.

[2] 'Hellenic' seems a better title than 'Graeco-Roman' for this society. The name is not only shorter and less clumsy but also really more accurate, since this society was originally created by the ancient Greeks or 'Hellenes' and the Romans only entered into the 'Hellenic' inheritance at a late date, when the Hellenic Civilization was already in decline. Accordingly, the term 'Hellenic' will be used in this sense in this Study hereafter. The term does, of course, beg the question—which the hyphenated compound 'Graeco-Roman' leaves open—of the relative importance of the roles which were played in the history of this civilization by the Romans and the Greeks respectively.

[3] The word 'proletariat' is used here and hereafter in this Study to mean any social element or group which in some way is 'in' but not 'of' any given society at any given stage of such society's history. That is, it is used in the sense of the Latin word *proletarius* from which it is derived. In Roman legal terminology, *proletarii* were citizens who had no entry against their names in the census except their progeny (*proles*). The following definition is given in the *Compendiosa Doctrina per Litteras* of Nonius Marcellinus: 'Proletarii dicti sunt plebeii qui nihil rei publicae exhibeant sed tantum prolem sufficiant.' (Quoted by Bruns, C.C., in *Fontes Iuris Romani Antiqui*, ed. 7 (Tübingen 1909, Mohr), Pars Posterior, p. 65.) To say that 'proletarians' contribute nothing to the community but their progeny is a euphemism for saying that the community gives them no remuneration for any other contributions that they may make (whether voluntarily or under compulsion) to the common weal. In other words, a 'proletariat' is an element or group in a community which has no 'stake' in that community beyond the fact of its physical existence. It is in this broad sense that the word 'proletariat' is used throughout this Study, and not in the specialized sense of an urban labouring population which employs the modern Western economic technique called 'Industrialism' and is employed under the modern Western economic régime called 'Capitalism'. This restricted usage of the word, which is current to-day, was given this currency by Karl Marx, as one of the technical terms which he coined in order to convey the results of his study of history. More than one of these Marxian coinages have become current even among people who reject the Marxian dogmas.

[4] For an examination of the phenomena of 'the internal proletariat' and 'the external proletariat', see the present Part, Division C (i) (a), pp. 53–62, below, and also Parts IV, V, VI, VII, and VIII, *passim*, especially V. C (i) (c) 2 and 3, vol. v, pp. 58–337.

had been permanently undermined and its character enfeebled by that great disaster; but the Hannibalic War, he would add, set a term to the creative period of Hellenic history. The student of Hellenic history who wishes 'to add to the knowledge of his own subject' should concentrate his attention on what went before. From the Hannibalic War onwards, it is his melancholy task to trace how the healthy native tissues of the stricken society were gradually eaten away by cancerous growths until death at last put an end to the victim's disorders. He is not called upon to study the physiology and the growth of these cancers themselves. It is sufficient for him to record the destructive results of their ravages. 'I have described the triumph of Barbarism and Religion', Gibbon writes as he brings his history to a close.[1]

Thus a student of Hellenic history and a student of Western history may both be studying the last phase of Hellenic history and yet their fields of study may show very little common ground. The reason is that they are concerned respectively with two histories which overlap in time but which are nevertheless distinct from one another. The student of Hellenic history, who is following up the social stratum that here still occupies the surface towards a point where this particular stratum disintegrates and disappears, is not primarily interested in the social stratum beneath it, which only appears on the surface beyond the point at which the object of his own study comes to an end. Conversely, the student of Western history, who is tracing this second stratum backwards from those sections of it which lie exposed on the surface to the section which is buried underground, regards the overlying stratum of the Hellenic Society, which can teach him little about the subsequent history of the Western Society, as so much useless rock, which has to be blasted away if he is to succeed in laying bare the subterranean section of the Western stratum which he is attempting to trace back to its starting-point.

This investigation enables us to draw a positive conclusion regarding the backward extension of our Western Society in Time. Just as we found that the spatial extension of this 'intelligible field', while wider than that of any single nation belonging to it, was narrower, even in its most extensive spatial cross-section, than the entire surface of the Earth and than the whole living generation of Mankind, so we now find that its backward extension in Time, while somewhat longer than that of any single nation belonging to it, is not so long, even when we take into account the length of its roots underground, as the span of Time during which the species of which it is a representative has been in existence. This conclusion

---

[1] *The History of the Decline and Fall of the Roman Empire*, chapter lxxi.

follows from the fact that, in the process of tracing the history of our Western Society backward towards its origins, we strike upon the last phase of another society of the same kind, the origins of which evidently lie considerably further back in the past.

This conclusion regarding the age and origins of the Western Society carries with it a corollary regarding 'the continuity of history'.

'The continuity of history' is the most attractive of all the conceptions which have been framed on the analogy of the 'classical' Western Physical Science by Western historians; yet, in view of its suspect origin, we must harden our hearts and criticize it in the light of the foregoing investigation. What, precisely, did the inventors of the term mean to imply? If they simply meant that 'the continuity of history' was a particular instance of the continuity of Life, then their formula is an unimpeachable but not very illuminating truism. Between all the manifestations of Life some kind of continuity is certainly discernible—between the amoeba and the vertebrate, between the ape and the human being, between parents and offspring in a family—but this continuity is so abstract that the apprehension of it only brings us to the threshold of understanding what Life is. We hardly begin to learn anything about the nature of Life until we succeed in distinguishing the points of relative discontinuity in the ever-rolling stream—the bends which intervene between the straight reaches, the rapids which isolate from one another the quiet navigable stretches, the crests and troughs of the waves which arise when the waters are troubled, the seracs and crevasses which are fashioned by age-long pressure into a myriad forms when the waters are frozen into a glacier. In other words, the concept of continuity is only significant as a symbolic mental background on which we can plot out our perceptions of discontinuity in all their actual variety and complexity. Let us apply this general observation concerning the study of Life to the study of History. Does the term 'continuity of history', as used by modern Western historians, tacitly imply that the mass, momentum, volume, velocity, and direction of the social stream of human life are constant, or, short of being literally constant, vary within such narrow limits that the variations have no historical significance? If the term carries any such implication as this, then however attractive it may seem at first sight it is seriously misleading, as is shown by the results of our inquiry into the backward Time-extension of our Western Society.

In studying Time-relations in History, our inquiry has demonstrated that we must distinguish sharply between two degrees of continuity: the continuity between successive chapters, or successive periods and phases, in the history of one and the same society, and the continuity between the lives of different societies. In the abstract, no doubt, the fact of continuity can be demonstrated in the latter case as well as in the former, however great the difference in the degree of continuity may be; but if we merely consider the two cases in the abstract and in isolation from one another, we shall not increase our understanding of either. We must consider them comparatively, and from this angle of vision it is the relative discontinuity in the second case which is the significant phenomenon.

We might express the qualitative difference between these two kinds of continuity by an analogy from the lives of human beings. The chapters in the history of one and the same society resemble the successive experiences of a single person; the 'affiliations' and 'apparentations' between one society and another resemble the relations between parent and child. First, the child physically inherits certain qualities from the parents at conception; then, after the crisis of birth has produced a violent separation between mother and child, the child's life is unconsciously moulded in infancy by the parental environment; next, after it attains consciousness, its childish imagination is dominated by parental emotions and images; and later, as it grows up, it educates itself by deliberately studying its parents' grown-up feelings and thoughts and imitating or eschewing their grown-up actions. The sum total of these parental influences upon the child is no doubt very great. Nevertheless, the child is in some sense a separate individual from the moment when it is conceived; and unless at maturity it makes itself independent of its parents and succeeds in solving the problems of life out of its own resources, it will not have become a new 'grown-up' person fit to procreate and educate children of its own. When we compare the continuity between the lives of parent and child with the continuity between the successive experiences in the life of one or other of these individuals, the relative discontinuity in the phenomena of 'apparentation' and 'affiliation' is the feature that strikes us as significant. Conception, birth, and death fix a great gulf between the lives of one individual and another:

> Inter enim iectast vitai pausa, vageque
> Deerrarunt passim motus ab sensibus omnes.[1]

V. SOME PROVISIONAL CONCLUSIONS

The first stage of our inquiry has now reached its term, and it may be convenient to sum up our provisional conclusions. They can be stated as follows:

(*a*) The 'intelligible fields of historical study', whose limits we

[1] Lucretius: *De Rerum Natura*, Book III, ll. 861-2.

have roughly established by working outwards and backwards from the standpoint of our own country in our own day, are societies which have a greater extension, in both Space and Time, than national states or city-states, or any other political communities.[1]

(*b*) Such political communities (national states, city-states, and the like) are not only narrower in their spatial extension and shorter-lived in their Time-extension than the respective societies to which they belong, but their relation to these societies is that of inseparable parts to indivisible wholes. They are simply articulations of the true social entities and are not independent entities in themselves. Societies, not states, are 'the social atoms' with which students of history have to deal.

(*c*) The societies of which national states like Great Britain or city-states like Athens are parts, while they are (unlike their parts) independent entities in the sense that each of them constitutes, by itself, an 'intelligible field of historical study', are at the same time related to one another in the sense that they are all representatives of a single species of society.

(*d*) No one of the particular societies which we have been studying embraces the whole of Mankind or extends spatially over the whole habitable and navigable surface of the Planet or is coeval with the species of which it is one representative. Our Western Society, for example, which is still alive, was not conceived until the Hellenic Society had passed its maturity, while the Hellenic Society—even if (as is not the case) it proved, on being traced back, to be one of the original representatives of the species—has been extinct for twelve and a half centuries, so that in any case its complete life-span would fall short of the still uncompleted life-span of the species by that much already.

(*e*) While the continuity between the histories of one society and another is very much slighter in degree than the continuity between different chapters in the history of any single society (indeed, so

[1] This conception of societies was already familiar, three-quarters of a century ago, to de Gobineau:

'Il est nécessaire de bien expliquer d'abord ce que j'entends par une société. Ce n'est pas le cercle plus ou moins étendu dans lequel s'exerce, sous une forme ou sous une autre, une souveraineté distincte. La république d'Athènes n'est pas une société, non plus que le royaume de Magadha, l'empire du Pont ou le Califat d'Égypte au temps des Fatimites. Ce sont des fragments de société qui se transforment sans doute, se rapprochent ou se subdivisent sous la pression des lois naturelles que je cherche; mais dont l'existence ou la mort ne constitue pas l'existence ou la mort d'une société. Leur formation n'est qu'un phénomène le plus souvent transitoire, et qui n'a qu'une action bornée ou même indirecte sur la civilisation au milieu de laquelle elle éclôt. Ce que j'entends par société, c'est une réunion, plus ou moins parfaite au point de vue politique, mais complète au point de vue social, d'hommes vivant sous la direction d'idées semblables et avec des instincts identiques. Ainsi l'Égypte, l'Assyrie, la Grèce, l'Inde, la Chine, ont été ou sont encore le théâtre où des sociétés distinctes ont déroulé leurs destinées, abstraction faite des perturbations survenues dans leurs constitutions politiques.' de Gobineau, le Comte J. A.: *Essai sur l'Inégalité des Races Humaines.* (Paris 1853-5, Firmin-Didot, 4 vols., vol. i, pp. 11-12.)

much slighter as virtually to differ in kind), yet in the Time-relation between two particular societies of different age—namely, the Western and the Hellenic—we have observed features which we may describe metaphorically as 'apparentation' and 'affiliation'.

In the light of these conclusions on matters of historical fact, we can draw certain other conclusions regarding History as a humane study. Its true concern is with the lives of societies in both their internal and their external aspects. The internal aspect is the articulation of the life of any given society into a series of chapters succeeding one another in time and into a number of communities living side by side. The external aspect is the relation of particular societies with one another, which has likewise to be studied in the two media of time and space.

This view of history may be supported by a further quotation from Lord Acton, one of the greatest minds among modern Western historians, in whose career the sterilizing influence of Industrialism upon historical thought is tragically apparent. Less daring than Mommsen, Acton did not write his great book before reaching middle age, and so he never wrote it at all. The spirit of the times, which transformed Mommsen into an editor of Latin inscriptions and an encyclopaedist of Roman Constitutional Law, established its ascendency over Acton also. Mommsen's *History of the Roman Republic* was safely published in 1856 before the author had completed his thirty-ninth year. The idea of a History of Liberty never faded out of Acton's mind as long as he lived, but after his death in 1902 no manuscript of such a work was found among his papers, and several volumes of essays were all that could be gleaned for posthumous publication by his literary executors. Acton's power of creative action was paralysed, partly perhaps by his inborn temperament, but almost certainly in larger measure by the unfavourable atmosphere of the times in which he lived. His 'History of Liberty' would assuredly have been committed to paper if he had been a contemporary of Voltaire or Gibbon or Turgot;[1] but in the industrial age his vision of the intelligible whole was perpetually being obstructed by the misapplied ideals of the

[1] Turgot's contributions to the study of history were juvenilia. At the threshold of maturity he was permanently diverted from study to administration, and it is as a philosophic administrator rather than as an effective philosopher that he has made his mark. Yet in these immature and fragmentary essays he has made a greater permanent contribution to the understanding of history than Acton succeeded in making by devoting a long and laborious life to historical industry. Turgot's essays on the study of history are: the two discourses 'Sur les avantages que l'établissement du Christianisme a procurés au genre humain', delivered at the Sorbonne on the 3rd July and the 11th September, 1750; the 'Esquisse d'un plan de géographie politique'; the 'Plan de deux discours sur l'histoire universelle'; and the 'Plan du second discours sur l'histoire universelle, dont l'objet sera les progrès de l'esprit humain'. These essays, together with some illuminating 'pensées et fragments', will be found on pp. 589–678 of the second volume of the edition of Turgot's collected works which was published at Paris in 1844 by Guillaumin.

exploitation of raw materials and the Division of Labour.[1] Just as Mommsen's name will always be associated with the *Corpus Inscriptionum Latinarum*, so Acton's name will be with *The Cambridge Modern History*—though, less fortunate than Mommsen in this again, he did not live to carry to completion the great composite work which he planned and initiated.

In his letter to the contributors to *The Cambridge Modern History*, dated the 12th March 1898, Acton gave this glimpse of the vision that was in him:

'By Universal History I understand that which is distinct from the combined history of all countries, which is not a rope of sand, but a continuous development, and is not a burden on the memory, but an illumination of the soul. It moves in a succession to which the nations are subsidiary. Their story will be told, not for their own sake, but in reference and subordination to a higher series, according to the time and degree in which they contribute to the common fortunes of Mankind.'

It was a tragedy that the great historian who gained this Pisgah sight of the Promised Land should not have lived to cross over at the head of the followers whom he had led to the threshold. Was not Moses a greater leader than Joshua? And was not David, who hewed and assembled and fashioned the materials for the building of the Temple, a greater hero than Solomon, who had simply to put together the laboriously wrought blocks and beams which his father had placed ready to his hand? Could Solomon ever have built the Temple if he had not been able to begin where David left off? Could Joshua ever have conquered the Promised Land if Moses had not shepherded the Israelites across the Wilderness to the brink of Jordan? Who are we to criticize our predecessors into whose labours we have entered? If Acton's career was a tragedy, is not our criticism of Acton and the other Western historians of his generation and his school an act of ingratitude and impiety?

[1] 'It was . . . the desire not to speak before he had read everything that was relevant, whether in print or manuscript, that hindered so severely his output. His projected *History of Liberty* was, from the first, impossible of achievement. It would have required the intellects of Napoleon and Julius Caesar combined, and the lifetime of the patriarchs, to have executed that project as Acton appears to have planned it. A *History of Liberty*, beginning with the ancient world and carried down to our own day, to be based entirely upon original sources, treating both of the institutions which secured it, the persons who fought for it, and the ideas which expressed it, and taking note of all that scholars had written about every several portion of the subject, was, and is, beyond the reach of a single man. Probably towards the close of his life Acton had felt this. The Cambridge Modern History, which required the co-operation of so many specialists, was to him really but a fragment of this great project.

'His life marks what, in an age of minute specialism, must always be at once the crown and the catastrophe of those who take all knowledge for their province.

'His achievement is something different from any book. Acton's life-work was, in fact, himself. . . . Those who are nice in comparisons may weigh against the book lost the man gained. Those who loved him will know no doubt.' (Introduction to *The History of Freedom and other Essays* by John Emerich Edward Dalberg-Acton, first Baron Acton, edited with an introduction by J. N. Figgis and R. V. Laurence (London 1907, Macmillan).)

Perhaps we may defend ourselves by pointing out that Acton and his contemporaries, in their day, were no less critical of their own predecessors—the Gibbons and the Voltaires. In the world of scholarship, to give and take criticism is all in the day's work; and, each in our day, we may criticize our predecessors without becoming guilty of presumption so long as we are able to look forward without rancour to being criticized in our turn by our successors when our day is past. This is simply one out of many applications of an ethical 'law' which is so fundamental that its classic illustrations are to be found in primitive ritual and mythology. In the ritual of the Golden Bough at Nemi, 'the priest who slew the slayer and shall himself be slain' was free from blood-guiltiness because he had paid for doing what his predecessor had done by dooming himself to suffer his predecessor's fate at the hands of his successor. In the mythology of Olympus, Cronos overthrew Uranus in order to be overthrown in his turn by Zeus.

ὃς δ' ἔπειτ' ἔφυ, τρια-
κτῆρος οἴχεται τυχών.[1]

Moreover, in the realm of thought, this inevitable destiny is no tragedy on a philosophic view, because the thinker who is surpassed is not thereby superseded. If the touchstone of criticism proves his thought true metal, this means that he has added one more burnished link to the golden chain. He has poured into the ever-rolling stream of thought one more bucketful of pure water which will swell the river's volume and flow onward in its current far beyond that point on the bank where the mortal who made his contribution has stood for a moment of Time, and long after his intervention has been forgotten.

Cedit enim rerum novitate extrusa vetustas
semper, et ex aliis aliud reparare necessest;
nec quisquam in barathrum nec Tartara deditur atra:
materies opus est ut crescant postera saecla;
quae tamen omnia te vita perfuncta sequentur:
nec minus ergo ante haec quam tu cecidere, cadentque.
sic alid ex alio nunquam desistet oriri
vitaque mancipio nulli datur, omnibus usu.[2]

Furthermore, these universal conditions—the three conditions of criticism, transitoriness, and succession under which the scholar has to do his work—are not mere arbitrary decrees, imposed from without, to which the wise man bows, as the Stoic Cleanthes bowed to the dictates of Zeus,[3] because he knows that they are ineluctable.

[1] Aeschylus: *Agamemnon*, ll. 171–2.
[2] Lucretius: *De Rerum Natura*, Book III, ll. 964–71.
[3] The passage will be found in von Arnim, J.: *Stoicorum Veterum Fragmenta*, vol. i, p. 118.

They are conditions that arise from the nature of scholarship itself, which makes its progress by a rhythmic alternation between two activities—the collection of materials and their arrangement, the finding of facts and their interpretation—just as a physical organism lives and grows by an alternation between eating and digestion. The old fable of the belly and the members points the moral that neither activity is superior or inferior, prior or posterior, primary or parasitic, but that each is inseparable from the other as a part of the same whole and complementary to the other as a phase in the same recurrent process. For the alternation perpetually recurs in virtue of the very nature of thought. When the mind is employed in finding facts, its sheer success inhibits it sooner or later from fact-finding uninterruptedly *ad infinitum*. Sooner or later it finds itself so formidably beleaguered by the mass of facts which it has gathered round it that, until it has sorted them out and arranged them in some kind of order, it can no longer sally out into the Universe to gather more. Then the mind changes its activity perforce and employs itself for a season in making syntheses and interpretations. Yet now, once again, its sheer success inhibits it from working, uninterruptedly and *ad infinitum*, at bringing order out of chaos. Sooner or later, it finds that it has reduced to order all those materials which it had collected in its last fact-finding reconnaissance. Fresh facts must now be found before the process of synthesis and interpretation can be carried further. And so, in due course, the mind changes its activity once more and issues out, by the new paths which it has cleared for itself, into the Universe that ever awaits its coming in order to gather facts there again, as before, until the time approaches for the next attempt at synthesis and interpretation on a new plan and perhaps on a larger scale. No collection of facts is ever complete, because the Universe is without bounds. And no synthesis or interpretation is ever final, because there are always fresh facts to be found after the first collection has been provisionally arranged.

This rhythm is native to thought in all its different channels. In the channel of Physical Science, we have seen that thought has recently passed out of a fact-finding phase into the next phase of synthesis and interpretation.[1] In the channel of historical thought,

---

[1] A clear-sighted recognition of this change of phase in the process of scientific thought will be found, for example, in the Harveian Oration which was delivered on the 19th October 1931 in London, at the Royal College of Physicians, by Dr. Robert Hutchison, as reported in *The Times* of the 20th October 1931:

'In the apparatus of knowledge, they had immense advantages compared with the men of Harvey's day. Our danger rather was that, owing to the accumulation of knowledge, Science might be suffocated in its own secretions; a remedy for that was one of the pressing needs of our generation. It was no longer possible for any man to take all knowledge for his province. Specialism was inevitable; but though favourable to the accumulation of facts, it was bad for the philosophy of knowledge. There was too little

we may foresee that a corresponding transition from the fact-finding to the synthetic and interpretative activity is destined to take place to-day or to-morrow.

'Data of one kind or another are not so difficult to obtain; but generalisation is another matter. The social scientist may resent the premature generalisations of his predecessors. He will himself not get very far unless he himself tentatively generalises; unless, in a word, he has ideas as well as data. Essays and investigations may be piled mountain-high; they will never by themselves constitute a science or a philosophy of economics, psychology or society. The two processes—the making of hypotheses and the gathering of data—must go on together, reacting upon each other. For in the social sciences, as elsewhere, generalisation is at once a test of and a stimulus to minute and realistic research. The generalisations will not endure; why should they? They have not endured in mathematics, physics and chemistry. But, then, neither have the data. Science, social or other, is a structure: "A series of judgments, revised without ceasing, goes to make up the incontestable progress of Science. We must believe in this progress, but we must never accord more than a limited amount of confidence to the forms in which it is successively vested." '[1]

As we pursue our Study of History, we shall find[2] that this rhythmic alternation between two antithetic yet complementary activities, which is native to thought in general and to historical thought in particular, is also native to History itself.

speculation and too little use of the imagination; and most scientific literature was barren in ideas. It might be a good thing if there were a close time in laboratory work for, say, five years, to enable them to digest the huge accumulation of knowledge they already possessed and to think out new lines of advance.'

[1] Flexner, Abraham: *Universities: American, English, German* (Oxford 1930, University Press), pp. 12–13, quoting Duclaux, E.: *Pasteur: the History of a Mind* (English translation: Philadelphia and London 1920, Saunders), p. 111.

[2] In Part II. B, below.

C. THE COMPARATIVE STUDY OF CIVILIZATIONS

I. A SURVEY OF SOCIETIES OF THE SPECIES

(a) A PLAN OF OPERATIONS

IN the preceding investigation[1] we have established the existence of societies which (unlike their articulations called states) are independent entities in the sense that each of them constitutes by itself an 'intelligible field of historical study', but which at the same time are all representatives of a single species. The next step in a study of History is to find out more about the species to which such societies belong; and the natural way to proceed is to make a comparative study of the societies belonging to it. The necessary prelude to this comparative study is to identify as many representatives of the species as we can.

For this preliminary survey, certain simple operations suggest themselves.

First, we start with five living representatives of the species—the Western, Orthodox Christian, Islamic, Hindu, and Far Eastern societies—which we have identified already.

Second, we may search for representatives of the species, belonging to an older generation, to which the other four of the living five may be 'affiliated' in the way in which our Western Society has been found to be 'affiliated' to a now extinct society which we have called the Hellenic.

Third, we may examine our two sets of what appear to be fossilized relics of societies now extinct: namely, the one set which includes the Monophysite Christians of Armenia, Mesopotamia, Egypt, and Abyssinia, the Nestorian Christians of Kurdistan and Malabar, the Jews, and the Parsees; and the other set which includes the Lamaistic Mahayanian Buddhists of Tibet and Mongolia and the Hinayanian Buddhists of Ceylon, Burma, and Siam, and the Jains of India. These fossils may either prove to be remnants of extinct societies which we have identified already, or they may give us clues to other representatives of the species on which we have not yet laid hand.

Fourth, we may trace back to its source the life-history of any extinct society which we have succeeded in identifying in this way, in order to find out whether it is 'affiliated' or otherwise related, in its turn, to some other society that is one generation older again.

Fifth, if the preceding operations succeed even so far as to enable us to double the number of specimens with which we start,

[1] Part I. B.

we may find ourselves in a position to pass over from the genealogical to the comparative method: that is to say, we may be able,
in a survey of our literary and archaeological records, to identify, by
analogy with the specimens identified already, some additional
representatives of the species which are neither themselves alive
to-day nor are related to any of the living representatives by
'apparentation' or any other kind of relation, either in the first or
in the second degree, and which have not left their trace on the
world of our day in the form of fossils.

Sixth and last, we may search (on the lines of the second of our
operations) for otherwise unidentified societies which may be
'apparented' or otherwise related to any of the societies which the
fifth of our operations may have brought to light.

Before we attempt to carry out this plan of campaign, there is
a question of procedure which we have to decide: What are the
tokens of Apparentation-and-Affiliation which we are to look out
for, and which we are to accept as valid if we find them, in operations two, four, and six?[1] Let us try, for working purposes, to
determine our tokens empirically by examining the particular
example of Affiliation-and-Apparentation which has come to our
notice already:[2] namely, the historical relation between the Western
Society and the Hellenic Society. In investigating the relation
between these two societies, we came across several social phenomena which were evidently of the essence of the relation and
which were also so distinct and striking in this instance that we
might reasonably expect to recognize other instances of them if
they occurred in our survey of relations between other societies.

The first of these phenomena was the Roman Empire: a 'universal state',[3] incorporating the whole of the Hellenic Society in a
single political community in the last phase of Hellenic history,
upon which we stumbled in trying to trace the history of the
Western Society back to its roots. This phenomenon of a 'universal state' is striking because it stands out in sharp contrast to the
multiplicity of local states—*peritura regna*[4]—into which the Hellenic Society had been articulated before the Roman Empire arose,
and in equally sharp contrast to the similar multiplicity of local
states into which our own Western Society has been articulated
ever since it emerged from the ruins in which the Hellenic Society

[1] In the life of the Hellenic Society, in which parents were permitted by social con-
vention, and not forbidden by law, to repudiate responsibility for new-born children
and to expose them either to perish or to be brought up by some compassionate passer-
by, it was the custom to leave with the exposed child some tokens of identity (γνωρίσματα),
in order that a possibility of re-establishing relations between child and parents might
be kept open to meet the perhaps improbable contingency of the child surviving.

[2] In I. B (iv), above.

[3] This phenomenon of 'Universal States' is examined further in Part VI, below.

[4] Virgil, *Georg.* ii, l. 498.

was left after the Roman Empire's fall.[1] The outlines of the Roman Empire in the time-dimension are still further sharpened by the qualitative difference between it and the dispensations which preceded and followed it immediately. We found that it was immediately preceded by what we may call a 'Time of Troubles',[2] going back at least as far as the Hannibalic War,[3] in which the Hellenic Society was no longer creative and was indeed patently in decline—a decline which the establishment of the Roman Empire arrested for a time but which proved in the end to be the symptom of an incurable and deadly disease that eventually destroyed the Hellenic Society, and the Roman Empire with it.[4] Again, the Roman Empire, when it fell, was immediately followed by a kind of 'interregnum' between the disappearance of the Hellenic Society and the emergence of our Western Society.

In that part of the former domain of the Roman Empire which eventually became the cradle of our Western Society, the vacuum in the time-dimension which is represented by this 'interregnum' was filled by two institutions which were alike in being transitional, though there was a vast difference in the degree of importance of their respective historical functions. These institutions were 'the Church' established by the spread of the Christian religion through the interior of the Roman Empire, and a bevy of ephemeral 'successor-states' arising on the former territory of the Empire out of the so-called Völkerwanderung[5] of 'the Barbarians' from the no-man's-land beyond the Imperial frontiers.

Placing ourselves at the standpoint of the Hellenic Society,[6] we have called the Christians 'the internal proletariat' and the Barbarians 'the external proletariat' of this society in its last phase, when the leaven of creativeness in the Hellenic culture had lost its power to transfigure Mankind, and when even the salt of the Hellenic tradition had lost its savour, so that 'the heirs of the kingdom'[7] of Hellenism had ceased to perform their fathers' function as pioneers in one of the great experiences of Humanity and had degenerated into a 'dominant minority', holding down by might

---

[1] This double contrast between the Roman Empire and the political formations by which it was preceded and succeeded respectively is brought out by Freeman in the eloquent passages quoted on pp. 342 and 344, below.

[2] The classical 'Time of Troubles', for which the name was originally coined, was a passage of Russian history at the opening of the seventeenth century of the Christian Era (the episode of 'the False Dmitri' and its sequel).

[3] On closer investigation, we shall find that this 'Time of Troubles' in the Hellenic World, immediately preceding the establishment of the Roman Empire, went back not merely to the Hannibalic War but to the Peloponnesian War, i.e. twice as far back as the Hannibalic War from the date of the establishment of the Empire, which for convenience we may equate conventionally with the date of the Battle of Actium, i.e. 31 B.C. (See IV. C (ii) (b) 1, vol. iv, pp. 62–3, below.)

[4] For the course of this decline, see further Part V, passim, below.

[5] 'The Wandering of the Nations'.

[6] See pp. 41–2, above.

[7] James ii. 5.

and main a proletarian underworld which no longer voluntarily followed their lead, as, in our own Western World in the eighteenth century of the Christian era, the English Protestant Ascendancy in Ireland held down the Catholic Irishry.

The progressive estrangement of the 'internal proletariat' of the Hellenic World from the 'dominant minority' in the course of the decline of the Hellenic Civilization has been vividly portrayed by a nineteenth-century French philosopher from whose work we have quoted already.

'On a admiré avec raison l'extrême homogenéité d'idées et de vues qui, dans les états grecs de la belle époque, dirigeait le corps entier des citoyens. . . . A Rome, avant les guerres puniques, il en était de même, et la civilisation du pays était uniforme, incontestée. Dans sa façon de procéder, elle s'étendait du maître à l'esclave; tout le monde y participait à des degrés divers, mais ne participait qu'à elle. Depuis les guerres puniques chez les successeurs de Romulus, et chez tous les Grecs depuis Périclès et surtout depuis Philippe, ce caractère d'homogénéité tendit de plus en plus à s'altérer. Le mélange plus grand des nations amena le mélange des civilisations, et il en résulta un produit extrêmement multiple, très savant, beaucoup plus raffiné que l'antique culture, qui avait cet inconvénient capital, en Italie comme dans l'Hellade, de n'exister que pour les classes supérieures, et de laisser les couches de dessous tout à fait ignorantes de sa nature, de ses mérites et de ses voies. La civilisation romaine, après les grandes guerres d'Asie, fut sans doute une manifestation puissante du génie humain; cependant, à l'exception des rhéteurs grecs, qui en fournissaient la partie transcendantale, des jurisconsultes syriens, qui vinrent lui composer un système de lois athée, égalitaire et monarchique, des hommes riches, engagés dans l'administration publique ou dans les entreprises d'argent, et enfin des gens de loisir et de plaisir, elle eut ce malheur de ne jamais être que subie par les masses. . . De sorte qu'au-dessous de ce qu'on pourrait appeler les classes sociales, vivaient des multitudes innombrables, civilisées autrement que le monde officiel, ou n'ayant pas du tout de civilisation. C'était donc la minorité du peuple romain qui, en possession du secret, y attachait quelque prix. Voilà un exemple d'une civilisation acceptée et régnante, non plus par la conviction des peuples qu'elle couvre, mais par leur épuisement, leur faiblesse, leur abandon.'[1]

The state of mind in which 'the dominant minority' lives out its life-in-death—a life which eventually becomes as burdensome to those who live it as it is for those who pay for it to be lived—has been described with profound psychological insight by a Roman poet of the last generation of the 'Time of Troubles', who knew

[1] De Gobineau, op. cit., vol. i, pp. 93-4. It is evident that we may regard 'the internal proletariat' and 'the external proletariat' of a declining civilization either as victims of or as parasites upon 'the dominant minority', according to the standpoint in which we place ourselves.

at first hand the distracted Roman masters of a devastated Hellenic World:

> Si possent homines, proinde ac sentire videntur
> pondus inesse animo quod se gravitate fatiget,
> e quibus id fiat causis quoque noscere et unde
> tanta mali tanquam moles in pectore constet,
> haud ita vitam agerent ut nunc plerumque videmus
> quid sibi quisque velit nescire et quaerere semper
> commutare locum quasi onus deponere possit.
> exit saepe foras magnis ex aedibus ille
> esse domi quem pertaesumst, subitoque [revertit],
> quippe foris nilo melius qui sentiat esse.
> currit agens mannos ad villam praecipitanter,
> auxilium tectis quasi ferre ardentibus instans;
> oscitat extemplo, tetigit cum limina villae,
> aut abit in somnum gravis atque oblivia quaerit,
> aut etiam properans urbem petit atque revisit.
> hoc se quisque modo fugitat, quem scilicet, ut fit,
> effugere haud potis est; ingratis haeret et odit
> propterea, morbi quia causam non tenet aeger.[1]

These lines of Lucretius may be capped by a passage from Goethe, in which the modern Western poet describes the same spiritual malady with the same masterly touch:

> Soll er gehen, soll er kommen?
> Der Entschluss ist ihm genommen;
> Auf gebahnten Weges Mitte
> Wankt er tastend halbe Schritte,
> Er verliert sich immer tiefer,
> Siehet alle Dinge schiefer,
> Sich und andre lästig drückend,
> Atem holend und erstickend;
> Nicht erstickt und ohne Leben,
> Nicht verzweifelnd, nicht ergeben.
> So ein unaufhaltsam Rollen,
> Schmerzlich Lassen, widrig Sollen,
> Bald Befreien, bald Erdrücken,
> Halber Schlaf und schlecht Erquicken
> Heftet ihn an seine Stelle
> Und bereitet ihn zur Hölle.[2]

This was the moral incubus against which 'the internal proletariat' and 'the external proletariat' of the declining Hellenic Society reacted each after its kind—'the internal proletariat' through the Christian Church[3] and 'the external proletariat' through the

---

[1] Lucretius: *De Rerum Natura*, Book III, ll. 1053-70.
[2] Goethe: *Faust*, ll. 11471-86.
[3] It is significant that Lucretius's cure for the spiritual malady which he describes in the passage here quoted is commended in language of such a Christian flavour that

Barbarian Völkerwanderung—and in the institutions through which these proletarian reactions were expressed we have two more phenomena which may serve our turn as tokens of Apparentation-and-Affiliation.

The Christian Church is, of course, as striking a phenomenon as the Roman Empire—in the first place by reason of the 'universality' which it acquired from the Empire by growing up within its framework and deliberately taking the Empire's organization as the basis of its own.[1] The Roman 'universal state' incorporated in itself the whole of the disintegrating Hellenic Society—'the dominant minority' which was maintaining itself on the surface, 'the internal proletariat' which was pressing up from below, and 'the external proletariat' which was pressing in from outside. The 'Catholic Church'[2] in its first phase conformed to the pattern of the Roman political universe by incorporating into itself the whole of 'the internal proletariat'. In this phase, the universality of the Church fell short of that of the Empire inasmuch as it embraced only one of the three elements which the Empire in some sense held together. On the other hand, the Church's hold over the affections and the allegiance of 'the internal proletariat' was far greater than the Empire's hold over either portion of the proletarian underworld, because the Church had been established by 'the internal proletariat' themselves out of their own spiritual and material resources in order to satisfy their own sense of their own needs, whereas the Empire presented itself to them as an alien institution imposed upon them by force.

Thus, while the Empire was a house built upon the sands, which collapsed at a touch when the waters of 'the external proletariat' came and went in the spate of the Völkerwanderung, the Church proved, under this ordeal, to be a house founded upon the rock. We might express the same contrast in another simile by comparing the Empire to an old tree whose roots gradually decayed until a breath of wind was enough to tear them up and overthrow the solid trunk which tempests could not bend, and the Church to a young sapling whose stem swayed in the breeze while its roots remained firmly planted deep in the soil. In short, during the time when the Empire and the Church coexisted as occupants of the same field, the Empire was dead-alive while the Church was

no reader who scanned these lines without knowing their authorship would guess that they were written by a pre-Christian poet. The passage proceeds:

> Quam bene si videat, iam rebus quisque relictis
> naturam primum studeat cognoscere rerum,
> temporis aeterni quoniam, non unius horae,
> ambigitur status, in quo sit mortalibus omnis
> aetas, post mortem quae restat cumque, manenda.

[1] For a general examination of the institution of universal churches, see Part VII, below.   [2] The Greek adjective καθολικός = the Latin adjective *universus*.

animated by a fresh vitality. And so, when the moribund Empire fell, the ensuing 'interregnum' gave the living Church an opportunity to perform an act of creation. The Church then played the part of a chrysalis out of which there emerged in the fullness of time a new society of the same species as the old society which had disappeared—but disappeared without carrying away the Church in its ruin as it carried away the Empire. Thus the Catholic Church, like the Roman God Janus, was a figure with two faces: in one aspect the refuge of 'the internal proletariat' of an old society in decline, and in another aspect the chrysalis of a new society in gestation. Since the two societies—the Hellenic and the Western—into whose histories the Church entered in these quite different ways stood to one another in the relation which we have called Apparentation-and-Affiliation, we may take the phenomenon of a universal church playing this dual role *vis-à-vis* any two given societies as one of our tokens that such a pair of societies are 'apparented-and-affiliated' to one another.

The essence of the Christian Church, which at once differentiates it as an institution from the Roman Empire and explains how it was able to go on living and growing when the Empire perished, was the germ of creative power which it harboured, under apparently unfavourable conditions, in a social environment where the once potent indigenous forces of creation had failed.[1] We have found that this spark of life which was afterwards fostered and fanned into a flame was in fact introduced into the Hellenic World by 'natives' of Oriental worlds from whose broken ranks 'the internal proletariat' of the Hellenic Society was forcibly recruited—expatriated Oriental slaves and Oriental populations that were subjugated *in situ* by Macedonian and Roman arms without being uprooted.[2] This alien origin of the spark of life latent in the Christian Church—alien, that is, from the indigenous tradition of the society by whose internal proletariat the Church was established—is another point which may possibly serve as a token for identifying other universal churches that have played an analogous role in the Apparentation-and-Affiliation of other societies. At the same time we need not treat the presence of this feature as essential, and need not rule out other churches from our category *a priori* if we happen to find that their 'sparks of life'—or 'germs of creative power'—are not alien from but indigenous to the societies among whose internal proletariats these churches have arisen.[3]

---

[1] Excessere omnes, adytis arisque relictis
Di quibus imperium hoc steterat. (Virgil, *Aeneid*, Book II, ll. 351-2.)
[2] See pp. 40-1, above.
[3] For a classification of universal churches on the criterion of the predominantly 'alien' or predominantly 'indigenous' origin of their inspirations, see V. C (iii), *Table III*, vol. vi, p. 329, below.

A third phenomenon which is associated with the Apparentation-and-Affiliation of the Hellenic and the Western Society is the Völkerwanderung in which 'the external proletariat' of the Hellenic Society came down in spate from the no-man's-land beyond the frontiers of the Roman Empire—Germans and Slavs from the forests of Northern Europe, Sarmatians and Huns from the Eurasian Steppe, Saracens from the Arabian Peninsula, Berbers from the Atlas and the Sahara. The ephemeral 'successor-states' which were set up on the former territories of the Roman Empire by these barbarian war-bands shared the stage of history with the Church during the interregnum between the disappearance of the Hellenic Society and the emergence of our Western Society—an interregnum which was the barbarians' 'heroic age'.[1]

We may observe, however, that in comparison with the role of the Church the role of the Barbarians during this interlude was insignificant. The Church, as we have seen, was intimately concerned and not just accidentally associated with the 'affiliation' of our Western Society to the Hellenic Society. Its role vis-à-vis the 'affiliated' society was creative. It was the chrysalis out of which our Western Society emerged. On the other hand, the Barbarian 'successor-states' of the Roman Empire were not the chrysalides of the local states into which the Western Society eventually articulated itself after its emergence. Almost all of them perished by violence before the interregnum following the fall of the Roman Empire came to an end.[2] The Vandals and Ostrogoths were overthrown by counter-attacks on the part of the Roman Empire itself. The last convulsive flicker of the Roman flame sufficed to burn these poor moths to cinders. Others were overthrown in fratricidal warfare: the Visigoths received the first blow from the Franks and the coup de grâce from the Arabs; the Gepids were exterminated by a concerted attack on the part of the Avars and the Lombards; the struggle for hegemony between the states of the Barbarian 'Heptarchy' in Britain ended in the overthrow of all the rest by Wessex. The few survivors of this Ishmaelitish struggle for existence incontinently degenerated and then vegetated on as fainéants until they were extinguished by new political forces which possessed the indispensable germ of creative power. Thus the Merovingian and the Lombard dynasties were brushed aside by the Carolingians in order to clear the ground at last for laying the political foundations of a new Western Society. The Umayyads were brushed aside by the 'Abbasids in order to resume, in the life of an old Oriental Society, an indigenous movement which had been interrupted, a

---

[1] This phenomenon of 'heroic ages' accompanied by Völkerwanderungen is examined in Part VIII, below.
[2] On this point see further Part VIII, below.

thousand years earlier, by the violent intrusion of the Hellenic Society through the conquests of Alexander the Great.[1] In fine, there are only two out of all the Barbarian 'successor-states' of the Roman Empire that can be shown to have any lineal descendants among the local states into which the Western World is articulated to-day. The first of these two states is Austrasia, a fragment of the Frankish 'successor-state' of the Roman Empire which was rescued from decay by the Church and was fashioned into the nucleus of the Carolingian Empire. Through this process of reconstruction, the Austrasian-Frankish 'successor-state' indirectly gave rise to the local states which arose in the West out of the Carolingian Empire's ruins. The second 'successor-state' that has left issue is Wessex, which incorporated itself into the Kingdom of England, which eventually incorporated itself in turn into the United Kingdom of Great Britain. This historical continuity between the Wessex of the interregnum preceding the emergence of our Western Society and the Great Britain of to-day may be regarded as one of those exceptions that prove a rule.[2]

Thus the Völkerwanderung and its ephemeral products—the Barbarian 'successor-states'—are tokens, like the Church and the Empire, of the 'affiliation' of the Western Society to the Hellenic; but, like the Empire and unlike the Church, they are tokens and no more. When we turn from the study of symptoms to the study of causes, we find that, whereas the Church belonged to the future as well as to the past, the Barbarian 'successor-states', as well as the Empire, belonged to the past wholly and exclusively.[3] The rise

[1] For the collisions between civilizations ('Contact in Space') see Part IX, below.

[2] Why was Wessex exceptional, among the Barbarian 'successor-states' of the Roman Empire, in having a future? At first sight the explanation might be expected to be geographical—the sheltered geographical situation of a state established in an *alter orbis* which was insulated from the European continent. Actually the real explanation is precisely the contrary of this. Wessex won a future for herself because she reacted successfully to an ordeal; and the challenge to which she responded was the intrusion into her *alter orbis* of invaders from Scandinavia. It was this that quickened her dry bones into life in King Alfred's day. On this point, see further II. D (v), vol. ii, pp. 195–6 and 198–200, below.

[3] 'Les Francs ont bien accepté le Christianisme, mais ils se montrent aussi incapables d'en faire la règle de leurs mœurs que de le propager autour d'eux.... La démoralisation et l'inertie du peuple valent celles de ses rois. Ce n'est pas la jeunesse mais la déchéance qu'atteste la société des temps mérovingiens et Grégoire de Tours (538–94), qui a vécu au milieu d'elle et en a été épouvanté, résume mélancoliquement son impression dans ces paroles découragées: *Mundus senescit.*' (Pirenne, H., in an article entitled 'Mahomet et Charlemagne', published in *La Revue Belge de Philologie et d'Histoire*, i (1927).) In this and other articles, as well as in a book entitled *Les Villes du Moyen Age* (Brussels 1927, Lamartin), Monsieur Pirenne puts forward at the same time the thesis that the long-distance maritime commerce which, under the Roman Empire, had linked together the whole circumference of the *Orbis Romanus* round the coasts of the Mediterranean, continued right through the ensuing interregnum and was only brought to an end by the Arab conquest of North-West Africa at the turn of the seventh and eighth centuries of our era, which was the last convulsion of the Völkerwanderung. In *The Journal of Roman Studies*, vol. xix, Part 2 (London 1929, Society for the Promotion of Roman Studies), pp. 230–3, Monsieur Pirenne's thesis is combated by Mr. N. H. Baynes, who submits that 'the unity of the Mediterranean world was broken', as early

of these 'successor-states' was merely the obverse of the Empire's fall, and that fall inexorably portended theirs. Their destruction had been decreed before their foundation fell to be recorded. When the house built upon the sands had been carried away by the spate of the Völkerwanderung, what expectation of life could there be for a collection of hovels heaped up on the same treacherous foundations out of the boulders and shingle which the flood happened to have deposited as it came and went?

This low estimate of the Barbarians' contribution to the life of our Western Society would have shocked our Western historians of the last generation, who were inclined to place the Barbarians almost on a par with the Church itself as creators of our Western culture. Their over-estimate of the importance of the Barbarians' role can be traced to the influence on their thought of features in their environment which we have studied in other instances already.

For instance, the conceit of historical continuity led them to view the modern Western institution of responsible parliamentary representative government in a sovereign national state as a development of certain institutions of self-government which the Teutons were supposed to have brought with them from no-man's-land. An unprejudiced study indicates that these 'primitive Teutonic liberties', if they existed at all, were rudimentary institutions which are characteristic of Primitive Man in almost all times and places; and that, such as they were, they did not survive the Völkerwanderung. The leaders of the Teutonic Barbarian warbands were military adventurers of the same type as the contemporary masters of the Roman soldiers who opposed them.[1] The constitution of the 'successor-states', like that of the Empire itself at the time, was a despotism tempered by revolution. And if, in certain cases, the substitution of one régime for the other brought a temporary alleviation for the miserable inhabitants of the warlord-ridden Roman provinces, that was only because the Barbarian rulers were less efficient than their Roman predecessors and not because they were more disposed to give their subjects freedom.[2]

as the middle of the fifth century of our era, 'by the pirate fleet of Vandal Carthage, and that the shattered unity was never restored'.

[1] 'La République fut asservie dès que le commandement des armées fut continué aux proconsuls pour plusieurs années, et qu'ils purent conserver sous le drapeau les mêmes soldats. Il se forma pour lors entre le proconsul et ses soldats une sorte d'association, un nouveau corps politique, une nation nouvelle, si l'on peut ainsi dire; et pour la République cette nouvelle nation ne ressemblait pas mal à un peuple barbare qui serait survenu' (*Œuvres de Turgot*, nouvelle édition (Paris 1844, Guillaumin, 2 vols.), vol. ii, p. 672). The encounter between Aetius's Romans and Attila's Huns 'presented the image of civil war' because the troops engaged on either side so much resembled one another (Adams, B.: *The Law of Civilisation and Decay*, 2nd edition (New York 1898, Macmillan), p. 40).

[2] See, for example, Sir Samuel Dill's account of the Merovingian 'successor-state' in *Roman Society in Gaul in the Merovingian Age* (London 1926, Macmillan), especially pp. 109-15.

The last of these Barbarian military despotisms was extinguished many centuries before the real beginning of the new growth which has gradually produced the political institutions that are now characteristic of the Modern Western World.[1]

The prevalent over-estimate of the Barbarians' contribution to the life of our Western Society can also be traced in part to the false belief that social progress can be explained by the presence of certain inborn qualities of race.[2] A false analogy from the phenomena that were being brought to light by the Physical Science of the day led our Western historians of the last generation to picture races as chemical 'elements' and their miscegenation as a chemical 'reaction' which might be presumed to release latent energies and so be expected to produce effervescence and change where there had been stagnation and immobility before. Self-hypnotized by the imagery of this misleading simile, our historians deluded themselves into believing that 'the infusion of new blood', as they metaphorically described the racial effect of the Völkerwanderung, could account for those long-subsequent manifestations of life and growth which constitute the history of the Western Society. In this pseudo-scientific delusion they were confirmed by the vanity of nineteenth-century Nationalism, which has indulged in the invention of genealogies for nations after the obsolete fashion of royal families and noble houses. This latter-day pedantry has borrowed from medieval heraldry its taste for fabulous beasts and its superstition that nobility derives from conquest; and hence we see half the peoples of modern Europe industriously striving to prove their descent from the Barbarians of the Völkerwanderung, in the mistaken belief that these casual war-bands from no-man's-land were 'pure races' of conquerors whose blood still invigorates and ennobles the bodies of their supposed descendants to-day.[3]

In reality, the Barbarians who were deposited in the Roman Empire by the Völkerwanderung were not the authors of our spiritual being. They were not even drones who were no longer permitted to cumber the hive after they had performed their sole function of fertilizing the queen bee; for the Church was already great with child when she encountered them, and the subsequent extirpation of the Barbarians had nothing to do with the genesis of our Western Society. The Barbarians made their passage felt by being in at the death of the Hellenic Society; but they cannot even

---

[1] On this point see further III. C (ii) (b), vol. iii, pp. 359–63, below.
[2] This fallacy is examined in II. C (ii) (a) 1, vol. ii, below.
[3] 'Les faits donnent le démenti le plus tragique au thème convenu de l'invasion germanique rajeunissant et vivifiant par un afflux de forces fraîches la décrépitude romaine.' (Pirenne, H., in La Revue Belge de Philologie et d'Histoire i (1922).)

claim the distinction of having delivered the death-blow;[1] for by the time when they overran the Roman Empire, the Hellenic Society was already moribund—a suicide slowly dying of wounds self-inflicted during a 'Time of Troubles' centuries before.[2] Thus the Barbarians were not the assassins of the mighty dead. They were merely the vultures feeding on the carrion or the maggots crawling in the carcass.[3] And the very process of dissolution which had brought them on to the scene determined the duration of their existence; since this transitory interregnum of corruption and decay was the only environment in which they were able to thrive. Their 'heroic age' was an epilogue to Hellenic history, not a prelude to ours. Their epic was a swan-song[4].

These considerations bring out a point of practical importance for our survey. The values of our three tokens, as evidence for the presence of the phenomenon of Apparentation-and-Affiliation, are not the same. The evidential value of 'universal churches' is absolute, because churches belong by nature to the future as well as to the past. The evidential value of 'universal states' and 'Völkerwanderungen' is conditional. Where we find one or both of these other tokens in conjunction with a church, we may take them as corroborative evidence for the instance of Apparentation-and-Affiliation which the existence of that church establishes. Where, however, we find one of these subsidiary tokens, or even both of them together, without finding a church there likewise, we cannot press the evidence so far. We can still infer the existence of an earlier society behind the horizon of the society in whose background the two subsidiary tokens appear; but since both 'universal states' and Völkerwanderungen belong by nature to the past wholly and exclusively, we cannot infer, from these tokens alone, that the earlier society is 'apparented' to the later. We must be content to establish the two facts of its existence and its chronological priority, and to recognize that, if it is related to the later society in any significant meaning of the term, this relation—as far as the evidence goes—is something less close than that which Apparentation-and-Affiliation imply.

There is one more symptom in the Apparentation-and-Affilia-

[1] The Barbarians 'n'ont vaincu l'empire romain que divisé, abattu, mal gouverné' (Œuvres de Turgot, nouvelle édition (Paris 1844, Guillaumin, 2 vols.), vol. ii, p. 672).

[2] 'So kann eine Kultur in sich selbst zu Grunde gehen, auch ohne dass sie dem Angriff äusserer Feinde erliegt, wie die antike Kultur im dritten Jahrhundert (denn nicht die Germanen haben sie zerschlagen, sondern sie haben nur das Werk der Zerstörung vollendet, als sie innerlich schon abgestorben war.' (Meyer, E.: Geschichte des Altertums, vol. i (i), 4th edition (Stuttgart and Berlin 1921, Cotta), p. 85. Cf. p. 248.)

[3] 'Le but des envahisseurs n'était pas d'anéantir l'Empire Romain, mais de s'y installer pour en jouir.' (Pirenne, Henri: Les Villes du Moyen Age (Brussels 1927, Lamartin), p. 11.)

[4] For their epitaph read Robert Bridges: The Testament of Beauty (Oxford, 1929, Clarendon Press), Book I, ll. 534–60.

tion between the Hellenic Society and the Western Society which we may notice before we make our attempt to identify other representatives of the same species; and this is the geographical displacement of the cradle or original home of the 'affiliated' society from the original home of the society which is 'apparented' to it. We have seen[1] that the base-line from which our Western Society has expanded—a line stretching from Rome across the Alps to Aachen and from Aachen across the Channel to the Roman Wall—coincides with a section of the frontier of the Roman Empire, and that this frontier marked the limit at which the expansion of the Hellenic Society in that direction came to an end. The original base from which the Hellenic Society itself had expanded to that north-western limit lay far away in the Aegean. In studying examples of the relation between an earlier and a later society elsewhere, we may obtain light upon the object of our study by taking the degree of such geographical displacement into account.

(b) OPERATIONS ACCORDING TO PLAN

The Orthodox Christian Society

After having observed these several distinctive features in that part of the landscape which is already within our view, we may now make the attempt to enlarge our field of vision by carrying out the several operations which we have planned. We were to begin by scanning the backgrounds of the histories of the other living societies of the same species as our Western Society, in the hope of recognizing features analogous to those which, in the background of our Western history, are recognizable tokens of the 'affiliation' of this Western Society to another society—the Hellenic—that lies beyond the horizon.

What lies, for example, in the background of the history of the Orthodox Christian Society? In this first reconnaissance we have an easy task, for here we find a universal state, a universal church, and a Völkerwanderung which are not only analogous to but identical with those which we have already found in the background of our own Western history: our familiar Roman Empire, Catholic Church, and Völkerwanderung of Teutons, Eurasians, Berbers, Arabs, and Slavs. From this we learn at once the particular fact that the Orthodox Christian Society as well as our own Western Society is 'affiliated' to the Hellenic Society, and the general fact that a society may be 'apparented' to more 'affiliated' societies than one. The phenomenon of geographical displacement explains how this is possible.

When we look for the original base-line of the Orthodox Christian World, we find that, like the base-line of the Western

---

[1] In I. B (iv), on pp. 37-41, above.

World, this shows a displacement from the original base of the
Hellenic World in the Aegean. It has been displaced, however, in
a different direction and to a slighter degree. While in the one case
the displacement is in a north-westerly direction from the Aegean
to Lotharingia, in the other it is in a north-easterly direction from
the Aegean to a base-line which runs diagonally across the interior
of Anatolia between Constantinople and Caesarea Mazaca. This
line is not only much less distant from the Aegean than the line
between Rome and the Roman Wall. It is also a much shorter line;
and the eventual expansion of the Orthodox Christian World from
this base has been on a decidedly smaller scale than the expansion
of our Western World, of which we have taken a bird's-eye view in
a previous chapter.[1]

In the expansion of the Orthodox Christian Society, the main
axis has coincided with the base-line itself, which has been produced in both directions in the figure of a crescent with its horns
pointing respectively north-east and north-west. North-eastward,
Orthodox Christendom first embraced Georgia, at the foot of the
Caucasus, and towards the beginning of the eighth century of the
Christian Era it leaped the range and secured a foothold beyond it
in Alania, as Western Christendom, before the end of the same
century, leaµed the Pyrenees and secured a foothold in the Iberian
Peninsula. Alania opened out on to the great Eurasian Steppe—
that arid ocean across which caravans can travel with the same
mobility as caravels across the face of the waters[2]—and from this
point of vantage the Orthodox Christian Society might conceivably have dominated the Steppe and have found fresh hinterlands to occupy on its further coasts, as, from the vantage-ground
of the Iberian Peninsula, our Western Society has eventually
mastered the South Atlantic and made itself at home in what has
since become Latin America.[3] At this juncture, however, while
Orthodox Christendom was still pausing at the northern foot of the
Caucasus on the brink of the Steppe, Judaism and Islam cut in—
Judaism captivating the Khazars who ranged between the Lower
Volga and the Don,[4] and Islam the White Bulgars on the Middle

---

[1] I. B (iii), above.   [2] For the Eurasian Steppe, see further Part III. A, vol. iii, below.
[3] It is noteworthy that Leo the Syrian, the first great statesman of Orthodox Christendom, began his career by pioneering in Alania, and made his mark there (for Leo's
personal history, see further III. C (ii) (b), vol. iii, pp. 274–6, below). Presumably he had
his eye on the openings for expansion in this direction; but he was called away to organize
the defence of Orthodox Christendom against the last assault of the Umayyads upon
Constantinople in A.D. 717, and he devoted the rest of his life to two other tasks: first,
the evocation of the ghost of the Roman Empire (a task which Leo accomplished in
Orthodox Christendom, while in Western Christendom Charlemagne attempted it and
failed: see Part II. D (vii), vol. ii, p. 344, and IV. C (iii) (c) 2 (β), vol. iv, pp. 322–3 and
340–7, as well as Part X, below); second, the promotion of the religious movement
which has come to be known by the misleadingly negative title of Iconoclasm (see V. C
(i) (d) 9 (β), vol. vi, pp. 116–17, below).
[4] For the conversion of the Khazars to Judaism, see further II. D (vi), Annex, vol. ii,
p. 410, and V. C (i) (c) 3, vol. v, p. 285, below.

Volga. This put a stop to the expansion of Orthodox Christendom along its main axis north-eastward.

Along the same axis north-westward, Orthodox Christendom leaped the Balkans and made a thrust towards Central Europe; but here it found itself in competition with Western Christendom, which enjoyed the double advantage of having started operations earlier[1] and of conducting them on a wider front. In the ninth century the two competing societies each sought to entrench itself at the gates of its rival's citadel. The Papacy made a bid for the ecclesiastical allegiance of the Bulgarians; the 'Byzantine' or 'East Roman' Empire—a ghost of the Roman Empire which was evoked with such success that it became the 'empire state' of Orthodox Christendom—sent its missionaries Cyril and Methodius to the Slavs of Moravia and Bohemia. The competition was interrupted by the irruption of the pagan Magyar Nomads from the Eurasian Steppe into the enclave of steppe-country which is now called the Alföld of Hungary. The boundary between Western and Orthodox Christendom in this quarter was eventually fixed at the turn of the tenth and eleventh centuries by the entry of the Hungarians (simultaneously with the Poles and the Scandinavians) into the society of the West.[2]

Orthodox Christendom also expanded along a transverse axis which intersected the main axis at Constantinople—the expansion along this transverse axis being not overland but oversea. The sea-route leading out of the Dardanelles into the Aegean carried Orthodox Christendom into the former homelands of the 'apparented' Hellenic Society; and here it followed the ancient track of Hellenic maritime expansion into Southern Italy, where it laboriously won a foothold between the Muslims and the Western Christians—only to lose it again in the eleventh century, when this Orthodox Christian outpost was captured for Western Christendom by the Normans. On the other hand, the production of this maritime axis in the opposite direction—out of the Bosphorus into

[1] The Irish and English missionary enterprises in Central Europe, which inaugurated the advance of Western Christendom on this front, were put in hand as early as the eighth century of the Christian Era (see II. D (vii), vol. ii, pp. 332 and 336, below). The corresponding operations in Orthodox Christendom—the conquest of the Slavonic settlers in Greece and the conversion of the Bulgarians by 'the East Roman Empire' (the ghost of the Roman Empire which had been evoked by Leo the Syrian)—were not carried out until the latter end of the ninth century.

[2] Thus the expansion of Orthodox Christendom along the line of its main axis was brought to a halt, by the more successful expansion of other societies of the same species, in both directions. Relatively, the expansion north-westward opened up more fruitful ground for the Orthodox Christian Society than its expansion towards the north-east, as is shown by the shifting of the centre of gravity of Orthodox Christendom in the former direction. In the tenth century the centre of gravity was unmistakably still on the Asiatic side of the Black Sea Straits. By the twelfth century it had come to be unmistakably on the European side. (On this point, see further Part II. D (iii), vol. ii, p. 79, below.)

and over the Black Sea—carried Orthodox Christendom much farther than the 'apparented' Hellenic Society had ever penetrated in that direction. Leaping the Black Sea and the strip of steppe that then skirted its northern shores,[1] Orthodox Christendom established itself in the eleventh century in Russia; and from this second home it expanded through the forests of Northern Europe and Asia, first to the Arctic Ocean and finally, in the seventeenth century, to the Pacific—outflanking the great Eurasian Steppe and making contact, round the corner, with another living society of the same species in the Far East.

This sketch of the expansion of Orthodox Christendom, in juxta-position to the sketch of the expansion of Western Christendom which has been given before,[2] explains in geographical terms how the Hellenic Society came to be 'apparented' to two separate 'affiliated' societies. In terms of life and growth, we can trace the differentiation of Western and Orthodox Christendom into two separate societies in the schism of their common chrysalis, the Catholic Church, into two bodies: the Roman Catholic Church and the Orthodox Church. The schism took rather more than three centuries to work itself out, and the final result was the cumulative effect of three crises. The first crisis was the conflict in the eighth century between the Iconoclasts and the Papacy over a matter of ritual—a conflict which immediately followed the successful evoca-tion of the ghost of the Roman Empire in Orthodox Christendom by Leo and immediately preceded the abortive evocation of the same ghost in Western Christendom by Charlemagne. The second crisis was the conflict in the ninth century between the Oecumenical Patriarchate of Constantinople and the Papacy over a question of ecclesiastical authority—a conflict which centred ostensibly upon the personality of the Patriarch Photius but fundamentally upon the competition between the Sees of Constantinople and Rome for the ecclesiastical allegiance of South-Eastern Europe. The third crisis was the fresh conflict and final rupture between the two sees in the eleventh century over a question of theological dogma—a conflict which was closely connected with the contem-porary political struggle in Southern Italy between the East Roman Empire, which was striving to maintain its rule over the local Latins, and the Norman adventurers who had come upon the scene as mercenaries of the East Roman Government and who were carving out a kingdom for themselves in the guise of knights errant for the Holy See.

The final rupture of A.D. 1054, which completed the schism of the

---

[1] See II. D (iii), vol. ii, p. 80, footnote 2, below.
[2] See I. B (iii) and (iv), above.

Catholic Church into two churches, the Roman and the Orthodox, likewise completed the fission of the social fabric which was growing up within the ecclesiastical chrysalis into the two new societies of Western and Orthodox Christendom; and this simultaneous separation of the two churches and the two societies was accompanied by a differentiation into two utterly different morphological types. The Catholic Church in the West had become centralized under the authority of the Roman See—a Great Power which succeeded in humiliating its only conceivable peer, the Holy Roman Empire, and in retarding for some centuries the articulation of the Western Society into the sharply defined and narrowly self-centred local states of the Modern Age. In the meantime, the Orthodox Church had become a department of state, first in the revived East Roman Empire and then in each of the other states which were brought into the circle of the Orthodox Christian Society by conversion; so that Orthodox Christendom, in the age corresponding to 'the Middle Ages' of the West, presented a spectacle which was most unlike medieval Western Christendom but not so unlike the Protestant part of the Modern Western World, where the map of ecclesiastical allegiances conforms to the map of political sovereignties[1] and where people of one faith, instead of being united in the bosom of one church, are divided between a number of local churches which are separate, not because they differ in practice or in creed, but because they are borne upon the establishments of separate sovereign states.

The Iranic and Arabic Societies

The next living society which we have to examine is Islam; and when we scan the background of Islamic history, we discern there a universal state, a universal church, and a Völkerwanderung which are not identical with those in the common background of Western and Orthodox Christendom but which are unmistakably analogous to them. The Islamic universal state is the 'Abbasid Caliphate of Baghdad.[2] The universal church is of course Islam itself. The Völkerwanderung which overran the domain of the Caliphate at its fall proceeded from the Turkish and the Mongol Nomads of the Eurasian Steppe, the Berber Nomads of the Sahara and highlanders of the Atlas, and the Arab Nomads from the Arabian Peninsula who raided 'Irāq under the leadership of the Carmathians and also flooded over North-West Africa—meeting and

---

[1] On the principle 'Cuius regio, eius religio'.

[2] The subsequent 'Abbasid Caliphate of Cairo was an evocation of a ghost of the 'Abbasid Caliphate of Baghdad, that is to say, it was a phenomenon of the same kind as 'the East Roman Empire' in Orthodox Christendom and 'the Holy Roman Empire' in the West. This phenomenon of the evocation, in 'affiliated' societies, of ghosts of the universal states of 'apparented' societies is examined further in Part X, below.

overcoming the corresponding movement of the Berbers—in the migration of the Banu Hilāl and the associated tribes of Arab *badu*.[1] The interregnum occupied by this Völkerwanderung and by the ephemeral lives of the barbarian 'successor-states' to the Caliphate extended over about three centuries which may be expressed in terms of the Christian Era by the conventional dates A.D. 975–1275.[2] The latter date represents approximately the *terminus post quem* the Islamic Society, as we find it living in the world to-day, has emerged.

Here, by all analogy, we have tokens of an 'apparented' society, beyond the horizon, to which the extant Islamic Society is 'affiliated'; and at first sight it looks as though we were in the presence of a relation between two parties only, in contrast to the tripartite relation involved in the double 'affiliation' of the Western Society and the Orthodox Christian Society to the Hellenic. On closer inspection, however, we find that this appearance of simplicity is an illusion. The single Islamic Society that exists to-day is not unique in origin but only in consequence of an act of union. That is to say, it is not the only society that has ever been 'affiliated' to the older society—still to be identified—of which the 'Abbasid Caliphate represents the last phase. If it is the only society with this 'affiliation' that survives, that is because in the course of its history it has incorporated into itself a sister society, with the same 'affiliation', which originally emerged from the same interregnum as an independent social entity.

When we look for the cradle of the society which is represented by the Islamic Society of to-day without any breach of continuity or change of identity as we trace its history back to the moment of its first emergence, we find this cradle in one particular part—and this a relatively small part—of the present Islamic World. The society that has become the Islamic Society of to-day first emerged in a zone of territory extending from the Asiatic hinterland of the Sea of Marmara to the delta of the Ganges. This zone was narrow relatively to its length. For the most part it consisted of a single chain of countries: Anatolia, Azerbaijan, Khurāsān, Afghanistan, and Hindustan (in the narrower usage of the name which covers the plains of Northern India from the Panjab to Bengal but excludes the Deccan). Only towards the middle this narrow zone swelled out north-eastwards to embrace the basin of the Rivers Oxus and

---

[1] i.e. people of the desert: plural *badu*, singular *badawī*. The word is more familiar to English readers in the Gallicized form *bedouin*. For the Völkerwanderung of the Banu Hilāl in Africa, see further III. C (ii) (*b*), vol. iii, pp. 322–4, and also V. C (i) (*c*) 3, vol. v, p. 247, below.

[2] When we thus transpose the post-'Abbasid Völkerwanderung on to our own time-scale, we find that there was an interval of about six centuries between it and the post-Hellenic Völkerwanderung, to which we may assign the conventional dates A.D. 375–675.

Jaxartes on the threshold of the Eurasian Steppe. The Islamic Society that began to emerge in this zone towards the end of the thirteenth century of the Christian Era eventually articulated itself into states from which almost all the states of the present Islamic World are derived—the only notable exception being the Sharifian Empire of Morocco.

There is not, however, any striking contrast in the Islamic World of to-day between Morocco on the one hand and all other Islamic countries on the other; and such a division of Dār-al-Islām into a Moroccan and a non-Moroccan section is certainly not the first that occurs to our minds. When we ask ourselves what is the main division in the Islamic World to-day, we find ourselves answering that it is the schism between Sunnīs and Shīʿīs; and when we translate this religious cleavage into geographical terms, we find that it cuts right across the zone which we have just plotted out as the original home of the society. Azerbaijan and Khurāsān, in the middle of the chain of countries of which that zone consists, are at this day provinces of Persia; and on the present map Shīʿism occupies the whole territory of Persia, with outposts in Trans-caucasia and ʿIrāq and Hasā and India and the Yaman. This wedge of Shīʿīs splits the Sunnīs into two groups which are geographically isolated from one another: to the east, the Sunnīs of Central Asia and India; to the west, the Sunnīs in the former territories of the Ottoman Empire in Asia, Europe, and Africa, from the western frontier of Persia to the eastern frontier of Morocco, together with the Sunnīs of Morocco itself.

This map of an Islamic World divided into Sunnī and Shīʿī portions has become so familiar that it needs an effort of imagination to recall how recent it is. Down to the year 1500 of the Christian Era, no Muslim would have been likely to anticipate that the zone which we have defined as the original home of this Islamic Society was about to be split into fragments by a religious schism. At that time Shīʿism was a minoritarian religion, endemic throughout the zone in question but dominant nowhere. The situation was transformed by a revolution which segregated the adherents of the Shīʿī and the Sunnī faiths and made Shīʿism locally dominant in one state; and this revolution was accomplished in the career of a single statesman, Ismāʿīl Shāh Safawī (*dominabatur* A.D. 1500–24).[1] Down to the year A.D. 1500, again, no Muslim observer would have been likely to anticipate that the Ottoman Empire was about to expand over those Muslim countries in Asia and Africa—from Syria southwards and westwards—in which Arabic had become the

[1] This revolution—which was really the evocation of a ghost from the life of the 'apparented' society—is examined further, in this aspect, in Part X, below.

current vernacular as well as the acknowledged classical language. Down to that time the Ottoman Empire had expanded entirely within the limits of the domain of Orthodox Christendom, as these limits have been sketched above; and if the expansion was to continue, the natural line of further Ottoman advance must have appeared at the time, to contemporary observers, to be either north-westward into Western Christendom or else south-eastward into Azerbaijan and the other countries of the zone which was the birth-place of the new Islamic society to which the 'Osmanlis themselves belonged. The Shī'ī revolution which suddenly debarred the Ottoman Empire from expansion in the latter direction also compelled the 'Osmanlis to extend their dominion over the Arabic countries in order to forestall an extension of the new Shī'ī Power in that quarter; and between A.D. 1516 and A.D. 1574 the structure of the Ottoman Empire was changed and its centre of gravity was shifted by the annexation of all the Arabic countries from Syria to the Yaman and from 'Irāq to Algeria inclusive.

This reminds us that, down to that time, these Arabic Muslim countries had lain outside the domain of the neighbouring Islamic society, in the zone to the north-east of them, to which the Safawīs of Gīlān belonged as well as the 'Osmanlis of Anatolia. And, when we look closer, we find that this Arabic World—and particularly Egypt and Syria—was the home of a different society which had emerged from the same interregnum independently and which was 'affiliated', likewise, to the older society—still to be identified—of which the 'Abbasid Caliphate represents the last phase.

Thus, after all, we find ourselves here in the presence of a relation between three societies, not two. Our pair of Islamic societies, both 'affiliated' to a single older society in the background, below the horizon, corresponds to the more familiar pair of societies—the Western and the Orthodox Christian—that are 'affiliated' to the Hellenic Society. And, comparing the two pairs of 'affiliated' societies with one another, we can see that the Islamic Society which emerged in what we may call the Perso-Turkish or Iranian zone bears a certain resemblance to our Western Society, while the other Islamic Society which emerged in what we may call the Arabic zone bears a certain resemblance to Orthodox Christendom.

For example, the ghost of the 'Abbasid Caliphate of Baghdad which was evoked by the Mamlūks at Cairo in the thirteenth century of the Christian Era reminds us of the ghost of the Roman Empire which was evoked at Constantinople by Leo the Syrian in the eighth century. The Mamlūks' political construction, like Leo's, was relatively modest, effective, and durable, by contrast with the Empire of Timur in the neighbouring Iranian zone—a vast, vague, ephemeral shape which appeared and disappeared like the Empire of Charlemagne in the West.[1] Again, the classical language which was the vehicle of culture in the Arabic zone was Arabic itself, which had been the language of culture in the society of the 'Abbasid Caliphate of Baghdad. In the Iranian zone, a new culture found a new vehicle for itself in Persian—a language which had been cultivated since the time of the Caliphate of Baghdad by grafting it on to Arabic, as Latin was cultivated by grafting it on to Greek. Latin, of course, has been the classical language of the Western Society and Greek that of the Orthodox Christian Society;[2] so that, in that matter again, the Islamic Society that emerged in the Iranian zone resembles the Western Society, while the Islamic Society that emerged in the Arabic zone resembles the Orthodox Christian Society.[3] Finally, we may notice that the conquest and

[1] Timur's Empire has a certain affinity with the Cairene 'Abbasid Caliphate—as 'the Holy Roman Empire' has a certain affinity with 'the East Roman Empire'—inasmuch as it was a deliberate and conscious attempt to revive the universal state which had broken up in the foregoing interregnum. Timur in Transoxania, like the Mamlūks in Egypt, was a champion of the Islamic tradition against the paganism and barbarism of the Mongol Nomads who had overrun the Iranian zone of the 'Abbasid Empire in the last convulsions of the post-'Abbasid interregnum. (For Timur's role as a Warden of the Marches of the Iranic World against Eurasian Nomadism, see further II. D (v), vol. ii, pp. 144–50, below.) In the Iranian zone for the best part of a century (*circa* A.D.1225–1325) beginning with the Mongol Conquest, political power had been in the hands of pagan Mongol feudatories of the Mongol Great Khan of Qaraqorum who were not merely non-Muslims but were positively anti-Islamic.

'The masterful descendants of Chingiz Khān were more ready to put forward descent from this world-conqueror as a justification for their exercise of authority than seek a diploma of investiture from the alleged descendants of that 'Abbasid Caliph whom their relatives had put to death in 1258.' (Arnold, Sir T. W.: *The Caliphate* (Oxford 1924, Clarendon Press), p. 109.)

[2] This statement has to be qualified, inasmuch as the break-up of the Orthodox Church into a bevy of local churches living on the establishments of the several states into which Orthodox Christendom came to be articulated was accompanied by the translation of the Liturgy and the Scriptures, for local use, from Greek into certain local languages. In this way, other classical languages (e.g. Classical Georgian and 'Old Slavonic') became established in Orthodox Christendom side by side with Classical Greek. Here, again, the evolution of the Orthodox Church in the Middle Ages resembled the evolution of Protestantism in the Modern Age of the Western Society.

[3] The fission of the derelict domain of the 'Abbasid Caliphate, in the course of the post-'Abbasid interregnum, into an Arabic and an Iranic World can be measured by the shrinkage of the area in which the Arabic language was in current use as the literary vehicle of culture—just as the fission of the derelict domain of the Roman Empire, in the course of the post-Hellenic interregnum, into an Orthodox Christian and a Western World can be measured by the shrinkage of the area of the literary use of Greek.

At the height of the 'Abbasid Caliphate, Arabic works of literature were written and read in every part of the 'Abbasid dominions; and men of letters, as well as men of business, circulated freely from one end of the Empire to the other (just as, at the height of the Roman Empire, Greek was written and read in every part of the Empire by cultivated people). The break-up of the 'Abbasid Caliphate, which was consummated by the Mongol invasion in the thirteenth century of the Christian Era, was followed by a reduction of the domain of literary Arabic to those regions in which Arabic was the current vernacular. Previously, a great Arabic writer might arise in the Oxus-Jaxartes Basin or Khurāsān or the Iberian Peninsula; but after the close of the thirteenth century of the Christian Era the field of secular Arabic literature came to be virtually confined to Egypt and Syria (with a few brilliant exceptions like Ibn Khaldūn (*vivebat* A.D. 1332–1404) in the Maghrib). Thenceforth, the only hold which the classical Arabic language retained in those parts of Dār-al-Islām in which the current vernaculars were non-Arabic was in virtue of its being the language of the Qur'ān. This ensured its

absorption of the Islamic Society of the Arabic zone by the Islamic Society of the Iranian zone, which occurred in the sixteenth century of the Christian Era, has its parallel in the aggression of Western Christendom upon Orthodox Christendom during the Crusades. When this aggression culminated, at the beginning of the thirteenth century, in the diversion of the Fourth Crusade to Constantinople, it looked for a moment as though Orthodox Christendom would be permanently conquered and absorbed by the sister society—the fate which actually overtook the Islamic Society of the Arabic zone some three centuries later, when the Mamlūk Power was overthrown and the 'Abbasid Caliphate of Cairo was extinguished by the Ottoman Pādishāh Selīm in A.D. 1517.

It would be out of proportion to study the histories of these two Islamic societies further in this place.[1] In distinguishing them from each other we have served our immediate purpose, and we have only to find names for them before we pass on. We may call them 'Iranic'[2] and 'Arabic', after the two geographical zones in which they respectively emerged.

The Syriac Society

Having thus paused to distinguish and name two Islamic societies—the Iranic and the Arabic—beneath the surface of the tardily and forcibly unified Islamic Society with which we started, we may now proceed towards our original objective of identifying the older society, 'apparented' to this 'affiliated' pair, whose existence in the background, below the horizon, is betokened by the three phenomena of the universal state represented by the 'Abbasid Caliphate of Baghdad, the universal church represented by Islam, and the Völkerwanderung in which the former domain of the Caliphate of Baghdad was overrun by barbarians within the three centuries between about A.D. 975 and A.D. 1275.

maintenance, throughout the Islamic World, as the vehicle of scholastic theology; but, outside the Arabic-speaking regions, Arabic ceased to be employed as the vehicle either of secular literature or of political administration; and in the Iranian zone its place was taken for these purposes by Persian. In the Iranian zone, during the post-'Abbasid interregnum, Persian gained the ground which Arabic lost (just as, in Western Christendom during the post-Hellenic interregnum, Latin secured a literary monopoly at the expense of Greek). It was Persian, and not Arabic, that became the culture-language of the Turkish-speaking barbarian invaders from the Eurasian Steppe by whom the Iranian zone was overrun (just as, in Western Christendom, it was Latin that became the culture-language of the Teutonic barbarians). In so far as the descendants of the Turkish barbarian invaders succeeded in creating new literatures in their own vernaculars, they moulded these on Persian rather than on Arabic models.

[1] A more detailed study will be found in I. C (i) (b), Annex I, below.
[2] 'Iranic' is less cumbrous than 'Perso-Turkish', and it is not really less accurate. 'Perso-Turkish' expresses the fact that most of the peoples in the original home of this society spoke either Persian or Turkish vernaculars (as one might coin the name 'Latino-Teutonic' to express a corresponding fact about Western Christendom). 'Iranic', however, expresses the more significant fact that the vehicle of the new culture which was emerging in this region was the classical language and literature of Iran.

Let us try to identify this unknown society by formulating an equation between its history, of which we know the latter end, and the history of the Hellenic Society, which we happen to know in all its stages. The universal state of the Hellenic Society was the Roman Empire, and the immediate antecedent phase of Hellenic history was a 'Time of Troubles' against which the régime of the universal state stands out in sharp contrast. The Hellenic 'Time of Troubles' was an age in which the Hellenic World was articulated into a multiplicity of states instead of being incorporated in one state; and these local states inflicted mortal wounds on Society in a series of ever more destructive wars which only ended in the overthrow of all the other contending states by one victorious survivor, the Roman Empire. If we peer into the immediate antecedents of the 'Abbasid Caliphate of Baghdad, do we find a similar situation?

The answer to this question is in the negative. The 'Abbasid Caliphate of Baghdad did not establish itself by the slow and laborious process that went to the making of the Roman Empire. It did not begin as one local state among many and then gradually grow into a universal state by conquering all its fellows in succession in a prolonged and internecine struggle for 'the survival of the fittest'. It won its position at a stroke, by capturing the greater part of the dominions of a single state which actually ruled over a somewhat larger area than the 'Abbasid Caliphate succeeded in acquiring from it. This single victim, out of whose ruin the 'Abbasid Caliphate of Baghdad made its fortune, was the Umayyad Caliphate of Damascus; and the Umayyad Caliphate of Damascus was one of the 'successor-states' of the Roman Empire.

Why did the Umayyads succumb to the 'Abbasids? And why was the change of dynasty followed by a transfer of the capital from Damascus in Syria to Baghdad in 'Irāq? The two breaks of continuity can be traced to one identical cause. While the Primitive Muslim Arab war-bands which prepared the ground for the establishment of the Umayyad Caliphate had been conquering the Roman provinces in Syria and Egypt with their right hands—breaking through this sector of the Roman Imperial frontiers from a no-man's-land in Arabia[1]—their left hands had been employed in conquering the entire domain of the adjoining empire of the Sasanidae. Since the Sasanian Empire covered the whole of 'Irāq and Iran, its annexation upset the balance and altered the nature of the Arab 'successor-state' to the Roman Empire which was

[1] Arabia lay south-east of the Roman dominions in Syria, and perhaps this was why the Muslim Arabs came to be known as 'Saracens' or 'Easterners'. The Greek adjective Σαρακηνός is derived from the Arabic substantive شَرْق = 'the East', and this etymology indicates that the name was coined by the western Arabs under the rule of the Banu Ghassān who were the Wardens of the Marches of the Roman Empire in this quarter at the time when the Muslim Arabs broke through.

organized from a base in Syria by the founder of the Umayyad Dynasty, Muʿāwiyah (*regnabat* A.D. 656–80);[1] and this casual inclusion of a huge extraneous member in the structure of the Umayyad Caliphate explains its peculiar end. While the other 'successor-states' of the Roman Empire ended in being either re-conquered by the expiring Empire or else conquered by one of their own kind,[2] the Umayyad 'successor-state' met the exceptional end of being superseded by another state of approximately the same extent—the ʿAbbasid Caliphate of Baghdad—which left an enduring mark on history. The ʿAbbasids left this mark because they made a social unity out of the two areas—one originally conquered from the Romans and the other from the Sasanids—which had been united politically under the preceding Umayyad régime. This process of social unification had indeed begun some time before the Umayyads fell and the ʿAbbasids reigned in their stead. It can be traced as far back as the time of the Umayyad Caliph Hishām (*imperabat* A.D. 724–43) or even to the reign of ʿUmar II (*imperabat* A.D. 717–20). But the process was consummated by the ʿAbbasids[3] and it was symbolized in the transfer of the capital to Baghdad— the true centre of gravity of an empire which extended from North Africa to Transoxania. Damascus, which the Umayyads had chosen for their capital, had been too eccentric, in the literal sense, to become the permanent seat of government of this immense empire (though Damascus was admirably placed for serving simply as the capital of an Arab 'successor-state' of the Roman Empire if Muʿāwiyah had been content to combine the former Roman provinces in Syria and Egypt with the no-man's-land in Arabia out of which he and his war-bands had come).[4] As it was, there were two alternative ends for the Umayyad Caliphate. Either it must break up into its two constituent parts, or if these parts were to be permanently held and fused together there must be a closer union of the kind which was actually consummated in the end after the Caliphate had been forcibly taken over from the Umayyads by the ʿAbbasids.

[1] Reckoning Muʿāwiyah's effective rule in Syria to have begun at the death of the Caliph ʿUthmān and not at the death of the Caliph ʿAlī, though it was not till the latter date that Muʿāwiyah assumed the title to the Caliphate. During the years when ʿAlī was ruling the former domain of the Sasanids from Kūfah, while Muʿāwiyah, from Damascus, was ruling the former Roman provinces in Syria and Egypt, the union of these territories, which had been brought about by the Arab conquest, was temporally dissolved.   [2] See p. 58, above.

[3] For an examination of the internal social evolution of the Caliphate in greater detail, see V. C (i) (c) 2, vol. v, p. 128, below.

[4] Mucāwiyah's domain was confined to these manageable limits so long as the Caliph ʿAli was ruling from Kūfah the former dominions of the Sasanidae in ʿIrāq and Iran. During this brief phase the Arab 'successor-state' of the Roman Empire which was being ruled from Damascus resembled, both in extent and in character, the premature and abortive 'successor-state' which had been ruled from Palmyra by Zenobia four centuries earlier.

The fact that this second alternative was the actual outcome indicates that there was something in the situation which told in its favour. The merely external union between the former Oriental provinces of the Roman Empire and the former dominions of the Sasanidae, which had been brought about casually by the primitive Muslim Arab conquerors and had been maintained under the Umayyad régime, was apparently unsatisfactory not because it was unwieldy but because it was superficial. Some social current was drawing the inhabitants of the two constituent parts of the Umayyad Caliphate towards union of a closer and a deeper kind; and it appears to have been this current that swept the House of Umayyah away and carried the House of 'Abbās into power in order that the new dynasty might do with a will the work of unification which the old dynasty had been doing only half-heartedly.

In setting out to discover whence this powerful trend towards unification came, we shall seek for a clue in the antecedent history of that division between the Roman and the Sasanian part of the Umayyad Empire which the 'Abbasids succeeded in effacing.

When the frontier between the Roman and Sasanian Empires was restored for the last time in A.D. 628, on the eve of the Arab conquest, it had been in existence for nearly 700 years, since the original organization of the Roman province of Syria by Pompey in 64 B.C. During those seven centuries the line had been singularly stable, varying within quite a narrow range; and in a more fluctuating condition it can be traced back as far as 140 B.C., when the Seleucid Monarchy, of which the Roman province of Syria was a kind of residuary legacy, had lost 'Irāq, as well as all its former dominions further east, in Iran, to the Arsacids who were the predecessors of the Sasanids. As soon as we recall the whole history of this dividing line,[1] we realize what its historical significance was. It was the line along which equilibrium was provisionally restored after the immense upheaval which attended the overthrow of the Empire of the Achaemenidae by Alexander the Great. Hellenism, following in the Macedonian conqueror's train, spread eastward over the former domain of the fallen Achaemenian Empire and established its ascendency from end to end of it for about two centuries.[2] Then the pendulum swung back towards the west with a violence proportionate to the original momentum of Alexander's stroke, so that there were times between the collapse of the Seleucid Monarchy and the Oriental campaigns of Pompey when it looked as though the insurgent Orientals might not only sweep Hellenism

[1] For a further examination of the line, see Parts IX and XI, below.
[2] i.e. from the overthrow of the Achaemenian Empire by Alexander in 334–330 B.C. to the discomfiture of Hellenism in Iran and 'Irāq during the latter part of the second century B.C.

out of Asia but might subjugate Greece itself.[1] The intervention of the Romans sent the pendulum swinging eastward again; but this time it was arrested, about half-way across the former Achaemenian domain, along the line which we are studying; and during the seven centuries preceding the Arab conquest the provisional balance along this line was never permanently upset either by the occasional insurrections of the Jews and other Orientals on the Roman side of the line or by the wars between the Romans and the Arsacidae and Sasanidae which occurred with increasing frequency and intensity from Crassus's inconclusive defeat to Heraclius's inconclusive victory.[2]

Thus, in tracing back to its historical origins the line which the 'Abbasid Caliphs ultimately effaced by fusing together the two territories which had been divided by it, we find that this line came into existence owing to the break-up of an earlier empire—the Empire of the Achaemenidae—in which these same territories had been united once before. In fact, the union of the territories under the 'Abbasid régime proves to have been a reunion; and this observation gives a hint of what the social current may have been which was making for this union so strongly at the time when the Umayyads gave way to the 'Abbasids. It may have been an impulse —mainly, no doubt, unconscious, yet certainly not less potent and probably more persistent than if it had been clearly envisaged—to join together again the parts of a whole which had been put asunder by force, and thereby to undo completely a deed which had been left in suspension—half undone and half still to undo—during those centuries in which an arbitrary line of division had cleft the former domain of the Achaemenian Empire in twain. In this light, the cataclysmic conquests of the primitive Muslim Arabs seem to respond antistrophically, in the rhythm of history, to the cataclysmic conquests of Alexander. Like these, they changed the face of the World in half a dozen years; but instead of changing it out of recognition, *more Macedonico*, they changed it back to a recognizable likeness of what it had been once before. As the Macedonian conquest, by breaking up the Achaemenian Empire, prepared the soil for the seed of Hellenism, so the Arab conquest opened the way for the later Umayyads, and after them the 'Abbasids, to reconstruct a universal state which was the equivalent of the Achaemenian Empire. If we superpose the map of either empire upon the map of the other, we shall be struck by the closeness with which

[1] e.g. in the years 87 and 86 B.C., during the first part of Sulla's operations against Mithradates of Pontus, when Greece was the theatre of war. In these campaigns the armies of Mithradates penetrated as far into continental European Greece as the armies of Xerxes had penetrated in 480–479 B.C.

[2] The rhythm of this series of wars is examined below in Part XI.

the outlines correspond, and we shall find that the correspondence is not simply geographical but extends to methods of administration and even to the more intimate phenomena of social and spiritual life.[1] We may express the historical function of the 'Abbasid Caliphate by describing it as a 'reintegration' or 'resumption' of the Achaemenian Empire—the reintegration of a political structure which had been broken up by the impact of an external force, and the resumption of a phase of social life which had been interrupted by an alien intrusion.

Is it fantastic to conceive the possibility of such a relation between two institutions which were separated in time by an interval of more than a millennium? If this seems fantastic at first sight, we may reflect that an interval which measured thirty-six generations of human lives was wholly occupied by a single historical event: the collision between the Hellenic Society and that other society—still to be identified—which manifested itself (as we suggest) alike in the Achaemenian Empire before the collision and in the 'Abbasid Caliphate after it. We must also allow for the fact that in this collision the non-Hellenic party was the victim. This society's career was suddenly and violently interrupted by the intrusion of an alien force; and such an abnormal interference with the course of life might be expected to produce an abnormal reaction in the shape of a paralysis lasting as long as the intrusion itself. As soon, however, as the alien intruder was expelled, we should expect the victim to reassume the posture out of which he had been shaken by the original impact and to resume the career which the intrusion had arrested.[2] If these expectations are reasonable, it does not seem fantastic to interpret the 'Abbasid Caliphate—a universal state which followed the interlude of Hellenic intrusion upon our still unidentified society's life—as a 'reintegration' or 'resumption' of the universal state which preceded the interlude, that is to say, the Achaemenian Empire. This is surely less fantastic than to dismiss as fortuitous coincidences the remarkable resemblances between two universal states which stand in this peculiar historical relation to one another.

[1] This correspondence is examined in greater detail in Part VI, below.

[2] When a hedgehog crawling across a field is attacked by a dog, it stops dead, curls itself up into a spiny ball, and remains motionless in this rigid defensive posture until the dog is tired of trying to find a weak spot in its armour. As soon as the dog gives up and goes away, the hedgehog uncurls itself, reassumes the crawling posture which the dog's attack had forced it to abandon, and resumes its journey across the field towards its original goal. It acts like this however long the interruption may have lasted. Yet there is no reason to suppose that any step in the action is purposive or even conscious. On this analogy, we may imagine a society to behave similarly in corresponding circumstances. This supposition does not involve the fallacy of interpreting the behaviour of a society as though it possessed the faculties of a rational self-conscious human being. 'Le passé n'a pas besoin d'être connu pour peser lourdement sur le présent. Il laisse au fond de l'inconscient des instincts, plus puissants que des souvenirs précis.' (Gautier, E. F.: Les Siècles Obscurs du Maghreb (Paris 1927, Payot), p. 414.)

This problem will be studied more closely in later chapters.[1] Our present concern is to identify further representatives of the species of society which we are studying; and, in our pursuit of this objective, we may here allow ourselves at least provisionally to regard the 'Abbasid Caliphate as a 'resumption' of the Achaemenian Empire, ignoring for our present purpose the Hellenic intrusion which intervened between them.[2] If we accept this postulate, we may now inspect the immediate antecedents of the Achaemenian Empire in search of that phenomenon which we failed to detect in the immediate antecedents of the 'Abbasid Caliphate: that is to say, a 'Time of Troubles' resembling the time which in Hellenic history immediately preceded the establishment of the Roman Empire. And this time our search is not in vain; for the Achaemenian Empire did arise out of a multiplicity of states which eventually disappeared in a series of ever more destructive wars.

The general similarity between the genesis of the Achaemenian Empire and the genesis of the Roman Empire is unmistakable. The chief difference of detail is that the Hellenic universal state grew out of the very state, among the superseded parochial states, which had been the principal agent of destruction in the foregoing struggle for existence, whereas in the genesis of the Achaemenian Empire the part of Rome was played by different parochial states in different acts of the tragedy. The Achaemenian Power which actually established the universal state in the last act was not the Power which, in previous acts, had prepared the ground by beating down its neighbours. That Power was Assyria; but when Assyria had been on the point of completing her work she had brought destruction upon herself by the very excess of her militarism.[3] Just before the grand finale, the protagonist had been dramatically struck down; and his role had been assumed unexpectedly by a performer who had hitherto been content to play a minor part in a sheltered corner at the back of the stage.[4] The Achaemenidae reaped where the Assyrians had sown. Yet this substitution of one performer for another at the eleventh hour did not change the plot;

[1] See Parts VI and IX below.

[2] There was, of course, an aspect of the 'Abbasid régime in which it came to fulfil Hellenism and not to destroy it; for under the 'Abbasid dispensation Oriental minds made the Hellenic philosophy and science their own far more thoroughly than they had ever assimilated Hellenic culture during the centuries when a large part of the ci-devant Achaemenian dominions were under Macedonian or Roman rule. For this cultural philhellenism of the 'Abbasids and their subjects, see further Part IX, below.

[3] For a further examination of Assyrian militarism, see IV. C (iii) (c) 3 (α), vol. iv, pp. 467–84, below.

[4] The Achaemenian Power started as a backward and unimportant local state in what is now the Persian province of Fars (Persis) on the south-western edge of the Iranian Plateau. The overthrow of Elam by Assyria in 655–639 B.C.—Assyria's last great act of destruction before she was destroyed herself—gave the Achaemenidae their first opportunity for aggrandizement. They descended into the derelict lowlands of Elam (in what is now the Persian province of Khuzistan) and established their capital in Susa, the former capital of the defunct Elamite State.

and we cannot compare the two performances which ended respectively in the establishment of the Achaemenian Empire and in the establishment of the Roman Empire without perceiving that the differences between them were mere variations on an identical theme.

Having thus discerned a 'Time of Troubles' antecedent to the Achaemenian Empire, we can now perhaps at last identify the society which lived through the successive experiences of this 'Time of Troubles' and the Achaemenian Empire and the Hellenic intrusion and the 'Abbasid Caliphate of Baghdad and the universal church of Islam and the Völkerwanderung that followed the fall of the 'Abbasid Empire and occupied the interregnum which the emergence of the Iranic and Arabic societies brought to an end.

Negatively, we can make out that this society was not identical with that to which the Assyrians belonged. In the history of this society, the Assyrians at an earlier stage, like the Macedonians at a later stage, played their part as intruders who came and went. Indeed, the culture which the Assyrians represented did not long survive the political *débâcle* in which Assyrian militarism ended. We can trace the process of its peaceful ejection from the culture upon which it had intruded by force in the gradual replacement of the Akkadian language and the cuneiform script by the Aramaic language and Alphabet.

The Assyrians themselves, in their latter days, employed the Aramaic Alphabet for writing on parchment as a supplement to the normal employment of their traditional cuneiform script, which they inscribed on stone or impressed on clay tablets. When they employed the Aramaic Alphabet, they may be presumed to have written the Aramaic language.[1] At any rate, after the destruction of the Assyrian State and of the short-lived Neo-Babylonian Empire which intervened between the fall of the Assyrians and the rise of the Achaemenidae, the Aramaic language and Alphabet, advancing concurrently, continued to gain ground upon both the kindred Akkadian language and the unrelated cuneiform script in which Akkadian was conveyed,[2] until, in the course of the last century before the beginning of the Christian Era, both of these

[1] This would have come natural to them, since the Aramaic language was a member of the same family—the Semitic family—as the Akkadian language in which the Assyrians expressed themselves in cuneiform.

[2] The cuneiform script was not an Alphabet but a phonetic syllabary combined with a collection of ideograms. It had been evolved originally to convey the Sumerian language, which had no affinity whatever with the Akkadian dialect of Semitic for which the script came to be used. The employment of cuneiform to convey two unrelated languages perhaps partly explains why the ideograms held their own side by side with the phonetic characters. The ideograms were written identically in Sumerian and Akkadian, though they were, of course, translated vocally into quite different words. Some characters which were used as ideograms in Akkadian had a phonetic value in Sumerian.

became extinct throughout their former homelands in Assyria and Babylonia.[1]

A corresponding process can be traced in the history of the Iranian language, which emerged suddenly from obscurity because it was the native language of the Achaemenidae and of their countrymen the Persians and the Medes, who were the ruling peoples in the Achaemenian Empire. Confronted with the problem of making records in a language which had evolved no script of its own, the Iranians of the Achaemenian Age adapted both the cuneiform script and the Aramaic Alphabet in order to convey their mother-tongue in the respective media of stone and parchment. The cuneiform inscriptions of the Achaemenidae themselves are the only monuments of the language that survive from this age; but during the Hellenic intrusion, when there was no Great King in Iran to carve a record of his deeds in cuneiform characters on the face of the mountains, the scriptures of the Zoroastrian Church, which were composed in an Iranian dialect akin to that of the Achaemenian inscriptions, continued to be copied on parchment rolls in Aramaic letters, with the result that in Iran, as in 'Irāq, the cuneiform characters became extinct and the Aramaic Alphabet prevailed. Moreover, in the train of the Aramaic Alphabet, the Aramaic language gained a lodgement in the body of the Iranian language—in spite of the fact that Iranian, which was a member of the Indo-European family, had none of that natural affinity with Aramaic which had assisted Aramaic in supplanting its own Semitic sister Akkadian. In 'Pehlevi'[2] some of the Iranian words were spelt out in the Aramaic Alphabet phonetically, but others were represented by the equivalent words in the Aramaic language. It is supposed that these Aramaic words were treated as ideograms which were rendered phonetically by their Iranian synonyms.[3] In the next stage, however, when 'Pehlevi' was transformed into what is now called 'Persian'[4] by the substitution of the Arabic Alphabet and Arabic loan-words for the Aramaic Alphabet and Aramaic loan-words in consequence of the Arab conquest,[5]

[1] See the present chapter, p. 119, and II D (v), vol. ii, p. 138, below.
[2] Literally 'Parthian'. The name indicates that this phase of the Iranian language, as spoken and written, came to maturity in the time of the Arsacidae, though the later age of the Sasanidae was the time when it most flourished.
[3] It seems strange that the Iranians should have lapsed into the use of ideograms for writing their language in an Alphabet which was free from ideograms, considering that they avoided the use of ideograms and used none but phonetic characters when they borrowed the cuneiform script, in which ideograms abounded.
[4] 'Farsi', that is to say, the dialect of Iranian current in the province of Fars (Persis).
[5] This substitution was easy because Arabic, like Akkadian, was a member of the same family of languages—the Semitic family—as Aramaic, while the Arabic Alphabet was derived from an earlier form of that Aramaic Alphabet which was employed for conveying Pehlevi.

these Arabic loan-words were pronounced as they were written, and became integral elements in the living speech.

Here we discern a process which was going on peacefully and steadily during and after and in the teeth of the successive intrusions of Assyrians and Macedonians: two elements of culture, one from Syria and the other from Iran, were asserting themselves contemporaneously and were at the same time entering into an ever closer association with one another. From the latter end of the 'Time of Troubles' preceding the establishment of the Achaemenian Empire, when the conquered Aramaeans were beginning to captivate their Assyrian conquerers, down to the time of the ʿAbbasid Caliphate of Baghdad, when the Persian language was being equipped with Arabic loan-words and was being transliterated into the Arabic Alphabet, we have been contemplating this process in the mirror of languages and scripts. If we wish to discern it at an earlier stage, we may look into the mirror of religion and observe how the same 'Time of Troubles' breathed the same inspiration into Zarathustra, the prophet of Iran, and into the contemporary prophets of Israel and Judah.[1]

In analysing this Syro-Iranian culture, can we determine whether it was the Syrian or the Iranian element that made the greater contribution? And can we perhaps push our analysis even further, and determine which of the two was the original contributor? The history of religion gives us no certain clue[2]; but the history of literature suggests that Syria and not Iran was the dominant partner.[3] And if we now try to extend our survey further into the

[1] It is now recognized on all hands that, during the four centuries or so that preceded the political union of the Iranians and the Syrians in the Empire of the Achaemenidae, the religions of Iran and Israel had been developing on certain remarkable lines which differentiated them both from all other contemporary religions and at the same time led them both into convergence towards one another. Was this convergence due to the influence of one party upon the other (e.g. the influence of Israelites who had been transplanted by the Assyrians to 'the cities of the Medes')? Or was it that an identical affliction, in the shape of Assyrian militarism, produced identical spiritual effects through independent but similar reactions in the souls of those who suffered under it? For our immediate purpose here, the question is immaterial. Whichever alternative may prove to be the truth, the Israelites and Iranians of this age were already going through the same spiritual experiences, and in virtue of that were already becoming members one with another in the same society.

[2] If there is some ground for suspecting a religious influence of Syria upon Iran in the Assyrian Age (see the preceding footnote), there is perhaps stronger ground for believing that in the Achaemenian Age the main current of religious influence flowed in the opposite direction. (See Gall, A. von: Βασιλεία τοῦ Θεοῦ (Heidelberg 1926, Winter).)

[3] In support of the view that the Syrian element is the predominant element in the Syro-Iranian culture, we can cite the high authority of Professor Edward G. Browne:

'Persians . . . have continued ever since the Muhammadan conquest—that is to say, for more than twelve hundred years—to use the Arabic language almost to the exclusion of their own in writing on certain subjects, notably theology and philosophy; while during the two centuries immediately succeeding the Arab invasion the language of the conquerors was, save amongst those who still adhered to the ancient national faith of Zoroaster, almost the sole literary medium employed in Persia. To ignore this literature would be to ignore many of the most important and characteristic manifestations of the

past behind the 'Time of Troubles' into an antecedent age of growth, we shall find that in this age Iran fades out of the picture, while we shall catch a glimpse of a society in Syria, in the generation of King Solomon and his contemporary King Hiram, which was just discovering the Atlantic and the Indian Ocean and had discovered the Alphabet already.[1]

Here at last we have identified the society, antecedent and 'apparented' to the Islamic, of which we have been so long in search. It remains to give this society a name. Perhaps the name 'Syriac' is the most convenient.[2]

In the light of this identification, let us look again at Islam—the

Persian genius, and to form an altogether inadequate judgement of the intellectual activity of that ingenious and talented people. . . .

'It is a remarkable thing how great at all periods of history has been Semitic influence on Persia: Arabian in the late Sasanian and Muhammadan time; Aramaic in earlier Sasanian and later Parthian days; Assyrian at a yet more ancient epoch. And indeed this fact can scarcely be insisted upon too strongly; for the study of Persian has suffered from nothing so much as from the purely philological view which regards mere linguistic and racial affinities as infinitely more important and significant than the much deeper and more potent influences of literary and religious contact. . . . If, as an adjunct to my equipment for the study of Persian thought and literature, I were offered my choice between a thorough knowledge of the Semitic and the Aryan languages, I should, from this point of view alone, unhesitatingly choose the former. A good knowledge of the Aramaic languages is essential for the study of Pahlawi, and a fruitful investigation of the post-Muhammadan literature and thought of Persia is impossible without a wide acquaintance with Arabic books; while in both these fields a knowledge of Sanskrit is practically of very little use, and even in the interpretation of the Avesta it must be employed with some reserve and due regard to the Pahlawi tradition.' (Browne, E. G.: *A Literary History of Persia*, vol. i (London 1908, Fisher Unwin), pp. 3–4 and 36–7.)

[1] For the origin of the Alphabet, see further the present section, p. 102, footnote 3; II. D (ii), vol. ii, pp. 50–1; and II. D (vii), vol. ii, p. 386, footnote 2, below.

[2] When a cross-section of this society is taken in the age of the Achaemenian Empire, the name 'Syro-Iranian' suggests itself, on the analogy of 'Graeco-Roman', which seems the natural name for the Hellenic Society when a cross-section of that is taken in the age of the Roman Empire. As between 'Graeco-Roman' and 'Hellenic', however, we have found the name 'Hellenic' preferable (see p. 41, footnote 2, above); and the same considerations recommend 'Syriac' in preference to 'Syro-Iranian'. It is not only less clumsy but also more accurate; since, when we trace back to its origins the 'Syro-Iranian' Society that came to be incorporated in the Achaemenian Empire, we find, as we see, that its original home was in Syria and that its original members were Syrian peoples—Phoenicians, Philistines, Israelites, and Aramaeans—whereas the Iranians did not enter into it until later.

The adjective 'Syriac' (from the Latin *Syriacus*) is more convenient than 'Syrian' (from the Latin *Syrus*), because 'Syrian' has come to be used in English in a geographical sense, to denote indifferently anything or anybody belonging to the territory called Syria at any time—e.g. at the present day or at the time when 'the Tell-el-Amarna Letters' were written in the fourteenth century B.C. Now at the present time the 'Syriac' Society is virtually extinct in its Syrian home. Except for a few Syriac fossils (Jews, Jacobite Monophysite Christians, and Maronite ex-Monotheletes) and a few Orthodox Christians (locally called Melchites), the soil of Syria is now occupied by a different society, related to the Syriac Society by 'affiliation', namely the Islamic Society. Again, in the fourteenth century B.C., the Syriac Civilization had not yet emerged and the soil of Syria was then occupied by the débris of a dead 'Sumeric' Society upon which two other societies—the 'Egyptiac' and the 'Hittite'—were at that time intruding. Hence the employment of the familiar adjective 'Syrian' to denote the 'Syriac' Society would be confusing. These considerations have led scholars already to employ the word 'Syriac' to denote a modification of the Aramaic language and script which emerged in the region between Aleppo and Mosul in the first century of the Christian Era and which eventually became the vehicle of the liturgy and literature of the Nestorian Dyophysite and the Jacobite Monophysite Christian Churches. It is simple and convenient to extend the usage of the word 'Syriac' to cover all aspects and ages of the society to which this Syriac language and literature belonged.

universal church through which our Syriac Society came to be 'apparented' to the Iranic and the Arabic societies. We can now observe an interesting difference between Islam and Christianity—the church through which the Hellenic Society came to be apparented to Western and to Orthodox Christendom. We have noticed[1] that the germ of creative power in Christianity was not of Hellenic but of alien origin (in fact of Syriac origin, as we can now identify it). By contrast we perceive that the germ of creative power in Islam was not alien from, but native to, the Syriac Society. The founder, Muhammad, drew his inspiration primarily from Judaism, which was a purely Syriac religion, and secondarily from Nestorianism, a form of Christianity in which the Syriac element had recovered its preponderance.[2] The subsequent development of Islam took place in the environment of a Syriac Society from which the intrusive culture of Hellenism had been expelled by the conquests of the Primitive Muslims. Of course a great institution like a universal church is never 'pure bred' from a single society, any more than a community is ever 'pure bred' from a single physical race. In Christianity, for example, we are aware of Hellenic elements—drawn from the Hellenic mystery religions and from Hellenic philosophy—which the original Syriac germ assimilated in building up the tissues of the Church, so that the Church, by the time when it reached maturity as an institution of the Hellenic internal proletariat, had come to be a syncretism of an alien Syriac germ with indigenous Hellenic accretions. Similarly, though to a slighter extent, in Islam we can detect alien Hellenic accretions to the original Syriac germ in the shape of influences from Hellenic philosophy upon Islamic theology. Broadly and substantially, however, it is correct to formulate an antithesis between Christianity as a universal church originating in a germ that was alien to the society in which the church played its part, and Islam as a universal church originating in a germ that was indigenous.[3]

Finally, before passing on, we may measure the respective degrees of displacement of the original homes of the 'affiliated' Iranic and Arabic societies from the original home of the 'apparented' Syriac Society. We see that the base-line of the Iranic Society, which we have traced within a zone extending from the Anatolian hinterland of the Black Sea Straits through Azerbaijan and Khurāsān to the Bay of Bengal, with a north-eastward protuberance in the basin of the Oxus and Jaxartes, was relatively far removed from the geographical nucleus of the 'apparented' society

---

[1] See p. 57, above.

[2] For Nestorianism as an abortive Syriac reaction against the intrusion of Hellenism upon the Syriac World, see II. D (vii), vol. ii, pp. 286–7, below.

[3] The causes of this antithesis are examined in Part IX, below.

in Syria. Even if we extend our conception of the nucleus of the Syriac Society to include the homelands of the Medes and Persians on the western rim of the Iranian Plateau, the zone in which the Syriac Society may be said to have emerged still does not overlap the zone in which the Iranic Society emerged subsequently.[1] On the other hand, we see that the original home of the Arabic Society, which we found in Syria and Egypt, not only overlaps the original home of the Syriac Society but includes the whole of it. In short, the displacement of the Iranic Society was relatively great and that of the Arabic Society relatively small; and in this point, again, the Iranic resembles the Western Society, while the Arabic Society corresponds to Orthodox Christendom.

The Indic Society

The identification of the Syriac Society is the first result which we have achieved in putting into execution our plan of campaign for adding to our muster-roll of societies of the same species as our own. In order to achieve this first result, we have had to spend some time and trouble in unravelling a perplexingly tangled skein of history. But now that we have successfully untied the last knot, we may take our success as a good omen and continue our operations with a good heart, without feeling that our trouble has been labour lost or that the complexity of the historical landscape is something that passes our understanding. The main cause of the complexity in Syriac history is to be found in the successive intrusions of two alien forces—Assyrian militarism and Hellenic culture—upon the Syriac World. These alien intrusions have interrupted the course of Syriac history, or at any rate they have overlaid it with a deposit of foreign detritus. But now that we have disinterred the *disiecta membra* of Syriac history and have pieced them together, we shall find that the peculiar complexity of this particular inquiry has served us well by introducing us to a new phenomenon—the contact and collision between different societies—which we have hardly had occasion to notice hitherto, but which will constantly occupy our attention hereafter as one of the most important of the phenomena which a study of history has to take into account.[2] Indeed, in our very next inquiry, it will provide us with a valuable clue.

The next living society which we have to examine is the Hindu, and here again we discern in the background our standard tokens

---

[1] Azerbaijan, of course, corresponds to Media Atropatene; but the homeland of the Medes was farther south in Media Magna, the region round Hamadan which the Arabs called Jibāl or 'Irāq 'Ajamī; and this region lay outside the original home of the Iranic Society.

[2] The contact in the Space-dimension between contemporary civilizations is the subject of Part IX.

of the existence of another, 'apparented', society beyond the horizon. The universal state in this case is the Empire of the Guptas (*imperabant circa* A.D. 375–475).[1] The universal church is Hinduism, which attained supremacy in India in the Gupta Age—expelling and supplanting Buddhism after Buddhism had been dominant for about seven centuries (since the time of Açoka) in the Indian 'sub-continent' which was the common cradle of both religions. The Völkerwanderung which overran the domain of the Gupta Empire at its fall proceeded from the Huns of the Eurasian Steppe, who were assailing the Sasanian and the Roman Empires simultaneously. The interregnum occupied by this Völkerwanderung and by the lives of the 'successor-states' to the Gupta Empire which the Huns and their associates the Gurjaras set up in North-Western India lies approximately within the dates A.D. 475–775.[2] Thereafter, there began to emerge on Indian soil that Hindu Society which is still alive. The father of Hindu philosophy, Šankara, flourished about A.D. 800; and in the ninth century of the Christian Era the society began to articulate itself into states on a pattern which can still be discerned in the political map of India to-day.

In seeking to identify the older society, 'apparented' to the Hindu Society, whose existence is betokened by these phenomena, we shall now find, as we have forecast, that our labours have been lightened by the foregoing investigation in which we have traced the 'affiliation' of the Islamic Society to the Syriac Society. That investigation was complicated by the presence of an abnormal phenomenon: the intrusion and subsequent eviction of an alien force, in consequence of a collision between the Syriac Society and the Hellenic. Now we know that the Hellenic Society also collided with that society in India—still to be identified and named—which eventually became 'apparented' to the Hindu Society; and so, if we find the antecedents of the Gupta Empire in a tangle, we may hope

---

[1] The Gupta Empire was actually founded about A.D. 350 and did not collapse till the death of Skandagupta in A.D. 480; but the Empire did not actually acquire the dimensions of a universal state until A.D. 390, and it had ceased to perform the functions of such a state before the second Hun invasion of India began in A.D. 470.

[2] The break in tradition in India at the time of the Hun and Gurjara invasions is emphasized by Mr. Vincent Smith in *The Early History of India* (3rd edition, Oxford 1914, Clarendon Press), p. 408. A number of facts which bear out Mr. Vincent Smith's view are mentioned by Mr. C. V. Vaidya in *The History of Mediaeval India*, vol. ii (Poona 1924, Oriental Book Supplying Agency). For example, by about the year 800 of the Christian Era, both Buddhism and the pre-Buddhist Indian ritual of the Vedic sacrifices had become extinct throughout the greater part of India (op. cit., p. 1). The ancient vernaculars (the so-called 'prakrits') had ceased to be spoken, and the modern vernaculars—Hindi, Bengali, Maratti, Gujarati, Panjabi, and so on—were already full-fledged (p. 3). The Rājput dynasties of the modern Rājputāna can mostly trace their genealogies back to this epoch but not beyond (p. 46). *Pace* Mr. Vaidya, this last fact supports Mr. Vincent Smith's view that the Rājputs are descended from the Huns and Gurjaras who entered India in the post-Gupta Völkerwanderung and were converted to Hinduism.

to unravel them, as we succeeded in unravelling the antecedents of the ʿAbbasid Caliphate of Baghdad, by taking the same abnormal phenomenon as our clue.

The first step is to make out when the Hellenic intrusion upon India began and ended. We cannot equate its beginning with Alexander's Indian campaign; for this raid, though justly celebrated in military history as a brilliant *tour de force*, had no effects which have made a mark in the history of culture. In India the Hellenic intrusion did not really begin until Demetrius the Greek King of Bactria—the Hellenic 'successor-state' of the Achaemenian Empire in the basin of the Oxus and Jaxartes—crossed the Hindu Kush in order to annex Indian territories to his kingdom about the year 190 B.C. On the other hand, this Hellenic intrusion did not come to an end when the last Greek principality south-east of the Hindu Kush was extinguished at some date in the first century of the Christian Era; for these Greek rulers were followed in India, as in Bactria whence they had come, by barbarian rulers of Nomadic origin from the Eurasian Steppe who took a veneer of Hellenic culture from the representatives of that culture whom they had supplanted. These 'Philhellenic', if not Hellenized, barbarians descended upon India in two waves: the Sakas and the Parthians in the last quarter of the second century B.C., and then, in the first century of the Christian Era, the Kushans. The Sakas ruled in Kathiawar from the last century B.C. to A.D. 390, when their dominions were annexed by the Guptas. 'Indo-Parthians' ruled in the Indus Valley, side by side with Greeks, until the Kushans supplanted them both simultaneously. The Kushan Empire—which bestrode the Hindu Kush like its predecessor the Kingdom of Bactria but surpassed the Greek Kingdom in extent and duration —lasted from the first century of the Christian Era into the third. It will be observed that the Hellenic intrusion upon India came to an end only just before the establishment of a universal state by the Guptas. On the analogy of the history of the Hellenic intrusion upon the Syriac Society, we should now look out for another universal state in India immediately preceding the Hellenic intrusion and standing to the Gupta Empire in the relation of the Achaemenian Empire to the ʿAbbasid Caliphate of Baghdad. When we look for this, we find it, at the point in history where we should expect, in the Empire of the Mauryas, which was established by Chandragupta in 323–322 B.C., was made illustrious by the reign of Açoka in the third century B.C., and was extinguished by the usurper Pushyamitra in 185 B.C., five years after the Hellenic intrusion upon India had been started by Demetrius's invasion. In the background of the Maurya Empire we catch glimpses of a 'Time of Troubles' in the familiar form of a series of destructive wars between a multiplicity of local states: for example, the conquest of Kosala and Vaisali by King Ajatasatru of Magadha,[1] the younger contemporary of Siddhārtha Gautama the Buddha, and the destruction, somewhat later, of Gautama's own city-state, Kapilavastu. Gautama's life, and attitude towards life, are the best evidence that the society of which he was a member was in a bad way in his time[2]; and this evidence is corroborated by the life and attitude of his contemporary Mahavira, the founder of Jainism, and by the host of less distinguished men of the age who were turning away from this world and seeking to find the way to another world through the practice of asceticism. In the furthest background of all, behind this 'Time of Troubles', we can make out a time of growth which has left its record in the Vedas. And so we have identified the society 'apparented' to the Hindu Society. Let us call it 'Indic'.

We can now observe that Hinduism—the universal church through which this Indic Society came to be 'apparented' to the Hindu Society of to-day—resembles Islam, and differs from Christianity, inasmuch as the germ of life in which it originated was native to, and not alien from, the society in whose history it played its part. No doubt, certain non-Indic accretions can be detected in Hinduism. The most prominent of these is the worship of deities in iconic form—a feature which is of the essence of Hinduism, though it was lacking in the primitive religion of the Indic Society as this is mirrored in the Vedas, and was lacking, likewise, in primitive Buddhism. It must therefore have been borrowed from the religion of some alien society—most probably from Hellenism through the medium of the modified Buddhism of the Mahayana. However, the chief differences between Hinduism and the Indic religion of the Vedas—and these differences are striking—are due to elements in Hinduism which were borrowed from Buddhism: that is, from a religion which was a reaction against the primitive Indic religion of the Vedas but a reaction of an entirely indigenous Indic origin. The most important elements, lacking in the religion of the Vedas, which Hinduism borrowed from Buddhism were its monasticism and its philosophy.

The original home of the Indic Society, as we know from its records, was in the valleys of the Indus and the Ganges; and from this base the society had expanded over the whole sub-continent of India before it came to the end of its universal state.[3] The area

---

[1] See Smith, Vincent: *The Early History of India* (3rd edition, Oxford 1914, Clarendon Press), pp. 28 and 35–7.
[2] For the life-history of Siddhārtha Gautama, see further III. C (ii) (*b*), vol. iii, pp. 270–2, below.
[3] The Maurya Empire at its greatest extent—at which it stood when Açoka renounced

which the Indic Society had thus come to cover at the close of its history was all embraced in the original home of the 'affiliated' Hindu Society, which occupied the whole sub-continent from the outset and afterwards expanded eastward overseas into Indonesia and Indo-China. Thus the geographical displacement of the Hindu Society from the domain of the Indic Society was comparable in degree to the displacement of the Arabic Society from the domain of the Syriac Society.

The Sinic Society

It remains to explore the background of the fifth of the living societies, which has its home in the Far East; and here our tokens are not difficult to distinguish. The universal state here is the empire that was established by Ts'in She Hwang-ti in 221 B.C. and was maintained for the next four centuries by the dynasties known as the Prior and Posterior Han. The universal church is the Mahayana—the variety of Buddhism which made its way into the Empire of the Posterior Han and so became the chrysalis of the present Far Eastern Society. The Völkerwanderung after the fall of the universal state proceeded from the Nomads of the Eurasian Steppe, who descended upon the basin of the Yellow River at a time when the dominions of the Han were reunited, after a century of disunion, under the rule of an indigenous 'successor-state', the so-called Western Tsin (*regnabant* A.D. 280–317). The interregnum preceding the emergence of the present Far Eastern Society must be reckoned to have set in at least a century before this Völkerwanderung took place. The universal state had really collapsed by A.D. 172, though the Posterior Han dragged out a shadowy existence until A.D. 221, so that the interregnum includes this half-century of impotence—and the ensuing half-century in which the dominions of the Han were divided between the indigenous 'successor-states' which are known as 'the Three Kingdoms'—as well as the age of the Barbarian 'successor-states', which did not begin until after the interlude of reunion in the time of the Western Tsin.[1]

If we turn now to the antecedents of the universal state which was established by Ts'in She Hwang-ti, we shall discern the lineaments of a 'Time of Troubles' here as clearly as we discerned them

War after the conquest of Kalinga—was practically conterminous with the present British-Indian Empire except that it did not include Burma but did include the greater part of what is now Afghanistan. It covered not only the whole basin of the Indus and Ganges but also the whole of India south of the Vindya Range except for the extreme tip of the peninsula. The Gupta Empire, which had the same capital as the Maurya Empire (at Pataliputra, in the present province of Bihar), never, at its largest, attained the same extension. Yet it exercised a hegemony over all India; and, thanks to the Mauryas' work, all India, North and South, constituted a social though not a political unity in the Gupta Age.

[1] The history of this interregnum is analysed further in V. C (i) (c) 3, vol. v, pp. 272–4; V. C (i) (d) 6 (α), vol. v, pp. 477–8; and Part X, below.

first in the antecedents of the universal state which was established by Augustus. They are stamped upon the very name—*chan kwo*: 'the [period of] contending states'—which Chinese historians have given to the two and a half centuries that intervened between the death of Confucius in 479 B.C. and the assumption of the title *She Hwang-ti*—'the first universal monarch'—by King Chêng of Ts'in in 221 B.C. The conquest of Ts'i by Ts'in in that year completed a long-drawn-out process by which a multiplicity of local states was converted into a single universal state through a struggle for existence in a series of destructive wars.[1] The two marks of the age—a suicidal statecraft and an intellectual vitality which was principally directed towards the philosophy of practical life—recall the age of Hellenic history between the generation of Zeno and Epicurus and the Battle of Actium. Moreover, in this case as in that, we can see that these last centuries before the establishment of the universal state were only the climax of a 'Time of Troubles' which had begun at some earlier date. The flame of militarism which burnt itself out in the post-Confucian Age was already alight before the great philosopher took his measure of human affairs. We hear of an abortive disarmament conference, attended by representatives of fourteen states, in 546 B.C.,[2] and we can read the same signs of the times in the mundane conservatism of Confucius and in the other-worldly quietism of Lao-Tse. The sun had already passed his zenith in the heavens when both these sages saw the light.[3] They both realized that, in the history of their society, the age of growth already lay behind them. What name shall we give to the society upon whose past the one sage looked reverently backward like Epimetheus while the other deliberately turned his back on it like Christian taking leave of the City of Destruction? We may perhaps conveniently call this society 'Sinic'.[4]

We can now observe that the Mahayana—the church through which this Sinic Society came to be 'apparented' to the Far Eastern Society of to-day—resembles the Christian Church, and differs

---

[1] It will be noticed that Ts'in, like Rome, fought her way through the struggle for existence until she issued from it as the sole survivor and incorporated herself into the universal state which replaced the multiplicity of states that she had destroyed. On the other hand, Ts'in resembled Assyria in collapsing, not indeed on the eve of complete victory, but on the morrow of it, so that the fruits of her militarism were reaped by the Han, as the fruits of Assyrian militarism were reaped by the Achaemenidae.

[2] Cordier, H.: *Histoire Générale de la Chine* (Paris 1920–1, Geuthner, 3 vols.), vol. i, p. 135.

[3] That is, if Lao-Tse ever did see the light—for he may be a fictitious character, invented to provide a founder for the school of philosophy that passes under his name.

[4] From the Latin names 'Sinae', denoting the inhabitants, and 'Sinica', denoting the territory, of the universal state which was brought into being by the sole survival of the state of Ts'in. The name is not altogether apt, since Ts'in did much to destroy, and little or nothing to create, the culture of the society which we are calling by its name. The work of creation was brought to an end by the destructive warfare in which Ts'in made its fortune—only to lose it to Han. Nevertheless, the name is convenient, since 'Sinae' is the original of our 'Chinese'.

from Islam and Hinduism, inasmuch as the germ of life in which it originated was not indigenous to the society in which it played its part, but was derived from elsewhere. Christianity was begotten in Syriac territories that had been incorporated into the Hellenic universal state, and it was introduced into the Hellenic World by Syriac 'Natives' who had been forcibly enrolled in the internal proletariat of the Hellenic Society. The Mahayana appears to have been begotten in Indic territories which were subject successively to the Greek Kings of Bactria and to their 'Philhellenic' successors the Kushans; and it had undoubtedly taken root in the provinces of the Kushan Empire in the Tarim Basin before these provinces were reconquered and re-annexed to the Sinic universal state by the Posterior Han towards the close of the first century of the Christian Era.[1] Through this door, the Mahayana entered the Sinic World and was there adapted by the internal proletariat of the Sinic Society to its own needs.

The original home of this Sinic Society was in the basin of the Yellow River, and thence the society expanded, in the course of its history, over the basin of the Yangtse. The basins of both rivers together were embraced in the original home of the 'affiliated' Far Eastern Society, which expanded from this base south-eastward on to what has since become the south-eastern coast-land of China[2] and north-eastward into Korea and Japan. Thus the geographical displacement of the Far Eastern Society from the Sinic was comparable in degree, not to the wide displacement of our Western Society from the Hellenic or of the Iranic Society from the Syriac, but rather to the narrower displacement of the Arabic from the Syriac and of the Hindu from the Indic.

'The Fossils'

The information which we have now obtained by investigating the 'affiliations' of all the living societies will enable us at once to identify the extinct societies which are represented to-day by certain 'fossils'.

The Jews and Parsees are manifestly fossils of the Syriac Society in the state in which this society was when it was developing under

---

[1] The Tarim Basin had been previously conquered and annexed at the close of the second century B.C. by the Prior Han, but had passed out of their control in the course of the last century B.C.

[2] This coast-land (the modern provinces of Chekiang, Fukien, Kwangtung, and Kwangsi) may have been incorporated politically into the Empire of the Han, but, even in this last phase of Sinic history, it never became an integral part of the Sinic World. To-day the people of these provinces call themselves 'T'ang people', in contrast to the 'Han people' of the rest of China. This nomenclature implies that the South China coast was not brought within the pale of Society until the age of the T'ang Dynasty (A.D. 618–907); that is, not until after the interregnum which intervened between the disappearance of the Sinic Society and the emergence of the 'affiliated' society that is still alive in the Far East to-day.

the Achaemenian Empire, before its normal development was suddenly and violently interrupted by the intrusion of the Hellenic Society in the wake of Alexander the Great. The Monophysite and Nestorian Christians are relics of the subsequent reaction of the Syriac Society against the alien intruder. They represent a stage of this reaction at which the internal proletariat of the submerged society was strong enough to resist complete assimilation to the internal proletariat of the intrusive society, but was not yet strong enough to expel the alien intruder altogether and to resume its own development at the point at which its course had been interrupted. The Nestorian and Monophysite 'heresies' were successive and alternative protests against a process of syncretism and adaptation which had been turning Christianity—a religion sprung from a Syriac germ—into an institution of the Hellenic internal proletariat and into a chrysalis from which new societies, 'affiliated' to the Hellenic Society, were to emerge. Nestorianism and Monophysitism were attempts to retain a religion which was Syriac in origin as an heirloom in the Syriac heritage. Christianity, however, in the fifth century of the Christian Era, was already too deeply imbued with Hellenic influences to serve as an effective instrument for an anti-Hellenic reaction. Hence the Nestorian and Monophysite movements were foredoomed to failure. The achievement of completing the expulsion of Hellenism from the Syriac World and providing the internal proletariat of the Syriac Society with a universal church of its own was reserved for Islam—a 'totalitarian' Syriac religion which was anti-Hellenic *au fond*.[1]

Similarly, the Jains of India and the Hinayanian Buddhists of Ceylon, Burma, and Siam can be seen to be fossils of the Indic Society in the state in which this society was when it was developing under the Maurya Empire,[2] before its normal development was interrupted by the intrusion of the Hellenic Society in the wake of the Greek conquerors from Bactria. The Lamaistic Mahayanian Buddhists of Tibet and Mongolia correspond to the Nestorians and Monophysites in representing a reaction that was abortive. The Lamaistic or Tantric form of the Mahayana is the relic of a vain attempt to turn the Mahayana back from the historic path along which this originally Indic religion, after travelling through the Kushan Empire and there becoming imbued with Hellenic influences, eventually fulfilled its great destiny in the Sinic World. The Tantric Mahayana was a half-hearted and therefore unsuccessful forerunner of Hinduism—the 'totalitarian' Indic religion out

---

[1] For the significance and the fortunes of the Nestorian and the Monophysite movement, see further I. C (iii) (*b*), vol. i, p. 155; II. D (vi), vol. ii, pp. 236–8; and II. D (vii), vol. ii, pp. 286–7, below.

[2] Legend ascribes the conversion of Ceylon to the Maurya Emperor Açoka's brother.

of which the internal proletariat of the Indic Society eventually fashioned its indigenous universal church.

These fossils have not given us clues to identifying any otherwise unknown members of the species of societies which we are studying; but they have given us some insight into the 'faults' and 'malformations' and 'stratifications' which occur when two or more societies of this kind collide. Later, we shall have occasion to examine this aspect of 'social geology' in detail.[1]

The Minoan Society

Let us go back to the extinct societies which we have identified, by several of our standard tokens, in the backgrounds of the living societies. If we now examine, in their turn, the backgrounds of these extinct societies, and if, in these older backgrounds, we discern the same tokens again, we may hope in this way to identify other extinct societies of an older generation which would prove to be related to the younger extinct societies as these are related to the living representatives of the species.

In the background of the Hellenic Society, certain tokens of the pre-existence of an older society stand out quite clear. The universal state is the maritime empire, maintained by command of the Aegean Sea from a base in the island of Crete, which left a name in Hellenic tradition as 'the thalassocracy of Minos'[2] and a mark on the face of the Earth in the topmost strata of the palaces at Cnossos and Phaestus which have been excavated, since the beginning of the twentieth century, by our Western archaeologists.[3] The Völkerwanderung after the fall of this universal state can be seen through a glass darkly in the oldest monuments of Hellenic literature, the *Iliad* and the *Odyssey*. These poems appear to be the remnant—or the quintessence—of an epic cycle which had gathered round two stories, 'the Siege of Troy' and 'the Seven against Thebes'. The final form in which the poems have come down to us seems to have been assumed as late as the sixth century B.C. and to be the last stage in a long process of literary evolution; but the Völkerwanderung which remotely inspired the poetry of 'Homer'—or the 'Homeridae'—is also known to us from the contemporary official records of 'the New Empire' of Egypt under

---

[1] In Part IX, below.

[2] For the possibility that the historical name of this Cretan imperial people may be preserved in the three names Μίνως, Μνωῖται, and Μινύαι, see I. C (i) (b), Annex II, below.

[3] The strata known as 'Late Minoan I and II' would appear to be the material remains that correspond in date to 'the thalassocracy of Minos'. The establishment of the 'thalassocracy' would appear to have been subsequent to the great catastrophe which devastated the Cretan palaces at the break between 'Middle Minoan II' (the age of the Kamáres pottery) and 'Middle Minoan III' (a time of transition which shades off gradually into 'Late Minoan I').

the Eighteenth, Nineteenth, and Twentieth Dynasties; and although these records do not refer to the particular incidents which 'Homer' professes to record, they do give a picture of a historical situation in which such incidents are quite in place, and which the archaeological evidence corroborates. The Völkerwanderung seems to have begun with an irruption of barbarians —Achaeans and the like—from the European hinterland of the Aegean, who took to the sea and overcame the Cretan 'thalassocrats' on their own element. The archaeological evidence of their handiwork is the destruction of the Cretan palaces at the end of the age which the archaeologists call 'Late Minoan II'.[1] The movement culminated in a kind of human avalanche in which the peoples of the Aegean—mainlanders and islanders, victors and vanquished—descended en masse upon 'the New Empire' of Egypt and upon the contemporary Empire of Khatti[2] in Anatolia. The Hittites were overwhelmed. The Egyptians survived to tell the tale to posterity. Scholars agree that the destruction of the Cretan palaces at the end of 'Late Minoan II' is to be dated about 1400 B.C.[3] The Egyptian records enable us to date the two supreme convulsions of the Völkerwanderung about 1230/1220 and 1200/1190 B.C. respectively. We can thus take 1425–1125 B.C. as the approximate span of the interregnum which intervened between the disappearance of the older society in the Aegean and the emergence of its Hellenic successor.

When we seek to trace the history of the older society back towards its origins, we find ourselves hampered by having no access to written records—a handicap from which we shall suffer until we succeed in reading the several varieties of Minoan script and interpreting the language or languages conveyed in them. At present, we are wholly dependent on archaeological evidence, which is notoriously difficult to translate into historical terms[4] and which, even when rightly translated, often fails to answer the questions which humanists are most concerned to ask. The

[1] The sack of the palace at Cnossos at the end of 'Late Minoan II' must have caused a shock like that which (as we know from the recorded evidence of contemporaries) was produced by the sack of Rome in A.D. 410.

[2] Khatti was the name, in its native form, of the people who appear in the Old Testament as the Children of Heth or Hittites.

[3] e.g. Meyer, E.: Geschichte des Altertums, vol. ii, part (i) (2nd edition, Stuttgart and Berlin 1928, Cotta), p. 238; Glotz, G.: La Civilisation Égéenne (Paris 1923, Renaissance du Livre), p. 61; Fimmen, D.; Die Kretisch-Mykenische Kultur (3rd edition, Leipzig 1929, Teubner), synchronistic table.

[4] e.g. Glotz interprets the archaeological evidence of 'Late Minoan II' as indicating that a universal state, governed by sea-power from Cnossos, was in existence during this period and this period only. M. P. Nilsson (Minoan-Mycenaean Religion and its Survival in Greek Religion (London 1927, Milford), pp. 25–7) argues from the same evidence that, during 'Late Minoan II', Cnossos was leading a parochial existence and was not at that time the capital of an empire extending to the coasts of Continental Greece.

geographical range of 'the thalassocracy of Minos' can be inferred from the fact that a material civilization, known to have been evolved in Crete, was suddenly propagated across the Aegean to the Argolid towards the end of the seventeenth century B.C.[1] and gradually spread over the whole of the Peloponnese and Central Greece during the two centuries preceding the catastrophe in which the fifteenth century closed.[2] In the opposite direction, we infer the maintenance of diplomatic relations between two Great Powers from the pictures of envoys from people called the Keftiu that appear in wall-paintings in Egyptian tombs of the first half of the fifteenth century B.C. The clothes which these envoys wear and the presents which they carry are recognized by archaeologists as being characteristic of Crete in 'Late Minoan II'.[3] If we seek to know the duration of the 'thalassocracy' we can perhaps equate its establishment with the building of new palaces at Cnossos and Phaestus at the beginning of 'Middle Minoan III', and can detect the culmination of a foregoing 'Time of Troubles' in the destruction of the earlier palaces at the close of 'Middle Minoan II', when Crete was overtaken by a catastrophe comparable in magnitude to that in which the 'thalassocracy' ended towards 1400 B.C.: that is, three or four centuries later. Below this particular archaeological stratum there lie others which carry the evidence for the existence of the society backwards—or, in archaeological terms, downwards—to the Neolithic Age. The most convenient name for this society in all its ages and all its works is perhaps 'Minoan'.[4]

The original home of the Minoan Society was in the islands of

[1] 'Tout d'un coup, vers la fin du XVIIème siècle, l'Argolide subit une transformation générale. On apprend à cultiver la vigne et l'olivier. Tout se crétise. Les femmes s'habillent à la mode de Cnosse. Dans des sanctuaires de type crétois s'installe la déesse crétoise, avec les animaux, les attributs, les objets rituels qui lui sont familiers. Toutes les cérémonies, tous les jeux célébrés en son honneur dans l'île l'accompagnent sur le continent. Les demeures princières s'ornent de fresques et se remplissent de vases précieux et de bijoux où ne se trahit plus guère l'inexpérience helladique.' (Glotz, op. cit., p. 55.)

[2] Glotz, op. cit., pp. 58–9.

[3] Fimmen, op. cit., pp. 184–5. It may be noted that this archaeological stratum called 'Late Minoan II' is equated by Glotz, op. cit. (synchronistic table), with the second half of the fifteenth century B.C., not the first.

[4] This name has already become so well established that it might seem pedantic to coin a new name: for example, 'Archipelagic' (to cover the twin starting-points in Crete and in the Cyclades). It seems simpler to extend the use of the name Minoan—which primarily describes the manifestations of the 'Archipelagic' culture in the single great island of Crete—to cover the 'Cycladic' manifestations of the same culture in the other islands of the Archipelago and the 'Helladic' manifestations in Continental European Greece. At the same time, 'Minoan' is open to the same objection as 'Sinic'. In using the word, we are naming a society after the people who established the universal state into which that society was incorporated in its last phase; and the analogies of the Ts'in and the Romans render it probable that these people did not make their mark on the history of the society until late in the day, and made it then as destroyers rather than as creators. Our use of the terms 'Middle Minoan' and 'Early Minoan' to denote the archaeological strata to which we apply them may be as much of a solecism as it would be to call the Parthenon a Roman building or the *Iliad* a Roman poem. The Muslims do use 'Rūmī' as an omnibus word for 'Graeco-Roman' or 'Hellenic'; and in our ears this sounds bizarre, e.g. 'Iskandar Rūmī' for Alexander of Macedon.

Crete and the Cyclades, and thence the society spread overseas through the Archipelago to the Aegean coast of Continental European Greece. The original home of the Hellenic Society embraced this coast, at which 'the thalassocracy of Minos' reached its limit, together with the western coast of Anatolia, along which the archaeological evidence for Minoan influence is singularly slight. Thus the geographical displacement of the Hellenic Society from the Minoan Society was considerable. In fact, when due allowance is made for the difference in scale between 'the thalasso-cracy of Minos' and the Roman Empire, the displacement of the Hellenic Society from the Minoan is comparable in degree to the displacement of Western Christendom, rather than to that of Orthodox Christendom, from Hellas.[1]

Before, however, we permit ourselves to make this comparison, we must ask ourselves the prior question: Are we warranted in treating the Minoan and the Hellenic Society as though they were related to one another in the way in which the Hellenic Society is related to Orthodox and to Western Christendom? Can we regard the Minoan and Hellenic societies as being 'apparented-and-affiliated' in any sense? In all the cases of Apparentation-and-Affiliation that we have investigated, the social link between the two parties has been a universal church, which has been created by the internal proletariat of the older society and has afterwards served as the chrysalis within which the younger society has come into existence and has gradually taken shape. In the 'apparentation' of the Hellenic Society to Orthodox and Western Christendom, this role was played by the Christian Church; in the 'apparentation' of the Syriac Society to the Arabic and the Iranic, it was played by Islam; in the 'apparentation' of the Indic to the Hindu, it was played by Hinduism; in the 'apparentation' of the Sinic to the Far Eastern, it was played by the Mahayana. Can we discern any universal church which has established a similar liaison between the Minoan Society and the Hellenic?

In order to answer this question in the affirmative, it is not enough to cite any and every instance of continuity between the religious histories of the two societies. For example, the temples of the state goddesses in the Hellenic city-states of Mycenae and Tiryns and Athens appear to have occupied the same sites as the chapels of the household goddesses in the 'Mycenaean'[2] palaces

[1] The respective functions of the Aegean coast of Continental Greece as a limit in the expansion of the Minoan Society and a base-line in the expansion of the Hellenic may be compared with the respective functions, in Hellenic and in Western history, of the line running across Western Europe from Rome to the Roman Wall. (See pp. 37–9, above.)
[2] The term 'Mycenaean' is used by archaeologists to denote the variant of the Minoan material civilization which maintained itself in Continental Greece from about the end of the seventeenth century B.C. until the cessation of the post-Minoan Völkerwanderung.

from which the same districts of Continental Greece had been governed in Minoan times.[1] For our purpose, however, this example of continuity is irrelevant; for the essence of these worships was their local character; and this distinctive feature, which suggests that they all survived because each was deep-rooted in its own soil, warns us that it is idle to look for the traces of a universal church in them. It is more to the point that a similar continuity can be detected in the sanctuaries at Delos, Eleusis, and Delphi[2]; for the worships in these sanctuaries were not local but 'Pan-Hellenic' in Hellenic times. Yet there was nothing Minoan about the principal expression of 'Pan-Hellenism' in Hellenic religion: that is, the Olympian Pantheon. This Pantheon took its classical form from the Homeric epic—an echo of the post-Minoan Völkerwanderung—and here we see Gods made in the image of the barbarians who descended upon the Minoan World from the European hinterland of the Aegean after 'the thalassocracy of Minos' had broken down. Zeus is an Achaean war-lord; the other Olympians are his war-band; and the divine adventurer has made his fortune, like any 'Zeus-born' king of men, by robbery under arms. Zeus reigns on Olympus as a usurper who has supplanted his predecessor Cronos by force; and he has divided the spoils of the Universe—giving the Waters and the Earth to his brothers Poseidon and Hades and keeping the Air for himself. This Olympian Pantheon is Achaean through and through and post-Minoan altogether.[3] We cannot even see a reflection of a Minoan Pantheon in the older divinities who are dispossessed; for Cronos and the Titans, as the Hellenic Mythology presents them, are simply projections into the past of Zeus and the Olympians themselves. We are reminded of the religion which had been abandoned by the majority of the Teutonic barbarians in the no-man's-land beyond the northern frontiers of the Roman Empire before their Völkerwanderung began,[4] and which was retained and refined by

---

[1] Nilsson, op. cit., pp. 405–17.

[2] Ibid., pp. 400–2 and 533–6.

[3] This derivation of Zeus and his Olympians from the barbarian war-lord of the post-Minoan Völkerwanderung and his war-band has been pointed out by Gilbert Murray in *Five Stages of Greek Religion*, 2nd edition (Oxford 1925, Clarendon Press), pp. 66–9. The Scandinavians appear to have re-made their ancestral gods in the corresponding image in the Viking Age (Grönbech, V.: *The Culture of the Teutons* (London 1931, Milford, 3 parts in 2 vols.), Part II, pp .252–3). M. P. Nilsson, in *The Mycenaean Origin of Greek Mythology* (Cambridge 1932, University Press), Chapter IV, argues, as against Murray, that the human prototype of Olympus is not the war-band of the Völkerwanderung but the grander and stabler Mycenaean monarchy which preceded the Völkerwanderung in Continental Greece in the sixteenth and fifteenth centuries B.C. Since, however, Nilsson is at pains to distinguish the Mycenaeans from the Minoans and to emphasize the links which connect the Mycenaeans with their Hellenic successors, his argument, even if it were accepted, would make no difference for our present purpose.

[4] Most of these barbarians were converted to the Arian form of Christianity in the course of the fourth century of the Christian Era, before they overran the Roman Empire, and were subsequently converted again to Catholicism—the religion of their subject

their kinsmen in Scandinavia—to be abandoned by these in turn in the course of their own Völkerwanderung five or six centuries later. If anything in the nature of a universal church existed in the Minoan World at the time when the barbarian avalanche descended it must have been something as different from the worship of the Olympian Pantheon as Christianity was from the worship of Odin and the Aesir.

Did such a thing exist? There are faint indications that it did, when we survey our scanty evidence.

From the archaeological evidence, which is at any rate at first hand, though it is not always easy to interpret, some striking conclusions are drawn by the greatest master of the subject:

'So far as it has been possible to read the evidences of the old Cretan worship, we seem to discern not only a prevailing spiritual essence but something in its followers akin to the faith that for the last two millennia has moved the adherents of successive Oriental religions: Iranian, Christian and Islamic.[1] It involves a dogmatic spirit in the worshipper far removed from the true Hellenic standpoint. . . . Broadly comparing it with the religion of the Ancient Greeks, it must be said that it had a more spiritual essence. From another aspect, it had a more personal bearing. On the "Ring of Nestor", where the symbols of resurgence are seen above her head in chrysalis and butterfly shape, she [the Goddess] has clearly the power of giving life beyond the grave to her worshippers. She was very near to her votaries. . . . She guarded her children even beyond the grave. . . . Greek religion had its Mysteries, but the Gods of both sexes, more or less on a par, by no means stood in such a close personal relation as is indicated by the evidences of the Minoan Cult. Their disunion, marked by family and clannish feuds, was as conspicuous as their multiplicity of form and attributes. In contrast to this, throughout the Minoan World, what appears to be the same paramount Goddess constantly reappears. . . . The general conclusion is that we are in the presence of a largely monotheistic cult, in which the female form of divinity held the supreme place.'[2]

This universal Goddess is also represented in Minoan art as the Divine Mother, holding up her infant child for adoration.[3]

populations. The English and the Franks were exceptional in carving out their 'successor-states' as pagans and in being converted thereafter to Catholicism without an intermediate Arian stage.

[1] The author cites archaeological evidence (in the same work, on p. 38) which seems to show that, in the period which 'corresponds with that of the great Minoan expansion in Mainland Greece', the Minoan religion 'had its propagandist side'. Stocks of Minoan religious emblems and furniture, dating from that age, have been unearthed in the quondam Minoan harbour at Niru Khani, on the north coast of Crete, near Cnossos. 'The inference is almost inevitable that we have here the evidence of an organized attempt to provide for the religious needs of co-religionists overseas. May there not even have been some actual propaganda *in partibus infidelium?*'

[2] Evans, Sir Arthur: *The Earlier Religion of Greece in the Light of Cretan Discoveries* (London 1931, Macmillan), pp. 37–41.

[3] Evans, op. cit., pp. 32–6.

And her symbols of immortality—the chrysalis and the butterfly—have been found in Minoan graves in the form of gold amulets.[1]

Another source of evidence for a Minoan belief in an after-life is to be found in Hellenic literature. For example, in one passage of Homer[2] there is a description of an after-life in 'Elysium' which is not compatible with the ordinary Homeric picture of the after-life in Hades. The shadow-world of Hades reproduces the unsubstantial fabric of barbarian life during a Völkerwanderung. The state of blessedness in Elysium looks like a cultivated seafaring people's idea of their own world made perfect.[3] Again, the Hellenic tradition has preserved the legend of a 'Zeus' in Crete who cannot really be the same divinity as the Zeus on Olympus. This Cretan 'Zeus' is not the leader of a war-band who comes on the scene, full-grown and fully armed, to take a kingdom by storm and reign happily ever after. He appears as a new-born babe, nursed by the nymphs and suckled by a beast of the field;[4] and he is not only born—he dies! Was his emblem the double-headed axe—a religious symbol which became as ubiquitous in the Minoan World as the cross in Christendom?[5] And were his birth and death re-enacted in the birth and death of Dionysus—the Thracian God with whom, in the course of Hellenic history, the God of the

---

[1] Evans, op. cit., p. 28.   [2] *Odyssey*, iv, ll. 561 seqq.

[3] Nilsson, op. cit. (on p. 93 above), pp. 540–4. He thinks that the Minoan idea of Elysium was coloured, if not originally inspired, by the imagery of the Osirian religion (op. cit., pp. 544–8). He interprets the Haghía Triádha Sarcophagus as a representation of the apotheosis of the dead with the external forms of the Osiris worship—e.g. the ritual garment of hide and the barque—supplemented by traditional Minoan religious symbols: double axe, pillar, bird, horns of consecration, and tree. 'The idea of the divinization of the dead, borrowed from Egypt and developed under Egyptian influence, has caused a superimposition of the divine cult upon the cult of the dead with some Egyptianizing details. It is only natural that those details were neither exactly understood nor applied in strict Egyptian fashion' (op. cit., p. 378). 'Whether the idea of the deification of Man was an original element in Minoan belief and developed under Egyptian influence, or whether it was borrowed from Egypt and remodelled in accordance with the forms of the Minoan religion—a borrowing, however, pre-supposing a congenial disposition of the Minoan religious temper—it is contrary to Greek ideas' (op. cit., p. 380). This conjecture is commended by the fact that the Haghía Triádha Sarcophagus belongs to the so-called 'Late Minoan' period—an age which included the Minoan universal state and the ensuing interregnum, and which was contemporary with the period of 'the New Empire' in Egypt. If the internal proletariat of the Minoan Society did create anything like a universal church, this is the age in which we should look for traces of it; and if the germ of life in the hypothetical new religion was derived from Osirism, this again, is the age in which we should expect Osirian influences to have spread to the Minoan World; for it was an age in which intercourse between Egypt and Crete was close; and in Egypt the Osirian religion had by then already asserted itself. It is also observed by Evans (op. cit., p. 41) that 'a certain moral ingredient—taken over, it may be, from Ancient Egypt—is perceptible in the idea of the weighing of the Soul in butterfly form, evidenced by the gold scales from the Mycenae tomb and by the scene on the "Ring of Nestor" where the deceased are led before the Griffin Inquisitor, enthroned before the Goddess'. For earlier connexions between the Minoan and the Egyptiac religion, going back to 'Pre-Dynastic' times, see op. cit., pp. 8–10.

[4] For this *motif*, see III. C (ii) (*b*), vol. iii, pp. 259–62, below.

[5] The comparison is made by Nilsson, op. cit., pp. 162 and 192. The cross itself appears to have been a Minoan religious symbol, as well as the double axe; but the comparative rarity of the examples that have been recovered in the process of archaeological research indicates that in this religion it was a symbol of minor importance.

Eleusinian Mysteries became identified? Were the Mysteries in Classical Greece, like witchcraft in Modern Europe, a survival from the religion of a submerged society?

If Christendom had succumbed to the Vikings—falling under their dominion and failing to convert them to its Faith—we can imagine the Mass being celebrated mysteriously for centuries in the underworld of a new society in which the prevailing religion was the worship of the Aesir. We can also imagine this new society, as it grew in wisdom and stature, failing to find satisfaction in the religious heritage of the Scandinavian Völkerwanderung and seeking for the bread of spiritual life in the soil on which, when the Völkerwanderung had subsided, the new society had found rest for the sole of its foot. In such a spiritual famine the remnant of an older religion, instead of being stamped out as in our Western history witchcraft was stamped out when it caught the attention of the Church, might have been rediscovered as a hidden treasure; and some religious genius might have met the needs of his age by an exotic combination of the submerged Christian rite with latter-day barbarian orgies derived from the Finns or the Magyars.

On the analogy of this imaginary religious history of the West, we might reconstruct the actual religious history of the Hellenic World: the revival of the ancient and traditional Mysteries of Eleusis and the invention of Orphism—'a speculative religion, created by a religious genius'[1]—out of a syncretism between the orgies of the Thracian Dionysus and the Minoan Mysteries of the birth and death and resurrection of Zagreus, the Divine Child.[2] Undoubtedly both the Eleusinian Mysteries and the Orphic Church did provide the Hellenic Society in the Classical Age with spiritual sustenance which it needed but could not find in the worship of the Olympians; and the vital element which the Olympian religion lacked and which the Mysteries and Orphism both contained was a transcendental other-worldly spirit such as we should expect to find in a religion which had been conceived in a 'Time of Troubles' and not in an age of youth and growth. It is a spirit that we recognize as characteristic of the universal churches, created by the internal proletariats of societies in decline, which we have been

---

[1] Nilsson, op. cit., pp. 510–11.

[2] If there really was a revival of Minoan religion in the Hellenic World in the seventh and sixth centuries B.C., the revivalists may not always have understood rightly the Mysteries which they were resuscitating. One of the great names with which this supposed revival is traditionally connected is that of the Cretan 'prophet' Epimenides of Cnossos; and the verse, abusing Epimenides' own Cretan countrymen, which St. Paul quotes from Epimenides' poem 'Minos' in his epistle to Titus i. 12, appears to have been evoked by Epimenides' indignation at the sacred pillar of the dying and re-arising Minoan 'Zeus'—a Bethel or habitat of the deity which the latter-day Hellenic religious reformer mistook for his tomb. (See Evans, Sir Arthur: The Earlier Religion of Greece in the Light of Cretan Discoveries (London 1931, Macmillan), pp. 17–18.)

passing in review: the Mahayana, Catholicism, Islam. And these churches bequeathed this vital element to the nascent societies for which they served as chrysalides. On this showing, when we see the same element of religion being communicated to another nascent society by a church which appears to spring suddenly from the ground in order to perform this office, we may speculate whether this Orphic Church is really new or old. The seed from which it is newly sprung may not have been newly sown but have been lying for ages underground, ready to germinate when a favourable moment arrived. It may have been like those seeds which have come to flower in the soil of English gardens after being buried with dead Pharaohs in Egyptian sands. Thus Shi'ism was raised from the dead by Ismā'īl Safawī in Iran, some four or five centuries after it had been buried in the grave of the Syriac Society with the Buwayhids and the Carmathians and the Fāti-mids.[1] And thus, in the days of St. Francis of Assisi, Manichaeism was suspected of covertly revisiting, in the guise of Catharism, a world in which it had hardly been heard of since the days of Augustine of Madaura.[2]

On these analogies it is not altogether fantastic to espy, in the Mysteries and Orphism, the ghost of a Minoan universal church which the Hellenic Society succeeded in conjuring up from the tomb. Yet even if this speculation hits the truth, this hardly warrants us in regarding the Hellenic Society as being 'affiliated' to the Minoan in the sense in which we have come to speak, in this Study, of the 'affiliation' of one society to another. For why did this church require resurrection unless it had been slain? And who were its slayers unless the barbarians who had overrun the Minoan World? In taking the Pantheon of these murderous Achaeans for its own, the Hellenic Society had proclaimed them its parents by adoption. It could not 'affiliate' itself to the Minoan Society without taking the blood-guiltiness of the Achaeans upon its head and confessing itself a parricide.

If we turn now to the background of the Syriac Society we shall find what we have found in the background of the Hellenic. On the surface, at any rate, we shall fail to detect any signs of a universal church; but we shall perceive a universal state and a Völker-wanderung; and, what is more, these will prove to be the identical universal state and Völkerwanderung which appear in the background of the Hellenic Society as the last chapters in Minoan history.

The final convulsion of the post-Minoan Völkerwanderung, which the Egyptian records enable us to date about 1200/1190 B.C.,

---

[1] See the present chapter, pp. 69–70, above, together with Annex I, below.
[2] These phenomena are examined in IV. C (iii) (c) 2 (β), vol. iv, pp. 368–71, and IV. C (iii) (c) 2 (β), Annex III, vol. iv, pp. 624–34, as well as in Part X, below.

was not a raid in quest of plunder but a migration in search of
new homes; and the migrants seem to have been a mixed multitude
of Achaeans and Minoans, driven pell-mell by the impetus of a
new human avalanche from the European hinterland of the Aegean:
the 'Dorians'.[1] The refugees—a mighty host of fighting men and
non-combatants, people and cattle, carts and ships—seem to have
descended upon the mainland of Asia and then travelled along the
Asiatic coast south-eastward—breaking, like a tidal wave, first
upon the Empire of Khatti in Anatolia and then upon 'the New
Empire' of Egypt. The Egyptian records inform us that the impact
broke the Empire of Khatti in pieces, while 'the New Empire'
withstood the shock in a great battle on the border between
Palestine and Egypt; but in both areas the sequel was the same:
the migrants failed to win a footing in the hinterland but made
permanent settlements in the coast-lands. On the north-western
coast of the broken Empire of Khatti they settled in the districts
which, as Aeolis and Ionia, became part of the original home of
the Hellenic Society.[2] On the north-eastern coast of 'the New
Empire' of Egypt (an empire which survived, dead-alive) the

[1] The names 'Minoans', 'Achaeans', and 'Dorians' are used here with no connotations of language and *a fortiori* none of race. By 'Minoans' are meant all people who were
members of the Minoan Society during its last phase when it was embodied in 'the
thalassocracy of Minos'. By 'Achaeans' are meant those members of the external
proletariat of the Minoan Society who descended from the European hinterland of the
Aegean at the end of the 'thalassocracy' and who made their mark in the sack of Cnossos
about 1400 B.C. By 'Dorians' are meant the backwoodsmen who followed in the foot-
steps of the 'Achaeans' at the turn of the thirteenth and twelfth centuries B.C. It is
likely that the Minoan Society, like other societies, included peoples belonging to
various races and speaking various languages. The members of the Society in Crete
and the Cyclades probably did not speak Greek. The 'Minoanized' inhabitants of
Continental Greece probably did speak Greek (of the dialects afterwards called Arcadian,
Ionic, and Aeolic) at the time when they first came within the orbit of the Minoan
Society; and they doubtless continued to speak it as their vernacular. Greek was also
almost certainly the vernacular language of both the 'Achaeans' and the 'Dorians' (and
they appear to have spoken dialects of the same group, which is now known as Doric and
North-Western). These linguistic affinities and differences are of more interest to the
philologist than to the historian; and a Western historian of the present day must take
care not to view them through the spectacles of a modern Western linguistic nationalism.
Unless he takes off these spectacles, he will be inclined to equate affinities and differences
of language with affinities and differences of culture and with the sympathies and anti-
pathies to which these cultural affinities and differences give rise. This equation, which
seems self-evident in our 'post-war' Western World, is quite invalid for the Aegean
World in the times of 'the thalassocracy of Minos' and the subsequent Völkerwanderung.
The Greek-speaking 'Mycenaeans' of Continental Greece about the year 1400 B.C.
assuredly regarded the non-Greek-speaking 'Minoans' of Crete and the Cyclades as
their brethren and the Greek-speaking Achaeans as barbarians beyond the pale. Again,
about the year 1200 B.C., the Doric-speaking 'Achaeans' who were the ruling element
in the 'successor-states' among which the former domain of the Minoan 'thalassocracy'
was partitioned from about 1400 to 1200 B.C., quite probably regarded the Doric-
speaking 'Dorians' very much as the 'Achaeans' themselves had been regarded by the
'Minoans' some two centuries earlier.

[2] For the original home of the Hellenic Society, see p. 95, above. When this home is
examined closely, it can be dissected into two nodes or nuclei. One of these is the
Aegean coast of Continental Greece, which had been the limit up to which the Minoan
Society had expanded in that direction. The other is the Aegean coast of Anatolia,
which the Minoans did not make their own until they settled there as refugees during the
interregnum which followed the breakdown of their 'thalassocracy'.

intruders settled in a district which, as Philistia[1] (Palestine), became part of the original home of the Syriac Society. Along the border between the coast-lands and the interior, between the low-lands and the highlands, the Philistine refugees from the Minoan World encountered the Hebrew Nomads who had been drifting into the Syrian dependencies of 'the New Empire' of Egypt out of a no-man's-land in Arabia. Farther north, the mountain-range of Lebanon set a limit to the simultaneous infiltration of the Aramaean Nomads and gave shelter to the Phoenicians of the coast, who had managed to survive the passage of the Philistines and had learnt to lean no longer on the broken reed of an Egyptian protectorate. Out of these elements, a new society—the society which we have already identified in the background of the Islamic Society, and which we have decided to call 'Syriac'—emerged slowly as the convulsion subsided.[2]

As far as the Syriac Society was related at all to any older member of the species, it was related to the Minoan, and this in the degree in which the Hellenic Society was related to the Minoan —neither more nor less. One heritage of the Syriac Society from the Minoan may have been the Alphabet;[3] another may have been the taste for long-distance sea-faring which declared itself in the exploration of the Red Sea and the Mediterranean and in the discovery of the Atlantic.[4] That the Syriac Society, too, should

[1] More accurately, 'Philistia and Teucria'. The Teucrians or Zakkari settled at Dor, under the lee of Mount Carmel; the Philistines or Prsta settled on the coast southward of Dor as far as Gaza. Another war-band of Teucri settled immediately to the north of the Aeolians, under the lee of Mount Ida in the Troad, on the ruins of Ilium.

[2] In the traditions of the Israelites, the genesis of this Syriac Society was accurately described in the form of a prophecy after the event. 'God shall enlarge Japheth [the mythical eponymous ancestor of the peoples of the Minoan World, who appears in the Hellenic Mythology as the Titan Iapetos], and he shall dwell in the tents of Shem [the mythical eponymous ancestor of the Hebrews and Aramaeans]; and Canaan [the eponym of the inhabitants of the Syrian dependencies of 'the New Empire' of Egypt] shall be his servant (Gen. ix. 27, cited by Meyer, E.: *Geschichte des Altertums,* vol. ii, part (i), 2nd edition, p. 561). 'La Palestine avait été convertie à la Civilisation Égéenne' (Glotz, G.: *La Civilisation Égéenne* (Paris 1923, Renaissance du Livre), p. 437). It will be seen that the geographical displacement of the Syriac Society from the Minoan was considerably greater than that of the Hellenic from the Minoan.

[3] Scholars have surmised that the Minoan scripts which Archaeology has brought to light may be the ancestors of the Alphabet, which first appears in history as a possession of the Syriac Society and which has since supplanted every other script that has ever been invented except the Sinic characters which are still employed in the Far East. This surmise is not ruled out by the discovery in the Sinai Peninsula of an inscription in an archaic form of the Alphabet which is believed to date from the sixteenth century B.C. This might only mean that the settlement of Minoan refugees in Syria at the beginning of the twelfth century B.C. had been preceded by an infiltration of Minoan culture during the foregoing centuries when Syria had formed part, first of the Hyksos Empire and then of 'the New Empire' of Egypt. (For the origin of the Alphabet, see further II. D (ii), vol. ii, pp. 50–1, and II. D (vii), vol. ii, p. 386, footnote 2, below.)

[4] There had been a local coastwise traffic between the ports of Phoenicia and the Delta of the Nile since the first half of the third millennium B.C., but the long-distance voyages of the Phoenicians to the Western Mediterranean do not seem to go back beyond the beginning of the first millennium B.C. On the other hand, during the second millennium B.C., the Minoans ventured to sail from Crete as far as Egypt in one direction and Sicily in the other. Was it this tradition of seamanship—brought to Syria by Philistines

stand in this relation to the Minoan is somewhat surprising. One would rather expect to discover that the universal state in the background of Syriac history was not 'the thalassocracy of Minos' but 'the New Empire' of Egypt, and that the Monotheism of the Jews was a resurrection of the monotheism of Ikhnaton. The evidence, however, as far as it goes, does not warrant the hypothesis of such an 'affiliation'. Nor is there any evidence that the Syriac Society was either 'affiliated' or related in any lesser degree to the society represented by the Empire of Khatti—the Anatolian Power which had been contending with 'the New Empire' of Egypt for the dominion over Syria during the two centuries before the great migration of 1200/1190 B.C. occurred. Finally, there is no evidence of any 'affiliation' of the Syriac Society to the society represented by an earlier empire to which Syria had belonged some centuries before her Egyptian and Hittite conquerors appeared on the scene: that is to say, the Empire of Sumer and Akkad which had been established by the Sumerian Dynasty of Ur (*imperabant circa* 2295–2180 B.C.) and had been restored by the Amorite Dynasty of Babylon in the reign of Hammurabi (*imperabat circa* 1947–1905 B.C.).[1] The culture of the society of which this empire was the universal state made a deep impress upon all the countries and peoples which it embraced; and for seven centuries after Hammurabi's death the Akkadian language, conveyed in the cuneiform script, continued to be the *lingua franca* of commerce and diplomacy through all South-Western Asia. The impress of this culture was as deep in Syria as in any other country outside the actual homeland of the culture in 'Irāq. It is stamped upon the manners and customs of the Syrian people as we see them, from the sixteenth century B.C. to the thirteenth, through Egyptian eyes. Yet this impress, though it lasted so long, was not destined to reproduce itself in a new order of society.[2] When the darkness which descends upon the history of Syria after the migration of 1200/1190 begins to lift, the old impress has disappeared. The cuneiform script has been superseded by the Alphabet without leaving a trace of its former currency in Syria. The Minoan influence has prevailed.

---

and Teucrians in the migration of 1200/1190 B.C.—that inspired the Phoenicians in the first millennium to emulate the Minoans and surpass themselves?

[1] The dates given in this work for events in Sumeric, Babylonic, Hittite, and Egyptiac history are those of Eduard Meyer in *Die Aeltere Chronologie Babyloniens, Assyriens und Aegyptens* (Stuttgart and Berlin 1925, Cotta), except where another authority is expressly cited.

[2] It is true that we can discern some faint traces of an incipient Syriac Society which was related, not to the Minoan Society, but to the society, still to be identified, of which the Empire of Sumer and Akkad was the universal state. This first attempt at a Syriac Society, however, was abortive. This first, abortive, Syriac Society is examined in II. D (vii), vol. ii, pp. 388–91, below.

The Sumeric Society

When we turn to the background of the Indic Society, the first thing that strikes us is that the religion of the Vedas, like the worship of the Olympians, shows evidence of having arisen among barbarians in the course of a Völkerwanderung, and bears none of the distinguishing marks of a religion that has been created during a 'Time of Troubles' by the internal proletariat of a society in decline.

In this case the barbarians were the Aryas, who appear in North-Western India at the dawn of Indic history as, at the dawn of Hellenic history, the Achaeans appear in the Aegean. On the analogy of the relation in which we have found the Hellenic Society standing to the Minoan, we should expect to discover in the background of the Indic Society some universal state with a no-man's-land beyond its frontier in which the ancestors of the Aryas were living as an external proletariat until the universal state broke down and left the way open for a Völkerwanderung to overrun its derelict provinces. Can that universal state be identified and that no-man's-land be located? We may perhaps obtain answers to those questions by first asking ourselves two others: Whence did the Aryas find their way to India? And did any of them, starting from the same centre of dispersion, arrive at a different destination?

The Aryas spoke an Indo-European language; and the historical distribution of this family of languages—one group in Europe and another group in India and Iran—shows that the Aryas must have entered India from the Eurasian Steppe, crossing the Hindu Kush from the basin of the Oxus and Jaxartes into the basin of the Indus and Ganges as the Bactrian Greeks crossed in the second century B.C. and the Kushans in the first century of the Christian Era and a succession of Turkish invaders, from Mahmūd of Ghaznah to Bābur of Farghāna, between the eleventh century and the sixteenth. Now when we study the dispersion of the Turks, during those centuries, from the common point of departure where they all broke out of the Steppe into Transoxania, we find that while some of them turned south-eastward and invaded India, others moved on south-westward across Iran and did not come to a halt until they had reached Anatolia and Syria. It was the advance of the Saljūq Turks from the Oxus to the Mediterranean and the Black Sea Straits in the eleventh century—at a time when other Turks were advancing from the Oxus to the Indus—that provoked the First Crusade. In the twelfth century the war-bands of Turkish Mamlūks in the service of Saladin passed on into Egypt; and in the thirteenth century the successors of these Mamlūks supplanted Saladin's descendants and took the dominion of Egypt and Syria for themselves.[1] The records of ancient Egypt give us evidence that, during the first half of the second millennium B.C., the Aryas, breaking out of the Eurasian Steppe at the point where the Turks broke out of it about 3,000 years later, anticipated the Turks in their subsequent dispersion. While some Aryas (as we know from Indian sources) crossed the Hindu Kush into India, others made their way across Iran and 'Irāq to Syria and thence overran Egypt towards the beginning of the seventeenth century B.C. The Hyksos, as the Egyptians called these barbarian war-lords,[2] ruled an empire, embracing Egypt and Syria and perhaps Mesopotamia[3] as well, which was probably as extensive as Saladin's and was certainly as ephemeral. When, about 1580 B.C., the Hyksos were expelled from Egypt by their vassal the native prince of Thebes, who thus became the founder of 'the New Empire', the war-bands of the petty rulers who entered into the Hyksos' inheritance[4] in Syria continued to be called by an Aryan name,[5] and the kings of Mitanni, in Mesopotamia, continued to worship Aryan Gods.[6]

What caused the Völkerwanderung of the Aryas? What carried them from the Oxus to the Indus and the Nile? We may reply by asking: What caused the Völkerwanderung of the Turks, 3,000 years later, and carried the Turks along the same divergent roads to the same distant goals? The answer to our last question is a matter of common knowledge. The ancestors of the Turks had been living as an external proletariat of the Syriac Society in the no-man's-land of the Steppe beyond the north-eastern frontier of the 'Abbasid Caliphate of Baghdad—the universal state of the Syriac Society in its last phase. When the Caliphate broke down, the Turks drifted in to take possession of its derelict territories, which now lay open to them from end to end. In one direction the provinces of the Caliphate extended continuously all the way from Transoxania to Egypt; but there was also a detached province in the valley of the Indus, extending from the coast up-river to Multan and beyond, which was accessible from Transoxania by

[1] They sought to legitimize their power by exercising it in the name of a line of nominal caliphs of 'Abbasid descent whom they maintained as their pensioners at Cairo. (See the present section, p. 70, with p. 71, footnote 1, above.)

[2] The Hyksos were probably a mixed multitude of Aryas and other adventurers (e.g. Kharrians) who had joined their ranks on their way across South-Western Asia, as the war-bands who entered Egypt with Saladin were a mixed multitude of Turks, Kurds, and Syrians.

[3] i.e. Mesopotamia in the strict sense, meaning the middle basin of the Euphrates and Tigris between Armenia on the north-west and 'Irāq on the south-east.

[4] The Aryan element among the Hyksos is inferred from the Aryan element among the successors of the Hyksos in Syria and Mitanni, for which we have direct evidence in the records of 'the New Empire' of Egypt from the sixteenth century B.C. onwards. For the whole subject see Meyer, E.: Geschichte des Altertums, vol. ii, part (i), 2nd edition, pp. 33-8.

[5] 'Maryanni' = 'men'. These Aryan 'maryanni' corresponded to the Turkish 'mamlūks' = 'property' (i.e. slaves brought up as fighting men).

[6] e.g. Mitra, Varuna, Indra, the Nasatyas.

way of the Hindu Kush. The political geography of the Caliphate thus explains the dispersion of the Turkish raiders very simply. They spread in every direction in which a province of the derelict universal state awaited the spoiler.[1] Does this explanation give us a clue to the corresponding dispersion of the Aryas 3,000 years earlier? Assuredly it does. For when we look at the political map of South-Western Asia in the first century of the second millennium B.C., we find it occupied by a universal state which, like the ʿAbbasid Caliphate of Baghdad, was governed from a capital in ʿIrāq, and whose territories extended in the same directions as the territories of the Caliphate from the same centre.

This universal state was 'the Empire of the Four Quarters of the World' or 'the Empire of Sumer and Akkad'—established *circa* 2298 B.C. by the Sumerian Ur-Engur of Ur and restored *circa* 1947 B.C. by the Amorite Hammurabi[2]—which we have encountered already as the empire to which Syria belonged some centuries before she became the battle-field of the Egyptians and the Hittites.[3] The interval between the break-up of Hammurabi's Empire, after his death about 1905 B.C., and the establishment of 'the New Empire' of Egypt in the sixteenth century B.C., was occupied in the history of Syria by the domination of the Aryan migrants who came to be known as the Hyksos. These Aryas must have migrated across South-Western Asia and made themselves masters of Syria before they used Syria as their base for conquering Egypt in the early years of the seventeenth century B.C. The dates indicate that the Empire of the Hyksos began as an Aryan 'successor-state' to the universal state of Sumer and Akkad in Syria—a 'successor-state' that afterwards lost its equilibrium and changed its character by incidentally conquering another country—Egypt—which had never been included in the Empire of Sumer and Akkad and which belonged to the domain of a different society.[4] Thus the

---

[1] The Turks who overran the ʿAbbasid Empire in the eleventh century of the Christian Era, like the majority of the Germans who overran the Roman Empire in the fifth century, did not cross the frontier of the universal state until they had become members of the universal church which had spread through the territories of the Empire and into the no-man's-lands beyond. The Muslim inhabitants of the ʿAbbasid Empire, finding their Turkish co-religionists from no-man's-land awkward guests, in spite of their conversion, tried to 'pass' these guests 'on' to their neighbours by encouraging them to take up the Holy War against the Unbelievers. The van-guard of the Saljūqs, after drifting right across the territory of the Caliphate, was successfully 'passed on' into the domain of Orthodox Christendom in Anatolia. (And the East Romans promptly retaliated by similarly 'passing on' the Normans from Apulia into Dār-al-Islām.) Mahmūd of Ghaznah was encouraged to turn his energies against the Hindu World by invading the Panjab; but when once he had descended into the Valley of the Indus, he did not respect the boundary of the ʿAbbasid province but overran Dār-al-Harb and Dār-al-Islām alike. Is it conceivable that the Hyksos were 'passed on' into the Egyptiac World by the statesmen of Sumer and Akkad?

[2] Hammurabi was consciously restoring the universal state, for he revived its style and title (Meyer, E.: *Geschichte des Altertums*, 3rd edition, vol. i, part (ii), p. 633).

[3] See p. 103, above.

[4] The history of the Hyksos Empire displays points of likeness to the history of the

political geography of the Empire of Sumer and Akkad explains the migration of some Aryas to Syria. Does it also explain the contemporary migration of other Aryas to India? Was there a province of the Empire of Sumer and Akkad in the Indus Valley to attract these other Aryas across the Hindu Kush, as some of the kinsmen of the Saljūq Turks were attracted in the same direction by the existence in the Indus Valley of a province of the 'Abbasid Caliphate?

A priori, this would be not unlikely. The 'Abbasid province in Sind was connected with the political centre of the 'Abbasid Caliphate in 'Irāq by the sea-route, down the Persian Gulf, from the estuary of the Tigris and Euphrates to the Delta of the Indus. The political centre of the Empire of Sumer and Akkad likewise lay in 'Irāq; its later capital was Babylon, at a point on the Euphrates corresponding to the position of Baghdad on the Tigris; its earlier capital was Ur, which in the third millennium B.C. was as near to the head of the Gulf as Basrah has been in this second millennium of the Christian Era. We know that the Sumerians were a seafaring people who navigated the waters of the Gulf. What more likely than that they should have explored it as far as its exit into the Indian Ocean and so have discovered the Delta of the Indus? And, if they did discover that, what more likely again than that they should have ascended a river so like the Tigris and Euphrates and have colonized a country so like their own—creating there a new land of Sumer overseas?[1] As it happens, these *a priori* surmises now find some support in the results of recent archaeological research in the Indus Valley.

At Mohenjo-Daro in north-western Sind and at Harappā in the Panjab, north-east of Multan, excavations carried out by the Archaeological Department of the Government of India have brought to light the material remains of an ancient culture which is closely related to the ancient culture of the Sumerians in 'Irāq. The affinity falls short of absolute identity. It recalls the affinity of the Mycenaean culture of Continental Greece to the Minoan

Umayyad Caliphate. The Umayyad Caliphate started as a 'successor-state' in Syria to the Roman Empire; the Hyksos Empire started as a 'successor-state' in Syria to the Empire of Sumer and Akkad. The Umayyad Caliphate lost its equilibrium by incidentally conquering the former domain of the Sasanian Empire; the Hyksos Empire lost its equilibrium by incidentally conquering the former domain of 'the Middle Empire' of Egypt (the empire of the Eleventh and the Twelfth Dynasty). The Umayyad Caliphate paid the penalty of being supplanted by the 'Abbasid Caliphate; the Hyksos Empire paid the penalty of being supplanted by 'the New Empire' of Egypt.

[1] The likeness of the Lower Indus Valley to the Lower Euphrates and Tigris Valley round about the turn of the fourth and third millennia B.C. appears to have been still greater than it is to-day; for at that time Sind, as well as 'Irāq, is believed to have been a land of two rivers. There are traces of a waterway, the so-called 'Great Mihran', which flowed from the Panjab to the Indian Ocean more or less parallel to the Indus, eastward of the latter river. (See Sir John Marshall in *The Times*, 5th January, 1928; and Childe, V. G.: *The Most Ancient East* (London 1922, Kegan Paul), p. 201.)

culture of Crete; and we may explain this in either of two ways. Either we may conjecture that 'the Indus Culture', like the Mycenaean, was a 'colonial' variation, produced by the transplantation overseas of a culture which had originated and grown up elsewhere—in this case, in the basin of the Tigris and Euphrates—or else we may see in it a sister-culture, derived from a common parent unknown, which grew up simultaneously and independently.[1] The two sites of 'the Indus Culture' which have been excavated up to date contain a number of successive strata; and this fact indicates that the duration of the communities which occupied them was considerable. Correspondences between stratified objects at Mohenjo-Daro and similar objects occurring in strata at Susa and Ur suggest that the life-span of the community at Mohenjo-Daro is to be dated between 3250 and 2750 B.C.[2]

In the Indus Valley, as in the Aegean, it is not easy to translate archaeological evidence into historical terms. Yet it is not unreasonable to suppose that a region in which a society propagated its culture—or held intercourse with a sister-society of kindred culture—in its age of expansion eventually became a province of the universal state into which the paramount society incorporated itself towards the end of its history. If we allow ourselves to suppose that the Indus Valley, in which the Indian variant or sister of the Sumeric culture took shape,[3] was eventually embraced in the Empire of Sumer and Akkad, we shall have found a possible answer to the question why some Aryas, like some Turks, crossed the Hindu Kush and descended upon India, while other Aryas, like other Turks, made their way westward as far as Syria. If this answer is right, it means that the Völkerwanderung of the Aryas and the creation of the Vedic religion were events of the inter-

---

[1] This second view is taken by Sir John Marshall and by Professor V. G. Childe. For Sir John Marshall's own exposition of his view, see further the present section, Annex III, below.

[2] For 'the Indus Culture' see the magnificent publication entitled *Mohenjo-Daro and the Indus Civilisation* (London 1931, Probsthain, 3 vols.) by the Director-General of Archaeology in India, Sir John Marshall. See also the articles by the same authority in *The Times* newspaper of London, issues of the 26th February, 1926, and the 4th and 5th January, 1928; and in *The Illustrated London News*, issues of the 20th and 27th September and the 4th October, 1924; the 27th February and the 6th March, 1926; the 7th and 14th January, 1928. The articles in *The Times* of the 26th February, 1926, and the 5th January, 1928, as well as those in *The Illustrated London News*, are accompanied by photographs.

[3] See Sir John Marshall: *Mohenjo-Daro and the Indus Civilisation*, vol. i, chapter vii: 'Extent of the Indus Civilisation'. There is direct evidence for the diffusion of 'the Indus Culture' over the whole of Sind and the Central Panjab. There is complete uniformity of culture between Mohenjo-Daro and Harappā, though the sites are 400 miles apart. 'We have no sufficient grounds as yet for affirming positively that this civilisation was limited to the Indus Valley and the plains of the Panjab' (op. cit., p. 91). The domain of the culture extended into Baluchistan; but Baluchistan was not an important seat of it, and there was a rival culture in Western Baluchistan and Seistan. In the opposite direction, there is no evidence yet forthcoming for the presence of 'the Indus Culture' in the Ganges Basin.

regnum after the fall of the Empire of Sumer and Akkad, and that the Indic Society is related to the society to which that empire belonged in the same manner and in the same degree in which the Hellenic Society and the Syriac are related to the Minoan.

Can we identify the society in whose history the Empire of Sumer and Akkad was the universal state? When we examine the antecedents of this universal state, we find symptoms of a 'Time of Troubles , in the form (with which we have become familiar) of a series of ever more destructive wars between local states. Immediately before the establishment of a universal state by Ur-Engur, the contending local states had exhausted themselves and one another to such a degree that the homeland of the society in 'Irāq had been overrun by barbarians from the foot-hills of the Iranian Plateau: the Gutaeans (*dominabantur* in 'Irāq *circa* 2429–2306 B.C.). The exhaustion which had made this calamity possible is explained by the foregoing careers of the two great military conquerors of the Dynasty of Akkad: Naramsin (*dominabatur circa* 2572–2517 B.C.) and his ancestor Sargon or Sharrukin (*dominabatur circa* 2652–2597). The Akkadian militarist Sargon of Agade began his career by overthrowing the Sumerian militarist Lugalzaggisi of Erech (Uruk) and Umma (*dominabatur circa* 2677–2653). Lugalzaggisi had begun by overthrowing Urukagina of Lagash, who had come into power by leading a kind of popular revolution against the local priesthood. Peering farther back into the past, we catch glimpses of earlier and apparently more temperate contests between Lagash and Umma and the other city states into which the society was by then already articulated. Before the wars became destructive, there was an age of growth and creation on which the recent excavations at Ur have thrown light. How far back into or beyond the fourth millennium B.C. this age extended we do not yet know.

What name shall we give to the society which has thus come into view? The title of its universal state—'The Empire of Sumer and Akkad'—commemorates the fact that, by the time when the society had reached this stage of its history, its homeland had come to consist of two regions inhabited by two peoples whose difference of origin—long transcended by the unity of their culture—was still betrayed by a difference of language. The Akkadians spoke a language of the Semitic family, the Sumerians a language with an utterly different structure and vocabulary which has no known affinities. In the time of the universal state and in the 'Time of Troubles' which preceded it, the two peoples stood upon so equal a footing in the society which embraced them both that, if we confined our attention to these ages, we should be inclined to name the society 'Sumero-Akkadian'. When, however, we examine the cuneiform script in which both the Sumerian and the Akkadian language was conveyed, we find, by conclusive internal evidence, that this script was originally evolved in order to convey Sumerian and was adapted to convey Akkadian subsequently. The adaptation remained imperfect, since the syllabic character of the cuneiform script, which was well suited to the 'agglutinative' structure of Sumerian, was at variance with the consonantal structure of a Semitic language. The history of the script proves to be an epitome of the history of the society; for when we dig down to the age of growth we find that the Akkadians recede into the background and leave the Sumerians in possession of the stage. Naming the society in accordance with its origin and not its end, we shall call it 'Sumeric'.[1]

The Hittite Society.

Having identified this Sumeric Society, we can go on to identify two others by proceeding, this time, not from the later to the earlier, but in the reverse order.

If we turn our attention again to the interregnum following the fall of the Sumeric universal state after the death of Hammurabi (*imperabat circa* 1947–1905 B.C.), we shall find that the Völkerwanderung which occupied this interregnum was not confined to the dispersion of the Aryas from the Eurasian Steppe into Syria and India. While the Sumeric Society, in the course of its long history, had propagated its culture westward round the Arabian Desert into Syria and perhaps also south-eastward down the Persian Gulf into the Indus Valley, as well as north-eastward over the Iranian Plateau as far as Transcaspia,[2] it had also been propagating it north-westward over the Taurus Range on to the eastern part of the Anatolian Plateau which was afterwards called Cappadocia. In the twenty-seventh century B.C., Sargon of Agade made a military expedition across the Taurus into Cappadocia in response to an appeal from Assyrian traders who had settled in the country and had fallen out with the local ruler. Clay tablets, impressed with business documents in cuneiform, which have been found in Cappadocia by Western archaeologists, prove that these Assyrian settlements north-west of Taurus survived and flourished and that, like Assyria itself,[3] they were included within the domain

---

[1] 'Sumeric' stands to 'Sumero-Akkadian' as 'Hellenic' to 'Graeco-Roman' and as 'Syriac' to 'Syro-Iranian'.

[2] Its expansion as far as Transcaspia—that is to say, up to the threshold of the gate through which the Aryas eventually broke out of the Steppe into the Sumeric World—has been revealed by the excavations of the Pumpelly Expedition at Anau.

[3] Assyria (Asshur) was the northernmost of the city-states into which the homeland of the Sumeric Society came to be articulated. Owing to its geographical position, its people naturally took the lead in pioneering in the wild north-west. Presumably they

of the Empire of Sumer and Akkad under the Dynasty of Ur
and probably again during the reign of Hammurabi. When, after
Hammurabi's death, the Sumeric universal state broke down
finally, its Cappadocian provinces were occupied by barbarians
from the no-man's-land beyond the north-western frontier; and
about 1750 B.C. the ruler of the principal barbarian 'successor-
state' in this quarter, King Mursil I of Khatti, raided and sacked
Babylon itself and overthrew the last descendant of Hammurabi.

The raiders from Khatti retired with their booty, but the political vacuum which they left behind them in 'Irāq was promptly
filled by the descent of other barbarians, the Kassites, from a no-
man's-land on the north-east, on the rim of the Iranian Plateau. The
Kassites founded a dynasty which ruled in Babylon from 1749 to
1173 B.C. After the double catastrophe of *circa* 1750–1749 B.C.,
which seems to mark the climax of the post-Sumeric interregnum
and the last convulsion of the Völkerwanderung,[1] a darkness soon
descends upon the history of the whole region which had once
been irradiated by the culture of the Sumeric Society and incorporated into the Sumeric universal state. From the middle of the
seventeenth century until after the beginning of the fifteenth, the
very names of the Hittite rulers in Cappadocia and the Kassite
rulers in Babylonia are lost. The darkness is first pierced by light
from Egypt: the records of the campaigns in which Thothmes III
(*imperabat solus circa* 1480–1450 B.C.) intruded upon the former
domain of the Sumeric Society by conquering Syria. As the light
grows, we begin to distinguish the outlines of two nascent societies
in South-Western Asia beyond 'the New Empire's' frontiers.[2]

The home of one of these two societies lay in the former

ascended the Tigris to its source, crossed the Euphrates Valley by the route of the modern
road from Kharput to Malaṭiyah, and mounted over the rolling hill-country which the
Turks call the Uzun Yayla into the Valley of the Halys (Qyzyl Yrmāq). In this age,
however, when the Assyrians were pioneers and traders, Assyria was not a military
power. It was to the distant King of Akkad, not to their own 'patesi' of Asshur, that the
Assyrian merchants appealed in the twenty-seventh century B.C. The militarism for
which Assyria has become a by-word belongs to a later phase of Assyrian history
which did not begin until long after the history of the Sumeric Society had come
to an end.

[1] There is no direct evidence as to whether the Hittite raid and the Kassite descent
upon Babylon occurred before or after the dispersion of the Aryas from the Eurasian
Steppe into India and Syria. Since the Hyksos' invasion of Egypt did not take place
before about 1680 B.C., it is chronologically possible that their migration from the Oxus
to Syria took place after 1749 B.C. Military considerations, however, make it seem more
likely that they traversed Iran and 'Irāq at a time when the Kassites were still confined
to their mountain fastnesses and when 'Irāq was under the feeble régime of the epigoni
of Hammurabi, rather than at a time when the passage was blocked by the Kassite
'successor-state' in Babylonia. Having acquired the choicest portion of the Empire of
Sumer and Akkad, the Kassites would assuredly have either fended off rival barbarian
claimants or perished in the attempt (as the Achaeans perished when they failed to fend
off the Dorians).

[2] Two, that is, in addition to the nascent Indic Society in the Indus Valley, which
may, as we have conjectured, have been an outlying province of the Empire of Sumer and
Akkad. (See pp. 107–9, above.)

provinces of the Empire of Sumer and Akkad in Cappadocia and in the adjoining Anatolian territories which had once been the no-man's-land beyond the Empire's Cappadocian frontier. This society borrowed freely from the Sumeric; yet we can hardly describe its relation to the Sumeric Society as 'affiliation'; for there is no indication that the two societies were linked together by the middle term of a universal church. The later society did indeed take over and assiduously practice the Sumeric system of divination. This illusory form of applied science must be regarded, however, as an offspring of magic rather than of religion; and in any case it was an elaboration of a primitive practice perpetuated by the dominant minority in the Sumeric Society and was not the product of a new religion developed by the internal proletariat—a development of which there is no trace.[1] When we turn to the later society's representation and worship of the Gods, we find here in general not a transmission or reflection of the Sumeric Pantheon and the Sumeric ritual,[2] but a religion with a distinctive character of its own which must have been derived either from elements indigenous in Cappadocia before the infiltration of the Sumeric culture in the third millennium B.C., or from elements introduced by barbarian invaders after the breakdown of the Sumeric universal state at the turn of the twentieth and nineteenth centuries B.C., or from some fusion or amalgamation of the two elements.

Again, when we study the scripts in which the later society made its records, we find that it began by employing cuneiform[3] but went on to invent a pictographic script of its own.[4] Moreover, while it began by taking over the Akkadian language together with the cuneiform script—and this for local records as well as for diplomatic correspondence—it afterwards adapted the cuneiform script to convey at least five of its own vernaculars, translating Akkadian and Sumerian texts as a nucleus for the development of vernacular literatures. By the time when these local vernaculars were conveyed in the new local pictographic script, the literary independence of the new society in Cappadocia from the Sumeric Society had become complete.

The diversity of local vernacular languages had its counterpart

[1] See footnote 1 on p. 115, below.
[2] There are, of course, exceptions to this general rule. For instance, the name, if not the ritual, of the Goddess Ishtar of Niniveh was perpetuated by the Hittites in the regions north-west of Taurus into which this worship had been introduced by the Assyrian colonists of Cappadocia in the third millennium B.C. (See Meyer, E.: *Geschichte des Altertums*, vol. ii (i), 2nd edition, p. 520.)
[3] In the style of the First Dynasty of Babylon (i.e. the imperial style of the Sumeric universal state in the age of Hammurabi), and not in the style of the former Assyrian commercial colonies in Cappadocia (i.e. the local style in the preceding age of the Dynasty of Ur).
[4] This pictographic script has so far defied the efforts of our Western scholars to decipher it.

in the multiplicity of local states. The oldest established of these languages seems to have been one with no known affinities which was called Khatti-li; and the same name—Khatti—was adopted by a local state which took the city of Khattusas (the present Boghazkiöi) as its capital in the course of an expansion that carried it to a position of predominance in its own world by the beginning of the fifteenth century B.C.[1] 'Khatti' is the original of the name 'Hittite' which appears in the Old Testament; and it will be convenient to use this latter name for the society that embraced all the states over which the Empire of Khatti exercised its hegemony[2] and all the languages which the peoples of these states employed.[3]

The destinies of this Hittite Society were decided by the history of the Khatti State. In the fourteenth century B.C., when 'the New Empire' of Egypt lost its grip upon its dominions in Syria, Subbilulyuma King of Khatti (*regnabat circa* 1380–1346 B.C.), the contemporary of Amenhotep IV Ikhnaton (*imperabat circa* 1370–1352 B.C.), did not resist the temptation to fish in troubled waters. Subbilulyuma substituted Khatti for Egypt as the paramount Power in Northern Syria by an adroit combination of fraud and force, and in Mesopotamia he extended his hegemony over the Kingdom of Mitanni; but he left a fatal legacy to his successors in a series of destructive wars between Khatti and Egypt, in which the Hittite Power, with its less substantial economic foundations, suffered relatively more severely than its adversary—to the point

[1] We may suppose that this Empire of Khatti, which dominated the Hittite World from some time before 1480 B.C. until 1200 B.C., stood to the Hittite 'successor-state' of the Empire of Sumer and Akkad, whose war-bands sacked Babylon about 1750 B.C., as the Carolingian Empire, which dominated the Western World from about A.D. 775 to 875, stood to the foregoing Merovingian 'successor-state' of the Roman Empire.

[2] This distinction of terms is suggested by Dr. D. G. Hogarth in *The Cambridge Ancient History*, vol. ii, pp 252–3.

[3] The official language of the Empire of Khatti was not the language called 'Khatti-li' but a quite different language which seems to have been called 'Nasian' or 'Kanisian'; and this 'Kanisian', as well as the closely related 'Luvian', turns out to belong to the Indo-European family. It does not, however, belong to the so-called 'Satem'-Group of Indo-European languages which includes Sanskrit (the language of the Aryan invaders of Syria and India) and Iranian, but to the so-called 'Centum'-Group, which is otherwise represented by the westernmost of the Indo-European languages (e.g. by all those that are alive in Europe now except the Letto-Lithuanian, Albanian, and Slavonic) and by one isolated language in the far north-east (the now extinct 'Tokharian', which has become known to Western scholars through the discovery in the Tarim Basin of documents in this language dating from the fourth and subsequent centuries of the Christian Era). From the geographical distribution it looks as though the 'Centum' and 'Satem' languages were dispersed successively from an identical centre on the Eurasian Steppe from which they spread in two concentric circles—the 'satem' wave following behind the 'centum' wave and eventually almost effacing it everywhere except in the remote peninsula of Europe. 'Kanisian', like 'Tokharian', is saturated with non-Indo-European elements, and this fact suggests that both these languages were on the forefront of the 'centum' wave; that they were, in fact, its broken crest of foam. (The Teutonic languages, which are also much modified from the Indo-European 'Ur-Sprache', may represent another 'breaker' at another point on the circumference of the circle.) The nearest affinity of 'Kanisian-Luvian' seems to be to Latin. This suggests that the language was brought into Anatolia from Central Europe, as the ('Satem'-Group) Thracian language was afterwards brought in by the Phrygians and the ('Centum'-Group) Celtic by the Galatians.

of permanently overstraining both itself and the society upon which it had become an incubus. When the two Powers at length made peace about the year 1278 B.C. on the basis of a partition of Syria, Khatti appears to have indulged a now ingrained habit of imperialism by conquering Western Anatolia up to the Aegean coast.[1] In this last adventure it merely blazed a trail for the great migration of 1200/1190 B.C., which brought the Khatti Empire down with a crash and buried the Hittite Society under the ruins.[2]

For about five centuries longer, the prematurely stricken society was represented on the map by settlements of refugees in Northern Syria and Cilicia—a sheltered nook between the cradles of the two new societies—the Syriac and the Hellenic—which were arising on either side. When the Phoenicians and the Greeks began to compete for the mastery of the Mediterranean, the remnant of the Hittite Society appears to have entered into the competition by sending out colonists who successfully established themselves overseas and became known in their new Italian home as the Etruscans.[3] Yet this transplantation failed to awaken the stricken society to new life. It only rendered the colonists more

[1] The monuments of this conquest are the Hittite sculptures overlooking the last stages of the roads that lead from the interior of Anatolia to the west coast. The most famous of these monuments is the rock-carved figure of the Hittite Mother-Goddess which is popularly known as the 'Niobe' of Mount Sipylus.

[2] The history of the Empire of Khatti during the two centuries which ended in this catastrophe may be compared with the history of the East Roman Empire during the century that ended in the catastrophe of Manzikert (A.D. 1071). After the overthrow of the Empire of Khatti by the great migration from the Aegean, the interior of Anatolia was silted up by two drifts of barbarians. The Phrygians (speaking a language belonging to the Thracian branch of the 'Satem'-Group of the Indo-European family) drifted in from South-Eastern Europe; the Moschians and Tibarenians drifted in from the Caucasus. These barbarians from the hinterland divided the heritage of the Empire of Khatti with the Minoan refugees (Teucrians, Aeolians, Ionians, Tramilae) and their 'Dorian' pursuers who occupied the west coast of Anatolia from the Troad to Lycia. (Compare the division of Syria between the Israelites and the Aramaeans on the one hand and the Philistines and the Teucrians on the other.)

[3] In a simpler form, the Etruscan name appears already as that of one of the sea-peoples in the Egyptian records of the great migration at the turn of the thirteenth and twelfth centuries B.C. (Tursha = Turs-sci or Etrusci = Turs-ani or Τυρρηνοί). Some scholars have inferred that this was the time when the Etruscans planted their colonies in Italy from their earlier home in the Levant; but this inference is not borne out by analogy. The same Egyptian records also mention the Aqaiwasha (Achaeans) in association with the Tursha (Etruscans); and at a later date we find Achaean settlements in Italy as well as Etruscan. We know, however, that these Achaean settlements in Italy were made, not at the time of the great migration during the post-Minoan interregnum, but at least four centuries later, in the course of the eighth century B.C. The Phoenician colonies in the Western Mediterranean appear to have been founded at a not much earlier date. It seems natural to suppose that the Etruscan settlements—the third group of Levantine settlements in the Western Mediterranean besides the Phoenician and the Greek—were contemporary.

Exactly whence the Etruscans sailed to Italy we do not know; but since the Asiatic coast of the Mediterranean was in Philistine, Teucrian, and Phoenician hands from the borders of Egypt as far north as Aradus, and in Greek, Lycian, and Teucrian hands from the eastern extremity of Pamphylia all the way round to the Dardanelles, the possible locus for the Etruscans' point of departure would appear to be reduced to the Asiatic coast of the Mediterranean between Aradus and Side.

The Tyrrhenians who were expelled by the Athenians from Lemnos in the sixth century B.C., but whose survivors still held their own in the fifth century on the Athos Peninsula, as well as under Macedonian rule in Crestonia and under Achaemenian rule

susceptible to assimilation; and, while the Etruscans were being Hellenized, the Hittite communities which remained in Asia were first ground to powder by the Assyrians and were then absorbed into the body of the Syriac Society by the Aramaeans.

The Babylonic Society

The other society which comes into view in Western Asia, side by side with the Hittite Society, when the darkness lifts in the fifteenth century B.C., had its home in the former homeland of the Sumeric Society in 'Irāq.

If we test the relation of this other society to the Sumeric by the criterion of religion, we shall again fail to find that middle term of a universal church which we have taken as the essential token of Apparentation-and-Affiliation. When, however, we examine what the religion of this other society was, we find that it was not, like the Hittite religion, of non-Sumeric origin. On the contrary, it was virtually identical with the state religion of the Empire of Sumer and Akkad in the time of the Amorite Dynasty of Babylon— a religion which had been created neither by the 'internal proletariat' nor by the 'external proletariat' of the Sumeric Society, but by the dominant minority.[1]

at Placia and Scylacē on the Asiatic coast of the Marmara, were presumably the representatives of an abortive attempt, on the Etruscans' part, to compete with the Greeks for the mastery of the Dardanelles and for the command of the Black Sea. (For these Lemnian Tyrrhenians, and their confusion with the Lemnian Pelasgi whom they appear to have overlaid and assimilated, see further I. C (i) (b), Annex II, below.)

From what is known of the culture which the Etruscans brought with them to Italy, it looks as though its affinities are with the Hittite culture; but the imprint cannot have been very strong, since after their arrival in Italy the Etruscans adopted the Alphabet from the Greeks, and there is no archaeological record of their having ever employed the Hittite hieroglyphic script, which remained in use among the Hittite refugees in Northern Syria. It may be conjectured that the Etruscans were a people living on the southwestern fringes of the Hittite World in the shelter of the Western Taurus, with an outlet on the Mediterranean in the neighbourhood of Western Cilicia. There is little to recommend the alternative conjecture that the Etruscans of Italy were an indigenous European people. (See further II D (iii), vol. ii, pp. 85–6, below).

[1] There is nothing in the religious life of the Sumeric Society that can be interpreted as a new religious movement—even a rudimentary or an abortive movement—proceeding from the 'internal proletariat' in the 'Time of Troubles' and in the universal state. We cannot so interpret either the cult of Tammuz or the Penitential Psalms—the two features of the Sumeric religion in which we find the nearest approach to the religious spirit of an 'internal proletariat' as we know it elsewhere—for there is no evidence that either of these features asserted itself as a reaction to the established religion of the 'dominant minority'. As for Tammuz, 'il suo nome ricorre soltanto—e non molto spesso —nei tempi più antichi, specialmente in documenti di Lagash: nel periodo assiro non se ne fa più menzione' (Furlani, G.: La Religione Babilonese e Assira, vol. i (Bologna 1928, Zanichelli), pp. 279–80). This chronological fact possibly supports the conjecture that the similarities between the cults of Tammuz, Attis, Adonis, and Osiris are due to the propagation of an originally Sumerian cult into Anatolia, Syria, and Egypt (see Langdon, S.: Tammuz and Ishtar (Oxford 1914, Clarendon Press), p. 1); but it certainly forbids us to be led by the suggestive meaning of the God's name (Dāmu-zi in Sumerian means 'faithful son': see Langdon, op. cit., p. 2) into regarding the Tammuz cult as either the rudiment or the vestige of a religion created in the Sumeric 'Time of Troubles' by the Sumeric 'internal proletariat'. As for the Penitential Psalms, there seems to be no clue to their date (Jastrow, M.: The Religion of Babylonia and Assyria (Boston 1898, Ginn), p. 317). Thus, in the present state of our knowledge, the question whether the 'internal proletariat' of the Sumeric Society ever created anything in the nature of a universal

The Babylonian pantheon reflects the life, and the attitude towards life, of the dominant minority in the Sumeric Society of that age as faithfully as the Olympian pantheon reflects the life and outlook of the barbarians who overran the Minoan World during the interregnum after the fall of the 'thalassocracy of Minos'. Here too, the relations between the Gods were simply a transposition of political facts into theological terms. In the Babylonian phase of the Empire of Sumer and Akkad, the political organization of the Sumeric Society into a universal state with its capital at Babylon entailed the subordination of all other Gods to the local God of Babylon, Marduk; and in the time of Hammurabi's immediate successor, Samsuiluna (*imperabat circa* 1904–1867 B.C.), Marduk's supremacy was confirmed by identifying him with Enlil the Lord (Bel) of Nippur—the God who, during the Sumeric 'Time of Troubles', had conferred a political hegemony upon whichever one of the contending states had been able, at any given moment, to establish a command over his shrine.

When we look at the society that was in existence in 'Irāq in the fifteenth century B.C., we observe that this political system of religion had been taken over from the past with the least amount of change that was required in order to adapt it to the political conditions of the day. The Society was now articulated into three states[1]—Babylonia, Assyria, and Elam—and in each state the local State-God was given the sovereignty over the pantheon without any other change in the names, number, and attributes of the Gods or any change at all in cult and ritual. Thus in Babylonia the sovereignty over the pantheon was retained by the Babylonian Marduk-Bel (masked under the Kassite name Kharbe so long as a Kassite dynasty remained on the throne),[2] while in Assyria the Assyrian God Asshur occupied Marduk-Bel's place; but in every other respect the religions of Babylonia and Assyria were

church has to be answered in the negative; but this answer cannot be regarded as definitive. 'Anche la religione babilonese-assira ha avuto, come tutta la civiltà mesopotamica, la sua storia e non v'ha dubbio che tra non molto si potrà scrivere anche una storia dello spirito religioso in Mesopotamia. . . . Pel momento conviene rinunciare a dare una vera e propria storia della religione babilonese-assira' (Furlani, op. cit., pp. 92–3). In Professor Langdon's opinion (op. cit., p. 183), the astral theology into which the myth of Tammuz and Ishtar—originally a vegetation myth (op. cit., p. 5)—was eventually taken up, presents 'all the essential conditions for the construction of a universal religion, based upon the sufferings of a divine son'.

[1] The Kingdom of the Sea-Land, under the so-called Second Dynasty of Babylon (which never ruled in Babylon), had been established in the time of Samsuiluna, Hammurabi's immediate successor on the throne of Sumer and Akkad, as an indigenous 'successor-state' of the Sumeric universal state, and it had been annexed to the barbarian 'successor-state', subsequently established by the Kassites at Babylon, at the turn of the eighteenth and seventeenth centuries B.C. Thus the Kingdom of the Sea Land was simply a phenomenon of the post-Sumeric interregnum. It is perhaps to be interpreted as a last attempt on the part of the Sumerians to preserve their distinctive nationality.

[2] The Kassite dynasty flickered out of existence in 1173 B.C.; but the date is of no historical importance, since the descendants of the barbarians had been 'Babylonicized' long before they ceased to rule.

identical both with one another and with the religion of the Sumeric universal state in its last phase.[1]

In the secular sphere, we do find certain important changes. For instance, the units of political articulation were no longer city-states—as they had been from the dawn of Sumeric history to the breakdown of the Empire of Sumer and Akkad[2]—but larger states which each contained a number of cities without political individuality. There were also changes in the currency of languages. Sumerian, which had begun to lose ground to Akkadian during the Sumeric 'Time of Troubles' but had still survived as a living language down to the end of the Sumeric universal state,[3] had now become extinct—though, as a dead language, it was still assiduously studied because the Akkadian Semitic language and the cuneiform script were instruments that could not be used without a grasp of the Sumerian classical background. In both Babylonia and Assyria, the Akkadian language still held its own as a medium for public and private records. On the other hand, in Elam, where Akkadian had acquired the same currency as in 'Irāq at the time when Elam had been a province of the Empire of Sumer and Akkad, the political independence of the country in the new era was expressed linguistically in the reinstatement of the vernacular language.[4]

These secular changes in the aspect of Society are considerable. Nevertheless, if we take the degree of continuity or change in religious life as our touchstone, we shall hesitate to describe the society of the later age as being 'affiliated' to the Sumeric Society; and our reason for hesitating will be the exact opposite of that which weighed with us when we were considering the relation

[1] See Jastrow, M.: *The Religion of Babylonia and Assyria* (Boston 1898, Ginn), p. 189.
[2] The Empire of Sumer and Akkad, like the Roman Empire, was a union of city-states in which the units did not lose their individuality and in which the Central Government confined its activities to functions which were beyond the local Governments' compass.
[3] The Sumerian language was already dying out in Hammurabi's time, and at the same time the geographical centre of gravity of the society was shifting from Sumer to Akkad: from Ur and Nippur and Isin to Babylon. (Meyer, E.: *Geschichte des Altertums*, 3rd edition, vol. i, part ii, pp. 630–2.)
[4] The Elamite language was a non-Semitic language with no known affinities. (It is noteworthy that it had no affinity with Sumerian.) Elam was the first region outside 'Irāq into which the Sumeric culture expanded. A monument of this expansion was the invention of an Elamitic script which was inspired by the Sumerian cuneiform but which struck out a new set of characters for conveying the Elamite language, instead of adapting the existing Sumerian characters, as these had been adapted to convey another non-Sumerian language: Akkadian. During the latter half of the third millennium B.C., however, the Elamitic script was supplanted by the Sumerian cuneiform after all; and after the establishment of the Empire of Sumer and Akkad, when Elam had become a province of the Sumeric universal state, the Elamite language itself was supplanted for purposes of record (though not as a spoken vernacular) by Akkadian—and this even in private transactions. By the time when our series of records from Elam begins again in the thirteenth century B.C., after the break during the interregnum, this process of linguistic assimilation had been not only checked but undone. (See Meyer, E.: *Geschichte des Altertums*, 3rd edition, vol. i, part ii, pp. 501–2, 560, and 662.)

between the Sumeric Society and the Hittite. In that instance the relation seemed too slight to be called Apparentation-and-Affiliation. In this instance it seems to be too intimate. We hesitate to say that the society which we find existing in 'Irāq in this later age is 'affiliated' to the Sumeric Society, because we are not sure that it may not be identical with it—that it may not, in fact, be the Sumeric Society itself in the act of attempting, after the play is over, to repeat its historic part on a derelict remnant of the stage. Here is a problem of identity which we must try to solve sooner or later. We may find ourselves in a better position to solve it when our present survey of societies has been completed. Provisionally, and without prejudice, let us treat the society which we find in possession in 'Irāq in the fifteenth century B.C. as a separate representative of the species in its own right, and let us lend it a name—for convenience 'Babylonic'.[1]

In Babylonic history—or the epilogue to Sumeric history, whichever title we may eventually decide to use—there was one portentous event: the militarization of Assyria. When the Empire of Sumer and Akkad broke up and the barbarians overran its territories—Aryas from one side, Hittites from another, Kassites from a third—Assyria was the only fraction of the Sumeric World that was not overwhelmed. By a superhuman effort the Assyrians kept successive invaders at bay; and their ordeal was prolonged for centuries. After surviving a Mitannian domination in the fifteenth century, they bore the brunt of the Aramaean expansion in the eleventh. Yet they never succumbed, and for this they had their reward and paid their penalty.[2] If the waters did not go over their soul, the iron did enter into it; and the Assyrian state emerged from the ordeal as a blade of tempered steel which would never allow the hand that held it to rest from shedding blood.[3] We have already encountered this Assyrian militarism as the scourge of the Syriac Society in its 'Time of Troubles'; but the injuries which it inflicted on an alien society were far exceeded by those which it inflicted on its own. An intermittent duel with Babylonia cul-

---

[1] 'Babylonic' (Latin *Babylonicus*) rather than 'Babylonian', in order to avoid the ambiguity that arises if an adjective with a geographical connotation is used as the label for a society. 'Babylonic' seems an apt name for this society on the analogy of 'Byzantine', since the city of Babylon played as dominant a part in its history as the city of Constantinople has played in the history of Orthodox Christendom. Babylon was not merely the capital of one of the states into which the society was articulated. It was the citadel of the common culture in which the people of all these states lived and moved and had their being; and political rancour did not diminish the city's cultural prestige. The Assyrians who made war on Babylonia in the eighth and seventh centuries B.C. could not escape the spell of Babylon, any more than the Bulgars who made war on the East Roman Empire in the ninth and tenth centuries of the Christian Era could escape the spell of Byzantium.

[2] For the reward, see II. D (v), vol. ii, pp. 133–6, and for the penalty, Part IV, below.

[3] Αὐτὸς γὰρ ἐφέλκεται ἄνδρα σίδηρος. (*Odyssey*, xix, l. 13.)

minated in the Hundred Years' War of the seventh century B.C., in which Babylon fell first, to rise again, and Nineveh next, to rise no more. Assyria's last great exploit before her annihilation was the overthrow of Elam; and Babylonia was so sorely stricken that she only survived her victory over Assyria for three-quarters of a century. The last survivor among the three states of the Babylonic World lost its independence when Cyrus entered Babylon in 538 B.C.; and though the Empire of the Achaemenidae was ruled from Babylon and Susa,[1] its ultimate mission was to serve as a universal state for the Syriac and not for the Babylonic Society.[2] In the course of five centuries, the Babylonic Society gradually faded away. Before the beginning of the Christian Era, it was extinct.[3]

The Andean Society

As far as this point in our survey of societies we have been identifying extinct representatives of the species that have left some monument or other in the world of our time, either in the shape of fossils or else in the shape of living societies to which they are 'apparented'—or related in a less intimate way—in the first or the second degree. In order to complete our survey up to the limits of our knowledge here and now, we must also try to identify, by analogy with the specimens identified already, those representatives of the species which are neither themselves alive to-day nor are related in any way to any of the living representatives nor have left their trace in the form of fossils, but which are known to us solely from our literary and archaeological records.

We know in this way of two societies in the New World which were both incorporated into our Western Society by conquest during the sixteenth century of the Christian Era, at the very time when in the Old World the Arabic Society was being incorporated by the same process into the Iranic Society to constitute the unitary Islamic Society of to-day.[4] At the time of the Spanish conquests in the New World one of these two indigenous societies occupied Central America, from the basin of the Mexican lakes to the peninsula of Yucatan. The other occupied the Andean Plateau, together with the lowlands between the western escarpment of the plateau and the Pacific Coast of South America, in a long narrow zone extending north and south from what is now the Republic of Colombia to what are now the north-eastern corner of Chile and the north-western corner of Argentina. In the quite different

[1] Susa—the capital of Elam—had been one of the three great cities of the Babylonic World.
[2] On this point, see pp. 80-1, above, and also II. D (v), vol. ii, p. 138, below.
[3] See pp. 79-80, above.
[4] See pp. 68-72, above, and I. C (i) (b), Annex I, below.

physical environments of the Pampas on the south and the tropical forests of the Amazon Basin on the east, the 'Andean' Society had failed to secure a footing.

Our knowledge of these two societies is derived partly from archaeological research and partly from literary records made by the Spanish conquistadores, or by members of the conquered societies at the instance of the conquistadores, on the morrow of the conquests, before the traditions of the conquered societies had been obliterated by the disappearance of the societies themselves.[1] From this evidence we can discern that at the respective moments when the histories of the two societies were interrupted by the shattering impact of an overwhelming alien force, the Andean Society had recently emerged from a 'Time of Troubles' into a universal state, while the Central American Society was in the last convulsions of a 'Time of Troubles' from which a universal state was about to issue.

The Andean universal state was the Empire of the Incas, which had already overthrown all the other Powers of the Andean World, had incorporated into itself the whole domain of the Andean Society except the northern extremity of the plateau beyond Quito, and had organized on a uniform plan the various peoples and territories that had come to be embraced within its frontiers.[2] As a result of the Spanish conquest, this indigenous Andean universal state was replaced by an alien universal state in the shape of the Spanish Viceroyalty of Peru. The prospective Central American universal state was the Aztec Empire of Tenochtitlan, which had been ruining the Central American Society since about A.D. 1375 by a career of militarism comparable, in its blood-thirstiness and destructiveness, to the militarism of Assyria. At the moment when the Spaniards arrived, the city-state of Tlaxcala was the only considerable Power in the Central American World which the Aztecs had not yet succeeded in overthrowing; and the Tlaxcalecs had their backs to the wall. It was by entering into an alliance with the Tlaxcalecs that Cortez overthrew the Aztecs and anticipated, at the eleventh hour, the transformation of the Aztec Empire into an indigenous Central American universal state by establishing in place of it an alien universal state in the shape of the Spanish Viceroyalty of Mexico.

---

[1] The disappearance of these two societies through their incorporation into our Western Society was a rapid process. The last surviving community of the Central American Society—a refugee community of Mayas who had migrated from Yucatan to the shores of Lake Peten—had become extinct before the close of the seventeenth century of the Christian Era. In the Andean Society, the last flicker of self-consciousness came and went in the rebellion of Tupac Amaru against the Spanish régime in Peru in 1780–3.

[2] For a description of the administrative organization of the Empire of the Incas, see Baudin, L.: *L'Empire Socialiste des Inka* (Paris 1928, Institut d'Ethnologie).

In attempting a retrospective reconnaissance of Andean and Central American history from our own date of entry into contact with these two societies at the moment of the Spanish Conquest, it may be convenient to deal with Andean history first, since its course is easier to survey than the course of Central American history on the whole.

The Empire of the Incas, which was suddenly and violently superseded by the Spaniards in A.D. 1530, had been fulfilling the functions of an Andean universal state for about a hundred years before its catastrophic overthrow in mid-career. At least, we may say that the Inca Empire could fairly lay claim to the title of an Andean universal state from the moment when it succeeded in incorporating the Kingdom of Chimu; for Chimu was not merely the second greatest Power in the Andean World, next to the Inca Empire itself, on the eve of the Inca conquest; it was also the foremost of the twin birth-places of the Andean culture, which had first emerged, and then risen to its zenith, partly in Chimu and partly in Nazca. Thus the conquest of Chimu by the Inca Power in the fifteenth century of the Christian Era established a political union between the oldest and the youngest elements in the Andean Society; for the rise of the Andean culture to its zenith in Chimu and Nazca appears to have taken place during the first five centuries of the Christian Era,[1] whereas the first Inca sovereign of the historical ten does not appear to have entered upon his reign at Cuzco until after the beginning of the twelfth century.[2] The conquest of Chimu by the Incas also consummated a political union between the lowlands of the coast and the highlands of the interior, which were the two different, and culturally as well as physically distinctive, areas which together constituted the Andean World; for Cuzco, which was the original nucleus of the Inca Empire, was a highland canton, while both Chimu and Nazca were lowland coastal states—Chimu being situated towards the northern and Nazca towards the southern end of the Peruvian coastline. For this combination of reasons, the conquest of Chimu by the Incas in the fifteenth century is perhaps to be taken as the epoch-making event that marks the establishment of the Andean universal state. The war in which this conquest was achieved was the culminating action in the military career of the Inca Pachacutec;[3] and, since Pachacutec reigned from about A.D. 1400 to A.D. 1448,[4] we shall not be far out in our reckoning if we date his annexation of Chimu not earlier than A.D. 1430, and if we therefore

---

[1] See the chronological tables on pp. 47-9 of Means, P.A.: *Ancient Civilisations of the Andes* (New York 1931, Scribner).   [2] Means, op. cit., p. 223.
[3] For this war, see Means, op. cit., pp. 260-1.   [4] Means. op. cit., p. 253.

allot a span of a century, or rather less, to the universal-state phase
of Andean history.

This conquest and annexation of Chimu by the Inca Power was
the climax[1] of a process of Inca empire-building which had begun,
three centuries earlier, in the reigns of the second and third of the
historical Inca sovereigns, Lloque Yupanqui (*imperabat circa* A.D.
1140–95) and Mayta Capac (*imperabat circa* A.D. 1195–1230).
These two Incas laid the foundations of the Empire by annexing
the basin of Lake Titicaca to their ancestral principality of Cuzco
and extending their dominions to the sea at Moquechua, towards
the southern extremity of the Peruvian coast.[2] And the ever
more intensive militarism through which the Inca Empire was
built up in the course of these three centuries, beginning in the
twelfth century of the Christian Era,[3] was one symptom of a
'Time of Troubles' which was to come to its close in the fifteenth
century and which appears to have had its beginning some time
between A.D. 900 and A.D. 1100.

When we peer back into the origins and antecedents of this
Andean 'Time of Troubles', several abiding features in the Andean
historical landscape begin to stand out clear. We perceive that the
'Time of Troubles' manifested itself on the Plateau and in the
Coast-lands simultaneously; we perceive that both regions were
already playing their historical parts in the age of growth by which
the 'Time of Troubles' was preceded; and finally we perceive that
the predominance of the Plateau over the Coast—a predominance
which eventually reached its zenith when an Inca Empire, with
its head-quarters on the Plateau, erected itself into an Andean
universal state embracing the Coast—was not the original relation
in which the Coast and the Plateau had stood to one another.

If we now project our thoughts right back to the beginning of
Andean history and then follow the growth of the Andean Society
forwards from the earliest point at which our archaeological
evidence begins to give us light, we find, as we have noticed by
anticipation, that this Andean culture originated in two districts
of the coastal lowlands—Chimu and Nazca—and that it was in
Chimu and in Nazca that the makers of this culture did their
creative work during the first five centuries of the Christian Era.
The art of early Chimu—in the modelling and painting of its
pottery and, above all, in its plastic portrayal of the human coun-

---

[1] The climax only, and not the term; for the reign of Pachacutec, while it marked the
zenith of the Inca Empire's greatness, did not see the end of its territorial expansion.
Both Northern Chile and the Ecuadorian section of the Andean Coast and Plateau were
added to the Empire by Pachacutec's successor Tupac Yupanqui (*imperabat circa* A.D.
1448–82).   [2] See Means, op. cit., pp. 227–9.
[3] For the vicissitudes in the fortunes of the Incas in their empire-building age, see
further II. D (iv), vol. ii, pp. 102–3, below.

tenance—is not unworthy to be compared with the art of early Hellas. In this creative age, the people of the Coast were the pioneers, while the people of the Plateau were backward. It was not till about the sixth century that the highlanders were stimulated into creative activity in their turn by a contact and conflict with the lowlanders in which it was the lowlanders that took the initiative. Thereafter, there was a second chapter in the growth-phase of the Andean Society in which the Plateau acquired the lead in art, and, above all, in architecture, as well as in politics and war. The outstanding monument of this and of all other ages of Andean history is the highland city of Tiahuanaco, at the south-eastern corner of Lake Titicaca, whose huge monoliths still defy the ravages of a cruel climate. But this first age of highland pre-dominance was followed by the beginning of the general 'Time of Troubles' of which we have already taken note; and when this common adversity fell upon both parts of the Andean World, it was the Plateau, on which the culture had a shorter history and shallower roots, that suffered the more severely. On the Plateau, after the onset of the 'Time of Troubles', there was a relapse to a level of culture which was scarcely above the primitive, whereas in the Lowlands a less depressing cultural set-back was followed, both in Chimu and in Nazca, by a revival of the old lowland culture at about the turn of the eleventh and twelfth centuries of the Christian Era. Thus the Lowlands reasserted their cultural superiority over the Plateau from the beginning of 'the Time of Troubles' onwards, and in this sphere they never yielded the palm to the Plateau again—not even when the military and political genius of the Incas imposed upon the lowlanders a highland pattern of an Andean universal state.

The Yucatec, Mexic, and Mayan Societies

By comparison with Andean history as we have sketched it above, the course of Central American history is complicated; for when we examine the home of the Central American Society as we find it at the time of the Spanish conquest, we observe that it had two distinct nodes, one on the Mexican Plateau and the other on the peninsula of Yucatan. And a closer examination reveals the fact that these nodes correspond to the former homes of two societies which were originally separate, and which we may call respectively the 'Mexic' and the 'Yucatec'. The Yucatec Society was apparently incorporated into the Mexic Society by conquest at about the turn of the twelfth and thirteenth centuries of the Christian Era;[1] and the Central American Society which the

[1] The Mexic conquerors of Yucatan at this juncture were not Aztecs but Toltecs. The Aztecs at that time were outer barbarians, living by hunting in the no-man's-land

Spaniards found in existence on their arrival in the New World was a composite society, brought into existence by this act of incorporation, as the composite Islamic Society that is extant in the Old World to-day has been brought into existence by the incorporation of the Arabic Society into the Iranic. The Mexic conquest of the Yucatec Society occurred (according to one view) because the city-states into which the Yucatec World was articulated had fallen into a state of internecine warfare and had sought to increase their military strength against one another by recruiting Mexic mercenaries who eventually made themselves their employers' masters.[1] In any case, the arrival of Mexic mercenaries in Yucatan and the outbreak of internecine warfare in Yucatan are both well-established historical facts, whatever their relation to one another. The warfare, too, was undoubtedly a sign that the Yucatec Society had fallen into a 'Time of Troubles'; and it appears to be generally agreed that, after the union of the Yucatec Society with the Mexic into a single Central American Society, the trouble eventually spread throughout the wider common weal and grew with time. By the middle of the fifteenth century of the Christian Era, at the latest, the social crisis in Central America had become acute;[2] and its denouement in the forcible establishment of a universal state through the agency of Aztec militarism was in sight when the Spaniards arrived.[3]

If we now trace the separate histories of the Yucatec Society and the Mexic Society back before the beginning of their common 'Time of Troubles' into their separate ages of growth, we shall find that they were related to one another, as the Iranic Society

to the north of the Mexic World. The Toltecs were the creators of the Mexic Society. The Aztecs did not gain a footing in the Mexic domain until the Toltecs had fallen into a 'Time of Troubles'. The creators of the Yucatec Society were Mayas.

[1] The other view is that the arrival of these Mexic mercenaries in Yucatan marks the beginning and not the end of the Yucatec age of peace and prosperity. (See the next footnote.)

[2] The experts are at present at variance over the chronology of Yucatec history. It seems to be agreed that there was a prosperous period, approximately two centuries long, during which the several Yucatec city-states were at peace with one another in virtue of the so-called 'League of Mayapan', and that this peace ended catastrophically in 'the War of Mayapan', which was a revolt of the other cities against the city of Mayapan's hegemony. Some scholars, however, place these two centuries of peace before the arrival of the Toltecs in Yucatan and others after it. This difference of view comes out in *The History of the Maya* (London 1931, Scribner) by T. Gann and J. E. Thompson. One of the two joint authors dates the two prosperous centuries between A.D. 1004 and A.D. 1201, and suggests that the 'multiplicity of small states, constantly at war with each other', which the Spaniards found in Yucatan in the sixteenth century, arose in A.D. 1201 (p. 18). The other author dates the same catastrophe A.D. 1451 (pp. 84–8).

[3] The Yucatec Society had originally been relatively pacific, the Mexic Society relatively warlike; and the reciprocal influence of the two spirits, at the time of the union of the two societies, is likely to have been disturbing and disintegrating (see *The Encyclopaedia Britannica*, ed. xiii, new volume i, p. 195). The union was followed by an infiltration of the Aztecs and other Chichimecs (that is to say, hunting tribes from a no-man's-land on the north); and these newcomers cultivated a peculiar vein of savagery, both in warfare and in religion, which reached its climax in the latter days of the Central American 'Time of Troubles', on the eve of the arrival of the Spaniards.

and the Arabic Society were related, through an identic relation
to a third society of an older generation. In their different homes,
they both emerged, before the beginning of the eleventh century
of the Christian Era, from an interregnum which had followed
the fall of a universal state into which this older society had incorporated itself in its last phase.[1] This universal state was the so-
called 'First Empire' of the Mayas,[2] which came to a rapid and
mysterious end in the seventh century of the Christian Era, after
having flourished for two or three hundred years.[3] The great
cities of this empire, which lay in the rain-soaked country to the
south of Yucatan, in what are now the Republic of Guatemala
and the British Colony of Honduras, were suddenly abandoned,
one after another, to the tropical forest,[4] in which their remains—
long since engulfed and overgrown—are being discovered in our
day by our Western archaeologists. The majority of the population
migrated northwards into Yucatan,[5] which had been a colonial
appendage of the older society's domain;[6] and the Yucatec
Society which emerged there eventually, after the interregnum,
was the creation of these refugees. As for the causes of the catastrophe in which the older society's history ended, it can only be
said—in the present state of our knowledge—that the triumph of
the tropical forest over the works of Man was probably a consequence of the catastrophe and not its cause;[7] since there is nothing
to suggest that there was at this time any change of climate which
might have given the tropical forest the upper hand at last over a

[1] This interregnum is dated *circa* A.D. 690–990 by Means, P. A.: *Ancient Civilisations
of the Andes* (New York 1931, Scribner), p. 38.

[2] The 'First Empire' appears to have been a genuine universal state, in which all the
Maya cities of the age obeyed a single Central Government. (For the archaeological
indications of this, see Gann and Thompson, op. cit., pp. 58–9.) The so-called 'Second
Empire' of the Mayas belongs to the history of the later Yucatec Society and was not
really an empire at all but an association of city-states, 'the League of Mayapan' (so
called after one of the three participating states). This League kept the peace in the
Yucatec World during the two centuries preceding the beginning of the 'Time of
Troubles'. For the controversy over the chronology, see p. 124, footnote 2, above.

[3] The 'First Empire' of the Mayas *floruit circa* A.D. 300–600 according to Spinden,
H. J.: *The Ancient Civilisations of Mexico and Central America* (New York 1922, Ameri-
can Museum of Natural History), p. 67; *circa* A.D. 400–600 according to *The Encyclo-
paedia Britannica*, ed. xiii, new volume i, p. 194; *circa* A.D. 450–700 according to Means,
P. A.: *Ancient Civilisations of the Andes* (New York 1931, Scribner), p. 35. On the other
hand, its fall is placed as late as the first half of the ninth century of the Christian Era by
Thompson, J. E.: *The Civilisation of the Mayas* (Chicago 1927, Field Museum of
Natural History), pp. 11–12.

[4] In *The History of the Maya* (London 1931, Scribner), Messrs. Gann and Thompson
—who follow Spinden's and not Thompson's own chronology in this joint work—
estimate that these successive sudden abandonments extended over about a century,
circa A.D. 530–630, from first to last (p. 60).

[5] A minority moved out in the opposite direction to Quen Santo, on the inland slope
of the Pacific Highlands.

[6] The first Maya colony in Yucatan is thought to have been Tuluum, on the east
coast. A monument at Tuluum bears a date which corresponds on Spinden's chronology
to A.D. 304. (Gann and Thompson, op. cit., p. 41. Cf. pp. 71–8.)

[7] For this victorious counter-offensive of the tropical forest, see further II. D (i),
vol. ii, pp. 3–4, and II. D (vii), vol. ii, pp. 304–6, below.

society which had been successfully keeping it at bay for many centuries. Here, as elsewhere, the catastrophe is more likely to have been due to some human failure in Society itself; but Archaeology gives us no clue to what this failure was.[1] It only tells us that the 'First Empire' of the Mayas did not perish by violence of any kind: not by revolution and not by war. Indeed, this older society seems to have been unusually pacific. The only evidence that it practised the art of war at all comes from the north-western fringe of its domain, where it had to deal with outer barbarians in the quarter in which the Mexic Society eventually emerged after the interregnum.[2] The arts in which the older society excelled were Astronomy (turned to practical account in a

[1] The problem is discussed systematically and critically but inconclusively by Messrs. Gann and Thompson in op. cit. on pp. 61–6.
'The abandonment of the area as a whole was a gradual one, and occupied approximately a century. It commenced in the extreme south, at Copan, and in the extreme west, at Palenque, extending thence eastward and northward till it reached the cities of north-eastern Peten, of which the group including Naranjo, Tikal, Uaxactun, Benque Viejo and Nakum was the last to be deserted. The exodus from each city was, however, apparently a sudden one, as the last created stelae are almost in the best style of the Great Period, and show no signs of any degeneration in the sculptor's art.
'A number of reasons have been assigned for this remarkable exodus, none of them, however, entirely satisfactory. They include:—1. National decadence; 2. Epidemic disease; 3. Earthquakes; 4. War, internecine or foreign, or both combined; 5. Climatic changes; 6. Exhaustion of the Soil; 7. Religious or superstitious reasons' (pp. 60–1).
The authors examine each of these suggested explanations in turn and find them all unconvincing, with the possible exception of a combination of nos. 6 and 7. As regards the possibility of soil-exhaustion, an observation of latter-day native agriculture in the area once covered by the 'First Empire' of the Mayas seems to show that a repeated clearing and burning-off of the tropical forest for the purpose of agriculture does tend eventually to exhaust the soil of the clearing and to end in its surface becoming covered with a tough mat of coarse grass. If this economic calamity occurred in the latter days of the Maya Empire on an unparalleled scale, and at a time when the Maya cultivators had given hostages to Fortune by being fruitful and multiplying and replenishing the Earth with a teeming population on the strength of an abundant food-supply which now unexpectedly began to fail, it is conceivable that the dominant minority of the Mayan Society—in which the ruling class appears to have been an esoteric priesthood—may have lost its nerve. In that event, the social effect of the exhaustion of the soil may have been reinforced and accentuated by religious terrors and tabus. The once fruitful and now barren corn-lands may have become an object of superstitious aversion as well as economic despair; and the two motives together may perhaps suffice to explain the wholesale trek into Yucatan.
The theory that an exhaustion of the soil may have been at least part cause of the trek is supported by the fact that, during the century (circa A.D. 530–630) during which the great cities of the 'First Empire' were being progressively deserted, the first step taken by their former inhabitants was to found a bevy of new small towns in their neighbourhoods. The purpose of this local change of residence may have been to bring the cultivators closer to the fringes of the cultivated areas that surrounded each of the great cities; for presumably the soil was less seriously exhausted on these fringes, where cultivation would previously have been less intense, than on the immediate outskirts of the previous centres of population. On this showing, the foundation of these small towns represents an attempt to compromise with 'economic necessity' by local decentralization—an attempt which proved vain and which was therefore followed, in the end, by an outright emigration to Yucatan. (See Gann and Thompson, op. cit., pp. 51–2 and 56–7.)
For a discussion of the fifth of Messrs. Gann and Thompson's alternative explanations—namely climatic changes—see II. D (vii), Annex I, vol. ii, below.
[2] There are only two sculptures that relate to war, and these have both been found at Piedras Negras (Gann and Thompson, op. cit., p. 63—where, however, the view is expressed that the Mayas and the Nahuas did not actually come into contact with each other). In this connexion it may be noted that two, at least, of the 'Old Empire' colonies in Yucatan, namely Tuluum and Ichpaatun, were walled cities (op. cit., pp. 40 and 42).

system of chronology which was remarkably exact in its calculations and painstaking in its records) and Calligraphy (in a grotesque pictographic script, carved on stone, which our Western scholars have not yet succeeded in deciphering). The people who created this society were the Mayas, and we may call the society 'Mayan'.[1]

What was the relation between the Mayan Society on the one hand and the Yucatec and Mexic Societies on the other? If we take as our touchstone the presence or absence of a middle term in the shape of a universal church, we shall hesitate to pronounce either the Yucatec Society or the Mexic Society to be 'affiliated' to the Mayan—and this for the reason that weighed with us when we were examining the relation of the Babylonic Society to the Sumeric. In the age of the Mayan universal state we can perceive no religious movement that can be confidently interpreted as the rise of a universal church created by an internal proletariat.[2] By that time, the dominant minority of the Mayan Society had organized its religious practices and beliefs into an elaborate and esoteric system; and this system appears to have been transmitted to the Yucatec Society and to the Mexic Society, as the somewhat similar religious system of the Sumeric dominant minority was transmitted to the Babylonic Society. The only change seems to have been that the Mexic Society failed to preserve the refinements of its Mayan heritage, in religion as in other aspects of culture, and even brutalized what it retained by lapsing into the practice of human sacrifice.[3] In a general way, the fortunes of the Mayan religion in Mexic hands resemble the fortunes of the Sumeric religion in the hands of the Assyrians.

When we turn to consider the relative displacement of the original homes of the Yucatec Society and the Mexic Society from the original home of the Mayan, the displacement of the Mexic Society—from a moist tropical plain to a dry plateau in the far

[1] The Mayas stand to the histories of the Mayan, Yucatec, and Mexic Societies as the Sumerians stand to the histories of the Sumeric, Babylonic, and Hittite Societies; moreover, there are certain material points of resemblance between the two groups: for instance, the turn for astronomy and the contrast between the unusually pacific character of the earlier society in either group and the unusually vicious militarism in which the history of the later societies culminated. In this, the early Mayas stand to the Aztecs as the early Sumerians stand to the Assyrians.

[2] In the Mayan religion, perhaps the nearest approach to the religious spirit of an 'internal proletariat', as we know it elsewhere, is the cult of the Plumed Serpent God Tutulcan or Kukulcan, which was transmitted to the Mexic Society (the God's name there being translated into the local Nahuan language as Quetzalcoatl). This Mayan Culture-God recalls the Sumeric Culture-God Ea. In considering the worship of Tutulcan, however, we are confronted with the difficulty which we encountered when we were considering the Sumeric worship of Tammuz. We are in ignorance of the historical relation of this cult to the organized religion of the dominant minority. (See the footnote on p. 115, above.)

[3] The Mayan religious system was possibly (though not unquestionably) innocent of human sacrifice, but it did contain a brutal element in the shape of outlandish and revolting penitential self-mortifications which recall those of Hinduism.

north-west—recalls the similar displacement of the Hittite Society from the Sumeric. The original home of the Mexic Society on the plateau was at, if not beyond, the extreme limit reached by the Mayan Society in this direction at the time of its greatest expansion. On the other hand, the peninsula which was the original home of the Yucatec Society appears to have been brought completely within the ambit of the Mayan Society in its latest age. At the same time, Yucatan lay right outside the region of tropical forest which was the birth-place of the Mayan Society; and although in actual distance it lay much nearer to the Mayan homeland than the Mexican Plateau lay, the essential differences in the physical environment were much the same on the peninsula as they were on the plateau. Whereas, in the Mayan homeland, the society had to contend with a superabundance of rainfall and of vegetation, Yucatan, like the plateau, was deficient in water and in trees.[1] Thus as far-reaching an adaptation of the material conditions of life to a new physical environment was demanded when the Yucatec Society was founded in an outlying province of the 'First Empire' by Mayan refugees as when the Mexic Society was founded by barbarians who had been irradiated by the Mayan culture in a no-man's-land beyond the frontier. In this respect the relation of the Yucatec Society to the Mayan was unlike that of the Babylonic Society to the Sumeric, for in this latter case the birth-place of the later society was coincident with the homeland of the earlier society and there was no geographical displacement at all.

The Egyptiac Society

Finally there is one representative of the species which has lived through a longer span than any other whose history we know, and this, apparently, without ever entering into the relationship either of 'affiliation' or of 'apparentation'. This is the society which emerged in the lower valley of the Nile, between the First Cataract and the Mediterranean, during the fourth millennium B.C., and which became extinct in the fifth century of the Christian Era[2] after existing, from first to last, at least three times as long as our own Western Society has existed so far.[3] This 'Egyptiac'[4] Society

[1] Yucatan is a low-lying shelf of limestone which has been elevated above sea-level without the strata being tilted out of the horizontal plane. In physical character the Yucatanian peninsula resembles the south-eastern extremity of Italy, from the plain of Foggia to the tip of the 'heel'.

[2] This is the extreme date down to which some vestiges of the Egyptiac tradition survived. As a 'going concern', the Egyptiac culture did not outlive the third century of the Christian Era.

[3] It is not yet thirteen centuries since our Western Society emerged from the interregnum which followed the fall of the Roman Empire. The span of Egyptiac history extends over at least four millennia.

[4] 'Egyptiac' (from the Latin *Aegyptiacus*), in order to avoid the ambiguity of the geographical adjective 'Egyptian' (from the Latin *Aegyptius*).

is not represented in the world of our day, as far as we can see, by any human heirs or assigns—not by any fossil of itself and not by any living society to which it might be either 'apparented' or related in some less intimate way. All the more triumphant is the immortality which it has sought and found in stone. It seems probable that the Pyramids, which have already borne inanimate witness to the existence of their makers for four or five thousand years without yielding to the ravages of Time, will continue steadfastly to perform their Atlantean task for hundreds of thousands of years to come. It is not inconceivable that they may outlast Mankind itself, and that, in a world where there are no longer human senses to receive their testimony or human minds to comprehend it, they will testify still of the Egyptiac Society that made them: 'Before Abraham was, I am.'

II. A PROVISIONAL CLASSIFICATION OF SOCIETIES OF THE SPECIES

In the foregoing survey we started with six representatives of the species of society which we are studying—five living representatives and one extinct specimen—and with two sets of fossils. As a result of the survey, we have succeeded in identifying thirteen representatives more. Thus we now have at our disposal nineteen representatives in all; and it may be convenient to run through their names in the order in which they have presented themselves. Our nineteen societies are the Western, the Orthodox Christian, the Iranic, the Arabic (now incorporated with the Iranic into the Islamic Society of to-day), the Hindu, the Far Eastern, the Hellenic, the Syriac, the Indic, the Sinic, the Minoan, the Sumeric, the Hittite, the Babylonic, the Andean, the Mexic, the Yucatec, the Mayan, and the Egyptiac.[1]

The practical operations by which we have carried out our survey suggest a basis for a provisional classification of the results that

---

[1] This list of nineteen societies may be compared with the list of ten societies which was compiled by Count J. A. de Gobineau nearly a century ago. (See vol. i, pp. 362–5, of the 1st edition of *L'Inégalité des Races Humaines* (Paris 1853–5, Firmin Didot, 4 vols.)). In introducing his list, de Gobineau declares:

'Du sein de ces multitudes de nations qui ont passé ou vivent encore sur la terre, dix seulement se sont élevées à l'état de sociétés complètes. Le reste, plus ou moins indépendant, gravite à l'entour comme les planètes autour de leurs soleils.'

The list itself is as follows. (N.B. Wherever one of de Gobineau's societies coincides with one of the societies identified in this Study, the name employed in this Study has been used to convey de Gobineau's description or title.)

    I. Indic [= our Indic+Hindu].
   II. Egyptiac.
  III. 'Assyriac' [= our Syriac approximately, since it is described as including the Jews, Phoenicians, Lydians, Carthaginians, Himyarites, and Zorastrian-

we have obtained. In exploring the background of a society we have sometimes come upon an earlier society which is 'apparented' to it through the middle term of a universal church or is related to it in some less intimate or more intimate way. Sometimes, on the other hand, we have explored the background of a society without striking upon any earlier representative of the species. Thus we can provisionally classify our nineteen societies according to whether they are unrelated to earlier societies or related in this or that degree. In attempting this provisional classification, we shall give first place to the criterion that we have employed in our survey when we have been identifying representatives of the species, namely the presence or absence of a universal church. We have also at our command a secondary criterion which we can apply in sub-dividing the set of 'related' societies, namely the degree of displacement, if any, of the original home of the later society from the original home of the earlier society.[1] By combining these two criteria, we may perhaps construct a 'yard-stick' with which we may be able to measure off all our societies on a single scale and assign them specific places in a continuous series.

In our primary religious classification, we may arrange our specimens in the following groups: first, societies that are not related in any way either to earlier or to later societies; second, societies that are not related in any way to earlier societies but are related to later societies; third, societies that are related to earlier societies, but in a less intimate way than by 'affiliation' through universal churches, the relation in this case consisting simply in the fact that the later society has been precipitated by a Völkerwanderung which has accompanied the fall of the earlier society's universal state;[2] fourth, societies that are 'affiliated' through universal churches to older societies that are 'apparented' to them through the same middle term;[3] fifth, societies that are related to

Iranians. The author remarks that this 'Assyriac' Society had its 'renaissance iranienne', and that this was the best thing about it].
  IV. Hellenic.
   V. Sinic [= our Sinic + Far Eastern].
  VI. Italic [= a fringe of our Hellenic].
 VII. Germanic [= our Western].
VIII. Alleghanian [= a fringe of our Mexic].
  IX. Mexic.
   X. Andean.
When we compare this list with ours, we find that nine of our societies are omitted. Of these nine, six (the Minoan, Sumeric, Hittite, Babylonic, Yucatec, Mayan) are societies whose existence has been rescued from oblivion by the discoveries of Western archaeologists since de Gobineau's day. The other three, however, are living societies (the Orthodox Christian and the two constituents of the Islamic). Either de Gobineau has deliberately ignored these societies or he has intended to include them respectively in his Hellenic and in his 'Assyriac'.
  [1] See pp. 62–3, above.
  [2] See p. 62, above.   [3] See pp. 56–7, above.

earlier societies, but in a more intimate way than by Apparentation-and-Affiliation, the relation in this case amounting to an inheritance of the organized religion of the dominant minority of the earlier society with little or no change.[1] Within the group of 'affiliated' societies, we can distinguish two sub-groups, according to whether the germ of creative power in the internal proletariat of the 'apparented' society, out of which the intermediary universal church has sprung, has been alien from the 'apparented' society or indigenous to it in origin.[2] This primary classification gives the following results:

Wholly Unrelated Societies

Egyptiac
Andean

Societies Unrelated to Earlier Societies

Sinic
Minoan
Sumeric
Mayan

Infra-affiliated Societies

Indic (?)[3]
Hittite
Syriac
Hellenic (?)[4]

Affiliated Societies I

(affiliated through a chrysalis church of the *alien-origin* type)
Western
Orthodox Christian
Far Eastern

---

[1] See pp. 115–18, above.   [2] See p. 57, above.

[3] On the assumption that the domain of the 'Indus Culture' was, at any rate latterly, an outlying province of the Sumeric universal state, and that this was the magnet that drew the Aryas on their Völkerwanderung to India from the Eurasian Steppe. (See pp. 104–9, above.) If this assumption is unwarranted, then the Indic Society ought to be placed in the preceding group of Societies Unrelated to Earlier Societies.

[4] On the view that the Mysteries and the Orphic Church which emerge in the course of Hellenic history represent no more than the rudiments of a universal church which the internal proletariat of the antecedent Minoan Society had attempted to create with only partial success (see pp. 95–100, above). If this view is mistaken, and if the Mysteries and Orphism are rather to be regarded as manifestations of a full-fledged universal church, then the Hellenic Society ought to be placed in the following group of Affiliated Societies. On the whole, however, it seems more probable that 'the memory of what she owed to her older population was effaced almost as effectually in Greece as it was in India'. (Marshall, Sir. J.: *Mohenjo-Daro and the Indus Civilisation* (London 1931, Probsthain, 3 vols.), vol. i, p. vii.)

Affiliated Societies II
(affiliated through a chrysalis church of the *indigenous-origin* type)
   Iranic
   Arabic
   Hindu

Supra-affiliated Societies
   Babylonic
   Yucatec
   Mexic

In our secondary geographical classification, which applies only to the 'related' societies, we may arrange our specimens in the following groups: first, societies whose original home is entirely non-coincident with the domain of the related earlier society at its widest range; second, societies whose original base-line coincides with a frontier of the universal state of the related earlier society, so that their original home lies partly in the former no-man's-land beyond that frontier but is also partly coincident with the domain of the related earlier society at its widest range; third, societies whose original home lies wholly within the domain of the related earlier society at its widest range but not wholly within the original home of the related earlier society; fourth, societies whose original home does lie wholly within the original home of the related earlier society. This secondary classification gives the following results:

| | Related Later Society | | | |
| Related Earlier Society | Non-coincident | Partly coincident | Wholly coincident | |
			With widest range	With original home
Sinic	Far Eastern in Korea and Japan		Far Eastern (main body)	
Minoan	Syriac	Hellenic		
Sumeric		Indic + Hittite		Babylonic [1]
Mayan		Mexic	Yucatec	
Indic			Hindu	
Syriac		Iranic	Arabic	
Hellenic	Orthodox Christian in Russia	Western	Orthodox Christian (main body)	

[1] The original home of the Babylonic Society was coincident with Sumer + Akkad + Assyria + Elam; and the two latter countries were not actually part of the original home

Let us now combine our two criteria of classification into a single 'yard-stick', retaining the groups established by our primary classification, but arranging the several societies within each group according to the order resulting from our secondary classification (so far as this secondary classification extends). In both the arrangements which are now to be combined we have proceeded always from the less intimate to the more intimate degree of relationship, so that, in our combined order, the 'direction' of the classification, from top to bottom of the list, will be the same. The series now works out as follows:

Egyptiac+Andean
Sinic+Minoan+Sumeric+Mayan
Syriac
Indic+Hittite+Hellenic
Western
Orthodox Christian (in Russia)+Far Eastern (in Korea and Japan)
Orthodox Christian (main body)+Far Eastern (main body)
Iranic
Arabic+Hindu
Mexic
Yucatec
Babylonic

As the result of our three classificatory operations, we have incidentally increased the number of our specimens from nineteen to twenty-one (the Orthodox Christian Society and the Far Eastern Society each falling into two parts which take different places in the series). We have arranged these twenty-one specimens in a series of twelve degrees, beginning with the degree represented by the Egyptiac Society and the Andean Society, which show no trace of being related in any way to any other society, either earlier or later than themselves, and ending with the degree represented by the Babylonic Society, which is related to the Sumeric Society so intimately that already we have asked ourselves the question whether the relation may not almost amount to identity.[1]

It may be opportune, before passing on, to ask ourselves this question again, and to seek this time for an answer; for after all

of the Sumeric Society, though they were embraced in its domain at so early a stage as to count as parts of its homeland. In so far, the original home of the Babylonic Society cannot be said to have been wholly coincident with that of the Sumeric Society in the strictest sense. On the other hand, it was far more nearly coincident with the original home of the Sumeric Society than with its widest range, which included not only Elam but possibly the Indus Valley as well, and not only Assyria but Cappadocia and Syria into the bargain.

[1] See pp. 117–18, above.

the equivocal status of the Babylonic Society is only an extreme case. The same question might arise over the status of a number of other societies in our list—all, in fact, that lie below the line occupied by the Western Society in our descending series. In the course of our Study down to this point, we have treated all these societies as distinct and separate representatives of the species, because in exploring their respective backgrounds we have found there some or all of the tokens with which we are familiar in the background of our Western Society—a universal state, a universal church, and a Völkerwanderung—and because we have found, again, that these tokens are phenomena in the decline and fall of some earlier society, as the Roman Empire and the Catholic Church and the Völkerwanderung in the background of our Western Society are phenomena in the decline and fall of the Hellenic Society. We took it for granted that our Western Society was a distinct and separate representative of the species. It did not occur to us to regard this society as identical with the Hellenic Society or to treat our Western history as a mere epilogue to Hellenic history on account of the relation between the two societies and between their two histories to which the familiar tokens bear witness. By analogy, we have assumed that all these other societies are distinct and separate likewise. We have made the assumption confidently in cases where we have found not only a universal state and a Völkerwanderung but also a universal church. We have made it, again, where instead of a universal church we have found a new religion introduced, in the Völkerwanderung, by barbarians. We have made it with some hesitation in three cases where the token of a universal church is lacking, but where we have found, instead, the organized religion of the dominant minority of the earlier society living on. Even in these cases, however, we have accepted the analogy provisionally. We now have to reconsider how all these societies stand to their predecessors.

If we begin with our Western Society and ask ourselves, in regard to it, the question which we have hitherto begged—Is our Western Society identical with the Hellenic Society, and is our Western history a mere epilogue to Hellenic history?—no doubt we shall abide by our previous assumption. We shall pronounce our Western Society to be a distinct and separate representative of the species on mature consideration. But this does not prejudge the answer to our question in the other cases in which we have to ask it. For while Analogy is a vastly suggestive and significant pointer, we cannot afford to follow its indications blindly and mechanically. It is open to critics to sweep our 'tokens' aside and to pronounce—if they choose, on subjective, intuitive grounds

—that, however our 'tokens' are to be interpreted, they cannot bring themselves to regard our 'Orthodox Christian' Society as independent of the Hellenic Society, or our 'Far Eastern' as independent of the Sinic, or our 'Iranic' and 'Arabic' as independent of the Syriac, or our 'Hindu' as independent of the Indic, or our 'Mexic' and 'Yucatec' as independent of the Mayan, any more than they can regard our 'Babylonic' as independent of the Sumeric. They may remind us that in this last extreme case we ourselves have hesitated; and they may refer us back to a simile which we have applied in a somewhat different connexion.

At an earlier point of our Study[1] we compared the Roman Empire to an old tree whose roots decayed until the wind tore them up and overthrew the solid trunk. The Roman Empire was a universal state, one of those institutions into which decaying societies incorporate themselves in the last phase of their lives. Why not extend the simile from a single institution to the whole life of a society *in extremis*?[2] Why not apply it, for instance, to the Sumeric Society *in extremis*? In this light, instead of viewing what we have called the Babylonic Society as a distinct and separate entity with a life of its own, we might view it rather as the dead trunk of the Sumeric Society—dead but not yet dissolved into dust, fallen but still cumbering the ground. Think how long a time it takes for a dead, fallen trunk to rot away. The time may be almost as long as the lifetime of the tree before it died and fell. If the lifetime of the Sumeric Society covered perhaps two thousand years (from the early centuries of the fourth millennium B.C. to the early years of the nineteenth century B.C.), there is nothing extravagant in the supposition that the carcass of the Sumeric Society should have cumbered the ground of 'Irāq for nearly two thousand years more (from the nineteenth century B.C. to the last). Are not the social phenomena which we observe in that region during that latter period of time more aptly described in these terms than on the hypothesis of a new society coming to birth, growing up, breaking down, and disintegrating in its turn?

[1] See p. 56, above.
[2] This very use of our simile has actually been made by Oswald Spengler (*Der Untergang des Abendlandes*, vol. i (Munich 1920, Beck), p. 154):

'When the goal and the idea [of a "culture"] are attained, when the entire range of its inner possibilities has been traversed in a series of external realizations, then the "culture" suddenly goes stiff; it dies off, its blood coagulates, its forces fail, it turns into a "civilization". In this condition it is capable, like a dead giant of the primeval forest, of keeping its withered branches outstretched for century after century. We see this in the cases of Egypt, of India, of China, of the Islamic World. In the same way, the Hellenic Civilization towered up in the Imperial Age, in gigantic dimensions and with all the appearance of youthful strength and exuberance—depriving the young Arabic Culture in the east of air and light.'

N.B. In Spengler's terminology, a 'culture' means what, in this Study, is meant by a 'civilization', while Spengler's 'civilizations' are the debris of dead 'cultures'.

Is it not misleading to treat these phenomena as though they were on a par with the preceding phenomena of Sumeric history and to lend them a distinctive name, as though they were the manifestations of a separate society existing in its own right? Would it not be better to wipe out the name 'Babylonic Society' and label the phenomena instead as the debris of the Sumeric Society? In principle we have already conceded that an extinct society may leave fossilized remains of its fabric behind. We have identified a number of fossil remnants of two extinct societies—the Syriac and the Indic—in the world of our own day. May not what we have labelled the 'Babylonic Society' be really just such another fossil of somewhat larger size and greater age?[1] And may not our 'Yucatec' and 'Mexic' and 'Hindu' and 'Arabic' and 'Iranic' and 'Far Eastern' and 'Orthodox Christian' societies be fossils likewise? If so, no less than ten[2] out of our twenty-one societies will have to be struck off the list and sent to limbo.

In meeting this criticism, we may admit at once that the conception of a society cumbering the ground as a carcass, long after the life has gone out of the body, is by no means absurd *a priori*. Indeed, we can assist our critics by pointing out an instance in which this conception is indisputably apt.

If we examine the history of the Egyptiac Society, we find that little more than a quarter of its vast time-span of four millennia was a period of growth. The impetus which manifested itself first in the mastery of a peculiarly formidable physical environment—in the clearing, draining, and cultivation of the jungle-swamp that originally occupied the lower valley and the Delta of the Nile to the exclusion of Man[3]—and which then displayed its increasing momentum in the precocious political unification of the Egyptiac World at the end of the so-called Predynastic Age, reached its climax in the stupendous material performances of the Fourth Dynasty. The Age of the Fourth and Fifth Dynasties was the zenith of Egyptiac history, by whatever criteria we measure the

---

[1] This view is forcibly expressed by Eduard Meyer in the following description of Babylonia under the rule of the Kassites:

'Business life maintains its movement in the traditional forms, and the culture and religion handed down from the past are spun out; but, in the sharpest contrast to Egypt, Babylonia failed to create anything new whatever through all these centuries. If we happened to possess monuments of the art of the age, the progressive decline of artistic power would doubtless leap to the eye. The fact is that the role of Babylonia in world history was played out by the end of the First Dynasty of Babylon' [i.e. during the interregnum after the death of Hammurabi]. 'Only the petrified forms preserve their existence without preserving any content.' (Meyer, E.: *Geschichte des Altertums*, vol. ii, 2nd edition (Stuttgart and Berlin 1928, Cotta), p. 154.)

[2] Reckoning the Orthodox Christian Society in Russia as distinct from the main body of Orthodox Christendom, and the Far Eastern Society in Korea and Japan as distinct from the main body of the Far Eastern Society.

[3] The setting and the significance of this achievement are discussed in II. C (ii) (b) 2, vol. i, on pp. 302-15, below.

curve of its progress and decline. It was the zenith in the characteristic achievement of the Egyptiac Society: the co-ordination of
human labour in great engineering enterprises ranging from the
reclamation of the swamps to the construction of the Pyramids.
It was also the zenith in the spheres of political administration
and of art. Even in the sphere of religion, where wisdom is pro-
verbially born of suffering,[1] the so-called 'Pyramid Texts' testify
that this age likewise saw the creation, the collision, and the
first stage in the interaction of the two religious movements—
the worship of the Sun and the worship of Osiris—which came
to their maturity after the Egyptiac Society had gone into its
decline.

The zenith was passed and the decline set in at the transition
from the Fifth Dynasty to the Sixth *circa* 2424 B.C.;[2] and at this
point we begin to recognize in Egyptiac history the familiar
symptoms of decline in the order in which they have presented
themselves to us in the histories of other societies. The break-up
of the Egyptiac United Kingdom into a plurality of local states
indulging in more and more destructive internecine warfare bears
the unmistakable stamp of a 'Time of Troubles'. This 'Time of
Troubles' entered upon its last and most acute stage about 2242
B.C., when the local princes of Heracleopolis brushed aside the
last legitimate Pharaohs of Memphis and usurped a title which
had long since become a vain pretension. The Egyptiac 'Time of
Troubles' was superseded, *circa* 2070/2060 B.C., by an Egyptiac
universal state. The founder was that member of the local dynasty
of Thebes[3] who commemorated his achievement by taking the
title 'Uniter of the two Lands'.[4] This Egyptiac universal state was
consolidated under the Twelfth Dynasty (*imperabant circa* 2000–
1788 B.C.); and that Egyptiac 'Age of the Antonines' was succeeded
in due course by an 'Age of the Thirty Tyrants'.[5] During the
century that followed the period of the Twelfth Dynasty, the
Egyptiac universal state broke down; and the consequent interregnum brought its Völkerwanderung in the shape of the invasion
of the Egyptiac World by the Hyksos.[6]

Here then, near the mid-point in the time-span of Egyptiac
history, we have found at any rate two of our standard 'tokens':
a Völkerwanderung and a universal state. Supposing that, in
our exploration of Egyptiac history, we had followed our usual

---

[1] The Aeschylean πάθει μάθος (*Agamemnon*, l. 177).
[2] This is Meyer's date in *Die Aeltere Chronologie Babyloniens, Assyriens und Aegyptens*
(Stuttgart and Berlin 1925, Cotta), p. 68.
[3] The so-called Eleventh Dynasty.
[4] See Meyer, E.: *Geschichte des Altertums*, vol. i (ii), 3rd edition, p. 257.
[5] This latter comparison is suggested by Meyer in op. cit., pp. 302–3.
[6] See I. C (i) (*b*), pp. 105 and 106, above.

procedure of starting at the latter end and working backwards chronologically instead of forwards, we should probably have paused at this point and said to ourselves: 'We have now traced the march of Egyptiac history back, from its last fading foot-prints in the fifth century of the Christian Era, through a span of twenty-one centuries, until, in the early part of the seventeenth century B.C., we have struck upon a Völkerwanderung following the fall of a universal state. By all analogy, we should infer that we have traced the history of the Egyptiac Society to its source, and have discovered, in its background, the tokens of the presence of an earlier society, related to the Egyptiac in some degree. Let us give this earlier society a name of its own and call it, let us say, "Nilotic" in order to distinguish it from its "Egyptiac" successor.' This is the path into which Analogy would lead us; yet we shall not only hesitate but positively refuse to take this path when we have considered the facts on their merits.

We shall refuse because, if we now resume our exploration of Egyptiac—or 'Nilotic'—history in the forward direction, we shall not find a new society emerging within the chrysalis of a universal church after the interregnum has run its course and the Völkerwanderung has played itself out. We shall find quite a different outcome. The barbarian 'successor-state' is overthrown; the Hyksos are expelled from Egypt; the interregnum is retrieved; the Egyptiac universal state is restored; and all this is done by another dynasty[1] from the Thebaid—the self-same locality that has previously sent forth the Eleventh Dynasty to found the Egyptiac universal state and the Twelfth Dynasty to maintain it. An Egyptiac universal state with its capital at Thebes is in existence once again; and the restoration of the old institution is not only exact; it is deliberate and self-conscious. In terms more familiar to us, it is as if Justinian had succeeded in exterminating not only the Vandals in Africa and the Ostrogoths in Italy but all the other barbarian invaders of the Roman Empire: the Visigoths in Spain, the Franks in Gaul, the Angles in Britain; and as if the Roman Imperial Restoration had been not only universal instead of local but also enduring instead of ephemeral. Indeed, the Egyptiac Imperial Restoration is a still more remarkable achievement than this imaginary parallel implies. In order to grasp its full magnitude we have further to imagine that in the fifth century of the Christian Era the Roman Empire had broken down completely everywhere —in the Greek and Oriental provinces as well as in the Latin

---

[1] The so-called Seventeenth Dynasty and Eighteenth Dynasty, which are really one single dynasty. The fiction that a new dynasty begins with Amosis, the expeller of the Hyksos, symbolizes the fact that in Amosis' reign and through Amosis' achievement a local state in the Thebaid is converted into the universal state of the Restoration.

provinces—and that thereafter the barbarians had all been exterminated and the Empire had been restored in its full extent by some descendant of 'Romulus Augustulus' who had been permitted to retain a local dominion over Rome itself by the contemptuous tolerance of an Odovacer and a Theodoric!

This extraordinary[1] restoration of the Egyptiac universal state was the sole significant historical event, in what had been the domain of the Egyptiac Society, that occurred between the sixteenth century B.C. and the fifth century of the Christian Era—the sole event, that is to say, except the abortive revolution of Ikhnaton (and that was evidently one of those exceptions which prove a rule). The duration of the restored universal state—its long Indian summer, its still longer autumn, its repeated overthrow and repeated rehabilitation—fills the whole span of these two millennia. When we examine these phases of existence, we cannot reasonably interpret them as the genesis, growth, breakdown, and disintegration of a new society, distinct and separate from the society which had passed through its 'Time of Troubles' between 2424 and 2070/2060 B.C. and had enjoyed the respite of a universal state from 2070/2060 B.C. until the early years of the seventeenth century and had fallen then into an interregnum accompanied by a Völkerwanderung. We cannot regard the phenomena that confront us, in the same geographical area, between the sixteenth century B.C. and the fifth century of the Christian Era in any other light than as an epilogue to the history of the society which had risen and fallen in the same area before. The object that occupied the field in the later age was not a new tree with a life of its own, but the old tree's dead trunk artificially re-erected, and many times re-erected again, during the ages that elapsed while its massive bulk was weathering away and its hard grain rotting into dust.

Now if we take this view of Egyptiac history; if we insist upon

---

[1] The restoration of the Egyptiac universal state is examined in IV. C (ii) (b) 2, vol. iv, p. 85; IV. C (iii) (c) 2 (β), vol. iv, p. 412; Part V. A, vol. v, pp. 2–3; and V. C (i) (c) 2, vol. v, p. 152, below. At this point it is sufficient to say that, like the resumption of the Syriac and Indic universal states (see pp. 76–7 and 86, above), the restoration of the Egyptiac universal state is to be explained by the exasperating effect of an alien intrusion. The Hyksos, by the time when they arrived at the borders of the Egyptiac World, were no longer quite indeterminate barbarians. They were members of the external proletariat of another society—the Sumeric—and they had taken a tinge of Sumeric colouring in their passage across the whole expanse of the Sumeric universal state (see II. D (vii), vol. ii, pp. 389–90, below). This tinge doubtless accounts for the fanatical hatred which the Hyksos inspired in the Egyptians; and this fanaticism was the stimulus which gave the Egyptians the energy to drive the Hyksos out. We may compare the similar hatred which was inspired in the Chinese, with similar consequences, by the tine of Nestorian Christian colouring which had been taken by the Mongols before they conquered the continental part of the Far Eastern World in the thirteenth century of the Christian Era. (For the influence of the Nestorian Christian culture upon the Mongols, see II. D (v), vol. ii, p. 122, footnote 2, and II. D (vi), vol. ii, pp. 237–8, below.)

the historical continuity of the social phenomena which occupy
the field here from the fourth millennium B.C. to the fifth century
of the Christian Era; if we refuse to regard the events that fill
this immense span of time as constituting the histories of two
distinct and separate societies and declare that they constitute the
history of an Egyptiac Society one and indivisible: our critics may
reasonably ask us why we take a different view of Sumeric history;
why we 'cut off its tail with a carving knife' for the pleasure of
calling the lifeless appendage a 'Babylonic Society' and making
believe that this is a distinct and separate living representative of
the species. If our 'Egyptiac Society' is one and indivisible, are
not our 'Sumeric' and 'Babylonic' societies one and indivisible by
the same token? And if it comes to tokens, have we not more
warrant for dividing Egyptiac history in two than for making our
division between Sumeric and Babylonic? What chiefly made us
hesitate to treat the Babylonic Society as an independent representative of the species in its own right was our observation that
the Babylonic religion was simply the religion of the dominant
minority of the Sumeric Society taken over practically unchanged,
and our failure to discover anything in the nature of a universal
church created by the internal proletariat of the Sumeric Society
and constituting a middle term between the Sumeric Society and
the Babylonic. If we study the religious history of the Egyptiac
Society, we find that here, too, after the interregnum, a religion
prevailed that had been taken over from the dominant minority
of the preceding age of decline. Yet it did not prevail definitively
here without a struggle; and it first secured its position by coming
to terms with a universal church which had been created in the
preceding age of decline by the Egyptiac internal proletariat out
of the worship of Osiris.

The Osiris worship came from the Delta. Originally it may have
come from farther afield, if there is any substance in the speculation that it was ultimately derived from the Tammuz worship of
the Sumerians.[1] At any rate, it did not spring from the soil of
Upper Egypt, where the political history of the Egyptiac Society
was made.[2] The main thread in the religious history of the Egyptiac
Society is the rivalry between this God of terrestrial and subterranean Nature—the spirit of the vegetation that alternately
appears above the ground and disappears beneath it; the spirit of
the Nile, whose waters cause the vegetation to appear—and the

---

[1] See p. 115, footnote 1, above.
[2] Eduard Meyer points out that the foundation of the United Kingdom *circa* 3200 B.C.,
.the foundation of the universal state *circa* 2070/2060 B.C., and the restoration of the
universal state *circa* 1580 B.C., were all accomplished by Powers arising in the south of
Upper Egypt. (*Geschichte des Altertums*, vol. ii (i), 2nd edition, pp. 60–1.) The point is
examined further in II. D (v), vol. ii, on pp. 114–15, below.

Sun-God of Heaven.[1] The essence of the rivalry was not the theological difference between two conceptions of the divine power, but a political difference between two sections of the Egyptiac Society in which the two worships respectively arose. In consequence of the political precocity of the Egyptiac Society —a precocity which showed itself in the foundation of the United Kingdom at the end of the Predynastic Age—the cult of Re, the Sun-God, was 'politicized'. The process was completed in the time of the Fifth Dynasty (*regnabant circa* 2564–2424 B.C.), when, under the influence of the priesthood of Heliopolis, the Pharaoh became the son of Re, while Re was re-conceived in the image of the Pharaoh.[2] On the other hand, the worship of Osiris was a popular religion.[3] 'In the solar faith we have a state theology, with all the splendour and the prestige of its royal patrons behind it; while in that of Osiris we are confronted by a religion of the people, which made a strong appeal to the individual believer.'[4]

The crucial difference between the two religions in their original forms, before the interaction between them began, was the difference in the prospects which they offered to their devotees after death. Osiris ruled the multitudes of the dead in a shadow-world underground or in the West.[5] Re—for a consideration—redeemed his devotees from death and raised them alive to the sky;[6] but this apotheosis was reserved for those who could pay the price; and since the material equipment in which the price was reckoned was steadily elaborated to the staggering proportions which it attained in the time of the pyramid-builders, the solar immortality was virtually a monopoly of the Pharaoh and those members of his court to whose immortalization-equipment he chose to contribute.[7] 'The Great Pyramids of Gīzah, while they are to-day the most imposing surviving witness to the earliest emergence of organized Man and the triumph of concerted effort, are likewise the silent but eloquent expression of a supreme endeavour to achieve immortality by sheer physical force.'[8] In the construction of the Pyramids, the organizing genius of the Egyptiac Society, which had drained the swamps and had established the United Kingdom, mobilized all the economic and political resources over which it had acquired command in an effort so tremendous that the structure of Society was irreparably overstrained.[9] The material

---

[1] Breasted, J. H.: *The Development of Religion and Thought in Ancient Egypt* (London 1912, Hodder and Stoughton), pp. 8–9.   [2] Breasted, op. cit., pp. 13–17.
[3] Breasted, op. cit., p. 29.   [4] Breasted, op. cit., p. 140.
[5] Breasted, op. cit., pp. 139 and 142.   [6] Breasted, op. cit., pp. 99 and 142.
[7] Breasted, op. cit., pp. 64–75 and 103.   [8] Breasted, op. cit., pp. 178–9.
[9] For the significance of the building of the Pyramids in the history of the Egyptiac Society, see further III. C (i) (a), vol. iii, p. 153, below.

consequences were the economic, political, and artistic decline which marked the Egyptiac 'Time of Troubles'. The spiritual consequences were complicated.

The first spiritual consequence seems to have been an increase in the power of Osiris owing to an increase in the devotion of the masses to the Osirian religion. The shadowy existence of their dead in the Osirian other-world might be a poor thing compared to the immortal life of the Pharaoh and his courtiers in Re's heaven. Yet it was the one consolation to which the masses could look forward under the grinding oppression to which they were being subjected in this life in order to secure the everlasting happiness of their masters in the life to come. The increase in the power of Osiris was a symptom that the oppression had become intolerable and that the Egyptiac Society was on the verge of fission into a proletariat and a dominant minority. Confronted with this danger, the solar priesthood of Heliopolis sought to render Osiris innocuous by taking him into partnership with their own God;[1] but in this transaction Osiris succeeded in taking far more than he gave. While he entered into the Pharaoh's solar cult, he captured the solar ritual of apotheosis, which had been a monopoly of the few, for the mass of Mankind.[2] The first stages of the process have left their mark in the so-called 'Pyramid Texts'[3]—'Osirianized' solar liturgies which were still, apparently, the exclusive possession of the Pharaohs of the Fifth Dynasty who inscribed them.[4] The monument of the completion of the process is 'the Book of the Dead'—an 'everyman's guide to immortality' which was already current under the Eighteenth Dynasty in the Restoration Period after the interregnum, and which dominated the religious life of the Egyptiac Society throughout the epilogue that occupied the last two millennia of its Time-span.[5]

The process was assisted by the disillusionment of the dominant minority themselves, who piled stone on stone up to the apex of the Great Pyramid without ever attaining that complete inward

---

[1] The dread which Osiris inspired in the votaries of Re is betrayed in the magical formulae for preventing Osiris from appropriating the royal pyramids. (Breasted, op. cit., pp. 74–5.)

[2] Breasted, op. cit., pp. 403 and 150–60. Compare the Hellenic myth of Prometheus, who stole fire from the Olympians for the use of Man. In the Aeschylean version of the Prometheus myth, Zeus is represented as an egotistical tyrant, who feels no concern for the welfare of Mankind and who is incensed with Prometheus for his revolutionary labour of love in imparting to Man some share in the Olympians' blessings, because, for Zeus, the essential value of these blessings consists in their being his own monopoly. For an interpretation of the contest between Prometheus and Zeus as a mythical representation of the cosmic conflict between Growth and Stagnation, see Part III. B, below.

[3] See p. 137, above.

[4] Breasted, op. cit., p. 99.

[5] A 'canonical redaction' of the Book of the Dead does not appear to have been made until the fourth century B.C. In the Book of the Dead, hardly anything from 'the Pyramid Texts' survived. (Breasted, op. cit., pp. 293–4.)

assurance of immortality for which they craved.[1] Under the Fifth Dynasty, the idea that Re demanded righteousness rather than big buildings began to prevail;[2] and this moralization of the God of the Pharaohs was extended in the 'Time of Troubles' to the God of their subjects. The temper of the Egyptiac 'Time of Troubles' is revealed in the surviving fragments of a prophetic literature[3] comparable to the literature of the Syriac 'Time of Troubles' which is familiar to us in the books of the prophets of Israel and in the Gathas of Zarathustra. We discern the same spiritual progress from scepticism through pessimism towards a new hope; and this new hope sprang from 'the democratisation of blessedness beyond the grave'.[4] Osiris had become a moral judge, in another world, of men's good and evil deeds in this world; the souls of all the dead must appear before his judgement-seat; and any soul whose good deeds outweighed its evil deeds in the balance became identified with Osiris himself and thus attained that blissful immortality which had once been the guerdon of material performances and the monopoly of Pharaohs who could command the labour of other men to perform them on a sufficient scale. The worship of Osiris—the God who died and rose again to endow the righteous dead with his own eternal life—was centralized in the time of the Twelfth Dynasty in a holy sepulchre at Abydos—the derelict tomb of some forgotten Thinite Pharaoh of the First or Second Dynasty of the old United Kingdom. This holy sepulchre became a place of pilgrimage and the scene of an annual passion-play.[5]

Here, under the Egyptiac universal state, we discern the lineaments of a universal church created by an internal proletariat. What would have been the future of this Osirian Church if the Egyptiac universal state had not been restored? If the interregnum had run its course, would the Osirian Church then have become the chrysalis of a new society, 'affiliated' to the Egyptiac Society

[1] This lack of assurance was justified by the event. During the Egyptiac 'Time of Troubles' the pyramids which had been built by the Pharaohs of the United Kingdom all became derelict, in spite of the endowments which had been left for their liturgical upkeep. By the time of the Eleventh and Twelfth Dynasties, these colossal monuments of their predecessors had become a by-word for the futility of mere material effort. (Breasted, op. cit., pp. 66-8, 83, 180-3.)

[2] Breasted, op. cit., pp. 170-9.

[3] The majority of the fragments, as we have them, appear to date from the time of the Twelfth Dynasty; that is to say, from the time of the Egyptiac universal state; but the spirit which they breathe and the historical setting in which they are placed belong to the foregoing 'Time of Troubles'. (Breasted, op. cit., p. 198.)

[4] Breasted, op. cit., p. 252.

[5] Breasted, op. cit., pp. 285-9. See further Schaefer, H.: *Die Mysterien des Osiris in Abydos unter Sesostris III nach dem Denkstein des Oberschatzmeisters I-cher-Nofret* (Leipzig 1904, Hinrichs = Untersuchungen zur Geschichte und Altertumskunde Aegyptens, herausgegeben von K. Sethe, vol. iv, Heft 2). According to Schaefer (in op. cit., pp. 28-9), the Pharaoh whose grave was appropriated by Osiris was the third king of Dynasty III. For a summary of the acts of the passion-play, see op. cit., p. 31.

but possessing a distinct and separate life of its own? First of all, we should have expected to see this religion of the Egyptiac internal proletariat captivate the external proletariat—the Hyksos—but this did not happen. The Hyksos remained faithful to the cult of their own God Set;[1] and the intrusion of this 'abomination of desolation' evoked an unnatural 'union sacrée' between the nascent religion of the internal proletariat of the Egyptiac Society and the moribund religion of the dominant minority. This defensive fusion of worships was one aspect—and ultimately the most important aspect—of that fanatical reaction against the Hyksos which also manifested itself in the restoration of the Egyptiac universal state by the Eighteenth Dynasty. The religious result of the Restoration was a permanent syncretism in which the Osirian religion was taken up by the priesthood of the dominant minority and was sterilized. The priests were prudent enough not to rob the internal proletariat of their hard-won Osirian immortality, but they were also shrewd enough to exploit the popular craving by making it easier to satisfy. Professional ingenuity was exercised —as of old, for a consideration—in teaching Man how to make up for deficiencies in righteousness by magical methods of taking the kingdom of Osiris by storm; and the magic was adroitly purveyed in guaranteed formulas at popular prices. The immortality which had once been bought by Pharaohs for the price of pyramids was now brought within the reach of every man for the price of a few texts written on papyrus rolls.[2] We may conjecture that, in this business as in others, the mass production of a cheap article for a small margin of profit brought the manufacturer the best return. At any rate, the priesthood profited more than any other class in the Egyptiac Society in the course of the two millennia that elapsed before the society became extinct. The religious syncretism of the age had its political counterpart in an alliance between Church and State; and in this partnership the priesthood steadily gained the upper hand, until in the eleventh century B.C. the chief priest of Amon-Re of Thebes dethroned the last Ramses and reigned in his stead.

Thus the Restoration of the sixteenth century B.C. was something more than a rehabilitation of the Egyptiac universal state. It was an amalgamation of the living tissues of the Osirian Church with the dead tissues of the Egyptiac Society into a single mass—a kind of social concrete that was far harder than any natural rock. Osiris, who had proclaimed to his worshippers 'I am the resurrection and

---

[1] More accurately, the cult of the Unknown God of the Hyksos whom the Egyptians identified with their Set. (See Meyer, E.: *Geschichte des Altertums*, vol. i (ii), 3rd edition, p. 315.)

[2] See Breasted, op. cit., pp. 281, 284, 290, 296, 308–9.

the life', had shown himself no better than a mummy. The Osirian Church, which had set out to lead a chosen people from a city of destruction to a promised land, had found an abomination of desolation in her path, and—fearing to look forward, lest the Gorgon's head might turn her to stone—had looked back and had been turned, like Lot's wife, into a pillar of salt. If this church was great with child, the child was petrified in the womb before ever it was due to be born.

The best proof that the restored figure of the Egyptiac Society was void of life is to be found in the utter failure of the solitary attempt that was made to awaken the dead. The Egyptiac restoration, as well as the foregoing Egyptiac decline and fall, had its abortive universal church; and this time one man, Ikhnaton,[1] sought to repeat, by an instantaneous gesture from above downwards, the miracle of religious creation which had been performed once already by the Egyptiac internal proletariat, in a gradual movement from below upwards, during the eight centuries of a 'Time of Troubles' and a universal state.[2] Ikhnaton was called to act, because that first time the miracle had been performed in vain and now could not be repeated by a people who had been content to accept a stone for bread and to relapse from a lofty religion to the magical practices of Primitive Man. Ikhnaton was driven to take drastic action by the desperate need of the age. Yet if there was no other way of retrieving the failure of the past, this fact proved the failure irretrievable, for universal churches cannot be created in Ikhnaton's way.[3] By sheer genius Ikhnaton did create a new conception of God and Man and Life and Nature[4] and expressed it in a new poetry and a new art; but a dead society could not be brought to life by the vicarious vitality of one individual, and even genius armed with the power and prestige of Pharaoh could not break through the serried phalanx of the priesthood[5] to reach the people marshalled in docile ranks behind. Clad in the whole armour of his faith and power, Ikhnaton leapt, like Curtius, into the abyss; and then the Egyptian earth closed over his head without leaving a trace of his passage. It swallowed him up as the Ocean might engulf some swimmer who had pre-

[1] Ikhnaton *imperabat circa* 1370–1352 B.C.
[2] For Ikhnaton's abortive Atonian Church, see further V. C (i) (d) 6 (δ), Annex, vol. v, pp. 605–6, below. [3] This point is discussed further ibid.

[4] Ikhnaton's solar monotheism was inspired by the worship of Re as this had been refined at Heliopolis. Ikhnaton was indifferent and perhaps hostile to the degenerate worship of Osiris. (Breasted, op. cit., pp. 321, 333, 340.)

[5] Ikhnaton's last predecessor but three, Thothmes III (*imperabat solus circa* 1480–1450 B.C.), had organized the priests of all the Gods in all the 'nomes' (provinces) of Egypt into a single corporation under the presidency of the chief priest of Amon-Re of Thebes. Hence Amon was singled out by Ikhnaton for his chief attack in the war which he waged against the united Egyptiac Pantheon on behalf of his own Jealous God Aton. (Breasted, op. cit., pp. 319 and 321–2.)

sumptuously cast himself upon the face of the waters where only the brooding spirit can move and live.

Ikhnaton's failure is conclusive evidence that we are justified in regarding the social phenomena which occupied the former field of the Egyptiac Society from the sixteenth century B.C. to the fifth century of the Christian Era as an epilogue to Egyptiac history rather than as the history of a distinct and separate society. Ought we, on this analogy, to refuse recognition to our 'Babylonic Society' and to the nine other societies on our list whose status we have allowed our critics to call in question? Ought we to regard their histories, too, as epilogues to the histories of societies and not as the histories of independent societies existing in their own right? When we make our comparative study of societies in their geneses, growths, breakdowns, and disintegrations, in their universal states and universal churches and heroic ages, in their contacts in Time and in Space, are we to leave these ten societies severely alone and rule it out of order to take their histories into account? No doubt our critics are entitled to an answer; but if they press for it we can only answer 'Wait and see'. Our method in this study is empirical; and there is no particular reason at this point for proceeding *a priori*. In our survey of societies, we have spent some time and trouble in rounding up twenty-one representatives of the species; and now that we are going to put our mustangs through their paces, are we to disqualify nearly half the stud before we have seen how they run? We prefer to let them alone and go ahead. If any of them are bad stock, they will fall by the way; but, until they fall, let us put them through their paces all together. Whatever may happen, we shall learn more about horseflesh by watching each and all of them in action, seeing how they shape, and comparing their performances than we can expect to learn if we make an arbitrary selection beforehand on points.

At any rate our provisional classification has established one general fact. The representatives of our species constitute a continuous series ranging between two extremes. At one extreme we find societies that are wholly unrelated to any others either earlier or later than themselves. At the other extreme we find societies that are related so intimately to their predecessors that the relation verges upon identity. Exactly which of the societies that we have identified fall fairly within these limits is a question that may be left to answer itself in the course of our study. *Solvitur eundo.*

III. THE COMPARABILITY OF SOCIETIES OF THE SPECIES

(a) THE DISTINCTION BETWEEN CIVILIZATIONS AND PRIMITIVE SOCIETIES

We have now identified twenty-one societies of the species to which our Western Society belongs and have classified them provisionally according to the criteria which we employed in surveying them. The next step in a study of history is to put these twenty-one societies through their paces and compare their performances in their geneses and growths, their breakdowns and disintegrations, their universal states and universal churches and heroic ages, their contacts in Time and in Space. First, however, before we begin to carry out a plan of operations which will occupy us almost to the end of this book, it may be well to forestall possible criticisms by debating the prior question: Are these twenty-one societies really comparable at all? For their comparability may be challenged on several different and partly contradictory grounds.

The first and simplest argument against the comparability of our twenty-one societies may be stated thus: These societies have no common characteristic beyond that of all being 'intelligible fields of historical study'; and this characteristic is so general and so vague that it cannot be turned to any practical account for our purpose.

The answer to this objection is to point out that societies which are 'intelligible fields of historical study' are a genus within which our twenty-one representatives constitute one particular species. Societies of this species are commonly called 'civilizations' in order to distinguish them from 'primitive societies', which are likewise 'intelligible fields of historical study' in the meaning of the term which we have worked out empirically at an earlier stage of this study.[1] If, when we started our inquiry by examining a single community, we had happened to take as our test case not Great Britain but some other community in the British Empire—for instance, the Todas of the Nilgiri Hills in the south of India or some tribe of Blackfellows in Central Australia—we should likewise have arrived empirically at a set of societies which were all 'intelligible fields of study', but they would all have been 'primitive societies' and not 'civilizations'.[2] These two terms correspond to

---

[1] See Part I. B, above.

[2] An empirical survey of our kind in this other field, resulting in a list of 'primitive societies', will be found in the introduction to *The Material Culture and Social Institutions of the Simpler Peoples: An Essay in Correlation*, by Hobhouse, L. T., Wheeler, G. C., and Ginsberg, M. (London 1915, Chapman and Hall; reprinted in 1930). In the remainder of their book the authors put their 'primitive societies' through their paces and compare their performances as we propose to do with our 'civilizations'.

a real specific difference within the genus 'societies'; and for the sake of clearness and accuracy we shall employ the terms in our study from this point onwards. Meanwhile, the fact that 'primitive societies' constitute a distinct species disposes of the first objection to our plan of operations by indicating that our twenty-one civilizations must have some specific distinguishing characteristic in common with one another over and above their generic characteristic of being 'intelligible fields of study'.

We can at once remark a specific difference of a purely quantitative kind. The number of known civilizations is small. In a survey of human societies in all parts of the World in every age from the present to the remotest past on which our modern Western Archaeology yet throws any light, we have succeeded in collecting only twenty-one specimens of civilizations, and we have been compelled to concede that no less than ten of these twenty-one may possibly turn out not to be distinct and separate specimens in their own right. The number of known primitive societies is vastly greater. In 1915 three Western anthropologists, setting out to make a comparative study of primitive societies, and confining their attention to societies about which they happened to find information that was sufficiently full and sufficiently trustworthy for their purpose,[1] drew up a list of about 650 societies of this species[2] for use in their work. Almost all the societies that found a place in this list were alive at the time; and the authors point out that 'the great bulk of anthropological inquiry dates from the last three or four centuries'. If we allow further for the (probably few) living primitive societies whose existence is unknown to modern Western observers; for the perhaps not very large number which, though known to exist, were omitted from the above-mentioned list for lack of sufficiently full and trustworthy information about them; and for the certainly immense number that have come into and passed out of existence, mostly unknown to us even by name, since Mankind first became human,[3] it becomes evident that the numerical preponderance of primitive societies over civilizations is overwhelming.

This preponderance of the primitive societies in numbers is obscured by the equally overwhelming preponderance of the civilizations in their individual dimensions. The two species stand to each other like elephants and rabbits. The primitive societies, in their legions, are relatively short-lived, are restricted to relatively narrow geographical areas, and embrace a relatively small number

---

[1] Hobhouse, Wheeler, and Ginsberg, op. cit., p. 2.
[2] List in op. cit., pp. 30–44.
[3] Sir James Jeans puts the present antiquity of Man at about 300,000 years (*The Universe around Us* (Cambridge 1929, University Press), p. 13).

of human beings either at any given moment or from first to last throughout their histories. The civilizations, whose muster-roll only just rises to double figures, are relatively long-lived, they spread from their original homes over relatively large areas, and the number of human beings that they embrace is relatively great. They spread by exterminating, subjecting, or assimilating other societies[1]—sometimes societies of their own species,[2] but primitive societies much more frequently.[3] Primitive societies, like rabbits, have their lives cut short by violence more often than not, and an encounter with some civilization is the way in which violent death commonly overtakes them. As for the disparity in the numbers of human beings that civilizations and primitive societies respectively embrace, it is probable that if we could take a census of the membership of the five living civilizations up to date, during the small number of centuries through which these have yet lived since they first emerged, we should find that each of our Leviathans, singly, has embraced a greater number of human beings already than could be mustered, in the aggregate, by all the primitive societies that have ever existed since the emergence of the Human Race. This counting of human heads, however, is irrelevant to the matter in hand. The individuals of the genus and the species that we are studying are not human beings but societies; and the significant fact for our purpose is that, when we compare the number of known civilizations with the number of known primitive societies, the latter number is vastly the greater of the two.

(b) THE MISCONCEPTION OF 'THE UNITY OF CIVILIZATION'

The second argument against the comparability of our twenty-one civilizations is the contrary of the first. Having answered the objection that our specimens are too heterogeneous for comparison, we may now be told that the homogeneity which we have established is too great; that the specific likeness amounts to identity; in fact, that there are not twenty-one civilizations but only one, which is no more susceptible of comparison than anything else that is unique of its kind.

This thesis of 'the Unity of Civilization' in this sense is a misconception into which our modern Western historians have been led by the influence of their social environment on their thought.[4]

[1] For a general examination of these alternative processes see V. C (i) (c) 2 and 3, *passim*, in vol. v, as well as Parts VIII and IX, below.

[2] For an examination of these processes in the contact in Space between two civilizations, see Part IX, below.

[3] For an examination of these processes in the contact in Space between a civilization and a primitive society, see Part VIII, below.

[4] See Part I. A, above.

There is, indeed, another sense in which our twenty-one civilizations are united with one another in virtue of their all alike being representatives of one single species of society; and it is, of course, in virtue of this specific unity that they lend themselves to a comparative study. On the other hand, the view that 'Civilization' is a species of society that has only one representative which is *ex hypothesi* unique of its kind is an error which can only be entertained by taking a distorted view of history.

The misleading feature in the social environment has been the fact that, in modern times, our own Western Civilization has cast the net of its economic system round the World and has caught in its meshes the whole living generation of Mankind and all the habitable lands and navigable seas on the face of the Planet.[1] This economic unification on a Western basis has been followed up by a political unification on the same basis which has gone almost as far; for though the conquests of Western armies and governments have been neither as extensive nor as thorough as the conquests of Western producers and manufacturers and carriers and technicians, it is nevertheless a fact that almost all the sixty or seventy states in the contemporary world, including the surviving states of non-Western origin, are now members—in various ways and in different degrees—of a single world-wide comity of states;[2] and this world-wide comity is a direct extension of the system of states into which our Western Society has articulated itself since the beginning of the modern age. These facts are remarkable (though by no means unparalleled or unprecedented),[3] and to Western observers they are gratifying; and this explains how Western historians have come to exaggerate both the range of these facts and their import.

They have exaggerated the range of the facts in two directions. First, they have assumed that the present more or less complete unification of the World on a Western basis on the economic plane and the large measure of unification on the same basis which has been accomplished on the political plane are together tantamount to a perfect unification on all planes. Secondly, they have equated unification with unity. They have assumed the pre-existence and the perpetuity of a state of affairs which has really come into existence only recently on any plane, which has not yet been established on all planes, and which may conceivably pass out of existence again without ever being established through and through. Having thus exaggerated the range in Time and Space of a phenomenon in their environment which is really still recent

[1] See pp. 27 and 30, above.   [2] See pp. 30-1, above.
[3] For parallels and precedents see Part IX, *passim.*

and superficial and which may prove to be transient, they have interpreted it to mean that Civilization (in the singular and with a capital 'C') is not merely a species of societies but is to be identified with a single particular society; that this concrete unique Civilization is in essence one and indivisible; that after a long probation it has fulfilled its destiny at last by attaining world-dominion in our day through our exertions; that the network of the Western economic system which now holds the whole of Mankind in its meshes is 'the glorious liberty of the children of God' for which 'the whole of creation groaneth and travaileth in pain together until now'; and that 'the sufferings of this present time are not worthy to be compared with the glory which shall be revealed in us' now that 'the manifestation of the sons of God'[1] has been made.

This thesis that the present unification of the World on a Western basis is the consummation of a single continuous process which accounts for the whole of human history requires a violent distortion of historical facts and a drastic limitation of the historian's field of vision.

In the first place, his vision of the contemporary world must be confined to the economic and political planes of social life and must be inhibited from penetrating to the cultural plane, which is not only deeper but is fundamental. While the economic and political maps of the World have now been 'Westernized' almost out of recognition, the cultural map remains to-day substantially what it was before our Western Society ever started on its career of economic and political conquest. On this cultural plane, for those who have eyes to see, the lineaments of the four living non-Western civilizations are still clear.[2] Even the fainter outlines of the frail primitive societies that are being ground to powder by the passage of the ponderous Western steam-roller have not quite ceased to be visible. How have our historians managed to close their eyes lest they should see?[3] They have simply put on the spectacles—or the blinkers—of their generation; and we may best apprehend what the outlook of this generation has been by examining the connotation of the English word 'Natives'[4] and the

---

[1] Paul: Epistle to the Romans, ix, 18–22. This translation of our modern Western concept of the consummation of human history into Pauline terms is not inappropriate, since the line of thought out of which this modern Western concept has arisen is actually of Syriac origin.

[2] See pp. 31 and 34–5, above.   [3] The Acts of the Apostles, xxviii, 26–7.

[4] The following extract from the *New English Dictionary* speaks for itself:

Native, substantive. 4. One of the original or usual inhabitants of a country, as distinguished from strangers or foreigners; now *esp.* one belonging to a non-European and imperfectly civilized or savage race.

1603 R. Johnson *Kingd. & Commw.* 153 He committed no lesse an error in suffering the Natiues to keepe their possessions and to inhabit all their townes. 1652–62 Heylin *Cosmogr.* iv (1673), 94 Inhabited by the Natives only, though the Portugals did some-

equivalent words in the other vernacular languages of the contemporary Western World.[1]

When we Westerners call people 'Natives' we implicitly take
the cultural colour out of our perceptions of them. We see them
as trees walking, or as wild animals infesting the country in which
we happen to come across them. In fact, we see them as part of
the local flora and fauna, and not as men of like passions with
ourselves; and, seeing them thus as something infra-human, we
feel entitled to treat them as though they did not possess ordinary
human rights. They are merely natives of the lands which they
occupy; and no term of occupancy can be long enough to confer
any prescriptive right. Their tenure is as provisional and precarious
as that of the forest trees which the Western pioneer fells or that
of the big game which he shoots down.[2] And how shall the
'civilized' Lords of Creation treat the human game, when in their
own good time they come to take possession of the land which,
by right of eminent domain, is indefeasibly their own? Shall they
treat these 'Natives' as vermin to be exterminated, or as domestic-
able animals to be turned into hewers of wood and drawers of
water? No other alternative need be considered, if 'niggers have
no souls'. All this is implicit in the word 'Natives', as we have
come to use it in the English language in our time.[3] Evidently

times endeavour a Plantation in it. 1695.Temple *Hist. Eng.* (1699) 5 The North-East
part of Scotland was by the Natives called *Cal Dun*. [&c.]. (*A New English Dictionary*,
edited by Sir James Murray, vol. vi (Oxford 1908, Clarendon Press).)

[1] e.g. 'indigènes' in French; 'Eingeborenen' in German.

[2] This point of view was translated into action by the Government of the United
Kingdom in A.D. 1932–3, when they threw open the Native Reserves in Kenya Colony to
European gold-diggers.

It may be observed that the Westerners of our age are not the only people who have
ever taken this view of the rest of Mankind. The Mongols once had the same outlook
on the World, as witness the following conversation which took place in the year 1254 of
the Christian Era, at Mangu Khan's Court at Qaraqorum, between the Great Khan's
secretaries and the envoy of St. Louis, King of France, the Friar William of Rubruck:

'And they began to question us greatly about the Kingdom of France, whether there
were many sheep and cattle and horses there, and whether they had not better go there at
once and take it all. And I had to use all my strength to conceal my indignation and
anger; but I answered: "There are many good things there, which you would see if it
befel you to go there".' (*Itinerarium fratris Willielmi de Rubruquis de Ordine Fratrum
Minorum, Galli, anno gratiae 1253, ad Partes Orientales*, chapter xxxiii, translated by
Rockhill, W. W., in the publications of the Hakluyt Society, Second Series, vol. iv
(London 1900, Hakluyt Society).)

This conversation must have confirmed our Western observer's first impression of the
Mongols as recorded in Chapter xi of his narrative, which is entitled '*Qualiter ingressi
sunt inter Tartaros, et de ingratitudine eorum*':

'Valde importunè et impudenter petunt quae vident. Et si dat homo eis perdit, quia
sunt ingrati. Reputant se dominos mundi, et videtur eis quod nihil debeat eis negari ab
aliquo.'

These passages are illuminating from more than one point of view. They show how
once a Westerner felt at being treated as a Native at a time when Westerners were
themselves exposed to a treatment which it is at present their privilege to inflict upon
others. We may also reflect that the Mongols, in their time, enjoyed the privilege for
not much more than one century. Is our own tenure of 'the Lordship of Creation'
likely to last much longer?

[3] The present derogatory connotation of the word is less than a century old. Its
original colour was neutral, and in that stage of its history it was given a laudatory con-

the word is not a scientific term but an instrument of action: an *a priori* justification for a plan of campaign. It belongs to the realm of Western practice and not of Western theory; and this explains the paradox that a classificatory-minded society has not hesitated to apply the name indiscriminately to the countrymen of a Gandhi and a Bose and a Rabindranath Tagore, as well as to 'primitives' of the lowest degree of culture, such as the Andaman Islanders and the Australian Blackfellows. For the theoretical purpose of objective description, this sweeping use of the word makes sheer nonsense. For the practical purpose of asserting the claim that our Western Civilization is the only civilization in the World, the usage is a militant gesture. It signalizes the fact that all the non-Western societies which are alive in the World to-day, from the lowest to the highest, have been swept up into our economic net, and it postulates the contention that this common predicament is the only important fact about any of them. In short, the word 'Natives' is like a piece of smoked glass which modern Western observers hold in front of their eyes when they look abroad upon the World, in order that the gratifying spectacle of a 'Westernized' surface may not be disturbed by any perception of the native fires which are still blazing underneath.

In the second place, the dogma of 'the Unity of Civilization' requires the historian to ignore the difference—of kind rather than mere degree—which distinguishes the continuity between the histories of two related civilizations from the continuity between two successive chapters in the history of a single civilization. The nature and extent of this difference have been investigated above[1] and may therefore be taken for granted for the purpose of the argument here. At this point we need only observe that, by shutting their eyes to this, our historians enable themselves to

notation as often as not: for instance, in such phrases as 'native land', 'native valour', 'native hue of resolution'. A solitary surviving instance of this laudatory usage is 'natives' = oysters bred in English oyster-beds! Apropos of the change in the Western attitude towards the Sinic and the Far Eastern Civilization between the time of Gibbon and the time of Freeman, it is suggested below (in I. B (iv), Annex) that the de-valuation of all non-Western culture in our Western estimation may have been a consequence of the rather sudden and sensational victory of our Western Society over all other contemporary societies on the economic and political planes. In this connexion it may be observed that the derogatory usage of the word 'Natives' became current about the same time as this condescending attitude, and it may be inferred that the attitude and the usage both reflect the influence of the same change in the social environment. In India, where the change in the economic and political relations of the parties within the same span of time was still more sudden and sensational than it was in the Far East, the change in the attitude of the Westerners was still more striking. Its extent can be measured by reading *The Travels of Mirza Abu Taleb Khan in Asia, Africa, and Europe during the years 1799–1803* (translated by Charles Stewart, Esq., London 1810, Long-man, Hurst, Rees, and Orme, 2 vols.). When this Indian gentleman visited the British Isles on the eve of the British conquest of India, it is evident from his narrative that he was received in 'Society' as an interesting and honoured guest, and his memoirs reveal no shadow of an 'inferiority complex'.

[1] See I. B (iv), above, and I. B (iv), Annex, below.

regard Hellenic history as just an earlier chapter in the history of
our Western Civilization (which they have already equated with
'Civilization' *sans phrase*), and Minoan history in the same way.
Thus they telescope three civilizations into one, and trace the
history of this singular 'Civilization' back in a straight line from
the ubiquitous Western Civilization of their own day to the
primitive society in the 'Neolithic' stage of material technique out
of which the Minoan Civilization emerged about the beginning
of the third millennium B.C., and thence, through the upper and
lower strata of the 'Palaeolithic' technique, to the pre-human
ancestors of Mankind. It is true that, in presenting the evolution
of Civilization in this figure of a single straight line, they are
compelled to admit the entrance of one tributary from a separate
source in order to account for the germ of creative activity, derived
from the Syriac Society, out of which the internal proletariat of
the Hellenic Society generated the Catholic Church.[1] Yet, however important they may acknowledge this contribution to be,
they insist upon treating it as exceptional; and in any case they
derive 'Modern Civilization' from no more than two sources:
the main stream from 'Greece and Rome', the tributary from
'Palestine'.[2]

In the third place, they ignore the histories, or the chapters in
the histories, of civilizations that do not happen to fit into the
frame within which they have confined their picture[3]—dismissing
them as 'semi-barbarous' or as 'decadent'[4] or as belonging to 'the

[1] See pp. 40 and 57, above.
[2] This manœuvre was denounced nearly a century and a half ago by Volney:
'On ne s'est occupé que des Grecs et des Romains, en suivant servilement une méthode
étroite et exclusive, qui rapporte tout au système d'un petit peuple d'Asie, inconnu dans
l'antiquité, et au système d'Hérodote, dont les limites sont infiniment resserrées; l'on
n'a voulu voir que l'Égypte, la Grèce, l'Italie, comme si l'univers était dans ce petit
espace; et comme si l'histoire de ces petits peuples était autre chose qu'un faible et
tardif rameau de l'histoire de toute l'espèce.' ('Leçons d'Histoire, Sixième Séance', *Œuvres
Complètes de Volney* (Paris 1876, Firmin Didot), p. 588.)
[3] The distortion which results from this third manœuvre is particularly violent, and a
startling loss of proportion may be the penalty for even a slight *penchant* in this direction
—as witness the classification of societies in Carr-Saunders, A. M.: *The Population
Problem* (Oxford 1922, Clarendon Press), p. 243. This example has been taken on
purpose from a work of fine scholarship, written from a broad point of view, which the
writer of this Study admires. If great scholars are subject to this infirmity of vision,
what can be expected from the small fry?
[4] This gesture is really incompatible with their main position; for if civilizations are
to be ruled out of account for being 'decadent' or 'semi-barbarous', it becomes impossible
to maintain the thesis of the absolute continuity between Western history and Hellenic
and between Hellenic history and Minoan—the thesis on which their main argument
rests. No one can deny that the Minoan and Hellenic civilizations were 'decadent' in
their last phases or that the Hellenic and Western civilizations were 'semi-barbarous' in
their first phases. If, however, these chapters of Minoan, Hellenic, and Western
history were for these reasons to be ruled out of account, then the three histories would
not only cease to be one history but would cease to have any relation with one another
at all. An ingenious attempt to escape from this dilemma was made by Saint-Simon.
He treated the histories of the Hellenic Civilization and our Western Civilization as
successive chapters in a single series, but he regarded the continuity of this series as
consisting in a rhythmic alternation of 'organic' and 'critical' periods. The first of his

Unchanging East' which is declared to be without significance for 'the History of Civilization'.[1]

On such grounds they ignore, to begin with, all those chapters in Syriac history which are subsequent to the fertilization of the internal proletariat of the Hellenic Society with the Syriac germ of the Catholic Church. They ignore, for example, the Nestorian and Monophysite movements in which the Syriac Society attempted to turn the Christian syncretism to its own account;[2] they ignore Islam, the universal church which the internal proletariat of the Syriac Society eventually succeeded in creating for itself out of indigenous elements after Hellenism had been expelled at length from the Syriac World;[3] they ignore the Umayyad and 'Abbasid Caliphates, the political instruments by which the final expulsion of Hellenism was accomplished and by which a barbarian 'successor-state' of the Roman Empire was then converted into a reintegration of the Syriac universal state of the Achaemenidae.[4] Again, they ignore the histories of the Egyptiac, Sumeric, Babylonic, and Hittite societies, except in so far as these civilizations influenced the Minoan or the Syriac or the Hellenic.[5] Finally, they ignore

critical periods covered the decadence of the Hellenic Civilization and the semi-barbarous beginnings of our Western Civilization. (See Part II. B, pp. 199–200, below.) The Minoan Civilization presented no problem to him because it had not yet been disinterred in his day.

[1] A classic example of this dismissal of the East may be found in Bazard's *Exposition de la Doctrine Saint-Simonienne* (a series of lectures delivered in 1829 and 1830):

'On a élevé quelques doutes sur la rigueur des démonstrations tirées de la série historique adoptée par notre école: on a demandé si cette série était assez longue, et s'il n'y avait pas imprudence à négliger toutes les traditions de l'Orient. A cette objection, nous répondons que l'histoire de la série de civilisation dont la société européenne est aujourd'hui le dernier terme embrasse environ trois mille ans, et que le développement de l'humanité pendant cette période, si vaste et si féconde, n'a pas seulement l'avantage de présenter une longue suite de termes, mais encore qu'aucune autre époque historique n'est mieux connue, et qu'elle est celle dont le dernier terme constitue l'état de civilisation le plus avancé. Les Orientalistes sont loin d'avoir rempli les lacunes de l'histoire de l'Asie, et comme à chaque pas, dans cette histoire, il y [a] solution de continuité, il est impossible d'y suivre un développement régulier; il en est de ces fragments historiques comme des lambeaux de terrain sur lesquels le géologue peut faire des hypothèses plus ou moins ingénieuses, mais où il ne porte jamais le cachet de certitude scientifique qu'il imprime aux contrées où les terrains se recouvrent successivement et sans interruption; il y a plus, on peut affirmer à l'avance que, si l'interpolation de cette série (celle de la civilisation orientale) est complétée, elle n'offrira dans son ensemble que l'un des termes qui nous sont connus. (Nous ne craignons pas même de dire que les Européens seuls sont capables d'apprendre aux Indiens leur propre histoire, et de voir dans leurs traditions, dans leurs monuments, des idées, des faits qui ne sauraient être découverts et compris par les Indiens eux-mêmes.) Remarquons en outre que la Grèce avait transporté chez elle tous les progrès épars chez les autres peuples, et qu'elle se présente comme le résumé de toutes les civilisations qui avaient grandi jusqu'à elle. On se souvient que, plus de six cents ans avant l'ère chrétienne, Thalès, arrivant de l'Égypte, étonna les Grecs par la prédiction d'une éclipse de soleil; on sait encore que les philosophes qui brillaient au Lycée avaient étendu leur savoir par de longs voyages dans les pays les plus éclairés de l'Orient.' (*Œuvres de Saint-Simon et d'Enfantin*, vol. xli (Paris 1877, Leroux), pp. 141–3.)

[2] See I. C (i) (*b*), p. 91, above, and II. D (vi), vol. ii, pp. 236–8, and II. D (vii), vol. ii, pp. 286–7, below.

[3] See p. 91, above.   [4] See pp. 73–7, above.

[5] This attitude of our Western historians towards these four civilizations is the more remarkable inasmuch as we do not feel towards them the animus which we undisguisedly display towards the four non-Western civilizations that are alive to-day. The existence

the histories of all the other civilizations completely. Orthodox Christendom, for instance, is either tacitly subsumed under Western Christendom on the strength of the common element in their names, or else it is disposed of, in terms of Western history, as a sort of temporary excrescence on the body of our Western Society which served it in its infancy as a shield against Oriental attacks and which afterwards atrophied and dropped off in the course of nature when its services had ceased to be necessary, as a tadpole's gills and tail disappear after the creature has turned into a frog.[1] As for the other three living non-Western civilizations—the Islamic, the Hindu, and the Far Eastern—they are refused recognition and their members are disposed of by being tied, as 'Natives', to our Western chariot wheels.[2] Moreover, Indic history is telescoped into Hindu history and Sinic history into Far Eastern history by the same high-handed manipulation that is applied to Minoan, Hellenic, and Western history; and thus the Indic and the Sinic civilizations are eliminated likewise. This only leaves the four civilizations of the New World—the Mayan, the Yucatec, the Mexic, and the Andean—and these are explained away as irrelevant phenomena of an *alter orbis*, or more bluntly

of these four living civilizations is unpalatable to Westerners because it is a standing challenge to the Western thesis that Civilization is one and indivisible and that this Civilization with a capital 'C' is identical with our Western Civilization in the contemporary world. On the other hand, the four extinct civilizations here in question are all in our good graces, partly for the negative reason that, just because they are now extinct, they do not challenge our claim to a monopoly of civilization in these latter days, and partly for the positive reason that their histories have been rescued from oblivion by the enterprise of our modern Western archaeologists, whose brilliant discoveries are a feather in our cap. On this account, we look upon these disinterred representatives of 'the Unchanging East' with less disfavour than we show to the living survivors. The mummies make no presumptuous claim to independence. They are our humble protégés, whose resuscitation is a perpetual monument to our archaeological skill.

[1] A characteristic expression of this view of 'Byzantium' will be found in *The Times Literary Supplement* of the 20th December, 1928, p. 1004, in a review of volume iv of *The Universal History of the World*. This metaphor of a shield—a thing which is no part of its owner's body yet at the same time has no use or significance apart from it—simply slurs over the question of what the relation between Orthodox Christendom and Western Christendom really is. The metaphor would be more apt apropos, not of Orthodox Christendom or of the East Roman Empire, but of the Danubian Hapsburg Monarchy, which really did come into existence in order to shield Western Christendom from the attacks of the 'Osmanlis and which did begin to atrophy as soon as the Ottoman pressure began to slacken—the decline and fall of the Ottoman and the Danubian Hapsburg Powers proceeding *pari passu* from the turn of the seventeenth and eighteenth centuries of the Christian Era down to the final disaster which overtook them both in the General War of 1914–18 (see II. D (v), vol. ii, pp. 177–88, below). Even here, however, the metaphor is inexact; for the relation of the Danubian Hapsburg Monarchy to our Western Society was not like that of a shield to a human being. The Hapsburg Monarchy was not, like a shield, a piece of matter external to and alien from the body which it was its function to protect. It was an excretion from the living substance of our Western Society—a special political articulation which was evoked by the need of guarding against a particular external attack. Thus it is strictly comparable not so much to a shield as to the carapace of a tortoise or an armadillo.

[2] There is already one significant exception. Few Westerners have had the effrontery to call the Japanese 'Natives' since the Japanese Empire has become one of the Great Powers. If the thesis of 'the Unity of Civilization' is to be preserved intact, it must be assumed that the Japanese have become Westerners by adoption. But can this assumption be made? The last word here lies not with us but with the Japanese themselves.

as abortive attempts at civilization which fell too far short of success to be taken into account.

By such Procrustean operations, the thesis of 'the Unity of Civilization' is maintained to this day. That a Freeman should have maintained it in a generation when seven of our twenty-one representatives of the species had not yet been disinterred by the archaeologist's spade was a venial error.[1] That a de Gobineau, at an earlier date and with less information at his command, should have perceived that civilizations are a species and that there is no such thing as a unique 'Civilization' with a capital 'C', was a brilliant feat of historical intuition.[2] That any Western historian in the year 1933 should follow Freeman and not de Gobineau in this matter, in the face of the facts as they have become apparent, is at first sight difficult to understand.[3] Perhaps this survival of the misconception of 'the Unity of History' is to be explained by the persistence of three underlying misconceptions: the ego-centric illusion, the catchword of 'the Unchanging East', and the misconception of growth as a movement in a straight line.

In examining the current Western view that the Western Society of our day is the consummation of human history and is synonymous with 'Civilization' itself, we have treated it as an instance of the influence of the social environment on historical thought and have seen in it a consequence of the world-dominion which this particular civilization has succeeded in establishing in modern times on the economic and political planes. On second thoughts, however, we may wonder whether this explanation is not, after all, too flattering to the human capacity for objective judgement.

If this world-dominion on these two planes happened to have been established by some living society other than ours of the West, and if Western observers held that the consummation of human history and the unique entity called 'Civilization' were to be found in this other society and not in ours, then their view would be entitled to respectful consideration; and although we should reject it still, on the same grounds on which we have rejected it above in its application to the Western Society, we should allow in these hypothetical circumstances that it might have an element of rationality and objectivity. We should make the same allowance, in the actual circumstances of the World in our day, if the current Western view regarding the role of the Western Society

[1] See the note at the end of I. B (iv), Annex, below. The figure becomes eight out of twenty-two if 'the Indus Culture' turns out to be an independent representative of the species. (See I. C (i) (b), Annex III, below.)

[2] See I. C (ii), footnote 1 on p. 129, above.

[3] For an effective protest against this misconception of 'the Unity of History', see the passage quoted from Headlam-Morley in I. B (iii) on p. 36, footnote 2, above.

were generally held by non-Western students of human affairs. It would be possible, no doubt, to find a number of non-Western observers who do take that view. Yet a census of opinions would almost certainly reveal that, in the actual circumstances of the World, there are still at least as many Orthodox Christian and Islamic and Hindu and Far Eastern observers who each regard their own respective society as the consummation of human history and as severally synonymous with Civilization itself, and who hold this view with the same assured conviction that sustains the corresponding but incompatible view among their Western contemporaries.[1] The same assurance proclaims itself in the utterances of all the extinct societies, in all the chances and changes of their mortal lives, wherever a record survives. The Pyramid-Builders of Egypt possessed this assurance in greater measure than the most triumphant captain of industry in the Western World of to-day; the revivalists of the Twenty-Sixth Dynasty, and the priesthood which continued to preserve the long-since petrified tradition of the Egyptiac culture under the Achaemenian and Ptolemaic and Roman régimes, inherited the assurance of the Pyramid-Builders, regardless of the fact that in their times the Egyptiac Society was in contact with other representatives of the species to which any unprejudiced observer would have given precedence over the Egyptiac Society unhesitatingly if he had been asked to pick out the Chosen People of the age. Doubtless the last scribe who knew how to write the hieroglyphic script and the last sculptor who knew how to carve a bas-relief in the Egyptiac style cherished the same illusion, when the Egyptiac Society was *in articulo mortis*, that had been cherished by their predecessors at the time when the Egyptiac Society was still holding its own among its kind and at the still earlier time when, for all that its members knew, it was the only society of the kind that ever had existed or was destined ever to exist in the World. All this suggests that the current Western misconception of 'the Unity of Civilization' through its assumed identity with the Western Society has deeper psychological roots than those which are grounded in the momentary state of our social environment. At bottom, the misconception is founded on an egocentric illusion which is always and everywhere ingrained in human minds.

Of course it is possible that the omnipresent illusion may accidentally coincide with reality in any given case. At any moment in the history of any civilization, so long as the society remains alive, its members may be right in believing that their own local

---

[1] For a further examination of the alternative psychological reactions towards a dominant alien civilization, see Part IX, below.

and temporary movement is in the main line of evolution—that it is on the point of vindicating its claim to be the consummation of human history by accomplishing the transformation of Sub-Man through Man into Super-Man.[1] Yet the chances in favour of this coincidence cannot ever be very great. We know of twenty-one cases in which the enterprise of civilization has been attempted hitherto. We know of no case in which the goal of human endeavours has been attained yet, while on the other hand we know of fourteen cases in which attempts to attain the goal are proved to have failed irretrievably by the fact that the societies which made them have become extinct. The possibility of attaining the goal is still an open question in the seven cases[2] of the civilizations that are still alive. While there is life there is hope; but in such a complicated and mysterious question it would be rash to prophesy —even on the most plausible appearances—that the prospects of any one of the seven still surviving candidates are assuredly better than those of any of its competitors; and it remains possible and indeed probable that none of the seven is destined to see the Promised Land. The goal of human endeavours may be attained, perhaps thousands or hundreds of thousands of years hence, by some society yet unborn; or the Human Race itself may become extinct without the goal ever having been attained at all.

Moreover, in the nature of the case, it is quite impossible for members of a living society to forecast, with any degree of probability whatever, the chances of this achievement being accomplished (if it is to be accomplished) by their own civilization.[3] Compared with the life-span of a human being, the time-span of a civilization is so vast that a human observer cannot hope to take the measure of its curve unless he is in a position to view it in a distant perspective;[4] and he can only obtain this perspective *vis-à-vis* some society that is extinct. He can never stand back sufficiently far from the history of the society in which he himself lives and moves and has his being. In other words, to assert of any living society, at any moment in its life, that it is the consummation of human history is to hazard a guess which is intrinsically unsusceptible of immediate verification. When we find that a majority of the members of all societies at all times make this assertion about their own civilizations, it becomes evident that

[1] See Part II. B, below.

[2] Seven and not five, if we count Orthodox Christendom in Russia as a separate society from Orthodox Christendom in South-Eastern Europe and Asia Minor, and if we look upon the Far Eastern Society in Korea and Japan as being likewise separate from the Far Eastern Society in China.

[3] On this point see I. B (iv), *init.*

[4] The curve is not only on an immense scale but is subject to abrupt and violent fluctuations which can be observed in retrospect but which it is beyond the wit of Man to predict. (See Parts IV and XI, below.)

their guesses have really nothing to do with any objective calculation of probabilities but are pure expressions of the egocentric illusion.

Now we have learnt to overcome this illusion in our study of the stellar universe. We no longer postulate a geocentric system because the Earth happens to be the stellar body whose surface we inhabit. We have taught ourselves to discount the false appearances arising from our accidental point of observation and to conceive of the Universe as a system of nebulae and galaxies in which our own planet and our own sun and even our own star-cluster is less conspicuous than a grain of dust in a cathedral. Again, in our personal relations with other human beings, we have learnt, if not to overcome the illusion, at least to be on our guard against it. In any human society, practising solipsists are treated as madmen and the tendency towards solipsism called egotism is regarded, according to its degree, as an absurdity or a vice. There are certain situations, however, in which the egocentric illusion still has the mastery over us.

On the political plane, for example, the illusion, projected as 'patriotism', is still 'the last infirmity of noble minds' as well as 'the last refuge of a scoundrel'. In the Western World of our day, almost every Englishman, Frenchman, Czechoslovak, and Lithuanian is influenced in his political feelings, thoughts, and actions by the irrational assumption that his own national state is a more precious institution than his neighbour's. Similarly, on the cultural plane, we have hardly yet begun to suspect that our own civilization may not, after all, be the consummation of human history or a synonym for Civilization itself. Indeed, we people of the West, so far from shaking ourselves free from the illusion as it besets us in this form, have apparently sunk deeper into this slough of error in the course of our history. In the so-called Middle Ages we portrayed one of the three Magi as a negro[1] and looked forward to the intervention of an Oriental champion of Christendom called Prester John. In the eighteenth century, when we had degraded the negro to the role of a slave, we were still capable of admiring the culture of the Far East.[2] To-day, after dismissing the artists and philosophers of China to the limbo—or corral—which we have constructed for 'Natives', we are apparently even losing our admiration for Hellenism, the civilization to which ours is 'affiliated'. When we have closed this last door against the humanities, we shall have touched the nadir of our fall from grace.

The best cure for such insanity is ridicule, and we can apply it

[1] The phenomenon of Race-feeling is examined in II. C (ii) (a) 1, vol. i, below.
[2] See the note at the end of I. B (iv), Annex, below, and p. 152, footnote 3, above.

by observing how exquisitely ridiculous our 'Anglo-Saxon attitude' looks when it is struck by other people. Consider, for instance, the following missive which was presented in A.D. 1793 by the philosophic Emperor Ch'ien Lung to a British envoy for delivery to his master the mad King George III of Britain:

'You, O King, live beyond the confines of many seas; nevertheless, impelled by your humble desire to partake of the benefits of our civilization, you have despatched a mission respectfully bearing your memorial. . . . I have perused your memorial: the earnest terms in which it is couched reveal a respectful humility on your part, which is highly praiseworthy.

'In consideration of the fact that your Ambassador and his deputy have come a long way with your memorial and tribute, I have shown them high favour and have allowed them to be introduced into my presence. To manifest my indulgence, I have entertained them at a banquet and made them numerous gifts. . . .

'As to your entreaty to send one of your nationals to be accredited to my Celestial Court and to be in control of your country's trade with China, this request is contrary to all usage of my Dynasty and cannot possibly be entertained. . . . If you assert that your reverence for Our Celestial Dynasty fills you with a desire to acquire our civilization, our ceremonies and code of laws differ so completely from your own that, even if your Envoy were able to acquire the rudiments of our civilization, you could not possibly transplant our manners and customs to your alien soil. Therefore, however adept the Envoy might become, nothing would be gained thereby.

'Swaying the wide world, I have but one aim in view, namely, to maintain a perfect governance and to fulfil the duties of the State. Strange and costly objects do not interest me. If I have commanded that the tribute offerings sent by you, O King, are to be accepted, this was solely in consideration for the spirit which prompted you to despatch them from afar. Our Dynasty's majestic virtue has penetrated into every country under Heaven, and kings of all nations have offered their costly tribute by land and sea. As your Ambassador can see for himself, we possess all things. I set no value on objects strange or ingenious, and have no use for your country's manufactures.'[1]

The Emperor's attitude evokes a smile to-day when we read his words in the light of all that has happened during the period of rather more than a century that has elapsed since those words were indited. It seems scarcely credible to us, here and now, that a Manchu philosopher-king, receiving a plain announcement of the approaching impact of the West newly armed with the tremendous weapons of Industrialism, should have shown himself so blind to the signs of the times. Yet there is no doubt that

---

[1] Quoted from Whyte, A. F.: *China and Foreign Powers* (London 1927, Milford), Appendix, p. 41.

Ch'ien Lung was an able and experienced statesman with a distinguished mind; and the sequel to the episode does not really expose him as a fool. Rather, it suggests that a contemporary Western statesman of equal ability, if he had been standing in Ch'ien Lung's shoes, would have reacted in the same way; and this suggests, in turn, that our own attitude towards 'Natives' may come to appear equally obtuse a century hence.

Again, we may recall the story of the Sharīf of Morocco who, returning home after a visit to Europe at some date which was later than the establishment of the French protectorate over his country, was yet heard to exclaim, as he sighted the Moroccan coast: 'What a comfort to be getting back to Civilization!' When our great-grandchildren make the same remark as their ship enters the Solent or the Mersey, will the joke be published in the comic papers of China and—Morocco?

We may also reflect upon a conversation which took place between a British statesman and a Persian visitor some time after the peace-settlement which followed the General War of 1914-18. The Persian was saying that he could not understand how the British Government, which he acknowledged to be intrinsically honourable and liberal-minded, had brought itself to pursue in Persia, from A.D. 1907 onwards, a policy which he could only describe as a cynical sacrifice of the rights and welfare of an innocent, friendly, and defenceless country on the altar of the Anglo-Russian *entente*. The British statesman, who had been largely responsible for the policy and who was of a frank, straightforward disposition, admitted to his visitor that Persia had been deliberately sacrificed; 'but', he added, 'the British policy which you criticize was not pursued by us in a cynical frame of mind. In matters of statesmanship, choices are usually limited; and in this case, with only two alternatives before us, we were simply choosing the lesser of two evils: the risk of allowing Russia to destroy the independence of Persia rather than the risk of seeing Russia remain neutral or even take the German side in the then imminent event of a European War. If, seven years later, Germany had started the Great War with Russia as an ally or indeed as a neutral, she would certainly have won the War; and that would not only have been the end of the British Empire. It would have been the end of Civilization. When Civilization was at stake, how could we act otherwise than we did? Put yourself in our place, and answer me with your hand on your heart.'

At this the Persian, who had at first been mildly puzzled and aggrieved, completely lost his temper. His heart burnt within him and a torrent of denunciation issued from his lips: 'Your policy was infinitely more wicked than I had suspected! The cynicism of it is beyond imagination! You have the effrontery to look me in the face and tell me complacently that you have deliberately sacrificed the unique treasure which Persia preserves for Humanity—the priceless jewel of Civilization—on the off-chance of saving your worthless Western Society from the catastrophe which its own greed and pugnacity were inevitably bringing upon its head! Put myself in your place, indeed! What should I have cared, and what do I care now, if Europe perish so long as Persia lives!' Therewith, he indignantly took his leave; and the British statesman found himself unable to feel certain that his visitor's indignation was unjustified or his point of view unreasonable. Was it Europe or Persia that held the seed from which the life of the future was to spring? Perhaps the answer to that question could not, after all, be taken for granted. Perhaps it could only be given by Time and only be read correctly by some historian looking back upon the year 1907 of the Christian Era from a distance of many centuries.

I will conclude these illustrations with a trivial incident which I witnessed myself at a meeting of the Board of Studies in History of a prominent and cosmopolitan Western university. We were considering the subjects for theses that were being offered by candidates for higher degrees, and I had fallen into a stupor as I listened to one title after another being recited and approved. Some of the subjects offered and accepted for research bore upon the minutiae of administration in the Kingdom of England and in one or two other parochial states of the Western World in the Middle Ages; others related to the diplomacy of the Western Balance of Power in more recent times. Suddenly I was roused by hearing the Secretary read out a proposal to investigate the social and political conditions of India in the age of the Guptas, and my mind immediately began to work. More light on one of those universal states that stand out as landmarks in the histories of civilizations; a study of the age in which Hellenism was finally expelled from the Indic World and in which the Buddha became a prophet without honour in his own country? Here at last was something on our agenda that might make our meeting worth while. This train of thought, which went through my mind in a flash, was cut short by a titter which ran round the Board. 'May we ask the Secretary to read that name again?' said a member on my left; and, at the repetition of the word 'Guptas', the titter turned to loud laughter. I found that I was laughing, too—at the laughter of my colleagues—and, glancing round the room, I caught the eye of an Orientalist, sitting opposite. Silently we signalled to each other that we were enjoying a private joke of our own.

In Western minds the egocentric illusion, illustrated above, is fortified by the catchword of 'the Unchanging East', which confounds the three living civilizations of Islam, Hinduism, and the Far East under the nondescript epithet 'Oriental', and which carries the assumption that they all differ in equal measure from the civilization of the West and that they are indistinguishable from one another and from any of the extinct civilizations except the Hellenic and perhaps the Minoan. In reality, Islam has less in common with either the Hindu or the Far Eastern Civilization than it has with the Orthodox Christian and the Western,[1] while the gulfs that divide the Hindu and the Far Eastern Civilization from ours are possibly not so wide as the gulf which divides them from one another. As for the extinct civilizations, we have found no evidence that any living civilization, either Western or non-Western, is in any way related to the Egyptiac; and it is certain that none of them are related to any of the four extinct civilizations of the New World.[2] The catchword of 'the Unchanging East' collapses at a touch; and we are left wondering how this vulgar error can ever have obtained its hold. It appears to be based on two confusions of thought, one general and the other particular.

In the first place, Western students of non-Western histories —unconsciously influenced in their historical thought by their social environment—have concentrated their attention upon the political plane because this is the plane on which the Western Society chiefly lives and in which Western minds are chiefly interested; and in many histories the political plane presents at first sight the appearance of a static condition of irresponsible despotism. This appearance is largely an illusion; and Western students might have seen through it if they had studied non-Western politics more thoroughly, even without looking deeper. If, however, their mental vision had penetrated through the political plane to the cultural plane beneath, they would have realized that, even if the first appearances on the political plane had been entirely confirmed by closer investigation, the static condition, on this plane, of the societies which they were studying was of little or no significance in view of the wealth and life which reveal themselves in the histories of these same societies as soon as the observer's attention is transferred from the superficial to the

[1] On this point, see two studies by C. H. Becker: 'Der Islam als Problem' and 'Der Islam im Rahmen einer allgemeinen Kulturgeschichte', which are both published in his *Islam Studien* (Leipzig 1924, Quelle und Mayer).

[2] *Pace* the 'Diffusionist School' of contemporary British anthropologists. For a discussion of the issue between the Diffusion Theory and the Uniformity Theory, see I. C (iii) (*b*), Annex, below.

fundamental plane of social existence. By ignoring the cultural plane[1] and by equating politics with Life, Western observers arrive at an opinion about non-Western histories which exposes the confusion of their thought as much as it ministers to their self-esteem.

The other confusion of thought that is responsible for the catch-word of 'the Unchanging East' arises from the historical accident of the origins of our Western religion. The germ of creative power from which the Christian Church has sprung was derived by the internal proletariat of the Hellenic Society from Syriac 'Natives' who were forcibly enrolled in its ranks;[2] these recruits contributed to the common stock not only their personal religious experience but an inherited religious literature which was adopted by the Church as its 'Old Testament'; for Westerners brought up in the Christian tradition, the 'Old Testament' came to stand for Oriental Literature *par excellence*; and no part of the 'Old Testament' has made such a general appeal to the Western imagination as the stories of the Hebrew Patriarchs. In these stories, the characters and events are mythical, but the social background against which they are set is the life along the border between the North Arabian Steppe and the cultivated lands of Syria as this life was actually lived by the Hebrew and Aramaean tribes in their heroic age (*circa* 1425–1125 B.C.), when they were just breaking out of the Desert into the Sown and were beginning to exchange a Nomadic for a sedentary system of economy. The conditions of this life in this age, as portrayed in the Book of Genesis, have made a deep impression on Western minds, partly owing to the great literary power of many of the passages[3] and partly because the conditions themselves are so picturesquely different from those of our Western life in any age. With their minds thus prepared, our modern Western travellers have visited the Holy Land of Christianity and have observed, with mingled feelings of astonishment and of delight, that, in the Transjordanian borderland between the Desert and the Sown, the life which is being lived to-day corresponds, in point after point, with the description in Genesis of the life of the Patriarchs. Since, in their tradition, the 'Old Testament' is tantamount to Oriental Literature and its scene of action to 'the East', they interpret these correspondences between their reading and their observations as evidences of an 'Unchanging

---

[1] For the Western habit of ignoring this plane, see pp. 151–3, above. For examples of societies which are static on the political and dynamic on the cultural plane, see the two passages quoted, in III. C (iii), vol. iii, on pp. 384–5 and 388, below, from Sir Charles Eliot.

[2] See pp. 40 and 57, above.

[3] This literary quality has not been lost in the translation of the Old Testament into Greek and Latin and the modern Teutonic vernaculars.

East', without reflecting that they are making a generalization about half the World on the strength of the local conditions in a small area with a peculiar character of its own.

In reality, our travellers have encountered, not an 'Unchanging East,' but an unchanging North Arabian Steppe. On the Steppe, the physical environment is so hard and so imperious a task-master to human beings that their ability to adapt themselves to it is confined within narrow limits. Life on the Steppe is a perpetual battle with Nature which is lost in a moment if ever the human combatants break their formation or relax their discipline; and there is only one kind of formation and one kind of discipline that enables them to hold their own. In other words, the North Arabian Steppe imposes upon all human beings in all ages who have the hardihood to be its inhabitants a rigid and unvarying way of life.[1] Yet this steppe, after all, is an infinitesimal fraction of an 'Unchanging East' which, in the popular Western imagination, is conceived as extending from the Mediterranean to the Pacific and perhaps from China to Peru. If the Old Testament had happened to contain equally minute and vivid descriptions of life in Ur, at the time when Abraham's father was supposed to have migrated thence to Haran,[2] or of life in Egyptian Thebes, at the time when Abraham was supposed to have visited Pharaoh's court,[3] the modern Western traveller, with these descriptions in his mind, would certainly not have found them reproduced with any remarkable closeness of correspondence in life as he saw it being lived in Baghdad and Cairo nowadays. It follows that, in all probability, he would not have been caught by the catchword of 'the Unchanging East' if an accident of his Western tradition had not focused his attention upon one small and unrepresentative fraction of the field.

Let us imaginarily invert the situation by constructing the intellectual history of a fictitious Baghdadī boy, who has been born since the arrival of the British at Baghdad in 1917 and whose father has determined to give him a thoroughly Western scientific education in order to fit him for making his way in the Westernized East of to-morrow. The father begins by giving the boy some direct insight into Western scientific methods by showing him Western scientists at work in his own country. He takes him to see the archaeological excavations at Ur. Let us assume that the boy is as intelligent as his father, and that this visit arouses in him a general interest in modern Western Archaeology, ranging over the whole field as far as it has been explored by Western scholars. Among other things, the life of the lake-dwellers in the Alps in the

[1] For a description of the Nomadic way of life, see Part III. A, vol. iii, pp. 7–22, below.
[2] Gen. xi. 31.
[3] Gen. xii. 10–20.

'Eneolithic Age' is sure to appeal to the Baghdadī boy for the same reasons which invest the conditions of life on the North Arabian Steppe with a special interest for Western readers of the Book of Genesis. The boy's interest in the lake-dwellers will broaden out into a study of all aspects of their life, including the manner in which they adapted themselves to the imperious conditions of the local terrain and climate in keeping their cattle. He will follow the ancient lacustrine herdsmen as they drive their cattle up from the lake-side to ever higher upland pastures with the advance of spring and then gradually down again from alp to alp to the water's edge with the retreat of summer. This study will become his hobby; and when the time comes for him to visit Europe, he will make a bee-line first for Switzerland. There, herded by some tourist agency into Alpine hotels, he will observe, with astonishment and delight, that the pastoral life with which he is familiar from the books about the ancient lake-dwellers which his father gave him to read at home is being lived, apparently unchanged, by the Swiss herdsmen of to-day. With what extraordinary persistence social phenomena perpetuate themselves in this strange and romantic Western World! How different from 'Irāq, where the disinterred vestiges of Ur and Babylon and Nineveh proclaim to any Baghdadī who sets eyes on them that, in his country, Life is a flux and history a synonym for change. And now this Baghdadī has discovered 'the Unchanging West'. What a tale to tell to his countrymen when he goes home again!

Of course our intelligent young man from Baghdad would not have rushed into this ludicrously erroneous generalization if the romance of the Alpine pastures had not absorbed his attention to the extent of preventing him from studying with equal thoroughness the histories of those sites on Western soil that are now occupied by the cities of Zürich and Lausanne—not to speak of Paris and London and Berlin and New York and Chicago. If he had studied these likewise, he could not conceivably have imagined that the West was 'unchanging' by comparison with 'Irāq (immense though the changes in 'Irāq have been, on every plane of social life, over the span of five or six thousand years within which we happen to know something about the country's history). He has been misled by a failure to realize that he has been making a generalization about half the World on the strength of local conditions in a small area with a peculiar character of its own. While the Alps impose upon all human beings in all ages who have the hardihood to be their inhabitants as rigid and as unvarying a way of life as is imposed by the North Arabian Steppe, it is likewise true that the Alps are as small a fraction of the Western World as the North Arabian Steppe is of the East. An extravaganza? Yet *quid rides?* For *mutato nomine de te fabula narratur*,[1] you Western traveller, whoever you may have been, who first brought home to us the catchword of 'the Unchanging East'.[2]

It is possible that neither this catchword nor its obverse, the egocentric illusion, would have sufficed in itself to support the misconception of 'the Unity of History' on a Western basis, without being reinforced by an underlying misconception of the process of growth as a movement in a straight line.

This is nothing but the primitive image of the magic bean-stalk in the fairy-story, which shoots up perpendicularly from the earth and grows on and on, without ever failing to draw the sap after it into its perpetually receding tendrils or ever crumpling under its perpetually increasing weight, until it strikes its head against the under side of the firmament. While our Western historians are still thinking in terms of this image, our Western physical scientists have long since discarded it, in their studies of evolution in non-human fields, in favour of what we may call the image of the pollarded willow. The workaday willow, like the magic bean-stalk, starts its growth perpendicularly in a single line; but, before it has time to grow top-heavy, a man comes along with an axe and pollards its head. The willow's upward movement in a single perpendicular line has been cut short violently by an external force. Will the tree die of the shock, or will it adapt its manner of growth to the new conditions that have been imposed on it from outside? Possessing the will to live, the tree chooses the latter alternative; and from its mutilated summit it now puts forth half a dozen shoots instead of one and sends these up in all directions, not perpendicularly but at a slant. Each of these shoots attempts, in its own growth, to overcome the effects of the blow which the trunk has received and to carry the life of the tree forward one stage farther. Most of the shoots come to nothing and wilt away; a minority—perhaps a single shoot—grows on until the man comes round with his axe and pays it the compliment of pollarding it in its turn; and so the story repeats itself: from its mutilated head the next cluster of shoots arises.

---

[1] Horace: *Satires*, i (i), ll. 69–70.
[2] It may be objected that even an ingenuous and unobservant Oriental traveller who visited the Alps to-day with a picture in his mind of the local conditions of life in the 'Eneolithic Age' could not really fail to notice, side by side with many points of correspondence, at least as many and as remarkable evidences of change. It can only be replied that Western travellers have contrived to ignore similar evidences on the North Arabian Steppe, where the conditions portrayed in the Book of Genesis have been changed profoundly, since that portrait was drawn, by at least two far-reaching innovations: the introduction of the horse and the introduction of fire-arms (not to speak of dry farming and motor-cars, which are both still too recent introductions to have had time to produce their full effects).

This is the true image of evolution as it has come to be conceived by our Western botanists and zoologists.[1] At an earlier point in this Study, we have already attempted to transpose it into terms of human history.[2] We have suggested that the histories of individuals and communities and societies fall into successive chapters, in each of which a number of representatives of whichever the species may be are confronted by some identical challenge which imposes an ordeal. Under each of these common ordeals, the parties react in different ways. The majority succumb outright; some just manage to survive, but at the cost of such wear and tear that they are good for nothing afterwards; others discover a response to the challenge which is so satisfactory that it not only carries them through the ordeal of the moment but puts them in a favourable posture for undergoing the next; others, again, follow these path-finders as sheep follow their leader into a gap which he has forced through a hedge. This seems to be a more illuminating conception of evolution than the old-fashioned image of the bean-stalk, and we shall be guided by this conception throughout our Study. Meanwhile, the old image still cramps the thought of many Western historians.

In their 'periodizations', our historians still dispose their periods in a single series end to end, like the sections of a bamboo-stem between joint and joint or the sections of the patent extensible handle on the end of which an up-to-date modern chimney sweep pokes his brush up a flue. On the brush-handle which our contemporary Western historians have inherited from their predecessors as part of their stock-in-trade, there were originally two joints only—the 'Ancient' and the 'Modern', corresponding to the 'Old Testament' and the 'New Testament' of the Bible and to the dual back-to-back reckoning by years 'before Christ' and by 'years of Our Lord' in our traditional Janus-faced system of chronology. This dichotomy of historical time was a relic of the

---

[1] Of course this conception is not altogether new. It has been conceived in flashes of insight by seers in other times and places: e.g. by Aeschylus, when he addresses Zeus as τὸν πάθει μάθος / θέντα κυρίως ἔχειν (*Agamemnon*, ll. 177–8), and by the author of the Epistle to the Hebrews, when he exclaims (xii, 6): 'For whom the Lord loveth He chasteneth, and scourgeth every son whom He receiveth.' These images represent the Power that wields the axe as pollarding the willow with the conscious purpose and expectation of making it grow better than it could grow if it were left to itself. That is to say, the pruner's policy is assumed to be directed towards the same end as the willow's instinctive *élan vital*. The blow which the tree dreads is struck for its good; the shock which it suffers is administered as a tonic to its vitality. This assumption, however, is not essential. The conception still holds good if we assume, instead, that the axe is wielded not with intent to invigorate but with intent to mutilate and stunt and kill. On this assumption, the Power that wields the axe manifests itself not as God but as the Devil, who does God's work in spite of himself 'und muss, als Teufel, schaffen'. Conversely, in the sight of the Devil, the willow transforms itself into the Hydra—the monster which baffles Hêraklês by sprouting two new heads in place of each head that the hero strikes off. This line of thought is followed up in II. C (ii) (b) i, vol. i, below.

[2] See I. B (ii), above.

Weltanschauung of the internal proletariat of the Hellenic Society, in which the proletariat expressed its sense of alienation from the Hellenic dominant minority by making an absolute antithesis between the old dispensation of the Hellenic Civilization and the new dispensation of the Christian Church, and succumbed to the egocentric illusion by treating the transition from the one dispensation to the other as the turning-point of all human history.[1] The retention of these two periods in our modern Western historians' conventional scheme is due to that consciousness of 'affiliation' to the Hellenic Society which still pervades all cultivated minds in a Western Society which has had the Christian Church for its chrysalis. The Primitive Christians, however, when they divided History into two periods and two only, were assuming that its origin was recent[2] and its end not far off. As time has gone on, our Western historians have found it convenient to extend their telescopic brush-handle by adding a third section, which they have called 'medieval' because they have chosen to insert it between the other two. They have not yet realized that they are the victims of a malicious trick. If only they would remove their heads from the chimney for a moment and take a walk round the house, they would observe that the builder is at work all the time on the roof and that he is heightening the chimney-stack faster than they are adding fresh sections to the handle of their brush. At this rate they have no more chance of ever poking their brush up to the top of the flue than the Danaïds have of filling their sieves or than Sisyphus has of planting his boulder on the summit of the mountain.

While the division between 'Ancient' and 'Modern' stands for the break between Hellenic and Western history, the division between 'Medieval' and 'Modern' merely stands for the transition from one chapter in Western history to another. The break (if there was one) which this transition involved was so much slighter than the other break that the difference in degree amounts to a difference in kind.[3] The formula 'Ancient+Medieval+Modern' is thus wrongly constructed. It should be rewritten 'Hellenic+ Western (Western=Medieval+Modern)'. Yet even this version is not altogether correct; for the transition from one chapter of

---

[1] This Christian scheme of history was not, of course, struck out in an instantaneous flash of thought. The point of view which it embodies had been gradually taking shape in the religious thought of Judaism and Zoroastrianism. (See Gall, Freiherr von: Βασιλεία τοῦ Θεοῦ (Heidelberg 1926, Winter), *passim*.)

[2] Archbp. Ussher's dating of the Creation in the year 4000 (or 4004!) B.C. and the Jewish and other varieties of the chronological reckoning by 'Years of the World' all placed the origin of the material universe at about the date at which we, with our rather greater knowledge, at present place the origin of the species of human societies called civilizations. How recently our greater knowledge has been acquired is pointed out by Mr. Lionel Curtis in the passage quoted at the end of this Part of the present Study (I. C (iii) (e), Annex, on p. 464, below).

[3] On this point, see I. B (iv) *ad finem* and I. B (v), above.

Western history to another about the year 1475 of the Christian Era which receives recognition in the division between 'Medieval' and 'Modern' is by no means the only transition of that kind and that degree which has occurred in the course of our Western history up to date. There is no warrant for laying greater stress on 1475 than on 1075 or on 1875. Round about each of these other dates, we can observe transitions which are not less strongly pronounced than that which we find in the neighbourhood of 1475;[1] and if, in working out a scheme for the internal 'periodization' of Western history, we decide to begin a new chapter about 1475 and to call this chapter by a special name, we must also begin other new chapters, with names of their own, about 1075 and 1875. The conventional formula will then have to be revised a second time and will come out as follows: 'Hellenic+Western (Western = Western I (*circa* A.D. 675–1075)+Western II (*circa* 1075–1475) +Western III (*circa* 1475–1875)+Western IV (*circa* 1875–x)).' The formula is now correct as far as it goes, but it is not yet complete. In order to complete it, we should have first to expand the term on the Hellenic side of the main copula by the operation which we have carried out already on the Western side. Then we should have to attach Minoan history by another copula in front of Hellenic history and expand this additional element in the same way; and after that we should have to treat the other civilizations on uniform lines. We should find it impossible to bring them all within a single comprehensive formula, however ingeniously we handled their relations. Fortunately, we need not pursue the fantasy further. It has served its turn in demonstrating that the conventional formula 'Ancient+Medieval+Modern' is not only inadequate but misleading.[2]

[1] For the transition in Western history round about A.D. 1875 see Part I. A *ad init.*, above, and III. C (ii) (*b*), vol. iii, p. 375, footnote 2, below. The equivalent transition round about A.D. 1075 was acutely felt by Westerners in that age. It produced in them a profound *malaise* which was really a form of growing pains, but which found expression, in terms of Christian theology, in a revival of the Primitive Christian belief that the end of the World was at hand. In the Primitive Church the Second Coming of Christ was expectedly immediately to follow His Ascension. At the transition from the first to the second chapter of our Western history, it was thought to be due on the thousandth anniversary of the Ascension.

[2] For a particularly effective as well as authoritative criticism of the conventional tripartite formula, see 'Der Gang der antiken Geschichte' by Eduard Meyer (printed in his *Kleine Schriften* (Halle 1910, Niemeyer)). For an attack upon the older dichotomy of history into 'Ancient' and 'Modern', see the passage from Freeman's essay on 'The Unity of History' (*Comparative Politics*, pp. 336–7) which is quoted on p. 341, below. The transition in the nineteenth century from the 'post-medieval' modern age to an 'ultra-modern' age whose beginning marks as much of a new departure as the transition to the 'post-medieval' age from the medieval is emphasized in the following passage by the late Professor J. B. Bury:

'The field of what we call "Modern History" has a roughly marked natural boundary at the point where it starts, towards the end of the fifteenth century. . . . But the phrase is used to cover all post-medieval history, and therefore the hither limit is always shifting. . . . The question arises whether this conventional nomenclature is any longer appropriate, whether all post-medieval history can be scientifically classified as a period, with

(c) THE PHILOSOPHICAL CONTEMPORANEITY OF ALL
REPRESENTATIVES OF THE SPECIES

We have now dealt with two incompatible objections to our plan of comparative study: on the one hand, that our twenty-one societies have no common characteristic beyond that of all being 'intelligible fields of historical study'; on the other, that 'the Unity of Civilization' reduces the apparent plurality of civilizations to the singular number. We have shown that the twenty-one societies which we have mustered in our survey are so many representatives of a single species of the genus. Yet our critics, though compelled to go with us thus far, may make a stand at this point and still deny that our twenty-one civilizations are comparable on the ground that they are not contemporary. While seven[1] of them are still alive, the other fourteen are extinct; and at least three of these fourteen—the Egyptiac, the Sumeric, and the Minoan—go back to 'the dawn of history'. These three certainly, and perhaps others, are separated from the living civilizations by the whole span of 'historical time'.

The answer to this objection is that Time is relative, and that the span of something less than six thousand years which bridges the interval between the emergence of those three earliest known civilizations and our own day has to be measured for the purpose of our study on the relevant time-scale: that is to say, not in terms of the lifetimes of human beings but in terms of the time-spans of the civilizations themselves. Now, in surveying the relations of civilizations in Time, the highest number of successive generations that we have met with in any case is three; and in each case these three between them more than cover our span of six thousand years, since the last term in each series is a civilization that is still

the same 'right and meaning as the Middle Ages. "Ancient History" is of course a merely conventional and convenient, unscientific term; is this true of "Modern History" also? It may be thought that the answer is affirmative. It may seem probable that the changes which began at the end of the eighteenth century, the great movements of thought which have thrilled the nineteenth century, the implications of the far-reaching vistas of knowledge which have been opened, mark as new and striking a departure as any to which our records go back, and constitute a *Neuzeit* in the fullest sense of the word; that in the nineteenth as in the sixteenth century Man entered into a new domain of ideas; that of the nineteenth as of the sixteenth are we justified in saying

Ab integro saeclorum nascitur ordo.

If so, our nomenclature should be altered. The three centuries after Columbus should be called by some other name, such as "post-medieval", and "modern" should be appropriated to the period ushered in by the French Revolution and the formation of the American Commonwealth, until in turn a new period shall claim a name which can never be permanently attached.' (Bury, J. B.: 'The Place of Modern History in the Perspective of Knowledge', in *Selected Essays* (Cambridge 1930, University Press), pp. 55–6.)

[1] Counting the Far Eastern Society in Korea and Japan and the Orthodox Christian Society in Russia as separate from the main bodies of the respective societies.

alive.[1] If we were to ask the opinion of recognized authorities on the study of any species of any form of Life as to whether, in principle, it is sound practice to compare with one another representatives of a species which are spread over as many as three successive generations, they would answer that it is incontestably sound practice to draw instances for comparison from a series of generations extending to many times that number, because it is one of the universal features of Life on this planet, as we know it by observation in any of its forms, that it takes many more generations than three for specific characters to change so far as to produce any specific difference.

The fact that, in our survey of civilizations, we have found in no case a higher number of successive generations than three, when read together with the fact that we have found no more than twenty-one representatives of the species altogether, means that this species is very young in terms of its own time-scale. Moreover, its absolute age up to date is very short compared with that of the sister species called 'Primitive Societies'. We have noted already that we cannot date the emergence of the earliest known civilizations quite as far back as six thousand years before our own time. On the other hand, we have reason to believe that the Human Race has been in existence for several hundred thousand years;[2] and primitive societies are coeval with Mankind itself—or rather, they are anterior to Mankind, since social life is a condition which the evolution of Man out of Sub-Man presupposes and without which that evolution could not conceivably have taken place.[3]

---

[1] The several series in question are Minoan–Hellenic–Western, Minoan–Hellenic–Orthodox Christian, Minoan–Syriac–Islamic, and Sumeric–Indic–Hindu (supposing that the relation which we have conjectured between the Sumeric and the Indic Civilization is established).

[2] The following figures are suggested by Sir James Jeans in *The Universe around Us* (Cambridge 1929, University Press), p. 13:

	Age of the Earth	about	2,000,000,000	years
,,	Life	,,	300,000,000	,,
,,	Man	,,	300,000	,,
,,	Civilizations	,,	6,000	,,

[3] This statement may be sufficiently supported by citing two authorities, one Hellenic and the other Western:

Ἄνθρωπος φύσει πολιτικὸν ζῷον, κα ἰδ ἄπολις διὰ φύσιν καὶ οὐ διὰ τύχην ἤτοι φαῦλός ἐστιν ἢ κρείττων ἢ ἄνθρωπος . . . ἡ πόλις καὶ φύσει καὶ πρότερον ἢ ἕκαστος . . . ὁ δὲ μὴ δυνάμενος κοινωνεῖν ἢ μηδὲν δεόμενος δι' αὐτάρκειαν οὐθὲν μέρος πόλεως, ὥστε ἢ θηρίον ἢ θεός.

'Man is by nature a social animal; and an unsocial person who is unsocial naturally and not accidentally is either unsatisfactory or superhuman. . . . Society is a natural phenomenon and is prior to the individual. . . . And any one who is unable to live a common life or who is so self-sufficient that he has no need to do so is no member of Society, which means that he is either a beast or a god.' (Aristotle: *Politics*, i. 1, 9–12 (p. 1253 A).)

'Man is precluded by both his bodily and his spiritual constitution from existing as an isolated individual. . . . Man really belongs to the gregarious animals: that is to say, to those races of animals in which the single individuals live permanently in fixed associations (*Verbände*). Such associations can be described as social associations (*soziale*

We can now see that the objection which we are answering rests on a simple mistake in reasoning. The 'historical time' which is represented as being so vast a span that it fixes a great gulf between the histories of civilizations which lie at opposite extremities of it is really a synonym for the time which has elapsed since the earliest date at which representatives of the species 'civilizations' are known to have existed. Therefore, *ex hypothesi*, some representatives of this species go back to 'the dawn of history' in this sense; and, with 'history' implicitly defined in this way, the statement is tautologous and its chronological implications are void of significance. The significant chronological measures are, first, the ratio between the time during which the species has existed up to date and the average duration of its representatives as indicated by the highest number of generations that we can find; and, second, the ratio between the time during which the species has existed up to date and the time during which primitive societies have existed since the date when, under their aegis, Sub-Man transformed himself into Man. If we take the antiquity of Man to be something like 300,000 years, then the antiquity of civilizations, so far from being coeval with human history, will be found to cover less than 2 per cent. of its present span: less than 6,000 years out of 300,000±. On this time-scale, the lives of our twenty-one civilizations—distributed over not more than three generations of societies and concentrated within less than one-fiftieth part of the lifetime of Mankind—must be regarded, on a philosophic view, as contemporary with one another.[1]

Verbände) in virtue of the fact that they unite a number of homogeneous single individuals in a fellowship.

'The entire spiritual development of Man presupposes the existence of group-associations with definite limits. First and foremost, it is impossible that Man's most important tool, speech—the first thing that makes him human and the first thing that created the conditions for building up our formulated thinking—can have been fashioned in the single human being or in the relation of parents to children. Speech grows out of the need for communication between equals who are bound together by common interests and by a regulated system of intercourse. Besides, the invention of tools, the acquisition of fire, the taming of domestic animals, the settlement in fixed habitations, and so on, are only possible within a group, or at any rate have only attained importance through something which began as the happy idea of some individual becoming the property of the whole association. That at any rate custom, law, religion, and every other kind of spiritual possession can only have arisen in such associations is a fact which needs no exposition. This means that organization in such associations (hordes, tribes), which we come across empirically everywhere where we find the presence of human beings, is not only coeval with Man but is far older than he is. It is the precedent condition without which the Human Race could not have come into existence at all.' (Eduard Meyer: 'Elemente der Anthropologie', *Geschichte des Altertums*, i (i), 4th edition: (Stuttgart and Berlin 1921, Cotta), pp. 5–8. Compare Bagehot, W.: *Physics and Politics*, 10th edition (London 1894, Kegan Paul), pp. 136–7.)

[1] The following illustration of the philosophic contemporaneity of civilizations is trivial but illuminating:

'Jamais, dans les variations continuelles de la mode, les Minoennes n'eurent la noblesse d'attitude que donneront aux Grecques et aux Romaines les plis des voiles flottants et la retombée naturelle des molles draperies. Ce qui les caractérise plutot, à la grande surprise de ceux qui les voient pour la première fois, c'est le cachet occidental

(d) THE PHILOSOPHICAL EQUIVALENCE OF ALL REPRESENTATIVES
OF THE SPECIES

At this point our critics may perhaps concede that civilizations are comparable, but they will probably object that this comparability is merely formal. Is not its scope confined to certain external characteristics? And when we take account of inner values, do we not find that the differences in value between one civilization and another are so vast that no comparative judgements of value can be made as between them? In respect of value, therefore, must we not draw an absolute distinction between the valuable civilizations and the valueless? And, supposing that the valuable category proved to be represented by not more than one specimen, would not that bring us back, by another road, to 'the Unity of Civilization' ('Civilization' in the singular being equated with the rare element of value in 'civilizations' in the plural)?

The first answer to this objection is one that we have given before, when 'the Unity of Civilization' was under discussion. Value is intrinsically subjective; and we shall find that the members of each civilization, if forced to abandon the assertion that their own civilization is the only civilization that exists, will fall back upon the assertion that it is the only civilization that possesses any value. This is simply the old egocentric illusion in a new form.

The second answer is that value, like Time, is relative. If we examine our species 'civilizations' *in vacuo*, we are bound *ex hypothesi* to arrange them on a value-scale on which they are distributed from extremity to extremity, just as we had to distribute them over the whole span of 'historical time' when 'historical time' was equated with the time during which the species

de toilettes qui semblent parfois copiées sur les derniers modèles de Paris. Certaines dames de Cnosse, de Haghia Triad[h]a ou de Pseira donnent d'abord une extraordinaire impression de luxe et d'élégante recherche par le bariolage des étoffes et la richesse des ornements: les couleurs s'harmonisent et s'opposent; les dessins les plus variés se combinent gracieusement, et l'étoffe est parsemée à profusion de plissés et de bouillonnés, de broderies et de passementeries multicolores. Mais plus étonnantes encore sont les formes qu'affectent les deux pièces dont se composent [? compose] le vêtement, la jupe et le corsage. Le coupe en rappelle à chaque instant les modes les plus singulières, parfois les plus extravagantes, qu'on ait imaginées depuis la Renaissance jusqu'à nos jours.

'De pareilles ressemblances seraient inexplicables, si elles ne provenaient pas d'une filiation commune et d'une évolution parallèle, quoique non synchronique. Il fut un temps, bien avant l'âge du métal, où les races destinées à vivre dans l'Égéide et celles qui devaient peupler l'Europe occidentale s'habillaient pareillement. Du costume néolithique et peut-être paléolithique sortirent, par un développement plus ou moins prompt, le costume minoen et le costume moderne. Avec les différences résultant de climats différents ou dues à des fantaisies individuelles, les Égéens ont, dans l'espace de deux millénaires, fait subir au costume féminin les modifications que les peuples septentrionaux, retardés par la longue prédominance des modes grecques et romaines, ont mis trois millénaires de plus à produire. Ayant à faire des costumes qui prenaient leur point d'appui à la taille, les couturières de l'époque minoenne et celles d'aujourd'hui n'ont pu satisfaire l'éternelle coquetterie des femmes qu'en donnant à des créations forcément indépendantes des formes semblantes et les mêmes accessoires.' (Glotz, G.: *La Civilisation Égéenne* (Paris 1923, La Renaissance du Livre), pp. 88–9.)

'civilizations' has been in existence. In order to obtain a value-scale for civilizations which, instead of being simply relative, is in some sense absolute, we must compare them, in respect of value, not only with one another, but also on the one hand with the common goal of their endeavours, and on the other hand with the primitive societies from which they are distinguished by a common specific difference. We must measure the degrees of value by which they all fall short of the goal of their own endeavours and likewise the degrees by which they all surpass the greatest common measure of value that the primitive societies have attained; and in making these several judgements of value we must assess the value of each civilization at the highest degree at which it is known to have stood at any time in its history.

This last proviso is important because civilizations are not static conditions of societies but dynamic movements[1] of an evolutionary kind. They not only cannot stand still, but they cannot reverse their direction without breaking their own law of motion, as motor-cars in a 'one-way street' break the traffic regulations if, instead of passing out through the prescribed exit at the farther end, they reverse their engines and try to back out through the prescribed entrance by which they have come into the street with full cognizance of the 'one-way' rule. If we apply this simile to our twenty-one civilizations, we see that none of them, to our knowledge, has ever yet succeeded in travelling over the whole length of the street and passing out through the exit; and that fourteen of them have come to grief by reversing, in defiance of the rule, before they had completed their transit and then either colliding with one another or being warned off the road as dangers to the public. As for the seven which are to be seen in the street at this moment, we will not attempt, off-hand, to ascertain which of them are already backsliding and which, if any, are still obeying the law of civilizations by moving forward.[2] We have followed out the simile far enough for our present purpose. It is clear that if we wish to measure, on an absolute scale of achievement, the respective performances of all the cars that have ever entered our street, then the points on their courses that have significance for us are the furthest points which they have ever reached respectively from first to last. These points give us the distances by which they have each fallen short of gaining the exit from the street, which is the

---

[1] This is implied in the form of the supposititious Latin word *civilisatio* from which the English word 'civilization' is derived. In Latin, abstract nouns formed from verbal roots by adding the stem '-*tion-*' always connote movements or processes or actions. For the significance of this characteristic of civilizations, see further Part II. B, below.

[2] This problem will be taken up in Part XII, below, after the phenomena of the geneses and growths of civilizations have been examined in Parts II–III and the phenomena of their breakdowns and disintegrations in Parts IV–VIII.

common goal of their endeavours, as well as the distances by which they have each advanced beyond the entrance to the street, which is the point where those old-fashioned horse-drawn vehicles called primitive societies have been compelled by the traffic regulations to halt. We should learn nothing about their relative achievements if we took our measurements from points in their courses after they had begun to backslide, when they would be re-traversing, in the reverse direction, the ground which they had once put behind them in their advance. Again, we should learn nothing if we took our measurements from points in their courses at such an early stage of their forward movements that they were still on ground which even the least successful car that had ever entered the street had managed to put behind it before its back-sliding began. Therefore, for our purpose of comparing per-formances, we must measure off our distances from the furthest points ever attained by the several entrants in their respective courses from first to last, and we must work out our calculations on this basis.

Now if we plot out these twenty-one points on a plan of our street, to scale, we shall discover that the points are not scattered up and down the whole length of the street from entrance to exit. We shall find them clustered together within the limits of a short section of the thoroughfare. Behind them there will be a relatively long stretch which all entrants, from the least to the most success-ful, have alike succeeded in putting behind them before they have reached the respective limits of their advance. In front of them there will be another stretch which no wheel has ever yet touched; and this stretch of virgin ground will be long not only by com-parison with the short section in which the twenty-one points of farthest attainment are concentrated, but also by comparison with the stretch of common ground at the lower end of the street. Of course, if we were to confine our attention to the section containing the twenty-one points and postulate that this section is to be regarded as being the whole length of the street, we should arrive at a different result; but no significance could be attached to calculations based on such an arbitrary excerpt from the plan. If we take account of the positions of the points in their complete setting—that is, in relation to the street-plan as a whole—we shall see that the greatest distance which separates any one of them from any other is inconsiderable by comparison with the distances which separate them collectively from the entrance to the street in one direction and from the exit in the other. On a philosophic view, they must be regarded as all approximately equal to one another in value.

(e) THE COMPARABILITY OF THE 'FACTS' ENCOUNTERED IN THE
STUDY OF CIVILIZATIONS

At this point our critics may shift their attack from the histories of civilizations to historical 'facts'. Conceding that civilizations are separate representatives of a particular species of societies which are all philosophically contemporary with one another and philosophically equal to one another in value, they may lodge the final objection that while a comparative study of civilizations may thus be proved possible in theory, it is rendered impossible in practice by the intractability of the materials. The histories of civilizations, they may assert (and we will let the assertion pass at the moment, for the sake of the argument) are nothing but strings of historical 'events' and 'facts'; and every historical fact is intrinsically unique and therefore essentially incomparable with any other fact.[1] The catchword that 'History repeats itself' has no truth in it.

To this criticism, which is perhaps the shrewdest of all that have been levelled at us yet, we shall return a soft answer. We shall merely ask our critics to agree with us that a given phenomenon may be unique and therefore incomparable in some respects, while at the same time in other respects it may be a member of a class and therefore comparable with other members of that class in so far as it is covered by the classification.[2] This duality in the nature of certain phenomena is reflected in the use of the word 'individual', which is not only ambiguous but has two at first sight diametrically opposite connotations. Sometimes it is used to convey the idea of uniqueness,[3] sometimes to convey the idea of a cipher about which nothing can be said except that it is a member of a class.[4] We may observe that this ambiguous word is not used of inanimate things. It belongs to the vocabulary of Life. And we will now concede to our critics, in return for the concession which they have made to us, that all the phenomena of Life are phenomena of this Janus-headed build which are at the same time, but in different aspects, both unique and comparable. Every manifestation of Life is in one sense unique, inasmuch as it contains within itself—and this as its essential characteristic—a capacity for variation and mutation which is uniquely creative and original. Yet certain manifestations of Life are shown to be in some sense comparable by the existence of the sciences of Physiology, Biology, Botany, Zoology,

[1] This objection really repeats, apropos of the supposed parts of the histories of civilizations, the objection which has been examined and rebutted in I. C (iii) (a), above, apropos of these histories taken as wholes.
[2] For an analysis, on these lines, of the nature of Rhythm, see IV. C (i), vol. iv, pp. 34-8, below.
[3] This is always the connotation of the word 'individuality'.
[4] In such phrases as 'a commonplace individual', 'a nameless individual', and so on.

and Anthropology. Physiology and Biology compare the material structures and mechanisms of Life statically and dynamically. Botany and Zoology compare individual living creatures in order to classify them and to discover how the classes are related to one another and in what chronological order they have emerged. Zoology includes in its field of comparative study the animal called Man; but, since this animal was gregarious before it became human, so that Mankind cannot exist and cannot be studied except in a social environment,[1] there is evidently room besides for a comparative study of human societies, which are manifestations of Life without being living creatures.[2] A science which makes a comparative study of primitive societies exists under the name of Anthropology;[3] and no one doubts that primitive societies are really susceptible of being studied in this way. There is, however, a widespread notion that the comparative method employed by Anthropology is applicable only to the study of 'the peoples that have no history'; and this notion rests on the assumption that comparative study and historical study are incompatible because 'History does not repeat itself'. If certain societies are being studied comparatively with success, this fact is assumed to imply that such societies are in some sense 'unhistoric'.

'The peoples that have no history', meaning primitive societies, is of course a question-begging phrase; for even if all extant primitive societies were shown to be in a completely static condition at the present day, that would not prove that they had always been in this condition from the beginning. In surveying the histories of civilizations we have found that, in the vicissitudes of societies of that species, an actionless epilogue sometimes follows the denouement of the plot; that the dead trunk sometimes remains intact after the sap has ceased to run.[4] May not primitive societies likewise cumber the ground with their mortal remains? And may not all the extant primitive societies, as we see them now, be the dead trunks of once living trees, and their static conditions be the epilogues of histories which were dynamic in their day? After all, these primitive societies cannot have been in motionless existence from eternity. This species of societies must have come into existence once upon a time; and we know that, after it had been brought into existence through the adoption of a gregarious way of life by a certain species of animal, this animal underwent—under the aegis of the primitive social environment which it had created

---

[1] See p. 173, footnote 3, above.
[2] The relation between societies and the human beings who are their members is discussed in III. C (ii), vol. iii, below.
[3] The application of this name to this science is rather arbitrary. One would expect Anthropology to mean the branch of Zoology that is concerned with the *Genus Homo*.
[4] See I. C (ii), above.

for itself—the mutation from Sub-Man into Man. Here we catch glimpses of a history of primitive societies which must have been as dynamic in its movements and has certainly been as momentous in its consequences as that history of civilizations which is sometimes asserted to be the only history worthy of the name.

Thus the description of primitive societies as 'peoples that have no history' proves to be a misnomer—our actual inability to study their history being due, not to some intrinsic quality of their nature, but to the external and accidental fact that their histories have left no records, or at any rate none that are at present accessible to us.[1] Yet the fact remains that these primitive societies are admittedly susceptible of comparative study as far as we know them. What warrant is there for assuming that the same method of study could not be extended to their past histories if ever the missing records were to come into our hands? And, on this analogy, what warrant is there for assuming that the histories of civilizations—which happen to have left records that are sometimes equated with 'History' *par excellence*—could not be studied comparatively likewise?

Seeing that so many different manifestations of Life do prove to be susceptible of comparative study, at least in certain respects, the onus of proof surely lies with those who assert that the 'facts' and 'events' in the histories of one particular manifestation of Life—the species of societies called civilizations—are exceptions to the prevailing rule in being incomparable not merely in some respects but in all respects whatsoever. *A priori*, the implied abnormality of civilizations appears improbable. Moreover, if we make an empirical investigation into the facts of human life as manifested in civilizations, we actually come across an element of regularity and recurrence, that is to say an aspect to which the comparative method of study can be applied. This element is particularly prominent at the present time in the life of that civilization of which we ourselves happen to be members. While our Western historians are disputing the possibility of making a comparative study of historical facts, our Western men of business are all the time making their living out of a comparative study of the facts of life around them. The perfect example of such a comparative study for practical ends is the collection and analysis of the statistics on which the business transactions of insurance companies are based; and some such study, in which statistics are collected and averages are taken for the purpose of making fore-casts, is at the basis of almost all profitable business enterprises in

[1] For this question of the lost histories of primitive societies, see further Part II. B, pp. 192–5, below.

the Western World nowadays. Now if, in practice, a comparative study of the facts of life in a civilization is being made with such effect that business transactions based on it yield profit, while business transactions that neglect to make it are apt to result in loss, this is surely conclusive and indeed superabundant proof that a comparative study of such facts is theoretically possible. Thus Western business men step in where Western scholars fear to tread; and in this adventure, at any rate, we need not hesitate to follow the lead of our latter-day masters.

We will begin forthwith, at the natural starting-point, by attempting a comparative study of the histories of civilizations in their geneses.

II

THE GENESES OF CIVILIZATIONS

A. THE PROBLEM OF THE GENESES OF CIVILIZATIONS

HAVING satisfied ourselves that societies of the species called civilizations are intrinsically comparable with one another, and having decided to attempt a comparative study of the twenty-one representatives of the species which we find at our command, we may now start our inquiry, at the natural starting-point, by considering how civilizations come into existence, or, in subjective terms, how they emerge above the lower limit of our mental field of vision. In this inquiry, we must take account of the different modes in which they emerge; and if we attempt to give some general description and explanation of the phenomenon, it must be such as to cover all the modes of emergence which we have observed.

When we were identifying representatives of the species,[1] our explorations revealed certain features in the backgrounds of civilizations which first served us as landmarks for a survey of the historical landscape and afterwards enabled us to make a provisional classification of the specimens which we had identified. This classification was determined by two criteria.

Our primary criterion was the origin of a society's religion; our secondary criterion was the original range of its geographical habitat. On the religious criterion, we classified our twenty-one civilizations into five groups: first, civilizations which carried on the traditions of earlier civilizations by taking over the religions of these earlier civilizations' dominant minorities; second, civilizations which 'affiliated' themselves to earlier civilizations by growing up within chrysalides constituted by churches which had been created by these earlier civilizations' internal proletariats. Such 'affiliated' civilizations fell into two sub-groups: one in which the germs out of which the chrysalis-churches had been created by the internal proletariats of the 'apparented' societies had been indigenous to these 'apparented' societies, and another in which those germs had been alien from them. The fourth group consisted of civilizations which were related to earlier civilizations by the looser tie of having derived their religions from these earlier civilizations' external proletariats. In the fifth place, we found civilizations

---

[1] In I. C (i), above.

which, so far as we could see, were not related to any earlier civilizations by any tie, however tenuous.

On the geographical criterion, we classified our twenty-one civilizations into four groups: first, civilizations whose original home lay wholly within the original home of some earlier civilization; second, civilizations whose original home lay wholly within the widest range which some earlier civilization had eventually attained, but not wholly within the area which that earlier civilization had occupied originally; third, civilizations whose original home lay partly within the widest range which an earlier civilization had eventually attained, but also partly outside it, on virgin soil; fourth, civilizations whose original home lay on virgin soil altogether.

By combining the results of these two systems of classification, we were able to arrange our twenty-one civilizations in a continuous series and to discern what the termini of this series were. At the one extremity we found societies which were so closely attached to certain earlier civilizations that we speculated whether we ought not to regard them as these earlier civilizations' 'dead trunks' (and their histories as epilogues to these earlier civilizations' histories) rather than as distinct and separate civilizations in their own rights. At the other extremity we found societies which appeared to have emerged in complete independence, without there being any traces of earlier civilizations in their backgrounds. In making a comparative study of the geneses of civilizations, we have to take all these various modes of emergence into consideration.

It is evident that the problem becomes more acute as we travel down the series. In the case of those societies whose distinct and separate existence is in doubt, it is possible that we may be relieved of the task of explaining their geneses by finding that they are merely survivals of earlier civilizations which have lost their vitality without having been rejuvenated by a second birth. In the case of those societies which show no traces of earlier civilizations in their backgrounds, we start with no clue to indicate how their geneses have occurred.

We may observe that the societies of this latter class—which we may call the 'unrelated' civilizations, in order to distinguish them from all those that are related to earlier civilizations in any manner and degree—are in a minority of six out of twenty-one[1] and belong chronologically to the infancy of the species. Of course, *ex hypothesi*, they include every civilization that stands at the head of any

---

[1] The six are the Egyptiac, Andean, Sumeric, Minoan, Sinic, and Mayan civilizations. If the Indic Civilization proves not to be related to the Sumeric, the number rises to seven; and it rises to eight if 'the Indus Culture' proves to have been independent of the Sumeric in its origin.

genealogical tree representing the relations between civilizations in the Time-dimension; but when we turn from relative to absolute dates, we observe further that no 'unrelated' civilization has emerged in the Old World within the last three, or in the New World (so far as we know) within the last two, of the six millennia during which the species has been in existence up to date.[1] On the other hand, we observe that no less than eight 'related' civilizations have emerged in the Old World, and two in the New World, within the three and the two millennia within which there have been no fresh emergences of 'unrelated' civilizations in the Old and in the New World respectively.[2] These chronological observations can be tabulated as on the following page.[3]

From this table it would appear that, both in the Old World and in the New, the mode of emergence of the 'unrelated' civilizations —that is, the mode, whatever it was, in which civilizations of the first generation emerged *ex hypothesi*—became obsolete almost as soon as certain of these civilizations had brought an alternative mode of emergence into operation through their own vicissitudes. In these 'unrelated' civilizations' break-downs and disintegrations, the earliest of the 'related' civilizations took their rise; and, under the conditions of our day, when the whole World has become emmeshed in the net of our Western Civilization, it is still quite possible to imagine this Western Civilization itself breaking down and disintegrating in its turn, but hardly possible any longer to imagine new civilizations emerging without their being related to the antecedent Western Civilization in some degree. In other words, the possibility of 'unrelated' civilizations ever emerging again seems now to be definitely excluded by the accomplished fact of the world-wide expansion of our Western Civilization on the economic and political planes; and this suggests what may have been the reason why the mode of emergence of the 'unrelated'

[1] In the Old World, the Egyptiac and Sumeric civilizations emerged in the fourth millennium B.C., the Minoan perhaps in the third, the Sinic perhaps in the second. In the New World, the Mayan Civilization appears to have emerged in the last millennium B.C.; and the Andean, as we find it at the moment of the Spanish conquest, has all the appearance of having had a long history, though we lack at present the necessary evidence for reconstructing its chronology with precision. (See, however, the table on p. 47 of Means, P.A.: *Ancient Civilisations of the Andes* (New York and London 1931, Scribner), where the emergence of the Andean Civilization is dated at least as far back as the beginning of the Christian Era.)

[2] The two related civilizations that are younger than any unrelated civilization in the New World are the Yucatec and the Mexic; the eight in the Old World are the Far Eastern (main body), the Far Eastern (in Korea and Japan), the Western, the Orthodox Christian (main body), the Orthodox Christian (in Russia), the Hindu, the Iranic, the Arabic. The civilizations related to the Sumeric and to the Minoan—that is, the Indic (?), the Hittite, the Babylonic, the Hellenic, and the Syriac—are excluded from the count because it is possible that they emerged earlier, or not later, than the Sinic.

[3] The names of the civilizations of the New World are printed in italics and those of the civilizations of the Old World in ordinary type in order to disentangle the two chronologies from one another.

	'Unrelated Civilizations'	'Related Civilizations'			
		related through external proletariats	'affiliated' through internal proletariats		
			with alien creative germs	with indigenous creative germs	attached through dominant minorities
B.C. 4000	Egyptiac+Sumeric				
B.C. 3000	Minoan				
B.C. 2000	Sinic (?)	Indic+Hittite			Babylonic
B.C. 1000	Mayan Andean (?)	Syriac+Hellenic			
B.C. 0000					
A.D.			Far Eastern (main body) Far Eastern (Korea and Japan) Western+Orthodox Christian (main body)	Hindu	Yucatec+Mexic
A.D. 1000			Orthodox Christian (Russia)	Iranic+Arabic	
A.D. 2000					

civilizations became obsolete in fact more than three thousand years ago in the Old World and probably more than two thousand years ago in the New World, at dates which in our age, when the species is still young, already seem to belong to its infancy. The reason is that the world-wide expansion which our Western Civilization has achieved on two planes of social life in modern times is merely the most conspicuous manifestation up to date of a tendency towards expansion which has been displayed in lesser measure by all civilizations that have ever come into existence. Apparently it is in the nature of civilizations to exert upon Mankind beyond their borders certain social influences which may be likened metaphorically to the physical pushes and pulls which, in scientific terminology, are called radiation and attraction. The forces of social radiation and attraction resemble their physical namesakes in their capacity for exerting effects at immense distances from their sources, even if only in minute degrees. We can observe this characteristic of their operation in the activities of the civilizations that are alive to-day; and our records show that the same powers were possessed and exerted by the earliest representatives of the species. Hence we may infer that, after the first few civilizations had emerged, it did not take long (on the time-scale of societies of this species) for the whole of Mankind to be affected by their existence—consciously or unconsciously, in greater measure or less. 'Verily their sound went into all the Earth and their words unto the ends of the World';[1] and the world-wide vibrations, by occupying the entire field of action, may have made it impossible for other vibratory movements of the same kind any longer to be generated independently at fresh centres in the manner in which these earliest vibrations, which had thus monopolized the field, had themselves been generated originally. This would explain why all the later vibratory movements that occurred were generated in a new way, by derivation. To drop our metaphor, it would explain why the mode of emergence of the 'unrelated' class of civilizations became obsolete and the mode of the 'related' class became the rule.

We have seen already[2] what the latter mode is. We have seen that, if and when a civilization begins to lose its creative power, the people below its surface and beyond its borders, whom it is all the time irradiating with its influence and attracting into its orbit, begin to resist assimilation, with the result that the society which, in its age of growth, was a social unity with an ever expanding and always indefinite fringe, becomes divided against itself by the sharp lines of division between a dominant minority and an

[1] Romans x, 18.   [2] In I. C (i) (a), pp. 55-7, above.

internal and an external proletariat. The minority, having lost
the power to influence and attract, seeks instead to impose itself by
force. The proletariat, inwardly alienated, remains in, but not of,
the disintegrating society until the disintegration has gone so far
that the dominant minority can no longer repress the efforts of the
proletariat to secede. In the act of secession, at length accomplished,
a new society is conceived.[1]

This, in brief, seems to be the mode of emergence of the 'related'
civilizations, in so far as we have investigated it yet; but how are
we to account for the emergence of the 'unrelated' civilizations?
Ex hypothesi, they did not emerge through secessions from older
societies of the same species. We can only suppose that they
emerged through mutations of societies previously belonging to
the sister species—that is, through mutations of primitive societies
into civilizations. The supposition is in accord with chronology;
for we know that the primitive species of societies had been in
existence hundreds of thousands of years before the first civilizations came into existence. Indeed, we know that primitive
societies were anterior to Mankind itself, which only became
human under their aegis.[2] The supposition is also in accord with
what we know about the general trend of Evolution, which normally
proceeds from the simpler to the more complex. Finally, the
supposition is virtually forced upon us by the absence of any
alternative possibility; οὐ γὰρ ἀπὸ δρυός ἐσσι παλαιφάτου οὐδ᾽ ἀπὸ
πέτρης;[3] and if the unrelated civilizations were derived neither
from other civilizations nor from primitive societies, they must
have originated in fortuitous concourses of non-social human
beings—*quod est absurdum*, since non-social human beings are
as fabulous as Cyclops or Leviathan. It would be as reasonable to
revive the fantasies of Mythology and to assert that the first
civilizations sprang from the earth or dropped from the skies.

Assuming, then, that the 'unrelated' civilizations have emerged
through mutations of primitive societies and the 'related' civilizations through secessions from pre-existent civilizations, we have to
explain how and why civilizations have emerged in terms which
apply to both the modes in which their emergence comes under
our observation.

---

[1] We have seen that it is sometimes an internal and sometimes an external proletariat
from which a new society, in the class of 'related' societies, derives its being; and we have
left it an open question whether a society which carries on the existence of a dominant
minority can be regarded as a distinct and separate society in its own right. (See I.C (ii),
above.)

[2] See pp. 173-4, above.   [3] *Odyssey*, xix, l. 163.

B. THE NATURE OF THE GENESES OF CIVILIZATIONS

IN setting out to inquire how civilizations have emerged, we have the choice of starting either with the mutation of primitive societies into 'unrelated' civilizations or with the emergence of 'related' civilizations through secessions of proletariats from pre-existent civilizations. The second of these modes of emergence has actually occurred more frequently than the former already; and we have seen reason to believe that the future belongs to it. On the other hand, the mutational mode might be expected, on the face of it, to involve a greater and therefore more conspicuous change; so that, if we examine this mode first, we may hope to find less difficulty, from this angle of approach, in obtaining some insight into the general nature of the phenomenon which we are studying in this place.

The measure of the mutation of primitive societies into civilizations will be given by the difference between the two species of societies now that they exist side by side. Hitherto, we have taken this difference for granted. Our next step is to look for the features in which it resides.

This difference does not consist in the presence or absence of institutions; for we find[1] that institutions, being the vehicles of the impersonal relations in which all societies have their existence, are attributes of the whole genus and therefore common properties of the two species. Primitive societies have their own characteristic institutions—the ἐνιαυτὸς δαίμων and his cycle; totemism and exogamy; tabus, initiations, and age-classes; segregations of the sexes, at certain stages of life, in separate communal establishments—and some of these institutions are certainly as elaborate and perhaps as subtle as those which are characteristic of civilizations.[2]

Nor are civilizations distinguished from primitive societies by the Division of Labour; for though in general this plays a more important part in their lives, and its importance tends to increase as they grow, we can discern at least the rudiments of the Division of Labour in the lives of primitive societies also. For instance, primitive kings, who seem like undifferentiated 'all-round men' by

[1] See I. C (iii) (e), Annex, pp. 454-5, below.
[2] The elaborateness and subtlety which primitive institutions sometimes display are illustrated in the Melanesian institution of the Kula, which is brilliantly described and studied in *The Argonauts of the Western Pacific* (London 1922, Routledge) by B. Malinowski.

contrast with the executive heads of political communities in societies which are in process of civilization, can be seen to be specialists when we observe them in their own social environment and compare them with the rank and file of their tribesmen. Primitive magicians and smiths and minstrels are specialists in the same degree.[1]

Indeed, the Division of Labour may be a necessary condition of the existence of institutions and therefore a generic feature in the lives of societies, since it is difficult to conceive how institutions could exist without in some way being embodied in the persons of particular human beings who are thus invested with special social functions. In primitive societies these incarnations are sometimes complete—the institutions and their human embodiments being absolutely identified with one another in the thoughts and feelings of those who participate in the social relations that are maintained by this means. In civilizations there is usually a greater ability to distinguish offices from office-holders and personalities from titles and uniforms; and there is sometimes a conscious endeavour to eliminate the personal factor and to place these essentially impersonal relations on an avowedly impersonal basis. Yet the tendency to make institutions incarnate dies hard. In the United States, where official titles have been abolished and official uniforms reduced to a minimum, the ingrained desire for these outward shows has found non-official outlets—for instance, the ceremonials of private associations like the Rotarians or the Elks or the Knights of Columbus or the Daughters of the American Revolution or the Ku-Klux-Klan. In the British Empire, where 'the Crown' has been piously preserved after its powers have been transferred to half a dozen parliaments, this medieval incarnation of political unity has latterly acquired a new and unforeseen institutional value as the *trait d'union* between the States Members of the British Commonwealth of Nations. The relation in which these nations stand, and wish to stand, towards one another involves a logical antinomy between the parliamentary self-government of each State Member and the political unity of the Commonwealth as a whole; and hence this relation cannot be expressed in the

[1] The most celebrated mythical representatives of these three professions—e.g. Merlin the magician, and Hephaestus the smith, and Homer the minstrel—were conceived in communities whose members, through contact with civilizations, had ceased to be altogether primitive and had been transformed from savages into barbarians. (For this transformation see V. C (i) (c) 3, vol. v, pp. 196–7, below.) The lameness of Hephaestus and the blindness of Homer indicate that in primitive societies, even of the more sophisticated kind, the tendency towards the Division of Labour is still so weak that it normally fails to assert itself except in people who are debarred from becoming 'all-round men' by insuperable physical defects. This negative condition has to exist before the positive forces of personal aptitudes and social needs can come into play in favour of specialization. For the stimulating effect of physical penalization, as illustrated by these examples, see further II. D (vi), *ad init.*, vol. ii, below.

logical terms of a constitutional relation between the parliaments that have severally inherited the powers once possessed by 'the Crown'. On the other hand, it can and does find expression in the incarnate institution of a personal monarch who 'reigns but does not govern' in each of his dominions.

Here we see an apparent anachronism acquiring a new value in a new age. Yet in every age of every society institutions depend for their maintenance upon the services of specialists in some measure; and in that measure these human beings become invested with symbolic significance and prestige in their fellows' hearts and minds. This happens even in spheres of life in which tradition is at a discount. While millions of human beings who think of themselves as British subjects find their incarnations of the British Empire in the King or in the Prince of Wales, other millions who think of themselves as American citizens find their incarnations of 'Americanism' in Edison or in Henry Ford. For almost all Westerners in our generation, the prowess of the Western Society in abstract science is incarnated in Einstein, its prowess in applied science in Marconi, its spirit of adventure in Lindbergh, its physical skill in its professional athletes, its physical strength in its professional pugilists, its physical beauty in its film-stars. It is a universal condition of social life that the majority of the members of any given society should be perpetually extending the narrow radius of their personal lives by living vicariously through the representative activities of a small number of their fellows; and the Division of Labour between this majority and this minority is inherent in the nature of Society itself.

The complement and antidote to the Division of Labour is social imitation or mimesis,[1] which may be defined as the acquisition, through imitation, of social 'assets'—aptitudes or emotions or ideas—which the acquisitors have not originated for themselves, and which they might never have come to possess if they had not encountered and imitated other people in whose possession these assets were already to be found. Mimesis, too, is a generic feature of social life.[2] Its operation can be observed both in primitive societies and in civilizations. It operates, however, in different

---

[1] In this Study, the Greek word (μίμησις from μιμεῖσθαι) is used in order to avoid the connotations of 'unintelligent imitation' or 'satirical imitation' which attach to the derivative English word 'mimicry'. Mimesis, as used here, denotes social imitation 'without prejudice'.

[2] The historical importance of mimesis was discerned by David Hume, as witness the following passage in his essay *Of National Characters*: 'The human mind is of a very imitative nature; nor is it possible for any set of men to converse often together without acquiring a similitude of manners and communicating to each other their vices as well as virtues. The propensity to company and society is strong in all rational creatures; and the same disposition which gives us this propensity makes us enter deeply into each other's sentiments and causes like passions and inclinations to run, as it were, by contagion through the whole club or knot of companions.'

directions in the two species. In primitive societies, as we know them, mimesis is directed towards the older generation of the living members and towards the dead ancestors who stand, unseen but not unfelt, at the back of the living elders, reinforcing their power and enhancing their prestige. In a society where mimesis is thus directed backward towards the past, custom rules and the society remains static. On the other hand, in societies in process of civilization, mimesis is directed towards creative personalities which command a following because they are pioneers on the road towards the common goal of human endeavours. In a society where mimesis is thus directed forward towards the future, 'the cake of custom'[1] is broken and the Society is in dynamic motion along a course of change and growth.

In this contrast between a dynamic movement and a static condition, we have come at last upon a point of difference between civilizations and primitive societies; but when we ask ourselves whether the difference thus empirically observed is permanent and fundamental, we find that the answer is in the negative.

We have noted already that, if we only know of primitive societies in a static condition, this is merely an accidental consequence of the fragmentariness of our knowledge.[2] All our 'data' for the study of primitive societies happen to come from representatives of the species which are in the last phases of their histories; but where direct observation fails us, a train of reasoning informs us that there must have been earlier phases in the histories of the primitive societies in which these were moving more dynamically than any civilizations have ever moved yet, as far as our knowledge goes. We have noted[3] that the primitive societies must be prior to Humanity, since Mankind could not have become human except in a social environment; and this mutation of Sub-Man into Man, which was accomplished, in circumstances of which we have no record, under the aegis of primitive societies, was a more profound change, a greater step in growth, than any progress which Man has yet achieved under the aegis of civilizations.[4]

Primitive societies, as we know them by direct observation, may

[1] Bagehot, W.: *Physics and Politics*, 10th edition (London 1894, Kegan Paul), pp. 27 and 35.

[2] See pp. 179-80, above, in I.C (iii) (*e*).

[3] See pp. 173-4, above.

[4] We cannot measure the degree of this change and growth unless and until we obtain more knowledge than we possess at present about 'the missing link' between Man and the earlier ancestor who is common to Man and to the anthropoid apes. We cannot reconstruct this 'Sub-Man' by analogy with the anthropoids, since these represent a divergent line of growth from the common ancestry. Yet, even in the present state of our knowledge, we can assert with confidence that there was a greater gulf between 'Sub-man' and Primitive Man than there is between Primitive Man and Man in process of civilization. Bagehot postulates a kind of 'pre-primitive' stage in which our ancestors were 'savages without the fixed habits of savages'. (Op. cit., pp. 112-13. Cf. pp. 134-5.)

be likened to people lying torpid upon a ledge on a mountain-side, with a precipice below and a precipice above; civilizations may be likened to companions of these 'Sleepers of Ephesus' who have just risen to their feet and have started to climb on up the face of the cliff; while we, for our part, may liken ourselves to observers whose field of vision is limited to the ledge and to the foot of the upper precipice and who have come upon the scene at the moment when the different members of the party happen to be in these respective postures and positions. At first sight we may be inclined to draw an absolute distinction between the two groups, acclaiming the climbers as athletes and dismissing the recumbent figures as paralytics; but on second thoughts we shall find it more prudent to suspend judgement.[1]

After all, the recumbent figures cannot be paralytics in reality; for they cannot have been born on the ledge, and no human muscles but their own can have hoisted them to this halting-place up the face of the precipice below. So far from being paralytics, they must be seasoned athletes who have successfully scaled the 'pitch' below and are still taking a well-earned rest from their recent labours.[2] On the other hand, their companions who are climbing at this moment have only just left this same ledge and started to climb the face of the precipice above; and, since the next ledge is out of sight, we do not know how high or how arduous this next 'pitch' may be. We only know that it is impossible to halt and rest before the next ledge, wherever that may lie, is reached. Thus, even if we could estimate each present climber's strength and skill and nerve and courage, we could not judge whether any of them have any prospect of gaining the unseen ledge above, which is the goal of their present endeavours. We can, however, be sure that certain of them will never attain it.

We are watching here, under a new guise, the same spectacle that we watched before when we saw civilizations in the likeness of drivers seeking to pass out through the exit from a one-way street.[3] We have simply to give this one-way street an up-hill gradient, and then to steepen the gradient until it becomes

---

[1] This point is made by Plato in *The Republic* (372 D–E), at the close of the first sketch of what a society (πόλις) involves (369 B–372 D). In this sketch, Plato makes the dramatis personae of his dialogue rough out the lineaments of a society of the primitive species. Thereupon, Glaucon complains that they have sketched 'a society of swine' (ὑῶν πόλιν)—with a possible reminiscence of a famous passage in the *Odyssey* (Book X, ll. 133–574) in which the companions of Odysseus are turned into swine by Circe. (This passage is quoted in II. D (i), vol ii, p. 23, below.) Socrates then consents to study a luxurious (τρυφῶσαν) or feverish (φλεγμαίνουσαν) society—i.e., in our terminology, a society in process of civilization—but' he remarks in passing that, in his opinion, the (primitive) society which they have just sketched is the genuine type of the genus, in the sense that it is representative of the genus when it is in a normal state of health.

[2] On this point see Bagehot, W.: *Physics and Politics*, 10th edition (London 1894, Kegan Paul), p. 42.   [3] In I. C (iii) (*d*), above.

precipitous, in order to transform the car-drivers of one simile into the climbers of the other. Just as the cars, when once they had entered the street, had no alternatives except to pass out through the exit or to backslide, so the climbers, when once they have started on the 'pitch', have no alternatives except to reach the ledge above or to fall; and as we saw many cars backsliding till they were warned off the road, and others till they met with fatal accidents, so we can see many of our climbers already falling—some to their death and others to an ignominious life-in-death on the ledge below. These others lie side by side with the decomposing corpses of their companions who—*felices opportunitate mortis*[1]—have escaped the pains of failure through annihilation, and also side by side with the recumbent forms of those apparent paralytics who have not yet essayed the 'pitch' by which these unfortunates have already been defeated. Disqualified from essaying the 'pitch' again and denied the *coup de grâce* of annihilation, they would lie 'fast bound in misery and iron',[2] enduring the torments of Prometheus with the vulture devouring his liver, if the Gods did not take pity on them and grant them insensibility by turning them into stone, to weather away, with the lapse of centuries, like Niobe on the flank of Mount Sipylus. By the time when we have come on the scene, a majority of the climbers on the precipice above our ledge have fallen to meet one or other of the penalties of defeat—petrifaction or annihilation—and there are only a few to be seen still working their way upward. If we could look down the face of the precipice below our ledge to the next ledge beneath, and translate ourselves back into the age when this lower 'pitch' was the scene of action, we should almost certainly discover that the mountaineers who have attained our ledge, to rest from their labours before essaying the 'pitch' next above, are in a still smaller minority by comparison with the unnumbered and unremembered casualties which the scaling of that 'pitch' likewise cost in its time.

We have now followed out our simile far enough to have ascertained that the contrast between the static condition of primitive societies, as we know them, and the dynamic motion of societies in process of civilization is not a permanent and fundamental point of difference, but an accident of the time and place of observation. All the primitive societies which we now observe at rest must once have been in motion; and all societies which have entered upon the process of civilization will come to rest sooner or later in one way or another. Some may eventually come to rest by attaining (though none has attained it yet) the goal of human endeavours: the mutation of Man into Superman. Others have come to rest already by

---

[1] Tacitus, *Agricola*, chap. 45.   [2] Psalm cvii. 10.

relapsing, long before the goal has been attained, to the level of primitive humanity from which they have started. The condition of these *ci-devant* civilizations which have failed in their endeavours is static like the condition of those primitive societies which are extant to-day because they have succeeded in theirs.[1] In every other respect, there is all the difference between them; and this difference—the difference between failure and success—is wholly in the primitive societies' favour. The primitive societies, as we see them to-day, are static because they are recuperating from the strain of a successful effort to attain the state in which they now persist. Their stillness is the stillness not of death but of sleep; and even if they may be destined never to awake, they are at least still alive. The *ci-devant* civilizations are static because they have lost their lives in an unsuccessful attempt to transcend the state into which they have now relapsed. Their stillness is the stillness of dead things in decay; and they are dead equally beyond doubt and beyond recall, whether they happen to be disintegrating as rapidly as a putrefying corpse or as slowly as a rotting tree-trunk or a weathering rock.

We have failed to find the immediate object of our search, a permanent and fundamental point of difference between primitive societies and civilizations; but incidentally we have obtained some light on the ultimate objective of our present inquiry: the nature of the geneses of civilizations. Starting with the mutation of primitive societies into civilizations, we have found that this consists in a transition from a static condition to a dynamic activity; and we shall find that the same formula holds good for the alternative mode of emergence of civilizations through the secession of proletariats from the dominant minorities of pre-existent civilizations which have lost their creative power. Such dominant minorities are static by definition; for to say that the creative minority of a civilization in growth has degenerated or atrophied into the dominant minority of a civilization in disintegration is only another way of saying that the society in question has relapsed from a dynamic activity into a static condition. Against this static condition, the secession of a proletariat is a dynamic reaction; and in this light we can see that, in the secession of a proletariat from a dominant minority, a new civilization is generated through the transition of a society from a static condition to a dynamic activity, just as it is in the mutation which produces a civilization out of a

[1] If we take the direction of mimesis as the test of whether a given society at a given moment is in a static condition or in a dynamic activity, we shall find that mimesis is directed backward towards the forefathers in the dominant minority of a *ci-devant* civilization, just as it is in an extant primitive society, in common contrast to the direction of mimesis forward—towards creative personalities—in a society in process of civilization which has not broken down.

primitive society. The geneses of all civilizations—the unrelated and the related class alike—could be described in a sentence written by a Western philosopher-statesman of our age one month after the close of the General War of 1914–18:

'There is no doubt that Mankind is once more on the move. The very foundations have been shaken and loosened, and things are again fluid. The tents have been struck, and the great caravan of Humanity is once more on the march.'[1]

Can we yet say anything more about the transition from a static condition to a dynamic activity in which the genesis of every civilization consists? We know this much more already: this instance of the transition is not unique. When we were studying it in our simile of the mountain-side, we realized that the ledge on which we saw the primitive societies lying dormant and the *ci-devant* civilizations lying dead, while the societies in process of civilization were scaling the face of the precipice above, was only one ledge in a series, the other terms of which were outside our field of vision. All extant primitive societies must have reached our ledge from an unseen ledge below, and all societies in process of civilization are endeavouring to reach an unseen ledge above; and, for all we know, the number of other ledges above this and below that may be infinite in both directions. The heights that tower above us are quite beyond our powers of estimation, but we have some inkling of the dizzy depths below. We know that we have to descend below the ledge from which Sub-man rose to Man in order to find the level of the common ancestor of Mankind and the anthropoids.[2] And how many hundreds and thousands of lower ledges should we have to leave behind us in our descent if we sought to trace the rise of mammals from the lowest vertebrates and of vertebrates from the rudimentary forms in which Life itself first emerged out of the abyss?

Without venturing down that dark descent or even allowing ourselves to speculate whether the alternating series of ledge and precipice, precipice and ledge, is infinite or finite, we can observe that the alternation between horizontal and perpendicular surfaces on the mountain-side repeats itself in a kind of pattern, and that the corresponding alternation between a static condition and a dynamic activity in the energies of the living creatures that are seeking to scale the mountain similarly recurs in a kind of rhythm. This rhythm has been pointed out by a number of observers, living

---

[1] Smuts, J. C.: *The League of Nations: A Practical Suggestion* (London 1918, Hodder and Stoughton), p. 71.
[2] See p. 192, footnote 4, above.

in different ages of different societies, who all agree in regarding it as something fundamental in the nature of the Universe.

It is pointed out, for example, by the contemporary Western philosopher-statesman whom we have just quoted, General Smuts, in an exposition of his philosophy of 'holism':

'Holism, as its very idea implies, is a tendency towards unity, a blending and ordering of multiple elements into new unities. From the more or less homogeneous to the heterogeneous; from heterogeneous multiplicity again to greater, more advanced harmony, to a harmonious co-operative ordered structural unity; such a formula may serve as a rough-and-ready description of the holistic process.'[1]

The same rhythm in the Universe is discerned, from his own standpoint, by a contemporary Western psychologist:

'In general terms we can say that all evolution is from the complex to the expressed, from the diffuse to the intense and back again to the resolved. Life is a constant process of focus and expansion. This is the systole and diastole of Time itself, the alternating current that drives the Universe. From co-consciousness has been evolved self-conscious individuality, and from individuality ought there not to be developed, in the course of evolution, a super-consciousness, a common self-consciousness?'[2]

We will take our third quotation from a contemporary Western anthropologist, and this at greater length, since this observer's standpoint is almost coincident with ours:

'An avenue of approach to the psychology of Primitive Man may be found in the principle of the Quest for Unity which, it appears to us, is fundamental in Human Nature. It is a tendency traceable and profoundly influential through all Man's thinking and practical life as soon as, and wherever, he is recognisably human. Its presence in the mental life of Civilised Man needs no demonstration. Mr. Bosanquet defined Reason as "the spirit of totality", and again as "the nisus towards the whole". Certainly, the characteristic activity of the mind, from the formation of a general idea to the great system of Philosophy, from the humblest perception to the laws of Science and the Uniformity of Nature itself, from the vaguest conception of spirit to the monistic unity of the Supreme Personality of Religion, is the endeavour to create "wholes" in thought, to organise experience into some form or other of coherent totality.

'It was one of the works of Herbert Spencer's genius for generalisation to show that this tendency in Man's mind is but a particular instance of the general course of the evolutionary process. This is evident from his illustrations of his famous definition of that process as a passage of matter from "an indefinite, incoherent homogeneity to a definite,

---

[1] Smuts, J.C.: *Holism and Evolution*, 2nd edition (London 1927, Macmillan), p. 241.
[2] Heard, Gerald: *The Ascent of Humanity* (London 1929, Cape), p. 260.

coherent heterogeneity"[1] through a continuous series of "integrations" and "differentiations". We shall find these latter terms useful in the exposition of the principle of the Quest for Unity; for we conceive that Man's progress towards and in civilisation proceeds by a series of integrations, by the formation of more and more comprehensive and yet more definite wholes, which are linked together by successive Differentiations. What happens is that Man with his unifying tendency forms a primitive integration, whether in his mental or practical life. This integration, on the emergence of some new power or idea in Man, is found inadequate, and is broken through by a differentiation which applies the new power or idea to wider areas of experience. Out of the more differentiated phenomena and relations thus arrived at, the mind with its determined search for unity creates a new integration, larger, richer and more organised than the former one. This again is followed by a differentiation; and so the process goes on, Man ever becoming more capable of more comprehensive, higher, and finer integrations both of his own inner life and of his outward social relations. . . .

'The transition between the integrations, inseparable from each as the trough of the wave from the crests before and after, is made by a differentiation, resulting from the pressure of some new necessity, or the acquisition of a new power, or whatever change of Man's inner life or outward circumstances compels his mind to grasp and organise, by its native hunger for unity, a wider range and content of experience. . . .

'In considering for a little the stage of Differentiation, it may be noted that its characteristic feature is that an earlier Integration has been broken up and a new one has not yet been formed. It is like the Children of Israel, released from Egyptian bondage, in which a certain unification of order and appointed task was imposed upon them from above by their masters, bursting out into the larger and freer life of the wilderness. It is to them, however, a life of wandering, more vague, more diffused, less organised than the more unified existence on the lower plane of slavery, upon which, indeed, they are more than inclined to lapse back at times, were it not that a higher integration beckons them onward to settlement in the Promised Land. . . . Any differentiation in this sense means that a larger range of phenomena and activity is opened to Man than before; and for a time they elude the grasp of his mind and of his practical endeavour to reduce them to some unity of mental comprehension or some form of unified life. He wanders about in the wide new field, trying many wrong paths and culs-de-sac, making many false integrations, before his unifying power is sufficiently developed to form the new and higher integration.'[2]

Looking back to the last generation in the age of Western history that immediately preceded our own, we find our rhythm pointed out—this time in the histories of civilizations—by a Western

---

[1] *First Principles* (4th edition), p. 307.
[2] Murphy, J.: *Primitive Man: His Essential Quest* (London 1927, Milford), pp. 24–5, 26, and 28–9.

sociologist, Saint-Simon. Saint-Simon saw these histories as a series of alternating 'organic' and 'critical' periods:[1]

'La loi du développement de l'humanité . . . nous montre deux états distincts et alternatifs de la société: l'un que nous appelons état organique, où tous les faits de l'activité humaine sont classés, prévus, ordonnés par une théorie générale; où le but de l'action sociale est nettement défini; l'autre, que nous nommons l'état critique, où toute communion de pensée, toute action d'ensemble, toute coordination a cessé, et où la société ne présente plus qu'une agglomération d'individus isolés et luttant les uns contre les autres.

'Chacun de ces états a occupé deux périodes de l'histoire. Un état organique précéda l'ère des Grecs que l'on nomme ère philosophique, et que nous préciserons avec plus de justesse par le titre d'époque critique. Plus tard, une nouvelle doctrine est produite, elle parcourt ses différentes phases d'élaboration et de perfectionnement, et établit enfin sa puissance politique sur tout l'Occident. La constitution de l'Église commence une nouvelle époque organique qui s'arrête au quinzième siècle, à l'instant où les réformateurs donnèrent le premier signal de la critique continuée jusqu'à nos jours.[2] . . .

'Quelle est la destination de l'homme par rapport à son semblable, quelle est sa destination par rapport à l'univers? Tels sont les termes généraux du double problème que l'humanité s'est toujours posé. Toutes les époques organiques ont été des solutions, au moins provisoires, de ces problèmes; mais bientôt les progrès opérés à l'aide de ces solutions, c'est-à-dire à l'abri des institutions sociales qui avaient été réalisées d'après elles, les rendaient elles-mêmes insuffisantes, et en appelaient de nouvelles; les époques critiques, moments de débats, de protestation, d'attente, de transition, venaient alors remplir l'intervalle par le doute, par l'indifférence à l'égard de ces grands problèmes, par l'égoïsme, conséquence obligée de ce doute, de cette indifférence.[3] Toutes les fois que ces grands problèmes sociaux ont été résolus, il y a eu époque organique; toutes les fois qu'ils sont demeurés sans solution, il y a eu époque critique. . . .

'Dans toutes les époques d'une même nature, organique ou critique,

[1] Through this *Anschauung*, he attempted to reconcile with the empirically observed phenomena of decadence and emergence the theory of the continuity of history as a single movement in a straight line. (See p. 155, footnote 2, above.)

[2] A more exact definition of these periods is given in a later passage of the same work: 'Deux périodes critiques nettement prononcées nous apparaissent dans la durée de vingt-trois siècles: 1° celle qui sépara le polythéisme du christianisme, c'est-à-dire qui s'étendit depuis l'apparition des premiers philosophes de la Grèce jusqu'à la prédication de l'Évangile; 2° celle qui sépare la doctrine catholique de celle de l'avenir, et qui comprend les trois siècles écoulés depuis Luther jusqu'à nos jours. Les époques organiques correspondantes sont: 1° celle où le polythéisme grec et romain fut dans la plus grande vigueur, et qui se termine aux siècles de Périclès et d'Auguste; 2° celle où le catholicisme et la féodalité furent constitués avec le plus de force et d'éclat, et qui vint finir, sous le rapport religieux, à Léon X, sous le point de vue politique, à Louis XIV.' (*Œuvres de Saint-Simon et d'Enfantin*, vol. xli (Paris 1877, Leroux), pp. 170-1.)
Saint-Simon believed that his own generation was on the eve of passing out of the prevailing 'critical period' into a new 'organic period'. (Op. cit., vol. xli, p. 179; vol. xlii, pp. 49-50.)

[3] 'Le cachet des époques critiques, comme celui des grandes déroutes, c'est l'égoïsme.' (Op. cit., vol. xli, p. 113.)

quels que soient le lieu et le temps, les hommes sont toujours occupés, dans la durée des premières, à édifier, pendant la durée des secondes, à détruire. . . .

'Dans les premières, de tous les points de la circonférence sociale on voit se diriger sympathiquement tous les esprits et tous les actes vers un centre d'affection; dans les secondes, au contraire, les vieilles croyances, signalées dans leurs vices par des sentiments, par des besoins que l'antique lien social n'avait pu comprendre, attaquées par un présent qui ne se lie plus aux traditions, et qui ne les rattache à aucun avenir, tombent en ruines de toutes parts.'[1]

Leaping, next, from Saint-Simon to Empedocles (a member of a society which is distinct and separate from, though 'apparented' to, ours), we again find our rhythm pointed out—this time, in the ebb and flow of the Physical Universe—by this Hellenic man of science.[2] Empedocles attributes the changes in the face of the Universe, of which we are empirically aware, to the alternate ebb and flow of two forces which are complementary to one another and at the same time antithetical: an integrating force which he calls 'Love' and a disintegrating force which he calls 'Hate':

'I will tell of a twofold [rhythm]. In one movement a unity builds itself up out of a plurality into sole existence; in another movement it disintegrates, to make a plurality out of a unity.[3] . . . This perpetual alternation never ceases. In one movement all things coalesce into a unity in Love; in another movement they all disperse apart in the enmity of Strife. Thus, inasmuch as a unity has learnt to grow out of a plurality and then, through the disintegration of this unity, a plurality arises again, they have a beginning and their existence is not eternal. Yet, in virtue of that perpetual never-ceasing alternation, they are also everlasting—immovable in their cycle.[4] . . . As it was aforetime, so it will be; nor ever, I trow, will Infinite Time be emptied of these two.[5] . . . [We see Love expelled from the Universe by Strife.] But as soon as great Strife has waxed fat upon the members [of the Universe] and has sprung to the place of honour in the fullness of the time which has been struck out for them, by a broad oath, to fulfil turn and turn about,[6] [Strife begins to recede and Love to advance again. In this reverse movement,] when Strife has touched the bottommost depth of the eddy and Love has penetrated to the centre of the vortex, then in Love all

---

[1] Bazard: 'Exposition de la Doctrine Saint-Simonienne', in *Œuvres de Saint-Simon et d'Enfantin*, vol. xli (Paris 1877, Leroux), pp. 86–7, 171–2, 177, 205.
[2] The thoroughly scientific nature of Empedocles' thought is sometimes overlooked, partly because of the brilliance of the imagery in which he conveys ideas which could not be expressed at all except through some kind of symbolism, and partly because, like Erasmus Darwin and Lucretius, he has chosen to expound his system of Natural Science in verse and has employed a traditional and highly mannered style which was originally created for dealing with wholly different subjects and can only be pressed into the service of Physical Science by a *tour de force*.
[3] Empedocles, Fragment 17, ll. 1–2. (This and the following references are to Diehls, H.: *Fragmente der Vorsokratiker*, vol. i: Empedokles.)
[4] Fragment 17, ll. 6–13.   [5] Fragment 16.   [6] Fragment 30.

things coalesce into a sole unity—not abruptly, but spontaneously coming into integration from different quarters. From this mixing flow innumerable families of mortal creatures. Yet many things remain unmixed in the interstices between those that are mingling—namely, all things that Strife still holds back in suspension. For Strife has not made a complete and blameless withdrawal to the uttermost limits of the circle,[1] but has partially continued to inhere while partially withdrawing from the members [of the Universe]. As fast as Strife accomplished each stage of his retreat, blameless Love followed him up in her gentle divine onset; and swiftly there grew into mortal things what before had learnt to be immortal, and there became fused what had formerly been separate: they made the alternation in their courses. From this mixing flow innumerable families of mortal creatures, manifold in their structures, a wonder to behold.[2] . . . [But Love only completes her conquest in order to be expelled from the Universe in her turn once more.] This is manifest in the members of the human body. In one movement they coalesce into a unity—all the limbs that have been embodied in the hey-day of lusty life; and then in another movement they are dismembered by the evil forces of Strife and are tossed about, each by itself, in the surf where the sea of Life breaks on Life's shore. So is it likewise with plants, and with fish that dwell in the waters, and with beasts that lurk in the mountains, and with birds that plunge on the wing.'[3]

The two alternating forces or phases in the rhythm of the Universe which Empedocles calls Love and Hate have also been detected—quite independently of the movement of Hellenic thought—by observers in the Sinic World, who have named them Yin and Yang.[4] The nucleus of the Sinic character which stands for Yin seems to represent dark coiling clouds overshadowing the Sun, while the nucleus of the character which stands for Yang seems to represent the unclouded Sun-disk emitting its rays. In the original every-day usage, Yin appears to have signified the side of a mountain or a valley which is in the shadow, and Yang the side which is in the sunshine.[5] Sinic philosophers conceived Yin and Yang as two different kinds of matter. As substances, Yin symbolized water and Yang fire.[6] As phases of the Universe, they symbolized the seasons; and the regular annual alternation of the

---

[1] Presumably 'circle' here means 'sphere', since Empedocles, like some Western men of science of our generation, conceives of the Universe as a finite sphere, though there is no evidence that he shares their further conception of this finite sphere as being unbounded.

[2] Fragment 35.

[3] Fragment 20. The only other relevant passage of Empedocles' poem that survives is Fragment 26, which describes the rhythm in identical terms (by repeating, verbatim, vv. 7–13 of Fragment 17) apropos of the production of living creatures through the rhythmical alternating interaction of the Four Elements.

[4] They are always mentioned in this order—Yin, the static condition, first, and Yang, the dynamic activity, second—and never the other way round (Forke, A.: *Die Gedankenwelt des chinesischen Kulturkreises* (Munich and Berlin 1927, Oldenbourg), p. 110).

[5] Maspéro, H.: *La Chine Antique* (Paris 1927, Boccard), p. 482.

[6] Compare the antithesis, in the conceptions of Hellenic physical science, between the damp, foggy, inert, cold ἀήρ, and the dry, clear, energetically circulating, fiery αἰθήρ.

seasons suggested the Sinic conception of how Yin and Yang are related to one another. Each in turn comes into the ascendant at the other's expense; yet even at the high tide of its expansion it never quite submerges the other, so that, when its tide ebbs, as it always does after reaching high-water mark, there is still a nucleus of the other element left free to expand, as its perpetual rival and partner contracts, until it arrives in due course at the opposite turning-point where the whole movement begins all over again.[1]

This Sinic conception of Yin and Yang was taken up and was worked out systematically in metaphysical terms[2] by the thinkers of the Far Eastern Society (the civilization 'affiliated' to the Sinic) at the intellectual renaissance which occurred in the age of the Sung Dynasty. According to the philosopher Shao Yung (*vivebat* A.D. 1011–77), at the beginning of motion Yang is produced, at its close, Yin; at the beginning of rest the soft is created, at its end, the hard; rest and motion, Yin and Yang, softness and hardness continually alternate and follow one another. According to the five Neo-Confucian philosophers (*vivebant* A.D. 1017–1200), whose thought was summed up by the last and greatest of the five, Chu Hsi (*vivebat* A.D. 1131–1200), the Yin-Yang rhythm is like the rhythmic movement of the lungs in breathing;[3] Yin and Yang are contraction and expansion; 'Yang emits and Yin transforms'; it is rare to find either in a pure state, and each brims over into the other;[4] they are not material substances but abstract correlates of the movement of the fundamental principle of the Universe, Li, which 'rests on Yin and Yang as a rider sits his horse'.[5]

'The Absolute (T'ai-chi) moves and engenders Yang. The movement having reached its climax, rest ensues. From rest springs Yin; and when rest has reached its utmost limit, again movement follows. So we have alternately now movement, now rest. They together form the basis from which by separation grow Yin and Yang, so that these are the two modes.'[6]

The conception, in its final form, is expounded by a gifted Western student of Sinic and Far Eastern thought as follows:

'The Ultimate Principie has operated from all eternity, and now

[1] For the Sinic conception of Yin and Yang, see Forke, A.: *The World-Conception of the Chinese* (London 1925, Probsthain), pp. 161–200.

[2] This metaphysical treatment, by Far Eastern philosophers, of a Sinic conception which had been applied originally to the Physical Universe, seems to have been suggested by the influence of the Buddhist thought which had entered the Far Eastern world in the vehicle of the Mahayana. (Hackmann, H.: *Chinesische Philosophie* (Munich 1927, Reinhardt), pp. 346–7.)

[3] Forke: *Die Gedankenwelt des chinesischen Kulturkreises*, p. 114

[4] Hackmann: *Chinesische Philosophie*, p. 335.

[5] Chu Hsi, quoted by Forke: *Die Gedankenwelt des chinesischen Kulturkreises*, p. 64.

[6] 'T'ai-chi t'u: Hsing-li ching-i', I. 5 v, quoted by Forke in *The World-Conception of the Chinese*, p. 201. The whole of the foregoing account of the Far Eastern elaboration of the concept of Yin and Yang is taken from Forke, op. cit., pp. 200–23, except where other references are given.

ceaselessly operates, by a dynamical process in virtue of which Animate and Inanimate Nature has existed from all eternity. This process is represented as pulsative, as a succession of active expansive and passive intensive states; which succession, as already indicated, never had a beginning. The Ultimate Principle, in its active expansive operation, constitutes and produces the Yang or Positive Essence; in its passive intensive operation it constitutes and produces the Yin or Negative Essence. When the active expansive phase of the process has reached its extreme limit, the operation becomes passive and intensive; and when the passive intensive phase has reached its extreme limit, the operation again becomes active and expansive: each phase roots in the other in the course of a sort of subjective vibration or twofold expansive and intensive action, which is, however, no motion in space. Not only did all material and mental existence of which we are cognisant originate by the process described—if we may speak of the origination of that which has existed from eternity—but all existences do now subsist in virtue of the same process, operating in ceaseless repetition.'[1]

Of the various symbols in which different observers in different societies have expressed the alternation between a static condition and a dynamic activity in the rhythm of the Universe, Yin and Yang are the most apt, because they convey the measure of the rhythm direct and not through some metaphor derived from psychology or mechanics or mathematics. We will therefore use these Far Eastern symbols in this Study henceforward; and we shall find that this notation lends itself readily to the music of other civilizations. In the *Magnificat* we shall hear Yin's song of joy at passing over into Yang:

My soul doth magnify the Lord, and my spirit hath rejoiced in God my Saviour;
For he hath regarded the lowliness of his handmaiden.

In the Chorus Mysticus which is the culmination of the Second Part of *Faust* we shall hear Yang's song of joy at passing back again, when his race is run, into Yin:

Alles vergängliche
Ist nur ein Gleichnis;
Das Unzulängliche,
Hier wird's Ereignis;
Das Unbeschreibliche,
Hier ist's getan;
Das ewig-Weibliche
Zieht uns hinan.[2]

---

[1] Meadows, T. T.: *The Chinese and their Rebellions* (London 1856, Smith, Elder), p. 343. Compare Eduard Meyer's 'Was zersetzt, baut auf; und was baut auf, führt wieder zur Zersetzung' (*Geschichte des Altertums*, vol. i (i), 4th edition (Stuttgart and Berlin 1921, Cotta), p. 161); and his 'Jede Idee, sobald sie sich verwirklicht, in ihr Gegenteil umschlägt; denn kein Gedanke vermag die Wirklichkeit in ihrer Totalität zu umfassen' (op. cit., p. 182).

[2] Goethe: *Faust*, ll. 12104-11.

In the self-revelation of the Spirit of the Earth to the scholar who evokes this mighty power by the vehemence of his mental strife, we shall hear the very beat of the alternating rhythm itself:

> In Lebensfluten, im Tatensturm
> Wall' ich auf und ab,
> Webe hin und her!
> Geburt und Grab
> Ein ewiges Meer,
> Ein wechselnd Weben,
> Ein glühend Leben,
> So schaff' ich am sausenden Webstuhl der Zeit
> Und wirke der Gottheit lebendiges Kleid.[1]

[1] *Faust*, ll. 501–9.

C. THE CAUSE OF THE GENESES OF CIVILIZATIONS

I. A POSSIBLE NEGATIVE FACTOR: *VIS INERTIAE*

WE have now ascertained the nature of the geneses of civilizations. They are particular beats of a general rhythmical pulsation which runs all through the Universe. Evidently this is as far as we can go in understanding how the geneses of civilizations occur. In this quest we have reached the Pillars of Hercules; τὸ πόρσω δ' ἔστι σοφοῖς ἄβατον κἀσόφοις. οὔ νιν διώξω· κεινὸς εἴην.[1] Yet we may still inquire why the geneses of civilizations have occurred when they have. Why did they not begin to occur until less than 6,000 years ago, when Man, after his ascent from Sub-Man, had been lying torpid on the level of Primitive Humanity for some 300,000 years? And if Man was content with his primitive condition so long, what has moved him, during these last six thousand years, to make a score of dynamic efforts to rise above himself and ascend to the level of Superman?

A negative factor which may account for the long pause on the primitive level, before the first attempts at civilization were made, is *vis inertiae*. The effect of this factor is well described by that contemporary Western anthropologist whom we have already quoted[2] apropos of Yin and Yang, or, as he calls them, 'integrations' and 'differentiations':

'The integrations . . . might with some truth be called resting-places, encampments, on [Man's] nomadic march. For in the evolution of Man, as in that of every other living thing, there are action and reaction between Inertia and Variability. Throughout all the range of Life, resting is easier than movement: there is economy of energy, which, other things being equal, makes for survival. Hence the tendency of organisms to remain in an integration which "works well", that is, in which there is more or less perfect equilibrium between the living creature and the conditions of its survival. So long as the adaptation of the organism to its surroundings is maintained, it may continue to exist unchanged for whole geological periods. This accounts for the persistence down to the present age of archaic forms of life, like Peripatus, almost an intermediate form between insect and worm, Amphioxus, a very primitive vertebrate, and the Marsupials. In like manner, Man may remain within a certain integration of his life for immense ages, provided the adaptation of his needs and powers to the environment continues substantially the same and no differentiation in his own life, or in that of his fellows, or in the external conditions of existence, calls

---

[1] Pindar's Third Olympian Ode, *ad fin.*   [2] On pp. 197–8, above.

for a new effort to secure survival or for an advance to a further stage in his development. Thus he remains for an enormous period at the Palaeolithic stage of culture, as regards his tools and weapons—no doubt because these unpolished flints are sufficient to ensure his survival against the natural conditions which threaten his existence, against the competing animals, and the members of his own species who are no better armed or equipped than he.'[1]

Our anthropologist calls this Yin-phase, in which Mankind was resting on the level of Primitive Humanity, 'the Integration of Custom', while he gives the name 'Integration of Instinct' to the preceding Yin-phase, in which Sub-Man was resting on his lower ledge before he embarked on his ultimately successful endeavour to achieve humanity.[2]

'The Integration of Custom, it is vital to observe, recovers much of the static nature and stability of the instinctive stage and of the Integration of Instinct, and thus resists differentiation to a remarkable degree, in virtue of its adaptation to immense variations of the environment—in other words, in virtue of its power of survival without the necessity of new departures. The stability and resistance to differentiation or change on the part of this Integration are so great that it retains a vast portion of uncivilised Mankind at the cultural stage of Tribal Custom through countless generations, and but for the irruption of civilised influences and conditions would, and in many cases does, keep these people in a state of arrested development, resembling those primeval forms of animal and plant life which survive down to the present age. The Integration of Custom is, however, broken through at last by inevitable differentiations. . . .'[3]

In detail, this observer describes the effect of *vis inertiae*, as operative in the customs of primitive societies, in the following terms:

'The strength of Custom, the custom of the tribe, lies . . . in its adaptation to a stage of mental development in which the effort of action is preferred to the more exacting effort of thought, especially if coordinative and prolonged. Its powerful appeal consists in its evasion, by practical solutions of life's problems, of the strain which reflection imposes upon

---

[1] Murphy, J.: *Primitive Man: His Essential Quest* (London 1927, Milford), pp. 26–7.
[2] Can we name the Yang-phases with which these two Yin-phases have alternated? 'The Integration of Custom' has been followed, in the geneses of civilizations, by a 'Differentiation of Intellectual Activity'. Were the two differentiations which respectively followed and preceded 'the Integration of Instinct' intellectual likewise? We have no data that enable us to answer this question in the line of evolution which has led to Man from the common ancestor of Mankind and the Anthropoid Apes. We are more likely to obtain an answer if we turn our attention to the line represented by the insects who still remain in 'the Integration of Instinct'. At least one student of insect life is inclined to think that 'Instinct began as a reasoned act' and that it 'became automatic'— that is, 'became instinctive'—only through a long process of repetition. (Hingston, R. W. G.: *Problems of Instinct and Intelligence* (London 1928, Arnold), p. 268.) This question is taken up again in Part III. A, below, vol. iii, on p. 110.
[3] Murphy, op. cit., p. 31.

the ill-developed co-ordinative powers of the savage brain. The result is the formation of a system of belief and practice which so dominates a great portion of Mankind in all ages down to the present, and is, in its own way, so deeply unified, that it deserves to be called the Integration of Custom. . . . Its supreme disadvantage is that the mental effort to break through tribal traditions and age-long practices is as difficult as for the individual to conquer ingrained personal habits, and indeed much more so, for the collective consciousness in the primitive state, and even beyond it, with the social instincts in the heart of it like the iron in reinforced concrete, is extremely resistant to alteration. The tendency to rest in what has proved safe is stronger by far than the adventurous impulse to launch out upon the new and the unknown. This accounts for the innumerable culs-de-sac in the history of the race, the stagnation in which so many tribes remain for long periods. Self-preservation seems all on the side of inertia. . . . This Integration of Custom, Man's next and prolonged resting-place after the Integration of Instinct, is an illustration of the difficulty of maintaining the erect posture of the mind, and of the tendency to relapse to various forms of rest from mental strain and fatigue, which are characteristic of Primitive Man.'[1]

Vis inertiae, thus entrenched in Custom, accounts well enough for Man's pause on the level of Primitive Humanity for something like 300,000 years; but why is it that, within the last 6,000 years, certain members of the Human Race, in certain societies, have so far overcome their inertia as to pass out of this Yin-state into a new fit of Yang-activity? The more weight we attach to *vis inertiae* as a negative retarding factor, the greater the momentum which we must ascribe to the positive factor, whatever it may be, which has set human life in motion again by its impetus. This unknown quantity must be the next object of our research.

II. POSSIBLE POSITIVE FACTORS

(a) RACE AND ENVIRONMENT

1. *Race*

The Race Theory and Race Feeling

We are now in search of the positive factor which, within the last 6,000 years, has shaken part of Mankind out of the Yin-state which we may call the 'Integration of Custom' into a Yang-activity which we may call 'the Differentiation of Civilization'. There are several alternative directions in which this positive factor may be looked for. It may be sought in some special quality in the human beings who have made this particular transition from

[1] Murphy, op. cit., pp. 82–3. Compare Bagehot, W.: *Physics and Politics*, 10th edition (London 1894, Kegan Paul), pp. 58–60.

Yin to Yang on the twenty-one occasions of which we have know-ledge; or it may be sought in some special feature in the environments in which the transition has taken place; or again it may be sought in some interaction between the microcosm and the macrocosm, in some prowess of the Race when confronted with some challenge from the Environment. Let us explore these alternatives one by one. Let us consider first the factor of Race, and second the factor of Environment, each in and by itself. If neither factor appears capable, in isolation, of generating the momentum for which, *ex hypothesi*, we have to account, then we must find our unknown quantity in some product of the two factors, if we are to find it at all. It may be that, when they interact under certain conditions, they produce effects which do not follow from their action under other conditions either separately or together—as air and petrol vapour, when mixed in a carburettor and introduced into a combustion chamber, produce explosions powerful enough to drive the engine of a motor-car, though the air in the atmosphere and the petrol in the petrol-tank remain inert.

Race is the term used to denote some distinctive innate quality in any genus or species or other class or group of living creatures. The racial elements which concern us here are distinctive psychic or spiritual qualities, possibly innate in certain societies of human beings, which may prove to be the positive factor impelling these societies towards civilization. Psychology, however, and particularly Social Psychology, is a study which is still in its infancy; and all discussions of Race, up to date, in which Race is considered from our point of view, depend on the postulate that there is a permanent and precise correlation between hypothetical racial characteristics of a psychic order in human beings and the racial characteristics which are manifest in our human bodily physique. The distinctive marks of Physical Race leap to the eye—even when the eye is untrained and the distinctions are subtle and minute. This general human sensitiveness to Race, in the physical aspect of Human Nature, may be an excrescence from the sexual faculty—though this suggestion is rather discredited by the fact that, within the *Genus Homo*, there are no differences of Physical Race which have the sexual effect of making cross-union sterile. Whatever the explanation of our sensitiveness to Physical Race may be, its undoubted existence as an element in our consciousness is apt to produce two intellectual consequences which are fertile in errors. It makes us assume that a phenomenon of which our perceptions are so acute must be proportionately plain to our understandings, whereas our scientific knowledge about Race in its physical aspect is really not appreciably greater than our knowledge about Race in its psychic aspect. In the second place, we are led into taking for granted—without proof and even without presumptive evidence—the postulate of a correlation between Physical Race and Psychical Race which we have mentioned just above. Before making these hazardous intellectual leaps in the dark, we seldom pause to reflect that we are setting out to explain one unknown quantity in terms of another.[1]

In the Western World of our day, 'racial' explanations of social phenomena are much in vogue. Racial differences of human physique, regarded as immutable in themselves and as bearing witness to likewise immutable racial differences in the human psyche, are supposed to account for the differences which we observe empirically between the fortunes and achievements of different human societies. These 'racial theories', which always start from the two assumptions to which we have drawn attention, are striking examples of one social phenomenon which we have now learnt to discount: to wit, the influence of social environment on historical study.

The belief that differences of Physical Race are immutable is not peculiar to our age of our society. The rhetorical question: 'Can the Ethiopian change his skin, or the leopard his spots?'[2] antici-pates, in poetic imagery, the modern Western racialist's travesty of the modern Western biologist's proposition that acquired charac-teristics are not transmissible—and the doctrine is not the more securely established for being formulated in prose. The present vogue of racialism in the West, however, has really little to do with current scientific hypotheses. A prejudice so strong as this cannot be accounted for by a cause so rational. Modern Western racial prejudice is not so much a distortion of Western scientific thought as a pseudo-intellectual reflection of Western race-feeling; and this feeling, as we see it in our time, is a consequence of the expansion of our Western Civilization over the face of the Earth since the last quarter of the fifteenth century of our era.

The feeling has been aroused by contact, often under untoward conditions, between societies whose members happen to stand at opposite extremes of the range of variety in Physical Race which is to be found in the *Genus Homo*. Our Western Civilization hap-pens to have emerged and developed among peoples in Western Europe who belong, in their physique, to certain varieties of 'the White Race' which our ethnologists have labelled 'Caucasian'. In

---

[1] 'Hier hat erst unsere Zeit dem äusseren Gegensatz eine innere Bedeutung beigelegt, und manche ins Absurde überspannte Theorien haben dem Rassenfaktor eine Bedeutung zugeschrieben, die ihm niemals zugekommen ist und aller geschichtlichen Erfahrung ins Gesicht schlägt.' (Meyer, E.: *Geschichte des Altertums*, vol. i (i), 4th edition (Stutt-gart and Berlin 1921, Cotta), p. 77.)

[2] Jeremiah, xiii. 23.

exploring the whole surface of the planet, these White Westerners have come across representatives of all the other physical races of Mankind; and in most of the permanent settlements which they have made, beyond the narrow borders of Western Europe, overseas, they have come to live intermingled geographically with members of one or more of these other races: in America, South Africa, and East Africa with African negroes; in the two latter regions with representatives of the dark-skinned races of India, as well; in Australia with the altogether primitive 'Blackfellows'; in New Zealand with the Polynesian Maoris; and in all parts of Australasia, as well as along the Pacific coast of North America, with representatives of the so-called Yellow Race from China and Japan.

In all these countries overseas where White people from Western Europe have settled cheek by jowl with representatives of other races, there are three elements in the situation which between them go far towards accounting for the strength and virulence of Western race-feeling in our time. First, the White people have established an ascendancy over the people of other races with whom they have come to share their new homes. Secondly, these White masters have almost everywhere abused their power in some way and in some degree. Thirdly, they are haunted by a perpetual fear that some day the positions may be reversed; that by weight of superior numbers or by more successful adaptation to the local climate or by ability to survive on a lower level of subsistence or by readiness to do harder physical or intellectual work, the Man of Colour may eventually bring the White Man's ascendancy to an end and perhaps even establish an ascendancy of his own over the White Man. The 'first shall be last, and the last first';[1] and, if ever this comes to pass, the White Man's children must expect to have the sins of their fathers visited on their heads, for, in the consciousness of 'under-dog', the past is ever present. These considerations enter into the race-feeling of Western settlers overseas; and it is the feeling of these frontiersmen on the subject of Race that determines the feeling of our Western Society as a whole.[2]

[1] Mark x. 31.
[2] In the homelands of our Western Society in Europe, which are thickly populated by White people with no appreciable admixture of other racial strains, no contact with members of other races in the experience of daily life, and no fear of Coloured people coming into Europe from abroad to swamp or subjugate the White Race here at home, race-feeling is dormant most of the time, and, even when aroused, is seldom excited to a high pitch. Yet, just on this account, public opinion among White people at home is prone to acquiesce in the attitude and the policy, with regard to Race, which are pressed upon them by White people who have settled in countries overseas. They acquiesce because they feel that, after all, Race is the overseas peoples' problem and not theirs and that they ought not to withhold support from their own kinsmen out in the wilderness, who, in enlarging the domain of the White Race at the expense of other races, are in some sense fighting the battle of all White Men, wherever they happen to be domiciled. Hence, in this matter, it is not the White Man in Europe but the European settler overseas who sets the tone.

The Protestant Background of our Modern Western Race-feeling

The race-feeling which is thus aroused in our Western Society by the present situation and temper of our settlers overseas also springs naturally from the religious background of those Western people who are of the Protestant persuasion.[1]

In our Western history, the Protestant movement started immediately before the movement of overseas settlement; and, in the eighteenth century of our era, the competition between the peoples of Western Europe for the command of the overseas world ended in the victory of the English-speaking Protestants, who secured for themselves the lion's share of those overseas countries, inhabited by primitive peoples, that were suitable for settlement by Europeans, as well as the lion's share of the countries inhabited by adherents of the living non-Western civilizations who were incapable at the time of resisting Western conquest and domination. The outcome of the Seven Years' War decided that the whole of North America, from the Arctic Circle to the Rio Grande, should be populated by new nations of European origin whose cultural background was the Western Civilization in its English Protestant version, and that a Government instituted by English Protestants and informed with their ideas should become paramount over the whole of Continental India. Thus the race-feeling engendered by the English Protestant version of our Western culture became the determining factor in the development of race-feeling in our Western Society as a whole.

This has been a misfortune for Mankind, for the Protestant temper and attitude and conduct in regard to Race, as in many other vital issues, is inspired largely by the Old Testament; and in matters of Race the promptings of this old-fashioned Syriac oracle are very clear and very savage.[2] The 'Bible Christian' of European origin and race who has settled among peoples of non-European race overseas has inevitably identified himself with Israel obeying the will of Jehovah and doing the Lord's work by taking possession of the Promised Land, while he has identified the non-Europeans

[1] As the following analysis of the historical relation between Protestantism and modern Western race-feeling might conceivably be misinterpreted as an expression of religious prejudice in the mind of the writer, it may be pertinent for him to mention that he was brought up as a Protestant and that he has not become a Catholic.—A. J. T.

[2] The Old Testament, of course, is only representative of the Syriac religious genius in its young and callow phase; and even in this phase, towards its latter end, there was an outburst of spiritual experience and spiritual creation—recorded in the Books of the Prophets—which points forward to the New Testament. It is in the New Testament, manifestly, that the Syriac religious genius is revealed at its zenith. It was an unfortunate perversity that led the founders of Protestantism in our modern Western Christendom to seek their main inspiration partly in the pre-prophetic books of the Old Testament and partly in the theology of one latter-day Syriac man of genius, St. Augustine of Hippo (a Syriac saint whose true spiritual legacy to Mankind was not the doctrine of Predestination).

who have crossed his path with the Canaanites whom the Lord has delivered into the hand of his Chosen People to be destroyed or subjugated.[1] Under this inspiration, the English-speaking Protestant settlers in the New World exterminated the North American Indian, as well as the bison, from coast to coast of the Continent, whereas the Spanish Catholics only exterminated the Indian in the Caribbean Islands and were content, on the Continent, to step into the shoes of the Aztecs and the Incas—sparing the conquered in order to rule them as subject populations, converting their subjects to their own religion, and inter-breeding with their converts.[2]

Again, the English Protestants took up the trade in negro slaves from Africa to the New World and afterwards obtained the monopoly of this trade as one of the perquisites in the Peace Settlement at Utrecht (A.D. 1713). The Spanish and Portuguese Catholic settlers bought the human merchandise which the Protestant slave-traders offered them; but the Spanish and Portuguese Empires and the 'successor-states' which eventually took their place as independent states members of the Western Society were not the fields in which the institution of plantation slavery, which had thus been introduced into the New World, struck deepest root and grew to the most formidable proportions. The stage on which the tragedy of negro slavery in the New World was played out on the grand scale was an English-speaking Protestant country: the United States.

Finally, in Continental India, where the English could not think of supplanting the conquered 'natives' as they had supplanted them in North America,[3] but could only impose their rule on them as the Spaniards had imposed theirs on the 'Natives' of Mexico and Peru, the sequel was not the same as it had been in the Spanish Indies. In British India, unlike Spanish America, only a negligible number of the 'Natives' were converted to the religion of the ruling race or were physically assimilated to it by interbreeding. For

---

[1] When the first translation of the Bible into a Teutonic language was made by Ulfilas, the apostle of the Goths, in the fourth century of our era, the translator wisely omitted the Books of Samuel and Kings, on the ground that war and bloodshed were too much in the minds of the Goths as it was, without their proclivity in this direction being consecrated and confirmed by the authority of the sacred book of their new religion. It is a pity that Luther and the English translators did not follow Ulfilas' example—or, indeed, improve on it by omitting Joshua and Judges as well! King James I's English Authorized Version of the Bible, which presents the Old Testament complete and unexpurgated, was published in A.D. 1611. A book called *The New English Canaan*, by Thomas Morton, was published in 1637!

[2] For the history of the vein of ruthlessness in English colonization, see II. C (ii) (a)1, Annex, below.

[3] The reasons are almost too obvious to need mentioning. In the first place, Europeans could not hope to make themselves at home in the Indian climate, even if they had found, or made, the soil of India free from other human occupants. In the second place, the existing 'Native' population of India was too numerous and too far advanced in civilization to be exterminated, even if our British Israelites had ever contemplated treating the Canaanite in India as they treated him in America.

good or evil, the English Protestant rulers of India have distinguished themselves from all other contemporary Western rulers over non-Western peoples by the rigidity with which they have held aloof from their subjects. They took to the Hindu institution of caste as readily[1] as if they had not found it established in India when they came but had invented it for their own convenience.

I once had an opportunity of seeing our old-fashioned Protestant zeal for the Lord through other Western eyes.

At a date some time after Signor Mussolini's march on Rome, I was lecturing at a summer school in a university in New England where one of my colleagues was a Senator of the Kingdom of Italy. The Senator's subject was the present position of Italy in the World—her achievements and her necessities, her claims and her grievances. This exposition was punctuated by rattlings of his sabre and tramplings of his jack-boots; and his English-speaking Protestant audience was neither impressed nor amused. As I watched their composed, disapproving countenances, I could read what was passing in their minds: 'Here is another foreigner, another naughty child—naughty, but not dangerous, because he cannot really act up to his parade; but it is shocking behaviour, and it shall have no encouragement from us.' I soon realized that the poor Senator read their minds as clearly as I did. (He had lived in England for years and understood the 'Anglo-Saxon' mentality.) In each successive lecture in the course, he struck his attitudes with less and less verve and breathed his fire and slaughter with less and less conviction. Undoubtedly he realized that his performance was producing just the opposite effect to what was intended; but, no less certainly, he was bound by precise instructions and had been warned to produce documentary evidence (in the shape of a short-hand record) that he had carried out these instructions to the letter, under pain of losing his head—or at any rate his senatorial *laticlavium*—on his return to his native land. I became quite sorry for the Senator as his unheroic self-martyrdom went on; and I could see that the President of the university—a kindly man—was sorry too. As a mark of courtesy and esteem, the President invited the Senator, who was a bibliophil, to inspect the university library one day when our session was drawing to a close, and I happened to be included in the party. The chief treasure of the library was a Bible printed in the seventeenth century in the language of the Red Indians who had inhabited this part of New England at that time;

[1] 'Readily', but not instantaneously, for the English in India did not fall into the practice of complete social segregation from 'the Natives' immediately upon their first arrival. During the seventeenth and eighteenth centuries there was a certain amount of social intercourse and racial intermixture between English and Indians which was discontinued in the nineteenth century and has not been renewed in the twentieth century on any considerable scale or with any noteworthy success.

and as the Senator handled the precious volume, his features relaxed and lighted up. 'This book is very rare, then?' he asked. 'There are not half-a-dozen copies known', replied the President proudly. 'Then the Indians do not read it nowadays?' the Senator went on. 'Why, no, you see', explained the President, 'the Indians are no longer there.' 'Why, what happened to the Indians?' asked the Senator brightly, with an innocent air—and at that question the President's speech became confused. He hummed and hawed, he stuttered and stammered, till at last the words came out like the knocks of the engine in a motor-car if you try to start it on top gear: 'What happened to the Indians? Well, the Indians, you know—the fact is, the Indians disappeared.' The Senator, listening politely, said never a word; but a smile appeared at either corner of his mouth and spread so broadly that I began to wonder whether, like the smile of the Cheshire Cat, it would meet round the back of his head. In that moment, weeks of suffering were revenged; and as I saw him savouring his revenge in his cultivated Latin way, I found myself repeating, under my breath, the ballad of those true-blue Protestant pioneers, the Walrus and the Carpenter, who wept with pity as the devouring Zeal of the Lord constrained them to eat up the devoted and defenceless oysters. Between this Protestant method of conversion by extermination and the methods of the Jesuit missionaries in Canada and Paraguay there is indeed a great gulf fixed.

Of course the fanaticism and ferocity of the race-feeling which the Old Testament once instilled into Protestant souls have both considerably abated as Protestantism itself has evolved through Rationalism towards Agnosticism. First the traffic in negro slaves, and finally the very institution of negro slavery in the New World, have been abolished by the English-speaking peoples themselves under the promptings of their own consciences and at the price of their own blood and treasure; and the attitude of the Englishman in India towards the people of India is no longer the attitude of unmitigated aloofness and superiority that it used to be. The improvement in feeling and conduct has certainly been very great. Yet even now this improvement is only partial and is still precarious.

The slavery once imposed nakedly on uprooted and transplanted Black Men by immigrant White Men of English speech and Protestant faith in the New World will be imposed under camouflage, in our generation, on other Black Men in the homeland of the Black Race by the Dutch and English settlers in South and East Africa, if these settlers once obtain a free hand to deal with the native African peoples at their discretion; and this revival of negro slavery—this time on the negro's native continent—will not be the less pernicious for being hypocritically disguised. The battle over negro slavery, which was fought out in the New World during the century ending with the end of the American Civil War, may have to be fought out in Africa once again; and even if Light discomfits Darkness for the second time, the sequel to the American battle over this issue shows how hard it is for the Light to drive the Darkness altogether off the field. In the United States, where negro slavery has been abolished at so great a cost, race-feeling remains to perpetuate the social evils of racial inequality and racial segregation. We can foresee that in Africa, too, the sequel, at the best, will be the same. The young communities of English-speaking White people in the United States and in the Union of South Africa and in Kenya Colony, upon whose future the more distant prospects of our 'Anglo-Saxon' version of Western culture very largely depend, are already in the grip of the paralysing institution of Caste.[1]

Meanwhile, the successive phases of Protestant race-feeling have left their mark on our Western thought in the form of various race-theories, as a slowly dying volcano leaves a record of successive eruptions in the petrified streams of lava that permanently disfigure its flanks.

Among English-speaking Protestants there are still to be found some 'Fundamentalists' who believe themselves to be 'the Chosen People' in the literal sense of the term as it is used in the Old Testament. This 'British Israel' confidently traces its physical descent from the lost Ten Tribes. We may leave it to dispute its claim to the title with the rival claimants, the most redoubtable of whom are the Afghans and the Abyssinians.[2]

There are other English-speaking Protestants—or ex-Protestants, for these would count themselves among the number of the intellectually emancipated—who hold the doctrine of 'British Israel' in a figurative or metaphorical sense. Without contending that the English-speaking peoples of the White Race[3] are descended from the Children of Israel after the flesh, these transcendentalist 'British Israelites' do maintain that they have succeeded to the Israelites' role of being 'the Chosen People' in a spiritual sense—that the mantle of Elijah has fallen upon Elisha, whether by some divine

---

[1] This institution is discussed in Parts VIII and IX, below.

[2] Perhaps the Abyssinians ought strictly to be regarded as *hors concours*, since they have 'gone one better' than their competitors. The Abyssinians have scorned the Ten Tribes and have claimed Judah for their father. The Negus Negusti styles himself officially, down to this day, 'the Lion of the Tribe of Judah' (see Genesis xlix. 9, and Revelations v. 5).

[3] This qualification has to be added for strict accuracy, since 'the English-speaking peoples' in the literal sense include nowadays some millions of Negroes and crossbreeds who speak English as their mother tongue, and many peoples, from India to Japan inclusive, for whom English is a second language, supplementing the mother tongue as an indispensable *lingua franca*.

sleight of hand or by the accident of which way the wind blew when the mantle was in the air. However it may have happened, the English-speaking peoples have become (on this view) the Heirs of the Kingdom, the depositories of the hopes and capacities of Mankind, the chosen vessels through whose instrumentality the Human Race is destined to attain to the goal of its endeavours. This doctrine is resonantly enunciated in Mr. Rudyard Kipling's *Recessional*.

There are others, again, who seek justification for their race-feeling in theories that purport to be objective, rational, and scientific. These rationalists are chasing a will-o'-the-wisp; for the race-feeling which is the *primum mobile* of their intellectual antics is an emotion fired by a religious spark, and any theory in which this emotion is reflected will prove, on analysis, to be emotional and religious like its original. The irrational nucleus can never be conjured away, however scientifically it may be fumigated or sterilized. *Tamen usque recurret.*[1] The most popular of the idols that have been set up by this rather priggish and pedantic school of superstition is 'Nordic Man': the xanthotrichous, glaucopian, dolichocephalic variety of *Homo Leucodermaticus* whose pet name (given him by Nietzsche) is 'the Blond Beast'. The votaries of this Racial God Incarnate maintain that all human achievements of any value in their eyes are his doing, and his alone. Before we bow down and worship this false god, let us see how far we may be able to account for his cult by the social environment in which it has arisen and maintained itself.

'Nordic Man' was first placed on his pedestal by a French aristocrat, the Count de Gobineau, who was active between the Restoration of A.D. 1815 and the Revolution of 1848.[2] De Gobineau's idolization of 'the Blond Beast' was an incident in the French political controversies of the age. In the Revolution of 1789, when the French nobility were being dispossessed of their estates by the peasantry and were emigrating as refugees to Coblentz, the pedants in the revolutionary ranks, who were never happy if they could not present the events of the day in classical guise, proclaimed that the Gauls, after fourteen centuries of subjection, were driving their Frankish conquerors back into the outer darkness beyond the Rhine from which they had originally emerged, and were resuming possession of the Gallic soil which, despite the long barbarian

---

[1] Horace: *Epistles*, Book I, Epistle 10, verse 24.
[2] It is noteworthy that David Hume (*vivebat* A.D. 1711–76), in his essay *Of National Characters*, deals with the problem of the empirically observed differences between one human society and another almost exclusively in terms of the question whether the physical environment or the social environment is the differentiating factor to which these differences are to be ascribed. In Hume's essay, the Race-theory is barely mentioned—except for one footnote in which the author records some considerations which incline him 'to suspect the Negroes to be naturally inferior to the Whites'.

usurpation, had never ceased to be rightfully their own. De Gobineau's cult of 'Nordic Man' was a reactionary 'scientific' counterblast to this revolutionary classical conceit.

'I accept your identifications', de Gobineau replied in effect to the revolutionary pedants of the generation before him. 'Let us agree that the populace of France is descended from the Gauls and the aristocracy from the Franks; that both races have bred pure; and that there is a definite and permanent correlation between their physical and their psychical characteristics. Well, now you have delivered yourselves into my hands. You imagine, do you, that your Gauls stand for civilization and my Franks for barbarism? Let me tell you that you have got hold of the wrong end of the stick. Whence came such civilization as your Gauls ever acquired? Of course, from Rome. And what made Rome grow great? Why, a primeval infusion of the same Nordic blood that flowed in my Franks' veins. The first Romans—and likewise the first Greeks, the Achaeans of Homer—were fair-haired, blue-eyed conquerors who descended from the invigorating North and established their dominion over the feebler natives of the enervating Mediterranean. As long as their blood remained pure, their civilization went from strength to strength; but, alas, climate and numbers were both working against them. In the long run, their blood was diluted and their race enfeebled, and *pari passu* their power and their glory declined. The Roman civilization of which the Gauls were privileged to partake was no longer the Roman civilization of the great age; and within five centuries of Caesar's conquest of Gaul the Roman stock was exhausted altogether. The time had come for another rescue-party of fair-haired, blue-eyed conquerors to descend from the invigorating North in order to set the pulse of civilization beating again. My Franks were the heroes who volunteered!'

This political *jeu d'esprit* was given countenance by a contemporary scientific discovery which de Gobineau was quick to take up and turn to account. It was discovered that almost all the living languages of Europe as well as ancient Greek and Latin, and the living languages of Persia and Northern India as well as the classical Iranian of the Avesta and the classical Sanskrit of the Vedas, were related to one another as members of a single vast linguistic family. It was rightly inferred that there must have been an *Ursprache*, a primeval 'Aryan' or 'Indo-European' language, from which all the known languages of the family derived their common descent. It was wrongly inferred that the peoples among whom these languages were current were physically related in the same degrees as the languages themselves, and that they were all descended from a primeval 'Aryan' or 'Indo-European' race which had spread conquering and to conquer, east and west and south and north, from its original home. A race which had brought forth the religious genius of Zarathustra and Gautama Buddha, the artistic genius of Greece, the political genius of Rome, and the all-embracing genius of our Western Society! Why, this race was responsible for practically all the achievements of human civilization. By comparison, anything that any other races had ever accomplished was negligible. The Indo-European stock must have some unique quality which distinguished it *in toto* from all other breeds of *Genus Homo*. It only remained to identify this hypothetical and almost certainly fabulous 'Indo-European Race' with the well-known fair-haired, blue-eyed, long-headed type of White Man, and the apotheosis was complete.

Starting from the pedantic polemics of revolutionary and counter-revolutionary French politics, and taking the Indo-European hypo-thesis in his stride, de Gobineau worked out a racial theory of history which he expounded in a brilliant book with the provocative title *Essai sur l'Inégalité des Races Humaines*. The following passage presents the gist of his thesis in clear and forcible terms:

'Il est donc établi:

'1° Que les tribus actuellement sauvages l'ont toujours été, quelque soit le milieu supérieur qu'elles aient pu traverser, et qu'elles le seront toujours; 2° que, pour qu'une nation sauvage puisse même supporter le séjour dans un milieu civilisé, il faut que la nation qui crée ce milieu soit un rameau plus noble de la même race; 3° que la même circonstance est encore nécessaire pour que des civilisations diverses puissent, non pas se confondre, ce qui n'arrive jamais, seulement se modifier forte-ment l'une par l'autre, se faire de riches emprunts réciproques, donner naissance à d'autres civilisations composées de leurs éléments; 4° que les civilisations issues de races complètement étrangères l'une à l'autre ne peuvent que se toucher à la surface, ne se pénètrent jamais et s'ex-cluent toujours.'[1]

De Gobineau's theory has been plagiarized, refurbished, elaborated, and popularized, but never reproduced in its original brilliance nor enriched with a single new idea, by a host of adepts since his time, each of whom has had his own axe to grind. The hare which the vivacious Frenchman had started was run by heavy-footed German philologists who improved the word 'Indo-European' into 'Indo-Germanic' and located the original home of the primeval 'Indo-Germans' on that portion of the North Euro-pean plain which happened to be occupied in their day by the Kingdom of Prussia. In the reign of the Emperor William II, an

---

[1] De Gobineau, le Comte J. A.: *Essai sur l'Inégalité des Races Humaines* (Paris 1853–5, Firmin Didot, 4 vols.), vol. i, p. 293.

English Germanophil joined in the chase with a 'zeal of the convert' which put the German devotees of 'Nordic Man' out of countenance. Houston Stewart Chamberlain's insatiable imagination ranged through the great civilizations and the great peoples and the great men and women of history, seeking whom it might devour, and it did not rest until it had swept them all into the Blond Beast's maw. Not content with finding a Nordic ancestry for Charlemagne and for 'fair-haired Menelaus', he found it for Dante and for Jesus Christ. Is it not written in *The Foundations of the Nineteenth Century*?[1] The fine flower of Nordicism, for Houston Stewart Chamberlain, was the Imperial Germany which was on the eve of coming to grief in the General War of 1914–18.[2]

Chevied out of Europe by the clash of arms, de Gobineau's hare audaciously leapt the Atlantic and created a furore in the United States, where 'top-dog' was just in the mood for the sport. In the Southern States, where the Nordic strain in the physical race of the White population is perceptibly strong, the Nordic Gospel brought its converts glad tidings of effortless superiority, not only over the despicable negro in their midst, but over the formidable Yankee in the North. In the rivalry between South and North, the Yankee had won the last round—the Civil War—but during the ensuing half century he had mixed his 'Nordic' gold with the 'Alpine' and 'Mediterranean' alloy of a stupendous immigration-from Southern and Eastern Europe which had given the South the go-by. Racially, the Yankee was no longer the man he once was, while the Southerner had been saved by misfortune from the temptation to sell his birthright. Through the days of adversity, he had kept intact the priceless heritage of the finest blood in the World. His heart beat faster as the Nordic Gospel proclaimed to his eager ears that he was not down-and-out after all, and that if ever he tried conclusions with the Yankee again, the verdict of the Civil War might be reversed. His lips hummed a new song: 'My strength is as the strength of ten, because my race is pure.' And meanwhile, in the North, where the immigrants from Europe were being reinspired by forgotten sentiments and recalled to discarded loyalties through the psychic effects of the European War, the same Gospel was producing, not elation, but a revival, in a terrifying guise, of that old Protestant fear of eternal damnation which had ceased to haunt the descendants of the Pilgrim Fathers in its primitive theological form.

'What shall we do to be saved? We had flattered ourselves, in our

---

[1] *The Foundations of the Nineteenth Century*, by Chamberlain, H. S.: English edition (London 1911, Lane, 2 vols.).

[2] This chapter was written before the cult of Nordic Man became part of the officially established creed of the German Reich as a result of the National-Socialist Revolution of 1933.

foolish pride, that the United States was a melting-pot in which any kind of Europeans could be turned into a-hundred-per-cent. Americans in any quantities. We were living in the same fool's paradise as those medieval alchemists who thought that they had discovered the art of transmuting base metal into gold; and now, under the test of the War, the futility of our social alchemy is exposed. We have not given the immigrant an American soul; we have only given him a hyphen; and when it comes to a tug of war between the two loyalties on either side of the line, it is the German- or the Irish- or the Polish- or the Italian-, and never the -American, that wins. And why have we failed to Americanize the immigrant's soul? Confronted with this vital question, we have opportunely discovered the new Science of Race, which supplies a convincing answer and indicates the action which we ought to take. We have failed to Americanize the immigrant's soul because Soul and Body are rigidly correlated by the first law of Race, while the second law of Race informs us that bodily characteristics are immutable. The descendants of the "Alpine" Jew from the Pale and of the "Mediterranean" peasant from Sicily will remain "Alpines" and "Mediterraneans" still unto the third and fourth and four-hundredth generation[1]; and, as far as they inter-marry with our own

[1] In the time immediately before the outbreak of the General War of 1914–18, when the volume of annual net immigration from Europe into the United States was at its maximum and the confidence of the American people in their own powers of assimilation was at its height, an American ethnologist, Professor Boas of Columbia University, conducted an investigation in New York at the instance of the United States immigration authorities and presented evidence purporting to show that the American-born children of the 'Alpine' Jewish immigrant from the Pale, with his brachycephalic skull, and of the 'Mediterranean' immigrant from Sicily, with his dolichocephalic skull, were both alike born with a skull which differed perceptibly from the skulls of the parents in each case, but tended in both cases to approximate towards the mesocephalic skull-type of the 'a-hundred-per-cent American' New Yorker. (See Hendrick, B. T.: 'The Skulls of our Immigrants', in *McClure's Magazine*, May 1910; and the following works by Professor Franz Boas himself: *Changes in Bodily Form of Descendants of Immigrants* (Washington, D.C. 1912, Govt. Printing Office = 61st Congress, 2nd Session, Senate Documents, vol. 64, Document No. 208); *Kultur und Rasse* (Leipzig 1914, Veit), chap. iii; *Materials for the Study of Inheritance in Man* = Columbia University Contributions to Anthropology, vol. vi (New York 1928, Columbia University Press, and London 1929, Milford). Compare also the belief, which was held by the Arabic philosopher Ibn Khaldūn, that Negro peoples which migrate northwards eventually turn white and that White peoples that migrate to the tropics eventually turn black (Ibn Khaldūn: *Muqaddamāt*, translated by de Slane, Baron McG., vol. i (Paris 1863, Imprimerie Impériale), p. 172. Ibn Khaldūn's view is upheld by one school of modern Western ethnologists. See, for example, Dixon, R. B.: *The Racial History of Man* (New York 1923, Scribner), pp. 479–81 and 494–5; and Taylor, Griffith: *Environment and Race* (Oxford 1927, University Press), pp. 33–4.)

Professor Boas's evidence produced a flutter in the dove-cots of Ethnological Science, since the majority of modern Western ethnologists had formed the opinion that the proportions between the length and breadth of the human skull were transmitted without change through any number of generations, and they had accordingly taken these skull-measurements as their chief criterion for classifying Mankind into races. It is not surprising to learn that Professor Boas's contention was rejected by the majority of his fellow-ethnologists as non-proven. In this controversy, we may be content, for our part, to be neutrals and agnostics. We will merely point out that, whereas Professor Boas's opponents regarded him as a subversive revolutionary who was proposing to destroy the whole basis on which the modern Western Science of Ethnology had been

American stock, they will merely contaminate our Nordic purity without eliminating those inalienable "Alpine" and "Mediterranean" qualities of body and soul which the immigrants have brought with them. In the language of our ancestral Calvinistic theology, it is impossible by human efforts to wash away the taint of original sin or to save a vessel of destruction. All that human providence can do—and it is common prudence to do it—is to exclude the lost soul and tainted body from the community of the just.'

This 'scientific' version of orthodox Protestant theology is expounded in the works of Mr. Madison Grant and Mr. Lothrop Stoddard. The efforts of a nation, converted to the Nordic Gospel wholesale, to save its 'a-hundred-per-cent Americanism', have gone into action in the United States Immigration (Restriction) Acts of 1921 and 1924.

The most ethereal of the intellectual forms in which our modern Western race-feeling has expressed itself is the theory of 'the Diffusionist School' of British anthropologists with which we deal in this Study in another chapter.[1] In this theory, the egocentric mania which stalks naked in the cults of 'British Israel' and 'Nordic Man' is so modestly clad and so scientifically presented that it gives us something of a shock to detect its presence here too. In each of the race-theories that we have examined so far, the monopoly of the unique magical quality, to which all human achievement is ascribed, is attributed to some fraction of Mankind in which the theorist himself is included. The 'British Israelites' claim this monopoly for British-born British subjects domiciled in the United Kingdom; the Nordicists claim it for all White Men with fair hair and blue eyes and a middling-shaped skull; others claim it for all White Men whatsoever. These theories differ only in regard to the size of the fraction of Mankind in which the monopoly of the magical quality is supposed to be vested. They all agree in selecting a fraction, large or small, which happens to include the people by whom the several theories are held. In

---

erected, he never challenged what is the fundamental postulate of all race-theories: that is, the postulate that physical and psychical characteristics are correlated. The assumption underlying Professor Boas's argument was that, if the children of immigrants turned out to have 'a-hundred-per-cent American' skulls, this meant that they also had 'a-hundred-per-cent American' souls. ('This fact [i.e. the alleged difference in skull-measurements between immigrants and their children] is . . . suggestive . . . because it shows that not even those characteristics of a race which have proved to be most permanent in their old home remain the same under the new surroundings; and we are compelled to conclude that when these features of the body change, the whole bodily and mental [sic] make-up of the immigrants may change'—Boas: Changes in Bodily Form of Descendants of Immigrants, p. 5. The postulate of a fixed correlation between bodily and mental changes is made with still greater emphasis on p. 76.) From this assumption it would follow logically that, if their skulls proved to have remained un-American after all, their souls must have remained un-American likewise. From our standpoint, Professor Boas and his opponents are in the same camp.

[1] In I. C (iii) (b), Annex, below.

contrast with all these vulgar egoists and 'low-brows', the 'British Diffusionists' bestow the priceless monopoly upon a fraction of Mankind which lived between four and five thousand years ago and from which the founders of this school are not themselves descended. In their view, 'the Chosen People', the uniquely gifted and creative race, were the ancient Egyptians of the age of the pyramid-builders. In their belief, the inhabitants of Egypt in that age invented 'Civilization', and their descendants, 'the Children of the Sun',[1] conveyed the invention at least half-way round the World: from Egypt to 'Irāq, from 'Irāq to India and China, from India to Indonesia, from China to Peru. The patrons of these *Kulturträger* maintain that their passage has left traces which, where found in combination, may be taken as sure evidence that 'the Chosen People' did once pass that way. The chief of these tokens are the techniques of agriculture and irrigation, the institutions of Caste and War, the art of carving the human form in stone, and the worship of the Sun.[2] Nowadays, however, these traces are mostly vestigial; for the civilization thus invented and propagated could not outlast the race of the propagators. While the advance-guard of this ever-advancing race has been perpetually carrying its 'heliolithic' civilization to fresh societies of primitive men, the garrisons which they have left behind at the successive halting-places on their march have been perpetually dying out; and, wherever this has happened, the primitive population whom the god-like strangers found when they came, and left behind them when they disappeared, have been unable to maintain the civilization which had been imparted to them—or imposed on them—by alien hands. Hence, in every successive zone in which it has been planted, the 'heliolithic' civilization has burst into sudden flower, enjoyed a brief bloom, and then degenerated, like the seed of the sower in the parable when it fell upon stony places.

The preachers of this 'diffusion theory' marshal, on behalf of it, such a mass of anthropological evidence that at first sight we may fail to perceive that they are simply showing off de Gobineau's 'Nordic Man' in a new suit of clothes, and that their anthropological frills are just as adventitious as de Gobineau's philological war-paint. Yet so it is. The lay figure employed in the staging of both theophanies is the same.

[1] How different from 'the Citizens of the Sun' who were led to die in a forlorn hope by Aristonicus of Pergamum. These were not a 'Chosen People' but proletarians who naturalized themselves as citizens of another heavenly body, because, on the surface of this planet, they had not where to lay their heads. (For these Heliopolites, see further Part V below.)

[2] The full list of fifteen culture elements which are alleged to be characteristic of 'the Children of the Sun' will be found in Perry, W. J.: *The Children of the Sun* (London 1923, Methuen), p. 406.

In placing their treasure in the ancient Egyptians instead of in 'Nordic Man', the 'British Diffusionists' have merely performed the psychical operation which psychologists call 'transference'. They have transferred their interests and affections and delusions from the living society of which they themselves are members to one of those extinct societies which their own society has adopted as its protégées[1]; but, in doing this, they have not exorcized the self-regarding emotion from which the impulse to spin a race-theory arises, and therefore have not escaped the intellectual errors to which all theories inspired by egoism are prone. 'The Children of the Sun', spreading the light of civilization, widdershins, from Suez to Panama, are wraiths of 'Nordic Man' spreading the same light southwards from the sunny shores of the Baltic to the Cimmerian darkness of the Mediterranean. The resemblance extends to details; for, in both theories, the illumination is ever ephemeral. The Sun of Civilization has to rise afresh day by day; the inferior races of Mankind have to be invigorated again and again with fresh grafts from Nordic or Egyptiac monkey-glands. What is to become of poor Humanity on the evil and inevitable day when the magic store of Simian vitality is exhausted?

We have now completed our examination of our modern Western race-feeling, the social environment in which it has arisen, and the theories in which it has expressed itself. We can discount the theories to the extent to which the environment accounts for them; and it accounts for them so largely that we might safely venture to discount them altogether. We prefer, however, to give them the *coup de grâce* by deploying certain positive facts against which they cannot stand.

The first of these facts is that our modern Western race-feeling—inspired, as we have seen it to be, by the spirit imbibed from the Old Testament by Protestantism—was unknown in our Western Society in earlier times and has failed to assert itself in certain sections of this Western Society down to this day. During the so-called 'Dark Ages' and 'Middle Ages'—that is to say, during the eight centuries ending about the last quarter of the fifteenth century of our era—the members of our Western Society, when they thought of Mankind as a whole, were accustomed to divide the human family into two categories, as we divide it nowadays. The principle of division, however, was utterly different. Instead of dividing Mankind, as we do, into White people and Coloured people, our forefathers divided it into Christians and Heathen; and

---

[1] For the indulgence shown by Western public opinion towards extinct civilizations which have been rescued from oblivion by the brilliant achievements of Western archaeologists, see above, I. C (iii) (*b*), p. 155, footnote 5.

we are bound to confess that their dichotomy was better than ours both intellectually and morally. It was better intellectually because a human being's religion is a vastly more important and significant factor in his life than the colour of his skin, and is therefore a vastly better criterion for purposes of classification. Again, the dichotomy into Christians and Heathen is better morally than the dichotomy into White and Coloured, because the gulf between religions, unlike the gulf between races, is not impassable. It is a division between sheep in the fold and sheep astray on the mountains, not between sheep and goats.

In the eyes of the medieval Western Christian, when he looked abroad upon the World, the Heathen, wandering unkempt in the wilderness, were neither incurably unclean nor irretrievably lost. Potentially, they were Christians like himself; and he looked forward to a time when all the lost sheep would be gathered into the fold. Indeed, he looked forward to this with assurance as the foreordained consummation of terrestrial history, the fulfilment of God's purpose in the World. In this spirit, medieval Western artists used to portray one of the three Magi as a Negro. How different from the spirit in which the white-skinned Western Protestant of modern times regards his black-skinned convert. The convert may have found spiritual salvation in the White Man's faith; he may have acquired the White Man's culture and learnt to speak his language with the tongue of an angel; he may have become an adept in the White Man's economic technique, and yet it profits him nothing so long as he has not changed his skin. Surely he can retort that it profits the White Man nothing to understand all mysteries and all knowledge and have skill so that he can move mountains, so long as he has not charity.[1]

This medieval Western freedom from the prejudice of race-feeling has survived among Western peoples who have remained more or less in the medieval phase of our Western Civilization: for instance, the Spaniards and Portuguese and the descendants of Spanish and Portuguese settlers who have established new Western communities in America.[2] Among these rather backward Western

---

[1] 1 Corinthians, xiii. 1–3.

[2] This is not to say that the condition of non-White populations under White rule in Spanish and Portuguese Africa and in Latin America is happier to-day than the condition of contemporary non-White populations under British or American rule. On the contrary, the condition of the non-White populations in the Hispanic countries and their present or former colonies, in the Old World and the New, is probably almost everywhere the less happy of the two at the present time. This, however, is because the Spanish and Portuguese-speaking peoples of the Western World are at present on the whole in a less happy condition themselves than the English-speaking peoples. As far as the non-White populations in the Hispanic countries suffer, they suffer equally with their White fellow-countrymen of the same social classes; that is to say, they suffer from the prevailing political disorders and economic injustices—but not from any racial discrimination.

peoples, the racial criterion has never superseded the criterion of religion[1]; but it is more interesting to observe the same freedom from race-feeling surviving among another Western people, the French, who have ever been in the forefront of Western progress and have distinguished themselves (for good or evil) by the radical thoroughness with which they have secularized their national life.

The French have discarded, as decidedly as the English-speaking peoples, the medieval Western dichotomy of Mankind into Christians and Heathen; but the dichotomy which they have substituted for it is one of the same humane and significant kind. When the modern Frenchman looks abroad upon the World, he divides the human family into people who possess, and people who lack, the modern French version of the Western culture; and in his eyes everybody, whatever the colour of his skin, is potentially a cultivated Frenchman. A negro from the Senegal who possesses the necessary qualities of intellect and character can rise, and does rise, to positions of power and honour in French society, without being made to feel that he is being enfranchised grudgingly or esteemed with reservations. The freedom of the French from race-feeling has been a fact of common knowledge all through the modern age of Western history. In the seventeenth and eighteenth centuries of our era, in North America, when the English settlers were expelling or exterminating the Red Indians, the French settlers were intermarrying with them and assimilating them. During the General War of 1914–18, the Negro citizens of the United States who were serving in the American Army in France were astonished at the social liberality with which the French Whites treated the African Negro subjects of the French Republic serving in the French Army, whose cultural level was much lower than that of the North American Negroes on the average. The justice of this observation can be verified by any English-speaking White man who takes the trouble to visit a garrison town in a French colony or in France itself and watch the White and Black soldiers of the Republic passing the time of day together when they are off duty.[2]

[1] The sense of religious solidarity and fraternity did not, however, restrain the Spaniards and the Portuguese in South America, a century and a half ago, from cold-bloodedly and brutally destroying—out of sheer greed for (non-existent) gold and for (to them, unutilizable) land—the wonderful society which had been conjured into existence, by the genius of the Jesuit missionaries, among the primitive peoples of Paraguay.

[2] Ardent 'Anglo-Saxon' racialists will argue that this fact of observation does not refute, but confirms, their racial theories. It is easy enough, they will say, for a 'Latin' to consort with a 'nigger', for a 'Latin' is a very doubtful sort of White Man. To speak frankly, he is half-way to being a 'nigger' himself, so it is a case of 'birds of a feather'! This gun can be silenced by a single shot. We have merely to point out that in the population of France to-day all the three conventional varieties of White Man—the 'Mediterranean', the 'Alpine', and the 'Nordic'—are well represented. Normandy and other districts of Northern France can supply pure specimens of 'the Blond Beast' as abundantly as Scandinavia or Appalachia themselves.

We may next point to the fact that while, in our Western Society, race-feeling was once unknown and is not now universal, there are other societies in which the prejudice has taken shape on different and sometimes diametrically opposite lines.

For instance, the Primitive Arabs who were the ruling element in the Umayyad Caliphate called themselves 'the swarthy people', with a connotation of racial superiority, and their Persian and Turkish subjects 'the ruddy people', with a connotation of racial inferiority: that is to say, they drew the same distinction that we draw between blonds and brunets but reversed the values which we assign to the two shades of White. Gentlemen may prefer blondes; but brunettes are the first choice of Allah's 'Chosen People'. Moreover, the Arabs and all other White Muslims, whether brunets or blonds, have always been free from colour-prejudice *vis-à-vis* the non-White races; and, at the present day, Muslims still make that dichotomy of the human family which Western Christians used to make in the Middle Ages. They divide Mankind into Believers and Unbelievers who are all potentially Believers; and this division cuts across every difference of Physical Race. This liberality is more remarkable in White Muslims to-day than it was in White Western Christians in our Middle Ages; for our medieval forefathers had little or no contact with peoples of a different colour, whereas the White Muslims were in contact with the Negroes of Africa and with the dark-skinned peoples of India from the beginning and have increased that contact steadily, until nowadays Whites and Blacks are intermingled, under the aegis of Islam, through the length and breadth of the Indian and the African Continent. Under this searching test, the White Muslims have demonstrated their freedom from race-feeling by the most convincing of all proofs: they have given their daughters to Black Muslims in marriage.

I had an opportunity to observe this Muslim freedom from race-feeling at first hand when I was an undergraduate at Oxford. At that time there were two Egyptian Muslim undergraduates in my college: one a grandee, the other a man of the same social class as the rest of us. Physically, this latter was a pure specimen of the Mediterranean Race. To look at him you could not have told that he was not a Sicilian or a Catalan or a Provençal. On the other hand, the young Egyptian grandee had a Negro strain in him which was not merely unmistakable but obtrusive. If this young man had been brought up in England, or *a fortiori* in the United States, he would have been made to feel his Negro traits as a crushing misfortune which would have permanently oppressed his spirits and undermined his self-confidence. Having been brought up in Egypt, he arrived at Oxford quite un-race-conscious. From his bearing, it was evident that he felt himself distinguished from other people, not at all by his Negro traits but by his noble descent. He bore himself accordingly, while the bearing of his socially less distinguished fellow countryman, who could easily have passed himself off to the United States immigration authorities as a full-blooded European, was modest and unassuming. This was not from lack of spirit—he has since made his mark by some particularly adventurous feats of exploration—but because, at Oxford, he felt himself to be living among his social equals, whereas the young grandee was evidently accustomed to regarding the people among whom he lived as his inferiors. How deeply outraged the grandee would have been if he had realized how his Negro traits were regarded by his English and American fellow undergraduates! The fact that he remained un-race-conscious during his years at Oxford speaks well, no doubt, for the manners of the English upper-middle class; but the more important fact that he had previously grown up un-race-conscious at home in Egypt speaks, surely, far better for the broad humanity of the spirit of Islam.

Race and Civilization

It is an established fact of Physiology that, in all human beings, the pigment secreted in the skin is qualitatively the same; and that the different shades of colour which strike the eye and affect the feelings and give rise to theories and classifications correspond to mere differences in the quantity in which this qualitatively uniform human pigment happens to be present beneath the skin of any given specimen of the Human Race.[1] We can verify this on the body of an African Negro; for the palms of his hands and the soles of his feet are of a different shade from the rest of his skin and of practically the same shade as the whole skin of a White man—the explanation being that, on his palms and soles, a Negro has about the same quantity of pigment that a White man has all over, while on the rest of his body the Negro has rather more. This fact indicates that our colour-prejudice has not a shadow of physiological justification and shows it up for what it is: a particular instance of the irrational but universal aversion from whatever is abnormal. 'Nordic Man', who rejoices in the rather low quantity of pigment in his skin, eyes, and hair which happens to be normal in human beings of his kind, is repelled by the abnormal case in which this quantity is reduced to zero and 'the Blond Beast' transformed into an albino, though logically, if colourlessness is the

[1] On this point see, for example, Taylor, Griffith: *Environment and Race* (Oxford 1927, University Press), p. 33.

pink of perfection, the rare albino ought to be hailed by his common-place Nordic relatives as a king of men. Again, even the relative lack of colour which is normal and therefore comely in the sight of a White man is abnormal and therefore unbecoming in the sight of a Red Indian, who expresses his aversion by calling the White man a 'pale-face'. It even happens that a human being comes to regard his own colour with aversion if he lives for some time in a minority of one among people of a different colour—the colour of the majority setting the norm. For example, it is said that David Livingstone, on one of his expeditions, after passing many months in Central Africa with no White companions and none but Negroes round him, began to find that the sight of his own naked skin turned him sick, as though he were looking at some deformity of nature.

This craving for the normal in physical appearance (whatever the normal may be in the particular circumstances) is not of course confined to the single feature of colour. For example, in the United States, where the physical appearance of the White people is the norm for the Coloured people,[1] the Coloured women try to lessen their unlikeness from the White women by straightening their hair. On the other hand, the White women, who have no fear of looking like Negroes, take pleasure, as White women do in other countries, in having their hair waved or curled. Thus, in the same American town at the same moment, some barbers may be busy straightening women's hair in the Negro quarter while others are busy curling women's hair in the White quarter—in both cases alike, for the satisfaction of the universal human craving to be 'in the fashion'.[2]

Hair, indeed, is just as good—or just as bad—a criterion of Race as pigment.[3] The North American Whites and Negroes are sensi-

[1] This is not because the Negroes are in a minority; for though they are in a minority of about 10 versus 90 per cent. in the United States as a whole, they usually live in a milieu of their own race owing to the tendency towards local segregation. The reason why the Coloured people aspire to resemble the White people is that the White people have the prestige of being the ruling race. Moreover, the Coloured population of the United States is crossed with White blood in all degrees; and the Coloured people who are seven-eights or fifteen-sixteenths White look forward to the possibility of 'passing' surreptitiously into the White community. It may be questioned, however, whether even if, in the course of generations, all visible traces of their Negro origin were bred out of the Coloured population of the United States, their descendants would be permitted by the descendants of the pure Whites to 'pass' wholesale and thus extinguish 'the colour-bar'. The precedent in India suggests that, even if the visible difference of colour eventually disappeared, the social barrier originally founded on this difference would survive, as rigid or more rigid than ever, in the form of Caste. In India to-day the caste divisions are reflected only slightly, or not at all, in any corresponding differences of colour; yet Philology shows that Caste—for which the Hindu word is Varna, meaning 'colour'—originated in a colour-bar such as exists in the United States to-day.

[2] It may be added that, in this generation, 'nigger' is a popular colour for White women's clothes, and that the colour of a Negro woman's skin is one of the favourite shades of White women's silk stockings, which are intended to convey to White men's eyes a suggestion of the naked flesh.

[3] Hair is taken as the primary basis of racial classification by Haddon, A. C., in *The Races of Man and their Distribution*, revised edition (Cambridge 1929, University Press).

tive to the straightness or curliness of the hair on the head. The Japanese are sensitive to the general hairiness of the human body, because, in Japan, this happens to be a more significant feature than the colour of the skin. The Japanese people (like almost every other people that has ever distinguished itself) is of mixed race; and its original racial components must have differed widely in colour; for there is a considerable diversity of colour among the Japanese people to this day. In the same district and in the same social class and in the same family you may find skins varying from copper-colour to what White people call white. Hence, the differences of colour within this range do not excite race-feeling among the Japanese any more than this is excited among Europeans by differences in the quantity of hair on their bodies. On the other hand, Japanese of all shades of skin are alike in being more or less hairless except on their heads, in contrast to the aboriginal inhabitants of the Japanese Islands who, like Nordic Man in the unshaven state of nature, have bushy beards and hairy chests.[1] For this reason, the Japanese call these aborigines (the remnant of whom are now philanthropically preserved, on the northern island of Hokkaido, in 'reservations') 'the Hairy Ainu'. In the local circumstances of Japan, it is just as natural to emphasize the hairiness of the inferior race as it is in the United States or in the Union of South Africa to emphasize their colour; and as the people of European origin apply the colour-classification, which suggests itself in their own local circumstances, to the whole of Mankind, so we might expect the Japanese to divide the human family, not into a 'White Race' and a 'Coloured Race' but into a 'Hairless Race' and a 'Hairy'.

Logically there is nothing to choose between one classification and the other; but it may be edifying for us to glance at the classification with which we are less familiar. It yields what, to our minds, are disconcerting results. It brackets 'Nordic Man' with the Hairy Ainu of Hokkaido and the Blackfellows of Australia and the Veddahs of Ceylon and the Todas of the Nilgiri Hills in Southern India, as one of the representatives of a race whose abnormal hairiness makes them not as other men are.[2]

'What nonsense', the indignant Nordic ethnologist exclaims. 'Is it likely that there is any racial relation between these tribes,

[1] The Ainu also resemble 'Nordic Man' in being white-skinned. In fact, their physical resemblance to him is so close that, if they choose to claim that they are his poor relations, he would find it difficult to disprove the embarrassing assertion.

[2] All the races mentioned in this sentence are bracketed together as members of the 'cymotrichous' or wavy-haired family by Haddon in op. cit. (e.g. in 'An Arrangement of the Main Groups of Mankind', on pp. 14–15). The author duly notes (in op. cit., on p. 6) that 'some cymotrichous peoples have very hairy bodies, e.g., Ainu, Toda, some Australians, some Europeans. The Xanthoderms [i.e. Mongoloid Asiatics, Bushmen, and Hottentots] usually have an almost hairless body, as have most Negroes.'

considering that their homes are separated by the whole breadth of Europe and Asia?' But the Japanese ethnologist has his answer up his sleeve. Courteously he points out to his Nordic colleague that 'the Hairy Race' is the nearest of all living races to the Apes in that feature which is fundamental for Japanese purposes of racial classification. It follows that 'the Hairy Race' is the nearest of all living breeds of Man to the common ancestor of Apes and Men. In other words, 'the Hairy Race' is the most primitive, rudimentary experiment in *Homo Sapiens* that survives; and it is natural enough that it should only survive in holes and corners. If we assume that the original breeding-ground of Mankind lay somewhere in the heart of the Old World, and that 'the Hairy Race' was one of the earliest human swarms to hive off, then we should expect to find *Homo Hirsutus* pushed outwards in all directions, to the ends of the Earth, to Australia and to Hokkaido and to Ultima Thule, by younger and superior races—*Homo Mediterraneus* and *Homo Dravidicus*, *Homo Alpinus* and *Homo Mongolicus*—which have issued from the common breeding-ground at later dates to multiply and replenish the Earth in their turns. Thus the vast distances which separate the several surviving tribes of *Homo Hirsutus* to-day are presumptive evidence for and not against the racial kinship of these tribes which their common shagginess betrays. Their present homes are not their respective cradles but their respective retreats from a common birthplace. They are fragments of the circumference of the circle in which *Homo Hirsutus* has spread—or has been chevied—over the face of the Earth from his original centre of dispersion. We may compare his now widely dispersed representatives with the disturbances which remain here and there on the surface of a pond when the last of the ripples produced by the fall of a stone into the water is dying away. If the Japanese ethnologist presents his case on these lines, it will be difficult for the Nordic ethnologist to rebut it.[1]

[1] Our more enterprising ethnologists seem inclined nowadays to explain the distribution of the Races of Man, as we find it at the earliest date to which our records extend back, by the hypothesis of successive waves of emigration, in all directions, from a common original centre. See, for example, Taylor, Griffith: *Environment and Race* (Oxford 1927, University Press), especially pp. 4–5 and chapter xx: 'The Migration-Zone Theory of Race Evolution'. The author's theory is summed up in the eight propositions on pp. 220–1, and is presented visually in the frontispiece.

Of course our *Homo Hirsutus* is not really the earliest breed of Man known. From fragments of skeletons, our palaeontologists have been able to reconstruct several much more rudimentary types, and indeed *Homo Hirsutus* is not quite the most primitive breed of Man that is still living. Beyond the Nordic remnant of *Homo Hirsutus*, which still clings to the north-western fringes of Europe and Asia, from the Normans in the lower valley of the Seine to the Eastern Finns in the lower valley of the Obi, we find a still more primitive race—the Lapps in Northern Scandinavia and the Samoyeds along the Arctic coasts of Russia, while in Arctic America we have the Esquimaux—who are supposed to be a remnant of the hunters that roamed over Europe in the Upper Palaeolithic Age. (See Dixon, R. B.: *The Racial History of Man* (New York 1923, Scribner), pp. 484–6.) Again, beyond the Ainu remnant of *Homo Hirsutus* in Hokkaido and Sakha-

Another racial feature which acts as a stimulus of race-feeling, no less powerfully that hairiness or colour, is smell.

'I hope you have been enjoying yourself', said an English dramatic critic to a celebrated Japanese actress who had been having a season in the West End of London. 'Yes, on the whole', the lady replied, 'but of course there have been hardships to put up with.' 'Hardships? I am sorry to hear that', the Englishman exclaimed (rather taken aback, for the Japanese artist had been received enthusiastically by the English public). 'Oh yes', she burst out. 'And the worst of all was the smell. The people in this country smell like lions and tigers. . . . But not you, of course', she added hastily, solicitous for her own manners and for her interlocutor's feelings, 'you only smell of mutton-fat and scented soap.' The truth is that the Japanese, whose national odour is kept sweet and wholesome by a mainly vegetarian diet, are considerably distressed by the rank and foetid odour of the carnivorous peoples of the West—an odour of which we are hardly conscious ourselves because we are living in the reek of it all the time.

It is not only the Japanese who are upset by the White Race's smell. A highly cultivated and fastidious English lady of my acquaintance once went to stay for several months in South Africa and engaged a staff of native servants—among them, a little Kaffir maid. It happened several times that the maid, on being summoned into her employer's presence, fell into a sudden faint; and the lady, who was kind-hearted, felt some concern. What could be the matter with the girl? Was it heart-disease? Or was it just acute nervousness at finding herself *tête-à-tête* with a member of the superior race? The lady questioned the other servants, only to have her questions parried and eluded in the usual provoking fashion; but at last an older servant, who saw that her mistress was becoming really upset and alarmed, succeeded in conquering her own reserve and embarrassment. 'You needn't worry, Madam', she assured my friend, 'there is nothing serious the matter with

lin, we find the still more primitive Palaeo-arctic peoples in the north-eastern corner of Continental Asia. Finally, beyond the Australian Blackfellows, we find (or, rather, found, before we exterminated them) the still more primitive natives of Tasmania.

All the same, this wave-theory of race-distribution leads to conclusions which must be horrifying for those of us who are addicts to race-feeling. A'National-Socialist'Mecklenburger who is thrilled to feel, coursing through his veins, the 'pure' blood of 'Nordic' Odin may be convicted by the expert of being a 'bleached' 'Proto-Australoid' or 'Proto-Negroid' (Dixon, op. cit., pp. 74–5), and may be grateful, in the circumstances, to the amateur who has been content to call our Mecklenburger nothing worse than a Germanized Slav. Nordic Man is firmly put in his place by Mr. Griffith Taylor: 'I have come to the conclusion that the so-called Nordic races do not stand out as the most advanced type of Man. . . . One result of the study of the distribution of Man is to lead the writer to the belief that the so-called 'yellow' or Mongolian type of Man is a later product of human evolution than many western members of the so-called 'white' or European type. In other words, the Eastern Asiatic is further from the primitive anthropoid stock, while the Negroid and West-European peoples are earlier, lower offshoots from the line of human evolution.' (Taylor, op. cit., pp. 336 and 337.)

the girl. The fact is, she has come straight from her village to you; this is her first place in White people's service, and she isn't yet quite used to the White people's smell. But don't you worry. She will get used to it soon enough. Why, look at us! We all used to faint at first, but now we have quite got over it. It will be the same with her, you'll see!'

Here, then, are three different physical features—colour, hairiness, and smell—which all excite race-feeling and are all equally suitable, or unsuitable, for being taken as bases for racial classifications. For our purpose it has merely to be pointed out that these alternative classifications, between which there is nothing to choose from a logical standpoint, yield results which are quite incompatible with one another.

Let us now take up the colour classification—a choice which is arbitrary in itself but apt for our argument, because this happens to be the currently accepted classification in the modern Western World. Let us briefly survey the contributions which peoples of the several races of Man, as classified by colour, have actually made to our twenty-one civilizations. We will confine our attention to active, creative contributions, leaving mere passive membership out of account (for, if we took account of that, we should have to inscribe, as contributors to the contemporary Western Civilization, the entire living generation of Mankind). Taking account, then, of creative contributions and of these alone,[1] we obtain the results set out in the following table:

Race	contributing to Civilizations
White ('Nordic')	Indic + Hittite (?) + Hellenic + Western + Orthodox Christian (in Russia)
White ('Alpine')	Egyptiac (?)[2] + Sumeric + Minoan (?)[3] + Hittite + Hellenic + Western + Orthodox Christian (main body) + Orthodox Christian (in Russia) + Iranic
White ('Mediterranean')	Egyptiac + Sumeric[4] + Minoan + Syriac + Hellenic + Western + Orthodox Christian (main body) + Iranic + Arabic + Babylonic
White ('Polynesian')	Far Eastern (in Korea and Japan)
Brown[5]	Indic + Hindu
Yellow[6]	Sinic + Far Eastern (main body) + Far Eastern (in Korea and Japan)
Red[7]	Andean + Mayan + Yucatec + Mexic
Black[8]	None

[1] The contributions, if any, which have been made to the 'related' civilizations by the external proletariats of the antecedent civilizations to which they are related, are not here counted as creative except in the cases of four related civilizations—the Indic, Hittite, Syriac, and Hellenic—in which the external proletariat, and not the internal proletariat, has been the living link through which the relation has been established.

For notes 2, 3, 4, 5, 6, 7, and 8, see the opposite page.

It will be seen that, when we classify Mankind by colour, the only primary race that has not made a creative contribution to any civilization is the Black Race (on the assumption that the Dravidians are, not 'black', but 'brown'). This single exception should not deter us from drawing the general inference which the remainder of the evidence suggests. If every primary race except one has made a creative contribution to at least one of the twenty-one civilizations which have emerged up to date, we must infer that the capacity for civilization is not a monopoly of any fraction or fractions of the human family, but is the universal birthright of Mankind; and there is no warrant for supposing that one particular fraction—the Black Race—has been born without this birthright and is congenitally incapable of civilization just because it has failed to make one of these creative contributions so far. In order to see the position and prospects of the Black Race in proper perspective, we must remind ourselves of a consideration which has been before our minds at an earlier stage of this Study.[1] The species of human societies called civilizations, which has been in existence less than 6,000 years so far, has an 'expectation of life' which is at least eighty-three million times as long as its present age, on the most 'conservative' estimate of astronomical probabilities.[2]

We can make the meaning of these figures intelligible to our minds if we think of the enterprise of civilization as a 'Marathon Race' in which a white, brown, yellow, red, and black man are

[2] For the evidence of the presence of an 'Alpine' as well as a 'Mediterranean' strain in the peoples who created the Egyptiac Civilization by mastering the physical environment of the Nile Valley below the First Cataract, see Smith, C. Elliot: *The Ancient Egyptians* (London and New York 1923, Harper), chapter vii, and *The Cambridge Ancient History*, vol. i, 2nd edition, pp. 33–4 and 244–5.

[3] For evidence of the presence of an 'Alpine' as well as a 'Mediterranean' strain in the people who created the Minoan Civilization by mastering the physical environment of the Aegean Archipelago, see Myres, J. L., in the *Proceedings of the British Academy*, 1906, pp. 700–1, and in *Who were the Greeks?* (Berkeley 1930, University of California Press), ch. ii, pp. 30–1.

[4] The Sumerians are supposed to have been 'Alpines'; but it is also supposed that the creation of the Sumeric Civilization, through the conquest of the physical environment of the lower valley of the Tigris and Euphrates, was the joint achievement of Sumerian immigrants and Semitic aborigines whom they found already squatting on the brink of the Tigro-Euphratean jungle-swamp; and these Semitic contributors to the creation of the Sumeric Civilization were presumably 'Mediterraneans'.

[5] The term 'Brown Race' is used here to cover both the Dravidian population of Continental India and the Malay population of Indonesia.

[6] The term 'Yellow Race' is a misnomer; for many members of this race in China and Japan are as white as any 'White Man'. The real distinguishing marks of this race are not the colour of its skin but the texture of its hair and the set of its eyes.

[7] The term 'Red Race' is no more appropriate than the term 'Yellow Race'. Here again, the real distinguishing marks are the texture of the hair and the set of the eyes; and, by these criteria, 'the Red Race' and 'the Yellow Race' ought perhaps to be classified as two branches of a single race which might be labelled the Mongolo-American.

[8] The term 'Black Race' is used here to cover the Australian Blackfellows, the Papuans and Melanesians, the Veddahs of Ceylon, and the Todas of Southern India, as well as the Negro population of Africa south of the Sahara.

[1] See I. C (iii) (c), p. 173, above.
[2] See I. C (iii) (e), Annex, below, *ad fin*.

competitors. The pistol has been fired; and an instantaneous photograph, taken at that instant, shows that the runners are off—that is, four of them are off out of the five, for the fifth still stands toeing the line. What is the matter with him? Is he in a day-dream? Is he paralysed? Is he out of the running? We can only answer that all these questions are premature; for the time which has elapsed between the moment when the signal was heard and the moment recorded in our instantaneous photograph is no more than one eighty-three-millionth part of the time which the five runners have to run. It is no doubt possible that the runner who has been this infinitesimal degree slower than his competitors in getting away may never get away at all; but there is no ground for this expectation in the position which our instantaneous photograph reveals, unless we wilfully ignore the time-factor which is of the essence of the situation. We have no more warrant for assuming that the black competitor will not get away, or that he will not eventually win the race, than we have for assuming that his red or yellow or brown or white competitor will be incapacitated, *en courant*, by some other kind of mishap—by failure of heart or wind, or by stumbling and breaking his leg. These contingencies are all just as possible as the contingency that the black competitor will remain toeing the line for eighty-three million times the infinitesimal length of time during which he has been toeing it so far since the moment when the starter's shot rang out.

As a matter of fact, there are certain features in the Negro's circumstances which convincingly account for his failure to take an active part in the enterprise of Civilization during these first five or six thousand years, without creating any presumption that this failure may be insurmountable and definitive. On this point, we will cite the opinion of an able, experienced, and sympathetic French observer:

'Lorsque nous disons des Nègres qu'ils sont de grands enfants, nous entendons que ce sont des adultes à mentalité puérile, et nous sous-entendons que la mentalité à laquelle nous assimilons la leur est celle de nos enfants à nous: en quoi nous retombons dans l'éternelle erreur qui nous fait juger des autres d'après nous-mêmes. C'est, si l'on veut, une définition comparative, basée sur des analogies plus ou moins super-ficielles, non sur des faits considérés en eux-mêmes.

'Elle est viciée à sa base, parce que reposant sur une pétition de principe. Nous supposons *a priori* que notre race est le prototype de la civilisation en soi, mais qu'elle ne réalise celle-ci que par l'organe de ses adultes, et nous voulons bien accorder à la race noire un pied de pseudo-égalité avec la nôtre, à condition de ne la mettre qu'au rang de nos enfants, c'est-à-dire de ceux d'entre nous auxquels nous refusons la faculté d'atteindre au niveau de la masse. C'est, en termes plus

aimables, mais non moins absolus, proclamer de nouveau cette infé-
riorité des races de couleur, soutenue avec plus d'âpreté, sinon plus
de logique, et en tout cas avec moins d'hypocrisie, par Gobineau et son
école. . . .'[1]

'Les Nègres africains forment-ils une race intellectuellement infé-
rieure aux autres races humaines? On l'a souvent affirmé, mais sans
jamais en donner de preuves convaincantes et en prenant généralement
un point de départ faux.

'On a dit que les Noirs seraient actuellement inférieurs, sous le
rapport du développement intellectuel, à ce que sont les autres types de
l'humanité. Il me paraît qu'on a, ce disant, confondu "ignorance" avec
"inintelligence". Le plus grand génie du monde, s'il n'était jamais allé
à l'école et n'avait jamais vécu qu'au milieu des sauvages, aurait été sans
doute dans la complète impossibilité de manifester sa haute intelligence naturelle, ce qui ne veut pas dire qu'il ne l'eût pas possédée
effectivement. . . .

'Or les Noirs de l'Afrique ont eu cette malechance funeste de ne
pouvoir évoluer comme l'ont fait les autres grandes races humaines, sans
qu'ils y aient été d'ailleurs pour rien. Alors que, depuis de nombreux
siècles, les descendants des Gaulois nos ancêtres se sont trouvés
constamment en contact avec des populations plus évoluées ou autrement évoluées qu'eux-mêmes, mais d'une civilisation contemporaine de
la leur, et ont pu, prenant aux unes, s'inspirant des autres, devenir les
Français d'aujourd'hui, les malheureux Nègres ont été, durant le même
période, à peu près complètement isolés du reste de l'humanité. . . .

'Les Nègres africains offrent ce spectacle, sans doute unique au
monde, de toute une race n'ayant jamais eu à compter que sur elle-
même pour progresser et n'ayant rien reçu de l'extérieur, ou en ayant
reçu autant de ferments de régression que d'éléments de progrès, sinon
plus. Aurions-nous fait mieux qu'eux si nous nous étions trouvés dans la
même situation?

'L'isolement dans lequel des barrières naturelles ont enfermé trop
longtemps leur habitat a fait des Nègres de l'Afrique, par rapport aux
Européens plus favorisés, des arriérés ou, plus exactement, des attardés:
ils ont perdu beaucoup de temps et ils ne sauraient le rattraper en un jour
ni même en un siècle. Mais ils n'ont certainement pas dit leur dernier
mot et leur histoire n'est pas finie. Peut-être ne fait-elle que commencer.'[2]

We may add that the Black Race is by no means the only fraction
of Mankind which has failed to take an active part in the enterprise
of Civilization up to date. The races which have made the most
numerous and the most brilliant contributions to those civilizations
which have emerged within the last 6,000 years are all of them still
represented, besides, in primitive societies which have not risen
above the level of barbarism or even above the level of savagery.
If we classify by hairiness, we can confront the Nordic specimens

---

[1] Delafosse, M.: *Les Nègres* (Paris 1927, Rieder), pp. 8–9.
[2] Delafosse, M.: *Les Noirs de l'Afrique* (Paris 1922, Payot), pp. 156–60.

of *Homo Hirsutus* who have helped to create the Indic and Hittite and Hellenic and Western civilizations, and the Orthodox Christian Civilization in Russia, with their poor relations the Hairy Ainu and the Australian Blackfellows and the Veddahs and the Todas, who have remained on the primitive level down to this day. If we classify by colour, we can confront the White Men who have helped to create perhaps half the civilizations of which we know, with our latter-day White barbarians: the fair-haired, blue-eyed highlanders of North-West Africa who have defied both the assaults and the blandishments of one civilization after another in the fastnesses of the Rīf and the Atlas and Kabylia; their Nomadic kinsmen in the Sahara, whose deficiency of pigment is betrayed in their hair and eyes even when their skins are tanned by a scorching sun; the fair-haired, blue-eyed highlanders of Albania, who have contrived to evade civilization in fastnesses which overlook the high road between Greece and Rome; the highlanders of the Caucasus, who are such magnificent specimens of the White Race that our Western ethnologists have taken their name in vain as a scientific term for the whole breed of *Homo Pallidus*; the highlanders of Kurdistan; the highlanders of the borderland between Afghanistan and India; and—once again—the Ainu who, despite the whiteness of the skin that peeps through their shaggy fur, have fought the losing battle of Barbarism against 'the yellow peril' of the Far Eastern Civilization in Japan. Again, we can confront the Yellow Men who have created this Far Eastern Civilization and its predecessor, the Sinic Civilization, with the Yellow barbarians who still survive, in a few scattered enclaves, among the mountains that divide the southern watershed of the Yangtse from the southern coast-line of China, and with the Yellow savages in the interior of the Indo-Chinese Peninsula. We can confront the Brown creators of the Indic and Hindu Civilizations with the wild tribes of Continental India—Bhils and Ghonds and the like—and with the head-hunters of Sumatra and Borneo. We can confront the Incas with the Araucanian barbarians of Chile and with the savages of Amazonia and of the Tierra del Fuego. We can confront the Mayas and the Toltecs with 'the Noble Savage' of North America who has established his fame as the Redskin *par excellence*.

If those who despair of the capacities of the Black Race were right in their thesis that a failure to make any creative contributions to the first twenty-one civilizations during the first six thousand years of the existence of the species is proof of an inherent and incurable incapacity, then it would be impossible to explain how other races, which still have their savage and their barbarous representatives to-day, have also produced the creators of all the civilizations that have emerged hitherto. The only way to reconcile the thesis and the facts would be to suppose that those White, Brown, Yellow, and Red populations which have helped to create civilizations are really of different race from the respective populations of the same colours which have never yet distinguished themselves in this fashion—that we can know them by their spiritual fruits, though we cannot tell them apart by their physical appearances. This way out of the impasse, however, could not be taken by the racialists, because it abandons the postulate of an absolute correlation between physical and psychical characteristics which is the indispensable foundation for all racial theories. Nor will it be taken by unprejudiced inquirers; for the ethnological evidence, considered objectively, does not at all suggest that the Yellow barbarians of Southern China are different in race, as well as in culture, from the Southern Chinese, or the White barbarians of Morocco, Albania, the Caucasus, Kurdistan, and the Indo-Afghan border from their White neighbours and contemporaries who are members to-day of the Western and Orthodox Christian and Islamic civilizations.

Indeed, in all these cases, our records show that the barbarians who still survive as such are a remnant of barbarian populations which the neighbouring civilizations have assimilated, and that this process of assimilation is still going on.[1] If we had taken our survey of White barbarians two centuries ago instead of to-day, our list would have included the Scottish highlanders, who have been so completely assimilated by our Western Society during the half-dozen generations that have come and gone between 1745 and 1933 that in this latter year a descendant of these barbarians is Prime Minister of one of the leading states of the Western World. If the survey is taken again two centuries hence, it may seem as strange then to our descendants that the Albanians and the Rīfīs should have been still barbarians in our time as it seems to us now that the Scottish highlanders should have been still barbarians in the reign of King George II. Similarly, a survey of Yellow barbarians taken about the year 1000 B.C. would have returned as barbarians almost the whole of the Chinese people of to-day except those living in two relatively small areas, in the lower and the middle basin of the Yellow River, to which the Sinic Civilization was confined in that early age.[2] The enlargement of the borders of civilizations and the recruitment of their 'man-power' by the assimilation of their barbarian neighbours has been one of the

---

[1] The assimilation of primitive societies by civilizations is examined further in Part VIII, below.

[2] On this point see Maspéro, H.: *La Chine Antique* (Paris 1927, Boccard), p. 11.

constant features in the lives and activities of civilizations since this species of society first came into existence.

If we assume that all human beings of all races are capable of civilization, this process of assimilation, which is an empirically established fact, is also a fact which presents no difficulties to the understanding. If, on the other hand, we assume that one whole race, and certain sections of other races, are incapable of civilization because they have failed to contribute to the creation of civilizations down to a certain date or dates, the process of assimilation ceases to be intelligible. How, on this showing, could the Cantonese become converted to the Far Eastern Civilization a dozen centuries ago, or the Scottish highlanders to our Western Civilization one century ago, when they had proved their inherent and incurable incapacity for civilization by having previously remained outside the pale? At the moment of their cultural conversion, did they undergo some kind of racial transubstantiation? Were they suddenly and mysteriously endowed with some inward spiritual grace of which no outward visible sign could be detected even by the trained ethnologist's eye? Such are the extravagances into which we find ourselves driven in the last resort if we proceed on the hypothesis that some fractions of Mankind are racially capable and others racially incapable of civilization *a priori*, and that a race stands convicted of inherent and incurable incapacity if it happens not to have contributed to the creation of any civilizations by the time in the history of the species when the censorious observer is moved to take his observations. No such *reductio ad absurdum* lies in wait for us if we adopt, instead, the hypothesis by which the French observer, quoted above, explains the failure of the Black Race to make creative contributions up to date, and if we apply this hypothesis to other races, or portions of races, which have played the same passive role as the Black Race during the whole or some of the time during which the species of societies called civilizations has been in existence. We can attribute these retardations to the interplay between a Human Nature which is common to all Mankind and certain exceptionally unfavourable circumstances in the local environments of some sections of the human family during certain periods of time; and we need seek no further than this in order to explain why it is that, within these first six thousand years, the Black Race has not helped to create any civilization, while the Polynesian White Race has helped to create one civilization, the Brown Race two, the Yellow Race three, the Red Race and the 'Nordic' White Race four apiece, the 'Alpine' White Race nine, and the 'Mediterranean' White Race ten.[1]

---

[1] See the table on p. 232, above.

The upshot of our inquiry is to discredit the hypothesis of a natural law in which the creation of civilizations is supposedly revealed as the peculiar racial function of particular branches of the human family. Indeed, the only vestige of a law relating civilizations and races which our inquiry has brought to light is one which puts a very different complexion upon the relation between them.

If we transpose the table of contributions of races to civilizations which we have given on p. 232, above, we obtain the following results:

Civilizations	contributed to by Races
Hellenic	White ('Nordic') + White ('Alpine') + White ('Mediterranean')
Western	White ('Nordic') + White ('Alpine') + White ('Mediterranean')
Egyptiac	White ('Alpine')+White ('Mediterranean')
Sumeric	White ('Alpine')+White ('Mediterranean')
Minoan	White ('Alpine')+White ('Mediterranean')
Indic	White ('Nordic')+Brown
Hittite	White ('Nordic')+White ('Alpine')
Far Eastern (in Korea and Japan)	White ('Polynesian')+Yellow
Orthodox Christian (main body)	White ('Alpine')+White ('Mediterranean')
Orthodox Christian (in Russia)	White ('Nordic')+White ('Alpine')
Iranic	White ('Alpine')+White ('Mediterranean')
Babylonic	White ('Mediterranean')
Syriac	White ('Mediterranean')
Arabic	White ('Mediterranean')
Hindu	Brown
Sinic	Yellow
Far Eastern (main body)	Yellow
Andean	Red
Mayan	Red
Yucatec	Red
Mexic	Red

Thus, on our classification, two civilizations have been created by contributions from three different races, nine by contributions from two different races, and ten by the unaided endeavours of a single race in each case. On this showing, nearly half the civilizations that have emerged hitherto have been created by a mixture of races; but our table considerably understates the frequency of this phenomenon in the creation of civilizations because our racial classification is imperfect. We have treated four varieties of White Man as separate races because that is the regular practice of our ethnologists; but we have not brought the rest of our classification into line with this section by subdividing the non-White races on the criteria employed in distinguishing the 'Nordic' White from the 'Alpine', the 'Alpine' from the 'Mediterranean', the 'Mediterranean' from the 'Polynesian'. If we had carried our racial analysis to this point all through,[1] we should certainly have found that several, at least, of the seven civilizations which here appear as created by the Brown or the Red Race exclusively had been created by two races ('Brown No. 1' and 'Brown No. 2') or by three ('Yellow No. 1' and 'Yellow No. 2' and 'Yellow No. 3'). The number of civilizations created by the unaided endeavours of a single race in each case would then turn out to be relatively so small that these cases would present themselves as exceptions to a prevalent law—a law to the effect that the geneses of civilizations require creative contributions from more races than one.[2]

The discovery of a law to this effect would not be surprising. Indeed, we might have discovered it, before this, as a corollary to another law which we have noted at an earlier stage in this Study:[3] the law that civilizations exert, upon Mankind beyond their borders, both a push and a pull—a centrifugal push in the nature of radiation and a centripetal pull in the nature of attraction. While a civilization is radiating out its material products as exports, its human members as traders, conquerors, colonists, and missionaries, and its culture in the shape of technique, institutions, ideas, and emotions, it is all the time drawing in other commodities and other beings and other techniques, institutions, ideas, and emotions from abroad. The roads which diverge from or converge upon it (whichever term we choose to employ) carry a two-way traffic— exports and imports, emigrants and immigrants, cultural influences emitted and cultural influences received. This simultaneous and perpetual movement in two contrary directions is the breath of Life, and we can observe it in operation wherever Life is being lived: in the circulation of the blood, with its outward movement from the heart to the limbs along the arteries and its return movement from the limbs to the heart along the veins; or in the economy of a Western industrial city, which draws its 'man-power' and its 'raw materials' from the ends of the Earth while it is sending out its manufactures to the ends of the Earth again.

---

[1] As is attempted by Mr. Griffith Taylor in his *Environment and Race* (Oxford 1927, University Press).

[2] There is a suggestion of this law in Taylor, op. cit., on p. 336. A distinguished Italian Orientalist regards 'il risveglio . . . morale e materiale che segue sempre al incrocio di varie razze' as a 'legge constante della genesi di civiltà nell' evoluzione dei popoli'. (Caetani, L.: *Studî di Storia Orientale*, vol. i (Milan 1911, Hoepli), p. 141.) Authority for the same view can be found in the works of the professional ethnologists. See, for example, Dixon, R. B.: *The Racial History of Man* (New York 1923, Scribner), pp. 514–16.

[3] See p. 187 in Part II. A, above.

In this setting, the subsidiary law that the geneses of civilizations require creative contributions from more races than one
becomes self-evident. We can catch a glimpse of this law in the
fragmentary picture of racial conditions in Egypt, during the ages
when the Egyptiac Civilization was being brought to birth, which
has been pieced together by the ingenuity of our Western archaeologists. The so-called 'Badarians', who in Upper Egypt made the
momentous transition from hunting to the rudiments of agriculture
and stock-breeding in the sixth millennium B.C., appear to have been
autochthonous representatives of the 'Mediterranean' variety of the
White Race who had acquired a Negroid strain.[1] The early Pre-
dynastic Egyptians, who succeeded the 'Badarians' and carried the
development of the Egyptiac Civilization a stage further, appear to
have been descendants of the 'Badarians' in whose racial composition the Negroid strain had been replaced by a 'Mediterranean'
strain, distinct from that of the Badarians themselves, which was
introduced into the Lower Nile Valley at this stage by an infiltration of 'Getulan' Nomadic hunters from North-West Africa.[2]
Thereafter, in the so-called Second Predynastic Age, we begin to
find evidence of a racial infiltration into the Lower Nile Valley
from South-Western Asia. The earliest evidence for this Asiatic
contribution is indirect: it is an inference from the appearance, in
Egypt, of Asiatic *motifs* in art and devices in technique[3]; of the cult
of Osiris, with its Asiatic affinities[4]; of domesticated breeds of
sheep and goats whose wild ancestors had their habitat not in
Africa but in Asia.[5] The direct evidence in the form of 'Alpine'
racial traits, of the so-called 'Armenoid' sub-variety, in skeletons
recovered from Egyptiac burials, is not found before the beginning
of the Dynastic Age.[6] Nevertheless, it will be seen that, in the
course of the period of two thousand years or so during which the
Egyptiac Civilization was in gestation, the population of the Lower
Nile Valley was recruited from at least four racial elements: a

[1] Childe, V. G.: *The Most Ancient East* (London 1928, Kegan Paul), pp. 51–2 and
60–2.
[2] Childe, op. cit., pp. 62–3 and 77.
[3] Childe, op. cit., pp. 94–5.
[4] Childe, op. cit., loc. cit.
[5] Newberry, P. E.: *Egypt as a Field of Anthropological Research* (British Association
for the Advancement of Science, Report of the Ninety-first Meeting, Liverpool 1923,
Presidential Address to Section H (London 1924, Murray), p. 187).
[6] 'If it be asked when this alien influence first made itself apparent in the physical
characters of the people of Egypt, it can be stated with certainty that there is no definite
trace of it in Upper Egypt in Predynastic times, and only rare sporadic instances before
the time of the Fifth Dynasty, when foreign traits became fairly common among the
aristocracy. Lower Egypt has not yet afforded much evidence of the archaic period; but
the information now in our possession seems to prove that Armenoid traits occurred in
some few skeletons of Protodynastic date and became common in the times of the Third
and Fourth Dynasties, i.e. long before they appeared in Upper Egypt.' (Smith, C.
Elliot: *The Ancient Egyptians* (London and New York 1923, Harper), pp. 42–3.)

'Mediterranean' element which was autochthonous; a Negroid element which was presumably drawn in from the south; a second 'Mediterranean' element from the north-west, and finally an 'Armenoid Alpine' element from the north-east.

This fragmentary evidence from the homeland of the Egyptiac Civilization is remarkable; and it is reinforced by the corresponding evidence from the homelands of the Sumeric Civilization and the Indus Valley Culture,[1] and likewise by the fuller evidence which presents itself in the field of Western Europe (the only region of the World in which scientifically accurate and statistically adequate racial surveys have yet been made). When we search here for 'pure' specimens of the three European White races, we can only find them on the peripheries or in holes and corners: 'pure Nordics' in Sweden,[2] 'pure Alpines' in Slovakia and Savoy and the Cevennes and Brittany; 'pure Mediterraneans' in Sardinia and Corsica.[3] Conversely, we find more than one of the European races represented in the central parts of Western Europe, and, in particular, in each of those four West European countries which at present rank as Great Powers. There are 'Mediterranean' as well as 'Nordic' strains in the population of Great Britain, 'Alpine' as well as 'Nordic' strains in the population of Germany, 'Alpine' as well as 'Mediterranean' strains in the population of Italy, and strains of all three races in the population of France. We find an equal or greater variety of racial strains in the populations of the other three Great Powers of the 'Post-War' World: a 'Polynesian' White strain as well as a Yellow strain in Japan, an 'Alpine' as well as a 'Nordic' White strain in Russia, and in-

---

[1] See Marshall, Sir J.: *Mohenjo-Daro and the Indus Civilisation* (London 1932, Probsthain, 3 vols.), vol. i, pp. 108–9. Cf. Meyer, E.: *Geschichte des Altertums*, vol. i (i), 4th edition (Stuttgart and Berlin 1921, Cotta), p. 80.

[2] There is a small but conspicuous dark Alpine strain in the populations of Denmark and Norway, and an English visitor to Sweden is surprised to find the Nordic traits less uniformly prevalent there than the ethnological handbooks have led him to expect *a priori*. Still more surprising is the well-attested racial mixture in the population of Iceland—an Ultima Thule in which the abortive Scandinavian Civilization (see II. D (vii), vol. ii, pp. 340–60, below) achieved its greatest triumphs (see II. D (iii), vol. ii, pp. 88–100, below). In the colonization of Iceland at the end of the ninth and tenth centuries of the Christian Era, Scandinavian freemen from many parts of Norway were mingled with Irish thralls; and we may assume that the Scandinavian stock was crossed with this Irish strain—even if no contribution to the racial composition of the Icelandic people was made by the Irish hermits who had found their way to Iceland before the Norsemen's arrival. (See Olrik, A.: *Viking Civilisation*, English translation (London 1930, Allen & Unwin), pp. 102–3 and 175–6.)

[3] The one Corsican family that has ever 'made history' (though this is by no means the same thing as 'making civilization') was not of Corsican origin. The Buonaparti are known to have come to Corsica from Florence—that is to say, from a district of the Italian mainland in which the several White races have been crossed and re-crossed an exceptional number of times: pre-Indo-European Neolithic 'Mediterraneans' with Bronze-Age Indo-European 'Alpines' speaking the Umbrian variety of the Italic branch of the Indo-European family of languages; these with Iron-Age non-Indo-European Alpines from the Levant (the Etruscans); and these, again, with 'Nordic' Lombards from the southern shores of the Baltic. With this Tuscan racial background Napoleon cannot be registered, either for good or for evil, as a 'pure Mediterranean'.

gredients from all the races of Europe in 'the melting-pot' of the United States.[1]

It is remarkable that this racial diversity in the populations of these countries, on which the ethnologists lay such stress, is of no significance to the people themselves. An 'Alpine' Cevenol is conscious of no special affinity with an 'Alpine' Piedmontese or an 'Alpine' Slovak. His sense of affinity has nothing whatever to do with the configuration of his skull and hardly anything to do with the colour of his hair and eyes. It is determined to some extent by language and to a still greater extent by citizenship. The 'Alpine' Frenchman from the Cevennes will feel himself alien to the 'Alpine' Italian from Piedmont and to the 'Alpine' Czechoslovak from Slovakia because these speak foreign languages and are citizens of foreign states. He will feel a greater affinity towards a 'Nordic' Belgian from Brussels whose mother-tongue is French, and a greater affinity still towards a 'Nordic' Frenchman from the Pas de Calais whose mother-tongue is Flemish. Here, in France, we observe a sense of common nationality precluding the consciousness of an objectively existing and empirically observed diversity of race.[2] If we turn from France to India, we there observe the converse phenomenon: a sense of caste distinction, originally corresponding to a diversity of race, which has perpetuated itself long after the diversity of race which first evoked it has actually been obliterated.[3]

In fine, the further our modern Western ethnologists push their analysis of Physical Race by determining the racial likenesses and

[1] This is without taking into account the representatives of the Black and Red Races in the U.S.A. or the representatives of the Yellow Race (not to speak of the rudimentary races represented by the Palaeo-arctics and the Samoyeds) in the U.S.S.R.

[2] It may be noted that France, which is the only European country in which all three of our ethnologists' three primary European races are represented in force, has also been the first European country in which the consciousness of a common nationality has asserted itself. Even at the present day, this consciousness of national unity and uniformity is less highly developed and less widely disseminated in Great Britain, Germany, and Italy, with their two races apiece, than it is in France with her three races.

[3] The racial origin of caste is proved by the etymology of the earliest name of the institution, 'Varna', which literally means 'colour' (see footnote 1 on p. 228, above). This original colour distinction between the castes has long since broken down—partly, no doubt, through surreptitious inter-breeding (which social tabus never effectively prevent between races, however different from one another in physique, which are living permanently cheek by jowl with one another). Another cause of the break-down of the colour distinction between the castes has been the deliberate policy of the Hindu Brahmans in recognizing as Brahmans the sacerdotal families of primitive societies which they were assimilating to the Hindu Civilization, and the deliberate policy of the Hindu Kshatriyas in recognizing as Kshatriyas the fighting men of non-Hindu tribes (e.g. the Huns and Gurjaras who overran North-Western India in the Völkerwanderung during the interregnum between the dissolution of the Indic Society and the emergence of the Hindu Society). By these various processes, the original colour distinction between Hindu castes has been almost completely broken down; yet this disappearance of the racial factor which originally evoked the sense of caste has not entailed the disappearance of caste-consciousness. In India to-day there is hardly a sign that the sense of caste divisions is yielding to any sense of common nationality, transcending caste, on the objective basis of a common country and a common race.

differences that are discernible both in Mankind as it exists to-day and in Primeval Man in so far as we have discovered his skeletal remains, the further does the resultant scientific conception of Race diverge from the popular notions about Race that are mirrored in the ordinary expressions of race-feeling. A perusal of the recent scientific literature on Race makes it evident that all serious ethnologists are arriving, by different paths, at a common conception of racial characters, in which these characters are reduced to mere factors that may actually be found in almost every possible permutation and combination but are never found 'pure' in a state of nature. Those ethnologists who have the courage to follow where the argument leads them are even beginning to ask themselves whether any concrete examples of 'pure' races would really be forthcoming, even if the fullest material evidence for the physique of the earliest types of Man were to be placed in their hands by some miracle. They are beginning to entertain the idea that the fundamental racial characters, when exhaustively analysed and defined, may prove to be nothing but an illuminating set of classificatory abstractions, which have never had any objective or independent existence at all 'in real life'.[1]

The foregoing considerations will perhaps be sufficient to guard us against the error of supposing that some special quality of Race in some fraction of Mankind is the positive factor which, within the last 6,000 years, has shaken part of Mankind out of the Yin-state which we call 'the Integration of Custom' into the Yang-activity which we have decided to call 'the Differentiation of Civilization'. We may add that even if Race had proved, on inquiry, to be the positive factor of which we are in search, we should have discovered no more than the occasion of the geneses of civilizations as opposed to the cause, which would still have remained the unknown quantity which it was when our inquiry started. We should have ascertained (on this supposition) that the geneses of our twenty-one civilizations were really due to a racial superiority of the people who created these civilizations over the common run of Mankind, only to find ourselves still confronted with our original question in a new form of words. Instead of asking why a fraction of Mankind had distinguished itself from the

[1] This question is discussed in the concluding chapter of R. B. Dixon's *The Racial History of Man* (New York 1923, Scribner), on pp. 501–6. This scholar's conclusion is that: 'The "types" whose distribution and hypothetical migrations we have . . . been attempting to trace are not races in the ordinary sense of the term, and are not to be confounded with the many more or less clearly differentiated racial groups into which we may divide the peoples of the World to-day. These various living races are each the result of some particular combination of the original "types" or elements; and the difficulty which we find in deciding just how many races there are is largely due to the fact that the elements have been blended so variously and in such varying proportions. Moreover, from this point of view, a race is not a permanent entity' (pp. 502–3).

rest of the human family by creating civilizations, we should have now to ask why the racial qualities which had enabled this fraction to distinguish itself in this way had been acquired at some previous time by one part of the human family and by one part only. We could not take this supposed prior diversity of racial endowment for granted, any more than the empirically observed diversity of cultural achievement which it was alleged to explain. Nor could we take it on trust as an inexplicable and unintelligible fact which had existed from all eternity, since it is evident that racial differences between branches of the human family cannot be older than Mankind itself, and Mankind, so far from having existed from all eternity, is a recent product of the evolution of Life on a planet which is one of the youngest bodies of the stellar universe. Thus we should not have genuinely solved the problem of finding an intelligible value for our original unknown quantity, the cause of the geneses of civilizations, but should have simply re-formulated the problem by presenting this original unknown quantity in terms of another unknown quantity, namely, the cause of the diversity of racial endowment within the human family. If we were clear-headed and intellectually honest, we should have had to admit that the operation which we had performed had made our equation more intricate without having brought us a single step nearer to working it out. In other words, the so-called racial explanation of differences in human performance and achievement is either an ineptitude or a fraud.[1]

It is noteworthy that the makers of the Jewish and Christian theological systems, from which all our modern Western 'race theories' are lineally descended, have faced the fact that the empirically observed differences between the performances and

---

[1] We have exposed this racial fallacy once before in the course of this Study (in I. B (ii), above, on pp. 25–6), when we were considering differences in performance and achievement between communities within a single society: e.g. the differences within the Hellenic Society, in the second period of its history, between the special part played by Athens and the special part played by Sparta and the ordinary part which was played by almost all the other city-states of the Hellenic World of that age with little or no variation. We saw that we should not be explaining the individuality of the initiatives which the Athenians and the Spartans respectively took, in circumstances which were the same for them and for their neighbours, if we ascribed this to a hypo-thetical pre-existing individuality in the Spartan and the Athenian 'racial' characters. We should either have to explain how these supposed prior differences of racial character between the peoples of the Hellenic World originally arose, or else admit that we had failed, after all, to explain the subsequent differences in their performances and achieve-ments in which the supposed prior differences of racial character were alleged to have unfolded themselves. What is sauce for the goose is sauce for the gander. If Race does not account for the special contributions of the Athenians and Spartans to the progress of the Hellenic Civilization, it is no use trying to account for the geneses of civilizations in general by the racial myths of 'Nordic Man' and 'the Children of the Sun'. The racial fallacy has been exposed succinctly by Monsieur Edmond Demolins: 'La race n'explique rien, car il reste encore à rechercher ce qui a produit la diversité des races. La race n'est pas une cause, c'est une conséquence.' (Demolins, E.: *Comment la Route crée le Type Social* (Paris no date, Firmin-Didot), p. vii.)

achievements of different fractions of the human family can neither be left unexplained nor yet be explained away, but have to be accounted for ultimately as effects of some differentiating act. Like Faust at the end of his soliloquy, they have divined that 'Im Anfang war die Tat '.[1]

The Jews have been intensely conscious of being not as other men are. In their view of the World, there is a great gulf fixed between them and the Gentiles; and they are as sincerely convinced as the English or the Americans of their own immeasurable superiority to 'the lesser breeds without the Law'. Yet they have not taken for granted this tremendous difference between one breed of human beings and another without postulating a correspondingly tremendous cause. In their belief, they are a peculiar people because they are a 'chosen people';[2] and the divine choice, which has made them what they are, is not irrevocable. It has been given effect in a covenant between their God Yahweh and their forefather Abraham; and the precariousness of the privileges which the Covenant confers is symbolized in the physical hall-mark which is its token; for this hall-mark is not a skin which cannot be changed nor a stature to which one cubit cannot be added, but the artificial and optional mark of circumcision.[3] Even so, the invidious racial conception that the privileges of the Covenant are immutable has crept into the Jewish consciousness. In the classic account of the Covenant in the Book of Genesis, Yahweh is made to declare:

'I will establish my Covenant between me and thee and thy seed after thee in their generations for an everlasting covenant;'[4]

and this proclamation of everlastingness is echoed in a hundred later passages in the Jewish scriptures.[5] Yet, in their heart of hearts, the Jews—unlike the English-speaking Protestants who claim to be their spiritual heirs—have ever been aware that Yahweh's choice is neither irrevocable like the Law of the Medes and Persians nor immutable like 'the Laws of Nature'; and their self-complacency was not impervious to John the Baptist's mortal thrust:

'Think not to say within yourselves: "We have Abraham to our father"; for I say unto you that God is able of these stones to raise up children unto Abraham.'[6]

---

[1] Goethe: *Faust*, Part I, l. 1237.
[2] Deuteronomy xiv. 2: 'The Lord hath chosen thee to be a peculiar people unto himself.'
[3] See the classical account of the Covenant in Genesis xvii.
[4] Genesis xvii. 7.
[5] e.g. in Psalm cv. 8-10.
[6] Matthew iii. 9. The point is elaborated in the Epistle to the Romans, ch. ix. Echoes of the same saying are placed in the mouth of Jesus himself in John viii. 33 and 39.

This text is a profound criticism of the fallacy of Race—a fallacy to which the Jews, to their credit, have never succumbed completely.

The Jewish dichotomy of Mankind into Jews and Gentiles was reproduced in the Pauline dichotomy into 'vessels of wrath fitted to destruction' and 'vessels of mercy afore prepared unto glory'.[1] The dividing line was now drawn no longer between communities but between individuals; yet the underlying conception remained unaltered. The distinction between Jews and Gentiles was ascribed to Yahweh's choice, the distinction between the Damned and the Elect to God's predestination; and, so long as an act of will was postulated as the first cause in the background, it was in vain for theologians to lay down that predestination was irrevocable, since it was logically impossible to believe that an omnipotent power was incapable of revoking its own decrees. Thus the Pauline doctrine was never completely stultified until, through the minds of Punic Augustine and Latin Calvin, it reached the mind of Nordic Man. Our modern Western racialists have rationalized their Calvinism by substituting Black and White skins for damnation and grace, and expurgated it by omitting the divine cause. The result is not science but fetishism.

The Jewish and Christian doctors have never fallen into the error of accepting Race as an explanation of the actual differences in human performance and achievement, whether between communities or between individuals; and they have satisfied their intellectual demand for an adequate cause by postulating an act of God. This postulate, which Syriac and Western theologians have made in all good faith, has been commended by a Hellenic philosopher as a pious fraud which is required by social expediency and is justified by *raison d'état*. In the half-humorous, half-cynical Spirit of Voltaire's *si Dieu n'existait pas il faudrait l'inventer*,[2] Plato, in a famous passage of *The Republic*, has propounded 'a noble lie' which is to reconcile the citizens of his utopia to the different stations in life to which it may please the Government to call them after having tested and brought out their innate abilities by a strenuously competitive course of education.

' "What we now need," I said, "is some dodge in the nature of an opportune lie: a single noble lie which will do the trick of convincing—if possible the Government themselves and in any case the rest of the community."

' "What do you mean?" he said.

' "Nothing out of the way," I said; "Just a *welsh*[3] which has been worked on ever so many occasions before now, as the poets credibly

[1] Romans ix. 22–3.
[2] Voltaire: Épîtres, xcvii, A l'Auteur du Livre des Trois Imposteurs (A.D. 1771), l. 22.
[3] Φοινικικόν τι.

inform us, though it has not been worked in our time and now could only be worked, if at all (of which I am not sure), at the cost of a great deal of tact and patience."

' "How shy you seem to be of your idea," he said.

' "You will feel," I said, "that I have every reason to be shy when I tell you what it is."

' "Speak out," he said, "and don't be afraid."

' "Here goes, then—though I don't know how I shall have the face to say it or whether I shall find words to say it in. Well, I shall try to convince first the Government and the Army and then the rest of the community that the upbringing and education which we gave them was all a dream and that all the time they were really being moulded and brought up underground in the bosom of the Earth, they and their arms and the rest of their equipment, which was likewise being manufactured there. Then, I shall tell them, when they had been completely finished off, their mother the Earth produced them—thus placing them under an obligation to defend their country, if she is attacked, with all their mind and all their strength, as their mother and their nurse, and also to look after their fellow-citizens as their brothers born of the same Mother Earth."

' "Really," he said, "how can you have the effrontery to go on and on with a lie like that?"

' "You have every reason to be shocked," I said, "but, all the same, do hear my fairy-story out. It goes on like this: 'All of you members of the community are brothers; but when God moulded you, he put a streak of metal into each at the moment of birth—gold into those of you who were fit to govern, because they were the most precious; silver into the soldiers; and iron and bronze into the peasants and the workmen. As you are all akin, you will generally breed true to type; but it will occasionally happen that the golden stock will have silver offspring and the silver stock golden offspring and so on, *mutatis mutandis*. Now the first and chiefest commandment that God lays upon members of the Government is this: the paramount call upon their honour and efficiency as guardians of Society is to be on the watch for any of these flaws in the psychic composition of the members of the rising generation and to take the proper action in each case. If it is a case of their own children showing traces of bronze or iron, they must have no mercy on them but must degrade them to the ranks of the workmen or the peasants to which they intrinsically belong. Conversely, if the children of peasants or workmen show traces of gold or silver, they must rate them at their intrinsic value and must promote them to be members of the Government or of the Army, as the case may be.' We must find scriptural authority for the prophecy that the community will come to grief on the day when a member of the iron race or the bronze race enters the Government. Well, can you think of any dodge for getting this fairy-story believed?"

' "Certainly not for getting it believed by grown-up people now alive; but we might manage it with their children and their descendants and the whole of posterity." '[1]

---

[1] Plato: *Respublica*, 414B–415D.

In this passage, Plato drives home the truth that the racial explanation of differences in human ability and achievement cannot be put forward by any rational mind except as a deliberate and cold-blooded piece of deception, in which the differentiating effects of 'upbringing and education' are mendaciously ascribed to pre-existing differences of a racial order—and this with the calculated object of producing certain effects in the practical field of social and political action.

In Plato's 'noble lie', the fallacy of Race thus receives its final exposure; and here we may leave it; for we can now see beyond the fallacy to an ulterior truth. In discarding the conception of racial powers that are supposed to be peculiar to this or that branch of the human family, we have attained the conception of one omnipresent power which manifests itself in the performances and achievements of all Mankind and all Life. We may conceive of this power as a transcendent first cause and call it God,[1] or as an immanent source of continuous creation and call it (as Bergson calls it) *Évolution Créatrice* or *Élan Vital*. On either view, our conception of its nature and activity and range of operation will be the same; and on either view we shall have to admit that, although the recognition of this power may illuminate the rest of our Study, it has not in itself brought us face to face with the immediate object of our research. We have still to find the positive factor which, within the last six thousand years, has shaken part of Mankind out of the Yin-state called 'the Integration of Custom' into the Yang-activity called 'the Differentiation of Civilization'. If Race is too trivial a phenomenon to be identified with this factor, God, who 'maketh his sun to rise on the evil and on the good, and sendeth rain on the just and on the unjust',[2] is too great. His action is ubiquitous and eternal; and a power which manifests itself in Life, or even merely in Humanity, at large cannot, in and by itself, be the unknown quantity which, in certain times and places, has given an impetus to a part of Mankind and not to the whole. We must continue our search.

2. *Environment*

We have next to see whether we can find our unknown quantity in the environments in which the geneses of civilizations have occurred.

The modern Western concept of Race, which we have now weighed in the balance and found wanting, was evoked, as we have

'Est deus in nobis. Agitante calescimus illo.
Impetus hic sacrae semina mentis habet.'
(Ovid: *Fasti*, Book VI, ll. 5–6 (quoted by David Hume in his essay *Of the Rise and Progress of the Arts and Sciences*).) [2] Matthew v. 45.

noticed, by the expansion of our Western Society over the World from the close of the fifteenth century of our era onwards. This expansion brought the peoples of the West into intimate contact with peoples of other physique and other culture; the differences, thus empirically observed, between human beings who were living on the surface of the same planet at the same time presented a problem to Western minds; and these minds solved that problem to their own satisfaction by improvising the concept of Race from the theological materials at their command. Hellenic minds were confronted with the same problem in consequence of a similar expansion of the Hellenic Society, which began towards the close of the eighth century B.C., and they solved the problem—also to their own satisfaction—by working out a theoretical explanation on quite different lines. It is noteworthy that although in Hellenic history this intellectual problem presented itself some four centuries earlier than in our Western history,[1] the Hellenic solution, instead of being the cruder, as might be expected *a priori*, was actually superior to the Western solution in all points. It was more imaginative, more rational, and more humane; and, above all, it was unprejudiced. The self-regarding element which is so general, so prominent, and so ugly a feature in our Western race-theories is conspicuous by its absence here. For, so far from being roused to race-consciousness by contact with human beings who were not as they were, the Hellenes drew an inference which made them more sceptical about Race than they had been before.[2] They explained the manifest differences between themselves and their newly-discovered neighbours as being the effects of diverse environments upon a uniform Human Nature, instead of seeing in them the outward manifestations of a diversity that was somehow intrinsic in Human Nature itself.[3]

[1] The Hellenic Society probably began to emerge before the close of the twelfth century B.C., and it began to expand before the close of the eighth. Our Western Society began to emerge before the close of the seventh century of the Christian Era, failed in its first attempt at expansion ('the Crusades'), and did not begin to expand successfully until the close of the fifteenth century: i.e. not until it had been in existence, in its original home, for some eight centuries, in contrast with the achievement of the Hellenic Society in expanding successfully within some four centuries of its first emergence.

[2] In the first age of Hellenic history Hellenic minds had passed through the stage of being under the dominion of the concept of Race, as is shown by the two facts that the earliest Hellenic institutions were based on kinship and that the earliest Hellenic efforts at historiography took a genealogical form.

[3] The fact that the same problem of the diversity of Mankind evoked a Race-theory in Western minds and an Environment-theory in Hellenic minds may be explained to some extent by the difference in the instances of human diversity with which the Western and the Hellenic voyagers were confronted respectively. The Westerners were first confronted with the problem of human diversity on the Guinea Coast of Africa and in the East and West Indies, where the physique of the indigenous populations was strikingly different from the European type, whereas there were no striking features in the local geographical environments which readily suggested themselves as causes of the particular turn which human life had taken there. In these circumstances, Western minds evolved the theory of Race. On the other hand, the Hellenes were first confronted with

The *locus classicus* in which the Hellenic 'environment theory' may be studied is a treatise entitled *Influences of Atmosphere, Water, and Situation* which dates from the fifth century B.C. and is preserved among the collected works of the Hippocratean School of Medicine. As the best exposition of the theory in any literature within our range, this monograph deserves quotation:

'The countries which have the greatest and the most frequent seasonal variations of climate also have the wildest and most highly diversified landscape and present the greatest array of mountains, forests, plains and meadow-lands, while in countries where the seasonal variations are slight the uniformity of landscape is at its maximum. Consideration will show that the same equations hold good for Human Nature. Human physiognomies may be classified into the well-wooded and well-watered mountain type, the thin-soiled waterless type, the meadowy marshy type, the well-cleared and well-drained lowland type. Here, too, there is the same effect of environmental variation upon physique; and if the variation is great, the differentiation of bodily type is increased proportionately. . . .

'Inhabitants of mountainous, rocky, well-watered country at a high altitude, where the margin of seasonal climatic variation is wide, will tend to have large-built bodies constitutionally adapted for courage and endurance, and in such natures there will be a considerable element of ferocity and brutality. Inhabitants of sultry hollows covered with water-meadows, who are more commonly exposed to warm winds than to cold and who drink tepid water, will, in contrast, not be large-built or slim, but thickset, fleshy and dark-haired, with swarthy rather than fair complexions and with less phlegm than bile in their constitutions. Courage and endurance will not be innate in their characters to the same degree, but will be capable of being produced in them by the coefficient of institutions. If there are rivers in the country which drain it of the stagnant water and the rainfall, the population will be healthy and in good condition; while, if there are no rivers and their drinking-water comes from stagnant lakes and marshes, their bodies will run to spleen and incline to be pot-bellied. Inhabitants of rolling, wind-swept, well-watered country at a high altitude will be large-built and un-individualized, with a vein of cowardice and tameness in their characters. Inhabitants of thin-soiled, waterless country without vegetation, where the seasonal climatic variations are abrupt and violent, will tend to have

this same problem of human diversity in the Delta of the Nile and along the north coast of the Black Sea on the fringe of the Eurasian Steppe—that is to say, in regions where the physique of the indigenous population was not strikingly different from the European type, while the local geographical environments did present certain striking features—the Nile in the one case and the Steppe in the other—which readily suggested themselves as causes of the particular turns which human life had taken in Egypt and in Scythia respectively. In these circumstances, Hellenic minds evolved the theory of Environment. The notion of a correlation between the Steppe and Nomadism or between the Nile and the Egyptiac Civilization was more obvious than any notion of a correlation between the tropical climate of the Guinea Coast and the primitive social life of the West African Negro. For the European explorer in the fifteenth century of the Christian Era, the colour of the Negro's skin was a more sensational novelty than the temperature of the atmosphere which the Negro was breathing.

bony, muscular bodies, fair rather than swarthy complexions, and head-strong, self-willed characters and temperaments. Where seasonal changes are most frequent and show the widest margin of variability, there you will find the greatest differentiation in the human body, character and organism.

'These are the most important varieties of organism; and then there is the effect of the country and the water which constitute the Human Race's environment. In the majority of cases, you will find that the human body and character vary in accordance with the nature of the country. Where the soil is rich and soft and well-watered, and where the water remains extremely near the surface, so that it is tepid in summer and chilly in winter, and where the climatic conditions are also favour-able, the inhabitants will be fleshy, loose-jointed, flaccid, unenergetic and poor-spirited as a general rule. Laziness and sleepiness will be prominent among their characteristics, and they will be clumsy instead of being neat or quick at skilled occupations. Where the country is rocky, waterless and without vegetation, and suffers from severe winters and from scorching suns, you will find the inhabitants bony and without spare flesh, with well-articulated joints and muscular, shaggy bodies. Such constitutions are instinct with energy and alertness, and their possessors have headstrong, self-willed characters and temperaments, with a tendency towards ferocity instead of tameness, and with a superior quickness and intelligence in skilled occupations and a superior aptitude for war. You will further find that the non-human fauna and flora of a given soil likewise vary according to the quality of that soil. I have now described the extreme contrasts of type and organism; and if you work out the rest for yourself on the analogy of these, you will not go wrong.'[1]

This passage is a commentary on the differences in physical structure and proportions and in psychological qualities which the Hellenes had observed among the inhabitants of Europe; but the favourite Hellenic illustrations of the 'environment theory' were taken from farther afield. They were the effect of life in the Lower Nile Valley upon the physique and character and institutions of the Egyptians, and the effect of life on the Eurasian Steppe upon the physique and character and institutions of the Scythians.[2]

[1] Hippocrates: *Influences of Atmosphere, Water, and Situation,* chs. 13 and 24. (English translation by A. J. Toynbee in *Greek Historical Thought from Homer to the Age of Heraclius* (London 1924, Dent), pp. 167–8.)

[2] For the effect of the climatic and topographical or hydrographical environment on the Egyptians, see Herodotus, Book II, *passim*, especially chapter 5 (Αἴγυπτος . . . ἐστὶ Αἰγυπτίοισι ἐπίκτητός τε γῆ καὶ δῶρον τοῦ ποταμοῦ) and chapter 35 (Αἰγύπτιοι ἅμα τῷ οὐρανῷ τῷ κατὰ σφέας ἐόντι ἑτεροίῳ, καὶ τῷ ποταμῷ φύσιν ἀλλοίην παρεχομένῳ ἢ οἱ ἄλλοι ποταμοί, τὰ πολλὰ πάντα ἔμπαλιν τοῖσι ἄλλοισι ἀνθρώποισι ἐστήσαντο ἤθεά τε καὶ νόμους); for the effect on two primitive peoples of the Black Sea Coast in what is now called Transcaucasia, the Macrocephali and the Phasians, see Hippocrates, op. cit., chs. 14–15; for the effect on the Scythians, see op. cit., chs. 17–22. See also a passage in Plato's *Republic* (435E–436A), where the writer gives, as illustrations of regional group-character-istics, the hot-temperedness of the peoples of Thrace, Scythia, and the North, the intellectual curiosity of Hellas, and the acquisitiveness of the Phoenicians and Egyptians. In a later work, *The Laws* (747D–E), Plato accepts, in general terms, the theory that the

The Environment-theory of the geneses of civilizations has none of the moral repulsiveness of the Race-theory, yet intellectually it is no less vulnerable. Both theories attempt to account for the empirically observed diversity in the psychical behaviour and performance of different fractions of Mankind by supposing that this psychical diversity is fixedly and permanently correlated, in the relation of effect to cause, with certain elements of diversity, likewise given by empirical observation, in the non-psychical domain of Nature. The Race-theory finds its differentiating natural cause in the diversity of human physique, the Environment-theory finds it in the diversity of the climatic, topographical, and hydrographical conditions in which different human societies live; but this discrepancy between the two theories is not fundamental. They are merely two different attempts to find a solution for the same equation by assigning different values to the same unknown quantity. The structure of the equation which is postulated in the two theories is identical; and neither can stand if the common underlying formula will not bear examination. The essence of the formula is a correlation between two sets of variations; and this correlation must be demonstrated to be fixed and permanent—it must maintain itself in every instance under all conditions—before any theories founded on it can claim the status of scientific laws. Under this test, we have already seen the Race-theory break down; and we shall now see the Environment-theory fare no better.

Let us start with the two favourite Hellenic illustrations of the Environment-theory: the supposed relations of cause and effect between the peculiarities of the environment on the Eurasian Steppe and in the Lower Nile Valley and the peculiarities of the Nomadic and the Egyptiac Society. In isolation, these two illustrations are no more than suggestive. They can only provide cogent evidence for the truth of the theory founded on them if we extend our survey to all the other specimens of either environment on the face of the Earth and find that every area resembling the Eurasian Steppe has become the seat of a society resembling the Eurasian Nomadic Society and every area resembling the Lower Nile Valley the seat of a society resembling the Egyptiac.

In attempting any such survey, we must take care to make our comparisons between areas which are genuinely distinct from one another. The Eurasian Steppe, for example, is a vast area extending

psychical as well as the physical characteristics of human beings are determined and differentiated by the physical environment; but, after enumerating various elements in this environment—winds, waters, foods—he suggests that πάντων μέγιστον διαφέροιεν ἂν τόποι χώρας ἐν οἷς θεία τις ἐπίπνοια καὶ δαιμόνων λήξεις εἶεν, τοὺς ἀεὶ κατοικιζομένους ἵλεῳ δεχόμενοι καὶ τοὐναντίον. In other words, he regards divine influences, or acts of God, as being the most potent creative forces in human affairs.

from the Arctic Circle to the 40th parallel of latitude and from
the 23rd degree of longitude, at the Iron Gates of the Danube, to
the passage of the Amur through the mountains a hundred degrees
to the east, with a girdle of outlying enclaves all round: the Hungarian Steppe beyond the Carpathians, the Manchurian Steppe
beyond the Khingan Range, the Seistan Steppe beyond the Hindu
Kush, the Azerbaijan Steppe beyond the Caucasus, the Thracian
Steppe beyond the Balkan. The Nomadic life which Hellenic
voyagers observed, from the eighth or seventh century B.C.
onwards, in the immediate hinterland of the northern coasts of the
Black Sea and the Sea of Azov, was being lived in a more or less
uniform way throughout the area which we have indicated, and it
has continued to be lived in the same way from then till now,
though nowadays it only maintains itself in a remnant of its former
domain and its complete extinction is in sight.[1] Within these
limits of Time and Space, the Nomadic life of the Eurasian Steppe
is a continuum; and it therefore proves nothing to our present
purpose to demonstrate that the life lived by one Nomadic people
on one portion of the Steppe in one age is the same as that lived
by another people on another portion in another age. We must
make our comparisons, not between different parts of the same
wholes, but between whole areas and whole societies that are
separate from and independent of one another. It is only under
these conditions that the emergence of similar societies in similar
environments can properly be taken as evidence for the truth of the
Environment-theory of the geneses of civilizations.

Taking, then, the Eurasian Steppe and its dependencies as one
whole, we may set beside it, first, the nearest area which offers a
similar environment for human life. This area extends from the
western shore of the Persian Gulf to the eastern shore of the Atlantic
and from the southern foot of the highlands of Iran, Anatolia,
Syria, and North-West Africa to the northern foot of the highlands
of the Yaman and Abyssinia and to the northern fringe of the
forests of Tropical Africa. We may call this steppe the 'Afrasian',
to give it a comprehensive name; and now we can put our test
question: Is the similarity between the environments offered by the
Eurasian and Afrasian steppes matched by any corresponding
similarity between the respective human societies that have
emerged in these two areas? The answer is in the affirmative. The
Afrasian Steppe has its Nomadism too—a Nomadism which displays just those resemblances to and differences from the Nomadism
of the Eurasian Steppe which, on the Environment-theory, we
should expect to find in view of the resemblances and differences

---

[1] See Part III. A, vol. iii, pp. 7–22, below.

between the two areas. This comes out when we compare the
Eurasian and Afrasian Nomads' domesticated animals. Both Nomadic societies have domesticated the camel (an animal which has all
but failed to survive on either steppe in the wild state)[1]; but the fact
that the domesticated Bactrian camel of the Eurasian Steppe and
the domesticated Arabian camel of the Afrasian Steppe represent
different breeds indicates that the two feats of domestication have
been achieved independently. Again, the herds on whose milk and
flesh the Eurasian Nomads live consist mainly of horses and cattle,
whereas the Afrasian Nomads, in their drier climate and on their
scantier pastures, have to content themselves with herds of sheep
and goats.[2]

In this first test, our survey of the Steppes and their inhabitants
has revealed the correlation between type of environment and type
of society which is demanded by the theory that similar environments always and everywhere produce similar societies, not by
mimesis, but on the principle of the Uniformity of Nature. Under
further tests, however, the correlation breaks down. For we find
that the other areas in the World which offer environments for
Nomad societies—the Prairies of North America, the Llanos of
Venezuela, the Pampas of Argentina, the Australian grass-lands in
Western Queensland and Western New South Wales—have not
fulfilled the requirements of the Environment-theory by producing
independent Nomadic societies of their own. Their potentialities
are not open to question. They have been realized by the enterprise of our Western Society in modern times; and the pioneering
Western stockmen—North American cowboys and South American
Gauchos and Australian cattlemen—who have won and held these
untenanted ranges for a few generations, in the van of the advancing
plough and mill, have captivated the imagination of Mankind as
triumphantly as the Scythian and the Tatar and the Arab. The
potentialities of the American and Australian steppes must have
been powerful indeed if they could transform into Nomads, if only
for a generation, the pioneers of a society which had no Nomadic
traditions, having lived by agriculture and manufacture ever since

[1] The problem of the desiccation of the Steppes, and its bearing upon the genesis of
the Nomadic societies and upon the almost complete failure of both the Bactrian and
the Arabian camel to survive on the Steppe except under the Nomad's aegis, is discussed
below in II. C (ii) (b), 2 on pp. 302–6, and in Part III. A, vol. iii, on pp. 8–13 and 23
and in Annex II.

[2] The horse was only introduced into South-Western Asia, South-Eastern Europe,
and North-Western Africa by the Eurasian Nomads who overran the domain of the
Empire of Sumer and Akkad during the post-Sumeric interregnum, *circa* 1875–1575 B.C.
(see I. C (i) (b), pp. 104–7, above). Even then it was only naturalized among the
sedentary societies in that part of the World. The Afrasian Nomads did not succeed in
making the horse at home on their steppe until perhaps 2,000 years later. For all his
fame, the Arab horse is a recent and exotic denizen of the Afrasian Steppe, and his
maintenance there has never ceased to be a *tour de force*. He is a luxury animal who is
spared hard labour and is nourished on camel's milk.

it first emerged. It is all the more remarkable that the peoples whom the first Western explorers found in occupation had never been stimulated by the potentialities of the environment into Nomadism, but had found no better use for these Nomads' paradises than to use them as hunting-grounds—remaining on the primitive hunting and food-gathering level of economy to the end.

If we next test the Environment-theory by a survey of areas resembling the Lower Nile Valley, our experience will be the same.

The Lower Nile Valley is, so to speak, a 'sport' in the landscape of the Afrasian Steppe. Egypt has the same dry climate as the vast surrounding area in which it is an enclave; but it has one exceptional asset—an ample and unfailing supply of water and alluvium, provided by a great river which rises, beyond the limits of the Steppe, in a different area which enjoys an abundant rainfall. The creators of the Egyptiac Civilization realized the potentialities of this asset by evolving a society which presents a sensational contrast, in every aspect of life, to the Afrasian Nomadism all round. Then is the special environment offered by the Nile in Egypt the positive factor to which the genesis of the Egyptiac Civilization is due? In order to establish that thesis we should have to show that in every other separate area in which an environment of the Nilotic type is offered, a civilization of the 'fluvial' type has independently emerged. Here, again, the Environment-theory stands the test in a neighbouring area in which the required conditions are fulfilled: that is to say, in the Lower Valley of the Euphrates and the Tigris. The conditions are substantially the same: the encompassing Afrasian Steppe, the dry climate, the ample supply of water and alluvium provided by great rivers which rise in rain-swept highlands in the back of beyond. And, sure enough, the independent 'fluvial' civilization, for which we are looking, is there—the Sumeric Civilization emerging in the Lower Valley of the Euphrates and the Tigris to match the emergence of the Egyptiac Civilization in the Lower Valley of the Nile.[1] When we extend our survey, however, the correlation breaks down, as it did when we were surveying the environments of the class represented by the Afrasian Steppe.

It breaks down, to begin with, in the Jordan Valley—an area,

---

[1] *Pace* the 'Diffusionist School' of British anthropologists, we take it for granted that the Sumeric and Egyptiac civilizations emerged independently of one another and that they did not come into effective contact until after each of them had developed its own individual character. This is not to deny that the contact really was effective, or that it can be traced back to a very early date. (On this matter see Childe, V. G.: *The Most Ancient East* (London 1928, Kegan Paul), especially pp. 112–22, 167–8, 196–8, 217–18, 221–4.)

situated nearer to Egypt than 'Irāq, in which the required conditions are fulfilled equally well on a miniature scale.

'The Jordan Valley below Betše'an and Pella, the Ghor, a broad deep rift between two mountain walls, with a glowing hot climate, lay completely desolate [in the sixteenth century B.C.] and has remained as good as uninhabited to this day. Much light is thrown on national character (*Volkscharakter*) by the fact that here the attempt has never been made—as it was made under the substantially similar conditions in the Nile Valley—to take advantage of the soil and to render it productive by systematic irrigation. It is only when we draw this comparison that we become able fully to appreciate the energy with which the Egyptians have made their country the most productive agricultural country in the World for thousands of years on end.'[1]

After our inquiry into Race, we may decline to accept—even at the hands of the great historian from whose pen this passage comes—the postulate that some hypothetical difference between 'the national characters' of the local populations accounts for the actual difference between the respective states of the Lower Nile Valley and the Jordan Valley during the last three or four thousand years; but, on Eduard Meyer's authority, we may accept this actual difference as a matter of fact and may recognize the historical acumen which has taken note of the fact and has brought it to our attention. In the Jordan Valley, the same environment has been offered as in the Lower Valley of the Nile and in the Lower Valley of the Euphrates and the Tigris, without having evoked the same response in the shape of another independent fluvial civilization.

The correlation may prove to break down again in the Lower Indus Valley, which is a 'sport' in the landscape of 'the Indian Desert' or 'Thar', as the Lower Nile Valley and the Jordan Valley and the Lower Valley of the Euphrates and the Tigris are 'sports' in the landscape of the Afrasian Steppe.[2] The Lower Indus Valley has not indeed suffered the perennial neglect which has been the fate of the Jordan Valley hitherto. Its potentialities have been turned to account; and this may prove to have been done, not by a local society on its own initiative, but by settlers from the Lower Valley of the Tigris and Euphrates who found the Indus Valley virgin soil and planted there, ready made, the Sumeric Civilization which they brought from home. In the present state of our knowledge,

---

[1] Meyer, Eduard: *Geschichte des Altertums*, vol. ii (i), 2nd edition (Stuttgart and Berlin 1928, Cotta), p. 96. In vol. i (i), 4th edition (Stuttgart and Berlin 1921, Cotta), p. 65, Meyer points out that the river-valleys of America have not become the cradles of any independent fluvial civilizations either, and that no independent archipelagic civilizations have arisen either in Indonesia or in the Caribbean.

[2] Climatically, the Indian Desert may be regarded as an outlying enclave of the Afrasian Steppe, if it receives such rainfall as it does receive from the Atlantic and not from the Indian Ocean. (See Childe, op. cit., pp. 23 and 201; but cf. the present volume, p. 303, footnote 2, below.)

it is perhaps not yet possible to decide between this explanation of the origins of 'the Indus Culture' and the alternative explanation of a related but still autonomous local growth.[1] Yet if, in the Indus Valley, the test does not, for the moment, yield a conclusive result, the conclusive result which it does yield in the Jordan Valley unmistakably repeats itself elsewhere. The defenders of the Environment-theory, after requiring us to suspend judgement in the case of the Indus Valley, may proceed to rule the Ganges Valley out of consideration as being too moist and tropical, and the Yangtse Valley as being too moist and temperate. On the latter grounds, they may rule out the Lower Mississippi Valley too, even though New Orleans, at the apex of the Mississippi Delta, lies in the very latitude of Egyptiac Memphis and Arabic Cairo at the apex of the Nile Delta. Yet the most captious critics cannot deny that the environment offered by the lower valleys of the Nile and of the Indus and of the Tigris and Euphrates is also offered by the valleys of the Rio Grande and the Colorado River in the South-Western United States. Under the hands of the modern European settler, equipped with the resources of a civilization which he has brought with him from the other side of the World, these rivers of America have performed the miracles which Nile and Euphrates once performed for Egyptiac and Sumeric irrigation-engineers; but this magic has never been taught by the Colorado or the Rio Grande, any more than it has been taught by the Jordan, to people who were not adepts in it already through having learnt it elsewhere.[2] In fine, we have half a dozen instances of the Nilotic type of environment[3] and only two or three separate and independent instances of the 'fluvial' type of civilization. The geneses of the Egyptiac and Sumeric civilizations in such environments thus turn out to be exceptions and not the rule; and it follows that the environmental factor cannot be the positive factor which has brought these two civilizations into existence.

We shall be confirmed in this conclusion if we examine the environments in which the geneses of other civilizations have occurred.

The Andean Civilization came into existence on a plateau of such

---

[1] For these alternative explanations of the origin of 'the Indus Culture' in the Lower Indus Valley, see I. C (i) (b), pp. 107–8, above, and Annex III, below.

[2] On the Colorado and the Rio Grande, the work of the European settlers was anticipated by that of the Pueblo communities; but the Pueblo culture was not an autochthonous product of the rivers on whose banks it found a footing. Like the European culture which eventually effaced it, it came in from outside—not, indeed, from the further shore of the Atlantic, but from the southern extremity of the Mexican Plateau.

[3] The number of instances would be greater if we allowed ourselves to take account of debatable cases like the Ganges Valley and the Yangtse Valley and the Lower Mississippi Valley—or, again, the Basin of the Murray and the Darling Rivers in Australia, where the modern European settler, bringing with him the technique of irrigation, has produced results which the previous inhabitants of Australia had never been moved to produce by the direct stimulus of the local environment.

an altitude that it offered a temperate climate and vegetation in
equatorial latitudes, in contrast to the tropical climate of the low-
lying basin of the Amazon, into which the waters of the plateau
found their way. There is a corresponding contrast between the
high level of culture which the Andean Society once attained and
the primitive savagery from which the tribes of the Amazonian
forest have not emerged.[1] Then was the Andean Plateau the cause
of the Andean Civilization? Before we answer in the affirmative,
let us extend our survey eastwards round the equatorial zone,
crossing the Atlantic, letting our gaze hover over the Amazon-like
basin of the Congo, and bringing it to rest on the Andean-like chain
of highlands which runs up the east side of Africa, south and north,
from Table Mountain to the Highlands of Abyssinia. In the low-
lying tropical forests of the Congo, we shall find persisting the same
kind of primitive savagery that has persisted in the low-lying
tropical forests of the Amazon; but the East African highlands can
show no civilization to match the civilization of the Andean
Plateau. In this case, the same offer of a temperate climate and
vegetation in equatorial latitudes has not met with the same
response. The indigenous societies of the East African highlands
have remained on a level of culture which is hardly less primitive
than that of the Congolese. The two civilizations which have a
footing on the highlands to-day—a fossil of the Syriac Civilization
in Abyssinia and a string of outposts of our Western Civilization
from Kenya to the Cape—have both been introduced ready-made
from overseas, our Western Civilization by settlers from Europe
and the Syriac by settlers from the Yaman.[2] Thus the correlation
breaks down again.

Similarly, we observe that the Minoan Civilization emerged in a
cluster of islands, situated in an inland sea and blessed with the
climate of the Mediterranean. Yet before we pronounce that the

---

[1] This contrast between Andean civilization and Amazonian savagery, great as it is,
tends to appear somewhat less extreme in the light of the latest archaeological and
ethnographical discoveries. 'The Indians east of the Andes, in their relations with the
higher civilization in the west, were not only receivers but also givers' (Nordenskiöld,
E.: *Modifications in Indian Culture through Inventions and Loans* (Göteborg 1930,
Elander), p. 63). Amazonia turns out to be the birthplace of a surprisingly large proportion of the original inventions of the New World (op. cit., p. 22). 'It is possible that
the Amazonas, if manioca was known there before maize, possessed a highly developed
civilization earlier than the Peruvian coastland. This is at all events a possibility to be
reckoned with' (Nordenskiöld, E.: *Origin of the Indian Civilisations in South America*
(Göteborg 1931, Elander), p. 52).

[2] We must not leave out of account the culture of Uganda, which is a primitive
culture of the highest level—a strikingly higher level than that of the surrounding
indigenous societies—although the progressive Baganda, like their savage neighbours,
are members of the Black Race and show no trace of any infusion of 'White' blood. This
enclave of exceptionally high native culture cannot be accounted for by immigration.
Is it a product of the radiation of the Egyptiac Civilization up the Nile? The radiation
of a civilization, like the radiation of star-light, may go on travelling through Space for
ages after the body which once emitted it has ceased to exist. (See Part II. A, p. 187,
above.)

Aegean environment was the cause of the Minoan Civilization, we must ask why a similar environment failed to evoke another civilization of the 'archipelago' type round the Inland Sea of Japan. We must ask why Japan never gave birth to an independent civilization, corresponding to the Japanese environment, but was eventually found vacant, and annexed, by the continental, non-maritime Far Eastern Civilization which had first emerged in the interior of China.

The Sinic Civilization, to which the extant Far Eastern Civilization is 'affiliated', is sometimes represented as being the offspring of the Yellow River, because it happened to emerge in the Yellow River Valley; but before this account of the genesis of the Sinic Civilization is accepted, it has to be explained why the Danube Valley, with much the same disposition of climate and soil and plain and mountain,[1] has failed to produce a sister-civilization of the same physiognomy.[2]

And what of the Mayan Civilization? Are we to regard the tropical rainfall and vegetation of Northern Guatemala and of British Honduras as the positive cause of the emergence of this civilization there? Then it has to be explained why human beings were stimulated into civilization in Central America by an environment which is still keeping them, more than two thousand years later, on the most primitive level of savagery in the basins of the Amazon and the Congo. It may be objected that while these two latter areas lie actually on the Equator, the original home of the Mayan Civilization lies on the 15th degree of latitude north, towards the outer edge of the tropical zone. In order to meet this objection, we will abandon the comparison with the Amazon and the Congo and will compare the country in which the Mayan Civilization emerged with another low-lying rain-sodden jungle-clad country in approximately the same latitude on the other side

---

[1] The geographical configuration of the Danube Valley, with a lower plain extending from the mouth of the river to the Iron Gates and an upper plain in Hungary, is singularly like the configuration of the Yellow River Valley, with its lower plain in Shantung and Honan and its upper plain, on the further side of a defile, in Shansi and Shensi.

[2] Modern Western archaeological research has, indeed, revealed traces of an incipient Danubian Civilization dating from the third millennium B.C.; but this was abortive. Unlike the Sinic Civilization, it did not succeed in striking out along an independent line of growth. It is possible that the difference in the fortunes of the Sinic Civilization and this abortive Danubian Civilization was due to the fact that although their climatic and topographical environments were similar, their human environments, in the shape of neighbouring societies, were different. The Sinic Society, at the time of its emergence during the second millennium B.C., seems to have had no direct contact with any societies that were above the primitive level. On the other hand, the abortive Danubian Civilization, at the time when it was in gestation, was probably within the range of both the Minoan Civilization and the Sumeric Civilization. The radiation and attraction exerted by these older and stronger civilizations upon the incipient Danubian Civilization in its embryonic state might account for its miscarriage. (For this abortive Danubian Civilization, see *The Cambridge Ancient History*, vol. i, ch. ii, 'Neolithic and Bronze Age Cultures', by J. L. Myres; and *The Danube in Prehistory*, by V. G. Childe (Oxford 1929, University Press).)

of the World. We plunge into the forests of Cambodia and discover, at Angkor Wat, as mighty a monument to the passage of a civilization as any which the forests of Central America have yielded up. What is the conclusion? That these low-lying rain-sodden tropical forests infallibly produce civilizations when their latitude happens to be round about 15 degrees? This conclusion might perhaps be forced on us, unconvincing though it seems *a priori*, if the civilization commemorated by the ruins of Angkor Wat, as well as the civilization commemorated by the ruins of Copan or Ixkun, were found to be indigenous.[1] Actually, the archaeological evidence tells us that the civilization which expressed itself so magnificently in Cambodia was not native to the soil but was imported ready-made from overseas. Cambodia was a colonial outpost of the Hindu Civilization, and not a region with an independent civilization of its own. The remains of the Hindu Civilization at Angkor Wat tell not for but against the hypothesis of a correlation, in the nature of cause and effect, between the existence of certain types of environment and the emergence of certain types of civilization. Angkor Wat testifies, first, that Cambodia did offer, like Central America, a tropical environment in which the existence of a civilization was possible; and, second, that in Cambodia the particular civilization which has proved that first point by establishing itself there cannot have been a spontaneous product of this environment, since its remains bear evidence that it originated far away, in India. In the light of this testimony, it is impossible to contend that because the Mayan Civilization happens to have been indigenous to Central America, the environment common to Central America and to Cambodia is the positive factor to which the genesis of the Mayan Civilization is due.[2]

By the same logic, the suggestion that the Russian variety of the Orthodox Christian Civilization is a product of the Russian forests, the Russian rivers, and the Russian cold can be rebutted by pointing out that no civilization has been generated by the similar environment of Canada. Or if it is suggested that the environment offered by Western Europe is the efficient cause of our Western Civilization, it may be pointed out that all the motley ingredients

---

[1] It is taken for granted here that the Mayan Civilization was indigenous to Central America, *pace* the 'Diffusionist School' of British archaeologists, and without intervening in the controversy as to whether one of the figures in a lost Mayan work of art, now only known at second hand from a drawing by a seventeenth-century French artist, represents an elephant or a macaw. (The Diffusionists' case in this controversy is presented in *Elephants and Ethnologists*, by G. Elliot Smith (London 1924, Kegan Paul). For a general discussion of the Diffusion Theory, see I. C (iii) (*b*), Annex, below.)

[2] Dr. Ellsworth Huntington contends that, in reality, the rain-soaked tropical jungle did not give birth to a civilization in Central America any more than in Cambodia. He seeks to show that the birthplace of the Mayan Civilization enjoyed a different climate, and was clad in a different vegetation, at the time when the Mayan Civilization arose there. For Dr. Huntington's views on this point, see further II. D (vii), Annex I, vol. ii, below.

of the West-European environment exist, without ever having combined to produce an independent civilization on their own account, within the present frontiers of the United States: another Norway in Maine, another Sweden in Minnesota, another England in New York State, another Riviera in Southern California, another Castile in Colorado, and so on to the end of the list. Why has a similarly compounded environment not begotten a similar civilization on both sides of the Atlantic?

At this point our critics may protest that, in our last two illustrations, we have not played fair. They may point out that the climatic and topographical environments of our Western Civilization and of the Russian variety of the Orthodox Christian Civilization, which we have just been comparing with similar climatic and topographical environments in the New World, are not the whole of the environment in which each of these two civilizations respectively emerged; and they may contend that the comparisons which we have made, being limited to a part of the environment which has been arbitrarily torn from its context by us, are illegitimate. The environment of any society, they may proceed, is always twofold. There is the non-human environment, consisting of the climate and topography and hydrography of the area in which the civilization originates and in which it expands; and it is this element in the environment that has been exclusively considered in this Study so far. There is also, however, a human environment, and this consists of all the other societies with which any given society has relations in either of the two dimensions of Time and Space.[1]

For instance, the environment in which the genesis of our Western Civilization took place includes the 'affiliation' of this Western Society to the Hellenic Society, as well as the climate and topography and hydrography of the geographical area which was the Western Society's original home. Moreover, they may proceed (pressing home their counter-attack), these two elements in the environment in which the Western Civilization emerged are bound up with one another. The Western Civilization, being 'affiliated' to the Hellenic, could not have arisen in some area which had lain quite beyond the horizon of the Hellenic Civilization even at its widest range; and it is therefore idle to point out an area in the New World in which all the features of the non-human environment of the Western Civilization can be found, unless it can also be shown that the human environment in which the genesis of the

[1] This duality of the Environment is taken into account in chapter 16 of the Hippocratean *Influences of Water, Atmosphere, and Situation*, and also in the second paragraph of David Hume's essay *Of National Characters*.

Western Civilization in Western Europe occurred was offering itself in North America contemporaneously. In other words, the proposition that an identical environment gave birth to a civilization on one side of the Atlantic and failed to give birth to one on the other is not proved by establishing the climatic, topographical, and hydrographical similarity of two geographical areas. It must also be proved that North America was as accessible as Western Europe to the radiation and attraction of the Hellenic Civilization in the age when the 'affiliation' of the Western Civilization to the Hellenic Civilization occurred; and on this point the case for the identity of the two environments breaks down. The horizon of the Hellenic World, which had expanded in the course of some twelve centuries from the coasts of the Aegean to the banks of the Ganges and the Elbe, remained bounded until the end by the coasts of the Atlantic. And when a latter-day poet, hailing from the Far West of the Hellenic *Orbis Terrarum*, divined, in a flash of inspiration, that the Atlantic was merely a vaster Mediterranean and that the Spirit of Man, which had triumphed over the estranging Sea, would one day conquer the Ocean,[1] no Hellenic Columbus arose to translate the poet's dream into the mariner's achievement. Thus there never was an opportunity for a civilization 'affiliated' to the Hellenic to emerge in the New World as well as in the Old; and, in the absence of this human environment, the climate and topography and hydrography of North America offered itself in vain as a cradle for a nascent civilization. Had not the similar non-human environment in Western Europe remained equally sterile until its frozen soil was touched and thawed by the last rays of the declining Hellenic sun?

On the same lines, it could be argued by our critics that the similarity of the non-human environment in Canada to the non-human environment in Russia does not confute the thesis that the Russian variety of the Orthodox Christian Civilization was a

---

[1] Nunc iam cessit pontus et omnes
patitur leges; non Palladia
compacta manu regum referens
inclita remos quaeritur Argo;
quaelibet altum cymba pererrat;
terminus omnis motus, et urbes
muros terra posuere nova;
nil qua fuerat sede reliquit
pervius orbis.

Indus gelidum potat Araxem,
Albim Persae Rhenumque bibunt.
Venient annis saecula seris,
quibus Oceanus vincula rerum
laxet, et ingens pateat tellus,
Tethysque novos detegat orbes,
nec sit terris ultima Thule.

(Seneca, *Medea*, ll. 364–79.)

product of the environment; for the whole environment must be taken into account, and, in confining our attention to the forests and the rivers and the cold, which Russia offers in common with Canada, we were attempting to make a part of the environment do duty for the whole. Why, the very name which we ourselves have given to this civilization ought to have guarded us against falling into that error. We have not named it 'the Russian Civilization', as though its affinities were solely with the geographical area in which it happens to have emerged. We have rightly called it 'the Orthodox Christian Civilization in Russia', in order to put on record the fact that it is an offshoot of a society whose original stem stands not in Russia but elsewhere; and this fact rigidly limits the range within which any civilization resembling the Orthodox Christian Civilization in Russia could have established itself. It limits it to the geographical radius within which it was possible for offshoots from the original stem to take root at the particular stage in the growth of the tree at which the actual offshoot did establish itself in Russian soil.[1] Since Canada lay far beyond this radius, it is incorrect and misleading to suggest that the identical environment which gave birth to a civilization in Russia existed in Canada likewise without giving birth to a civilization there. The Canadian environment lacked one of the essential elements of the Russian environment taken as a whole.

Against such assaults from our critics we are not entirely defenceless. For instance, we might concede that the area, now occupied by the United States, which offered substantially the same non-human environment as Western Europe for the genesis of a civilization, but offered it in vain, was not able to offer exactly the same human environment as Western Europe inasmuch as North America was never subject to social radiation from the Hellenic World. Having made this concession with a good grace, we could point out to our critics that, even when both elements in the environment are taken into account, the difference between the two environments, in their geographico-social totality, turns out after all to be not so great as might appear at first sight. Though the rays of Hellenism never played upon any part of the New World, the section of North America between the Rio Grande and the Great Lakes was no more immune than Western Europe from the radiation of any

[1] The process by which the Orthodox Christian Civilization in Russia and the Far Eastern Civilization in Korea and Japan respectively became self-supporting and independent of the main bodies of the two societies may be likened to the process by which the branches of banyan trees strike roots of their own and so draw sustenance from the soil on their own account. It is clear that the range of these subsidiary roots lies within limits which are narrow and rigid. These roots cannot strike in soil which lies beyond the furthest spread of the branches, however suitable the chemical composition of the soil at some greater distance from the main stem.

civilization whatsoever. The New World, as we have seen, has
indigenous civilizations of its own; and by the time when the first
modern European explorers reached the Atlantic sea-board of
what is now the United States, the Mexic Civilization had already
radiated that far from its home on the Mexican Plateau—at any
rate on the economic plane, as is proved by the fact that the Pilgrim
Fathers found the Red Indian tribes of Massachusetts practising
the Mexic art of maize cultivation. If the non-human environment
which is common to Western Europe and to the United States did
successfully combine in Western Europe with the human environment which is represented by the radiation of the Hellenic
Civilization, in order to give birth to a new civilization 'affiliated'
to the Hellenic, why, in North America, did a similar non-human
environment not combine with the corresponding human environment which was provided by the radiation of the Mexic Civilization
in order to give birth to another new civilization 'affiliated' to the
Mexic?

Thus, the test which we have been applying to the theory that
Environment is the positive factor in the geneses of civilizations
may not, after all, be invalidated by the broader conception of the
Environment which our critics have put into the field. At the
same time, it remains true that the human environment in North
America, while comparable to both that in Western Europe and
that in Russia, is not identical with either of them; and there are
also other elements of difference—for instance, the Time-factor[1]—

[1] A non-correspondence, in the Time-factor, between the radiation of Hellenism over
Western Europe and the radiation of the Mexic Civilization over North America may
suggest the answer to the question asked at the end of the last paragraph: Why, in North
America, did not the non-human environment combine with the human environment
which was provided by the radiation of the Mexic Civilization, in order to give birth to
another new civilization 'affiliated' to the Mexic? The Pilgrim Fathers landed in Massachusetts not quite a hundred years after Cortez had conquered Mexico; and, at the moment
of the Spanish Conquest, the Mexic Society was still in the last convulsions of a 'Time of
Troubles' which had not yet reached its apparently inevitable end in the foundation of a
universal state by the Aztec Empire of Tenochtitlan. (See I. C (i) (b), p. 124, above.)
On this showing, if we reduce the chronology of Mexic history to the Time-scale of
Hellenic and Western history, Mexic 1521 of the Christian Era corresponds approximately to Hellenic 100 B.C. Now by 100 B.C. Hellenism was not yet radiating more
widely or more vigorously over Western Europe than the Mexic Civilization was
radiating over North America by A.D. 1521. From the beginning of the last century B.C.
some seven or eight centuries—during which the Hellenic universal state came into
existence and passed out again into an interregnum—had still to run before, in Western
Europe, a new civilization, 'affiliated' to the Hellenic, began to emerge. Supposing that
the Spaniards, English, French, and Dutch had never set foot in Central and North
America, and that Mexic history had run its course to the end without ever being exposed
to the impact of our Western Civilization, who can say that its radiation over North
America, which had reached Massachusetts before A.D. 1620, might not by 1933 have
produced effects which would have enabled European observers at this date to forecast
that, though the disintegration of the Mexic Civilization itself might be beyond repair,
some new civilization or civilizations, 'affiliated' to the Mexic, might be expected to
emerge, in about the twenty-third century of the Christian Era, in the basins of the
Mississippi and the St. Lawrence? As things have turned out, we cannot tell whether the
human environment of the Mexic Civilization might not eventually have combined
with the non-human environment of North America to generate a new civilization, as the

to be taken into account. Accordingly, in order to be on the safe side, we will now rule out of account all applications of our test except those in which the civilization playing the part of the human environment in either case is one and the same.

Confining our attention to such cases, we may still ask, for example, whether the genesis of the Hittite Civilization is completely accounted for by the non-human environment of the Anatolian Plateau in combination with the human environment provided by the Sumeric Civilization, to which the Hittite Civilization is related through the Sumeric Society's external proletariat. If a plateau exposed to the radiation of the Sumeric culture was really the positive factor by which the genesis of the Hittite Civilization was brought about, then the advocates of the Environment-theory have to explain why it was that a sister-civilization, related to the Sumeric Civilization in the same manner and in the same degree, did not emerge contemporaneously on the Iranian Plateau. The plateau of Iran offers the same non-human environment as the plateau of Anatolia; it is geographically nearer than the latter to the homelands of the Sumeric Society from which the radiation of the Sumeric culture was emitted; and there cannot be anything in the Iranian environment which is inimical to civilizations *a priori* and in perpetuity, for we know that Iran became the second home of the Syriac Civilization a dozen centuries or so after it had failed to make a home for a sister-civilization to the Hittite Civilization of Anatolia.

We may ask just the same question about the genesis of the Mexic Civilization on the Mexican Plateau. If a plateau exposed to the radiation of the Mayan culture was really the positive factor by which the genesis of the Mexic civilization was brought about, then why did no sister-civilization emerge contemporaneously on those Central American highlands, overhanging the coast of the Pacific from Southern Guatemala to Panama, which adjoin the homelands of the Mayan Civilization in Northern Guatemala on

human environment of Hellenism actually did combine with the non-human environment of Western Europe to bring our Western Civilization to birth. We cannot tell, because the intrusion of our Western Civilization into the New World deprived North America of the Mexic radiation and subjected it to a Western radiation instead, long before the Mexic radiation could have been expected to produce in North America the results which were produced eventually by the long and never interrupted radiation of Hellenism over Western Europe. (For an expert discussion of this problem, see Huntington, Ellsworth: *Civilisation and Climate*, 3rd edition (New Haven 1924, Yale University Press), pp. 369-72. Dr. Huntington points out that the material apparatus of the Mexic Civilization did not include either tools of iron or beasts of burden, and that, without these two equipments, any human attempt to overcome the North American forest and transform it into fields would have been more difficult than we can readily imagine. To this it may be replied that, in spite of that handicap, the Mayan Civilization, to which the Mexic was 'affiliated', had actually performed this very feat upon the Central American forest—a tropical monster which was assuredly not less formidable to cope with than the temperate forest of the Mississippi and St. Lawrence basins.)

the south-west, and are actually nearer to them than the Mexican Plateau is? Why did a civilization related to the Mayan emerge on the more distant Mexican Plateau and not on the less distant Central American highlands? For the environment in these highlands was no more inimical *a priori* to civilizations than the environment in Iran, as is proved by the fact that, a dozen centuries or so after the Central American highlands had failed to make a home for a sister-civilization to the Mexic Civilization of the north-western plateau, they were occupied by the Spanish pioneers of an intrusive civilization from overseas whose descendants are the ruling element in the six Central American Republics of our day.[1]

And what of the environment which gave birth to the Syriac Civilization? The non-human environment here was provided by the climate and topography of the Syrian coast-lands, the human environment by the Minoan Civilization—inasmuch as the Syriac Civilization emerged among Minoan refugees who secured a footing on the coast of Syria during the post-Minoan interregnum and there encountered the Hebrew and Aramaean barbarians who were drifting into Syria out of its North-Arabian hinterland.[2] If a Mediterranean coast-line, exposed to the radiation of the Minoan culture, was really the positive factor by which the genesis of the Syriac Civilization was brought about, then why did no sister-civilization emerge contemporaneously along the opposite coast-line of Southern Italy and Sicily and North-West Africa from Taranto to Gabes? These coasts offer the same peculiar and distinctive climate and topography, of the Mediterranean type, that are offered by the coasts of Syria; they are no more distant, or more difficult to reach, than the Syrian coasts are from the homelands of the Minoan Civilization in Crete and the Cyclades; and the researches of our modern Western archaeologists seem to bear out the traditions of Hellenic Mythology by informing us that the Minoan Society, in its last days, was radiating its culture not only eastwards on to the coasts of Syria but also westwards as far as the coasts of Sicily and perhaps farther still. Why was it then that, during the post-Minoan interregnum, when one swarm of Minoan refugees settled on the Syrian coasts and sowed the seed of the Syriac Civilization among Hebrew and Aramaean barbarians from the Arabian hinterland, another swarm did not sow the seed of a sister-civilization by hiving off in the opposite direction and settling on the South Italian and Sicilian and North-West African coasts, where Libyan and Italic barbarians from the hinterlands were

---

[1] On this, see further II. D (ii), vol. ii, pp. 34–6, below.
[2] See I. C (i) (*b*), pp. 100–2, above.

waiting to receive the same seed and to bring forth, in due course, a similar harvest. There was certainly nothing about these western coast-lines that was inimical to civilizations *a priori*. They were the very fields which brought forth so abundantly when they were taken in hand by Syriac and Hellenic settlers eventually, a few centuries later. If Southern Italy was capable of becoming a 'Magna Graecia' and Sicily and Africa of becoming foster-mothers to a Syracuse and a Carthage,[1] why did they all lie fallow during the post-Minoan interregnum, when, in Syria, precisely the same geographico-social environment was bringing a new civilization to birth?

And what of the 'transplantation' of the Far Eastern Civilization to Korea and Japan? If this phenomenon of 'transplantation' is wholly accounted for by the presence of soil of a certain quality at a certain range from the main stem of the tree, then why did not another offshoot of the Far Eastern Civilization take root simultaneously in the Malay Peninsula and in Indonesia? For the Far Eastern Society did expand some distance in this direction too. At the very time when it was advancing north-eastwards upon Korea and Japan, it was also advancing south-eastwards upon the long coast-land which is now occupied by the four Chinese provinces Chekiang, Fukien, Kwangtung, and Kwangsi[2] and the two French possessions Tongking and Annam. This advance of the Far Eastern Civilization on a south-eastern front was as fruitful, as far as it went, as the advance in the north-easterly direction; for, if the one movement has produced the modern Japanese, the modern Cantonese are a product of the other. Then why did the south-eastward movement stop dead at the coast instead of taking to the sea and passing over into Indonesia, as the north-eastward movement of the Far Eastern Civilization actually took to the sea and passed over from the Asiatic mainland into Japan? Geographically, Indonesia is not more distant than Japan is from the homelands of the Far Eastern Civilization in Central China. Nor is it more difficult to reach. The Philippines can be reached from Central China by way of Formosa as easily as Japan by way of Korea; and the access to Sumatra by way of the Malay Peninsula is easier still. Nor, again, can there be anything in the Indonesian environment which is inimical to civilizations *a priori*; for this field, in which the Far Eastern Civilization neglected to strike root, was successfully occupied and cultivated by the Hindu Civilization, though Indonesia is sundered from the Coromandel

---

[1] Hellenic Syracuse and Syriac Carthage each surpassed and put out of countenance her mother-city in 'the old country'—Syracuse her mother Corinth, Carthage her mother Tyre.

[2] Kwangsi does not actually touch the coast.

Coast by half the breadth of the Indian Ocean. Striking out boldly across this gulf, the Hindu mariners called into existence in Indonesia a new Hindu World of such power and splendour that its ruins—a Cambodian Angkor Wat and a Javan Boroboedoer—are not put out of countenance by any monuments of Hindu Art that survive in Continental India. But why is it the Hindu Civilization, and not the Far Eastern Civilization, that has left its mark upon an archipelago which the Far Eastern mariners could have reached without ever having to venture out of sight of land?

These illustrations perhaps suffice to show that even the total geographico-social environment, in which the human as well as the non-human element is taken into account, cannot be regarded as the positive factor by which our twenty-one civilizations have been generated. It is clear that a virtually identical combination of the two elements in the environment may give birth to a civilization in one instance and fail to give birth to a civilization in another instance, without our being able to account for this absolute difference in the outcome by detecting any substantial difference in the circumstances, however strictly we may define the terms of our comparison. Conversely, it is clear that civilizations can and do emerge in environments which are utterly diverse. The non-human environment may be of 'the fluvial type' which has given birth to the Egyptiac and Sumeric civilizations and perhaps to an independent 'Indus Culture' as well; or it may be of 'the plateau type' which has given birth to the Andean and the Hittite and the Mexic civilizations; or it may be of 'the archipelago type' which has given birth to the Minoan and the Hellenic civilizations, and to the Far Eastern Civilization in Japan; or it may be of 'the continental type' which has given birth to the Sinic and the Indic and the Western civilizations, and to the Orthodox Christian Civilization in Russia; or it may be of 'the jungle type' which has given birth to the Mayan Civilization. This catalogue suggests that any kind of climate and topography is capable of serving as an environment for the genesis of a civilization if the necessary miracle is performed by some positive factor which still eludes our search. And when we turn to the human environment, in the shape of other civilizations, we see that the diversity of possible conditions is just as great here. Of the twenty-one civilizations which have come to birth so far to our knowledge, six show no trace of being related to any earlier civilizations in their backgrounds, while the remaining fifteen all appear to be related to certain earlier civilizations in various manners and degrees. Moreover, two of these fifteen are offshoots which have taken separate root and have grown up side by side with the main stems of which they once were branches. It seems as though the genesis of a civilization can take place in any kind of human environment or—on the evidence of the 'unrelated' civilizations—without any human environment at all.

We have now drawn the covert of Environment, and we have had the same experience as when we drew the covert of Race. We have not found the quarry which we are hunting; but we have fought our way through the thicket and have come out on the other side into open country again. We have seen through the Environment-theory as we saw through the Race-theory before. We have seen it for what it is: the hallucination of a wanderer lost in the forest, who has turned and turned again in an ever narrowing circle till he cannot see the wood for the trees. When we struggled clear of the first thicket in our path we found that we had liberated ourselves from the conception of racial powers peculiar to this or that branch of the human family and had attained the conception of an omnipresent power, manifesting itself in the conduct and achievements of all Mankind and all Life, in which we recognize the philosopher's *Élan Vital* or the mystic's God. Looking back now upon the second thicket from which we have just broken out into the daylight, we shall find that, this time, we have shaken ourselves free from the conception of environmental stimuli, peculiar to this or that climate and area, or this or that human background, or this or that combination of the two. The Environment resolves itself into an omnipresent object confronting the omnipresent power which manifests itself in Life. We may conceive of this object as an obstacle lying across the path of the *Élan Vital* or as an Adversary challenging a living God to halt or do battle. On either view, we shall have to admit, once again, that we are not here face to face with the immediate object of our research. We have not yet found the positive factor which, within the last six thousand years, has shaken part of Mankind out of the Yin-state which we have called 'the Integration of Custom' into the Yang-activity which we have called 'the Differentiation of Civilization'.[1] An object which presents itself perpetually in every part of the field of Life cannot, in and by itself, be the unknown quantity which, in certain times and places, has given an impetus to part of Mankind and not to the whole. Our hunt must go on; and, with two coverts drawn, only one possibility remains open. If our unknown

---

[1] 'Deutlich zeigt sich . . . dass die Natur und die Geographie nur das Substrat des historischen Lebens der Menschen bildet, dass sie nur Möglichkeiten einer Entwicklung bietet, nicht Notwendigkeiten. . . . Die Geschichte ist keineswegs in der Natur eines Landes vorgezeichnet . . . sondern das Entscheidende sind überall im menschlichen Leben die geistigen und individuellen Faktoren, welche das gegebene Substrat benutzen oder vernachlässigen.' (Meyer, E.: *Geschichte des Altertums*, vol. i (i), 4th edition (Stuttgart and Berlin 1921, Cotta), p. 66; cf. p. 84.)

quantity is neither Race nor Environment, neither God nor the Devil, it cannot be a simple quantity but must be a product of two: some interaction between Environment and Race, some encounter between the Devil and God. That is the plot of the Book of Job and the plot of Goethe's *Faust*. Is it, perhaps, the plot of Life and the plot of History?

(b) CHALLENGE-AND-RESPONSE

1. *The Action of Challenge-and-Response*

In searching for the positive factor which, within the last six thousand years, has shaken part of Mankind out of 'the Integration of Custom' into 'the Differentiation of Civilization', we have so far been employing the tactics of 'the classical school' of our modern Western Physical Science. We have been thinking in abstract terms and experimenting with the play of soulless forces: *Vis Inertiae* and Race and Environment. Now that these manœuvres have ended, one after another, in our drawing blank, we may pause to consider whether our successive failures may not point to some mistake in method. Perhaps, under the insidious influence of the spirit of an outgoing age, we have fallen victims to 'the Apathetic Fallacy' against which we took warning at the outset of our inquiry.[1] Have we not been guilty of applying to historical thought, which is a study of living creatures, a scientific method of thought which has been devised for thinking about Inanimate Nature? In making a final attempt to solve the riddle that has been baffling us, let us follow Plato's lead and try the alternative course. Let us shut our eyes, for the moment, to the formulae of Science in order to open our ears to the language of Mythology.[2]

So far, by the process of exhaustion, we have made one discovery: the cause of the geneses of civilizations is not simple but multiple; it is not an entity but a relation. We have the choice of conceiving this relation either as an interaction between two inhuman forces—like the petrol and the air which interact in the engine of a motor-car—or as an encounter between two superhuman personalities. Let us yield our minds to the second of these two conceptions. Perhaps it will lead us towards the light.

An encounter between two superhuman personalities is the plot of some of the greatest stories and dramas that the human imagination has conceived. An encounter between Yahweh and the Serpent is the plot of the story of the Fall of Man in the Book of Genesis; a second encounter between the same antagonists (transfigured by a progressive enlightenment of Syriac souls) is the plot

---

[1] See Part I. A, pp. 7–8, above.
[2] For the nature of Mythology, see I. C (iii) (*e*) Annex, p. 442, below.

of the New Testament which tells the story of the Redemption; an encounter between the Lord and Satan is the plot of the Book of Job; an encounter between the Lord and Mephistopheles is the plot of Goethe's *Faust*; an encounter between Gods and Demons is the plot of the Scandinavian *Voluspà*[1]; an encounter between Artemis and Aphrodite is the plot of Euripides' *Hippolytus*.

We find another version of the same plot in that ubiquitous and ever-recurring myth—a 'primordial image', if ever there was one—of the encounter between the Virgin and the Father of her Child. The characters of this myth have played their allotted parts on a thousand different stages under an infinite variety of names: Danae and the Shower of Gold; Europa and the Bull; Semele the stricken Earth and Zeus the Sky that launches the thunderbolt; Creusa and Apollo in Euripides' *Ion*; Psyche and Cupid; Gretchen and Faust. The theme recurs, transfigured, in the Annunciation. In our own day in the West, this protean myth has re-expressed itself as the last word of our astronomers on the genesis of the Planetary System, as witness the following *credo*:

'We believe . . . that, some two thousand million years ago, . . . a second star, wandering blindly through Space, happened to come within hailing distance of the Sun. Just as the Sun and Moon raise tides on the Earth, this second star must have raised tides on the surface of the Sun. But they would be very different from the puny tides which the small mass of the Moon raises in our oceans; a huge tidal wave must have travelled over the surface of the Sun, ultimately forming a mountain of prodigious height, which would rise ever higher and higher as the cause of the disturbance came nearer and nearer. And, before the second star began to recede, its tidal pull had become so powerful that this mountain was torn to pieces and threw off small fragments of itself, much as the crest of a wave throws off spray. These small fragments have been circulating round their parent Sun ever since. They are the Planets, great and small, of which our Earth is one.'[2]

Thus, out of the mouth of the mathematical astronomer, when all his complex calculations are done, there comes forth, once again, the myth of the encounter between the Sun Goddess and her ravisher that is so familiar a tale in the mouths of the untutored children of Nature.

The parable is taken up by the modern Western biologist. His speech bewrays him, however vehemently he may deny that there is any mythological content in his thought:

'Darwin assumed two operative factors in the organic world: Variation in the reproduction and inheritance of living beings and Natural

---

[1] The genius who conceived 'The Sibyl's Vision' has not chosen to reveal his name.
[2] Jeans, Sir James: *The Mysterious Universe* (Cambridge 1930, University Press), pp. 1–2.

Selection, or the survival of the fittest, as Herbert Spencer called it. . . .
There is no doubt that both Variation and Natural Selection are essential
elements in the Darwinian theory. Darwinism, in fact, implies two
factors: an internal factor, operating mysteriously in the inmost nature
and constitution of living organisms, and an external factor working
along independent lines on the results achieved by the internal factor.
The inner factor, Variation, is positive and creative, producing all the
variations which are the raw material for progress. The external factor,
Natural Selection, is essentially negative and destructive, eliminating the
harmful or less fit or useful variations and leaving the more fit or useful
variations free play to continue and multiply, and in this process fitting
and adapting the individual to the character of its environment. As de
Vries has phrased it, the inner factor explains the arrival, and the
external factor the survival, of the fit or useful variation or organism.'[1]

The presence and potency of the internal as well as the external
factor is admitted by the modern Western archaeologist, whose
studies begin with a concentration of attention upon the environment and end with an intuition of the mystery of Life.

'Environment . . . is not the total causation in culture-shaping. . . . It
is, beyond doubt, the most conspicuous single factor. . . . But there is
still an indefinable factor which may best be designated quite frankly as
x, the unknown quantity, apparently psychological in kind. . . . If x be
not the most conspicuous factor in the matter, it certainly is the most
important, the most fate-laden.'[2]

Even in our present study of history, this insistent theme of the
superhuman encounter has asserted itself at least twice already.
At an early stage we observed that 'a society . . . is confronted in
the course of its life by a succession of problems' and that 'the
presentation of each problem is a challenge to undergo an ordeal'.[3]
We were feeling our way towards an expression of the same idea
when we attempted to conceive Evolution through the simile of an
encounter between a growing tree and a man with an axe: 'the
image of the pollarded willow'.[4]

Let us try to analyse the plot of this story or drama which
repeats itself in such different contexts and in such various forms.
We may begin with two general features: the encounter is

[1] Smuts, J. C.: *Holism and Evolution*, 2nd edition (London 1927, Macmillan),
pp. 195–7.
[2] Means, P. A.: *Ancient Civilisations of the Andes* (New York and London 1931,
Scribner), pp. 25–6. It should be noted, however, that while this scholar agrees with
the other scholars here quoted in finding the cause of genesis in a relation between two
factors, he differs from them in regarding this relation, not as a collision or an encounter,
but as a harmony. The last of the passages omitted in the present quotation from Mr.
Means runs as follows: 'If x be in harmony with the environment factors—and it is so
comparatively rarely—culture will progress and civilization will be constructed, to
continue, we may suppose, until x ceases to be in harmony with the environment
factors. From this it follows that . . .'.
[3] I. B (ii), pp. 22–3, above.   [4] I. C (iii) (*b*), pp. 168–9, above.

conceived as a rare and sometimes as a unique event; and it has consequences which are vast in proportion to the vastness of the breach which it makes in the customary course of Nature.

Even in the easy-going world of the Hellenic Mythology, where the Gods saw the daughters of men that they were fair, and had their way with so many of them that their victims could be marshalled and paraded in poetic catalogues,[1] such incidents never ceased to be sensational affairs and invariably resulted in the births of heroes. In the versions of the plot in which both the parties to the encounter are superhuman, the rarity and the momentousness of the event are apt to be thrown into stronger relief. In the Book of Job, 'the day when the sons of God came to present themselves before the Lord, and Satan came also among them', is evidently conceived as an unusual occasion; and so is the encounter between the Lord and Mephistopheles in the 'Prologue in Heaven' (suggested, of course, by the passage in the Book of Job) which starts the action of Goethe's *Faust*.[2] In both these dramas, the consequences on Earth of this unusual encounter in Heaven are tremendous. The single ordeals of Job and Faust represent, in the intuitive language of fiction,[3] the infinitely multiple ordeal of Man; and, in the language of theology, the same vast consequence is represented as following from the superhuman encounters that are portrayed in the Book of Genesis and in the New Testament. The expulsion of Adam and Eve from the Garden of Eden, which follows from the encounter between Yahweh and the Serpent, is nothing less than the Fall of Man; the passion of Christ in the New Testament is nothing less than Man's Redemption.

In the New Testament, the uniqueness of the divine event is of the essence of the story; and this has been a stumbling-block to the Western intellect ever since the geocentric conception of the material universe was first impugned by the discoveries of our modern Western Astronomy. Milton, who was acquainted with, and probably convinced by, the heliocentric system of Copernicus, avoided this stumbling-block by deliberately following the geocentric system of Ptolemy when he set the stage for *Paradise Lost*. And in our generation, when the Sun itself has been dwarfed by comparison with an ever-expanding Universe to a still more overwhelming degree than the Earth by comparison with the Sun, astronomical facts have been invoked to confound theological dogmas. 'You tell us that your God, who by definition is the maker of our Universe, took flesh and suffered and died in order to redeem

---

[1] e.g. the catalogue in the *Odyssey*, Book XI, ll. 225–330, a passage which is probably a fair sample of the lost Hesiodic *Ehoiai*.

[2] *Mephistopheles*: 'Von Zeit zu Zeit seh' ich den Alten gern' (*Faust*, l. 350).

[3] See I. C (iii) (*e*) Annex, pp. 452–3, below.

the Human Race on Earth? If the Earth were the centre of the Universe and Man the image of his Maker, your myth might not be contradicted by common sense, though it would still remain incapable of verification. But what happens to this myth in a Universe in which the Earth is one of a myriad myriad floating specks of dust, and life on Earth an accident? If God chose this speck for the scene of the unique divine event, His choice was infinitely capricious and therefore infinitely frivolous. How do you conceive that He made it? By drawing lots or by throwing dice? The only alternative is to suppose that the divine event was not unique after all, and that the tragedy of the Incarnation and the Crucifixion has been enacted on every speck of dust in the Universe. But then does not the very multiplication of the performance somehow rob it of its sublime and awful significance? A myriad myriad crucifixions on a myriad myriad earths? We make non-sense of them by the simple process of writing out the astro-nomical figure in arabic numerals, as the Shakespearian hyperbole of the 40,000 brothers is made nonsense of by Straker in Mr. Bernard Shaw's *Man and Superman*.'[1]

Yet this modern astronomical conception of immensity, which appeared, only yesterday, to confute the ageless myth of the unique divine event, may appear to rehabilitate it to-morrow; for the immensity of the reputed extent of empty space is out of all proportion to the immensity of the reputed number of the stars; and it follows from this that the encounter between the Sun and a star unknown, which is supposed to have given birth to our Planetary System, 'is an event of almost unimaginable rarity '.[2]

'Millions of millions of stars wandering blindly through Space for millions of millions of years are bound to meet with every sort of acci-dent, and so are bound to produce a certain limited number of planetary systems in time. Yet the number of these must be very small in com-parison with the total number of stars in the sky.

'This rarity of planetary systems is important, because, so far as we can see, Life of the kind we know on Earth could only originate on planets like the Earth. It needs suitable physical conditions for its appearance, the most important of which is a temperature at which substances can exist in the liquid state.

'The stars themselves are disqualified by being far too hot. We may think of them as a vast collection of fires scattered throughout Space,

---

[1] This *reductio ad absurdum* of the myth of Christianity is of course by no means absolute (even granting the astronomical hypothesis which is its premiss). It may carry conviction to Syriac and Western minds, but it would leave a Platonist or a Mahayanian Buddhist unmoved. In the scriptures of the Mahayana, 'we remain dazzled by an endless panorama of an infinity of universes with an infinity of shining Buddhas, illuminating infinite space' (Sir Charles Eliot: *Hinduism and Buddhism* (London 1921, Edward Arnold), vol. ii, p. 26).

[2] Jeans, op. cit., p. 1.

providing warmth in a climate which is at most some four degrees above absolute zero—about 484 degrees of frost on our Fahrenheit scale—and is even lower in the vast stretches of Space which lie out beyond the Milky Way. Away from the fires there is this unimaginable cold of hundreds of degrees of frost, close up to them there is a temperature of thousands of degrees, at which all solids melt, all liquids boil.

'Life can only exist inside a narrow temperate zone which surrounds each of these fires at a very definite distance. Outside these zones Life would be frozen; inside, it would be shrivelled up. At a rough computation, these zones within which Life is possible, all added together, constitute less than a thousand million millionth part of the whole of Space. And even inside them Life must be of very rare occurrence, for it is so unusual an accident for suns to throw off planets, as our own Sun has done, that probably only about one star in 100,000 has a planet revolving round it in the small zone in which Life is possible.'[1]

Thus, in this portrayal of the encounter between two stars which is supposed to have led to the appearance of Life on Earth, the rarity and the momentousness of the event turn out to be almost as much of the essence of the story as they are in the Book of Genesis and in the New Testament, where the encounters are between God and the Devil and the consequences are the Fall and the Redemption of Man. The traditional plot of the play has a way of reasserting itself in exotic settings.

The play opens with a perfect state of Yin. In the Universe, Balder keeps all things bright and beautiful through keeping himself alive. In Heaven,

> Die unbegreiflich hohen Werke
> Sind herrlich, wie am ersten Tag.[2]

On Earth, Faust is perfect in knowledge; Job is perfect in goodness and prosperity;[3] Adam and Eve, in the Garden of Eden, are perfect in innocence and ease; the virgins—Gretchen, Danae, Hippolytus—are perfect in purity and beauty. In the astronomers' universe, the Sun, a perfect orb of incandescent matter, is travelling on an unimpeded course through Space. In the biologist's universe, the Species is in perfect adaptation to its environment.

When Yin is thus complete, it is ready to pass over into Yang. But what is to make it pass? A change in a state which, by definition, is perfect after its kind can only be started by an impulse or motive which comes from outside. If we think of the state as one of physical equilibrium, we must bring another star to raise a tide on the spherical surface of the Sun, or another gas to evoke an explosion from the inert air in the combustion-chamber of the motor-engine. If we think of the state as one of psychic beatitude

---

[1] Jeans, op. cit., pp. 4–5.   [2] *Faust*, ll. 249–50.   [3] Job i. 1–5.

or nirvana, we must bring another actor on to the stage: a critic to set the mind thinking again by suggesting doubts; an adversary to set the heart feeling again by instilling distress or discontent or fear or antipathy; in fact, an enemy to sow tares in the field;[1] an access of desire to generate karma. This is the role of the Serpent in the Book of Genesis, of Satan in the Book of Job, of Mephistopheles in Goethe's *Faust*, of Loki in the Scandinavian Mythology, of Aphrodite in Euripides' *Hippolytus* and Apollo in his *Ion*, of the passing star in Sir James Jeans's cosmogony, of the Environment in the Darwinian theory of Evolution. In the language of our modern Western Science, 'the inner creative factor in a measure acts directly under the stimulus of the external factor, and the variations which emerge are the result of this intimate interaction'.[2]

The role is interpreted most clearly when it is played by Mephistopheles. First, the Lord propounds it in the Prologue in Heaven:

> Des Menschen Tätigkeit kann allzuleicht erschlaffen,
> Er liebt sich bald die unbedingte Ruh';
> Drum geb' ich gern ihm den Gesellen zu
> Der reizt und wirkt und muss, als Teufel, schaffen.[3]

Afterwards, Mephistopheles gives the same account of his role in introducing himself, on Earth, to Faust:

> Ich bin der Geist, der stets verneint!
> Und das mit Recht; denn alles, was entsteht,
> Ist wert, dass es zugrunde geht;
> Drum besser wär's, dass nichts entstünde.
> So ist denn alles, was ihr Sünde,
> Zerstörung, kurz das Böse nennt,
> Mein eigentliches Element.[4]

Finally Faust explains the adversary's role, by implication, from his own experience, in his dying speech:

> Nur der verdient sich Freiheit wie das Leben
> Der täglich sie erobern muss.[5]

In prose we may put it that the function of 'the external factor' is to supply 'the inner creative factor' with a perpetual stimulus of the kind best calculated to evoke the most potently creative

---

[1] Matthew xiii. 24–30.
[2] Smuts, *Holism and Evolution*, 2nd edition (London 1927, Macmillan), p. 227.
[3] *Faust*, ll. 340–3. In the oddly different language of Rationalism, precisely the same idea is expressed by Turgot in his *Plan de Deux Discours sur l'Histoire Universelle*: 'La Raison et la Justice, mieux écoutées, auraient tout fixé, comme cela est à peu près arrivé à la Chine. . . . Le genre humain serait resté à jamais dans la médiocrité. . . . Mais ce qui n'est jamais parfait ne doit jamais être entièrement fixé. Les passions tumultueuses, dangereuses, sont devenues un principe d'action, et par conséquent de progrès.' (*Œuvres de Turgot*, nouvelle édition (Paris 1844, Guillaumin, 2 vols.), vol. ii, p. 632.)
[4] *Faust*, ll. 1338–44.   [5] *Faust*, ll. 11575–6.

variations. If we take, as a sample of 'the external factor', the climatic and geographical environment of human life, we shall find that our proposition agrees with Dr. Ellsworth Huntington's thesis 'that a relatively high degree of storminess and a relatively long duration of the season of cyclonic storms have apparently been characteristic of the places where civilization has risen to high levels both in the past and at present'.[1] The converse of Dr. Huntington's equation between 'the cyclone belt' and the habitat of civilizations[2] is the thesis, which he likewise propounds, that all monotonous climates are unfavourable to civilization by very reason of their monotony, however greatly they may differ from one another in every other feature. According to this thesis, the various monotonies of Central Asian summers and winters,[3] with their extremes of heat and cold, or of Tropical lowlands and highlands,[4] with their extremes of humidity and dryness, all produce on human spirits the same uniformly depressing and deadening effects.[5] Supposing, again, that we reckon our bodily physique among the components of 'the external factor' which acts upon 'the inner creative factor' in the human psyche, then, in the light of what we have come to regard as 'the external factor's' function, we shall see the reason for a 'law' which we have stumbled upon empirically[6] —the law that the geneses of civilizations require contributions from more races than one. If the mongrel is found by experience to be more apt for civilization than the thoroughbred, we may attribute his prowess to the stimulus administered to his psyche by the physical disturbance that results from the crossing of two distinct physical strains.

To return to the language of Mythology, the impulse or motive which makes a perfect Yin-state pass over into a new Yang-activity comes from an intrusion of the Devil into the universe of God. The event can best be described in these mythological images because they are not embarrassed by the contradiction that arises when the statement is translated into logical terms. In logic,

[1] Huntington, Ellsworth: *Civilization and Climate*, 3rd edition (New Haven 1924, Yale University Press), p. 12. The passage here quoted gives the main theme of the book. See especially chapter x: 'The Ideal Climate', where the author suggests that the best climate, for work and for health, is determined by three factors. It is a climate 'in which the mean temperature rarely falls below the mental optimum of perhaps 38°, or rises above the physical optimum of about 64°', but varies seasonally to the full extent of these limits. It is a climate in which the daily changes of temperature are numerous and extreme. In the third place it is a climate with the maximum of storminess (i.e. the greatest number of cyclonic storms, not the greatest number of inches of rainfall) (op. cit., pp. 398–9).

[2] For a graphic visual presentation of this equation, see op. cit., the pair of maps on p. 295.

[3] Op. cit., p. 226.   [4] Op. cit., pp. 226–7.

[5] See op. cit., pp. 235–8, for further illustrations of the same thesis apropos of Greenland and Siberia.

[6] See II. C (ii) (a) 1, pp. 239–43, above.

if God's universe is perfect, there cannot be a Devil outside it, while, if the Devil exists, the perfection which he comes to spoil must have been incomplete already through the very fact of his existence. This logical contradiction, which cannot logically be resolved, is intuitively transcended in the imagery of the poet and the prophet,[1] who give glory to an omnipotent God yet take it for granted that He is subject to two crucial limitations.

The first limitation is that, in the perfection of what He has created already, He cannot find an opportunity for further creative activity. If God is conceived as transcendent, then

> Die unbegreiflich hohen Werke
> Sind herrlich, wie am ersten Tag[2];

the works of creation are as glorious as ever they were, but they are not 'changed from glory to glory'.[3] At this point, the principle that 'where the spirit of the Lord is, there is liberty'[4] fails; and, if God is conceived as immanent, the same limitation still holds:

> Der Gott, der mir im Busen wohnt
> Kann tief mein Innerstes erregen,
> Der über allen meinen Kräften thront,
> Er kann nach aussen nichts bewegen.[5]

The second limitation upon God's power is that when the opportunity for fresh creation is offered to Him from outside, He cannot but take it. When the Devil challenges Him, He cannot refuse to take the challenge up. 'Live dangerously', which is the Nietzschian Zarathustra's ideal, is God's necessity. This limitation is illustrated in the Parable of the Tares:

'So the servants of the householder came and said unto him: "Sir, didst thou not sow good seed in thy field? From whence, then, hath

---

[1] The contradiction cannot be resolved by translating its terms into impersonal and abstract language, as they are translated by General Smuts in the following passage of his *Holism and Evolution* (2nd edition, pp. 180–1):

'Science has made clear . . . that the physico-chemical system is a structure, a structure composed of elements in more or less of equilibrium. . . . The equilibrium of the structure is . . . only approximate; were it complete, little room would be left for change; the physical world would be a stereotyped system of fixed stable forms, and little or no room would be left for those changes and developments which make Nature a great system of events, a great history moving onward through Space-Time. The fundamental structures of Nature are thus in somewhat unstable equilibrium.'

In this passage, the contradiction between the perfection of God's universe and the existence of a Devil outside it lurks in the formula 'unstable equilibrium', which is, in fact, a contradiction in terms. To say that events in Space-Time are accounted for by an 'unstable equilibrium' is equivalent to saying that the creation of the World is the work of a supreme being called 'Devil-God'. An 'unstable equilibrium' is the same monstrosity in logic as a 'Devil-God' would be in Mythology. The only difference is that our minds are slower to protest when the monstrosity is presented to them in the terminology of our modern Western Physical Science, because this terminology, being brand-new, has not yet become so highly charged with meaning as the ancient language of poetry and prophecy. In translating our thoughts from more into less significant terms, we needlessly increase the danger—to which we are always exposed—of being led astray by words.   [2] *Faust*, ll. 249–50, quoted above.

[3] 2 Corinthians iii. 18.   [4] 2 Corinthians iii. 17.   [5] *Faust*, ll. 1566–9.

it tares?" He said unto them: "An enemy hath done this." The servants said unto him: "Wilt thou then that we go and gather them up?" But he said: "Nay; lest, while ye gather up the tares, ye root up also the wheat with them. Let both grow together until the harvest." [1]

God is bound to accept the predicament that is thrust upon Him by the Devil because He can only refuse at the price of renouncing His own purposes and undoing His own work—in fact, at the price of denying His own nature and ceasing to be God, which is either an impossibility or another story.

If God is thus not omnipotent in logical terms, is He still mythologically invincible? If He is bound to take up the Devil's challenge, is He equally bound to win the ensuing battle? In Euripides' *Hippolytus*, where God's part is played by Artemis and the Devil's by Aphrodite, Artemis is not only unable to decline the combat but is foredoomed to defeat. The relation between the Olympians—all peers of one another in a barbarian war-lord's war-band[2]—is anarchic:

> 'Twas the will
> Of Cypris that these evil things should be,
> Sating her wrath. And this immutably
> Hath Zeus ordained in heaven: no God may thwart
> A God's fixed will; we grieve but stand apart.[3]

And Artemis can only console herself by making up her mind that one day she will play the Devil's role herself to Aphrodite's hurt:

> My hand shall win its vengeance, through and through
> Piercing with flawless shaft what heart soe'er
> Of all men living is most dear to her.[4]

Thus, in Euripides' version of the plot, the victory in the battle falls to the Power which assumes the Devil's role, and the outcome is not creation but destruction. In the Scandinavian version, destruction is likewise the outcome of Ragnarök—when 'Gods and Demons slay and are slain'[5]—though the unique genius of the author of *Voluspà* makes his Sibyl's vision pierce the gloom to behold the light of a new dawn beyond it. On the other hand, in another version of the plot, the combat which follows the compulsory acceptance of the challenge takes the form, not of an exchange of fire in which the Devil has the first shot and cannot fail to kill his man, but of a wager which the Devil is apparently bound to lose. The classic works of art in which this wager-*motif* is

---

[1] Matthew xiii. 27–30.
[2] See I. C (i) (*b*), pp. 96–7, above.
[3] Euripides: *Hippolytus*, ll. 1327–30, Gilbert Murray's translation.
[4] Op. cit., ll. 1420–2.
[5] Grönbech, V.: *The Culture of the Teutons* (London 1931, Milford, 3 parts in 2 vols.), part II, p. 302.

worked out are, of course, the Book of Job and Goethe's *Faust*; and
it is in *Faust*, again, that the points are made most clear.

After the Lord has accepted the wager with Mephistopheles[1] in
the Prologue in Heaven, the terms are agreed on Earth, between
Mephistopheles and *Faust*, as follows:

> *Faust.* Werd' ich beruhigt je mich auf ein Faulbett legen,
> So sei es gleich um mich getan!
> Kannst du mich schmeichelnd je belügen
> Dass ich mir selbst gefallen mag,
> Kannst du mich mit Genuss betrügen—
> Das sei für mich der letzte Tag!
> Die Wette biet' ich!
> *Mephistopheles.* Topp!
> *Faust.* Und Schlag auf Schlag!
> Werd' ich zum Augenblicke sagen:
> 'Verweile doch! Du bist so schön!'
> Dann magst du mich in Fesseln schlagen,
> Dann will ich gern zugrunde gehn!
> Dann mag die Totenglocke schallen,
> Dann bist du deines Dienstes frei,
> Die Uhr mag stehn, der Zeiger fallen,
> Es sei die Zeit für mich vorbei![2]

The bearing of this mythical compact upon our problem of the
geneses of civilizations can be brought out by identifying Faust,
at the moment when he makes his bet, with one of those 'awakened
sleepers' who have risen from the ledge on which they had been
lying torpid, and have started to climb on up the face of the cliff,
in our simile of the climbers' pitch.[3] In the language of our simile,
Faust is saying: 'I have made up my mind to leave this ledge and
climb this precipice in search of the next ledge above. In attempting this, I am aware that I am courting danger and deliberately
leaving safety behind me. I am aware that if once I pause I shall
fall, and that if once I fall I shall fall to destruction. Yet, for the sake
of the possible achievement, I am ready to take the inevitable risk.'

In the story as told in this version of the plot, the intrepid
climber, after an ordeal of mortal dangers and desperate reverses,
succeeds in the end in scaling the cliff triumphantly. In both *Job*
and *Faust*, the wager is won by God; and again, in the New Testament, the same ending is given, through the revelation of a second
encounter between the same pair of antagonists, to the combat
between Yahweh and the Serpent which, in the original version
in the Book of Genesis, had ended rather in the manner of the
combat between Artemis and Aphrodite in the *Hippolytus*.[4]

[1] *Faust*, ll. 312–17.   [2] *Faust*, ll. 1692–1706.
[3] See this Part, Division B, pp. 192–5, above.
[4] The hint of a future reversal of fortune, which is darkly conveyed in 'it shall bruise

Moreover, in *Job* and *Faust* and the New Testament alike, it is suggested, or even declared outright, that the wager cannot be won by the Devil; that the Devil, in meddling with God's work, cannot frustrate but can only serve the purpose of God, who remains master of the situation all the time and gives the Devil rope for the Devil to hang himself. This seems to be implied in Jesus's words to the chief priests and captains of the Temple and the elders: 'This is your hour and the power of darkness';[1] and in his words to Pilate: 'Thou couldst have no power at all against me, except it were given thee from above'.[2] And the implication is worked out in the following passage from the pen of a modern Christian theologian:

'Not *through* pain and defeat and death does Christ come to victory—and after Him all we who are Christ's because of Him—but . . . these things are the victory. . . . It is . . . in the Risen Christ that we can see how Evil, against which we yet must strive, runs its course and is found at the end to be the good which it seemed to be resisting and destroying: how God must abandon us in order that He may be the more sure of us.'[3]

So, in Goethe's *Faust*, in the Prologue in Heaven, after the wager has been offered and taken, the Lord declares to Mephistopheles:

> Du darfst auch da nur frei *erscheinen*,[4]

and announces that He gladly gives Mephistopheles to Man as a companion, because he

> reizt und wirkt und *muss*, als Teufel, *schaffen*.[5]

Stranger still, Mephistopheles, when he opens his attack upon Faust, introduces himself to his intended victim as

> Ein Teil von jener Kraft
> Die stets das Böse will und stets das Gute schafft.[6]

In fact, Mephistopheles, notwithstanding the fearful wickedness and suffering which he manages to produce, is treated throughout the play as a buffoon who is destined to be a dupe. This note is struck by the Lord Himself in the passage just quoted from the Prologue in Heaven, where He proceeds:

> Ich habe deinesgleichen nie gehasst.
> Von allen Geistern die verneinen
> Ist mir der Schalk am wenigsten zur Last.[7]

---

thy head and thou shalt bruise his heel', is hardly more comforting than Artemis' assurance to Hippolytus that he shall become the object of a cult and the hero of a song (*Hippolytus*, ll. 1423–30).   [1] Luke xxii. 53.   [2] John xix. 11.

[3] Steuart, R. H. J. (S.J.): *The Inward Vision* (London 1930, Longmans), pp. 62–3. An expression of the same truth, in remarkably similar language, from the standpoint of a contemporary psychologist, will be found in Jung, C. G.: *Modern Man in Search of a Soul* (London 1933, Kegan Paul), pp. 274–5.

[4] *Faust*, l. 336.   [5] *Faust*, l. 343, quoted above.
[6] *Faust*, ll. 1335–6.   [7] *Faust*, ll. 337–9.

The same note persists throughout the first part of the play and is intensified in the second, until, in the scene of his final discomfiture,[1] which is written in a deliberately comic vein, Mephistopheles is turned into a positive figure of fun. Faust repeats, in his dying speech, the very words

> Verweile doch, du bist so schön

on which his wager with Mephistopheles turns; and Mephistopheles gloats over the corpse in the belief that he is the winner; but he has congratulated himself too soon; for Faust has recited the crucial formula not affirmatively apropos of the present, but only conditionally apropos of the future:

> Zum Augenblicke *möcht'* ich sagen
> 'Verweile doch, du bist so schön!' . . .
> Im Vorgefuhl von solchem hohen Glück
> Geniess' ich *jetzt* den höchsten Augenblick.[2]

Mephistopheles has not won the wager after all; and he is ignominiously pelted off the stage with volleys of roses strewn by a chorus of *putti*, who distract him with their sensuous charms while they spirit away the dead Faust's immortal part from under his nose. In his mingled self-pity and self-contempt for so much labour lost, Mephistopheles cuts a poorer figure than the discomfited Shylock in the denouement of *The Merchant of Venice*.

These ludicrously discomfited villains who have been created by our two great modern Western dramatists have their prototype in the Scandinavian Loki: a figure who played his part in a traditional and anonymous drama which was performed as a religious rite before it crystallized into a myth. In this ritual drama, Loki

'was the sacral actor whose business was to draw out the demon, to bring the antagonism to a head, and thus to prepare for victory—hence the duplicity of his nature. . . . Such a figure has to bear the blame of the tricks and feints necessary to provoke the conquest of Life, he becomes a comic figure—the trickster who is predestined to be overreached.'[3]

Has the Devil really been cheated? Did God accept a wager which He knew all the time that He could not lose? That would be a hard saying; for, if that were true, the whole transaction would have been a sham. God would have been risking nothing; He would not have been 'living dangerously', after all; and, surely, 'Nothing venture, nothing win.' An encounter that was no encounter could not produce the consequence of an encounter— the vast cosmic consequence of causing Yin to pass over into Yang.

---

[1] *Faust*, ll. 11167–843.
[2] *Faust*, ll. 11581–2 and 11585–6.
[3] Grönbech, V.: *The Culture of the Teutons* (London 1931, Milford, 3 parts in 2 vols.), part II, pp. 331 and 332.

Perhaps the explanation is that the wager which the Devil offers, and which God accepts, covers not the whole of God's creation but only a part. The part, not the whole, is at stake; yet the chances and changes to which the part is thus exposed cannot possibly leave the whole unaffected. In the language of our modern Western Physical Science:

'A change in equilibrium does not mean an alteration in the position and activity of one element of the structure only; there is a redistribution which affects all the elements. It is the very nature of the structure in changing its equilibrium to distribute the change over all its component elements. No demon is at work among these elements to transpose them, to rearrange them, and to vary their functions slightly so as to produce the new balance or equilibrium of the whole. It is an inherent character of the physico-chemical structure as such, and is explicable on purely physical and chemical principles which do not call for the intervention of an extraordinary agent.'[1]

In the language of Mythology, when one of God's creatures is tempted by the Devil, God Himself is thereby given the opportunity to recreate the World. By the stroke of the Adversary's trident, all the fountains of the great deep are broken up. The Devil's intervention has accomplished that transition from Yin to Yang, from static to dynamic, for which God had been yearning ever since the moment when His Yin-state became complete, but which it was impossible for God to accomplish by Himself, out of His own perfection. And the Devil has done more for God than this; for, when once Yin has passed over into Yang, not the Devil himself can prevent God from completing His fresh act of creation by passing over again from Yang to Yin on a higher level. When once the divine equilibrium has been upset by the Satanic instability, the Devil has shot his bolt; and the restoration of equilibrium on a new plan, in which God's purpose is fulfilled, lies wholly within God's power. In this act of creation, which is the sole permanent and significant result of the transaction between God and the Devil, 'no demon is', or can be, 'at work'.

Thus the Devil is bound to lose the wager, not because he has been cheated by God, but because he has overreached himself.[2] He has played into God's hands because he would not or could not deny himself the malicious satisfaction of forcing God's hand.

---

[1] Smuts, J. C.: *Holism and Evolution*, 2nd edition (London 1927, Macmillan), p. 181.
[2] This is the *motif* of the Syriac myth (preserved in Genesis xxxii. 24–32) of the mysterious being—man or angel or demon or God himself—who assails Jacob before dawn and, in doing so, goes out of his way to bring about his own discomfiture. The assailant, in virtue of his nature, must be gone before dawn; and when he fails to overcome Jacob's resistance and break free—even after using his supernatural power in the hope of putting Jacob out of action—he is driven to confess that Jacob has prevailed and to comply with Jacob's terms: 'I will not let thee go except thou bless me.'

Knowing that God would not or could not refuse the wager if it were offered, the Devil did not observe that God was hoping, silently but eagerly, that the offer would be made. In his jubilation at obtaining an opportunity to ruin one of God's choicest creatures, the Devil did not foresee that he would be giving God Himself an opportunity to renew the whole work of creation. And so God's purpose is fulfilled through the Devil's instrumentality and in the Devil's despite.[1]

It will be seen that this denouement of the plot turns upon the role of God's creature who is the object of the wager; and here again we find ourselves beset by logical contradictions on all sides. A Job or a Faust is at once a chosen vessel and a vessel of destruction; and, in the fact of being subjected to his ordeal, he has already fulfilled his function, so that it makes no difference to the drama in Heaven whether he, on Earth, is blasted by the fire or whether he emerges more finely tempered. Even if the Devil has his way with him—even if his destruction is complete—God's purpose is nevertheless fulfilled and the Devil's purpose frustrated; for, in spite of the sacrifice of the creature, the Creator lives, while, through the sacrifice of the creature, the work of creation proceeds:

'Of old hast Thou laid the foundation of the Earth, and the Heavens are the work of Thy hands.

'They shall perish, but Thou shalt endure. Yea, all of them shall wax old like a garment; as a vesture shalt Thou change them, and they shall be changed.

'But Thou art the same, and Thy years shall have no end.'[2]

Again, this chosen vessel of destruction which is the object of the wager between God and the Devil is their common field of action, the arena in which they do battle, the stage on which they play; but he is also the combatants as well as the arena and the dramatis personae as well as the stage. Created by God and abandoned to the Devil, he is seen, in the prophet's vision, to be an incarnation of both his Maker and his Tempter, while, in the psychologist's analysis, God and the Devil alike are reduced to conflicting psychic

---

[1] It would seem to follow that, if the Devil had known his business, he would have played just the opposite game. Instead of naïvely vaunting his own ability to ruin one of God's creatures—a Faust or a Job—he would have hypocritically chimed in with the Archangels in hymning the omnipotence of God and the perfection of His works. His song would have been not a candid satire on God's chief creation, Man:

'Der kleine Gott der Welt bleibt stets von gleichem Schlag,
Und ist so wunderlich als wie am ersten Tag',

but a disingenuous

'God's in His Heaven,
All's right with the World'.

Perhaps the Devil does play this game sometimes. We shall recur to this, apropos of the breakdowns of civilizations, in studying the myth of 'the Envy of the Gods'. (See IV. C (iii) (c) 1, vol. iv, pp. 245–61, below.)

[2] Psalm cii, 25–7.

forces in his soul—forces which have no independent existence apart from the symbolic language of Mythology.

The conception that the object of the wager between God and the Devil is an incarnation of God is familiar. It is the central theme of the New Testament; and it is readily translated into the language of our modern Western Physical Science:

'The individual and its parts are reciprocally means and end to one another; neither is merely self-regarding, but each supports the other in the moving dynamic equilibrium which is called Life. And so it happens that the central control of the whole also maintains and assists the parts, and the functions of the parts are ever directed towards the conservation and fulfilment of the whole.'[1]

The conception that the object of the wager is at the same time an incarnation of the Devil is less familiar but perhaps not less profound. It is expressed in the encounter between Faust and the Earth Spirit, who prostrates Faust by proclaiming Faust's likeness to the spirit whom he understands—the still unmanifested Mephistopheles:

> *Faust.* Der du die weite Welt umschweifst,
> Geschäftiger Geist, wie nah fühl' ich mich dir!
> *Geist.* Du gleichst dem Geist den du begreifst,
> Nicht mir! (*Verschwindet*).
> *Faust* (*zusammenstürzend*). Nicht dir!
> Wem denn!
> Ich Ebenbild der Gottheit!
> Und nicht einmal dir![2]

It remains to consider the role of this 'Devil-God', this part and whole, this creature and incarnation, this arena and combatant, this stage and player; for, in the wager version of the plot, the encounter between the Powers of Hell and Heaven is only the prologue, while the passion of a human figure on Earth is the substance of the play.

In every presentation of this drama, suffering is the keynote of the human protagonist's part, whether the part is played by Jesus of Nazareth, or by Job, or by Faust and Gretchen, or by Adam and Eve, or by Hippolytus and Phaedra, or by Hoder and Balder. 'He is despised and rejected of men; a man of sorrows, and acquainted with grief.'[3] 'He will be scourged, racked, shackled, blinded with hot irons and be put to every other torment, ending with being impaled.'[4] Faust makes his entry in a state of utter disillusionment with his mastery of human knowledge[5]; turns to magic only to

---

[1] Smuts, J. C.: *Holism and Evolution*, 2nd edition, pp. 218–19.
[2] *Faust*, ll. 510–17; cf. lines 1744–7.
[3] Isaiah liii. 3.
[4] Plato: *Respublica*, Book II, 361E–362A.   [5] *Faust*, ll. 354–417.

receive a shattering rebuff from the Earth Spirit;[1] and then accepts from Mephistopheles an initiation into the life of sense and sex which leads him to the tragic moment in Margaret's prison, at the dawn of her dying day, when he cries, like Job,[2] in his agony: 'O, would that I had never been born.'[3] Gretchen, entering carefree,[4] is made to pass through the Valley of the Shadow of Death:

> Mein Ruh' ist hin,
> Mein Herz ist schwer;
> Ich finde sie nimmer
> Und nimmermehr.[5]

The subjective experience of the human being who is cast for this part is conveyed with unusual vividness and poignancy in the following dream of a woman undergoing an operation under insufficient ether, which is cited by William James:

'A great Being or Power was travelling through the sky, his foot was on a kind of lightning as a wheel is on a rail, it was his pathway. The lightning was made entirely of the spirits of innumerable people close to one another, and I was one of them. He moved in a straight line, and each part of the streak or flash came into his short conscious existence only that he might travel. I seemed to be directly under the foot of God, and I thought he was grinding his own life up out of my pain. Then I saw that what he had been trying with all his might to do was to *change his course*, to *bend* the lightning to which he was tied, in the direction in which he wanted to go. I felt my flexibility and helplessness, and knew that he would succeed. He bended me, turning his corner by means of my hurt, hurting me more than I had ever been hurt in my life, and at the acutest point of this, as he passed, I *saw*. I understood for a moment things that I have now forgotten, things that no one could remember while retaining sanity. The angle was an obtuse angle, and I remember thinking as I woke that had he made it a right or acute angle, I should have both suffered and "seen" still more, and should probably have died.

'If I had to formulate a few of the things I then caught a glimpse of, they would run somewhat as follows:

'The eternal necessity of suffering and its eternal vicariousness. The veiled and incommunicable nature of the worst sufferings;—the passivity of genius, how it is essentially instrumental and defenceless, moved, not moving, it must do what it does;—the impossibility of discovery without its price;—finally, the excess of what the suffering "seer" or genius pays over what his generation gains. (He seems like one who sweats his life out to earn enough to save a district from famine, and just as he staggers back, dying and satisfied, bringing a lac of rupees to buy grain with, God lifts the lac away, dropping one rupee, and says, "That you

---

[1] *Faust*, ll. 418–517. [2] Job, ch. iii. [3] *Faust*, l. 4596.
[4] *Faust*, ll. 2607–8. [5] *Faust*, ll. 3376–413.

may give them. That you have earned for them. The rest is for ME.")
I perceived also, in a way never to be forgotten, the excess of what we
see over what we can demonstrate.'[1]

Objectively, the ordeal consists of a series of stages which the
sufferer has to pass through in order to serve God's purpose.

In the first stage, the human protagonist in the drama takes
action—in reaction to an assault from the tempter—which sets up
a change from passivity to activity, from rest to motion, from
calm to storm, from harmony to discord, in fact from Yin to Yang.
The action may be either dynamically base, as when the Ancient
Mariner shoots the Albatross or Loki shoots Balder with the blind
God Hoder's hand and the mistletoe shaft; or dynamically sublime,
as when Jesus, in the temptation in the wilderness which immediately follows his baptism in Jordan, rejects the traditional Jewish
role of the militant Messiah who was to raise the Chosen People
to dominion in this world by the sword.[2] The essence of the act
is not its moral character but its dynamic effect. The Ancient
Mariner's act changes the fortunes of the ship and her crew;
Jesus's act gives the conception of the Messiah a new turn and
therewith a power which had not resided in it before.[3] The corresponding act in the ordeal of Job is his cursing of the day of
his birth[4]—a protest which raises the whole issue of Job's deserts
and God's justice. In the ordeal of Faust, the point is elaborated
and brought out more clearly.

Before Mephistopheles intervenes, Faust is already making efforts
on his own account to break out of his Yin-state—his unsatis-
fyingly perfect mastery of human knowledge. He seeks escape
from his spiritual prison through the arts of magic and is repelled
by the Earth Spirit;[5] he seeks escape through suicide and is
checked by the song of the choir of angels;[6] he is driven back from
action to meditation; yet his mind still runs upon action and
transposes 'Im Anfang war das Wort' into 'Im Anfang war die
Tat'.[7] At that moment, already, Mephistopheles is present in a
theriomorphic disguise; but it is not till the tempter stands before
him in human form that Faust performs his dynamic act by
cursing the whole moral and material universe.[8] Therewith, the
foundations of the great deep are loosed; and an invisible choir of

---

[1] Dream of a woman undergoing an operation under insufficient ether, cited by
William James in *The Varieties of Religious Experience*, 33rd impression (London 1922,
Longmans), pp. 392–3.

[2] Matthew iii. 13–iv. 11; Mark i. 9–13; Luke iii. 2–22 and iv. 1–13.

[3] The non-violence of Jesus and his followers, and its contrast with the militancy of
the abortive messianic movements of a Theudas or a Judas of Galilee, did not escape the
observation of Gamaliel (Acts v. 34–40).

[4] Job iii.   [5] *Faust*, ll. 418–521.   [6] *Faust*, ll. 602–807.

[7] *Faust*, ll. 1224–37.   [8] *Faust*, ll. 1583–1606.

spirits laments and exults that the old creation is shattered and a new creation begun.

> Weh! Weh!
> Du hast sie zerstört,
> Die schöne Welt
> Mit mächtiger Faust;
> Sie stürzt, sie zerfällt!
> Ein Halbgott hat sie zerschlagen!
> Wir tragen
> Die Trümmern ins Nichts hinüber,
> Und Klagen
> Über die verlorne Schöne.
>
> Mächtiger
> Der Erdensöhne,
> Prächtiger
> Baue sie wieder,
> In deinem Busen baue sie auf !
> Neuen Lebenslauf
> Beginne
> Mit hellem Sinne,
> Und neue Lieder
> Tönen darauf.[1]

In the song of these spirits, whom Mephistopheles claims as his own,[2] the first note of Yang resounds. The hymn of the Archangels—

> Die unbegreiflich hohen Werke
> Sind herrlich, wie am ersten Tag—

is now transcended.

So, too, in the Scandinavian universe, when, at Loki's prompting, blind Hoder performs his unwittingly dynamic act, and Balder is slain,

'Life is blighted and the curse spreads from the Gods to the dwelling-place of human beings. The thoughts of men are darkened and confused by the upheaval in Nature and the tumult of their own minds, and in their distraction men violate the very principles of Life. The bonds of kinship give way to blind passion: brothers fight with one another, kinsmen shed their own blood, no one trusts his fellow; a new age dawns: the age of swords, the age of axes; the ears of men are filled with the din of shields being splintered and of wolves howling over the bodies of the slain.'[3]

[1] *Faust*, ll. 1607–26.   [2] *Faust*, ll. 1627–8.
[3] Grönbech, V.: *The Culture of the Teutons* (London 1931, Milford, 3 parts in 2 vols.), part II, p. 302. There is a curious congruity between the language of the anonymous author of the *Voluspá* and Virgil's language in the First Georgic, ll. 505-11 :

> Quippe ubi fas versum atque nefas; tot bella per orbem,
> tam multae scelerum facies, non ullus aratro
> dignus honos, squalent abductis arva colonis,
> et curvae rigidum falces conflantur in ensem. . . .
> vicinae ruptis inter se legibus urbes
> arma ferunt; saevit toto Mars impius orbe.

In the story of the Fall of Man in the Book of Genesis, the dynamic act is Eve's eating of the fruit of the Tree of Knowledge at the Serpent's prompting; and here the application of the myth to the geneses of civilizations is direct. The picture of Adam and Eve in the Garden of Eden is a reminiscence of the Yin-state to which Primitive Man attained in 'the food-gathering phase' of economy, after he had established his ascendancy over all the rest of the flora and fauna of the Earth—the state which is remembered in the Hellenic Mythology as 'the Times of Cronos'.[1] The Fall, in response to the temptation to taste the fruit of the Tree of the Knowledge of Good and Evil, symbolizes the acceptance of a challenge to abandon the achieved integration and to venture upon a fresh differentiation out of which another integration may—or may not—arise. The expulsion from the Garden into an unfriendly outer world in which the Woman must bring forth children in sorrow and the Man must eat bread in the sweat of his face, is the ordeal which the acceptance of the Serpent's challenge has entailed. The sexual intercourse between Adam and Eve, which follows, is an act of social creation. It bears fruit in the birth of two sons who impersonate two nascent civilizations: Abel the keeper of sheep and Cain the tiller of the ground.[2]

The equation of civilization with agriculture, and progress with toil, is also to be found in Hellenic literature in the famous line of Hesiod

τῆς δ' ἀρετῆς ἱδρῶτα θεοὶ προπάροιθεν ἔθηκαν[3]

which is echoed in Virgil's

Pater ipse colendi
haud facilem esse viam voluit, primusque per artem
movit agros, curis acuens mortalia corda,
nec torpere gravi passus sua regna veterno.[4]

In more general terms and with less poetic imagery, the same story is retold by Origen—a thinker who, in the second century of our era, became one of the fathers of the Christian Church without ceasing to be a Hellenic philosopher:

'God, wishing Man's intelligence to be exercised everywhere, in

---

[1] ὁ ἐπὶ Κρόνου βίος. (See, for example, Plato, Leges, 713C-D, where the myth is adapted to illustrate the philosopher's social theory.)

[2] The story of Cain and his descendants, which is given as an epilogue (Gen. iv. 16–25) to the story of Cain and Abel (Gen. iv. 1–15), represents Cain as the father of civilization in general and all its works. In this epilogue, Cain himself builds a city and his descendant, Lamech, has two sons, Jubal and Tubal-Cain, who are respectively 'the father of all such as handle the harp and organ' and 'an instructor of every artificer in brass and iron'. Here we have the picture of a civilization with an agricultural basis evolving an urban life and industry. At the same time, Jubal and Tubal-Cain are given a brother, Jabal, who is 'the father of such as dwell in tents and such as have cattle', so that Cain's descendant, Lamech, is made progenitor of the Nomadic stock-breeding civilization and the sedentary agricultural and industrial civilizations alike.

[3] Hesiod: Works and Days, l. 289.   [4] Virgil, Georg. i, ll. 121-4.

order that it might not remain idle and without a conception of the arts, created Man with needs, in order that sheer need might force him to invent arts for providing himself with food and providing himself with shelter. It was better for those who would not have used their intelligence in seeking after a philosophic knowledge of God that they should be badly enough off to use it in the invention of arts, rather than that they should be well enough off to leave their intelligence altogether uncultivated.'[1]

In the language of our modern Western rationalism, the same theme has been expounded by the eighteenth-century French philosopher Volney:

'L'on s'apperçoit que toute activité, soit de corps, soit d'esprit, prend sa source dans les besoins; que c'est en raison de leur étendue, de leurs développemens, qu'elle-même s'étend et se développe; l'on en suit la gradation depuis les élémens les plus simples jusqu'à l'état le plus composé. C'est la faim, c'est la soif qui, dans l'homme encore sauvage, éveillent les premiers mouvemens de l'âme et du corps; ce sont ces besoins qui le font courir, chercher, épier, user d'astuce ou de violence: toute son activité se mesure sur les moyens de pourvoir à sa subsistance. Sont-ils faciles; a-t-il sous sa main les fruits, le gibier, le poisson: il est moins actif, parce que en étendant le bras il se rassasie, et que, rassasié, rien ne l'invite à se mouvoir, jusqu'à ce que l'expérience de diverses jouissances ait éveillé en lui les désirs qui deviennent des besoins nouveaux, de nouveaux mobiles d'activité. Les moyens sont-ils difficiles; le gibier est-il rare et agile, le poisson rusé, les fruits passagers: alors l'homme est forcé d'être plus actif; il faut que son corps et son esprit s'exercent à vaincre les difficultés qu'il rencontre à vivre; il faut qu'il devienne agile comme le gibier, rusé comme le poisson, et prévoyant pour conserver les fruits. Alors, pour étendre ses facultés naturelles, il s'agite, il pense, il médite; alors il imagine de courber un rameau d'arbre pour en faire un arc; d'aiguiser un roseau pour en faire une flèche; d'emmancher un bâton à une pierre tranchante pour en faire une hache: alors il travaille à faire des filets, à abattre des arbres, à en creuser le tronc pour en faire des pirogues. Déjà il a franchi les bornes des premiers besoins, déjà l'expérience d'une foule de sensations lui a fait connaître des jouissances et des peines; et il prend un surcroît d'activité pour écarter les unes et multiplier les autres.'[2]

---

[1] πανταχοῦ τὴν ἀνθρωπίνην σύνεσιν γυμνάζεσθαι βουλόμενος ὁ θεὸς ἵνα μὴ μένῃ ἀργὴ καὶ ἀνεπινόητος τῶν τεχνῶν, πεποίηκε τὸν ἄνθρωπον ἐπιδεῆ, ἵνα δι' αὐτὸ τὸ ἐπιδεὲς αὐτοῦ ἀναγκασθῇ εὑρεῖν τέχνας, τινὰς μὲν διὰ τὴν τροφήν, ἄλλας δὲ διὰ τὴν σκέπην· καὶ γὰρ κρεῖττον ἦν τοῖς μὴ μέλλουσι τὰ θεῖα ζητεῖν καὶ φιλοσοφεῖν τὸ ἀπορεῖν ὑπὲρ τοῦ τῇ συνέσει χρήσασθαι πρὸς εὕρεσιν τεχνῶν, ἥπερ ἐκ τοῦ εὐπορεῖν πάντῃ τῆς συνέσεως ἀμελεῖν. Origenes contra Celsum, iv. 76, xix, p. 116, ed. Lommatzsch (cited by Nock, A. D., in his edition of Sallustius, Concerning the Gods and the Universe (Cambridge 1926, University Press), p. xlv).

[2] Volney, C. F.: Voyage en Syrie et en Égypte pendant les Années 1783, 1784 et 1785, 2ᵉ édition (Paris 1787, Desenne et Volland, 2 vols.), vol. ii, pp. 428–9.

In our own generation, one of our most distinguished and original-minded students of the physical environment of human life takes up the parable:

'Ages ago a band of naked, houseless, fireless savages started from their warm home in the torrid zone and pushed steadily northward from the beginning of spring to the end of summer. They never guessed that they had left the land of constant warmth until in September they began to feel an uncomfortable chill at night. Day by day it grew worse. Not knowing its cause, they travelled this way or that to escape. Some went southward, but only a handful returned to their former home. There they resumed the old life, and their descendants are untutored savages to this day. Of those who wandered in other directions, all perished except one small band. Finding that they could not escape the nipping air, the members of this band used the loftiest of human faculties, the power of conscious invention. Some tried to find shelter by digging in the ground, some gathered branches and leaves to make huts and warm beds, and some wrapped themselves in the skins of the beasts that they had slain. Soon these savages had taken some of the greatest steps toward civilisation. The naked were clothed; the houseless sheltered; the improvident learned to dry meat and store it, with nuts, for the winter; and at last the art of making fire was discovered as a means of keeping warm. Thus they subsisted where at first they thought that they were doomed. And in the process of adjusting themselves to a hard environment they advanced by enormous strides, leaving the tropical part of Mankind far in the rear.

'To-day, Mankind resembles these savages in certain respects. We know that we are limited by climate. As the savages faced the winter, so we are face to face with the fact that the Human Race has tried to conquer the arctic zone, the deserts, and the torrid zone, and has met with only the most limited success. Even in the temperate zone he has made a partial failure, for he is still handicapped in hundreds of ways. Hitherto we have attributed our failure to economic conditions, to isolation and remoteness, to racial incapacity, or to specific diseases. Now we see that it is probably due in part to lack of energy or to other unfavourable effects produced directly upon the human system by climate. There is no reason for despair. We ought rather to rejoice because, perhaps, we may correct some of the evils which hitherto have baffled us.'[1]

Finally, a contemporary classical scholar translates the story into the orthodox scientific terminology of our age:

'It is . . . a paradox of advancement that if Necessity be the mother of Invention, the other parent is Obstinacy, the determination that you will go on living under adverse conditions rather than cut your losses and go where life is easier. It was no accident, that is, that Civilisation, as we know it, began in that ebb and flow of climate, flora and fauna

---

[1] Huntington, Ellsworth: *Civilisation and Climate*, 3rd edition (New Haven 1924, Yale University Press), pp. 405–6.

which characterises the four-fold 'Ice Age'. Those primates who just 'got out' as arboreal conditions wilted retained their primacy among the servants of Natural Law, but they forwent the conquest of Nature. Those others won through, and became men, who stood their ground when there were no more trees to sit in, who "made do" with meat when fruit did not ripen, who made fires and clothes rather than follow the sunshine; who fortified their lairs and trained their young and vindicated the reasonableness of a world that seemed so reasonless.'[1]

The first stage, then, in the human protagonist's ordeal is a transition from Yin to Yang through a dynamic act—performed by God's creature under temptation from the adversary—which enables God Himself to resume His creative activity. But this progress has to be paid for; and it is not God—a hard master, reaping where He has not sown, and gathering where He has not strawed[2]—but God's servant, the human sower, who pays the price.

The second stage in the human protagonist's ordeal is the crisis. He realizes that his dynamic act, which has re-liberated the creative power of his Master and Maker, has set his own feet on a course which is leading him to suffering and death. In an agony of disillusionment and horror,[3] he rebels against the fate which, by his own act, he has brought upon himself for God's gain. The crisis is resolved when he resigns himself consciously to be the instrument of God's will, the tool in God's hands; and this activity through passivity, this victory through defeat, brings on another cosmic change. Just as the dynamic act in the first phase of the ordeal shook the Universe out of Yin into Yang, so the act of resignation in the second phase reverses the rhythm of the Universe—guiding it now from motion towards rest, from storm towards calm, from discord towards harmony, from Yang towards Yin again.

---

[1] Myres, J. L.: Who were the Greeks? (Berkeley 1930, University of California Press), pp. 277–8.

[2] Matthew xxv. 24.

[3] This agony, arising out of a spiritual conflict, may be suffered on the unconscious plane of the psyche; and there, unless and until it is transcended, it produces the psychic phenomena which our modern Western psycho-analysts call neuroses.

'The challenge of Life asks different things of each individual. It may be marriage or celibacy, staying at home or going abroad, self-assertion or self-effacement: the problem takes countless different forms. Often the intolerable situation against which the neurosis is a defence appears outwardly safe and attractive; and the victim of the neurosis accepts other people's estimate of it and is entirely unaware of his own resistance and fear. In general, however, these varied problems can be reduced to simple terms of the choice between growing up and remaining children: the choice between a progressive and a repressive reaction to Life. In so far as progress means self-help, and in so far as self-help is incompatible with self-pity, it is obvious that the neurosis which gives an opportunity to self-pity is an effective barrier to progress.' (Crichton Miller, H.: The New Psychology and the Teacher (London 1921, Jarrolds), pp. 139–40.)

Compare the quotation from Joseph Conrad—'Neither his fellows, nor his gods, nor his passions will leave a man alone'—in op. cit., p. 128, and the passage in The New Psychology and the Preacher (London 1924, Jarrolds), pp. 162–3, on the challenge of Religion.

In the cry of a Hellenic poet, we hear the note of agony without a note of resignation to follow:

μηκέτ' ἔπειτ' ὤφελλον ἐγὼ πέμπτοισι μετεῖναι
ἀνδράσιν, ἀλλ' ἢ πρόσθε θανεῖν ἢ ἔπειτα γενέσθαι.[1]

The tragedy rises to a higher level in the Scandinavian vision of Odin, on the eve of Ragnarök, mentally striving with all his might to wrest the secret of Fate from the powers that hold it—not in order to save himself alive but for the sake of the universe of Gods and Men who look to him, the All Father, to preserve them. In the passion of Jesus, we are initiated into the whole psychological experience.

When Jesus first realizes His destiny, in the course of His last journey from Galilee to Jerusalem, He is master of the situation; and it is His disciples, to whom He communicates His intuition immediately before,[2] and again immediately after,[3] His transfiguration, who are perplexed and dismayed. The agony comes upon Him, on the eve of His passion, in the Garden of Gethsemane,[4] and is resolved in the prayer: 'O my Father, if this cup may not pass away from me except I drink it, Thy will be done.'[5] Yet the agony recurs when the sufferer is hanging on the Cross, where the final cry of despair—'My God, My God, Why hast Thou forsaken me?'[6]—precedes the final words of resignation: 'Father, into Thy hands I commend my spirit',[7] and 'It is finished.'[8]

The same experience of agony and resignation is presented—here in purely psychological terms—in the Epistle to the Romans, where the cry—'O wretched man that I am! Who shall deliver me from the body of this death?'—is followed by the antiphony: 'I thank God through Jesus Christ our Lord. So then with the mind I myself serve the law of God, but with the flesh the law of sin.'[9]

The same experience, again, is narrated to the Wedding-Guest by the Ancient Mariner, who has brought upon himself the ordeal of 'Life-in-Death' by his criminal yet none the less dynamic act of shooting the Albatross:

> Alone, alone, all, all alone,
> Alone, on a wide wide sea!
> And never a saint took pity on
> My soul in agony.

---

[1] Hesiod: *Works and Days*, ll. 174–5.
[2] Matthew xvi. 13–23; Mark viii. 27–33; Luke ix. 18–22.
[3] Matthew xvii. 10–12; Mark xi. 11–13.
[4] Matthew xxvi. 36–46; Mark xiv. 32–42; Luke xxii. 39–46. Compare John xii. 23–8.
[5] Matthew xxvi. 42.
[6] Matthew xxvii. 46; Mark xv. 34.
[7] Luke xxiii. 46.   [8] John xix. 30.
[9] Romans vii. 24–5. The whole of chapters vii and viii is a lyrical meditation upon this theme.

> The many men, so beautiful!
> And they all dead did lie:
> And a thousand thousand slimy things
> Lived on; and so did I.

In this ordeal, the curse is lifted when the sufferer resigns himself
to the consequences of his act and has a vision of beauty where he
had only perceived hideousness so long as his heart remained hard:

> O happy living things! No tongue
> Their beauty might declare:
> A spring of love gushed from my heart,
> And I blessed them unaware:
> Sure my kind saint took pity on me,
> And I blessed them unaware.

> The self-same moment I could pray;
> And from my neck so free
> The Albatross fell off, and sank
> Like lead into the sea.

This is the turning-point in the Romantic Odyssey. The divine
powers which had magically becalmed the ship now magically waft
her to port and bring the villain—or the hero—of the ballad home
to his own country.

So, too, Job humbles himself to God at the end of his colloquy
with his friends, when Elihu has shown how God is just in His
ways and is to be feared because of His great words in which His
wisdom is unsearchable, and when the Lord Himself, addressing
Job out of the whirlwind, has challenged the sufferer to continue
the debate with Him.

Then Job answered the Lord and said:
'Behold, I am vile. What shall I answer thee? I will lay mine hand
upon my mouth.
'Once have I spoken, but I will not answer; yea, twice, but I will
proceed no further. . . .
'I know that Thou canst do everything, and that no thought can be
withholden from Thee. . . .
'I have uttered that I understood not—things too wonderful for me,
which I knew not. . . .
'I have heard of Thee by the hearing of the ear, but now mine eye
seeth thee.
'Wherefore I abhor myself, and repent in dust and ashes.'[1]

In this Syriac poem, the psychology is crude. The resignation
comes, not through a spiritual intuition in the soul, but through
a physical manifestation to the eye of God's irresistible force. In
Goethe's version of the drama, the sequence of agony and resignation

---

[1] Job xl. 3–5 and xlii. 2–6.

holds its place as the crisis and the culmination of the plot—Gretchen passes through it in the last scene of Part I[1] and Faust, in his turn, at the climax of Part II[2]—but the êthos is transformed beyond recognition.

In the scene in Gretchen's prison, in the grey dawn of her last day, Mephistopheles seeks to take advantage of Gretchen's agony in order to induce her to forgo her salvation by escaping her doom. It seems the easiest enterprise that he has yet essayed. His victim is distraught with horror at the imagination of what lies before her; it is the hour at which human vitality is at its lowest ebb; the pains of death are imminent; the prospect of escape is offered suddenly and unexpectedly; and it is Gretchen's lover Faust himself who implores her to flee with him through the magically opened prison doors. Yet Gretchen, raving in her agony, seems insensible to Faust's appeal, until at last Mephistopheles, in his impatience, intervenes himself. That is the moment of the tempter's defeat; for Gretchen, recognizing him for what he is, awakes from her frenzied trance and takes refuge in the judgement of God—no longer rooted to the spot in a nightmare like the Aeschylean Cassandra, but deliberately rejecting, like the Platonic Socrates, a possibility of escape of which she is fully aware:

> *Margarete.* Was steigt aus dem Boden herauf?
> Der! Der! Schick' ihn fort!
> Was will er an dem heiligen Ort?
> Er will mich!
> *Faust.*   Du sollst leben!
> *Margarete.* Gericht Gottes! Dir hab' ich mich übergeben!
> *Mephistopheles (zu Faust).*
> Komm! Komm! Ich lasse dich mit ihr im Stich.
> *Margarete.* Dein bin ich, Vater! Rette mich!
> Ihr Engel! Ihr heiligen Scharen,
> Lagert euch umher, mich zu bewahren!
> Heinrich! Mir graut's vor dir.
> *Mephistopheles.* Sie ist gerichtet!
> *Stimme (von oben).*   Ist gerettet!
> *Mephistopheles (zu Faust).*   Her zu mir!
> *(Verschwindet mit Faust).*
> *Stimme (von innen, verhallend).* Heinrich! Heinrich.[3]

---

[1] *Faust*, ll. 4405–612.   [2] *Faust*, ll. 11384–510.
[3] *Faust*, ll. 4601–12. This is, psychologically, the end of the play; for Mephistopheles' defeat is irrevocable; and although the light which has broken upon Gretchen's soul in this dawn does not enlighten Faust till many more years have passed over his head, yet his ultimate salvation is ensured by hers, and the labyrinthine second part of the play is therefore psychologically as well as artistically superfluous. By comparison with the last scene of Part I, the corresponding scene in Part II, in which Faust confronts and defies the four grey women—Want and Guilt and Care and Need—is an anti-climax. The last ten lines of Part I already convey the mystery—'Das ewig Weibliche / Zieht uns hinan'—which is uttered, in the last two lines of Part II, by the Mystic Choir. The poet had no need to point his meaning by an epilogue which almost quadruples the length of his work.

In the third stage, the reversal of the cosmic rhythm from Yang towards Yin, which was initiated in the second stage, is carried to completion. At the climax of Ragnarök, when Thor has met the Dragon and Odin the Wolf,

'The Sun is darkened, the Earth sinks back into the waves, stars rain down, and the flames leap up and lick the heavens.' But then 'the barking' of the Wolf 'is heard for the last time as the world-fire flickers down'. And 'when the roar and the voices are stilled, the Earth once more rises out of the sea in evergreen freshness; brooks leap down the hills; the eagle wheels on high, peering into the streams. The Gods meet among self-sown fields, they call to mind the tale of deeds and former wisdom, and in the grass before their feet the golden tables are found lying. A new hall rises golden-roofed and fairer than the Sun. Here a race of true-hearted men will dwell and rejoice in their heart's desire. Then from above descends the mighty one, all-powerful. The dusky dragon flies past, brushing the ground with his wings weighted down by dead bodies; he sinks into the abyss and disappears.'[1]

In this new creation, which the ordeal of one of God's creatures has enabled God to achieve, the sufferer himself returns to a state of peace and harmony and bliss on a higher level than the state which he left behind when he responded to the tempter's challenge. In the Book of Job, the achievement is startlingly crude—the Lord convinces Job that He is answerable for His acts to no man—and the restoration is naïvely material: 'the Lord blessed the latter end of Job more than his beginning' by giving him fairer daughters than those that he had lost and twice as many sheep and camels and oxen and asses.[2] In the New Testament, the agony and resignation and passion of Jesus achieve the redemption of Man and are followed by the Redeemer's resurrection and ascension. In the Scandinavian Mythology, Odin returns to life after hanging upon a tree, and has keener vision in his one eye than he had before he plucked out his other eye and cast it from him as the purchase-price of wisdom.[3] In Goethe's *Faust*, the last scene of the second part, in which the Virgin Goddess, with her train of penitents, grants an epiphany to the pilgrims who have scaled the rugged mountain to its summit, is the counterpart of the Prologue in Heaven with which the first part of the play opens. The two scenes correspond, as, in the Christian version of the myth, Man's state of blessedness after the Redemption corresponds to his state of innocence before the Fall. The cosmic rhythm has come round, full circle, from Yin

---

[1] Grönbech, op. cit., Part II, pp. 302–3. Compare Virgil's Fourth Eclogue.
[2] Job xlii. 12–17, compared with i. 2–3.
[3] Contrast the fable of Solomon's choice (1 Kings iii. 5–15), in which the hero merely forbears to ask for long life or riches for himself, or for the life of his enemies, in order to ask for an understanding heart to judge the people, yet is rewarded by being given, not only a wise and understanding heart, but riches and honour into the bargain.

through Yang to Yin; but the latter Yin-state differs from the
former with the difference of spring from autumn. The works of
creation, which the Archangels hymned[1] and which Faust's curse
shattered,[2] arise in splendour again, to be hymned by the Pater
Profundus;[3] but this time they are in the tender shoot instead of
being ripe for the sickle. Through Faust's dynamic act and
Gretchen's act of resignation, the Lord has been enabled to make
all things new; and, in this new creation, the human protagonists
in the divine drama have their part. Gretchen, whose salvation had
been proclaimed by the voice from Heaven at the dawn of her
last day on Earth, appears, transfigured as Una Poenitentium, in
Mary's train, and the *visio beatifica* is vouchsafed to Faust, who
rises to join her, transfigured as Doctor Marianus.

> Das Unzulängliche,
> Hier wird's Ereignis;
> Das Unbeschreibliche,
> Hier ist's getan.[4]

Thus the manifestation of God as a hard master proves not to have
been the ultimate truth. The ordeal of God's creature appears in
retrospect as a revelation, not of God's callousness or cruelty, but
of His love.

> So ist es die allmächtige Liebe
> Die alles bildet, alles hegt.[5]

'For whom the Lord loveth He chasteneth, and scourgeth every
son whom He receiveth.'—'Πάθει μάθος.'[6]
Finally, the sufferer triumphant serves as a pioneer. 'Strait is
the gate and narrow is the way which leadeth unto life, and few
there be that find it.'[7] The human protagonist in the divine drama
not only serves God by enabling Him to renew His creation, but
also serves his fellow-men by pointing a way for others to follow.[8]
Job's intercession averts the Lord's wrath from Job's friends.[9]
Gretchen's intercession wins for Faust the *visio beatifica*.[10] When
Jesus first foreshadows his ordeal to his disciples, he proclaims, 'If
any man will come after me, let him deny himself and take up his
cross and follow me';[11] and on the eve of his passion he adds: 'And
I, if I be lifted up from the Earth, will draw all men unto me.'[12]

---

[1] *Faust*, ll. 243-70. [2] *Faust*, ll. 1583-1606.
[3] *Faust*, ll. 11866-89. [4] *Faust*, ll. 12106-9.
[5] Pater Profundus, in *Faust*, ll. 11872-3.
[6] For these last two quotations, see I. C (iii) (*b*), p. 169, footnote 1, above.
[7] Matthew vii. 14.
[8] In the Hellenic story of Prometheus, the two services are incompatible, and the
hero suffers because he has served Man in God's despite. For an interpretation of
Aeschylus's version of the Prometheus Myth, see Part III. B, below.
[9] Job xlii. 7-10. [10] *Faust*, ll. 12069-111.
[11] Matthew xvi. 24-8; Mark viii. 34-8; Luke ix. 23-7. [12] John xii. 32.

Democritus's intellectual pilgrimage breaches the walls of the prison house in which Superstition had incarcerated the human spirit:

> Humana ante oculos foede cum vita iaceret
> in terris oppressa gravi sub religione
> quae caput a caeli regionibus ostendebat
> horribili super aspectu mortalibus instans,
> primum Graius homo mortalis tollere contra
> est oculos ausus primusque obsistere contra,
> quem neque fama deum nec fulmina nec minitanti
> murmure compressit caelum, sed eo magis acrem
> inritat animi virtutem, effringere ut arta
> naturae primus portarum claustra cupiret.
> ergo vivida vis animi pervicit, et extra
> processit longe flammantia moenia mundi
> atque omne immensum peragravit mente animoque,
> unde refert nobis victor quid possit oriri,
> quid nequeat, finita potestas denique cuique
> quanam sit ratione et alte terminus haerens.
> quare religio pedibus subiecta vicissim
> opteritur, nos exaequat victoria caelo.[1]

In this magnificent passage of Lucretius, the feat of the pathfinder is extolled in the language of the intellect; but the paean must be transposed into the language of the soul if the victor-victim is to reveal himself in his ultimate sublimity:

'Let not your heart be troubled: ye believe in God; believe also in me.

'In my Father's house are many mansions. . . . I go to prepare a place for you.

'And if I go and prepare a place for you, I will come again and receive you unto myself, that, where I am, there ye may be also.

'And whither I go ye know, and the way ye know. . . .

'I am the way, the truth and the life.'[2]

2. A Survey of Challenges and Responses in the Geneses of Civilizations

The Unknown God

By the light of Mythology, we have gained some insight into the nature of challenges and responses. We have come to see that creation is the outcome of an encounter, or—to re-translate the imagery of myths into the terminology of Science—that genesis is a function of interaction. Let us now return to our immediate quest: our search for the positive factor which has shaken part of Mankind out of 'the Integration of Custom' into 'the Differentiation of Civilization' within the last six thousand years. Let us look

---

[1] Lucretius: *De Rerum Natura*, Book I, ll. 62–79.   [2] John xiv. 1–6.

again into the origins of our twenty-one civilizations in order to ascertain, by an empirical test, whether the conception of Challenge-and-Response answers to the factor of which we are in search any better than the hypotheses of Race and Environment, which we have already weighed in the balance and found wanting.[1]

In this fresh survey, we shall be concerned with Race and Environment once more, but we shall regard them in a new light and shall place a different interpretation upon the phenomena. We shall no longer be on the look-out for some simple cause of the geneses of civilizations which can be demonstrated always and everywhere to produce an identical effect. We shall no longer be surprised if, in the production of civilizations, the same race, or the same environment, appears to be fruitful in one instance and sterile in another. Indeed, we shall not be surprised to find this phenomenon of inconstancy and variability in the effects produced, on different occasions, by one and the same cause, even when that cause is an interaction between the same race and the same environment under the same conditions. However scientifically exact the identity between two or more situations may be, we shall not expect the respective outcomes of these situations to conform with one another in the same degree of exactitude, or even in any degree at all. In fact, we shall no longer make the scientific postulate of the Uniformity of Nature, which we rightly made so long as we were thinking of our problem in scientific terms as a function of the play of inanimate forces. We shall be prepared now to recognize, *a priori*, that, even if we were exactly acquainted with all the racial, environmental, or other data that are capable of being formulated scientifically, we should not be able to predict the outcome of the interaction between the forces which these data represent, any more than a military expert can predict the outcome of a battle or a campaign from an 'inside knowledge' of the dispositions and resources of both the opposing general staffs, or a bridge expert the outcome of a game or a rubber from a similar knowledge of all the cards in every hand.

In both these analogies, 'inside knowledge' is not sufficient to enable its possessor to predict results with any exactness or assurance, because it is not the same thing as complete knowledge. There is one thing which must remain an unknown quantity to the best-informed onlooker, because it is beyond the knowledge of the combatants, or the players, themselves; and their ignorance of this quantity makes calculation impossible, because it is the most important term in the equation which the would-be calculator has to solve. This unknown quantity is the reaction of the actors to the

1 See II. C (ii) (*a*), above.

ordeal when it actually comes. 'Les causes physiques n'agissent que sur les principes cachés qui contribuent à former notre esprit et notre caractère.'[1] A general may have an accurate knowledge of his own man-power and munition-power and almost as good a knowledge of his opponent's; he may also have a shrewd idea of his opponent's plans; and, in the light of all this knowledge, he may have laid his own plans to his own best advantage. He cannot, however, foreknow how his opponent, or any of the other men who compose the force under his opponent's command, will behave, in action, when the campaign is opened and the battle joined; he cannot foreknow how his own men will behave; he cannot foreknow how he will behave himself. Yet these psychological momenta, which are inherently impossible to weigh and measure and therefore to estimate scientifically in advance, are the very forces which actually decide the issue when the encounter takes place. The military genius is the general who repeatedly succeeds in divining the unpredictable by guesswork or intuition; and most of the historic military geniuses—commanders of such diverse temperament and outlook as a Cromwell and a Napoleon—have recognized clearly that man-power and munition-power and intelligence and strategy are not the talismans that have brought them their victories. After estimating all the measurable and manageable factors at their full value—insisting that 'God is on the side of the big battalions', that 'God helps those who help themselves', that you should 'trust in God and keep your powder dry'— they have admitted frankly that, when all is said and done, victory cannot be predicted by thought or commanded by will because it comes in the end from a source to which neither thought nor will have access. If they have been religious-minded, they have cried 'Thanks be to God which giveth us the victory';[2] if they have been sceptical-minded, they have ascribed their victories—in superstitious terms—to the operations of Fortune or to the ascendancy of their personal star; but, whatever language they have used, they have testified to the reality of the same experience: the experience that the outcome of an encounter cannot be predicted and has no appearance of being predetermined, but arises, in the likeness of a new creation, out of the encounter itself.

With this preface, we will now survey the origins of our twenty-one civilizations once more—taking note of any challenges which we may find to have been presented by the environment and of any responses which we may find to have been evoked, and contenting

---

[1] 'Turgot: 'Plan de Deux Discours sur l'Histoire Universelle', in *Œuvres de Turgot*, nouvelle édition (Paris 1844, Guillaumin, 2 vols.), vol. ii, p. 647. Cf. Meyer, E.: *Geschichte des Altertums*, vol. i (i), 4th edition (Stuttgart and Berlin 1921, Cotta), pp. 83 and 174.   [2] 1 Corinthians xv. 57.

ourselves with observing, empirically, the phenomena of Challenge-and-Response in each particular instance, without postulating uniformity or expecting to discover a scientific law.

The Genesis of the Egyptiac Civilization

Let us proceed in the same order as before, taking first the challenges presented by the physical environment and afterwards those presented by the human environment at the geneses of the several societies by which the species called civilizations has been represented so far.

On this plan of operations, the first challenges which we have to consider are those presented by the valleys of certain rivers—the Nile, the Jordan, the Tigris and Euphrates, and the Indus with its once existent sister-stream—which traverse, as rare exceptions and at wide intervals, the otherwise riverless expanse of what is now the Afrasian Steppe.[1] The first responses which we have to consider are those made to the Nile Valley at the genesis of the Egyptiac Civilization, to the valley of the Tigris and Euphrates at the genesis of the Sumeric Civilization, and to the valley of the Indus and its former companion at the genesis of the so-called 'Indus Culture', supposing that this culture proves not to have been a colonial offshoot of the Sumeric Civilization but to have had an independent origin.[2]

Our reference to the sister-stream of the Indus which has now ceased to flow calls our attention to an element in the situation which we have not taken into account so far. Up to this point, we have assumed that the physical environment presented by the Afrasian Steppe, with its exceptional river-valleys, is static. We have made this assumption because there has actually been no appreciable change in its state within the twenty-four centuries or so which lie between our time and the time when this environment became familiar to those Hellenic observers whose speculations first gave us occasion, in a previous chapter,[3] to study the Afrasian environment ourselves. In going back, however, some two or three thousand years further, towards the origins of the civilizations which have arisen in this environment, we have already found one notable difference in the landscape. In a place where there is no river to-day there was a river then. In other words, the environment has changed, in at least one place, within the last four or five or six thousand years, and it has changed in a particular direction:

[1] See II. C (ii) (a) 2, pp. 256–8, above.
[2] For the openness of this question in the present state of our knowledge, see I. C (i) (b), p. 108, above, and Annex III, below, as well as II. C (ii) (a) 2, pp. 257–8.
[3] II. C (ii) (a) 2, pp. 249–53, above.

from humidity towards aridity.[1] As a matter of fact, we know that this phenomenon of the drying-up of the Indus's sister-stream has not been an isolated or an exceptional occurrence. It has been an incident in a process of desiccation which has manifested itself in all parts of our Afrasian area since the last glacial and pluvial paroxysm in that period of geological time which is popularly known as 'the Ice Age'.

'While Northern Europe was covered in ice as far as the Harz, and the Alps and the Pyrenees were capped with glaciers, the Arctic high pressure deflected southwards the Atlantic rainstorms. The cyclones that to-day traverse Central Europe then passed over the Mediterranean basin and the northern Sahara and continued, undrained by Lebanon, across Mesopotamia and Arabia to Persia and India.[2] The parched Sahara enjoyed a regular rainfall, and farther east the showers were not only more bountiful than to-day but were distributed over the whole year, instead of being restricted to the winter. On the Iranian Plateau the precipitation, although insufficient to feed extensive glaciers, filled the great hollows that are now salt deserts with shallow inland seas whose presence tempered the severity of the climate. . . .

'We should expect in North Africa, Arabia, Persia and the Indus Valley parklands and savannahs, such as flourish to-day north of the Mediterranean, at a time when much of Europe was tundra or wind-swept steppe on which the dust was collecting as loess. While the mammoth, the woolly rhinoceros and the reindeer were browsing in France and Southern England, North Africa was supporting a fauna that is found to-day on the Zambesi in Rhodesia. . . .

'The pleasant grasslands of North Africa and Southern Asia were naturally as thickly populated by Man as the frozen steppes of Europe, and it is reasonable to suspect that in this favourable and indeed stimulating environment Man would make greater progress than in the ice-bound north. In fact it is somewhere in this region that many would locate the first cradle of *Homo Sapiens*. Lower Palaeolithic men have left their hand-axes all over North Africa from Morocco to Egypt, in Somaliland, in Palestine and Syria and in many parts of India. These agree so exactly in form with those made in Western Europe during the last interglacial [period] and before it that one assumes a more or less uniform population, of course very sparse and physically very primitive, common to Western Europe, Africa, and Southern Asia . . . a loose chain of interrelated bands of hunting folk ranging all along the temperate

[1] For the evidence of this climatic change, within this period of time, in the domain of 'the Indus Culture', including Baluchistan as well as Sind and the Lower Panjab, see Marshall, Sir J.: *Mohenjo-Daro and the Indus Civilization* (London 1931, Probsthain, 3 vols.), vol. i, chapter i: 'The Country, Climate and Rivers.' The sister-stream of the Indus seems not to have dried up completely until the fourteenth century of the Christian Era (op. cit., loc. cit., p. 5); and its latter-day name is known to have been Mihran.

[2] Sir John Marshall (in op. cit., vol. i, pp. 4–5) suggests that the more abundant rain which gave Baluchistan and the Indus Valley a moister climate in the third millennium B.C. than they enjoy to-day is more likely to have been monsoon rain from the Indian Ocean than cyclone rain from the Atlantic.—A. J. T.

grassland of North Africa and Arabia and extending even into India on the one hand and into South-Eastern Spain on the other.'[1]

After the close of 'the Ice Age', our Afrasian area began to experience a profound physical change in the direction of desiccation; and simultaneously two or more civilizations arose in an area which had previously been occupied solely by primitive societies of the Palaeolithic order. Our archaeologists encourage us to look upon the desiccation of Afrasia as a challenge to which the geneses of these civilizations were responses.

'Now we are on the brink of the great revolution, and soon we shall encounter men who are masters of their own food-supply through possession of domesticated animals and the cultivation of cereals. It seems inevitable to connect that revolution with the crisis produced by the melting of the northern glaciers and consequent contraction of the Arctic high-pressure over Europe and diversion of the Atlantic rainstorms from the South Mediterranean zone to their present course across Central Europe.

'That event would certainly tax the ingenuity of the inhabitants of the former grassland zone to the utmost. . . .

'Faced with the gradual desiccation consequent upon the re-shift northward of the Atlantic cyclone belt as the European glaciers contracted, three alternatives were open to the hunting populations affected. They might move northward or southward with their prey, following the climatic belt to which they were accustomed; they might remain at home eking out a miserable existence on such game as could withstand the droughts, or they might—still without leaving their home-land—emancipate themselves from dependence on the whims of their environment by domesticating animals and taking to agriculture.'[2]

In the event, those hunting and food-gathering communities of the Afrasian grasslands that changed neither their habitat nor their way of life when they were challenged by the change in the climate, paid the penalty of extinction for their complete failure to respond. Those that avoided changing their habitat by changing their way of life and transforming themselves from hunters blindly wandering in pursuit of their game into shepherds skilfully leading their flocks on a seasonal orbit of migration, became the Nomads of the Afrasian Steppe. Their achievement and their fate will demand our atten-

---

[1] Childe, V. G.: *The Most Ancient East* (London 1928, Kegan Paul), ch. ii.

[2] Childe, op. cit., ch. iii. Cf. the same work, chapter ii, 'The Setting of the Stage', and chapter iii, 'The Oldest Farmers', *passim*. See further Huntington, Ellsworth: *Civilisation and Climate* (New Haven 1924, Yale University Press), ch. xiv, 'The Shifting of Climatic Zones'; and Caetani, Leone: *Studî di Storia Orientale*, vol. i (Milan 1911, Hoepli), ch. ii: 'L'Arabia Preistorica e il progressivo Essiccamento della Terra'. The link between the particular Egyptian and Sumeric responses to the particular challenge constituted by the desiccation of the Afrasian Steppe and the general conception of Challenge-and-Response will be found in the story of the Fall of Man in the Book of Genesis, with the quotations from Hesiod, Virgil, Origen, Volney, Huntington, and Myres which have been made, apropos of the story of the Fall, in II. C (ii) (b) 1, pp. 290-3, above.

tion hereafter.[1] Of those that elected to change their habitat rather than change their way of life, the communities which avoided the drought by following the cyclone belt as it shifted northward exposed themselves, unintentionally, to a new challenge—the challenge of the northern cold—which evoked a new creative response in such as did not succumb to it;[2] while the communities which avoided the drought by retreating southward into the monsoon belt[3] came under the soporific influence emanating from the climatic monotony of the Tropics.[4] Finally, there were communities that responded to the challenge of desiccation by changing their habitat and their way of life alike, and this rare double reaction was the dynamic act which created the Egyptiac and Sumeric civilizations out of the primitive societies of the vanishing Afrasian grasslands.

The change in these creative communities' way of life was the thoroughgoing transformation of food-gatherers into cultivators. The change in their habitat was small in point of distance but vast if measured by the difference in character between the grasslands which they abandoned and the new physical environment in which they made themselves at home. When the grasslands overlooking the lower valley of the Nile turned into the Libyan Desert and the grasslands overlooking the lower valley of the Tigris and Euphrates into the Rubʿ al-Khāli and the Dasht-i-Lūt, these heroic pioneers—inspired by audacity or by desperation—plunged into the jungle-swamps of the valley-bottoms, never before penetrated by Man, which their dynamic act was to turn into the Land of Egypt and the Land of Shinar. To their neighbours, who took the alternative courses described above, their venture must have seemed a forlorn hope; for, in the outlived age when the area that was now beginning to turn into the inhospitable Afrasian Steppe had been an earthly paradise,[5] the Nilotic and Mesopotamian jungle-swamp had been a forbidding and apparently impenetrable wilderness. As it turned out, the venture succeeded beyond the most sanguine hopes in which the pioneers can ever have indulged. The wantonness

---

[1] In Part III. A, vol. iii, pp. 7–22, below.

[2] See Dr. Ellsworth Huntington's parable, quoted in II. C (ii) (b) 1, on p. 292, above.

[3] For the traces left by these southward emigrants in the Great Rift Valley in East Africa, see Leakey, L. S. B.: *The Stone Age Cultures of Kenya Colony* (Cambridge 1931, University Press), especially chs. x and xi. For their supposed descendants who still survive, nearer home, in the tropical part of the Sudan, see the present chapter, pp. 312–13, below.

[4] See II. C (ii) (b) 1, p. 278, above, and II. D (i), vol. ii, pp. 26–8, below.

[5] 'Paradise' in the literal meaning of the Greek word παράδεισος, which is the transliteration of a Persian word signifying a stretch of savannah—a mixture of grassland and woodland abounding in game—which was artificially preserved in its virgin state in order to enable the dominant minority in an agrarian and urban society to enjoy, as a sport, the primitive occupation of hunting.

of Nature was subdued by the works of Man; the formless jungle-swamp made way for a pattern of ditches and embankments and fields; the Lands of Egypt and Shinar were reclaimed from the wilderness; the Egyptiac and Sumeric civilizations were created.

The simultaneous creation of the Egyptiac Civilization and of the Land of Egypt itself in the Lower Nile Valley, in response to the challenge presented by the gradual desiccation of the once hospitable regions round about, has been portrayed as follows by a distinguished Egyptologist:

'We are accustomed to regard Egypt as a paradise, as the most fertile country in the World, where, if we but scratch the soil and scatter seed, we have only to await and gather the harvest. The Greeks spoke of Egypt as the most fit place for the first generations of men, for there, they said, food was always ready at hand, and it took no labour to secure an abundant supply. But there can be no doubt that the Egypt of to-day is a very different place from the Egypt of pre-agricultural times. There has been a great, but gradual, change in the physical condition of the whole country. In the mortuary chapels of tombs of the Old and Middle Kingdoms, as well as in many of the Empire, are scenes of papyrus swamps and reed marshes; in these swamps and marshes are figured the animals and birds that then frequented them. Among the animals are the hippopotamus and the wild boar, the crocodile, the ibis, and a great variety of water-fowl. These animals, and some of the birds, have now disappeared from the region north of the First Cataract.[1] . . .

'Much is known about the ancient fauna of the desert wadies from the paintings and sculptured scenes in the tombs of the Old and Middle Kingdoms and of the Empire. On the walls of many of these tombs are depicted hunting scenes, and among the wild animals figured in them are the lion, leopard, Barbary sheep, wild ass, wild ox, hartebeest, oryx, ibex, addax, dorcas gazelle, fallow deer, giraffe, and ostrich. As several of these animals are not now known in Egypt it has been argued that the scenes do not faithfully represent the ancient fauna of the country. But I can see no reason to doubt that the scenes depict actual hunts that took place in the Arabian and Libyan Deserts not far from the localities in which the tombs figuring them are found. . . .

'At the present day all but one of the animals represented in these ancient hunting scenes are found in the Nubian Deserts to the south of Egypt. The exception is important; it is the fallow deer, which belongs

---

[1] Similarly, in the Indus Valley, there is evidence that, in the age when the city of Mohenjo-Daro was 'a going concern' (i.e. from the turn of the fourth and third millennia down to the middle of the third millennium B.C.), the region was inhabited by a moist-country fauna—the tiger, the rhinoceros, the elephant, but not the lion—which is not to be found there to-day. (Marshall, Sir John: *Mohenjo-Daro and the Indus Civilisation* (London 1931, Probsthain), vol. i, p. 2.) The works of Man tell the same story. At Mohenjo-Daro and the other sites of 'the Indus Culture', kiln-dried bricks have been employed at all exposed points (op. cit., loc. cit.). In the sites of this culture in Baluchistan, there are traces of dams in places where there is nowadays no water to catch (op. cit, vol. i, p. 3). In the Indus Valley itself, 'if there is one fact that stands out clear and unmistakable, it is that people must have lived in ever-present dread of the river'. (Op. cit., vol. i, p. 6).—A. J. T.

to the Holarctic, not to the Ethiopian, zoological zone. Although most of the animals that were hunted by the dynastic Egyptians have now disappeared from their northern home, many have been recorded in recent years as occurring in the Arabian and Libyan Deserts. We can, in fact, follow them gradually receding southwards. . . .

'Now the appearance of all these animals in Egypt and in its bordering deserts in dynastic times presupposes that the vegetation of the wadies was much more abundant then than now, and this again presupposes a greater rainfall than we find at present. . . .

'The characteristic wild trees of the dynastic flora of Egypt, as we know from the remains of them that have been found in the ancient tombs, were the heglik (*Balanites aegyptiaca*), the seyal (*Acacia seyal*), the sûnt (*Acacia nilotica*), the tamarisk (*Tamarix nilotica*), the nebak (*Zizyphus spina-Christi*), the sycomore-fig (*Ficus sycomorus*), and the moringa (*Moringa aptera*). The dom palm (*Hyphaene thebaica*) and the Dellach palm (*H. argun*) were also common. The heglik does not now grow wild north of Aswân, and, of the other trees, only the sûnt and the tamarisk are really common in the Lower Nile Valley. All these trees, however, now grow in abundance in the region north of the Atbara, and it is here, in what is called the Taka country, that we find also the fauna that was once so abundant in more northerly regions.

'But if the fauna and flora of the Arabian and Libyan Deserts in dynastic times approached more closely to that now seen in the Taka country, we have to go further south again for the earliest pre-dynastic fauna and flora of the Lower Nile Valley. This pre-dynastic fauna is particularly interesting, because, in addition to several of the animals already mentioned as occurring in dynastic times, we meet with others, such as the elephant, the kudu (*Streptoceros kudu*), the gerenuk gazelle (*Lithocranius walleri*), a species of *Sus* (which is certainly not the wild boar, i.e. *Sus scrofa*), and the marabou stork (*Leptoptilus crumenifer*). From the nature and habits of these mammals and birds it is evident that there must have been a considerable rainfall in the Valley of the Nile north of Aswân when they frequented Egypt. Dr. Anderson has referred to this subject in his monograph on the Reptilia of Egypt.[1] He notes that the physical features on both sides of the Nile "indicate the existence of a period long antecedent to the present, in which a considerable rainfall prevailed, as in the eroded valleys of the desert may be observed rocky ravines which have been carved out by the action of water, which has left behind it dry channels over which waterfalls had once precipitated themselves, and others down which cataracts once raced. The rainfall of the present is not sufficient to account for such a degree of erosion." This evidence sanctions the conclusion that a material change in the character of the climate of North-Eastern Africa, so far as its rainfall is concerned, has taken place since pre-dynastic days. The flora of the valley of the Lower Nile also points to the same conclusion. Dr. Schweinfurth has drawn attention to the fact that many plants, now known in Egypt only under cultivation, are found in the primeval

[1] A. Anderson, *Zoology of Egypt* (Reptilia), p. xlvi.

swamps and forests of the White Nile. He not unreasonably draws the inference that in ages long ago the entire Nile Valley exhibited a vegetation harmonising in its character throughout much more than at present. The papyrus swamps and reed marshes that lined the Lower Nile Valley in pre-agricultural days have been changed into peaceful fields, in which now grow the cereal grains, wheat and barley, and the other crops that have made Egypt famous as an agricultural country. It was the canalisation of the Valley, carried out by Man, and the consequent draining of the swamps and marshes, that displaced the ancient flora from its northern seat, and made it, as at the present day, only to be found hundreds of miles higher up the river. The land of Egypt has, in fact, been drained by Man; each foot of ground has been won by the sweat of his brow with difficulty from the swamp, until at last the wild plants and animals which once possessed it have been completely exterminated in it. The agricultural Egypt of modern times is as much a gift of Man as it is of the Nile.

'I have dwelt at some length on the ancient fauna and flora because I want to bring out as clearly as I can two facts concerning the Egypt of pre-agricultural days—the Egypt of the time before Man began to win the alluvial soil for the purposes of agriculture. (1) The aspect of the Lower Nile must have been very different from what it is now; it was a continuous line of papyrus swamps and marshes inhabited by hippopotami, wild boars, crocodiles, and immense flocks of wild-fowl of all kinds; it was singularly destitute of trees or plants that could be put to any useful purpose, and timber-trees were non-existent; its physical conditions resembled those prevailing on the banks of the White Nile to-day. (2) The deserts bordering the Lower Nile Valley on both sides were much more fertile, and their fauna and flora resembled that of the Taka country in Upper Nubia. Of the animals that frequented the wadies only the ass and the wild ox were capable of domestication. If Man inhabited Egypt in pre-agricultural times—and there is no valid reason to suppose that he did not—he probably lived a wandering life, partly hunter, partly herdsman, in the fertile wadies that bordered the valley, only going down to the river to fish or to fowl or to hunt the hippopotamus. In the valley itself there was certainly no pasture-land for supporting herds of large or small cattle.

'It was probably also in these wadies that agriculture was first practised in Egypt. Even at the present day a considerable number of Ababdeh roam the wadies of the Arabian Desert between Keneh and the Red Sea, where, at certain seasons of the year, there is fair pasturage for small flocks of sheep and goats. I have myself seen many of these people in the course of several journeys that I have undertaken to the Red Sea coast. Some of these Nomads sow a little barley and millet after a rainstorm, and then pitch their tents for a while till the grain grows, ripens, and can be gathered. They then move on again with their little flocks. What the Ababdeh do on a very small scale the Hadendoa of the Taka country do on a much greater one. If we turn to the Taka country we see there people living under much the same physical conditions as those which must have prevailed in the Arabian and Libyan Deserts in early times. The inhabitants of the Taka country are Hamite; and, as Professor Seligman has pointed out, the least modified of these people are physically identical with the pre-dynastic Egyptians of Upper Egypt. I would suggest that they, like the fauna and flora of ancient Egypt, receded southwards under the pressure of the advance of civilisation, and that the physical conditions of the country have preserved them to a great extent in their primitive life and pursuits. The picture of the Taka as Burckhardt draws it[1] would, I believe, describe almost equally well the earliest pre-dynastic Egyptians.'[2]

The foregoing testimony from an archaeologist may be supported by the following testimony from a physiographer, who, in the light of his own science, reconstructs as follows the original state of the lowest section of the Nile Valley, from Assuan to Cairo, and the original state of the Nile Delta:

'Where a silt-laden river inundates its flood-plain the greatest amount of deposition takes place along the banks, where the velocity is first checked, so that these are raised, and beyond them the country slopes away from the river; this is well shown in Upper Egypt, where there is a difference of up to 3 metres in height between the land by the river and that along the edge of the desert. Branches which leave the main stream flow out along this lower country, which in the natural state of the valley contains swamps and lagoons which are filled with water in the flood season and, being imperfectly drained, remain as waste tracts covered with swamp-loving plants. At an earlier period of the Nile Valley's history there must have been a belt of such land along the edge of the western desert which bounds it, and here and there traces of it still exist; the present Sohagia canal probably occupies the line of one of the branches of an earlier time, and the Bahr Yusef is certainly one, as it has all the characteristics of a stream meandering in its flood-plain.'[3]

'In the early times of ancient Egyptian history the delta was largely an area of marsh; the main arms, of which seven are recorded by Greek authors, divided into numerous branches and followed meandering courses to the sea. In the flood season all these overflowed their banks, depositing their load of silt to raise the delta and fill the low-lying depressions with water so that they remained as water-logged marshes throughout the year; the river arms and smaller water channels, until they were trained and embanked in much later times, eroded their banks, and cut across their bends to leave deep crescent-shaped lakes where their channels had formerly been, as is to be seen in all deltas of rivers which periodically rise in flood. At this period the larger settlements

---

[1] Burckhardt, *Travels in Nubia*, pp. 387 seqq.
[2] Newberry, P. E.: *Egypt as a Field for Anthropological Research* (British Association for the Advancement of Science, Report of the Ninety-first Meeting, Liverpool 1923, Presidential Address to Section H (London 1924, Murray), pp. 176–80). See also Meyer, E.: *Geschichte des Altertums*, 3rd edition, vol. i, part (ii) (Stuttgart and Berlin 1913, Cotta), pp. 57–8.
[3] Lyons, H. G.: *The Physiography of the River Nile and its Basin* (Cairo 1906, National Printing Department), p. 312.

must have been in the neighbourhood of the larger branches where sufficient high ground had been formed to provide areas of cultivable land, until the marshes became silted up, forming a plain suitable for cultivation.'[1]

Since a river can only have one delta, the state of Nature which the works of Man have effaced in the Delta of the Nile cannot be found extant now in any other part of the Nile Basin. On the other hand, the section of the Nile Valley which human interference with Nature has made into Upper Egypt is not without its counterparts farther up-stream, in regions where Nature still wears her original aspect to-day either because Man has never yet attempted to transform her or because she has succeeded, here, in defying his efforts and frustrating his purpose. The pre-human aspect of Nature along the Lower Nile, above the Delta, may be inferred to some extent from her present aspect along the Bahr-al-Jabal and the Bahr-az-Zaraf; and even her pre-human aspect in the Delta may perhaps be reflected, in some of its features, in the present aspect of the region round Lake No, where the Bahr-al-Jabal and the Bahr-al-Ghazal now mingle their 'Sudd'-laden waters.

'North of Gondokoro the Bahr-al-Jabal passes from its mountain tract to its plain tract and henceforth flows as a meandering stream in the flood plain which occupies the valley. . . . In this old flood plain the Bahr-al-Jabal has eroded a very shallow valley which it has since partially refilled, while the Bahr-az-Zaraf has carved out no valley but only the channel that it flows in. . . . The Bahr-al-Jabal flows down its valley with a very low slope . . . and all the features which it presents are those characteristic of such low grade streams carrying a small load of silt and situated in a tropical climate. The length of the Bahr-al-Jabal from Gondokoro to Lake No is about the same as that of the Nile Valley from Esna to Cairo, and . . . on the whole their respective valleys do not differ greatly in area.'[2]

The following description of the Bahr-al-Jabal Valley as it is to-day gives some idea of what the Lower Nile Valley must have been like when its terrors were first braved by the fathers of the Egyptiac Civilization:

'The scenery of the Bahr-al-Gabal throughout its course through the 'Sudd' region is monotonous to a degree. There are no banks at all, except at a few isolated spots, no semblance of any ridge on the water's edge. Reedy swamps stretch for many kilometres upon either side. Their expanse is only broken at intervals by lagoons of open water. Their surface is only a few centimetres above that of the water-level in the river when at its lowest, and a rise of half a metre floods them to an immense distance. These marshes are covered with a dense growth of water-weeds extending in every direction to the horizon. Of these reeds the

---

[1] Lyons, H. G., op. cit., p. 338.   [2] Lyons, H. G., op. cit., pp. 91–2.

principal is the papyrus, which grows in extreme luxuriance. The stems are so close together that it is difficult to force a way through them, and the plants reach a height of from 3 to 5 metres above the marsh. . . .

'Throughout this whole region, more especially between Bor and Lake No, it is extremely rare to see any sign of human life. Even hippopotami, which in the White Nile swarm, appear to shun the swamps of the Bahr-al-Gabal. Beyond a few night herons bird life is unrepresented, especially in the lower part of its course. The water, on the contrary, teems with fish, and crocodiles are constantly to be seen. The Bahr-al-Gabal has an evil name for mosquitoes, and one that is well deserved. With the disappearance of the sun they come forth in countless myriads, and make life a burden until the luminary reappears above the horizon. The whole region has an aspect of desolation beyond the power of words to describe. It must be seen to be understood. The dark-green masses of the papyrus which hedge in the channel, although possessing a certain gloomy beauty, become monotonous to the eye, when kilometre after kilometre is passed without any change in the aspect of the landscape. Even on the rare occasions when it is possible to see over this hedge no relief is experienced. In every direction the sea of vegetation extends without a break. An occasional stunted mimosa is welcomed as a landmark. The air is hot and steamy, while the whole region is malarious to a degree. No one can remain long in this portion of the river without experiencing a feeling of depression. Through these dreary marshes the river winds in a continual succession of loops and curves. As soon as one is passed another commences.'[1]

This picture may be supplemented by another which is equally graphic:

'The "sudd" (in Arabic *sadd* = block)[2] is a generic name by custom applied to the huge marshes through which the Bahr-al-Jabal, Bahr-al-Ghazal, Bahr-az-Zaraf and the lower portion of their tributaries wind their way. It forms an irregular triangle of which the northern base extends about 200 miles west from the mouth of the Bahr-az-Zaraf, and the southern apex lies about Bor, 250 miles S.S.E. of Lake No. It is difficult to estimate the area of these vast marshes, but it cannot be much less than 35,000 [square] miles. . . .

'A great part of this area is covered with a shallow sheet of water, over almost the whole extent of which thick reeds and swamp-grasses have sprung up. Except in the actual river channels this water is probably nowhere more than 2 to 6 feet deep.

'To the eye the effect is one of a vast extent of brilliant green papyrus, feathery reeds and sword grass, 5 to 15 feet above the water, broken by occasional patches of light ambach trees, with channels of water, pools and lagoons dotting the "swamp-scape", and here and there a sparse tree

---

[1] Garstin, Sir William: *Report upon the Basin of the Upper Nile*, enclosed in a dispatch from His Majesty's Agent and Consul-General at Cairo = Egypt No. 2 (1904) = Cmd. 2165 (London 1904, H.M. Stationery Office), pp. 98–9.

[2] For an expert account of the formation of the 'Sudd', see Sir W. Garstin, op. cit., pp. 117–18.—A. J. T.

or two on the horizon. Occasionally, and more especially towards the south, ridges, or patches of mud or solid ground, are visible, and in such parts there is much bird and animal life. In the lower (northern) reaches of the Sudd nearly all signs of life—except the brilliant little bee-eater, an occasional heron, fish-eagle, or "anvil-bird", the ubiquitous crocodile, and, of course, the insects—disappear; but in the more southerly parts are found many varieties of game.

'On the Bahr-al-Jabal, for the first 150 miles south of Lake No there are no human inhabitants visible. Thereafter occasional Dinkas and their villages are seen up to about Bor (384 miles); whilst beyond this the Bari country commences, the population as the Lado Enclave is approached being considerably thicker on the east than on the west bank. The Bahr-al-Ghazal swamps and banks are almost uninhabited.'[1]

They are uninhabited because the people who live on their out-skirts are not confronted here and now, as the fathers of the Egyptiac Civilization were confronted when they were squatting on the borders of the Lower Nile Valley some five or six thousand years ago, with the hard choice between plunging into the for-bidding 'Sudd' and clinging to an ancestral habitat in process of transformation from an earthly paradise into an inhospitable desert. If our scholars are right in their surmise, the forefathers of these people who now live on the margin of the 'Sudd' were living, in what is now the Libyan Desert, cheek by jowl with the fathers of the Egyptiac Civilization, at the time when these responded to the challenge of desiccation by making their momentous choice. At that time, it would seem, the forefathers of the modern Dinka and Shilluk parted company with their heroic neighbours and followed the line of least resistance by retreating southwards to a country where they could continue to live, without changing their way of life, in physical surroundings partly identical with those to which they were accustomed.[2] They settled in the tropical part of the Sudan, within the range of the treacherously genial equatorial rains; and here their descendants remain to this day, living, on the out-skirts of the Bahr-al-Jabal 'Sudd', the self-same life that their forefathers lived, on the outskirts of the Lower Nile 'Sudd', in com-mon with the fathers of the Egyptiac Civilization, some thousands of years ago, before the Afrasian paradise was turned into a desert

[1] Gleichen, Lord Edward: *The Anglo-Egyptian Sudan: A Compendium prepared by Officers of the Sudan Government* (London 1905, H.M. Stationery Office, 2 vols.), vol. i, pp. 299–300.

[2] The identity was partial and not complete; for while the climate, past and present, of the Equatorial Zone resembles the prehistoric climate of the zone which has now become the Afrasian Steppe in respect of enjoying that sufficiency of rainfall with which the Afrasian area has now ceased to be blessed, there are also differences which are no less important in their effects on human life—and this altogether to the disadvantage of the inhabitants of Equatoria. The rain-bringing cyclones which used to pass over Afrasia during 'the Ice Age' gave the local climate a stimulating rigour and variety which must have been the antithesis, in its effects on Human Nature, to the soporific monotony of the rain-bringing monsoons. (See above, pp. 303–4.)

by Nature and the Lower Nile 'Sudd' into a cradle of civilization by Man.

In their new home, the sluggish and unambitious emigrants found what their soul desired. They had successfully transferred their habitat from a changing environment to a static environment in which nothing was destined to happen to them or to their descendants for the next five or six thousand years:

'On the Upper Nile there dwell to-day people allied to the oldest Egyptians in appearance, stature, cranial proportions, language and dress. These are ruled by rain-maker magicians or by divine kings who were until recently ritually slain, and the tribes are organised in totemic clans. The Shilluk, ruled by a centralised king with animal (i.e. totem) ancestry who was ritually slain, illustrate a stage immediately prior to the divine monarchy of Menes. A still older phase is seen among the Dinka: they are a congeries of autonomous totemic clans, often at war with one another, and each ruled by a "rain-maker" who was ceremonially killed before old age overtook him. It really looks as if among these tribes on the Upper Nile social development had been arrested at a stage that the Egyptians had traversed before their history began. There we have a living museum whose exhibits supplement and vivify the prehistoric cases in our collections.'[1]

This living museum, furnished by the Shilluk and Dinka societies of to-day, stands next door to the inanimate museum, constituted by the jungle-swamp of the Bahr-al-Jabal and the Bahr-al-Ghazal, which we have just been studying; and here again, in this juxtaposition of Primitive Man and Virgin Nature, the present faithfully reproduces the past. Just so, some five or six thousand years ago, the fathers of the Egyptiac Civilization (perhaps accompanied by the forefathers of the Dinka and the Shilluk before the parting of their ways) were squatting on the edge of the jungle-swamp which at that time occupied the Lower Nile Valley and the Delta.

This parallel between earlier conditions in one part of the Nile Basin and present conditions in another part invites certain speculations. Supposing that the challenge of desiccation had never been presented to the human inhabitants of the Nile Basin in those parts of it which, under our present climatic conditions, are beyond the pale of the equatorial rains: in that event, would the Delta and the Lower Valley of the Nile have been left in that original state of Nature—a wilderness of jungle and swamp and 'Sudd'—from which the valleys of the Bahr-al-Jabal and the Bahr-al-Ghazal have never been redeemed? And would Egypt never have been made nor the

[1] Childe, V. G.: *The Most Ancient East* (London 1928, Kegan Paul), pp. 10–11. For a detailed description of the life of these primitive Nilotic peoples at the present day, see Seligman, C. G. and B. Z.: *Pagan Tribes of the Nilotic Sudan* (London 1932, Routledge).

Egyptiac Civilization have arisen? What would have happened, then, to the descendants of those heroic pioneers who actually made themselves the fathers of the Egyptiac Civilization by descending, in response to the challenge of desiccation, into the valley of the shadow of death? Would nothing have happened to them at all? Would they be squatting, still, upon the edges of an untamed Lower Nile Valley, in that primitive state of society in which the Shilluk and the Dinka are living, now, upon the edges of an untamed Bahr-al-Jabal? And there is another line of speculation which concerns not the past but the future. We may remind ourselves that, on the time-scale of the universe or of our planet or of Life or even of the *Genus Homo*, a span of five or six thousand years is an almost negligible lapse of time—as brief as the twinkling of an eye.[1] Supposing that another challenge, as formidable as that which presented itself to the inhabitants of the Lower Nile Basin yesterday, at the end of 'the Ice Age', were to present itself to the inhabitants of the Upper Nile Basin to-morrow: is there any reason to believe that these are incapable of responding, on this hypothetical occasion, by some equally dynamic act which might have equally creative effects?

We need not require that this hypothetical challenge to the Shilluk and the Dinka in our time shall be the same in kind as the historic challenge which was presented some five or six thousand years ago to the fathers of the Egyptiac Civilization. Indeed, there seems no reason to expect, in any near future, a desiccation of Equatorial Africa which might challenge the inhabitants of the tropical Sudan to master the Bahr-al-Jabal 'Sudd' and there to re-enact the genesis of the Egyptiac Civilization by creating a second Egypt on the upper reaches of the same great river. So let us imagine that, this time, the challenge in the Nile Basin comes not from the physical but from the human environment—not from a transformation of the local climate but from the intrusion of an alien civilization. Is not this very challenge actually being presented, under our eyes, to the primitive societies of Tropical Africa by the impact of our own Western Civilization—a human agency which, in our generation, is playing the mythical role of Mephistopheles towards every other extant civilization and towards every extant primitive society on the face of the Earth? This challenge is still so recent in our time that we cannot yet forecast the ultimate response that any of the challenged societies will make to it. All that we can tell for certain is that they are being subjected to an impact of immense dynamic energy. Assuredly the Shilluk and the Dinka have never been exposed to any challenge of the

[1] On this point, see I. C (iii) (e), Annex, *ad fin.*, and II. C (ii) (a) 1, pp. 233-8, above.

same order of magnitude since the time, some five or six thousand years ago, when their forefathers (if our modern Western scholars have guessed aright) evaded the challenge of desiccation by migrating towards the Equator through fifteen or twenty degrees of latitude. How will these primitive societies respond this time? We can only say (in contradiction to the doctrine of 'Original Sin') that the failure of the fathers to respond to one challenge, even if such failure were proven, would not predispose the children to fail in face of another challenge when their own hour came. It is not inconceivable that the challenge of Westernization may evoke from the Shilluk and the Dinka in our day a response as creative in its effects, though not necessarily of at all the same kind, as the response which the challenge of desiccation evoked from the fathers of the Egyptiac Civilization in the fifth or the fourth millennium B.C.

The Genesis of the Sumeric Civilization

Having studied the genesis of the Egyptiac Civilization at some length, we shall find ourselves able to deal with the genesis of the Sumeric Civilization much more briefly; for we shall be dealing with a challenge which was identic and with a response which was the same in kind. The desiccation of Afrasia, which impelled the fathers of the Egyptiac Civilization to penetrate the jungle-swamp of the Lower Nile Valley and transform it into the Land of Egypt, likewise impelled the fathers of the Sumeric Civilization to come to grips with the jungle-swamp in the Lower Valley of the Tigris and Euphrates and transform it into the Land of Shinar. The material aspects of these two geneses of civilizations almost coincide. In both challenges we find the same two material elements: the increasing inhospitality of the Afrasian grasslands as they changed into steppe and desert, and the ever forbidding wilderness of rank vegetation and treacherous water. In both responses we find the same material results: a new landscape of ditches and embankments and fields, in which the original face of Nature has been utterly transfigured by the works of Man. The spiritual characteristics of the two resultant civilizations—their religion, their art, and even their social life—display much less similarity: another indication that, in the field of our studies, identic causes cannot be presumed, *a priori*, to produce identic effects.

The ordeal through which the fathers of the Sumeric Civilization passed is commemorated in Sumeric legend. The slaying of the dragon Tiamat by the God Marduk and the creation of the World out of her mortal remains signifies the subjugation of the primeval wilderness and the creation of the Land of Shinar by the canalization of the waters and the draining of the soil. The story of the Flood records Nature's revolt against the shackles which Man's audacity had placed upon her. In the Biblical version (a literary heritage of the Jews from their exile by the waters of Babylon), 'the Flood' has been a household word in our Western Society ever since its genesis. It has remained for our modern Western archaeologists first to unearth and decipher the original version of the legend as it crystallized in its homeland, and latterly to find direct material evidence of a particular flood of abnormal severity in a thick layer of flood-laid clay which intervenes between the earliest and the later strata deposited by human habitation on the sites of certain historic seats of the Sumeric culture.

Besides this direct material evidence for an exceptional calamity, in the shape of a flood, with which the fathers of the Sumeric Civilization once had to contend, the Basin of the Tigris and Euphrates, like the Basin of the Nile, displays for our observation a museum in which we can study the normal aspect of inanimate Nature in the wilderness which Man has transformed into the Land of Shinar, as well as the life that was lived in this wilderness by the first Sumeric pioneers. In the Land of the Two Rivers, however, this museum is not to be found, as in the Nile Basin, by travelling up-stream.[1] On the contrary, it lies in a new delta, at the head of the Persian Gulf, which has been laid down by the confluence of the sister streams in times posterior not only to the genesis of the Sumeric Civilization but to its extinction, and also to the extinction of its Babylonic successor. The marshes which have come into existence gradually, during the last two or three thousand years, in the triangle of territory in Lower 'Irāq between 'Amārah on the Tigris and Nāsirīyah on the Euphrates and Basrah on the Shatt-al-'Arab, have remained in their virgin state because, from their formation down to this day, no human society with the will or the power to master them has appeared on the scene. The marshmen by whom they are haunted have learnt to adapt themselves to this forbidding environment in a passive way (as witness their nickname, 'the web-feet', which they received from the British soldiers who encountered them during the General War of 1914–18), but they have never yet girded themselves for the task,

[1] In the geography of the Tigris and Euphrates Basin, 'Irāq, from the head of the Persian Gulf up to the neighbourhood of Hit on the Euphrates and a point in the same latitude on the Tigris, corresponds to Egypt from the coast of the Mediterranean to Assuan; the barren tract through which the two rivers run between reaching these points and leaving the Armenian highlands corresponds to Nubia; the highlands of Armenia and Kurdistan, in which the two rivers and their principal tributaries take their rise, correspond to the highlands of Abyssinia and British East Africa; but there is nothing in the Basin of the Tigris and Euphrates that corresponds to the 'Sudd'-choked valleys of the Bahr-al-Jabal and the Bahr-al-Ghazal.

which the fathers of the Sumeric Civilization accomplished in the immediate vicinity some five or six thousand years ago, of transfiguring the marshes into a network of canals and fields.

Here is a description, by a recent Western observer, of this latter-day wilderness and its human denizens:

'Soon branching off from our arrow-straight waterway, we began to wind once more among reeds which grew taller, until we were surrounded by *mardi*, the giant of the marshes, which provides the *Ma'dan* with their long *mashhuf*-poles; here it towered above our heads to a height of twenty-five feet. Slowly we threaded our way among these silent, stately monarchs of the waste, until, suddenly breaking through the gloom, we came out upon a wide sea of sunny open water, blue as the Mediterranean and covered with white-crested waves. The wind, which in the shelter of the *mardi* we had not felt, was here blowing freshly, and Haji Rikkan had doubts as to the wisdom of attempting to cross; for the loss of a marsh boat in these squalls of wind is by no means infrequent. In the end he decided to skirt the edge of the reeds, and with a pious "We are in the hands of Allah" gave the word to cross. Rocking and tossing, and shipping a good deal of water, we reached the other side in safety, and slid into the calm waters of a channel which wound between walls of *shabab*, the stout but pliable reed from which the marshman makes the arched frame-work of his hut. Only the waving of their silver feathery heads showed that above the shelter of our little channel the wind blew as strongly as before.

'Always changing from hour to hour as we penetrated more and more deeply into its heart, yet always the same, the quiet marsh opened its waterways to receive us. Like some Belle Dame sans Merci, it seemed to beckon us on and on, ever revealing fresh beauties, yet closing fast the way of retreat. Its towering ramparts rose silently behind us as though, having once laid bare the wonders of its inmost hidden life, the marsh would keep us for ever in its embrace, lest we should go forth again and tell the secret of its winds and waters to the world outside. . . .

'In front, the friendly reeds seemed to open of themselves to provide a way for us; behind, they closed their ranks in dark and threatening masses against the sky, as though prepared to oppose our return. The scream of an unseen bird might echo across the stillness, or a startled beating of wings die away as suddenly as it had arisen; then once more silence held the marsh. Here the reeds were taller; old, thick, and towering masses, so far from any marsh settlements that they had never been disturbed by Man seeking material for hut-building, for buffalo fodder, or for mats. The solitude was intense—more intense than that of the desert. There countless tracks reveal the presence of man or beast, but here the flowering weeds close up again, leaving no trace. Only very rarely did we come across a few reeds twisted together and bent—a landmark or wordless message from a marshman to his fellows, seeming only to intensify the lonely silence of the wilderness.

'When at last we came upon a settlement of marsh-dwellers, it was a village so small, so remote from the river, that at first sight of us the men seized their rifles and leapt in among the reeds, from the shelter of which they could best defend their homes. . . .

'The ground on which I stepped was covered with broken pottery, some unglazed, some a bright sky-blue. Fragments of all shapes and sizes lay jumbled together, with here and there a flat square brick inscribed with cuneiform symbols.'[1]

Those relics of the Sumeric Civilization in the untamed wilderness bore silent but eloquent witness to the dynamic acts which, in the language of Sumeric Mythology, were once performed by the god Marduk who slew the dragon Tiamat,[2] and by the hero Uta-Napishtim who built his ark in anticipation of the Flood and kept her afloat on the waste of waters when the great inundation came.

The Genesis of the Sinic Civilization

If we consider, next, the genesis of the Sinic Civilization in the Lower Valley of the Yellow River, we shall find its explanation in a human response to a challenge from Physical Nature which was perhaps even more severe than the challenge of the Two Rivers or the challenge of the Nile. In the wilderness which Man once transfigured into the cradle of the Sinic Civilization, the ordeal of marsh and bush and flood was capped by the ordeal of a temperature which varied seasonally to severe extremes of summer heat and winter cold. The fathers of the Sinic Civilization do not seem to have differed in race from the peoples occupying the vast region to the south and south-west which extends from the Yellow River to the Brahmaputra and from the Tibetan Plateau to the China Sea.[3] If certain members of this wide-spread race created a civilization while the rest remained culturally sterile, the explanation may be that a creative faculty, latent in all alike, was evoked in those particular members, and in those only, by the presentation of a challenge to which the rest did not happen to be exposed. The challenge and response which gave birth to the Sinic Civilization are depicted by a distinguished Western Sinologist as follows:

'The Chinese would appear to be the northernmost branch of the sedentary agricultural peoples whose western branch is formed by the Tibeto-Burman tribes of Tibet, Sechwan and Yunnan (Tibetans, Lolos, Mossos, Burmans, &c.), its southern branch by the Thai in the south of China and in the north of Indo-China, and its central branch by the Miao-tse of Hunan and Kweichow.

---

[1] 'Fulanain': *Haji Rikkan, Marsh Arab* (London 1927, Chatto & Windus), pp. 24–5 and 249–50.
[2] The superhuman effort of breaking in the River with embankments and forbidding the angry waters to break their way out again is vividly conveyed in the story of Abu Mā'itayn ('The Father of Two Dead Men') in op. cit., pp. 85–93.
[3] On this point, see II. C (ii) (a) 1, p. 236, above.

'None of these related peoples with a more southerly habitat are likely to have had so rough a life as the Chinese must have had since the dawn of the historical period. It was probably in the great plain of the North-East, between the sea and the escarpment which forms the [eastern] boundary of the Shansi Plateau, that the Chinese began to develop their civilisation. It was from there that this civilisation hived off, at that remote epoch, towards the west into the fine valley of the Wei and thence along the Fen into the little basins of Shansi, and towards the south in the direction of the Hwai and the River Han and the mountains leading over into the immense basin where the River Han falls into the Yangtse.

'The climate of this region was extremely severe: sultry in summer, icy in winter, while the spring was ushered in by storms of chilly wind, laden with sand, which were even more cruel than the great winter cold. The rivers, which all through the winter were frozen or at any rate choked with floating ice, thawed rapidly at the first fine weather and became transformed almost immediately into torrents; and all this combined to make communications difficult during more than a third of the year. The great artery, the Yellow River, with its rapids and sandbanks, is dangerous to navigate; its innumerable branches wandered off capriciously across the low, level plains, where there is hardly any fall. This was the country which was called the Nine Rivers, because, it was said, the Yellow River had there nine principal branches. It extended over a broad zone at the foot of the Shansi Plateau; for its course at that time was different from its present course, and it proceeded, after a long detour, to flow out into the sea along the present course of the Pei-ho, in the neighbourhood of Tientsin.

'Every year, moreover, the floods changed the river's course and sought new channels; the shallows became water-logged and turned into great swamps . . . some of which still remain in existence to-day. These swamps were jungles of water plants, giving shelter to wild geese and cranes and swarming with fish. They were surrounded by belts, varying in width, of land which was too wet for agriculture and which was covered with a tall grassy vegetation broken by thickets of white elms, plums and chestnuts. This was not real forest: that was only to be found on the periphery of the region, on the slopes of the mountains, on the east in Shantung, on the west in Shansi; and the line where the forest began marked the beginning of the domain of the barbarians. [The Sinic wilderness was not a forest but] was a thick bush, haunted by wild beasts—tigers, panthers, wild cats, leopards, bears, wild cattle, even elephants and rhinoceroses, wolves, wild boars, foxes—as well as by game of all kinds, herds of stags and antelopes, monkeys, hares, rabbits and birds of every species. . . .

'Only the fringes were "broken in" (*aménagées*)—either into pastures for domesticated horses and cattle or into mulberry-plantations for breeding silk-worms. The best lands, which were protected against the floods by dykes and were regularly cultivated, produced millet and sorghum in Chihli, rice to the south of the Yellow River, and some wheat more or less everywhere. Haricot beans, gourds, indigo, and hemp were also made to grow. . . .

'It was not without toil and trouble, however, that the Chinese countryside had been successfully "broken in" like this, in face of the extreme difficulties with which Nature confronted the pioneers. All these fine fields of millet, rice, and wheat had had to be conquered by the pioneers, in the sweat of their brow, from the bush and from the waters. . . . The process had been long and cruel. Dykes had had to be built as bulwarks against the floods, canals had had to be dug to drain the swamps and turn them into dry land. All these works were so ancient that the memory of them was lost in the fog of Legend. They were attributed to the heroes of remote antiquity. At the beginning of things, the heroes had come down from Heaven to Earth to set the Earth in order, in accordance with the instructions of the Lord above, and to make it possible for Mankind to inhabit it.'[1]

If we want to see with our own eyes what the future site of China once looked like before China herself was brought into existence by Chinese labour, we may catch a glimpse of this long-vanished scene by travelling northwards from the basin of the Yellow River to the basin of the Amur—the next, in this direction, of the great river-systems of Eastern Asia—and alighting among the swamps that fringe Lake Khanka, at the head-waters of the River Ussuri. For this swampy valley, hemmed in by forest-clad mountains, remains to-day not far removed from the virgin state in which the Chinese found the valley-bottoms of Shensi when they first won them for the plough from the woodland barbarians.

'The Ussuri District is mainly woodland. Open plains are to be found only in the valleys of the larger rivers: on the banks of the Ussuri itself and along the lower courses of its right-bank tributaries and on the shores of Lake Khanka. The higher one goes up into the mountains, the rarer become the patches that are suitable for agricultural settlement. There are merely isolated clearings, at long distances from one another; and beyond these there stretches the gloomy Taiga, unending, wild, and desolate.

'In these woods the day dawns late and the sun only penetrates feebly through the thick lace-work of branches. The perpetual twilight of this wilderness exhales a damp chill, and the forest prison-house oppresses the spirit. In these surroundings the eye soon grows weary and longs for a free field of vision.

'Even the most audacious hunter and forester who dives into the gorges of the Sikhote Alin Range feels, in spite of himself, a secret terror in face of these uncanny, gigantic tracts of primeval forest. The endlessness and tracklessness of the Taiga, the storms, the floods, the intolerable plagues of insects, the wild beasts, the occasional dearth of game, and a host of other dangers—mostly encountered without warning

[1] Maspéro, H.: *La Chine Antique* (Paris 1927, Boccard), pp. 20–6.

—often seal the doom of isolated adventurers who have the hardihood to take up the struggle with Nature in a region where Nature interposes her veto.

'In the southern part of the Ussuri District the flora of the Taiga is extraordinarily rich in variety and magnificent in the spectacle which it presents. The spectator is taken by surprise at the intermingling of tropical and northern species. His vision is overwhelmed and confounded by the exuberance of this luxuriant growth and by the sight of butterflies hovering round flowers and blossoms: a feature which a European hardly expects to see here in this corner of Siberia. The tangled thickets of this virgin primeval forest are almost impassable. They catch and crush the explorer at every step as he painfully edges his way through them; and they hide the game from his eyes until he has come within a few paces of it, when the creature starts up from its lair and tears away before the startled wanderer's face, through crackling sticks and rustling bush.'[1]

The Geneses of the Mayan and Andean Civilizations

While the Egyptiac and Sumeric and Sinic civilizations were responses to the challenges of drought and flood and swamp and thicket, the challenge to which the Mayan Civilization was a response was the luxuriance of the tropical forest:

'The Mayan culture was made possible by the agricultural conquest of the rich lowlands where the exuberance of Nature can only be held in check by organized effort. On the highlands the preparation of the land is comparatively easy, owing to scanty natural vegetation and a control vested in irrigation. On the lowlands, however, great trees have to be felled and fast-growing bushes kept down by untiring energy. But when Nature is truly tamed she returns recompense many fold to the daring farmer. Moreover, there is reason to believe that the removal of the forest cover over large areas affects favourably the conditions of life which under a canopy of leaves are hard indeed.'[2]

This challenge of the tropical forest, which called the Mayan Civilization into existence in one part of the New World, was offered to no effect on the other side of the Isthmus and the Equator. The civilization which arose in South America was a response, not to a challenge from the forests of the Amazon Basin,[3]

---

[1] Arsenjew, W. K.: *Russen und Chinesen in Ostsiberien* (German translation: Berlin 1926, Scherl), pp. 14–15.
[2] Spinden, H. J.: *Ancient Civilisations of Mexico and Central America* (New York 1917, American Museum of Natural History, Handbook Series, No. 3), p. 65. The fact that 'the highest native American civilization grew up in one of the worst physical environments of the whole Western Hemisphere' is likewise noted by Dr. Ellsworth Huntington (in *The Climatic Factor as illustrated in Arid America* (Washington 1914, Carnegie Institution of Washington, Publication No. 192), on p. 220). For Dr. Huntington's attempt to explain this fact—which in his view is a paradox—by the hypothesis of a periodical shifting of climatic zones, see II. D (vii), Annex I, vol. ii, below.
[3] See, however, II. C (ii) (a) 2, p. 259, footnote 1, above, for the actual cultural achievements of the inhabitants of Amazonia.

but to the two quite different challenges of the Andean Plateau and the adjoining Pacific Coast.

'In no other region of the World have the forces of Nature played a more formative part in human history. . . . In the Andean area Man has always been if not the slave at any rate the pupil of that exigent mistress, Mother Nature; and his history has largely consisted of varyingly successful struggles against many of her enactments.'[1]

The modern observer from the United States, here quoted, thus describes the upland basin of Lake Titicaca in the neighbourhood of Tiahuanaco—the deserted city whose stupendous masonry is the most notable of all the earlier monuments of the Andean Civilization on the Plateau:

'The locality is not, at any rate to-day, one that seems propitious to the development of high civilisation. A flattish valley, gray to red in hue, sodden with stagnant water in many places, hemmed in by rounded hills, grim in their sterile grayness, a zinc-coloured sky that seems to weigh upon one's very head, and a prevailing sombreness and faintness of daylight—these go to make up the scene in the vicinity of Tiahuanaco as I saw it. . . . Far off to the west and south, snow-clad peaks of the Eastern Cordillera—Sorata, Huayna Potosí and Illampu—bite into the sky with glistening white teeth. The traveller looks upon it all and sees that the keynote of that land is majesty, distinctly cold and grim, but majesty all the same, and very seldom tempered by any softer or more genial note.'[2]

The same observer thus describes the Coast, as seen first from the sea and then from the air:

'Lengthwise of the sea-board, where long, unhurrying rollers ceaselessly roar amid a haze of their own making, stretch fifteen hundred miles of barren desert, interspersed with westward-dipping streaks of green, nestling in valley-bottoms. . . . The traveller voyaging along this weirdly exquisite shore gazes long upon the somewhat awful grandeur of these plains, half-unconsciously begins to seek, and with satisfaction finds evidences of Man's presence and of his industry, crowded for the most part into richly verdant valleys wherein winding rivers flow tranquilly through fields of cotton, maize and other crops, and through groves of fruit trees, all of which combine to make a little world hemmed in by high bright bluffs, margins of the deserts beyond. . . . In order really to grasp the essential character of that wondrous sea-board, one must view it from the air. Seen from aloft, its conformation, so bewildering to earth-bound wanderers, becomes exquisitely simple; the puzzling jumble of hills, bluffs and hillocks smooth themselves out into sand-clad

---

[1] Means, P. A.: *Ancient Civilisations of the Andes* (London 1931, Scribner), p. 415.
[2] Means, op. cit., pp. 129-30. The writer qualifies his description by suggesting that 'perhaps at seasons of the year other than November, when the rainy-season is on, the landscape is less forlorn and repellent'.

undulations of merely local importance and combine to form a westward-tilted desert plain crossed frequently from east to west by river-nurtured strips of green—the justly celebrated coastal valleys of Peru.'[1]

Thus, on the Plateau, the fathers of the Andean Civilization were challenged by a bleak climate and a grudging soil; on the Coast they were challenged by the heat and drought of an almost rainless equatorial desert at sea-level, which could only be made to blossom as the rose by the works of Man. The pioneers of civilization on the Coast conjured their oases out of the desert by husbanding the scanty waters that descended from the western scarp of the Plateau and giving life to the plains by irrigation.[2] The pioneers on the Plateau transformed their mountain-sides into fields by husbanding the scanty soil on terraces preserved by an ubiquitous system of laboriously constructed retaining walls.[3]

The Genesis of the Minoan Civilization

We have now explained, in terms of responses to challenges from the physical environment, the geneses of five out of our six 'unrelated' civilizations. The sixth, which we have called the Minoan Civilization, was a response to a physical challenge which we have not yet encountered in this survey: the challenge of the Sea.

The map shows at a glance that the region in which the Minoan Civilization arose has experienced, in an age not very remote from the present on the scale of geological time, a physical catastrophe from which the regions round about have been exempt. The Aegean lies in a zone of exceptional geological formation, and within that zone the Aegean itself is an exception to the local rule.

In the zone to which the Aegean belongs, the crust of the Earth has been folded into mountain ranges, like some giant's blanket which has been ruckled up by the uneasy movements of the sleeper beneath. Starting from the Pamir Plateau—'the Roof of the World' and the navel of Asia—the folds run westward, now diverging and now converging, now straightening out and now bending back upon themselves, until the furthest range reaches the remote Atlantic. One fold runs through the Suleyman Mountains and the Zagros and the Taurus and the Pindus and the Dinaric Alps; another through the Hindu Kush and the Elbruz and the northern escarpments of the Armenian and Anatolian plateaux, to reappear in Thrace as the Istranja; yet another runs through the Balkans of Transcaspia and through the Caucasus and the Crimea and the Balkans of Europe and the Carpathians and the Alps and the Appennines and the Atlas, recoils from the Ocean at the Pillars of

---

[1] Op. cit., pp. 7–9.   [2] See Means, op. cit., pp. 11 and 24.
[3] See Means, op. cit., fig. 145, opposite p. 241.

Hercules, and sweeps back, right round the geologically older core of Spain, through Granada and the Balearic Islands and the Pyrenees, before it reconciles itself to finding its term at last at Cape Finisterre.

This long-drawn-out and tortuous bunch of folded mountains stands out in contrast to the comparatively featureless Eurasian and Afrasian regions, north and south of it, in which the strata are tilted here and there out of the horizontal plane but are nowhere contorted. On the north, the great Eurasian plain stretches from the Kirghiz Steppes to the Netherlands with a hardly perceptible undulation at the Urals; on the south, the Afrasian terrace runs parallel to the zone of folding like a loosely-laid pavement of huge, uneven, ill-fitting slabs: the Deccan, Arabia, Libya. By contrast to these planes and peneplanes on either flank, the zone of folding presents, on a bird's-eye view, an appearance of homogeneity and continuity throughout its length from the Pamirs to the Atlantic; but this appearance breaks down under a practical test; and the sector in which it breaks down is the Aegean.

Let us now imagine that some primitive society has made itself at home among the mountain-folds towards the eastern end of the zone, in Iran; and let us imagine, further, that, having adapted themselves to this particular physical environment, these people are then impelled or compelled to expand or migrate. In what direction will they seek an outlet? Presumably they will follow the line of least resistance; and this will not lead them into the low-lands, where their special asset of adaptation to a highland environment would give them no advantage in a contest with the peoples already in possession. If they follow the line of least resistance they will move neither northward nor southward into the plains but either eastward or westward along the mountain-zone itself, where they can change their dwelling-place without changing their environment. If, however, they move eastward, they will soon be brought to a halt by the blank wall which bears up 'the Roof of the World'. By a process of elimination, therefore, we are left to imagine them moving through the mountain-zone in a westerly direction: from Iran into Armenia and from Armenia into Anatolia. In these first stages of their movement they will find themselves everywhere at home; they will meet with no challenge from Physical Nature which they have not already met and mastered in their Iranian homeland; but when they gird up their loins for the next stage in their westward march, which should lead them on from the mountain-folds of Asia Minor into those of South-Eastern Europe, they will stumble, in the Aegean, upon a barrier which has never stood in their path before.

In the Aegean, by contrast with the two continents between which it intervenes, the process of folding has not been the last event in geological history. A second process, the process of subsidence, has here come into play. The exact relation between these two geological phenomena has not yet been quite clearly established by our modern Western scientists; but it seems probable that it is a relation of cause and effect and that subsidence is an outcome of folding where folding has gone to extremes. Apparently the strain imposed by an extreme degree of folding upon the upheaved and contorted strata of the Earth's crust cracks and snaps the crust along lines transverse to the lines of folding, until the pressure is relieved by the subsidence of an entire cross-section to a level which permits an overlap between its broken edges and the corresponding broken ends of the undisturbed strata on either side of the rift. The still upstanding sections expand into, without closing, the void which the collapse of the intermediate section has created; and the first impression which the resulting formation makes upon the eye is as if these upstanding sections, which now face one another across a gulf, had originally been in contact, end to end, and had afterwards drawn apart. The same mountain-folds that traverse the face of the Earth in Asia from the Pamirs to the east coast of the Aegean are seen to traverse it in Europe from the west coast of the Aegean to the Atlantic. Each range that breaks off abruptly at one coast can be identified with some range that begins with equal abruptness at the other. The pattern stands out clear; but the very features which make it clear are also evidence that the first visual impression of an original contact between the two continental coasts is an illusion. We are able to identify range with range in Asia and in Europe just because the intervening sections of these ranges, which have subsided below sea-level in the Aegean, have not vanished without leaving a memorial. The missing link is supplied by the mountain peaks which still hold their heads above water in chains of islands to point the way from continent to continent. Thus the eye is carried from Asiatic Taurus to European Taenarum over the island-chain of Rhodes and Carpathos and Crete and Cythera; from Mycale to Pindus over Samos and Euboea; from Tmolus to Pelion and Ossa and Olympus over Chios and Scyros; from Ida to Athos over Tenedos and Lemnos.

These chains of islands, with the sea-passages between them and the continental mountain ranges on either side, bring the fact of subsidence to the eye; and the ancient inhabitants of the Aegean described this geological phenomenon in mythological imagery as the work of the Earth-Shaker Poseidon, who cleft the mountains

with his trident in order to make way for the waters to pass.[1]
Poseidon did not rest from his labours until he had pierced the last
range and led the salt waters of the Mediterranean through the
breaches and out beyond to lave the skirts of the Eurasian Steppe in
the Sea of Azov.[2]

In this exercise of his power, which divided Europe from Asia
and transformed the submerged section of the continent into the
Aegean Archipelago,[3] the Earth-Shaker was presenting a challenge.

> The islands feel the enclasping flow,
> And then their endless bounds they know. . . .
>
> O then a longing like despair
> Is to their farthest caverns sent!
> For surely once, they feel, we were
> Parts of a single continent.
> Now round us spreads the watery plain—
> O might our marges meet again!
>
> Who order'd that their longing's fire
> Should be, as soon as kindled, cool'd?
> Who renders vain their deep desire?—
> A God, a God their severance rul'd;
> And bade betwixt their shores to be
> The unplumb'd, salt, estranging sea.[4]

The poet who has taken the severance of isle from isle as a
symbol of the isolation of human souls assumes that the challenge
remains unanswered, that the deep desire for communion is
rendered vain. Yet in reality, though the islands themselves have
remained in that state in which it once pleased the primeval Earth-

---

[1] Compare the similar exploits of the Sinic culture-hero Yu. (Maspéro, op. cit.,
pp. 27–8.) In the age of Hellenic rationalism, Poseidon was recognized by men of
science to be a mythological presentation of a natural force. See, for example, Herodotus,
Book VII, ch. 129.

[2] The present fantastic configuration of the successive basins and straits through
which the Medjterranean communicates with the Sea of Azov becomes explicable if we
make the assumption that these land-locked seas cover the submerged estuary of a great
river, in which the narrower reaches alternated with wide-spreading lakes. On this
hypothesis, the former lakes would be represented now by the Sea of Crete, the Aegean,
the Marmara, the Black Sea, and the Sea of Azov; the narrower reaches by the channels
through the Archipelago and by the Dardanelles, the Bosphorus, and the Straits of
Kertch. When this great river flowed into the Mediterranean round the eastern or
western end of the former continental mountain range which now survives as the Island
of Crete, it will have numbered among its tributaries many streams which have won
their subsequent renown as independent rivers: the Maeander, Cayster, and Hermus;
the Peneus and Axius and Strymon and Hebrus; the Simois and the Scamander; the
Halys and the Phasis; the Kuban and the Don; the Dniepr and Dniestr and Danube.
As the salt waters of the Mediterranean flooded up the subsiding bed of the main river,
these former tributaries gained their independence one after another by coming to discharge directly into the sea and thereby becoming each a river in its own right.

[3] Archipelago = ἅγιον πέλαγος: 'Sacred Sea'. This formal consecration has been
conferred upon the Aegean by Christian piety; but the Archipelago remains the
inalienable domain of the pre-Christian divinity who is its mythical creator.

[4] Matthew Arnold: Isolation.

Shaker to leave them, the challenge which has intimidated the Goddess Nature has met with a victorious response from Mortal Man. 'The unplumb'd, salt, estranging sea' has been changed into a medium of human communication by the art and audacity of the navigator[1]—a greater transformation of Nature than any which Poseidon's trident is capable of producing by its barbaric strokes.

> Illi robur et aes triplex
> Circa pectus erat, qui fragilem truci
>   Commisit pelago ratem
> Primus nec timuit praecipitem Africum
> Decertantem Aquilonibus. . . .

> Nequicquam deus abscidit
> Prudens Oceano dissociabili
>   Terras, si tamen impiae
> Non tangenda rates transiliunt vada.[2]

By what men, in what age, was Poseidon's challenge taken up? When our hypothetical primitive society which had adapted itself to life in the mountain-zone at some point in Asia eventually stumbled upon the Aegean in the course of its hypothetical westward march, we may imagine that it no more attempted to make itself at home in the inhospitable Archipelago than the primitive societies of the Afrasian grasslands attempted—before the challenge of desiccation impelled them—to make themselves at home in the jungle-swamps of the Nile or of the Tigris and Euphrates. We may conjecture that at the forbidding shores of the Aegean the highlanders turned aside and reconnoitred the western coasts of the Asiatic mainland until they struck the shores of the Bosphorus or the Dardanelles, where an opposite continent in full view heartened them to hazard the easy transit of the Straits. We may also conjecture that, by this passage, they had made their way from the highlands of Asia into the highlands of Europe before they embarked upon the Aegean, and had ensconced themselves among the Alpine Lakes before they set foot on Delos or on Santorin. If so, the highlanders really evaded Poseidon's challenge instead of responding to it; and indeed our ethnologists and archaeologists tell us that the challenge presented in the Aegean Archipelago was first taken up, not by the occupants of the immediately adjoining continents, but by more distant adventurers who, in order to reach the landlocked sea, had first to cross the open waters of the Eastern Mediterranean.

---

[1] In the language of Greek Mythology, the Black Sea was transformed from 'the inhospitable' (ἄξεινος) into 'the hospitable' (εὔξεινος) sea by the heroic enterprise of the Argonauts.

[2] Horace: *Carm.* i. 3, ll. 9–13 and 21–5. For the significance of the epithets 'prudens', 'impiae', and 'non tangenda', see the passage on 'the Envy of the Gods' in IV. C (iii) (c) 1, vol. iv, pp. 245–61, below.

The oldest trace of human habitation in the Archipelago which is yet known to our archaeologists is the Neolithic stratum on the site of Cnossos in Crete.

'Crete was discovered and occupied by people from elsewhere at a time which cannot be fixed precisely but cannot be less than many hundreds of years, and was probably some thousands, before this Neolithic community and its culture were superseded by those of the Minoan Bronze Age. . . . In the Cycladic Islands . . . nothing has been found hitherto of purely Neolithic culture.'[1]

Whence came these earliest human occupants of Crete? On this question, Ethnology is able to throw some light; for it appears to be established that, among the earliest known inhabitants of the continents surrounding the Aegean, there were certain clear distinctions of physical type. The earliest known inhabitants of the highland-zone of folded mountains were 'broad-heads'; the earliest known inhabitants of the Afrasian grasslands were 'long-heads'; and an analysis of the oldest relics of human physique in Crete seems to indicate that the island was first occupied wholly or mainly by 'long-heads', while the 'broad-heads', though they eventually became predominant, were originally either not represented in the population of Crete at all or only in a small minority.[2] This ethnological evidence points to the conclusion that the first human beings to secure a footing in any part of the Aegean Archipelago were immigrants from the Afrasian grasslands on the far side of the Eastern Mediterranean.[3] The challenge of desiccation could not be evaded by the people of the Afrasian grasslands, as the challenge of population pressure could be evaded by the Asiatic highlanders in virtue of the easy passage from the Asiatic to the European highlands which was afforded by the constriction of the estranging waters at the Dardanelles and the Bosphorus. And this inexorable challenge, to which some Afrasian communities had responded by plunging into the jungle-swamps of the Nile and the Tigris and the Euphrates, impelled other kindred communities to brave the terrors of the salt, estranging sea and make themselves at home in the Aegean Archipelago. The genesis of the Minoan

---

[1] Myres, J. L.: *Who were the Greeks?* (Berkeley 1930, University of California Press), p. 215.

[2] Myres, op. cit., pp. 44–5.

[3] Theoretically, the evidence offered by long skulls is ambiguous, since 'dolichocephaly' is a trait which the 'Mediterranean' variety of the White Race shares with the 'Nordic' variety—the differentia between the two varieties being given by pigmentation and not by skull-form. Thus, in theory, any given 'dolichocephalic' skull may be attributed—in the absence of evidence as to the pigmentation of the human being to which the skull once belonged—either to a 'Mediterranean' or to a 'Nordic' physique. In practice, however, geographical and historical considerations allow us to rule out the theoretical alternative that the 'dolichocephalic' aborigines of Crete were not 'Mediterranean' immigrants from the Afrasian grasslands but were 'Nordic' immigrants from the Eurasian Steppe.

Civilization can thus be traced back to the same first cause as the geneses of the Egyptiac and Sumeric civilizations.

If this analysis is correct, it offers a fresh illustration of the truth that, in the geneses of civilizations, the interplay between challenges and responses is the factor which counts above all others—in this case, for example, above proximity. If proximity had been the determining factor in the human occupation of the Archipelago, then the inhabitants of the nearest continent—that is to say, the 'broad-headed' highlanders in the Asiatic portion of the zone of mountain-folding—would have been the first occupants of the Aegean islands. In point of proximity, they had a notable advantage over the 'long-headed' inhabitants of the Afrasian grasslands, who were separated from the Aegean Archipelago by the whole breadth of the open Mediterranean. Apparently, however, the determining factor was not proximity but Challenge-and-Response. The peoples of the Afrasian grasslands had to respond to the inexorable challenge of desiccation at a time when the peoples of the Asiatic highlands were still able to evade the challenge of population pressure by following the line of lesser resistance which led them across the Dardanelles and the Bosphorus into the adjacent highlands of Europe. Hence it was the distant Afrasians and not the neighbouring Asiatics who first braved, under duress, the terrors of the sea and so became the fathers of the Minoan Civilization. It was only in the later stages of the human occupation of the Archipelago that the 'broad-headed' highlanders from the adjoining continents came to play a prominent part. In Crete, which appears to have been the first of the islands to be occupied, the 'broad-heads', as we have seen, were later comers than the 'long-heads'. On the other hand, the Cyclades, which apparently were not occupied until a much later date than Crete,[1] appear to have been occupied by 'long-heads' and 'broad-heads' concurrently[2]; and the ethnological evidence on this point is confirmed by Archaeology, which finds in the Cyclades a mingling of techniques and *motifs* derived from Libya[3] and from Anatolia.[4]

[1] Myres, op. cit., pp. 214–15, summarizes the archaeological evidence up to date. 'At present the only coherent series of material illustrating the Aegean Stone Age comes from the stratified deposit of village debris, from twenty to twenty-five feet deep, which underlies the "palace" building at Cnossos. Even this long series begins with material arts, pot-making, implement-grinding, and adobe-building, which are far from primitive. Crete, therefore, was discovered and occupied by people from elsewhere, at a time which cannot be fixed precisely, but cannot be less than many hundreds of years, and was probably some thousands, before this neolithic community and its culture were superseded by those of the Minoan Bronze Age. . . . In the Cycladic islands . . . nothing has been found hitherto of purely neolithic culture.'   [2] Myres, op. cit., p. 43.

[3] e.g. there is a type of decoration on early Cretan and Cycladic pottery which proclaims its derivation from grass-woven basketry of a kind that is still plaited to this day in North Africa (Myres, op. cit., pp. 216–17). Again, the earliest known Cycladic boats seem to have been modelled on the boats of the pre-dynastic age in Egypt (Myres, op. cit., pp. 217–18).   [4] Myres, op. cit., pp. 228–33, apropos of 'red ware'.

Broadly, it may be said that the first response to Poseidon's challenge in the Aegean was made by Afrasian 'long-heads' single-handed; but that the work which had been begun by these Afrasian pioneers was carried on and completed by convergent movements into the Archipelago from the other side of the Mediterranean and from the adjoining continents[1]—the 'broad-headed' continental highlanders participating in the later stages partly, perhaps, in sheer imitation of the 'long-headed' Mediterranean navigators and partly, perhaps, because the saturation of the highlands on the European as well as the Asiatic side of the narrow seas eventually forced the 'broad-heads', in their turn, to seek a new outlet upon the waters of the Aegean from which they had always hung back so long as any other outlet lay open to them.

Physical Challenges at the Geneses of the 'Related' Civilizations

We have now surveyed the interplay between challenges from the physical environment and responses to these challenges in the geneses of the six 'unrelated' civilizations. When we pass on to the 'related' civilizations, we find our problem complicated *a priori* by the very fact that here, *ex hypothesi*, there is in every case an older civilization in the background and that this older civilization has been in occupation of a geographical area within which the original home of the 'related' civilization may be included, either partly or wholly.[2]

In the extreme case—illustrated by the geographical relation of the Babylonic Civilization to the Sumeric—in which the original home of the 'related' civilization is included not merely within the widest eventual range but actually within the original home of its predecessor, it is evident that a challenge from the physical environment cannot have entered into the genesis of the 'related' civilization at all—except, perhaps, in so far as, during the interregnum between the disappearance of the older civilization and the emergence of its successor, their common cradle may have relapsed into its primitive state of nature and thus have challenged the fathers of the 'related' civilization to fight a repetition of the same battle with the physical environment that the fathers of the antecedent civilization had once fought out on the same spot. There are, however, other cases in which we can see that the fathers of the 'related' civilization responded to some challenge from the physical environment with which the fathers of the antecedent civilization had never been confronted. In the case of the Yucatec Civilization, for instance, we can see that, although the original home of the

[1] Myres, op. cit., pp. 234–5.
[2] For a conspectus of the geographical relations between the several 'related' civilizations and their predecessors, see the table in Part I. C (ii), on p. 132, above.

'related' civilization was wholly included within the domain of the antecedent Mayan Civilization at its widest range, it was not only non-coincident with the original home of the Mayan Civilization but also presented a challenge of an entirely different character: the challenge of the waterless, treeless, and almost soil-less limestone shelf of the Yucatan Peninsula (a magnified counterpart of the Italian Tavole di Puglia),[1] as contrasted with the challenge of the deep-soiled rain-soaked country to the south of it, where agriculture had to wage a never-ceasing warfare against the luxuriance of the tropical forest.[2]

In thus being exposed, at its genesis, to the stimulus of a new and still unmastered physical environment, the Yucatec Civilization would appear to be unique among the 'related' civilizations of its own group. In the cases of all the other four members of this group—the Hindu Civilization, the Far Eastern Civilization (main body), the Orthodox Christian, and the Arabic—even that part of the original home of the 'related' civilization which was not included in the original home of the antecedent civilization no longer presented the challenge of virgin soil, since it had been mastered and broken in, some time before the genesis of the 'related' civilization, either by the antecedent civilization itself or by some alien civilization which the antecedent civilization had encountered and assimilated in the course of its expansion. For instance, the Yangtse Basin, which fell within the original home of the Far Eastern Civilization (main body), though not within that of the antecedent Sinic Civilization, had been broken in by the Sinic Civilization before the Far Eastern Civilization came into being.[3] The Deccan and the tip of the Indian Peninsula, which fell within the original home of the Hindu Civilization, though not within that of the antecedent Indic Civilization, had been broken in by the Indic Civilization before the Hindu Civilization came into being.[4] The Anatolian Plateau, which fell within the original home of the Orthodox Christian Civilization, though not within that of the antecedent Hellenic Civilization, had been broken in, before the Orthodox Christian Civilization came into being, not by the Hellenic Civilization itself but by the Hittite,[5] the debris of which, after its premature downfall,[6] had been encountered by the Hellenic Civilization and assimilated. The Lower Valley of the Nile, which fell within the original home of the Arabic Civilization,[7] though not within that of the antecedent Syriac Civilization,

[1] See I. C (i) (b), p. 128, above.
[2] See I. C (i) (b), pp. 125–6, and also the present section, p. 321, above.
[3] See I. C. (i) b, p. 90, above.   [4] See p. 87, above.
[5] See p. 112, above.   [6] See pp. 101 and 113–15, above.
[7] See p. 70, above.

had been broken in, long ages before the Arabic Civilization came into being, not by the Syriac Civilization itself, but by the Egyptiac, which had been encountered and eventually assimilated by the Syriac.

Thus none of these four 'related' civilizations happened to be exposed, at their geneses, to a challenge from a new and still unmastered physical environment in that part of their original home which was not included within the original home of the antecedent civilization in each case; and when we turn to the next group—namely, the 'related' civilizations whose original home was only partly coincident with that of the antecedent civilization, even at the latter's widest range—we find the same absence of a physical challenge at the genesis of one representative: namely, the Iranic Civilization. Those parts of the original home of the Iranic Civilization which lay wholly outside the domain of the antecedent Syriac Civilization, even at its widest range, were Anatolia at one extremity and Hindustan at the other[1]; and both these regions— which had been captured by the nascent Iranic Civilization from Orthodox Christendom and from Hinduism respectively, and which had previously been taken over by these civilizations from the Hittite Civilization and from the Indic—had naturally been broken in long ages before.

In this absence, however, of a fresh physical challenge at its genesis, the Iranic Civilization appears to be as exceptional, within its own group, as the Yucatec Civilization appears to be, in the foregoing group, on the opposite account. When we survey the other five civilizations which belong to the same group as the Iranic—that is to say, the Mexic, the Western, the Indic, the Hittite, and the Hellenic—we find that they differ from the Iranic Civilization, and agree with the Yucatec, on the point with which we are at present concerned. For instance, the Mexic Civilization agrees with the Yucatec, not only in being 'related' to the Mayan, but also in having been exposed at its genesis to a physical challenge —the challenge of the Mexican Plateau—which was as different as the challenge of the Yucatan Peninsula from the challenge of the tropical forest with which the Mayan Civilization had been confronted. Again, our Western Civilization was exposed at its genesis to a challenge from the forests and the rains and the frosts of Transalpine Europe which had not confronted the antecedent Hellenic Civilization. The Indic Civilization, at its genesis, was exposed, in the Ganges Valley, to a challenge from the moist tropical forest which was to confront the Mayan Civilization, centuries later, on the other side of the globe, but which had not confronted the Indic

[1] See pp. 68–9, above.

POSSIBLE POSITIVE FACTORS 333

Civilization's predecessor in the Indus Valley.[1] The Hittite Civilization, at its genesis, was exposed, in Anatolia, to a challenge from the plateau which had not confronted the antecedent Sumeric Civilization, though, in later times and in distant places, this new challenge was likewise to confront both the Andean Civilization and the Mexic. It is true that the highland environment, which was so strange to the internal proletariat of the Sumeric Civilization in its home on the alluvial plains of the Land of Shinar, may have been the native environment of that external proletariat, coming from beyond the Cappadocian frontier of the Sumeric universal state, which probably played the leading part in bringing the Hittite Civilization into existence[2]; and, in so far as the Hittite Civilization is to be regarded as this external proletariat's handiwork, the likelihood of a contribution to the genesis of this civilization having been made by a physical challenge from a new and unmastered physical environment has to be discounted on the assumption that the barbarian fathers of the Hittite Civilization may have been at home on the Anatolian Plateau already, before their Völkerwanderung carried them into the Anatolian provinces of the Sumeric World in Cappadocia. In the case of the Hellenic Civilization—in the genesis of which, the influence of the external proletariat was apparently predominant likewise[3]—the situation is inverted. The challenge to which the Hellenic Civilization was exposed at its genesis—the challenge of the sea[4]—was precisely the same as that which had confronted the antecedent Minoan Civilization.[5] At the same time, this challenge of the sea was entirely new to the external proletariat beyond the European land-frontier of 'the Thalassocracy of Minos'; and these continental barbarians—Achaeans and the like—were facing and surmounting as great an ordeal, when they took to the sea in the post-Minoan Völkerwanderung, as the pioneers of the Minoan Civilization themselves had faced and surmounted when they made the first human conquest of the Aegean Archipelago.

Finally, we come to those 'related' or 'transplanted' civilizations,[6] at the opposite end of the series from the Babylonic, whose original home was altogether non-coincident with the domain of the antecedent civilization, even at its widest range; and here we find, as we should expect, that a challenge from a new and still unmastered physical environment was presented, at their geneses, in all cases.

---

[1] For the present purpose, it is immaterial whether 'the Indus Culture' was a civilization in its own right or a colonial offshoot of the Sumeric Civilization. (On this question see I. C (i) (b), pp. 107-8, above, and Annex III, below.)
[2] See pp. 111-12, above. [3] See pp. 96-100, above. [4] See p. 93, above.
[5] See II. C (ii) (a) 2, p. 259, and the present chapter, pp. 323-30, above.
[6] For the distinction between 'related' civilizations and 'transplanted' civilizations or 'offshoots', see I. C (ii), p. 133, and II. C (ii) (a) 2, pp. 269-70, above.

For instance, the Orthodox Christian Civilization in Russia was exposed, at its transplantation, to a challenge from forests and rains and frosts which was even more severe than the similar challenge to which the Western Civilization in Transalpine Europe was exposed at its genesis.[1] Thus, in Russia, the Orthodox Christian Civilization not only received a fresh physical stimulus, like our Western Civilization in Transalpine Europe, but it actually received the same stimulus in a higher degree which made it still more different from any physical challenge that had ever confronted these two civilizations' common Hellenic predecessor. Again, the Far Eastern Civilization in the Korean Peninsula and in the Japanese Archipelago was exposed, at its transplantation, to a challenge from the sea which resembled the challenge that had once confronted both the Afrasian pioneers and the Continental European supplanters of the Minoan Civilization in the Aegean,[2] but which was utterly different from any challenge that had ever confronted the first Far Eastern navigators' own predecessors who had created, in a continental environment of swamp and bush, the antecedent civilization which we have called the Sinic.[3]

Similarly, the Philistine refugees from the Minoan World who found asylum on the Syrian coast, and the Hebrew and Aramaean Nomads who simultaneously drifted into the interior of Syria out of the Afrasian Steppe, at the genesis of the Syriac Civilization,[4] were both exposed to the challenge—new in different ways to each —of having to make the desert bear fruit by irrigation (the same challenge that, at the genesis of the Andean Civilization, was to confront the occupants of the Peruvian coast-land).[5] The Philistines, when they came to Syria from the Aegean, were already well acquainted with agriculture; but they had acquired the art in a climate which yielded the tiller of the soil the easy return of rain-grown crops, and they were novices in the practice of husbandry in an arid environment. Conversely, the Hebrews and Aramaeans, when they came in from the North Arabian Steppe, were already inured to life in an arid environment, but this as Nomadic stock-breeders and not as sedentary husbandmen. Thus both the intrusive human elements out of whose arrival in Syria, and encounter there, the Syriac Civilization eventually arose,[6] had to

---

[1] In Transalpine Europe, the rigours of the northern climate are tempered by the proximity of the Atlantic Ocean and by the flow of the Gulf Stream, which washes the European coasts from Portugal to Norway. As one moves eastward from the coast into the interior, from Europe into Russia, one finds the influence of these moderating climatic factors steadily diminishing until it reaches vanishing point.

[2] See II. C (ii) (a) 2, p. 259, and the present chapter, pp. 323–30 and 333, above.

[3] For the physical challenge encountered at the genesis of the Sinic Civilization, see the present chapter, pp. 318–21, above.

[4] See I. C (i) (b), pp. 101–2, above.

[5] See the present chapter, pp. 322–3, above.　　　[6] See I. C (i) (b), p. 102, above.

make a formidable effort of adaptation to unfamiliar physical conditions before they 'dwelt safely, every man under his vine and
under his fig tree',[1] in the oases watered by the springs of Beersheba and Baalbek and Jericho and by the rivers of Aleppo and
Hamath and Damascus, as their predecessors in the land had
dwelt before them.[2] Indeed, the ordeal was so severe that it left
a permanent mark on Syriac 'folk-memory'; and the successful
response to it, out of which the Syriac Civilization arose, was
ascribed by latter-day poets not to the heroism of their human
ancestors but to the might and mercy of their God, who

'gathered them out of the lands, from the east and from the west, from
the north and from the south.

'They wandered in the wilderness in a solitary way; they found no
city to dwell in.

'Hungry and thirsty, their soul fainted in them.

'Then they cried unto the Lord in their trouble, and he delivered
them out of their distresses.

'And he led them forth by the right way, that they might go to a city
of habitation. . . .

'He turneth the wilderness into a standing water, and dry ground into
watersprings.

'And there he maketh the hungry to dwell, that they may prepare a
city for habitation;

'And sow the fields and plant vineyards, which may yield fruits of
increase. . . .

'O that men would praise the Lord for his goodness, and for his
wonderful works to the children of men!'[3]

Challenges from the Human Environment

This concludes our survey of challenges from the physical
environment at the origins of our twenty-one civilizations. We
have detected the operation of physical challenges at the geneses of
a certain number of 'related' civilizations, as well as at the geneses
of all the civilizations of the 'unrelated' category; but it is in this
latter category, which we examined first, that the role played by
physical challenges has come out the most clearly. We have now
to complete the task which we have set ourselves in this chapter
by considering the phenomenon of challenges from the human

---

[1] 1 Kings iv. 25.

[2] Before the emergence of a distinctive Syriac Civilization, Syria had received the
cultural impress of the Sumeric Civilization and had been included politically first in the
Sumeric Universal State (the Empire of Sumer and Akkad); then in the local 'successor-
state' founded, during the post-Sumeric Völkerwanderung, by the Hyksos; and finally in
'the New Empire' of Egypt. (See I. C (i) (b), pp. 103 and 105, above.) For the abortive
Syriac Civilization, related to the Sumeric Civilization, which the Hyksos might have
brought to birth if they had not been diverted by the attraction of the Egyptiac World,
see II. D (vii), vol. ii, pp. 388–91, below.

[3] Psalm cvii. 3–7, 35–7, and 8.

environment; and here we shall find it convenient to begin our examination with the 'related' civilizations and to consider the 'unrelated' civilizations afterwards.

At the genesis of every 'related' civilization, a challenge from the human environment is given and taken *ex hypothesi*. This challenge is implicit in the relation itself, which begins with a differentiation and culminates in a secession.[1] The differentiation takes place within the bosom of the antecedent civilization when that civilization begins to lose the creative power through which, in its period of growth, it has once upon a time inspired a voluntary allegiance in the hearts of people below its surface or beyond its borders. When this happens, the ailing civilization pays the penalty for its failure of vitality by becoming disintegrated into a dominant minority which attempts to find a substitute for its vanishing leadership in a régime of force, and a proletariat (internal and external) which responds to this challenge by becoming conscious that it has a soul of its own and by making up its mind to save its soul alive. The dominant minority's will to repress evokes in the proletariat a will to secede; and the conflict between these two wills continues[2] while the declining civilization verges to its fall, until, when it is *in articulo mortis*, the proletariat at length breaks free from a *ci-devant* spiritual home which has been transformed first into a prison-house and finally into a city of destruction. In this conflict between a proletariat and a dominant minority, as it works itself out from beginning to end, we can discern one of those dramatic spiritual encounters which renew the work of creation by carrying the life of the Universe out of the stagnation of autumn through the pains of winter into the ferment of spring.[3] The secession of the proletariat is the dynamic act, in response to the challenge, through which the change from Yin to Yang is brought about;[4] and, in this dynamic separation between the proletariat and the dominant minority of the antecedent civilization, the 'related' civilization is born.

Thus, in the geneses of the 'related' civilizations, the factor of response to a challenge from the human environment is not merely visible but prominent. With this aid to our vision, can we now discern a challenge from the human environment, and a response to it, in the geneses of the 'unrelated' civilizations likewise?

In this quarter, the state of the evidence makes the investigation

[1] See above, I. B (iv), p. 41; I. C (i) (*a*), pp. 53–6; I. C (ii), pp. 130–2; II. A, pp. 187–8; II. B, p. 195.
[2] The successive phases and moods of this conflict are analysed in Part V, below.
[3] See II. C (ii) (*b*) 1, above.
[4] See Part II. B, above, pp. 201–4, for the symbolism of Yin and Yang; for the secession of the proletariat, see I. B (iv), pp. 41–2, and I. C (i) (*a*), pp. 53–6.

more difficult. In the case of the 'related' civilizations, we have seen that the presence of an antecedent civilization in the historical background produces contrary effects upon the field of investigation in different spheres. In the sphere of the physical environment, it tends to obscure the operation of physical challenges at the geneses of 'related' civilizations, while on the other hand in the sphere of the human environment it throws the operation of human challenges into relief. In the case of the 'unrelated' civilizations, the absence of any antecedent civilization likewise has contrary effects upon the field of investigation in the human ard in the physical sphere, but in this case the contrast is inverted. When we are surveying the genesis of an 'unrelated' civilization, it is the response to some challenge from the physical environment that leaps to the eye, because the physical environment is virgin soil when the 'unrelated' civilization encounters it (the contingency that it may have already been broken in by some antecedent civilization being ruled out *ex hypothesi*). When, however, we pursue our study of the geneses of 'unrelated' civilizations into the human sphere, and seek light on the role which challenges from the human environment may have played here, we find that the very absence of an antecedent civilization, which has facilitated our investigation in the physical sphere, becomes a handicap which may turn out to be insurmountable.

Let us consider once again, for a moment, the origins of the six 'unrelated' civilizations in our catalogue: the Egyptiac, Sumeric, Sinic, Mayan, Andean, and Minoan. The physical environment in which the miracle of genesis occurred has proved here to be ascertainable in every instance. At each attempt, we have always found ourselves able to reconstruct the face of Physical Nature, as it must have appeared at that remote time in the past, by scanning its aspect in the present. In following this line of investigation, we have never failed to discover sufficient clues—either on the actual scene of the historic event or else in some adjoining region where Nature, left in peace by God and Man, remains down to this day as she was then. On the other hand, if we now seek to reconstruct the human environments in which the geneses of these six civilizations took place, we shall be pulled up short, at the outset of our inquiry, by the dearth or indeed almost complete absence of direct evidence. Here, instead of the historically recorded secession of a proletariat from a dominant minority, such as is presented to us at the geneses of the 'related' civilizations, we find nothing more substantial to work upon than the hypothetical mutation of a primitive society into a civilization.[1]

[1] See Part II. A, p. 188, above.

Assuming the truth of the hypothesis, shall we venture to build, on this airy foundation, the further hypothesis that 'mutation' and 'secession', being morphologically equivalent, are also spiritually akin to one another? Shall we conjecture, for example, that the pioneers of the Egyptiac Civilization, when they responded to the physical challenge from the jungle-swamp of the Nile Valley, were also responding simultaneously to a human challenge from the older generation of their fellows, whose static primitive way of life had to be thrown to the winds if the pioneers were to gird themselves for their great adventure?[1] We do know for a fact[2] that when the pioneers of our Western Civilization were responding to the physical challenge which was presented to them by the forests and rains and frosts of Transalpine Europe, they were also responding simultaneously, in their role as the proletariat of the Hellenic Society, to a human challenge from the Hellenic dominant minority, whose way of life—which was as static, in its decline, as the way of any primitive society in its Yin-phase[3]—had undoubtedly to be thrown to the winds if these Western pioneers were to embark on their enterprise unencumbered. Does the analogy hold? Perhaps we can only say that it casts, into this dark corner of our present field of inquiry, a ray of light which at least indicates the limit beyond which it would hardly be possible to push conjecture further. At this point, accordingly, we will desist from our survey of challenges and responses in the geneses of civilizations and will attempt to draw some provisional conclusions from the results which we have obtained so far.

[1] This conception of a human challenge from the older generation, which the younger generation have to overcome before they can take up the challenge from the physical environment effectively, appears in the Syriac Mythology in the legend of the forty years' wandering in the wilderness, which was imposed upon the Children of Israel by Yahweh when, on the threshold of Canaan, their resolution failed them and they desired to return to the flesh pots and task-work of Egypt rather than try conclusions with the gigantic sons of Anak. The forty years' delay was neither a punishment nor a probation but a purgatory. Yahweh's purpose in decreeing it was to give time for the whole adult generation to die out save only for the two stalwarts, Caleb and Joshua. The Chosen People would not be fit to enter into the Promised Land until the older generation had passed away and the younger generation had grown to manhood. (Numbers xiv, especially vv. 28–34.)

[2] See I. C (i) (a), pp. 53–6, above.

[3] See the present Part, II. B, pp. 194–5, above.

ANNEXES

ANNEX TO I. B (iv)

E. A. FREEMAN'S CONCEPTION OF 'THE UNITY OF HISTORY'

THE conception of 'the Continuity of History' which is criticized on pages 42–4, above, is sometimes associated with the name of E. A. Freeman; and some readers may perhaps have interpreted what is really an impersonal criticism of a debatable formula as an implicit disparagement of a great historian. There was no thought of this in the writer's mind; for, as far as he knows, Freeman did not conceive 'the Continuity of History' in the sense in which it is criticized here; but, before leaving the subject, it may be opportune to inquire what Freeman's own conception actually was. For one thing, any point of historical study upon which the light of Freeman's genius has been directed is likely to have been illuminated by it. Apart from this, the present writer is moved by a personal consideration. For a smaller mind to make light of a greater is always presumptuous and in bad taste; and for the writer of this Study to make light of Freeman would be an act of ingratitude as well, since he owes a greater debt than he can repay to the reading of Freeman's *Historical Essays* as a boy. A brief examination of his relevant works will suffice to make Freeman's view clear.

The *locus classicus* in which Freeman's view appears is his lecture on 'The Unity of History'. And it is to be noted that, in his title, he employs the word 'Unity' and not the word 'Continuity', and that the lecture is printed in the same volume as a set of lectures entitled *Comparative Politics*.[1] Moreover, in the phrase 'the Unity of History' Freeman is using the word 'History' in the original subjective meaning of an inquiry (the Ionic ἱστορίη)[2] and not in the derived objective meaning of a field of inquiry consisting of events in a time-series.[3] Freeman means, by his phrase, 'the Unity of the Study of Historical Facts'; and, though one of the cases which he discusses is that in which the unity of study depends on the continuity of the objective events studied, he also includes

---

[1] Freeman, E. A.: *Comparative Politics* (London 1873, Macmillan).
[2] Herodotus calls his work ἱστορίης ἀπόδεξις, 'the exhibition of his inquiry'. (Herodotus, Book I, *ad init.*)
[3] In the vernaculars of the Modern West, the words 'History', 'Histoire', 'Storia', 'Geschichte', and so on are used ambiguously sometimes in the objective sense and sometimes in the subjective. In Herodotus's Ionic this ambiguity is avoided; and in translating into it the title of the present work—'A Study of History'—it would be 'Study' and not 'History' that would have to be represented by the Ionic word ἱστορίη.

in his conception of 'the Unity of History' the comparative method of studying analogies and parallels.

'We might carry out the same doctrine of the unity of history into many and various applications. I have as yet been speaking of branches of the study where its oneness takes the form of direct connexion, of long chains of events bound together in the direct relation of cause and effect. There are other branches of history which proclaim the unity of the study in a hardly less striking way, in the form of mere analogy. Man is in truth ever the same; even when the direct succession of cause and effect does not come in, we see that in times and places most remote from one another like events follow upon like causes.'[1]

He explicitly commends the comparative method of study both in this lecture[2] and in the set of lectures on *Comparative Politics*. At the beginning of these, he speaks of the invention of the method in Philology and Mythology as 'the greatest intellectual achievement of our time';[3] and in another passage he affirms that

'to master analogies, . . . to grasp the laws which regulate the essential likeness and not to be led away by points either of likeness or unlikeness which are merely incidental, is the true philosophy of history.'[4]

More than that, he perceives the implications of these principles of study for the policy of the historian.

'Of some branches he must know everything, but of every branch he must know something.'[5]

Freeman thus had the insight and the courage to go against the fashion—dictated by Industrialism and Nationalism—into which most of his contemporaries were falling in obedience to the law of the relativity of historical thought.[6] Freeman was great enough to rise above that law, though its influence upon his generation was so powerful that it mastered historians of the heroic build of an Acton and a Mommsen.

At the same time Freeman, like all historians and all human beings, was to some extent governed in his thinking by the mental environment of his time, and particularly by the current intellectual controversies in which he was a protagonist; and, as happens to critics, he was sometimes led by the impetuosity of his attack upon his opponents' errors to fall into opposite errors himself. In 'The Unity of History', for example, he was attacking that arbitrary division of historical studies into water-tight compartments which was an established tradition in the Western World of his day.[7] In

---

[1] Freeman, E. A.: 'The Unity of History' in *Comparative Politics* (London 1873, Macmillan), pp. 332–3.　　[2] Op. cit., pp. 301–2.　　[3] Op. cit., p. 1.
[4] Op. cit., pp. 32–3.　　[5] Op. cit., p. 308.　　[6] See Part I. A, above.
[7] The vogue of this myopic view, like that of 'the Continuity of History', is explained by the relativity of historical thought. It was a 'function' (in the mathematical sense) of

detail he was attacking, first, a division of studies between a Greek and a Roman 'classical period' of 'Ancient History' (a division which still prevailed in the School of Literae Humaniores at Oxford in A.D. 1933, sixty years after the publication of Freeman's lecture!). In the second place he was attacking the division between the study of 'Classical Greece' and 'Classical Rome' on the one hand and the study of the Western Society on the other. This disposition of the battle-field in which Freeman was breaking his lance caused him, in his struggle to attain true insight, to fall into certain mistakes of proportion and perspective.

He victoriously attained a perception of the truth that Hellenic and Western history are philosophically contemporary—an insight which, by implication, rules out the misconception of growth as a movement whose track is a straight line.[1]

'Forget, if we can, the whole line of thought implied in the distinctions of "ancient", "classical", and "modern", to proclaim boldly that no languages are more truly living than those which are falsely called dead, that no portions of history are more truly "modern" than the history of the times which in mere physical distance we look upon as "ancient".'[2]

At the same time, Freeman was led by the *élan* of his onslaught to pass the line at which the relation between the Hellenic Society and the Western Society could be seen in its true perspective as one of 'apparentation' and 'affiliation', and to take up a position in which he expressed his vivid realization and his inevitably propagandist assertion of the link between them in terms of absolute continuity. No doubt, if the prevailing error of Freeman's contemporaries had been (as that of his successors is) precisely the assumption that the continuity between Hellenic history and Western history was absolute, that the rhythm of the tune was unbroken and the tempo unchanged in the transition, then Freeman would have emphasized (and perhaps even over-emphasized) the element of discontinuity in the relation between an 'apparented' and an 'affiliated' society in comparison with the degree of the continuity obtaining between successive chapters in the history of one

the aesthetic and intellectual renaissance which had occurred in the sub-society constituted by the city-states of Northern Italy at the close of the Western 'Middle Ages' and which had been communicated, at the opening of 'the Modern Age', to the rest of the Western World. Under the influence of this renaissance, history was approached from the standpoint of Greek and Latin philology, and all the activities of Mankind were charted, for study or neglect, in accordance with the classical stylist's chart of the history of literature—a picture in which two brief 'golden ages', with silver fringes, stood out against a dark background of literary vulgarism and linguistic impurity. (For the Italian renaissance as a ghost of the Hellenic Society evoked by the 'affiliated' Western Society, see further Part X, below.)

[1] This misconception is dealt with above in I. C (iii) (*b*). The philosophical contemporaneity of all societies of the species to which the Hellenic Society and the Western Society belong is dealt with in I. C (iii) (*c*).

[2] Op. cit., pp. 336-7.

and the same society. Actually, of course, Freeman was contending against contemporaries who, so far from exaggerating the degree of continuity involved in 'apparentation' and 'affiliation', ignored the existence of the relation altogether. Hence Freeman was led to emphasize its reality and importance, and so was led on to exaggerate the degree of continuity implied in his own thesis. A fair example of this exaggeration (and of its context in Freeman's thought) is offered by the following passage:

'We are learning that Greek and Roman history do not stand alone, bound together by some special tie, but isolated from the rest of the history of the World, even from the history of the kindred nations. We are learning that European history, from its first glimmerings to our own day, is one unbroken drama, no part of which can be rightly understood without reference to the other parts which came before and after it. We are learning that of this great drama Rome is the centre, the point to which all roads lead, and from which all roads lead no less. It is the vast lake in which all the streams of earlier history lose themselves, and from which all the streams of later history flow forth again. The world of independent Greece stands on one side of it; the world of modern Europe stands on the other. But the history alike of the great centre and of its satellites on either side can never be fully grasped, except from a point of view wide enough to take in the whole group, and to mark the relations of each of its members to the centre and to one another.'[1]

This over-statement of the degree of continuity between Hellenic history and Western history betrayed Freeman into two misjudgements.

First, he dismissed, as a hallucination, the phenomenon of the evocation of 'ghosts' from the life of an 'apparented' society into the life of an 'affiliated' society—a phenomenon which is one of the outstanding traits in the morphology of history, but a trait that does not come into focus unless the nature of 'apparentation' and 'affiliation' is rightly apprehended.[2] He reveals this blindness in a passage like the following:

'[The] position [of Rome] in the history of the World . . . is unintelligible to those who break up the unity of history by artificial barriers of "ancient" and "modern". Much that in a shallow view of things passes for mere imitation, for mere artificial revival, was in truth abiding and unbroken tradition.'[3]

The very language of the second sentence displays a strange bias. The creative effort of re-evoking something that has passed away is represented as a less noble and less valuable activity than the

[1] Freeman, E. A.: 'The Unity of History', in *Comparative Politics* (London 1873, Macmillan), p. 306.
[2] For an examination of this phenomenon, see Part X, *passim*, below.
[3] Op. cit., pp. 325–6.

retention of something that has never ceased to be there. Yet 'tradition', after all, is itself merely a form of imitation which is of a more passive and more feeble kind than the imitation which Freeman belittles; and if one were to replace this word 'tradition' by its synonym 'survival', to point the antithesis to 'revival', it would become apparent that in Freeman's sentence the true values are actually reversed. Perhaps, unconsciously, Freeman and his school preferred 'survivals' to 'revivals' for the subjective reason that 'survivals' afforded them the intellectual and aesthetic pleasure of tracing—as they imagined—the continuity of this thread and that, as its colour flashed out and vanished and flashed out again in the shot-silk texture of historical sequences. This pleasant exercise of the fancy has sometimes led historians who have indulged in it into irrelevant conceits and barren controversies.

A brilliant example of such a conceit is the eloquent opening passage of *The Holy Roman Empire*:

'Of those who in August, 1806, read in the English newspapers that the Emperor Francis II had announced to the Diet his resignation of the imperial crown, there were probably few who reflected that the oldest political institution in the World had come to an end. Yet it was so. The Empire which a note issued by a diplomatist on the banks of the Danube extinguished, was the same which the crafty nephew of Julius had won for himself, against the powers of the East, beneath the cliffs of Actium; and which had preserved almost unaltered, through eighteen centuries of time, and through the greatest changes in extent, in power, in character, a title and pretensions from which all meaning had long since departed. Nothing else so directly linked the old world to the new— nothing else displayed so many strange contrasts of the present and the past, and summed up in those contrasts so much of European history.'[1]

Bryce presents the institution which came to an end in A.D. 1806 as bone of the bone and flesh of the flesh of the institution which had been established in 31 B.C. after the Battle of Actium, and introduces the last Hapsburg Holy Roman Emperor as the lineal successor of Caesar and Augustus. The author insists that this ostensible continuity is the theme of his book; yet the book itself expounds in the reader's mind a theme that is the exact contrary of the author's thesis. It renders the history of the Holy Roman Empire intelligible by making it apparent that this shade flitting across the stage of Western history was not, after all, the Roman Empire's self, but the Roman Empire's ghost; and it explains the paradox of the Emperor Francis being the legitimate successor of the Emperor Augustus by showing that he was so by a far-fetched legal fiction. Bryce had a great book to write, and he wrote

---

[1] Bryce: *The Holy Roman Empire* (7th edition, London 1884, Macmillan), p. 1.

it in the grand manner of his age. Yet it is great in spite of, and not because of, the current conceit of continuity which had captivated his imagination and perhaps actually inspired him to take up his pen.

Examples of barren controversies into which the will-o'-the-wisp of 'Continuity' inveigled historians in Freeman's time are the dispute over the question whether the self-governing communes which emerged in the cities of Northern Italy at the transition from 'the Dark Ages' to 'the Middle Ages' of Western history were survivals, or 'mere revivals', of the self-governing municipalities which were known to have existed in those same cities under the early Roman Empire; and the not less acrimonious dispute over the question whether the Greeks who fought the War of Independence against the Turks in 1821–9 were physically descended from the Greeks of the Periclean Age or from 'mere graecized Slavs' who had supplanted the ancient population of Greece in the Dark Ages. In both these controversies, the historical evidence, such as it is, appears to tell decidedly in favour of the hypothesis of 'revival'; but under the influence of the prejudice that 'mere imitation, mere artificial revival', is somehow a poorer thing than 'abiding and unbroken tradition', the 'revivalists' were denounced by Greek and Italian scholar-patriots as foreign enemies who were maliciously seeking to despoil two ancient nations of some of the most valuable properties in their lumber-rooms; and a hypothesis of 'survival' was intrepidly brought into action, in the teeth of the historical evidence, as a counterblast.

The second misjudgement into which Freeman was betrayed by his over-statement of the continuity of history was that he equated with 'Universal History' the histories of the two particular societies, the Hellenic and the Western, which he had fused together in his imagination through failure to apprehend the exact relation in which they really stood to one another. He enunciated this judgement with characteristic vigour:

'The history of Rome is the history of the European World. It is in Rome that all the earlier states of the European World lose themselves; it is out of Rome that all the states of the later European World take their being. The true meaning of Roman history as a branch of universal history, or rather the absolute identity of Roman history with universal history, can only be fully understood by giving special attention to those ages of the history of Europe which are commonly most neglected.'[1]

Yet, notwithstanding such passages as the above, Freeman was not given over to this second error completely. In the back of his mind he was aware all the time that other worlds with other histories did exist outside the limits of the Hellenic and the

---

[1] Freeman, op. cit., p. 327.

Western World and beyond the range of Hellenic and Western history. Moreover, he realized that, in this broader historical landscape, 'the Unity of History' could still be discerned and that here it was discernible not at all in the form of a continuity of objective events but wholly in the form of similarities in tendency and structure.[1]

'European history forms one whole in the strictest sense, but between European and Asiatic history the connexion is only occasional and incidental. The fortunes of the Roman Empire had no effect on the internal revolutions of the Saracenic Caliphate, still less effect had they on the momentary dominion of the House of Jenghiz or on the Mogul Empire in India. Yet the way in which the European Empire and its several kingdoms broke in pieces had its exact parallel in those distant Eastern monarchies.'[2]

From this passage we may conjecture that if, in Freeman's time, Western historians had had at their disposal as much knowledge of the history of other societies besides the Hellenic Society and the Western Society as we have in our generation, Freeman would have realized that Hellenic and Western history only covered a fraction of the field of universal history, and that in equating the relation between them with 'continuity' *sans phrase* and endeavouring to stretch the two histories, thus erroneously fused together, into covering the whole field, he was falling into a misconception of growth, as a movement whose track is a straight line, from which his appreciation of the comparative method of study ought to have emancipated him.

So much in justice, and in tribute of admiration, to Freeman.

Additional Note

It may be observed that in Freeman's time the histories of two out of the four living non-Western societies—namely the Islamic and the Hindu—and also the histories of two extinct societies—the Syriac and the Indic—which were respectively 'apparented' to these, were considerably less well known than they are to-day; that the knowledge of the histories of the Egyptiac, Sumeric, Babylonic, Mayan, Central American, and Andean societies was in his time still so rudimentary as to be practically useless for the purpose of comparative study; and that the existence of the Minoan and the Hittite societies was not only unknown but unsuspected (as was also the existence of 'the Indus Culture', if this turns out to be an independent representative of the species). On the other hand, Freeman possessed, and made use of, the materials for studying Byzantine history without apparently appreciating their significance for the morphology of universal history. Moreover, he ignored Sinic history and Far Eastern history, though, had he cared to study these, they were almost as accessible to him as they are to a Western

---

[1] In this context, however, he rather disparages 'mere analogy' by contrast with 'long chains of events bound together in the direct relation of cause and effect'. (Op. cit., p. 333, quoted above.)

[2] Op. cit., p. 333. On pp. 333–5 he discusses another parallel: the tendency for the prestige of 'universal states' like the Roman Empire and the Arab Caliphate to outlast their material power in such strength that the very 'successor-states' which have forcibly taken the material power to themselves are unable to dispense with some form of legitimation at the hands of the nominal 'world-rulers' whom they have supplanted *de facto* but who remain *de jure* the sole founts and dispensers of lawful authority.

historian in 1933; for the materials which had been communicated to Western scholars by the magnificent researches and publications of the Jesuit missionaries in China during the century *circa* A.D. 1675–1775 have not been appreciably increased or improved from that day to this. (On this point, see Hudson, G. F.: *Europe and China* (London 1931, Arnold), pp. 326–7.)

Why was it that Freeman did not turn this great body of accessible knowledge about Sinic history and Far Eastern history to account for the purpose of comparative study? His neglect of this valuable resource is thrown into relief by the good use that had been made of it, immediately after it had been opened up, by his predecessors Voltaire and Gibbon. Voltaire gives the Sinic and Far Eastern Society the place of honour in his *Histoire des Mœurs*; and it is impossible to read *The History of the Decline and Fall of the Roman Empire* without becoming aware that a contemporary empire of equal scale and pretensions was declining and falling in another quarter of the World—and this though the Celestial Empire only enters into Gibbon's story incidentally, apropos of the migrations of the Huns and the Mongols. Thus, among Western scholars a hundred years before Freeman's time, as among Western scholars to-day, an interest in Sinic history and Far Eastern history was 'in the air'. Why was this interest in suspense in Freeman's time? Was the eighteenth-century *penchant* towards Sinology replaced by the nineteenth-century *penchant* towards Sanskrit studies? Or is the explanation to be found in the sensitiveness of movements on the cultural plane to movements on the political plane? Was the change in the attitude of Western scholars towards the Sinic and Far Eastern culture, from a mood of respect and curiosity to a posture of contempt and indifference, an indirect effect of the revolution in the political relations between the Manchu Empire and the Western Powers which had occurred between Gibbon's and Freeman's times?

In the interval, 'the Barbarians from the South Sea' had taken the Celestial Empire by storm, opening Chinese ports to Western trade by force of arms and compelling the Manchu Imperial Government to grant to Western Governments and their nationals those extra-territorial privileges in the newly opened 'treaty-ports' of China which the Ottoman Imperial Government already accorded to them in the *Échelles du Levant*. Before the wars and treaties of 1839–61 the Celestials had been accepted by 'the South Sea Barbarians' more or less at their own valuation as superior persons. In less than a quarter of a century the roles had been reversed, and the Westerners had established themselves in China as a privileged minority among a herd of 'Natives'. Could Western historians who had seen the hand of the Lord revealed in their day in this discomfiture of the heathen be expected to waste their time in exploring 'native' footpaths when they might be mapping out the great highway along which the Chosen People had travelled from Greece through Rome to the Promised Land in the West? *Ex Oriente lux?* An exploded fallacy. After all, 'can any good thing come out of Nazareth?'

Some such change of outlook, induced by the triumph of Nationalism and Industrialism in Western historians' minds, may perhaps explain the paradox that a Freeman should have neglected a field of comparative historical study which had been assiduously cultivated by a Gibbon and a Voltaire.

For an authoritative discussion of 'the eclipse of Chinese cultural prestige' in the nineteenth century, see further Hudson, op. cit., pp. 327–8.

THE SCHISM IN THE IRANIC WORLD AND THE INCORPORATION OF THE ARABIC SOCIETY INTO THE IRANIC

The Differentiation of the Iranic and Arabic Worlds during the Post-Syriac Interregnum

ON pages 68–72, above, we have observed that after the post-'Abbasid interregnum, in which the Syriac Society went into dissolution, two new societies, both 'affiliated' to the Syriac, arose in different parts of the derelict Syriac domain. We have called these two sister societies the Arabic and the Iranic respectively; and we have drawn a comparison between this pair of Islamic societies 'affiliated' to the Syriac Society and the pair of Christian societies—the Orthodox and the Western—that are 'affiliated' to the Hellenic Society. Our comparison, however, has brought out an important point of difference between the respective histories of these two pairs of societies of the second generation; and while this difference was not strictly relevant to the purpose of the chapter in which it came to light, it may prove to have some bearing on our Study of History nevertheless. On this account it may be convenient to pursue the investigation in the present Annex.

This difference in the histories of the pair of Christian and the pair of Islamic societies may be recapitulated as follows. The two Christian societies, when once they had become differentiated and segregated from one another during the interregnum, continued thereafter to follow separate paths. The attempt made by our Western Society to incorporate Orthodox Christendom into itself by main force during the Middle Ages, in the course of the Crusades, was unsuccessful; and it is only within the last two centuries and a half that the enterprise has been attempted again (and attempted, this time, with greater success, inasmuch as the West has been wise enough to refrain, on this second occasion, from imposing itself upon Orthodox Christendom by violence and has been content to win its way peacefully and gradually through the attraction which our modern Western culture has exercised upon Orthodox Christian hearts and minds). In this respect, the history of the relations between the Iranic and the Arabic Society has taken a markedly different turn. For, as early as the first quarter of the sixteenth century of the Christian Era, about two hundred and fifty years after the emergence of the two Islamic societies from the post-ʿAbbasid interregnum, the Iranic Society took the offensive against the Arabic Society and won a decisive victory.

This Iranic offensive was taken, and this Iranic victory was won, by one particular state among those into which the Iranic Society had come to be articulated; and this state was the Ottoman Empire. As a result of the Ottoman conquests of Syria and Egypt (in A.D. 1516–17) and Algeria (in A.D. 1512–19), almost the whole of the Arabic World with the exception of Morocco was incorporated into the Iranic World. The Ottoman occupation of Cairo in A.D. 1517 was the analogue, in Islamic history, of the capture of Constantinople by the Crusaders in A.D. 1204; but there was a vital difference in the sequel, since the Ottoman act of aggression in the sixteenth century of the Christian Era resulted in the annexation of the sister-society for a period of no less than four hundred years, whereas the Fourth Crusade was as ineffectual as it was discreditable. Thus, while Orthodox Christendom enjoyed a thousand years of independent life between its emergence from the post-Hellenic interregnum towards the end of the seventh century and its pacific incorporation into 'the Great Society' of our latter-day Westernized World since the latter part of the seventeenth century, the Arabic Society only enjoyed its independence for some two centuries and a half (approximately A.D. 1275–1525) before it was forcibly incorporated into the Iranic Society by the ʿOsmanlis in order to be merged in the united Sunni Islamic World which has existed from the sixteenth century of the Christian Era down to the present day.

This sharp divergence between the respective histories of the two Islamic and the two Christian societies evidently requires explanation. Why was it that the Ottoman offensive against the Arabic World in the first quarter of the sixteenth century was successful? In a previous passage (on pp. 69–70) we have mentioned by anticipation that the conquest of the Arabic World at this juncture was virtually forced upon the ʿOsmanlis in consequence of a religious schism within the bosom of the Iranic Society to which the ʿOsmanlis themselves belonged; and that this schism arose through the unexpected and revolutionary resuscitation of Shiʿism as a militant political force by Ismāʿīl Shāh Safawī (*dominabatur* A.D. 1500–24). In other words, the incorporation of the Arabic World into one part—that is to say, the Ottoman part—of the Iranic World was the consequence of a sudden and violent and disruptive social convulsion by which the Iranic World itself was first overtaken. In the present Annex, we have to trace out, in greater detail, the concatenation of events which thus abruptly and surprisingly deflected the course of Islamic history.

We may preface this investigation by pointing out, once again, how completely unexpected the sixteenth-century course of Islamic history really was.

Down to about the year A.D. 1500, the segregation and differentiation between the infant Arabic and Iranic societies showed every sign of persisting and indeed of becoming more sharply accentuated. Geographically, a clearly defined frontier had arisen between the two worlds; and this frontier extended continuously from the waters of the Indian Ocean in the Persian Gulf to the waters of the Mediterranean in the Gulf of Alexandretta. The province of 'Irāq, which had been the metropolitan province of the 'Abbasid Caliphate, had lain waste since the sack of the Imperial City of Baghdad by the Mongols in A.D. 1258; and in consequence the lower valley of the Tigris and the Euphrates had become a positive barrier, instead of being a link, between the regions on either side of it. Farther to the north-west, the line of the Euphrates, in the sector between the North Arabian Steppe and the Taurus Range, had become once again the military frontier that it had formerly been, for some seven centuries, in the Roman Age. From the first century B.C. to the seventh century of the Christian Era, the Romans had held the line of the Euphrates first against the Arsacids and then against the Sasanids. From the latter part of the thirteenth century onwards, the Mamlūks of Egypt held the same river-line against the Mongols and their successors. Finally, between the Euphrates and the Mediterranean, the Arabic World was insulated by the barrier of the Taurus from the territories which the nascent Iranic Society had conquered from Orthodox Christendom in Anatolia,[1] while Anatolia itself was linked up with the main body of the Iranic World through Azerbaijan.

Thus the geographical frontier between these two worlds was clearly defined from one end to the other by A.D. 1500; and the geographical insulation of the two regions on either side of this line had been accompanied, as we have seen, by a divergence in the political and cultural development of the two societies which were growing up separately in these two different geographical cradles. In politics, the Arabic Society looked back to the 'Abbasid Caliphate while the Iranic Society looked back to the Eurasian Nomad

[1] This Iranic conquest of Anatolia had begun, during the post-'Abbasid and pre-Iranic interregnum, with the irruption of the Saljūq Turkish barbarian invaders into Anatolia from the Eurasian Steppe, via Iran, in the latter half of the eleventh century of the Christian Era. The process was completed in the fourteenth and fifteenth centuries by the Turkish successor-states of the Anatolian Saljūqs and first and foremost by the 'Osmanlis (who were spoken of by their co-religionists, in consequence, as 'the Ghāzis of Rūm': the periphrasis by which the 'Osmanlis are commonly described in the memoirs of the Emperor Bābur (*vivebat* A.D. 1483–1530). See Bābur, Zahīr-ad-Dīn Muhammad: *Memoirs*, translated by Beveridge, A. S. (London 1922, Luzac, 2 vols.), vol. ii, p. 564).

Empire of Chingis Khan. In culture, the Arabic Society remained faithful to the Classical Arabic language, while the Iranic Society had discarded Arabic in favour of Persian as its secular literary vehicle. In fact, in every important aspect of social life, the differentiation between the Iranic and the Arabic Society appeared, by A.D. 1500, to be definitive.

Moreover, although both societies were expanding geographically with great vigour, neither showed any inclination to trespass seriously upon the other's ground. The Arabic Society was directing its expansion across the Sahara into Tropical Africa and across the Indian Ocean into Indonesia. The Iranic Society was expanding out of Anatolia into South-Eastern Europe and out of Hindustan into the Deccan and out of Transoxania over the Eurasian Steppe; but until the close of the fifteenth century of the Christian Era the two sister-societies stood, so to speak, back to back, and rarely collided with one another. Their mutual trespasses down to that date can be counted on the fingers of one hand. The invasions of Syria by Mongol armies in the years 1260, 1281, 1299–1300, and 1303, and by Timur in 1400–1, may be reckoned as Iranic incursions into the Arabic domain; and we may count it as an Arabic incursion into the Iranic domain when the Mamlūk Sultan Beybars defeated the Mongols at Abulusteyn in the fastnesses of the Taurus and occupied Caesarea on the Anatolian Plateau in A.D. 1277. But these incursions were exceptional. For the most part, the two societies steered clear of one another from the middle of the thirteenth century of the Christian Era until the opening of the sixteenth.

The next point to observe is that although, during this period, the Arabic and Iranic worlds were more or less isolated from one another, the intercommunication between the different parts of each of these two worlds was actively maintained. In the Arabic World in the fourteenth century of the Christian Era, the statesman and philosopher Ibn Khaldūn moved freely from his birth-place at Tunis to Fez and Granada in one direction and to Cairo and Damascus in the other; and he appears to have found himself almost equally at home in any of these local seats of the Arabic culture.[1] Similarly, in the Iranic zone, the poet and philosopher Muhammad Jelāl-ed-Dīn (*vivebat* A.D. 1207–73) found no difficulty in migrating from his birth-place at Balkh, in the Oxus-Jaxartes Basin, to Qonīyah in Anatolia, where he made himself so thoroughly at home that he is remembered at this day not as Balkhī but as Rūmī. With equal facility, a Turkish soldier of fortune like Ertoghrul, the father of 'Osmān the eponym of the 'Osmanlis, could traverse

---

[1] For Ibn Khaldūn's career, see further III. C (ii) (b), vol. iii, pp. 321–8, below.

the Iranic World from the Transoxanian fringe of the Eurasian
Steppe to the north-western escarpment of the Anatolian Plateau,[1]
while other Eurasian adventurers, turning their faces in a different
direction, were able as easily to traverse Afghanistan, in order to
seek and find their fortunes in India, from the days of Mahmūd
of Ghaznah to the days of Bābur of Farghana. In fact, down to
the generation of Bābur the Timurid (*vivebat* A.D. 1483–1530) and
Ismāʿīl Shāh Safawī (*dominabatur* A.D. 1499/1500–1523/4) and the
Ottoman Sultan Selīm I (*imperabat* A.D. 1512–20), this active social
intercommunication between the different parts of the Iranic
World—a healthy circulation of the blood in the body social—
continued without intermission.

From the remote domain which they had carved out for them-
selves in the European provinces of Orthodox Christendom, the
Ottoman 'Ghāzis of Rūm' still looked to the heart of the Iranic
World for intellectual light and leading. The Ottoman Sultan
Bāyezīd II (*imperabat* A.D. 1481–1512), who was the father of
Selīm I and the son of Mehmed the Conqueror, was in correspondence with the divines and the men of letters of Khurāsān,
including the poet Jāmī and the Sunni doctor Farīd-ad-Dīn
Ahmad-i-Taftāzānī: the Shaykh-al-Islam of Herat who was put to
death by Shāh Ismāʿīl in A.D. 1510 for refusing to pay lip service
to the Shīʿī creed.[2] The Timurid ruler of Herat, Sultan Husayn
b. Mansūr b. Bayqarā (*regnabat* A.D. 1468–1506), was Jāmī's patron,
and his patronage was not confined to Persian literature. For it was
Sultan Husayn's minister of state Mīr ʿAlī Shīr Nawāʾī (*decessit*
A.D. 1501) who gathered round him a literary circle which created
a new Turkī literature on the Persian model; and, while this
Turkish literary movement in Khurāsān was an artificial and
ephemeral plant, which did not long survive the ensuing political
and religious storms to which Khurāsān was exposed, it had a
permanent effect in stimulating the growth of another Turkish
literature, in the kindred Ottoman Turkish language, at the
opposite extremity of the Iranic World.[3]

In return for these cultural gifts,[4] the Court of Constantinople
gave asylum to the prince Badīʿ-az-Zamān, the son of Sultan
Husayn Bayqarā, after the overrunning of Khurāsān, about A.D.

---

[1] For Ertoghrul's trek, see further II. D (v), vol. ii, p. 151, below.

[2] Browne, E. G.: *A Literary History of Persia*, vol. iv (Cambridge 1928, University Press), p. 69. Letters addressed by Bāyezīd to Jāmī, Farīd-ad-Dīn, and other leading lights in Khurāsān are preserved in the first volume of Firīdūn Bey's *Munshaʾāt-i-Salātīn*: a collection of state papers which was compiled in A.D. 1574 and printed at Constantinople in A.D. 1858.

[3] For the influence of Mīr ʿAlī Shīr Nawāʾī's literary circle at Herat upon Ottoman Turkish literature, see Browne, op. cit., vol. iii, pp. 398–9 and 422–3.

[4] For the cultural achievements of the Timurids, see further II. D (v), vol. ii, pp. 148–50, below.

1507, by the Uzbeg Nomad invaders from the Eurasian Steppe.[1]
And there are other instances, besides, of a reciprocal give-and-
take between the two extremities of the Iranic World. While
literary inspirations and political refugees were travelling westward
from Khurāsān to Rūm, Rūmī technique and technicians were
travelling eastward from South-Eastern Europe to Khurāsān and
Transoxania. The Timurid Emperor Bābur repeatedly refers in
his Memoirs to his employment of the Rūmī battle array: a formation of wagons, linked to one another by chains, with firing-parties
of artillery and musketeers posted in the intervals.[2] These tactical
arrangements were superintended for Bābur by a Rūmī soldier of
fortune named Mustafā,[3] who incurred the jealousy of Bābur's
official master of arms, Ustād ʿAlī Qūlī.[4] Nor was the Ottoman

[1] For the Uzbeg invasion see pp. 371–7, below. Badīʿ-az-Zamān found asylum with
Shāh Ismāʿīl in the first instance, and was brought from Tabrīz to Constantinople by
Sultan Selīm when the ʿOsmanlis evacuated Tabrīz after their momentary occupation
of the Safawī capital in A.D. 1514. (See pp. 385–6, below.)

[2] This self-same military formation was employed in the fifteenth century of the
Christian Era by the Hussites in Bohemia; and the resemblance in detail between the
Hussite and the Mughal 'lagers' is too close to be fortuitous—in spite of the remoteness
of the Bohemian plains from those of Northern India. Since we know, on Bābur's own
evidence, that this formation, as used by him in India, was derived from an Ottoman
source, we may conjecture that the Hussites, on their side, derived it from the same
quarter. The channel of communication in this case was doubtless Hungary: Bohemia's
south-eastern neighbour, who, throughout the fifteenth century, was in intimate
political and military relations with Bohemia on the one side and with the Ottoman
Empire on the other. In any case, the Rūmī battle-formation was as novel, and therefore
as effective, when it was introduced by the Hussites into Western Europe as when it
was introduced into India by Bābur. It was designed, of course, to baffle the heavy
cavalry which at that time were the staple arm in the Western and the Iranic worlds
alike. The combination of wagons with artillery and musketeers was just what might
be expected from the ʿOsmanlis with their Nomadic tradition and their aptitude for
Western technique.

Count Lützow gives the following account of the lager-tactics which were employed
by the Hussite forces in Bohemia, during their warfare with the anti-Hussite Crusaders
(bellum gerebatur circa A.D. 1419–36), on the initiative of the Hussite leader Žižka
(vivebat circa 1378–1424):

'The hradba vozová ('Wagenburg', wagon-fort or lager of wagons), if not absolutely
Žižka's invention, became, entirely through him, a serious feature in Bohemian warfare.
From the scanty and contradictory accounts that have reached us it appears that the
wagons or chariots of the Bohemian armies were linked together by strong iron chains,
and were used not only for defence, but also for offensive movements. All the warriors,
except the few horsemen as well as the women and children who accompanied the
armies, found shelter in these wagons, which in time of battle were generally formed in
four lines or columns. The wagons were covered with steel or iron—iron-clad, to use a
modern term—and the best marksmen were placed next to the driver of each of them.
In case of defeat, the wagons formed what was practically a fortified entrenchment.
When an offensive movement was undertaken, the drivers of the wagons at one end
of the line of battle attempted to outflank the enemy, and after Žižka's men had become
accustomed to warfare, often succeeded in doing so. It may be noticed that the wide
plains of Bohemia, which then—as now—were little intersected by ditches or fences,
offered every advantage to this novel system of warfare. Žižka also seems to have given
his attention to fire-arms, as the picked marksmen whom he placed next to the drivers
of the wagons soon became the terror of the Germans, through the precision of their
fire, whilst the few and unwieldy field-pieces which accompanied the Bohemian armies
were yet far superior to anything the Germans and other enemies could then bring to
battle against them.' (Lützow, Count Francis: Bohemia: An Historical Sketch (London
1896, Chapman & Hall), pp. 184–9.)

[3] For Bābur's references to Mustafā Rūmī or to the Rūmī battle-formation, see the
Memoirs, ed. Beveridge, vol. ii, pp. 469, 550, 564, 635.

[4] Bābur, ed. cit., vol. ii, p. 550. From ʿAlī Qūlī's name and profession, one might

technique which found its way eastward exclusively military.
Bābur mentions a Rūmī medical remedy[1]; and, three generations
earlier,[2] a certain Salāh-ad-Dīn Mūsā Qādi-zāda-i-Rūmī[3] was one
of the savants who compiled for the Timurid prince Ulugh Beg
the famous set of astronomical tables that were completed in
A.D. 1437/8.[4]

It must be added that there was not, within the interior of either
of our two worlds, any regional segregation of communities on
the basis of language; for though Turkish as well as Persian was
current in the Iranic World, and Berber as well as Arabic in the
Arabic World, the Berber and the Turkish vernaculars were simply
the vulgar tongues of camp and court; and they did not dispute the
claims of Arabic and Persian, in their respective geographical
spheres, to be the vehicles of official transactions and of literary
works of art. In the Iranic World, at the turn of the fifteenth and
sixteenth centuries of the Christian Era, the literary use of the
Turkish language was still in its infancy; and this infant literature
in the vulgar tongue was not a symptom of linguistic or regional
nationalism in the modern Western sense. It is a remarkable fact
that the two grim antagonists Ismā'īl Shāh Safawī and Selīm
Pādishāh 'Osmanlī were both poets as well as men of blood. But
in Western eyes it is perhaps still more remarkable that Ismā'īl, the
political founder of 'Modern Persia', followed the new fashion of
Mir 'Alī Shīr Nawā'ī in writing his verses almost exclusively in the
Turkish idiom which was his native vernacular, whereas Selīm,
the sovereign of 'Turkey', persisted in writing almost exclusively
in Persian.[5]

Thus, down to about A.D. 1500, the Arabic and Iranic worlds were
more or less isolated from one another, while at the same time
either world was substantially a unity in itself. This state of affairs,
however, was radically and permanently upset by the career of
Ismā'īl Shāh Safawī, the resuscitator of Shī'ism as a militant
political force.

The Eclipse of the Shī'ah

In order to understand the revolutionary character of Shāh
Ismā'īl's work, it is necessary to remind ourselves of the history
of the Shī'ah before Shāh Ismā'īl's time.

hazard the guess that he was a refugee Shī'ī from Anatolia who had entered Shāh
Ismā'īl's service and afterwards transferred into Bābur's.
[1] Bābur: Memoirs, ed. cit., vol. ii, p. 657.
[2] Bābur was Timur's great-great-great-grandson, Ulugh Beg his grandson.
[3] Browne, op. cit., vol. iii, p. 386.
[4] For Ulugh Beg's patronage of astronomical research, see further II. D (v), vol. ii,
p. 149.
[5] Browne, op. cit., vol. iv, pp. 12–13.

Down to the moment of Shāh Ismāʿil's dramatic entry upon the stage, the survival of Shiʿism in the Iranic and Arabic worlds must have seemed to intelligent Sunnī observers to be really nothing more than one of the curiosities of history: a relic of the past which could have little or no significance for the future. The Shiʿism which had survived the post-ʿAbbasid interregnum in the crannies and corners of Dār-al-Islām was in fact the flotsam and jetsam of a movement which belonged to the last chapter in the history of the extinct Syriac Society and which reflected the social conditions of that now obsolete age.

In its origin, the Shīʿah was the faction of one of the rival Meccan houses that laid claim to the Caliphate in a domestic quarrel over the spoils of victory among the primitive Arab Muslim conquerors, who had reunited under one rule the vast territories that had once been embraced in the Achaemenian Empire before the Hellenic intrusion upon the Syriac World. Thereafter, when the House of ʿAlī had been worsted in the competition for the Caliphate, first by the House of Umayyah and finally by the House of ʿAbbās, the Shīʿah still perpetuated its own existence, in its already stereotyped role as an embodiment of frustrated ambitions, by broadening its basis and identifying itself with the reaction of the non-Arab subjects of the Caliphate against the Arab ascendancy. The most important of these non-Arab communities were the Iranians in the eastern and the Berbers in the western provinces of the Arab Empire; and, of these two, the Iranians were the more highly cultivated and the more self-conscious party. Accordingly, under the ʿAbbasid régime at Baghdad, from the latter part of the eighth century of the Christian Era onwards, we find Shiʿism perpetually seeking to propagate itself into Iran in the one direction and into the Maghrib in the other direction from its original stronghold in Lower ʿIrāq, which was a meeting-place of the Aramaic, Iranian, and Arabic elements of the Syriac culture.[1]

In Iran, it was the (Zaydī) Shīʿī and not the Sunnī version of Islam that was adopted by the outlying Iranians in the fastness of the Caspian Provinces when they tardily abandoned their ancestral Zoroastrianism in the ninth and tenth centuries of the Christian Era;[2] and in the tenth century these recently converted Daylamīs

---

[1] See the note by Professor H. A. R. Gibb at the end of this Annex.

Compare the conversion of the Teutonic barbarians in the no-man's-land beyond the European frontiers of the Roman Empire to Arian instead of Catholic Christianity in the fourth century of the Christian Era. In both these cases we may detect the result of two convergent tendencies: a tendency on the part of trans-frontier dissidents or barbarians to maintain some show of individuality in the form in which they eventually succumb to an expanding civilization, when they cannot avoid succumbing to some extent; and the tendency for a discountenanced or persecuted minoritarian religion to abandon the interior of the world to which it belongs and to seek compensation by winning new converts on the periphery. (For this latter tendency, compare the centri-

produced a Shī'ī dynasty, the Buwayhids, who overran the whole of Western Iran and descended upon 'Irāq and imposed their will upon the 'Abbasid Caliphs at Baghdad.[1] In the Maghrib, a Shī'ī principality which held its own for nearly two centuries (A.D. 788–985) between the remnant of the Umayyad Caliphate in the Iberian Peninsula and the 'Abbasid dominion over the rest of the Syriac World was founded in Morocco in A.D. 788 by an 'Alid, Idrīs b. 'Abdallāh, after he had tried and failed to make head against the 'Abbasids at Medina. At about the same time, a Khārijī ['Dissident'] principality which endured for a century and a half (A.D. 761–908) was founded in the hinterland of Ifrīqīyah by a Persian adventurer named Rustem who won the allegiance of the Zenāta Berbers.[2] The Rustemids extended their rule or influence from the coast of Algeria to the hinterland of Tripoli, and severed the communication by land between the 'Abbasid Caliphs at Baghdad and their Aghlabid lieutenants in Tunisia.[3] Finally, in A.D. 909, both the Sunnī Aghlabids and the Khārijī Rustemids were supplanted in Ifrīqīyah and its hinterland by the Fātimids, who made their fortunes by winning the allegiance of the Katāma Berbers, as the Rustemids had made theirs by winning the allegiance of the Zenāta.[4] The actual founder of the Fātimid Power in Ifrīqīyah was the head of a Shī'ī propaganda organization in Syria who styled himself al-Mahdī Abu Muhammad 'Ubaydallah and claimed descent from 'Alī and Fātimah through the Seventh Imām —though his real name was said by the opponents of the Fātimids to be Sa'īd b. al-Husayn b. 'Abdallah b. Maymūn al-Qaddāh, and his grandfather 'Abdallah, who had created the propaganda organization which al-Mahdī had inherited, was reputed to have been no true descendant of 'Alī but merely the son of an oculist who was a native of the town of Ahwāz in the Iranian province of Khuzistan.

In A.D. 969 the Fātimids, at the head of their Katāma henchmen, succeeded in conquering Egypt and Southern Syria (a country which was apt to share the political fortunes of Egypt in this age);

---

fugal movements of the Russian Orthodox Christian 'Old Believers' from the centre to the circumference of the Russian Empire, of the Pilgrim Fathers overseas, and of the Mormons into Utah (see II. D (vi), vol. ii, pp. 221–2, below), and the expansion of the Syriac religions—Judaism, Christianity, Islam—in concentric waves (see II. D (vi), vol. ii, Annex, below).)

[1] See II. D (vii), Annex (viii), vol. ii, p. 448, below.

[2] For the 'Ibādī sect, which is a survival of the Khārijī Power that once created and maintained the Rustemid principality, see further II. D (vi), vol. ii, p. 239, below.

[3] The confederates of the Rustemids in the hinterland of Tripoli were their fellow-Khārijīs the Berbers of Jabal Nafūsah. (See Gautier, E. F.: Les Siècles Obscurs du Maghreb (Paris 1927, Payot), pp. 294–6.) Compare the hemming in of the Carthaginian dominions from sea to sea by the Numidian Power in the second century B.C.

[4] For the recurrent common features of these Shī'ī and Khārijī principalities in the Maghrib—the arrival of an adventurer from the Levant and his adoption as a leader by some local Berber people—see Gautier, op. cit., p. 312.

and for a time it seemed as though not only the 'Abbasid Caliphate at Baghdad but Sunnism itself might be overwhelmed by a convergence of victorious Shī'ī Powers from all quarters of the compass. The Carmathians, who were co-religionists of the Fātimids,[1] had built up a military, and militant, Power in Arabia which terrorized the fringes of Syria and 'Irāq for about a century (*circa* A.D. 890–990). In A.D. 930 the Carmathians actually sacked Mecca and carried off the Black Stone from the Ka'bah. At the same time, 'Irāq and Western Iran were under the dominion of the Shī'ī Buwayhids, who dictated the policy of the 'Abbasid Caliphs at Baghdad. There were actually forty weeks, in A.D. 1058–9, when, in Baghdad itself, the Khutbah was recited in the name of the Fātimid Caliph Mustansir.[2] This was not, however, the outcome of any fraternization between the Daylamī Iranian Shī'ī henchmen of the Buwayhids and the Katāma Berber Shī'ī henchmen of the Fātimids in an *union sacrée* against the 'Abbasid Caliphate and the Arab ascendancy. For the momentary master of Baghdad who gave this fleeting recognition to the Fātimids' pretensions was not a Buwayhid but an ephemeral Turkish war-lord who temporarily occupied Baghdad after the overthrow of the Buwayhids, in A.D. 1055–6, by the Saljūqs. The Buwayhids differed in religion from the Fātimids, as well as from the Carmathians, inasmuch as they belonged to the Zaydī or Six-Imām and not to the Seven-Imām branch of the Shī'ah;[3] and, apart from religious considerations, they found their political interest in keeping the 'Abbasid Caliphs on their throne in Baghdad as puppets manipulated by Buwayhid hands; and therefore the Buwayhids, so long as they remained in power, were steadfast in refusing to recognize the Fātimids' claims to the Caliphate. Indeed, these claims were not even recognized by the Carmathians, who contested the possession of Syria with the Fātimids by force of arms. Through this failure to make common cause, the three Shī'ī Powers that had arisen simultaneously in the tenth century of the Christian Era threw away the opportunity for securing the triumph of Shi'ism which offered itself between the entry of the Fātimids into Cairo in A.D. 969 and the entry of the Saljūqs into Baghdad in A.D. 1055. Thereafter, the political power of Shi'ism receded in the Syriac World as rapidly as it had previously advanced.

[1] The Fātimids and the Carmathians were co-religionists in the most exact sense, since they were both adherents of the Ismā'īlī or Seven-Imām form of Shi'ism which had been created by 'Abdallah b. Maymūn. The founder of the Carmathians, Hamdān Qarmat, was one of 'Abdallah's missionaries, while the founder of the Fātimids was 'Abdallah's grandson.

[2] Lane-Poole, S.: *A History of Egypt in the Middle Ages*, 2nd edition (London 1914, Methuen), pp. 138–9.

[3] The Shī'ī missionaries who had converted Daylam from Zoroastrianism in the ninth and tenth centuries of the Christian Era had been Zaydīs.

This political collapse of Shiʿism was an accomplished fact before the end of the interregnum (*circa* A.D. 975–1275) which intervened between the break-up of the ʿAbbasid Caliphate and the emergence, from its ruins, of the nascent Arabic and Iranic societies which stood to the defunct Syriac Society in the relation of 'Apparentation-and-Affiliation'. In Ifriqīyah, Sunnism regained the ascendancy over Shiʿism *circa* A.D. 1044–6, when the chieftain of the Sanhāja Berbers, to whom the Fātimids had delegated their authority in their original dominions after their conquest of Egypt, revolted against his overlord, renounced the Shīʿī doctrine, and accepted investiture from the hands of the ʿAbbasid Caliph at Baghdad. The subsequent Berber masters of the Maghrib and Andalusia—the Murābits (*circa* A.D. 1056–1147) and the Muwahhids (*circa* A.D. 1130–1269)—followed the established Berber practice of expressing their political self-consciousness in a religious form; but, among these outer barbarians from the Sahara and the Atlas, the form which this expression took was not Shiʿism but an exaggeration of the Sunnī Orthodoxy.[1] In Iran, again, the Turkish Saljūqs from the Eurasian Steppe, who overthrew and superseded the Iranian Buwayhids from Daylam, were as faithful to Sunnism and as hostile to Shiʿism as their Murābit Berber contemporaries and counterparts in the Maghrib. The final blow to Shiʿism was struck when the Fātimid Caliphate was snuffed out in Egypt itself by Saladin in A.D. 1171, as the result of a competition for the mastery of Egypt between the Frankish Kingdom of Jerusalem and the successors of the Saljūqs in Syria and the Jazīrah.[2]

Thereafter, it was only in the crannies and corners of Dār-al-Islām that Shiʿism survived as a political force.

In the highlands of the Yaman, for example, the Zaydī form of Shiʿism asserted itself at an early date, and has maintained itself down to the present day, as a religious expression of local particularism: the reaction of the highlander against the lowlander, of the cultivator against the Nomad, and of the ancient culture of the Yaman against the *parvenue* culture of the Hijāz.[3] The present Zaydī Imāms, who have reigned at Sanʿā since the end of the first Ottoman occupation in A.D. 1633, are the successors of the Rassid Imāms who founded a Shīʿī principality in the more remote fastness of Saʿdah as early as A.D. 893; and, at the moment when

---

[1] This contrast between the Shiʿism of the relatively cultivated Katāma and the Sunnism of their more barbarous kinsmen and successors the Murābits and Muwahhids may be compared, in the history of the Teutonic Völkerwanderung during the post-Hellenic interregnum, with the contrast between the Arianism of the Goths and the Catholicism of the Franks and Angles.

[2] This competition had begun with the invasion of Egypt by King Amaury of Jerusalem in A.D. 1163.

[3] It will be seen that the role of Shiʿism in the Yaman has been not unlike its role in Iran.

Shi'ism was collapsing politically in the Maghrib and in Iran, the whole of the Yaman, including the San a, was conquered by the short-lived Shi i dynasty of the Sulayhids (*circa* A.D. 1037–1101).

On the other hand, the Ismā'īlī or Seven-Imām sect of the Shī'ah, which had been politically paramount in fully half of Dār-al-Islām when the Fāṭimids and the Carmathians were at the height of their power, was restricted, before the end of the twelfth century of the Christian Era, to two groups of fastnesses—one in Northern Iran on the southern slopes of the Elbrūz Range, and the other in Northern Syria in the Jabal Ansarīyah—which were held by a remnant of the 'Ismā'īlīs who made themselves notorious under the name of the Assassins.[1] And the Assassins barely outlasted the post-'Abbasid and pre-Iranic interregnum. Their Iranian fastnesses were reduced to submission by the Mongol conqueror Hulāgū about A.D. 1255; and the temporary recovery of the citadel of Alamūt by the last 'Grand Master' of the 'Order', Rukn-ad-Dīn Khurshāh, in A.D. 1275–6, simply resulted in the extirpation of the sect in Iran by Hulāgū's successor Abāqā. The Syrian fastnesses of the sect were reduced by the Egyptian Mamlūks in A.D. 1270. Since then, the Ismā'īlīs have been represented by the Syrian branch of the sect, which survived the loss of its independence and has lived on in obscurity, and by a diasporà in India, where, under new social and psychological conditions, the descendants of the Assassins have undergone their astonishing transformation into the mild 'nation of shopkeepers' who pay Peter's Pence to the Agha Khan under the name of Khwājas.[2] Their last surving fastness is in Hunza, between Gilgit and the Pamirs.

In the last quarter of the thirteenth century of the Christian Era, when the post-'Abbasid interregnum was drawing to its close and the nascent Arabic and Iranic societies were beginning to emerge, almost the only overt adherents of Shi'ism that were still to be found within the boundaries of Dār-al-Islām were the Zaydīs in the Yaman and the Imāmīs—that is to say, the followers of the Twelve-Imām sect of the Shī'ah, as opposed to the Seven-Imām Ismā'īlīs—who were maintaining themselves here and there: for example in the Jabal 'Āmil at the southern end of the Lebanon

---

[1] The Assassins were a militant branch of the Ismā'īlīs who were organized by Hasan-i-Sabbāh about A.D. 1090. Their method of action was the assassination of princes; and they did their work impartially, for the list of their victims includes their fellow-Ismā'īlī the Fāṭimid Caliph al-Āmir, whom they assassinated in A.D. 1130, as well as a host of Sunnīs and Christians. The word 'assassinate' itself is derived from the name of the Assassins, and their name is derived in turn from the *hashīsh* or hemp-fumes with which their desperadoes used to intoxicate themselves before making their *attentats*. For Hasan-i-Sabbāh and the Assassins, see Browne, E. G.: *A Literary History of Persia*, vol. ii (London 1906, Fisher Unwin), pp. 201–11, and Yule, Sir Henry: *The Book of Ser Marco Polo*, 3rd edition (London 1903, Murray, 2 vols.), vol. i, pp. 139–48.)

[2] For the Khwājas, see further II. D (vi), vol. ii, pp. 238–9, below.

Range in Syria, in the East Arabian provinces of Bahrayn and Hasā, and at Hillah in the neighbourhood of the Shīʿī holy places in the original stronghold of Shiʿism in Lower ʿIrāq.[1] One reason why these Imāmīs survived when the Ismāʿīlīs went under was that, in striking contrast to the Ismāʿīlīs, the Imāmīs were committed to non-violence by the very nature of their special beliefs;[2] and they therefore did not invite persecution at the hands of the Sunnī majority among whom they had to live. At this time, no observer could have suspected that this Imāmī sect of the Shīʿah was destined to achieve by violence a great political renascence of Shiʿism two centuries later.

During the two hundred years or so which elapsed between the emergence of the Arabic and Iranic societies out of the interregnum and the opening of Ismāʿīl Shāh Safawī's career in the last year of the fifteenth century of the Christian Era, Shiʿism must have seemed a lost cause both on external evidence and *a priori*—*a priori* because, as we have observed already, the social conditions on which it had thriven during the first few centuries after the Hijrah had been completely transcended, and on external evidence because it was manifest that in point of numbers the Shīʿah, which at its strongest had never been more than a strong minority, had now dwindled to an insignificant fraction of the Islamic community.

In regard to the *a priori* consideration, our survey of the history of Shiʿism to this point has brought out the fact that, by the end of the thirteenth century of the Christian Era, the motives which had evoked and sustained the Shīʿī movement during the first three centuries of Islam had been put out of action by radical changes of circumstance. The personal appeal to right the wrongs of the disinherited and persecuted House of ʿAlī had lost much of its effect by the time when a line of Caliphs who at any rate laid claim to an ʿAlid and Fātimid ancestry had enjoyed two centuries of power and prosperity as rulers of Egypt, which was the most desirable province in the whole heritage of the primitive Arab Muslim conquerors with the one possible exception of ʿIrāq. By the year A.D. 1171, in which the Fātimid rule in Egypt was extinguished by Saladin, the usurping House of Umayyah had already been extinct for 160 years, even in its last refuge in Andalusia, while the usurping House of ʿAbbās was only lingering on at Baghdad as a puppet Power whose strings were pulled by Iranian

[1] For a daily ritual which was performed at Hillah by the Imāmī Shīʿis in the fourteenth century of the Christian Era, see III. C (ii) (b), Annex I, vol. iii, pp. 463–4, below.
[2] The central point in the Imāmī doctrine was the duty (symbolized in the daily ritual which is referred to in the preceding footnote) of waiting passively for the advent of 'the Expected Imām', instead of attempting to bring the Millennium about (as the Ismāʿīlīs attempted) by human force.

Shī'īs or by Turkish barbarians. After the overwhelming catastrophe of the Mongol sack of Baghdad in A.D. 1258, it was altogether impossible to feel that, at the end of the story, the House of
'Abbās had profited appreciably, in comparison with the fortunes of
the House of 'Alī, by that usurpation of the Caliphate in A.D. 750
which had embittered the Shī'ah so grievously at the time. The
ghost of the 'Abbasid Caliphate, which was maintained at Cairo
by the Egyptian Mamlūks for their own convenience from A.D.
1261 onwards, was no object of envy but rather an object of pity
as a token of the depths to which the once mighty House of 'Abbās
had fallen.

And if the personal or dynastic appeal of Shi'ism had been
effectively estopped by these complete changes in family fortunes,
the racial or national appeal had become every whit as obsolete.
By the year A.D. 1300, the ascendancy of the Arabs over the Iranian
and the Berber populations in the domain of the *ci-devant* Arab
Empire had been over and done with for fully five centuries; and,
in the course of these centuries, the parts of 'top-dog' and 'under-
dog' had actually been reversed. Under the Idrisid and Rustemid
and Fātimid régimes in the west, and the Tāhirid and Saffārid and
Sāmānid and Buwayhid régimes in the east, the former Berber and
Iranian subjects of the Arabs had enjoyed their turn of ruling over
their former Arab masters. By A.D. 1300 even this chapter of
history was a thing of the past,[1] and all the peoples of the derelict
Caliphate—Arabs and Berbers and Iranians alike—were being
ruled by intrusive barbarians from the no-man's-land beyond the
frontiers: Nomad Turks and Mongols from the Eurasian Steppe
and wild Berbers from the Sahara and the Atlas. Thus the entire
political and psychological situation which had first evoked and

---

[1] The actual political ascendancy of Iranian dynasties in the eastern provinces of the
'Abbasid Caliphate, between Baghdad and the coasts of the Eurasian Steppe, lasted for
hardly more than two centuries (*circa* A.D. 825–1025) round about the transition from the
universal state to the ensuing interregnum; but this Iranian political revival was only
one manifestation, and a superficial manifestation, of a cultural revival which was far
deeper and far more enduring. The great age of Persian literature set in at the very time
when, on the Iranian Plateau as well as in the Oxus-Jaxartes Basin, Iranian rulers were
yielding up the sceptre to Turkish Eurasian Nomads. But in these alien Turkish-
speaking princes, from Mahmūd of Ghaznah in the eleventh century of the Christian
Era down to the Timurids in the fifteenth, the great Persian men of letters found their
most appreciative patrons, with the result that the new civilization which emerged in
these regions after the interregnum was fundamentally 'Iranic' in its cultural background. It is one of the ironical curiosities of history that the great age of Persian literature, which began at the moment when the political régime of the Iranian Sāmānids and
Buwayhids was supplanted by the rule of Turkish barbarian adventurers, should have
come to an end at the moment when, at the turn of the fifteenth and sixteenth centuries
of the Christian Era, the rule of the Turkish Timurids was replaced by that of the
Safawīs, which heralded an Iranian political restoration (in spite of the fact that the
Safawīs themselves were apparently Türkmens). On the empirical evidence, it looks as
though the Iranians were incapable of achieving greatness simultaneously in literature
and in politics. (For the historical role of the great Persian literature of the post-Syriac
and pre-Iranic interregnum as an aftermath of the Syriac culture, see further II. D (iii),
vol. ii, p. 77, footnote 1, below.)

then sustained Shiʿism in the early centuries of Islam had now passed away; and, by the same token, Shiʿism might now be deemed to have become an anachronism.

It might also be written off as a mere lingering relic of the past on the test of numbers. In the Maghrib, Shiʿism had left no trace of its former political dominance. In Egypt, where the Fāṭimids had reigned for two full centuries with every opportunity to turn their political power to account for religious propaganda and with every inducement for their subjects to consult their material interests by adopting the religion of the reigning dynasty, Shiʿism appears to have gained a singularly small foothold among the population.[1] At any rate, there is no record of any formidable or persistent local religious opposition to the eviction of the last Shīʿī Fāṭimid Caliph by the Sunnī intruder, Saladin, and no trace of any lingering subterranean survival of Shiʿism in the country when once the Shīʿī dynasty had been brushed aside. So far from that, the trouble which was taken by the Ayyūbid conquerors of Egypt to obtain the blessing of the ʿAbbasid Caliphs at Baghdad, and the elaborate fiction of governing Egypt in the name of a refugee ʿAbbasid Caliph, which was promptly introduced and sedulously maintained by the Ayyūbids' Mamlūk successors, are historical facts which suggest that, on the morrow of the overthrow of the Fāṭimids, Egypt not only acquiesced passively in the substitution of a Sunnī for a Shīʿī régime but was positively Sunnī rather than Shīʿī in sentiment.[2]

A still more striking historical fact is the numerical weakness of the Shīʿah in Iran on the eve of Shāh Ismāʿīl's conquest of Iran during the first decade of the sixteenth century of the Christian Era. This fact is attested by several convergent lines of evidence. For example, in the time of the poet Jāmī (vivebat A.D. 1414–92), the province of Khurāsān appears to have been predominantly Sunnī, as it had been in the age of the Sāmānids and the Saljūqs (though Baghdad was now perhaps predominantly Shīʿī);[3] and when the Timurid prince of Herat, Sultan Husayn b. Mansūr b. Bayqarā (regnabat A.D. 1468–1506) displayed a proclivity towards Shiʿism, he was restrained by his minister of state the Turkī man

---

[1] The only Fāṭimid Caliph of Egypt who seems to have exerted himself in religious propaganda was Ḥākim (imperabat A.D. 996–1020); and the peculiar version of Ismāʿīlī Shiʿism which Ḥākim put into circulation, with his own personality in the centre of the picture, survives to-day not in Egypt but in Syria, as the religion of the Druses. (For the Druses see further II. D (vi), vol. ii, p. 258, below.)

[2] There was a movement for a Fāṭimid restoration in A.D. 1184, which Saladin crushed. Professor H. A. R. Gibb, who has brought this fact to the writer's attention, suggests that 'probably the imminent danger of the Crusades weighed more than religious enthusiasm in winning popular support for Saladin and his dynasty (as a fear of the Byzantines may have played a part in the Egyptian acceptance of the Fāṭimids' two centuries earlier).

[3] See Browne, op. cit., vol. iii (Cambridge 1928, University Press), pp. 510–11.

of letters Mīr 'Alī Shīr Nawā'ī (*decessit* A.D. 1501).[1] Again, when Ismā'īl conquered the city of Tabrīz, the capital of Azerbaijan, in A.D. 1501/2, he was informed by the local Shī'ī divines that two-thirds of the population were Sunnīs; and these Shī'ī divines themselves attempted (though without success) to dissuade their militant co-religionist from imposing public conformity to Shī'ism upon the Sunnī majority of their fellow citizens at the sword's point.[2] When Ismā'īl conquered the province of Fārs in A.D. 1503, a number of the Sunnī doctors of the law in the city of Kāzarūn were put to death[3]; and their colleagues at Herat (including the local Sunnī Shaykh-al-Islam himself) shared the same fate when the province of Khurāsān was conquered by Ismā'īl in A.D. 1510.[4] The numerical weakness of the Shī'ah in Iran at this date is also attested in another way by the dearth of Shī'ī theological works at Tabrīz in A.D. 1501/2 when these were required for the instruction of the forcibly converted Sunnī majority;[5] and, still more strikingly, by the dearth of Shī'ī divines throughout the territories of the Safawī Empire that was brought into existence by Ismā'īl's conquests. This dearth was so extreme that, during the sixteenth century of the Christian Era, the Safawī Government found it necessary to import Shī'ī divines into Iran from the two Imāmī Shī'ī fastnesses in the Jabal 'Āmil and in Bahrayn, in spite of the linguistic barrier that divided these Arabic-speaking exponents of Shī'ism from the Persian-speaking converts whom it was their mission to instruct.[6] And if Shī'ism was as weak as this, at the beginning of the sixteenth century, in Iran, it was weak *a fortiori* in the outlying regions in which the young Iranic Civilization had recently propagated itself. In Anatolia, for example, when the Ottoman Pādishāh Selīm (*imperabat* A.D. 1512–20) retorted to Ismā'īl Shāh Safawī's forcible extirpation of the Sunnah in Iran by a wholesale massacre of the Shī'ī element in the Ottoman dominions, the number of the victims is estimated by contemporary authorities at the low figure of 40,000.[7]

Nor was Shī'ism weak in numbers only during the five centuries ending in the generation of Shāh Ismā'īl. During this long intermediate period, as during the first four centuries of Islam, it was not—as it was to be from Shāh Ismā'īl's generation onwards—the

---

[1] Browne, op. cit., vol. iii, p. 456, following Bābur, ed. Beveridge, vol. i, p. 258.
[2] Browne, op. cit., vol. iv (Cambridge 1928, University Press), pp. 22 and 53–4.
[3] Browne, op. cit., vol. iv, p. 55.
[4] Browne, op. cit., vol. iv, p. 63; see also Haydar Dūghlāt, Muhammad: *Tarīkh-i-Rashīdī*, English translation by Elias, N., and Ross, E. D. (London 1895, Sampson Low & Martin), pp. 235–6.
[5] Browne, op. cit., vol. iv, p. 54.
[6] See Browne, op. cit., vol. iv, pp. 360 and 427–8.
[7] See Browne, op. cit., vol. iv, pp. 71–3. Sultan Selīm's massacre of the Anatolian Shī'is appears to have been perpetrated in A.D. 1514.

principal expression of an Iranian social consciousness. During this intermediate period, the Iranian social consciousness found its expression not in religion but in literature; and, at least ostensibly, the leading lights of Persian literary history, from Firdawsī (*vivebat circa* A.D. 930–1020)[1] to Jāmī (*vivebat* A.D. 1414–92)[2] inclusive, were not Shīʿīs but Sunnīs.[3] While Shiʿism remained endemic in Iran, and indeed became endemic throughout the whole Iranic World, beyond the narrow limits of the Iranian Plateau, it was apparently regarded during these centuries as an obsolete faith which reflected the vanished conditions of a past age rather than anything vital in the contemporary life of the young Iranic body social.

The same tale is told by the nature of the relations between Shiʿism and Sunnism in the Iranic World after the emergence of the new society from the post-ʿAbbasid interregnum, in so far as the nature of these relations can be ascertained; for they appear, on the whole, to have been both static and tolerant. Between the close of the thirteenth and the opening of the sixteenth century of the Christian Era, records of conversions to Shiʿism from Sunnism, or of militant Shīʿī outbreaks in the traditional style of the Khārijīs and the Carmathians and the Assassins, are few and far between. A certain proclivity towards the Shīʿah appears to have been shown by the Mongol Il-Khan Ghāzān (*regnabat* A.D. 1295–1304), who was the first convert to Islam in his dynasty,[4] and by Ghāzān's brother and successor Uljaytū (*regnabat* A.D. 1305–16).[5] But this *penchant* may be accounted for partly by the psychological bent towards empiricism and eclecticism in religion which was characteristic of all branches of the House of Chingis Khan, and partly by the political enmity between the Mongol Il-Khans and the Egyptian Mamlūks. Since the Mamlūks had proclaimed their Sunnī orthodoxy ostentatiously by setting up at Cairo, in A.D. 1261, a ghost of that ʿAbbasid Caliphate which the Mongols had overthrown at

---

[1] Firdawsī was accused of Shiʿism by his enemies.

[2] From the story cited by Browne in op. cit., vol. iii, pp. 510–11, it would appear that Jāmī himself, like his patron Sultan Husayn Bayqarā, had certain Shīʿī proclivities.

[3] It will be seen that the Golden Age of Persian literature coincides with the period during which Shiʿism was under eclipse, as well as with the period during which the political power in Iran was in Turkish and Mongol but not in Iranian hands (see p. 360, footnote 1, above). These two chronological coincidences can hardly be accidental; and they are susceptible of a psychological explanation. We may perhaps venture to suppose that the Iranian spirit insisted upon finding some medium of self-expression in all ages and therefore resorted to different alternatives at different times according to the circumstances of the day. From the eleventh to the fifteenth century of the Christian Era, when Shiʿism was under eclipse, and when a political outlet was precluded by the political ascendancy of the Eurasian barbarian invaders, the whole power of the Iranic genius was concentrated upon literature. Conversely, Persian literature wilted as soon as the military triumph of Shāh Ismāʿīl had opened new political and religious outlets for the Iranian spirit by asserting in Iran the political ascendancy of the Iranians over the Turks and of the Shīʿah over the Sunnah. For the positive inclemency of the Safawī régime towards intellectual culture, see an extract, quoted on pp. 393–4, below, from a letter by a Persian friend of Professor Browne's in op. cit., vol. iv, pp. 26–8.

[4] Ghāzān was converted in A.D. 1295.   [5] Browne, op. cit., vol. iii, pp. 44 and 50–1.

Baghdad in A.D. 1258, it was natural that the Mongol masters of Iran and 'Irāq, when they decided to adopt the religion of their subjects, should think of adopting it in a form which was opposed to the Mamlūks' form of it, and which could not be taken to imply any recognition of the shadowy 'Abbasid Caliphate which the Mamlūks were maintaining in Egypt for their own political purposes. The fact that the Il-Khans eventually became Sunnīs and not Shī'īs after all is another indication of the weakness of the Shī'ah and the strength of the Sunnah in Iran at this time. The Shī'ite proclivities of Sultan Husayn Bayqarā of Herat (*regnabat* A.D. 1468–1506) have been referred to already.[1] In the early part of the fifteenth century of the Christian Era and at the other end of the Iranic World, there seems to have been at least a tinge of Shī'ism, as well as Christianity, in the social revolutionary movement in the Ottoman Empire which came to a head in the revolt of Sheykh Bedr-ed-Dīn of Simāv against the Ottoman Government in A.D. 1416.[2] This movement, however, was abortive. In fine, the only effective and permanent conversion from Sunnism to Shī'ism of which there is a record in the Iranic World in this age is the conversion of the Safawī House: a family which possessed the hereditary headship of a religious order with its head-quarters in the Caspian Province of Gīlān.[3] The conversion of the Safawis was of course an event of supreme historical importance, since these were the ancestors of Shāh Ismā'īl.

It is certainly one of the curiosities of history that Shaykh Safīyu'd-Dīn, the founder of the Safawī House (*vivebat circa* A.D. 1252–1334), should not have been a Shī'ī. Yet there is no evidence of his having held Shī'ī tenets or even of his having had Shī'ī proclivities, while he is positively asserted to have been a Sunnī in a letter addressed to Shaykh Safī's descendant Tahmāsp Shāh Safawī by the Uzbeg Prince 'Ubaydallah Khan.[4] The first head of the Safawī House whose Shī'ism is beyond question is Shaykh Safī's grandson and second successor, Shaykh Khwāja 'Alī (*pontificali munere fungebatur* A.D. 1392–1427). The conversion of the House to the Imāmī (i.e. the Twelve-Imām) version of Shī'ism—whether abruptly or gradually (as is perhaps more probable)—must have taken place between the pontificates of the grandfather and the grandson.[5]

---

[1] On p. 361, above.

[2] The revolt was started by a disciple of Bedr-ed-Dīn's at Qaraburun in Aydin, whereupon Bedr-ed-Dīn himself raised his standard in Rumelia (Deli Ormān). For Bedr-ed-Dīn see Babinger, Fr.: 'Schejch Bedr-ed-Din', in *Der Islam*, vols. xi and xii.

[3] The modern Gīlān corresponds approximately to the ancient Daylam.

[4] See Browne, op. cit., vol. iv, pp. 43–4. The letter, which was written in A.D. 1529/1530, is preserved in a contemporary historical work.

[5] Khwāja 'Alī's contemporaries the Qāra Qōyūnlū lords of Western Iran and 'Irāq (see p. 369 below) were also Shī'īs according to Minorsky, V.: *La Perse au xve siècle entre la Turquie et Venise* (Paris 1933, Leroux), p. 4.

This exceptional case of conversion from Sunnism to Shiʿism round about the fourteenth century of the Christian Era does not appear to have occasioned, on either side, any immediate outbreak of either aggressive or defensive fanaticism. Indeed it is Shaykh Khwāja ʿAlī, the first of the Safawī line who was unquestionably a Shīʿī, who is reported to have prevailed upon Timur Lenk to liberate a number of his ʿOsmanlī prisoners of war, notwithstanding the fact that the ʿOsmanlis were a Sunnī community.[1] And the tolerant and humane attitude towards the adherents of the opposite sect, which this story ascribes to an enthusiastic Shīʿī, appears to have been also the attitude of the Sunnīs in this age towards the Shīʿah. The tolerance of the Ottoman Government, which was one of the principal Sunnī Powers of the day, is attested by the fact that Shāh Qūlī, who was a propagandist of the Shīʿī faith in the Ottoman dominions and a political agent of the Safawī Power into the bargain, was receiving a pension from the Ottoman Sultan Bāyezīd II (*imperabat* A.D. 1481–1512), and was in friendly relations with Bāyezīd's son Qorqūd, who was the Sultan's viceroy at Mānysa, down to the eve of the great rebellion of A.D. 1511–12, in which Shāh Qūlī sought to overthrow the Sunnī Ottoman Power in order that the Shīʿī Safawī Power might reign in its stead. In fact, the normal relation between the Sunnah and the Shīʿah, during the two centuries ending in the first decade of the sixteenth century of the Christian Era, seems to have been the relation of 'live and let live' which still tempers the feud between them in India at this day.[2]

---

[1] Browne, op. cit., vol. iv, p. 46. The liberated ʿOsmanlī prisoners and their descendants, the Sūfiyān-i-Rūmlū, became, of course, pious Shīʿīs as well as devoted adherents of the Safawis.

[2] In India, too, relations were often bad, and in the tribal areas of the North-West Frontier Province they were apt to rankle into warfare. Nevertheless, the recrudescence of the feud seems to have been less violent in India than elsewhere, and this difference—if such there was—may have had several causes. For one thing, the subversive effect of Shāh Ismāʿīl's career upon the life of the other Iranic countries did not extend to Hindustan; for although Ismāʿīl's career affected Indian history indirectly by leading (as will appear below) to the invasion of India by Bābur, Bābur (as will also appear) was a Laodicean in his attitude towards the Sunnī-Shīʿī quarrel. Another manifest ground for the relative tolerance shown by Shīʿīs and Sunnīs towards each other in India is the common consciousness of being members of an Islamic diasporà among a numerically overwhelming majority of Hindus to whom both forms of Islam are equally anathema. Though Bābur reverted to Sunnism after his final expulsion from Transoxania (see p. 379, below), and though his descendants in India remained Sunnis thereafter, the paramount concern of the Mughals, as of all other Islamic Powers in India, was to maintain as large as possible an inflow of Muslim recruits from Dār-al-Islām to sustain the Islamic ascendancy in Hindustan; and they did not inquire too narrowly into the religious views of the Muslims who responded to their call. Since Iran was the nearest part of Dār-al-Islām to India, and since Iran had become an exclusively Shīʿī country in consequence of the Safawi conquests and the Safawī policy, the Shīʿī contingent in the Muslim immigration into India was considerable. On the other hand, it is noteworthy that although the Muslim masters of Orthodox Christendom were likewise a small minority dispersed among a numerically stronger non-Muslim subject population, this state of affairs did not here deter the Sunnis from extirpating their Shīʿī co-religionists. The reason for this Ottoman ruthlessness towards the Shīʿis in Anatolia was that Anatolia was far more dangerously exposed than India was to attack by Shāh Ismāʿīl and his successors

This amiable and reasonable relation between the two ancient sects of Islam in the Iranic World augured well for the prospects of the rising Iranic Civilization. Unhappily, persecution was substituted for toleration and hatred for indifference or goodwill by the action of two princes: the Safawī Shāh Ismāʿīl (*dominabatur* A.D. 1499/1500–1523/4) and the ʿOsmanlī Sultan Selīm I (*imperabat* A.D. 1512–20)—an adversary in whom the violent and implacable character of Ismāʿīl found its match, to the undoing of the Iranic Society which had given birth to both these men of blood. In this savage encounter, which changed the course of Islamic history by reopening a breach which has only begun to close again within living memory, the initiative was taken by Ismāʿīl; and it continued to remain with him even after his signal discomfiture by Selīm in A.D. 1514. Accordingly, the career of Ismāʿīl, and not the career of Selīm, is the guiding thread which we have to follow.

The Career of Ismāʿīl Shāh Safawī down to A.D. 1511

Ismāʿīl's career provokes two questions: First, how was it that the heir to the headship of a religious order—and an order which was committed to non-violence by its tenets[1]—now burst upon the World as a military conqueror and became the founder of a political empire? And, second, what was Ismāʿīl's ultimate military and political aim?

The answer to the first question is that the metamorphosis of the Safawī organization from a religious order propagating itself by pacific missionary enterprise[2] into a political power extending its dominion by military force had been accomplished already by Ismāʿīl Shāh's grandfather Shaykh Junayd (*militabat* A.D. 1447–56), who was the grandson of Shaykh Khwāja ʿAlī and the great-great-grandson of Shaykh Safī. Shaykh Junayd was evidently tempted to abandon Imāmī principles, revolutionize Safawī practice, and try his fortune in the political and military arena by the political vacuum that was created in Iran and ʿIrāq by the utter disintegration of the Timurid Empire after the death of Shāh Rukh—an event which occurred in the very year of Shaykh Junayd's accession. Shaykh Junayd raised a military force of ten thousand 'Saints Militant' (Ghuzāt-i-Sūfīyah); and his son and successor Shaykh Haydar (*militabat* A.D. 1456–88), who was the father and predecessor of Shāh Ismāʿīl, gave the Safawī troops their distinctive uniform, the scarlet cap of twelve gores, which gained them their nickname of 'Red Heads' (*Qyzyl Bāsh*). Both Shaykh

---

[1] On this point see p. 359, above.

[2] By the time of Shaykh Junayd, who was the head of the House from A.D. 1447 to A.D. 1456, the Safawis had gained adherents throughout the Iranic World, 'from the remotest West to the limits of Balkh and Bukhārā'. (See Browne, op. cit., vol. iv, p. 51.)

Junayd and Shaykh Haydar fell in battle.[1] It will be seen that the Safawī military tradition was inherited and not created by Ismāʿīl, though Ismāʿīl himself was the first of his line to pursue the military career with success. For weal or woe, however, the Safawī House had taken decisively to militarism between Junayd's accession in A.D. 1447 and Ismāʿīl's in A.D. 1499/1500.[2]

When we inquire into Ismāʿīl's ultimate aim when in A.D. 1499/1500, at the age of thirteen, he started to turn his inherited military power to account, we find that he aimed at nothing less than the military conquest of the entire Iranic World and that he proposed to use his power in order to impose the faith of the Shīʿī minority of the Iranic Society upon the consciences of the Sunnī majority by sheer force. The two objectives have to be distinguished, because the second was a sensational and deplorable departure from the Iranic practice of 'live and let live', whereas the former was a natural reflection of the social unity of the Iranic World, which had remained unbroken down to Ismāʿīl's day.[3]

Ismāʿīl's oecumenical ambitions are revealed in the organization of his army. Two of his army corps bore the names of Türkmen tribes—the Avshārs and the Qājārs[4]—and this Turkish tribal element was perhaps the nucleus,[5] since the Safawī battle-cry was in the Turkish language,[6] and a Turkish vernacular was Ismāʿīl's own mother-tongue, as is testified by the evidence of his poetical works.[7] The majority of the corps, however, bore geographical names which corresponded to the dominions of various Sunnī Powers of the day.[8] Presumably the soldiers who served in each of these Safawī corps were actually recruited from the respective countries after which the corps were named; and the names were tantamount to an announcement of Ismāʿīl's intention to extend his rule over each of these countries through the military prowess of his local adherents who had already rallied to his banner. If this

---

[1] For Shaykhs Junayd and Haydar, see Browne, op. cit., vol. iv, pp. 47–8.

[2] The history of the Safawis is one example of the historical phenomenon of a would-be universal church becoming militant and paying the penalty of military success by turning into a local state. Other examples are the transformation of the Zoroastrian Church into the Sasanian Empire, and the history of the Sikhs. This phenomenon is examined further in Part VIII, below.

[3] See pp. 350–3, above.

[4] Sections of the Avshārs ranged as far afield as the Uzun Yayla (the watershed between the Euphrates and the Halys) on the west and Khurāsān eastward. The Khurāsānī Avshārs gave birth, two centuries later, to Nādir Shah. The Qājārs, who had established themselves in the Caspian Provinces, gave birth to the Turkish dynasty that ruled the Empire of Iran from A.D. 1779 (officially from 1796) to A.D. 1925.

[5] Mirza Haydar Dūghlāt calls the Safawī troops 'Türkmens' in the Tārīkh-i-Rashīdī, and Mirza Haydar's cousin Bābur gives them the same name in his Memoirs (e.g. on pp. 635–6 of vol. ii of Beveridge's edition).

[6] Browne, op. cit., vol. iv, p. 15.

[7] For Ismāʿīl's Turkish verses, see the citation from Browne on p. 353, above.

[8] For the names of Ismāʿīl's army corps, see Browne, op. cit., vol. iv, pp. 14 and 52, footnote 1.

interpretation is right, the names tell their own tale. The Rūmlū corps was presumably recruited from the descendants of those 'Osmanlī prisoners of war whose liberty had been obtained from Timur Lenk by one of Ismā'īl's ancestors.[1] The Hāmyd-lȳ and the Tekke-lī were presumably recruited from the South-West Anatolian principalities of Hāmyd and Tekke[2]: two Turkish 'successor-states' of the Anatolian Saljūq Empire which had been conquered, in A.D. 1381–91 and A.D. 1450 respectively, by the 'Osmanlis, after the 'Osmanlis had grown to be a match for all the other 'successor-states' of the Saljūqs combined, in consequence of their conquests in Europe. Hāmyd and Tekke had submitted, perforce, to the Ottoman yoke; but their people had never forgotten that their new 'Osmanlī masters had been the least among the successors of the Saljūqs in the beginning; and their consequent restiveness under Ottoman rule apparently found expression in Shi'ism. The Hāmyd-lȳ and the Tekke-lī fought for Ismā'īl Shāh Safawī as their future liberator from their present Ottoman masters. Another of Shāh Ismā'īl's corps, the Dhu'l-Qadar,[3] were presumably recruited from the principality of that name in the highlands of South-Eastern Anatolia which was the buffer-state between the 'Osmanlis and the Egyptian Mamlūks. The Shāmlū were presumably recruited from the Mamlūk dominions in Shām or Syria (e.g. from among the Imāmī Shī'īs of the Jabal 'Āmil). The Mawsyl-lȳs must have been Arab or Kurdish recruits from Mawsil (Mosul): a key-point on the line of march between Ismā'īl's base of operations in Gīlān and the Shī'ī holy cities in 'Irāq.

While this list of names reveals Ismā'īl's ambitions, his prospects of success, when he started on his career of conquest in A.D. 1500, can hardly be appreciated without a preliminary glance at the political state of the Iranic World in that year.

The two governing factors in the situation were, first, the collapse and disintegration of the empire which had been established over the Oxus-Jaxartes Basin and Iran and 'Irāq, a century earlier, by Timur Lenk;[4] and, second, the settled policy of the 'Osmanlis, which was to concentrate all their energies upon making conquests in Europe and to limit their action in Asia to the minimum necessary in order to cover their rear.

---

[1] For this incident, see p. 365, above.

[2] Hāmyd-lȳ recruits in Ismā'īl's army are mentioned by Babinger in op. cit. (*Der Islam*, vol. xi, p. 85). In A.D. 1534, at the moment when the Ottoman Sultan Suleymān invaded 'Irāq, a Tekke-lī garrison was holding Baghdad for Shāh Ismā'īl's son and successor, Shāh Tahmāsp. (See Longrigg, S. H.: *Four Centuries of Modern 'Iraq* (Oxford 1926, Clarendon Press), p. 23.)

[3] An Ilyas Beg Dhu'l-Qadar was Ismā'īl's first governor of Shīrāz (Browne, op. cit., vol. iv, p. 56).

[4] For Timur's career as a response of the Iranic Society to the challenge of Eurasian Nomadism, see II. D (v), vol. ii, pp. 144–50, below.

Timur's Empire had proved ephemeral.[1] In Western Iran and
'Irāq, it had not outlasted its founder's lifetime. In these regions,
the dominion had passed in A.D. 1405, the very year of Timur's
death, to Türkmen tribes of the same breed as Ismāʿīl's Avshārs and
Qājārs. From A.D. 1405 to 1411, Western Iran and 'Irāq had been
partitioned between the Qāra Qōyūnlū and the Jalayrs, while since
A.D. 1411 the two territories had been dominated by a single Türkmen tribe: the Qāra Qōyūnlū from A.D. 1411 to 1469, and the Āq
Qōyūnlū thereafter. In Khurāsān and the Oxus-Jaxartes Basin, the
Timurid Empire had held together, in a ramshackle fashion, for half
a century longer; but, after the death of Shāh Rukh in A.D. 1447, it
had fallen to pieces even in its homelands. During the last half of
the fifteenth century of the Christian Era, the Timurid domain in
these regions was partitioned among a multitude of small, shifting,
warring Timurid principalities which presented as melancholy a
contrast to the Empire of Timur as was presented to the Empire of
Charlemagne by the Carolingian principalities after the Partition
of Verdun in A.D. 843.[2]

This collapse of the Timurid Power had given the 'Osmanlis
relief without tempting them either to take their revenge for the
wanton blow which Timur had dealt them, or again to indulge
their ambitions by occupying the new vacuum on their Asiatic
frontier. They contented themselves with restoring their Asiatic
dominions to the limits at which they had stood before Timur
intervened in Anatolia: and when, half a century after the overthrow of Bāyezīd I by Timur at Angora in A.D. 1402, Bāyezīd's
successor Mehmed the Conqueror (*imperabat* A.D. 1451–81) found
the Ottoman Power sufficiently recuperated to go into action again,
he deliberately pursued the established policy of his House. In
spite of his name and fame, Mehmed Pādishāh 'Osmānlī was not a
'conqueror' in the same sense as either Timur Lenk or Ismāʿīl Shāh
Safawī; for he was not aiming at an oecumenical dominion. He is
famous because he set himself with success to round off an empire
which had expanded steadily within definite limits. The 'Osmanlis
were an Iranic community which had started life in the borderland
between the Iranic and the Orthodox Christian worlds and had
acquired an empire by conquering Orthodox Christian territories.[3]

[1] The main cause of Timur's failure was the perversity with which he repeatedly
turned aside from his mission of imposing the Iranic Civilization upon the Eurasian
Steppe in order to wage an internecine warfare in the interior of the Iranic World
against other Iranic Powers. (On this point, see further Part IV, below.) Timur's
waywardness contrasts strikingly with the steadfastness of the 'Osmanlis in confining
themselves to their own mission of conquering Orthodox Christendom.
[2] For the tripartite partition of the Carolingian Empire in A.D. 843 and its historical
significance, see I. B (iv), above.
[3] For the growth of the Ottoman Empire as a response to the challenge which confronts a warden of the marches, see II. D (v), vol. ii, pp. 150–4, below.

The historical function of the Ottoman empire-builders was to bring the Orthodox Christian Society's 'Time of Troubles' to a close by uniting the whole of the main body of Orthodox Christendom politically into one universal state under an alien Pax Ottomanica.[1] And this Ottoman task, which had been interrupted, on the verge of completion, by Timur's tempestuous passage, was duly completed by Sultan Mehmed II.

Mehmed spent his life in wiping out those enclaves of territory in the Balkan and Anatolian peninsulas which had not yet fallen under Ottoman sovereignty; and with one or two exceptions— e.g. the Hungarian stronghold in Belgrade and the stronghold of the Knights of St. John on the Island of Rhodes and a few Venetian strongholds in the Aegean—he had substantially achieved his life-work before his death in A.D. 1481. The conquest of the East Roman Imperial City of Constantinople in A.D. 1453 was simply the most conspicuous achievement in this limited and definite series. On his Asiatic land-frontier, Mehmed's programme included the annexation of the Greek principality of Trebizond and the Turkish principality of Qāramān (the senior 'successor-state' of the Anatolian Saljūq Empire, and a more formidable adversary than the shadow of the East Roman Empire).[2] And when he had conquered Trebizond in 1461 and Qāramān in 1465, he refused to be drawn on farther eastward. His non-expansion policy in this quarter became apparent when he was threatened with an attack on the part of Uzun Hasan, the prince of the Āq Qōyūnlū Türkmens who was alarmed at the fall of Qāramān and Trebizond and at the same time elated by his own succession to the lordship of 'Irāq and Western Iran. Mehmed forestalled this danger by an offensive defensive, invaded Uzun Hasan's territory, and inflicted a defeat on the Türkmen at Bayburt in 1473. But he made no motion to follow this victory up. It is true that Mehmed's death on the 3rd May 1481 overtook him marching eastward again; but his objective on this occasion was probably limited to the buffer-state of Dhu'l-Qadar in South-Eastern Anatolia; and before his death he had dispatched another expeditionary force, in exactly the opposite direction, to occupy Otranto in the heel of Italy.[3] When these two simultaneous military enterprises at the end of Mehmed the Conqueror's reign are taken together, they give the impression that Death found him still at work upon his precise and limited pro-

[1] For the means by which the 'Osmanlis equipped themselves for performing this function, see Part III A, vol. iii, pp. 28–44, below.
[2] For the rivalry between the 'Osmanlis and the Qaramanlis, which ended, after continuing for two centuries, in the definitive Ottoman victory of A.D. 1465, see further II. D (v), vol. ii, pp. 151–3, below.
[3] This force had duly occupied Otranto in July 1480; but, after Mehmed's death, it was soon withdrawn by Mehmed's unenterprising successor Bāyezīd II.

gramme of making the Ottoman Empire conterminous with the area once covered by the East Roman and Bulgarian Empires; and the Taurus Range and Trebizond marked the historical limits of the East Roman Empire in Asia. Until the appearance on the scene of Ismāʿīl Shāh Safawī, with his programme of oecumenical conquest and forcible conversion to Shiʿism, there is no indication of any Ottoman ambition to expand in Asia, outside the historical limits of Orthodox Christendom, at the expense of other Islamic Powers, just as there is none of any Ottoman intolerance towards the Shīʿah. The military and religious aggressiveness of Ismāʿīl eventually forced a profound change of policy upon the ʿOsmanlis on both these heads.

At the outset, however, the persistent and deliberate passivity of the Ottoman policy in Asia worked together with the disintegration of the Timurid Power to give Ismāʿīl Shāh Safawī's ambitions a free field. The derelict Timurid domain was virtually at the disposal of the first comer; and the portion of the prize that lay nearest to Ismāʿīl's base of operations in Gīlān was the western half, in which the Timurid régime had not only broken down but had disappeared altogether. The Āq Qōyūnlū Türkmens, who had squatted, in the Timurids' place, in ʿIrāq and in Western Iran, were no match for the Avshār and Qājār Türkmens of Ismāʿīl, whose native Nomad hardihood and energy were fortified by religious fanaticism as well as by hereditary devotion to the family of their leader, and whose numbers were reinforced by recruits from the Shīʿī minority in the dominions of the Shīʿite paladin's Sunnī adversaries. Ismāʿīl's first military success was the defeat and slaughter of the King of Shīrwān (the slayer of Ismāʿīl's father Haydar) in A.D. 1500. The decisive victory in this first stage of Ismāʿīl's career was the overthrow of the Āq Qōyūnlū at the Battle of Shurūr in A.D. 1501/2: a triumph which was followed by the crowning of Ismāʿīl in Tabrīz and by the sensational inauguration of his religious policy of wholesale conversion by force. Between A.D. 1500 and A.D. 1508 (the year of his conquest of Baghdad), Ismāʿīl had eliminated all powers and principalities, great or small, that challenged his mastery over an area which extended from the province of Shīrwān, at the south-eastern foot of the Caucasus, to the province of Kirmān on the south-western border of the Dash-i-Lūt, the Central Desert of Iran.

What were to be Ismāʿīl's relations with the petty Timurid princes who still retained a precarious hold upon Khurāsān and Transoxania between the north-eastern border of the Central Desert of Iran and the southern fringe of the Eurasian Steppe? This question was answered for Ismāʿīl by the apparition of a rival

aspirant to the Timurid inheritance who had been conquering the
north-eastern half of it while Ismāʿīl had been similarly engaged
in the west. This competitor was a new Eurasian Nomad intruder
upon Iranic soil, in the shape of Shaybāk or Shaybānī Khan, the
leader of the Uzbegs.

This fresh invasion of the Islamic World by a Eurasian Nomad
horde within less than a century after the death of Timur Lenk
was a signal proof that Timur's life-work was utterly undone. It
had been Timur's mission to liberate the oases of Transoxania
from Nomad domination and to establish an Iranic military and
political ascendancy over the Eurasian Nomadic World.[1] But
Timur had turned aside from the completion of this constructive
task in order to exhaust the energies of the Iranic Society in barren
fratricidal conflicts with the contemporary Iranic Powers in
Western Iran and ʿIrāq and Hindustan and Anatolia.[2] The return
of the Nomadic tide within less than a century was the nemesis for
the wanton misdirection of aim which had wrecked Timur's career.
The Uzbeg invasion of Transoxania and Khurāsān in the first
decade of the sixteenth century of the Christian Era was the more
portentous inasmuch as it was not, apparently, occasioned by any
deterioration in the physical environment of the Nomadic life on
the Uzbegs' Eurasian ranges. The physical pressure resulting
from a desiccation of the Steppe accounts for many of the most
violent and sensational eruptions of Nomadic conquerors from 'the
Desert' into 'the Sown'; but 'the Pulse of Asia' appears to beat in
a rhythmical alternation of aridity and humidity; and the turn of
the fifteenth and sixteenth centuries of the Christian Era appears to
fall within what was a relatively humid period in the alternating
rhythm. Thus the Uzbegs' irruption into the Iranic World at
this date can hardly be accounted for by a physical push from
behind; and it must therefore be attributed to a social pull
from in front.[3] The political vacuum left by the collapse of the
Timurid Empire was drawing in the Uzbegs from one quarter
at the moment when it was drawing in the Qyzyl-Bāsh from the
other.

The horde which thus undid Timur's work within a century of
his death was not one of those hordes that Timur himself had
encountered and chastised. Timur had crushed the Chaghatāy
horde of Mughalistan or Zungaria who had been the previous

[1] See II. D (v), vol. ii, pp. 144-50, below.
[2] See IV. C (iii) (c) 3 (α), vol. iv, pp. 491-501, below.
[3] For these two alternative external agencies which apparently account, between
them, for all the recorded eruptions of the Nomads from the Eurasian and the Afrasian
Steppe alike, see further Part III. A, Annex II, vol. iii, below. There does, however,
appear to be some evidence for at least a subsidiary and temporary fluctuation in the
direction of aridity round about A.D. 1500 (see vol. iii, pp. 439 and 447).

Nomad suzerains of Transoxania; and he had crushed the Jūjī hordes of Qipchāq, whose vast appanage had embraced a suzerainty over Khwārizm at one extremity and over Russia at the other.[1] Though Timur had harried the Eurasian Steppe victoriously from coast to coast—a feat which many sedentary Powers had attempted but which none had achieved before him[2]—there were other tenants of the vast Steppe whose ranges were so remote from Samarqand that they had lain beyond the reach of even Timur's arm; and one of these was the horde whose alternative eponyms were Shaybān and Uzbeg and whose proper ranges were in Western Siberia.

In the middle of the fifteenth century of the Christian Era these Uzbegs, who had escaped unscathed by Timur's passage, attempted to dispossess their neighbours and cousins the White Horde, who had received the full shock of the impact. The White Horde's ranges lay on the Steppes of Eastern Qipchāq, between the western foot of the Altai and the east bank of the Lower Volga: a less inclement region than' the Uzbegs' sub-arctic appanage on the banks of the Irtish and the Ob. This enterprise, which was undertaken about A.D. 1428 by the Uzbeg Khan Abu'l-Khayr, was unsuccessful; for after the Uzbeg leader's death in A.D. 1469/70 the White Horde, whom he had temporarily driven out of Qipchāq into Mughalistan, surged back westward into their hereditary domain and forcibly incorporated the majority of the Uzbeg intruders into their own tribal organization. Towards the close of the fifteenth century, Abu'l-Khayr's grandson, Muhammad Shaybānī, found himself—with only a remnant of an Uzbeg horde that he could call his own—constrained to seek a livelihood, off the Steppe, in the service of some sedentary Power.

Muhammad Shaybānī had the choice of seeking his fortune in either of two alternative directions. He might turn towards Russia or turn towards Transoxania; and, if he had come upon the scene a century or so earlier, he would probably have chosen the former objective, for Russia had been one of the easiest as well as the widest conquests of 'the Sown' which the Eurasian Nomads had made in their latest and greatest eruption out of 'the Desert', under Mongol leadership, in the thirteenth century of the Christian Era. At the close of the fifteenth century, the Mongol Khanate of Jūjī's appanage which had exercised this Nomad dominion over Russia was still in existence at the Saray on the left bank of the Volga, just below the elbow where that river's course approaches closest to the

---

[1] Chaghatāy and Jūjī were sons of Chingis Khān whose descendants and followers had received these domains as their appanages (see II. D (v), vol. ii, pp. 144-5 and 146-7, below).

[2] See II. D (v), vol. ii, p. 146, below.

course of the Don.[1] But Saray now offered no attractive prospect to a Nomad soldier of fortune; for Russia had become more than a match for the Nomads after the union of the two strongest Russian states—the Grand Duchy of Muscovy and the Republic of Novgorod—in A.D. 1478; and the Russians did not wait long before they passed over to the offensive. In 1502, when Muhammad Shaybānī was busy carving out a kingdom for himself at the expense of his fellow Muslims in Transoxania, Saray was annexed by Russia; and this was the first step in a Russian advance which only found its term, four centuries later, on the coast of the Pacific and on the summit of the Pamirs.[2]

Meanwhile, Shaybānī Khān Uzbeg had made better provision for his own fortunes—though not for the interests of the Iranic Society or of Islam—by turning his face in the other alternative direction. He repaired to Transoxania; took service with the Timurid Government at Bukhārā; changed sides in a battle between his Timurid master and the Chaghatāy Khan of Western Mughalistan; was rewarded by his new patron with the governorship of Tāshqand; and used this post as 'a jumping-off ground' for springing, on his own account, upon the Timurid dominions of Bukhārā and Samarqand.[3]

Muhammad Shaybānī's conquest of the two chief cities of Transoxania was achieved in the same year—A.D. 1500—in which Ismāʿīl Safawī made his military début at the opposite end of the *ci-devant* Timurid Empire by conquering the Transcaucasian province of Shīrwān;[4] and thereafter the two conquerors pushed

---

[1] The Khans who ruled at Saray at the close of the fifteenth century of the Christian Era were descendants of Toqatmysh, the Khan of the White Horde who had momentarily united all the hordes of Jūjī's appanage under a single leadership in A.D. 1381—for the first and last time—and had sacked Moscow in 1382 (in reprisal for the first Russian attempt to shake off the Tatar yoke), before he crossed the path of Timur. (For the collision between Toqatmysh Khan and Timur, see further II. D (v), vol. ii, pp. 146–8, below.)

[2] The fate which overtook the Khanate of Saray in A.D. 1502 was shared, in 1552 and 1554 respectively, by the sister-Khanates of Qāzān and Astrakhān; and the Khanate of the Crimea was only saved by its previous acceptance of an Ottoman protectorate. Even the ʿOsmanlis were defeated by the Russians when they attempted, in 1568–70, to seize the isthmus between the Don and the Volga in order to link the two waterways by a canal. (For this incident, see further II. D (vii), Annex VII, vol. ii, below.) The Russians consolidated their victory by building the fortress of Cherkask on the River Don, almost within sight of the sea of Azov. In the subsequent Russian advance, the pioneers were the Cossacks, who duly accomplished the feat, which Timur had brilliantly essayed, of being the first sedentary Power to bring the Eurasian Nomadism into lasting subjection. (See II. D (v), vol. ii, pp. 154–7, below.) The homeland of the Uzbegs in Western Siberia was overrun by the Cossacks before the end of the sixteenth century.

[3] Muhammad Shaybānī's residence at Tashqand as governor on behalf of the Western Chaghatāy Khan appears to have lasted at least a decade; for the battle in which he deserted from the Timurids to the Chaghatayids seems to have been fought about 1488–9, while Shaybānī's conquest of Bukhārā and Samarqand did not take place till A.D. 1500. He may have spent the interval in gathering round him the scattered sheep— or wolves—of his ancestral Uzbeg horde. For Muhammad Shaybānī's career down to A.D. 1500, see Muhammad Haydar Dūghlāt: *Tarīkh-i-Rashīdī*, English translation by Elias and Ross, cited above, *passim*, and especially pp. 82, 92, 115–16, 158–60, 166, 272–3.

[4] See p. 371, above.

forward into Iran with equal speed from the north-east and the north-west towards 'the natural frontier' of the Central Desert. The Timurids were as utterly outmatched by the Shaybānī as the Āq Qōyūnlū were by the Safawī. In A.D. 1501–2, the young Timurid prince Bābur, who had inherited the small and out-of-the-way province of Farghānā, made his first entry upon the stage of history in a gallant attempt to retrieve for his House their lost Transoxanian dominions. He actually recovered Samarqand for a moment—only to be driven out and to lose his own patrimony of Farghānā into the bargain. Thereafter, in A.D. 1502–3, Bābur persuaded the Chaghatāy Khans of Western and Eastern Mughali-stan to join forces with each other and with himself in an attempt to drive the Uzbegs out of Farghānā; but the Shaybānī was stronger than the coalition. He took the two Khans prisoner and annexed the greater part of the Chaghatay Horde's ranges, as well as the province of Tāshqand, which he had formerly governed as their agent, while Bābur fled to Afghanistan. Thereupon, in A.D. 1505–8, the Shaybānī conquered Khwārizm with one hand and Khurāsān with the other, until, of all the House of Timur, Bābur, and Bābur only, was left in the field; and Bābur was a fugitive from his home.

Muhammad Shaybānī's next enterprises, however, were less successful. In A.D. 1509, when he turned on his tracks and invaded the Qipchāq Steppe, he was roughly handled by the White Horde and the *ci-devant* Uzbegs whom they had incorporated;[1] and in 1510 he committed the folly of poaching upon Ismāʿīl Safawī's preserves. In this year he crossed the Iranian desert, raided the province of Kirmān,[2] and sent 'a most insulting letter in reply to Ismāʿīl's politely worded remonstrance'.[3] The Safawī retorted to this provocation by marching against the Shaybānī and bringing him to battle at Tāhir-ābād, near Merv. In this second decisive battle in Shāh Ismāʿīl's career, which was fought on the 1st or 2nd December 1510, the Uzbegs were heavily defeated by the Qyzyl Bāsh, and Muhammad Khān Shaybānī himself was among the slain.

This victory doubled Ismāʿīl's power at one stroke; and the events which followed played still further into his hands. Upon the news of Tāhir-ābād, Bābur promptly issued out of his fastness in Afghanistan and attempted once again to recover Transoxania with the aid of 20,000 Chaghatāy Mughals who had been transplanted from Zungaria to Khurāsān by Muhammad Shaybānī. The Uzbegs,

[1] Muhammad Haydar Dūghlāt: *Tarikh-i-Rashīdī*, translation by Elias and Ross, pp. 230–1.
[2] Perhaps this raid was executed in the same campaign as an unsuccessful expedition (likewise attributed to the year 1510) against the Hazaras, a stray Mongol tribe which had been left stranded on the south side of the Hindu Kush.
[3] Browne, op. cit., vol. iv, p. 64.

however, had been defeated by Ismā'īl without being annihilated; and Bābur found that they were still too strong for him when he measured his strength against them once more in January 1511. At this juncture, when Bābur was marking time, baffled, at Qūndūz, on the south side of the Oxus, Ismā'īl intervened. He sent an embassy to Bābur bringing Bābur's sister (she was Shaybānī's widow) and an offer of friendship; and this courtly gesture on Ismā'īl's part seems to have been followed by negotiations between the heir of the Safawis and the heir of the Timurids over which the later historians of Bābur and his orthodox Sunnī descendants have discreetly drawn a veil.[1] The fact seems to be that the two princes struck an unholy bargain. Bābur, on his part, seems to have asked for, and received, a promise of military assistance from Ismā'īl; while Ismā'īl, on his part, seems to have made his military assistance conditional upon Bābur's conversion to Shi'ism, and to have received Bābur's assurance that he would accept Ismā'īl's help on Ismā'īl's terms.[2]

Whatever the understanding may have been, there is no question about the sequel.

The first result was that, in October 1511, Bābur returned to the attack with a Qyzyl Bāsh army supporting him; and that, with this support, he achieved in the autumn what he had failed to achieve in the preceding winter. He successfully reoccupied Samarqand and drove the Uzbeg invaders out of the Transoxanian oases into their native steppes. This victory, won with Ismā'īl's aid by a fugitive prince who had become Ismā'īl's lieutenant, was Ismā'īl's own victory in effect; and thereafter, during the interval between the campaigning seasons of A.D. 1511 and A.D. 1512, Ismā'īl stood at the height of his power. He had crowned the conquests of the past twelve years by assuming the position of Warden of the North-Eastern Marches of South-Western Asia over against the Great Eurasian Steppe; and two thousand years of history bore witness that, time and again, the effective wardens of these marches had derived from their wardenship the title to be the ruling, or at any rate the paramount, Power in the region which they were defending, as far south as the Indian Ocean and as far west as the Mediterranean. The Medes had won this power by expelling the Scyths; the Achaemenids by keeping out the Massagetae; the Umayyads by expelling and the 'Abbasids by keeping out the Türgesh; Timur Lenk by expelling the Mughal 'jātah'; and at other times there had

---

[1] We do not know how Bābur handled this delicate and dubious transaction himself, since the relevant section of his *Memoirs* is lost.

[2] The lukewarmness, to say the least of it, towards the Sunnah, which this reputed bargain presupposes on Bābur's part, may perhaps be brought into relation with the reported Shi'ite proclivities of a kinsman of Bābur's in the preceding generation, Sultan Husayn Bayqarā (see p. 361, above).

been other wardens of the same marches—the Greek princes of
Bactria and the Sāmānids and the Khwārizm Shāhs—who, short
of being the masters of all South-Western Asia, had been the
foremost Powers in the South-Western Asia of their day.[1] In
the winter of A.D. 1511-12, the Imperial mantle conferred by this
wardenship, which had been worn last by Tīmūr a century back,
appeared to have descended upon the shoulders of Shāh Ismāʿīl in
virtue of the mutually advantageous compact between the Safawī
empire-builder and the last of the Tīmūrids, Bābur. At this point,
however, which was the zenith of his career, Shāh Ismāʿīl was
overtaken by the nemesis of his dual ambition: the ambition to win
an oecumenical empire by conquest and to use this political power
in order to impose the minoritarian religion of Shiʿism upon a
Sunnī majority by main force.

The Career of Ismāʿīl Shāh Safawī after A.D. 1511

The first chapter in the story of Ismāʿīl Shāh Safawī's discomfiture (which also involved the temporary and local discomfiture of
Bābur Pādishāh Tīmūrī) is plainly set out in the following passages
in the *Tarīkh-i-Rashīdī*:

'Now when the Emperor [Bābur] arrived in Bokhārā, he sent back the
auxiliaries of Shāh Ismāʿīl, after praising them for their services and
bestowing upon them adequate rewards, while he himself, victorious
and covered with glory, proceeded to Samarqand. All the inhabitants of
the towns of Mā-warā-an-Nahr[2]—high and low, nobles and poor men,
grandees and artizans, princes and peasants—alike testified their joy at
the advent of the Emperor. He was received by the nobles, while the
other classes were busy with the decoration of the town. The streets and
the bazaars were draped with cloth and gold brocades, and drawings and
pictures were hung up on every side. The Emperor entered the city in
the middle of the month of Rajab in the year 917,[3] in the midst of such
pomp and splendour as no one has ever seen or heard of, before or
since. The angels cried aloud: "Enter with peace", and the people
exclaimed: "Praise be to God, Lord of the Universe." The people of
Mā-warā-an-Nahr, especially the inhabitants of Samarqand, had for
years been longing for him to come, that the shadow of his protection
might be cast upon them. Although, in the hour of necessity, the
Emperor had clothed himself in the garments of Qyzyl Bāsh (which was
pure heresy; nay, almost unbelief), they sincerely hoped, when he
mounted the throne of Samarqand (the throne of the Law of the Prophet), and placed on his head the diadem of the holy Sunnah of Muhammad, that he would remove from it the crown of royalty (Shāhī), whose
nature was heresy and whose form was as the tail of an ass.

---

[1] This wardenship of the marches, and the political perquisites which it was apt to
bring with it, are dealt with further in II. D (v), vol. ii, on pp. 138-44, below.
[2] i.e. Transoxania.—A. J. T.   [3] i.e. the October of A.D. 1511.—A. J. T.

'But the hopes of the people of Samarqand were not realised. For, as yet, the Emperor did not feel able to dispense with the aid of Shāh Ismāʿīl; nor did he consider himself sufficiently strong to cope single-handed with the Uzbeg; hence he appeared to overlook (mudāra) the gross errors of the Qyzyl Bāsh. On this account, the people of Mā-warā-an-Nahr ceased to feel that intense longing for the Emperor which they had entertained while he was absent—their regard for him was at an end. It was thus that the Emperor began (already) to flatter the Türkmens [i.e. the Qyzyl Bāsh], and associate himself with them. . . .

'When the Emperor, in Rajab 917,[1] mounted the throne of Samarqand, as has been stated above, the learned men and nobles of Mā-warā-an-Nahr were indignant at his attachment to Shāh Ismāʿīl and at his adoption of the Türkmen style of dress. When that winter had passed and spring had set in (the plentiful drops of her rain having clothed the earth in green raiment) the Uzbeg advanced out of Turkistan. Their main body marched against Tāshqand, while ʿUbaydallah[2] went to Bukhārā by way of Yati Kuduk. As the citadel of Tāshqand had been fortified by Amir Ahmad Qāsim Kuhbur, (the Emperor) sent him some rein-forcements, under the command of such men as Amir Dust Nāsir, Sultan Muhammad Dulādī,[3] and others, while he himself (the Emperor) advanced on Bukhārā. When he neared the town, news of his approach reached ʿUbaydallah Khan, who (becoming alarmed) immediately drew his bridle and returned along the road by which he had just come. The Emperor pursued him, overtook him at Kūl Malik, and compelled him to retreat. ʿUbaydallah Khan had 3,000 men with him, while the Emperor had 40,000. ʿUbaydallah Khan having repeated to the end of the verse: "And how often has not a small force defeated a large one, by the permission of God?" (faced the Emperor), and a fierce battle began to rage. God, the most high, has shown to the peoples of the Earth, and especially to kings and rulers, that no boast is to be made of, no reliance to be placed in, the numbers of an army nor [in] their equipment; for He in His might gives victory to whomsoever He will.

'Thus ʿUbaydallah Khan, with 3,000 shattered (rikhta) men, who eight months previously had retreated before this same force, now entirely defeated an army of 40,000, perfectly equipped and mounted on fine horses (tupchāq).[4] This event occurred in Safar of the year 918.[5] The Emperor had reigned eight months in Samarqand.

'When the Emperor returned to Samarqand, he was unable to get a firm footing upon the steps of the throne, and so, bidding farewell to the sovereignty of Samarqand, he hastened to Hisār. He sent one ambassador after another to Shāh Ismāʿīl, to inform him of what had passed, and to beg for succour. Shāh Ismāʿīl granted his request, and sent Mīr Najm, his commander-in-chief, with 60,000 men, to his aid. Thus at the beginning of the winter succeeding that spring, (the allies)

---

[1] i.e. the October of A.D. 1511.—A. J. T.
[2] 'Ubaydallah was the nephew of Muhammad Khān Shaybānī, and his successor in the leadership of the Uzbeg Horde.—A. J. T.
[3] ? Dūldā'ī.—A. J. T.   [4] ? Tīpūchāq.—A. J. T.
[5] i.e. the April and May of A.D. 1512.—A. J. T.

once more marched against the Uzbeg. On reaching Qarshī, they found that Shaykhīm Mīrzā, the uncle of 'Ubaydallah Khan, had strengthened the fort of Qarshī. They, therefore, began by laying siege to the fort, which they quickly reduced. Then they put to death Shaykhīm Mīrzā, and massacred the whole of the people of the fort, killing both high and low—the sucklings and the decrepit.[1]

'Of the Uzbeg Sultans, each one had fortified himself in his own castle. Thus Jānī Beg Sultan had stood on the defensive in the fort of Ghajdavān. When the Türkmens had finished with Qarshī they asked the Emperor about the condition of all the fortified cities of Mā-warā-an-Nahr, and he described them one by one. It appeared that the easiest of all to take was that of Ghajdavān; towards it, therefore, they marched. The Uzbeg Sultans heard of their coming, and entered the fort on the same night that the Türkmens and the Emperor, who were encamped before the place, were busy preparing their siege implements. At dawn they arranged their forces in the midst of the suburbs, and stood facing (the enemy). On the other side, too, preparations were made for a fight. Since the Uzbeg were in the midst of the suburbs, the field of battle was narrow. The Uzbeg infantry began to pour forth their arrows from every corner, so that very soon the claws of Islam twisted the hands of heresy and unbelief, and victory declared for the True Faith [i.e. for the Sunnah]. The victorious breezes of Islam overturned the banners of the schismatics. (The Türkmens) were so completely routed that most of them perished on the field; all the rents that had been made by the swords of Qarshī were now sewn up with the arrow-stitches of vengeance. They sent Mīr Najm and all the Türkmen Amirs to Hell. The Emperor retired, broken and crestfallen, to Hisār.'[2]

Every line of this passage breathes an implacable Sunnī hatred of the Shī'ah and the Qyzyl Bāsh and the Safawī and all their works; and this fanatical spirit is the more remarkable when we recall the fact that the author, Mīrzā Haydar Dūghlāt, was the son of a Chaghatāy beg who had been murdered by 'Ubaydallah Khān Uzbeg's predecessor Muhammad Khān Shaybānī,[3] and that Bābur, who had thrown in his lot with Shāh Ismā'īl in order to retrieve his ancestral dominions from the common enemies of the Mughal and the Timurid, was Haydar's cousin, benefactor, and hero. Indeed, Mīrzā Haydar was actually in Bābur's service at this time (though he was not present at all the military actions here recorded); and he shared the unpleasant consequences of Bābur's discomfiture. For, after the making of peace between Shāh Ismā'īl and 'Ubaydallah Khān in A.D. 1513,[4] the Chaghatāys as well as the Timurids gave up the struggle to save their Central Asian heritage from passing under

---

[1] Among their victims was the poet Bannā'ī (Browne, op. cit., vol. iv, p. 63).—A. J. T.

[2] Haydar Dūghlāt, Mīrzā Muhammad: *Tarīkh-i-Rashīdī*, English translation by Elias, N., and Ross, E. D. (London 1895, Sampson Low & Marston), pp. 245-6 and 259-61.

[3] Bābur: *Memoirs*, ed. Beveridge, vol. i, p. 22.   [4] See p. 381, below.

the Uzbegs' dominion. In A.D. 1514, the Chaghatāys abandoned
Tāshqand and turned their energies to the enterprise of recouping
themselves by reasserting their authority in the Tarim Basin[1]—a
movement which eventually carried Haydar himself into Tibet and
Kashmir and placed him on the throne of the latter country from
A.D. 1541 to his death in 1551. Thus Haydar's career was upset
as violently as Bābur's career by the outcome of the decisive battle
which had been fought at Ghajdavān (Ghujduwān) on the 12th
November 1512; and, at the time when he was writing the *Tarīkh-i-Rashīdī*, the memory of that disastrous defeat was not softened
for Haydar by Bābur's consolations; for the throne of Kashmir was
not a dazzling reward for a forced migration across the Tibetan
Plateau, whereas Bābur won a consolation prize in India which
almost eclipsed the empire of his ancestor Timur when, in A.D.
1519, he finally turned his back upon the Oxus-Jaxartes Basin for
ever and descended, from his Afghan fastness, upon the Basin of the
Indus and the Ganges. Thus every personal consideration must
have militated, in Mīrzā Haydar's mind, against his rejoicing in
Bābur Pādishāh's defeat and in 'Ubaydallah Khān's victory; and if
Mīrzā Haydar's religious feelings, as a Sunnī, were strong enough
to override these personal interests and to cause him to rejoice in
his own side's defeat all the same, we may infer that the rest of
Haydar's Central Asian Sunnī co-religionists, who had no comparable personal interests at stake, must have rejoiced at the outcome
of the Battle of Ghujduwān *a fortiori*.

We may also infer that the hostility of the Sunnī population of
Transoxania to the Safawī, and therefore, at second hand, to
Bābur for having consented to put on the Safawī's Qyzyl Bāsh
uniform, was the decisive military factor in the Transoxanian campaign of A.D. 1512. For the wardens of the Transoxanian marches
of South-Western Asia had never held the frontier by the unaided
strength of their own arms. They had merely been the leaders of
the warlike frontiersmen of the Transoxanian oases. The Achaemenidae had been able to rely upon those Soghdian barons who
offered such a strenuous resistance to Alexander the Great after the
fall of the last Darius;[2] and Timur had only succeeded in expelling
the Chaghatāy Nomads from Transoxania in the six hard-fought
campaigns of A.D. 1362–7 because he, likewise, had been the
leader of a popular movement.[3] Indeed, at the crisis of this struggle
between Transoxania and the 'jātah', when the Battle of the Mire
had resulted in as severe a defeat for Timur and his braves as Bābur

---

[1] *Tarīkh-i-Rashīdī*, translation by Elias and Ross, pp. 284–5.
[2] For this resistance, see further II. D (v), vol. ii, pp. 139–40, below.
[3] See II. D (v), vol. ii, p. 146, and footnote 1, below.

and his Qyzyl Bāsh auxiliaries suffered at Ghujduwān in A.D. 1512, a military disaster which left the Nomad invader in possession of the open country was actually retrieved by the indomitable resistance of the townspeople of Samarqand under the leadership of their 'ulamā. This repulse of the Nomad besiegers of Samarqand by the townspeople themselves in A.D. 1365 had been the turning-point of this previous Central Asian war between 'the Desert' and 'the Sown'; and there is no reason to suppose that in A.D. 1512 the townspeople and peasantry of Transoxania were any less averse from the prospect of falling again under Nomad dominion than they had been in A.D. 1365. The difference between the two situations was that, on the earlier occasion, these Transoxanian Sunnīs had not been torn in two directions between two conflicting loyalties; for their champion, Timur, was Sunnī like themselves, as well as their enemy the 'jātah'. On the other hand, in A.D. 1512 their descendants had to choose between acquiescing in the dominion of a Eurasian Nomad barbarian who was their co-religionist and striking a blow for their own hereditary champion and ruler the Timurid Bābur when Bābur had thrown in his lot with the Shī'ī heretic Ismā'īl and when Ismā'īl had shown unmistakably his determination to impose Shi'ism upon his Sunnī subjects by force. In this painful dilemma, the Transoxanians appear to have taken the line of least resistance and to have accepted the outcome of the Battle of Ghujduwān as the judgement of God. And their un-willingness to step into the breach, as their ancestors had stepped in 147 years before, actually sealed the discomfiture of Bābur and his Qyzyl Bāsh allies and the victory of the Uzbeg Khan 'Ubaydallah.

If Shāh Ismā'īl's hands had now still been free, it is conceivable that he might have retrieved the disaster of Ghujduwān unaided by driving the Uzbegs out of Transoxania again once and for all and converting the Sunnī townspeople and peasantry of the Oxus-Jaxartes Basin to Shi'ism by main force as he did succeed in con-verting their neighbours and kinsmen on the Iranian Plateau. As it was, he not only launched no further campaign in this quarter, but in the autumn of A.D. 1513 he made peace with 'Ubaydallah Khān Uzbeg on a basis of *uti possidetis*—the Uzbegs retaining their conquests in the Oxus-Jaxartes Basin while the Safawīs retained Khurāsān. This admission of failure in the east was forced upon Shāh Ismā'īl because, in the meantime, his fixed policy of oecu-menical conquest combined with religious intolerance had com-mitted him to a life-and-death struggle with his Western neighbours, the 'Osmanlis.

Shāh Ismā'īl need have found no difficulty in keeping his hands free in the west, if he had wished, in order to concentrate his energies upon objectives in Central Asia; for, of his two western neighbours, the 'Osmanlis, as has been explained already, had no further Asiatic territorial ambitions, while the Egyptian Mamlūks had no territorial ambitions at all. Fortune had further favoured Ismā'īl by preserving on the Ottoman throne, for the first twelve years of Ismā'īl's reign, a *roi fainéant*, in the person of Sultan Bāyezīd II (*imperabat* A.D. 1481–1512), whose character and conduct were in utter contrast to those of his immediate predecessors and successors. It may have been the very incompetence and complacency of Sultan Bāyezīd that tempted the headstrong Ismā'īl to rouse the sleeping Ottoman lion and provoke a reversal of the established Ottoman policy of non-aggression in Asia. At any rate, Ismā'īl did offer such provocation, intentionally or unintentionally, by promoting—or at any rate countenancing—a subversive Shī'ī propaganda in the Ottoman Sultan's Asiatic dominions in Anatolia; and in the campaigning season of A.D. 1511, when Ismā'īl was far away on the Oxus, preparing to reap the fruits of his recent victory over the Shaybānī Muhammad Khān Uzbeg by restoring the Timurid Bābur to the Transoxanian throne of his fathers as Ismā'īl's vassal, the Shī'ī movement in Anatolia came suddenly and violently to a head. Whether this happened in spite of, or in accordance with, Shāh Ismā'īl's instructions we do not know, but it is certain that, in the spring of 1511, his agent in Anatolia, Shāh Qūlī,[1] rose in arms against the Ottoman Government.

The rising, which turned into a general Shī'ī insurrection, was a formidable affair, and a punitive column of Janissaries, led by the Grand Vizier in person, was routed, and their leader killed in battle, before the Ottoman Government eventually recovered control of the situation. Considering the fact that Sultan Bāyezīd's son and viceroy at Manysa, Qorqūd, had been in friendly relations with Shāh Qūlī,[2] and that there was already a keen competition between the several sons of the old and incompetent Sultan for the succession to the Ottoman throne, it is not altogether inconceivable that, if Shāh Qūlī had been able to receive, in A.D. 1511, the military support which was actually given by Ismā'īl to Bābur, the Shī'ī insurrection in Anatolia might have triumphed and might then have carried on to the Ottoman throne a new Sultan who would have been bound to the Safawī Empire by the same political and religious bonds that Bābur was actually forced to accept. Such an event would probably have changed the course of history. But as it was, with Shāh Ismā'īl engaged at the opposite extremity of the Iranic World and unable to come to the rescue of his Anatolian

---

[1] This Shāh Qūlī was a native of the Anatolian Turkish principality of Tekke whose father, Hasan Khalīfah, had been a disciple of Shāh Ismā'īl's father, Shaykh Haydar Safawī. (Browne, op. cit. vol. iv, p. 70.) [2] See p. 365, above.

supporters now that they had put their fortunes, and their master's fortunes, to the touch, Shāh Qūlī's rising was really a forlorn hope, notwithstanding its initial success; and it was also a stroke which could not be repeated. Shāh Qūlī himself appears to have lost his life; and all that his lieutenant, Ustādjÿ Oghlu, could do was to cut his way through to Tabrīz with the remnant of his followers. These survivors of the abortive Shī'ī insurrection in Anatolia were not well received by their Safawī master;[1] and indeed Shāh Ismā'īl had good reason to be displeased; for in the Ottoman dominions, as it had turned out, the master-stroke of the Safawī policy had miscarried; and the baffled Safawī empire-builder had now to await a counter-stroke from the most formidable military Power in the contemporary world, whose hostility had been wantonly provoked by his own henchmen.

Indeed, before Ustādjÿ Oghlu had been driven out of the Ottoman dominions in Asia, Shāh Ismā'īl's great Ottoman adversary, Sultan Bāyezīd's son Selīm, was already on the move.

This Ottoman Prince Selīm—a poet who was as competent and as ruthless in politics and war as his father was good-natured and inefficient—had long before made up his mind that the traditional Ottoman policy of non-aggression in Asia was not adequate for dealing with the new problem presented by the emergence, on the Asiatic frontiers of the Ottoman Empire, of the new Safawī Power, with its formidable tactics of preparing the ground for a military offensive by religious and political propaganda. His father, who shrank from Selīm's militant ideas, had marooned him in the governorship of Trebizond; but in the self-same year in which Shāh Qūlī raised his Shī'ī standard of revolt in Anatolia, Selīm likewise took the law into his own hands.[2] He sailed from Trebizond to Caffa, won over the Janissary garrison there, and obtained troops and supplies from his father-in-law the Khan of the Crimea (a successor-state of the Mongol appanage of Jūjī which had avoided Russian conquest by accepting Ottoman suzerainty). Thereupon, Selīm marched upon Constantinople down the west coast of the Black Sea; reached Chorlu in Thrace before he was intercepted and defeated by the Government troops; was allowed by his father, after the battle, to escape to the Crimea by sea; and was then bold enough to present himself in Constantinople, unaccompanied by an army, in the winter of 1511–12.

[1] They appear, however, to have been enrolled in the Qyzyl Bāsh forces. At least, the so-called Ustādjÿlÿ corps of the Safawī Army (for the name, see Browne, op. cit., vol. iv, p. 52, note 1) may be presumed to have been formed out of Ustādjÿ Oghlu's Anatolian recruits.

[2] The exact dates are uncertain, so that it is impossible to say whether Selīm made his move in the hope of forestalling Shāh Qūlī, or whether he was goaded into making it by the bankruptcy of his father's policy, after this had been exposed by Shāh Qūlī's stroke.

His boldness was justified by the event; for by this time the shock produced by Shāh Qūlī's revolt—which had revealed in a flash both the gravity and the imminence of the danger with which the Ottoman Power was now confronted in the militant policy of the Qyzyl Bāsh—seems to have had its effect upon the minds of the Ottoman Pādishāh's administrative and military slave-household, which was the ultimate ruling power behind the Ottoman throne.[1] They had made up their minds that Selīm, with his energy, his ruthlessness, and his militancy against the Qyzyl Bāsh (which was quite as vehement as Shāh Ismā'īl's militancy against the Sunnah), was the man of the hour. In the spring of A.D. 1512, before 'Ubaydallah Khān Uzbeg had driven Bābur out of Transoxania for the second time, the Janissaries at Constantinople had compelled Sultan Bāyezīd II to abdicate and had placed Sultan Selīm I on the Ottoman throne in his stead. By the end of the campaigning season of A.D. 1513, Selīm had secured his personal position at home by extirpating all his brothers and nephews except one nephew who escaped to Shāh Ismā'īl's court at Tabrīz and two who escaped to the Mamlūk Sultan's court at Cairo. Shāh Ismā'īl had no choice now but to make peace on his eastern front with 'Ubaydallah Khān, for on his western front he was now threatened for the first time in his career by an adversary of his own temper.

The now inevitable collision between the Safawī and the Ottoman Power duly occurred in the campaigning season of A.D. 1514. Shāh Ismā'īl took the offensive by sending Selīm's refugee nephew Murād—to whom the Shāh had given his own daughter in marriage—on a cavalry raid into Anatolia, accompanied by the late Shāh Qūlī's lieutenant Ustādjȳ Oghlu. But the prospects of this manœuvre—which depended for its success upon a responsive Shī'ī uprising in the Anatolian countryside—had been prejudiced in advance by the failure of Shāh Qūlī's insurrection three years before; and Selīm now made assurance doubly sure by extirpating the Shī'ī remnant in the Anatolian population—massacring some of them and deporting the rest to the Ottoman territories in Europe.[2] Murād and Ustādjȳ Oghlu penetrated no farther west than Sivās before they were compelled to retreat; and Selīm now marched

[1] For some account of this Ottoman slave-household, see further Part III. A, vol. iii, below.
[2] For Selīm's extirpation of the Shi'ah in Anatolia, which seems to have been carried out in A.D. 1514, see p. 362, above. Compare the massacre and deportation of the Armenians in the same region, by the orders of a latter-day Ottoman Government, in A.D. 1915–16, during the General War, when the 'Osmanlis were once again engaged in a life-and-death struggle with another Great Power—this time Russia—for the possession of their Asiatic dominions. In 1915, as in 1514, the Ottoman Government's purpose in committing its atrocities against a subject minority in the interior of its own dominions was to forestall the risk of being attacked in the rear by insurgents acting in concert with the foreign invader.

eastward with the Ottoman Regular Army, while Ismā'īl assumed the defensive (for the first time in his career)—devastating the western provinces of his empire through which the Ottoman in-vaders' route lay, and awaiting their arrival, with the main body of his army, in a position covering his own capital, Tabrīz.

Selīm, whose literary tastes had acquainted him with the Alexander Romance in its Persian version, now dreamed of emulat-ing the exploits of this legendary European conqueror of Asia; for Selīm was a Rūmī like Iskender himself, and he was aware that his own 'Osmanlis, like Alexander's Macedonians, had not their match as a fighting force in the world of his day. As far as fighting-power went, Selīm's expectations were not disappointed; for when the Ottoman Army made contact with the Safawī Army at Chāldirān, on the 22nd August 1514, the 'Osmanlis won the day, in spite of having to encounter an unharassed enemy after their own long and harassing march across a zone that had been purposely laid waste. From behind the regular 'Rūmī' battle-lager,[1] the Ottoman musketry and artillery swept the Qyzyl Bāsh cavalry away; and in little more than a fortnight after the battle Selīm marched into Ismā'īl's capital city of Tabrīz as a conqueror.

Ismā'īl's ignominious retreat from the traditional capital of North-Western Irān, after his heavy defeat at Chāldirān, bade fair to extinguish the prestige which the Safawī had first acquired, a dozen years earlier, when he was solemnly crowned king in Tabrīz after his resounding victory at Shurūr.[2] And Selīm was able to enter Tabrīz not merely as a conqueror but as a liberator; for his first act was to reconvert to the service of the Sunnah the mosques which had been arbitrarily converted to the service of the Shī'ah when Ismā'īl had signalized his original triumph by imposing his own religion by main force upon the Sunnī majority of the Tabrīzīs. With Shāh Ismā'īl discredited by his first great military disaster, and with the majority of his subjects waiting to welcome Ismā'īl's conqueror as the victorious champion of their own persecuted faith, Selīm, at this moment, had the entire Iranic World at his feet. He might have marched on, eastward, unopposed by hostile arms and warmly received by public opinion, from Tabrīz to Merv, along the road trodden by Ismā'īl four years before; and if the 'Osmanlī had now appeared in place of the Safawī on the borders of Transoxania and had offered himself to the Transoxanians, in his turn, as a saviour of the Iranic Civilization from the barbarism of the Eurasian Nomad Uzbegs, it is certain that the Transoxanians would have greeted Selīm with open arms as a second Timur; for when Sunnī

---

[1] For the use of this Rūmī battle-lager by Bābur, see p. 352, above.
[2] See p. 371, above.

Orthodoxy was united in the same person with cultural superiority and military invincibility, their allegiance to such a prince could hardly be in doubt. But the temper of Selīm's invincible troops was fatal to this brilliant prospect of Asiatic conquest; for, if Selīm had the talent and ambition of an Alexander, his Janissaries were by no means as amenable to their prince's will as Alexander's Phalangites had been.

The Macedonian peasants who served in Alexander's army were Europeans who had been born and bred on the very threshold of Asia; and they did not strike against being led into the interior of the familiar neighbouring continent till they had reached the bank of the Ganges. On the other hand, the Serb and Bosniak peasants who were the raw material of Selīm's Janissaries were Europeans through and through. Their nativewaters were theAdriatic and the Danube, not the Bosphorus or the Aegean. They could not make themselves at home on Asiatic soil; and when they were marched eastward beyond the ancient bounds of Orthodox Christendom in Anatolia, they were utterly *dépaysés*. They had mutinied already on the march from Amāsīyeh to Chāldirān; and, after the occupation of Tabrīz, they refused point-blank to go into winter quarters in the Qārabāgh, where Tīmur's mobile Transoxanians had wintered contentedly at least three times in an earlier chapter of Iranic history.[1] This intractability of Selīm's military machine settled Selīm's plans for him inexorably. He found himself compelled to start on his march back westward after having stayed in Tabrīz for little more than a week; and this Ottoman retreat from Tabrīz threatened at times to turn into the same kind of disaster as the French retreat from Moscow, before the army regained Amāsīyeh in mid-winter. Thus the homesickness of the Janissaries gave the Qyzyl Bāsh a reprieve; and this reprieve decided that Ismāʿīl Shāh Safawī's life-work should have permanent results. These results, in their turn, were to be decisive for the destinies of the Iranic World. But the destinies of the Iranic World were not the Janissaries' business. Their duty, as they felt it, was to be the apostate policemen of Orthodox Christendom, not the champions of the Sunnah against the Shīʿah.

[1] Sultan Selīm's European troops did not always show themselves as fastidious as this about being quartered in alien continents. For example, in A.D. 1520, only six years after the Chāldirān campaign, Selīm sent a force of Bosniak troops up the Nile into Nubia as a corollary to his conquest of Egypt in A.D. 1516–17 (see pp. 387–8, below). The landscape and climate of Nubia presumably seemed more exotic to these Dinaric highlanders than the landscape and climate of Armenia and Azerbaijan. Yet for the next three centuries the descendants of these Europeans maintained themselves in the section of the Nile Valley between the First Cataract at Aswān and the Third Cataract a little below (i.e. north of) Dongola. Nor was their continued residence there forced upon them, for they soon made themselves virtually independent of the Ottoman Empire. (See Budge, E. A. Wallis: *The Egyptian Sudan, its History and Monuments* (London 1907, Kegan Paul, 2 vols.), vol. ii, pp. 207–8.)

Thus the first round in the conflict between the Safawis and the 'Osmanlis had ended in a stalemate; and, just because it had ended in this way, this internecine struggle between the two foremost Powers of the Iranic World was bound to have, as its sequel, an Iranic movement of aggression against the Arabic World. At first sight it may seem paradoxical that the division of the Iranic Society against itself—a division which was manifestly draining the strength and sapping the vitality of the Iranic body social—should be accompanied by an apparently wanton attack upon inoffensive neighbours. But on closer inspection the paradox is resolved; for this apparently aggressive movement against a third party, so far from being superfluous, turns out to have been an inevitable incident in the trial of strength between the two Iranic Great Powers.

The truth was that the stalemate between the Ottoman and the Safawī Power could not be resolved by any further direct attack on either combatant's part upon the home territory of the other. By the end of the campaigning season of A.D. 1514 it had been proved by trial and error that the Safawī could make no permanent conquests in Anatolia and the 'Osmanlī none in Iran. On this showing, the even balance could only be upset, in one party's favour or in the other's, by aggrandisement at the expense of some third party which would be too weak to defend itself against an attack from either of the two Iranic belligerents. The two weakest states that lay nearest to Constantinople and Tabrīz, and approximately equidistant from the 'Osmanlī and from the Safawī capital, were the buffer-state of Dhu'l-Qadar in the highlands of South-Eastern Anatolia and the Empire of the Mamlūks in Syria and Egypt, and this Mamlūk Empire was the leading state in the Arabic World. Accordingly, after the indecisive outcome of the campaign of A.D. 1514, the next stage in the struggle between the 'Osmanlī and the Safawī Power was bound to be a race between these two Iranic Powers for the conquest of the adjacent Arabic provinces. Either the Safawī Empire would spread to the shores of the Mediterranean and hem the 'Osmanlis into the Anatolian Peninsula as the East Roman Empire had once been hemmed in by the 'Abbasids, or else the Ottoman Empire would advance to the line of the Euphrates and bar the Safawis out from the Levant as the Arsacid and Sasanian Empires had once been barred out by the Romans.

In this race, Shāh Ismā'īl had a certain start over Sultan Selīm; for the Imāmī Shī'īs had an ancient Syrian stronghold in the Jabal 'Āmil, and the Imāmī Shāh already had his eye on Syria, as is shown by the fact that one of the Qyzyl Bāsh army-corps was called 'the Syrian Corps' or Shāmlū. Accordingly, Selīm had to act

quickly if he was to steal a march on his Safawī rival; and he lost
no time, indeed. In A.D. 1515, which was the season following the
year of Chāldirān, Selīm occupied and annexed the buffer-state of
Dhu'l-Qadar (thus bringing his Asiatic frontier up to the line of the
Euphrates one hundred and twenty-two years after the date at
which the European frontier of the Ottoman Empire had reached
the line of the Danube). In the next season, A.D. 1516, Selīm proceeded to invade the Mamlūk dominions; overthrew the Mamlūk
Army on the plain of Marj Dābiq, in North Syria, on the 24th
August 1516; and occupied the Mamlūk capital Cairo itself on the
26th January 1517. Selīm's entry into Cairo, unlike his entry into
Tabrīz, was definitive. It established a political connexion between
the Ottoman Empire and the Arabic provinces of Syria, Egypt, and
the Hijāz which—sometimes in the form of direct Ottoman rule
and at other times in the form of an Ottoman suzerainty—was to
last altogether for three hundred years. Ismā'īl proved unable
either to prevent or to undo this last piece of Selīm's work. And
thus, before Selīm died in 1520 and Ismā'īl in 1524 (and they both
died young), the results of their collision had changed the face of
the Arabic as well as the Iranic World beyond recognition.

The Historical Consequences of Shāh Ismā'īl's Career

We may now bring this excursus to a close by attempting to sum
up and appraise these changes, including both the immediate
effects and the ultimate consequences.

The most conspicuous tangible effect, which was not only
immediate but was also enduring, was the abrupt and violent
break-up of the former Iranic World into three separate fractions:
one consisting of Transoxania and the Iranic 'colonial' domain in
India, the second consisting of Iran proper, and the third consisting of the other Iranic 'colonial' domain which had been
created by the Turkish conquests in Orthodox Christendom.
These three fractions of the former Iranic World were prised
asunder and held apart by two new frontiers: a new frontier between
Iran and Transoxania which ran from the north-western face of the
Hindu Kush northwards to the Qāra Qūm Desert or alternatively
to the south-eastern corner of the Caspian Sea; and a new frontier
between Iran and the Ottoman domain which ran from the southern
face of the Caucasus southwards to the Syrian Desert or alternatively to the head of the Persian Gulf.

Strictly, these two new frontiers were not fresh cuts but ancient
wounds which had broken open and begun to bleed again along the
lines of the old scars, under the stress of a tremendous social shock.
The frontier which now divided the Safawī Empire from the Uzbeg

Empire had once divided the Seleucid and Arsacid and Sasanian and Umayyad Empires in Iran from a series of Hellenic and barbarian principalities in the Oxus-Jaxartes Basin over a span of about a thousand years extending from the third century B.C. into the eighth century of the Christian Era.[1] Similarly, the frontier which now divided the Safawī Empire from the Ottoman Empire had once divided the Arsacid and Sasanian Empires from the Roman Empire over a span of about seven hundred years extending from the last century B.C. into the seventh century of the Christian Era.

The Ottoman Government of Rūm began to reorganize this ci-devant frontier of its eponym the Roman Empire as early as A.D. 1514,[2] when the temper of the Janissaries made it apparent to Selīm that he had no prospect of driving Ismāʿīl beyond the horizon and annexing the whole of the Safawī Empire to his own; for this made it evident that he must content himself with the more modest alternative of carrying the existing defensive frontier of the Ottoman Empire in Asia a few degrees farther eastward. The temper of the Janissaries also made it evident that, in making and maintaining even this modest eastward advance, the Ottoman Government would have to rely upon securing the loyalty of one of the local 'martial races', rather than attempting to induce its own regular European soldiery to do garrison duty against the grain in this (to them) outlandish region. For this purpose, the Ottoman Government picked out the Kurds: a local race of pugnacious highlanders who were linked with the ʿOsmanlis by their common Sunnī faith and were no more cut off from these new Turkish partners by their Persian patois than they were from the Qyzyl Bāsh Türkmens, while they were up in arms against Shāh Ismāʿīl's attempt to dragoon them into becoming Shīʿīs.

The Ottoman Government appointed a Kurdish Sunnī 'cleric', Mawlā Idrīs of Bitlis—an ex-secretary of Ismāʿīl's former victim Yaʿqūb Khān Āq Qōyūnlū—to act in Kurdistan as an agent of the Sunnī faith, in much the same way as Shāh Qūlī had once acted for Shāh Ismāʿīl and for the Shīʿah in Anatolia. Mawlā Idrīs was either more competent himself, or else more effectively supported by his principals, than Shāh Qūlī had been, for he appears to have performed his function without disaster from A.D. 1514 to A.D. 1535. Under Mawlā Idrīs's guidance or advice, a number of measures were taken for turning the Kurds into a bulwark of the Ottoman Empire in Asia. As an inner line of defence against future

---

[1] See II. D (v), vol. ii, p. 141, footnote 2, below.

[2] The account of this organization which is given here is taken from a passage in an unpublished work on Armenians and Kurds by Mr. A. S. Safrastian, which the author has been kind enough to show to the present writer.

Safawī invasions, Kurdish military colonies were settled astride the east-and-west routes between Iran and Anatolia on the north side of the Anti-Taurus. As an advanced line, the Kurdish tribal chiefs in Kurdistan proper (i.e. on the western face of the Zagros Range which formed the western escarpment of the Iranian Plateau) were nominally incorporated into the Ottoman feudal system—receiving the styles and titles of Ottoman feudatories without being asked to renounce their hereditary tenures. In the religious sphere, the Kurds were fortified in their Sunnī faith by the importation, into the principal Kurdish centres, of Arab Sunnī Shaykhs, who were distinguished by the title of Saʿdat from the native Kurdish ʿulamā.[1]

This Kurdish frontier effectively covered the Ottoman dominions in Anatolia; but it did not completely preclude the Safawī Power from striking at the new Ottoman provinces in Syria and Egypt so long as the Safawīs remained masters of ʿIrāq; and therefore the ʿOsmanlis, like the Romans before them, had to choose between the shorter but vaguer line running from the Caucasus to the North Arabian Desert and the longer but more definite line that ran from the Caucasus to the Persian Gulf. Sultan Selīm's son Sultan Suleymān rounded off his work by annexing Baghdad in A.D. 1534 and Basrah in A.D. 1546, as Pompey's work had been rounded off by Trajan. The ʿOsmanlis differed from the Romans in preferring the longer line to the shorter after having made a trial of both; but, in both cases alike, the price paid for the drawing of the frontier along either line was a series of recurrent, and progressively more devastating, wars between the opposing Powers on either side of the barrier.[2]

As for the other frontier of the Safawī Empire over against the Uzbegs, the role of frontiersmen, which was played for the Ottoman Empire by the Sunnī Kurds, was here played for the Uzbeg principalities by the Sunnī Türkmens of the Transcaspian oases, who were as violently up in arms against Shāh Ismāʿīl's Qyzyl Bāsh Türkmens as the Kurds were. On this frontier, social conditions eventually relapsed so far towards barbarism that the opposing forces on either side of the barrier became incapable of waging formal wars like those which were fought periodically between the Safawis and the ʿOsmanlis. In the borderland between Iran and

---

[1] Compare the importation of Arab Shīʿī Shaykhs from the Jabal ʿĀmil and Bahrayn into the Safawī dominions, which has been noticed in another connexion on p. 362, above. Presumably these two applications of an identical religious propaganda policy were not thought out by the Ottoman and the Safawī Government independently, but there seems to be no means of ascertaining which one of the two Governments was copying the other.

[2] For the rhythm of such recurrent wars along frontiers of such a kind, see further Part XI, below.

the Oxus-Jaxartes Basin, the warfare between Safawī and Shaybānī, or between Shī'ī and Sunnī, degenerated into raids; and, after the collapse of the Safawī Power in the first quarter of the eighteenth century of the Christian Era, the Sunnī Türkmen slave-raiders took the offensive and ranged almost at will over Iran until their lairs in Transcaspia were captured by the Russian Army, and their criminal activities suppressed by the Russian Government, between 1863 and 1886.

On both fronts, however, the warfare was uniformly bitter, because the hostility which inspired it was not merely political but was also religious. For these two new frontiers not only divided the Safawī Empire from the Uzbeg principalities on the one hand and from the Ottoman Empire on the other. They also now divided the domain of the Imāmī Shī'ah from the domain of the Sunnah.[1]

As a result of the partial success and partial failure of Shāh Ismā'īl's work, the relations between the Sunnah and the Shī'ah in the Islamic World had been changed out of recognition without being changed *in toto*. Before Shāh Ismā'īl started on his career, the adherents of the two sects had been living cheek by jowl, geographically intermingled with one another, from end to end of the Iranic World, with the Shī'ah everywhere in a decided minority and with a tolerant spirit of 'Live and let live' presiding over the relations between the two sects. Shāh Ismā'īl had set out to reduce this religious dualism of the Iranic World to a unity by imposing the minority's religion upon the majority of the Iranic Society by sheer military force; and this *tour de force* had finally proved to be beyond his powers. At the end of his career, as at the beginning, both sects were still in being in the Iranic World side by side; and, although the Shī'ah had obtained a net numerical increase through the excess of Ismā'īl's forcible conversions of Sunnīs to Shī'ism over Selīm's forcible conversions of Shī'īs to the Sunnah, the Shī'ah still remained in a minority on the whole. In these two fundamental points, the situation was still what it had been before. The great change—and this was not only a change out of all recognition, but was also a change that was wholly for the worse—consisted, first, in the forcible sorting out and geographical segregation of the two sects by the violent means of massacre and deportation and compulsory conversion, while the second new feature was the fiery

---

[1] Compare the situation in the age of the Sasanidae, when the frontier between the Sasanian Empire and the Roman Empire had also been a frontier between Zoroastrianism and Nestorian Christianity on the one side and Catholic and Monophysite Christianity on the other, while the frontier between the Sasanian Empire and the Ephthalite and Turkish principalities in the Oxus-Jaxartes Basin had then been a frontier between Zoroastrianism and Buddhism. (For this latter religious frontier, see further Part II. D (vii), vol. ii, pp. 371-5, below.)

hatred between Sunnī and Shī'ī which had flamed up on both sides owing to the introduction of these 'methods of barbarism'—first on the Shī'ī side by Ismā'īl, and then on the Sunnī side by Selīm. This schism of the Iranic Society on the moral and religious as well as the political plane severed all the threads that had previously knit the Iranic social fabric together; and this 'sawing asunder' took the life out of the Iranic Civilization and stopped its progress dead.

When we examine the subsequent condition of each of the three fragments, we observe, in different forms, the unmistakable symptoms of the same moral sickness.

To take the central or Iranian fragment first, it is manifest that the new Imāmī Shī'ī Empire, as Shāh Ismā'īl left it, fell far short of its founder's ambitions and intentions. It was indeed a great empire within which the Shī'ah was the only religion that was permitted to exist; and its frontiers did embrace all the principal Imāmī Shī'ī holy places: the martyrs' tombs at Najaf and Karbalā and Kāzimayn and the mosque of the Expected Imām[1] at Hillah in the Arab 'Irāq; the holy cities of Qumm and Qāshān in the Achaemenian 'Irāq;[2] and the Mashhad of the Imām Riza at the opposite corner of the Safawī dominions, in Khurāsān. Yet, even so, this was not the oecumenical Shī'ī Empire that Shāh Ismā'īl had dreamed of; and the increase in the numbers of the Shī'ah which he had secured by the forcible conversion of the Sunnī majority in the territories which he had succeeded in conquering was partly set off by the loss of the Shī'ī minority which was exterminated, in retaliation, by the Uzbegs in Transoxania and by the 'Osmanlis in Anatolia. In fact, Ismā'īl fell so far short of establishing a world empire that the state which he formed became a kind of hermit kingdom, whose internal uniformity and solidarity as the earthly domain of Imāmī Shi'ism was counterbalanced by its isolation from a Sunnī World which still hemmed it in on either side. It was the deliberate policy of the Safawī Government to keep their Shī'ī subjects both materially and spiritually insulated from Sunnī contagion by discouraging pilgrimages to Holy Places outside the Safawī dominions. This policy applied not only to the Pan-Islamic Holy Places—Mecca and Medina and Jerusalem—but even to the specifically Shī'ī Holy Places when these were under Sunnī rule. It applied, for example, to Najaf and Karbalā and the Kāzimayn at times when the Arab 'Irāq was in Ottoman and not in Safawī hands.[3] Under this régime, the Imāmī Shi'ism which Shāh

---

[1] See III. C (ii) (b), Annex I, vol. iii, pp. 463–4, below.
[2] 'Irāq 'Ajamī, otherwise known as the Jibāl, in Western Iran.
[3] On this point, see Browne, op. cit., vol. iv, pp. 29–30.

Ismāʿīl had made into the exclusive regional religion of Iran dwindled from a would-be world religion into something which may be called a 'national' religion without any serious mis-application of our Western terminology. Moreover, in modern Shīʿī Iran, as in the Protestant parts of our modern Western Christendom, the national religion has become the matrix of a secular or political national consciousness.[1]

It will be seen that Ismāʿīl Shāh Safawī's Shīʿī Revival in the Iranic World resembled the contemporary Protestant Reformation in Western Christendom both in the violence with which it was carried out and in the political consequences which eventually fol-lowed from it. A third point of resemblance is that, in both cases, the violent religious change was accompanied by a disastrous set-back in culture. This cultural set-back in modern Iran is described and explained in the following terms by a Persian correspondent of the late Professor Browne, Mirzā Muhammad Khān of Qazwīn:

'There is . . . no doubt that during the Safawī period literature and poetry in Persia had sunk to a very low ebb, and that not one single poet of the first rank can be reckoned as representing this epoch. The chief reason for this . . . seems to have been that these kings, by reason of their political aims and strong antagonism to the Ottoman Empire, devoted the greater part of their energies to the propagation of the Shīʿah doctrine and the encouragement of divines learned in its principles and

[1] For this analogue of our modern Western Nationalism in the modern êthos of Shīʿī Iran, see further II. D (vi), vol. ii, pp. 254–5, below. It is perhaps worth noting that this indigenous Iranian Nationalism also resembles our Western Nationalism in the fact that its original basis was religious and dynastic but not linguistic. The factors which produced the modern Persian national consciousness were the two common bonds of Safawī government and Shīʿī faith, and not any community of mother-tongue. We have noticed already that Turkish, not Persian, was the mother-tongue of Shāh Ismāʿīl, and that the nucleus of his army was formed, not of Persians, but of Türkmens. Tabrīz, which he chose for his capital, was a Turkish-speaking city situated in the Turkish-speaking province of Azerbaijan. And Tabrīz remained the second city of the Empire, and the seat of the heir-apparent, even after the capital had been moved to Isfahān—a move which was made because Isfahān was less exposed to Ottoman attack and was also nearer the centre of the Safawī Empire after its expansion had been cut short on the west. Even then, the Safawis seem still to have retained their Turkish mother-tongue to the end, in spite of the fact that Isfahān was a Persian-speaking city in a Persian-speaking region. (See the anecdote of the last Safawī, Shāh Husayn (regnabat A.D. 1694–1722), which is recounted by Browne in op. cit., vol. iv, p. 113.) Moreover, Nādir Shāh Avshār (dominabatur A.D. 1730–47) was also a Turk by race and mother-tongue; and so were the Qājārs, who were the rulers of Persia from A.D. 1779 to A.D. 1925. The Qājār Dynasty had a private law that no member of the family could qualify for succeeding to the throne of Persia unless his mother were a Qājār princess—unless, that is to say, he were descended on both sides from the same Turkish tribe. Perhaps the greatest paradox of all is the fact that the new-fangled form of Persian Nationalism, alla Franca, arose first in the Turkish-speaking province of Azerbaijan—the reason being that Azerbaijan, through its geographical situation, was more exposed than other parts of Persia to Western influences. In fact, the ultra-modern type of Western Nationalism, in which the linguistic factor is paramount, did not really capture Persia until after the rise of Shāh Rizā. This parvenu ruler's adoption of the dynastic name Pahlawī is quite in the manner of our nineteenth-century Western political Romanticism; and it is also note-worthy that, in conscious opposition to the dynastic law of the Qājār Dynasty, the founder of the Pahlawī Dynasty has enacted that his descendants must be born of Persian mothers in order to qualify for succeeding to the throne. (For this enactment, see Toynbee, A. J.: Survey of International Affairs, 1925, vol. i (London 1927, Milford), p. 537, footnote 6.)

laws. Now although these divines strove greatly to effect the religious unification of Persia (which resulted in its political unification), and laid the foundations of this present-day Persia, whose inhabitants are, speaking generally, of one faith, one tongue, and one race, yet, on the other hand, from the point of view of literature, poetry, Sūfī-ism, and Mysticism, and, to use their own expression, everything connected with the "Accomplishments" (as opposed to the "Legalities"), they not merely fell far short in the promotion thereof but sought by every means to injure and annoy the representatives of these "Accomplishments", who were generally not too firmly established in the Religious Law and its derivatives. In regard to the Sūfīs particularly, they employed every kind of severity and vexation, whether by exile, expulsion, slaughter, or reprimand, slaying or burning many of them with their own hands or by their sentence. Now the close connexion between poetry and Belles Lettres on the one hand, and Sūfī-ism and Mysticism on the other, at any rate in Persia, is obvious, so that the extinction of the one necessarily involves the extinction and destruction of the other. Hence it was that under this dynasty learning, culture, poetry and Mysticism completely deserted Persia, and the cloisters, monasteries, retreats, and rest-houses of the *darwīshes* were so utterly destroyed that there is now throughout the whole of Persia no name or sign of such charitable foundations, though formerly, as, for instance, in the time of Ibn Battūtah,[1] such institutions were to be found in every town, hamlet, and village, as abundantly appears from the perusal of his *Travels*, wherein he describes how in every place, small or great, where he halted, he alighted in such buildings, of which at the present day no name or sign exists. Anyone ignorant of the circumstances of the Safawī period might well wonder whether this Persia and that are the same country, and the creed of its inhabitants the same Islām; and, if so, why practically, with rare exceptions, there exists now not a single monastery throughout the whole of Persia, while in those parts of Turkey, such as Mesopotamia, Kurdistan, and Sulaymānīyah, which did not remain under the Safawī dominion, there are many such buildings, just as there were in Ibn Battūtah's days.'[2]

The 'Iconoclastic' or 'Calvinistic' spirit[3] which wrought this havoc in Iran when it incarnated itself in the person of Ismāʻīl Shāh Safawī did not ravage Turkey until some four centuries later, when it found its incarnation there in President Mustafā Kemāl.[4]

[1] *Peregrinabatur* A.D. 1325–53.—A. J. T.
[2] Letter, dated the 24th May 1911, from Mirzā Muhammad Khān to Professor E. G. Browne, quoted in Browne, op. cit., vol. iv, pp. 26-7.
[3] In a further sentence, Mirzā Muhammad Khān describes the Shīʻī theologians who now took the place of the great poets and philosophers in Iran as 'great indeed' themselves, 'but harsh, dry, fanatical, and formal'—a combination of qualities which is equally characteristic of the êthos of their Calvinist contemporaries in Western Christendom.
[4] The source of Mustafā Kemāl's inspiration with this spirit is manifest. He is a palpable convert to our modern Western Nationalism with its fanatical, barbarizing vein. The source of Ismāʻīl Safawī's inspiration with the same spirit, four centuries earlier, remains mysterious; for, although Ismāʻīl's Shīʻī Revival was contemporary with the Protestant Reformation in Western Christendom, there seems to be no trace of any direct connexion between the two movements.

Nevertheless, the sudden impoverishment of culture in Iran, which
Ismāʿīl brought about, dealt the Iranic culture of the ʿOsmanlis a
deadly blow by cutting its roots; and during the following four
centuries the ʿOsmanlis lived a cultural life-in-death until, in our
time, they have thrown off the cerements of their dead Iranic
culture and have sought to adopt our Western culture, like a suit
of ready-made clothes, as a counsel of despair. We have observed
already that the territories which were conquered from Orthodox
Christendom by the Saljūqs and the ʿOsmanlis successively were
a kind of 'colonial' extension of the Iranic World; and that the
representatives of the Iranic Society in these *partibus infidelium*,
like its representatives in Hindustan, depended for the maintenance
of their culture upon a steady inflow of arts and ideas, and of
immigrants to import them, from the homelands of the Iranic
Civilization in Iran itself. The last of these immigrant *Kulturträger* were the fugitive Timurid prince Bādīʿ-az-Zamān[1] and the
seven hundred families of indigenous skilled artisans whom the
Ottoman Sultan Selīm brought home with him from Tabrīz in
1514 as the sole substantial souvenir of his one week's sojourn in
that great home of Iranic culture. Thereafter, the ancient channels
of intercourse along which the vivifying stream of culture had been
flowing into Anatolia from Iran for the past four hundred years
were blocked by the new frontier between the Ottoman and the
Safawī Empire and between the segregated domains of the Sunnah and the Shīʿah—a frontier which was established by the
ʿOsmanlis themselves. Yet, even if they had forborn to choke up
the channel, the waters would still have ceased to flow; for, as we
have seen, the Shīʿī Revival in Iran was now drying up the springs
of Iranic culture at their source.

Nor did the ʿOsmanlis find equivalent compensation for this
cultural drought by tapping fresh waters in the Arabic World in
which they had now for the first time obtained a footing through
their conquest of Syria and Egypt and the Hijāz. The Arabic
culture was incapable of taking the place of the Iranic culture in
Ottoman life for two reasons: first because it was alien, and second
because it was only half alive. The contemporary culture of the
Arabic World was alien to the ʿOsmanlis in the sense that they had
drawn hitherto through a Persian, and not through an Arabic,
medium upon the Classical Arabic version in which the ancient
culture of the antecedent Syriac Society had been cultivated, in its
last phase, in the age of the ʿAbbasid Caliphate of Baghdad. It
would hardly have been possible for the ʿOsmanlis to take an
Arabic in exchange for a Persian medium of communication with

[1] See pp. 351-2, above.

this cultural past, even if the contemporary Arabic culture had been as vital as the contemporary Iranian. But, as a matter of fact, the Arabic culture of Egypt, at the turn of the fifteenth and sixteenth centuries of the Christian Era, was sadly cut-and-dried. The genius of the Maghribī Ibn Khaldūn had proved to be a *lusus Naturae*, a flash in the pan.[1] The Egyptian version of the Arabic Civilization had prevailed; and this Egyptian Arabic culture stood to the Iranian culture of a Jāmī and a Hāfiz and a Saʿdī and a Firdawsī rather as the Byzantine culture of medieval Orthodox Christendom stood to the contemporary Latin culture of the West. The Arabic Civilization had acquired in Egypt an Epimethean instead of a Promethean outlook; and this rearward stance was not confined to the things of the spirit. It was also adopted in the field of politics, where the Byzantine resuscitation of an 'East Roman Empire' had its analogue in the Cairene ghost of the ʿAbbasid Caliphate.

It is true that our modern Western scholarship has exploded the legend that a formal transfer of the Caliphate to the Ottoman Sultan Selīm I was made by the last ʿAbbasid puppet of the Egyptian Mamlūks after the last Mamlūk Sultan himself had been over-thrown by Selīm. It appears that the Ottoman Sultans had long since made play with the title of Caliph and had also long since ceased to value a faded title which had been likewise usurped by every other contemporary Islamic Dynasty.[2] Yet this fact does not mean that the conquest of Egypt and the Hijāz was without effect upon the Ottoman Government's political and religious outlook. For the same scholarship has shown[3] that Sultan Selīm I did take over—not from the Cairene ʿAbbasid Caliphs, but from their masters the Mamlūk Sultans—the title of 'Servant of the two Holy Sanctuaries' [of Mecca and Medina], and that he valued this title very highly.

In fact, the annexation of the principal provinces of the Arabic World did affect the ʿOsmanlis profoundly in their politics and in their religion and in their culture. And the effect was not for good; for the Ottoman and the Arabic Society were ill-assorted partners,[4] and the partnership always remained uncomfortable and unfruitful so long as it lasted. The ʿOsmanlis were compelled to annex this great Arabic domain in order to forestall its annexation by the Safawīs; but the Arabic half of their dominions hung like a mill-stone round their necks.[5]

---

[1] For Ibn Khaldūn, see further III. C (ii) (b), vol. iii, pp. 321–8 with Annex III, below.
[2] This is shown by Sir T. W. Arnold in *The Caliphate* (Oxford 1924, Clarendor Press), chapters xi and xii.
[3] See Arnold, op cit., loc. cit.
[4] The spirit and structure of the Ottoman Society are examined in Part III. A vol. iii, pp. 22–50, below.
[5] The ʿOsmanlis might, no doubt, have reaped a dazzling economic reward from these

It remains for us to glance at the fate of the third of the fragments into which the *ci-devant* Iranic World had been broken up. This third fragment was the Oxus-Jaxartes Basin; and its fate may be summed up in the one word 'barbarization'. Transoxania had depended almost as much as the Ottoman Empire upon the inflow of culture from Iran, and it suffered still more severely from the blocking of the channels and the drying-up of the springs; for at this moment Transoxania had need of an additional cultural stimulus in order to leaven the barbarism of her Uzbeg conquerors who now sat on the thrones of the cultivated Timurids. When the stimulus, so far from being intensified, was removed altogether, the Iranic culture of Transoxania was doomed to decay.[1]

The bare chance remained that the Transoxanians and the 'Osmanlis might save their relics of Iranic culture by putting them into common stock, if they could succeed in getting into touch with one another again by somehow circumventing the obstacle of the hostile and alien Safawī Empire that now intervened between them. Now that the direct line of communication south of the Caspian was closed, the only alternative was to open up a new route, north of the Caspian, across the Eurasian Steppe. The western end of a potential northern passage was already in the

Arabic conquests if only they had pushed them a little bit farther. For the Arabic World—extending, as it did, from the Arabian and Egyptian coasts of the Persian Gulf and the Red Sea to a Moroccan seaboard on the Atlantic—commanded the interior lines of the new Oceanic highway between Europe and India which was just being opened up, at this very time, by the Portuguese. The 'Osmanlis gained possession of Suez in A.D. 1517; they held the Yaman from 1517 to 1633; and they occupied Basrah in 1546; while in the opposite direction they established themselves in Algeria in A.D. 1512–19. But they never pushed on across Morocco to the Atlantic, they never seriously contested the supremacy of the Portuguese on the west coast of India, and they never made effective use of the incomparable combination of strategic and commercial points of vantage which they had actually acquired. It was the Dutch and English and French, and not the 'Osmanlis, who challenged the Spanish and Portuguese monopoly of the Overseas World. (On this point, see further II. D (vii), Annex VII, vol. ii, below. See also Kahle, P.: *Die Verschollene Columbus-Karte von 1498 in einer türkischen Weltkarte von 1513* (Berlin and Leipzig 1933, de Gruyter.)

[1] During the span of a thousand years extending from the third century B.C. to the eighth century of the Christian Era, during which Transoxania had been divided by a political frontier from Iran, the country had also been overrun by Eurasian Nomad barbarians—Sakas, Yuechi, Ephthalites, Turks—on at least four occasions. But in this epoch the situation had never been entirely comparable to that in which Transoxania found herself during the period which intervened between the Uzbeg and the Russian conquest; for in the earlier epoch Transoxania, even when she was under a barbarian yoke, had never been entirely insulated from the radiation of culture from outside. For one thing, the political frontier dividing Transoxania from Iran had only been a religious frontier in this epoch during the lifetime of the Sasanian Empire; and throughout those thousand years Transoxania had never been cut off from Buddhist cultural influences emanating from India. It is true that, under the Uzbeg régime, Transoxania was likewise in cultural contact with India, while culturally isolated from Iran. But, unhappily for Transoxania in these latter days, the only culture from India which was now accessible to her was no indigenous Indian civilization with its roots in Indian soil. It was merely the 'colonial' version of the Iranic culture which had been transplanted to India as an incidental consequence of Turkish military conquests; and this exotic Iranic culture in India was just as dependent upon Iran for sustenance as was the Iranic culture of Transoxania itself; so that Transoxania could derive no culture from India at second hand when once the springs in Iran had been dried up.

'Osmanlis' hands; for the Ottoman Empire had taken over the
Genoese maritime stations of Caffa in the Crimea and Tana at the
head of the Sea of Azov as far back as A.D. 1475, and the Crimean
'successor-state' of the Mongol appanage of Jūjī had also passed
under Ottoman suzerainty. From this base of operations an Ottoman expeditionary force actually attempted, in A.D. 1569, to take
possession of the isthmus between the elbows of the Don and
the Volga, with the intention of opening up an all-Ottoman inland
waterway from the Black Sea to the Caspian.[1] But they had taken
action too late; for the Muscovites had just secured control of the
line of the Volga by conquering Qāzān in A.D. 1552 and Āstrakhān
in 1554. The Ottoman expeditionary force withdrew ignominiously without having achieved anything; the Ottoman outpost of
Tana was masked by the new Muscovite foundation of Cherkask-
on-Don;[2] and the insulation of Transoxania from the Ottoman
World was thus consummated by the combination of a Muscovite
with a Safawī barrier: a dual barrier which it was quite impossible
to turn, since it extended, south and north, from the Indian to the
Arctic Ocean. By this stroke, the Russians virtually put Transoxania 'into cold storage' until they found it convenient to annex
this derelict fragment of the Iranic World to the Russian Empire
some three hundred years later.

These were some of the portentous historical consequences of
Ismāʿīl Shāh Safawī's extraordinary career. And it is the sum of
these consequences that accounts for the break-up of the former
Iranic World and the formation of 'the Islamic World' as we know
it to-day. It will be seen that this latter-day Islamic World is really
not an organic unity but a pile of wreckage; and that the wreck was
the consequence of a collision between *two* former Islamic worlds
—the Iranic and the Arabic—which occurred some four hundred
years ago as the after-effect of a great social explosion in which one
of these two worlds—the Iranic World—had burst into fragments.
The explosion was produced by Shāh Ismāʿīl; and it would be
difficult to find any other public character in history who has been
so highly 'explosive' as this, with the possible exception of Lenin.

[1] This Ottoman enterprise of A.D. 1569 has a remarkably close historical precedent
in the contact which had been established, exactly a thousand years before, between the
Imperial Roman Government at Constantinople and the Transoxanian city-states of the
day, via this self-same northern passage across the Eurasian Steppe north of the Caspian.
The motive, too, was the same; for, in the sixth century of the Christian Era, the direct
land-route between the Roman Empire and Transoxania, south of the Caspian, as well
as the water-route to China via the Indian Ocean, was being deliberately blocked by the
Iranian Empire of the Sasanids, just as the direct route was being blocked in the sixteenth century by the Iranian Empire of the Safawis. In the sixth century, the northern
route was actually opened up with success, since at that time the paramount Power on the
Steppes was not a hostile Muscovy but a friendly Turkish Great Khan, who was
anxious to foster the commerce of his Transoxanian vassals. (See Hudson, G. F.:
Europe and China (London 1931, Arnold), pp. 122–33.)
[2] For this episode, see further II. D (vii), Annex VII, vol. ii, below.

There is, in fact, an obvious parallel between the sudden schism of the Iranic World, in the sixteenth century of the Christian Era, into a Shīʿī and a Sunnī camp, divided by a virulent and implacable mutual hatred, and the sudden schism of our latter-day 'Great Society', in the twentieth century, into a Communist and a Capitalist camp, with an equally great gulf of hatred fixed between them.

This recrudescence of the ancient feud between the Shīʿah and the Sunnah in the heart of the former Iranic World has received very poor compensation in that uneasy union of part of the Iranic World with part of the Arabic World which has been brought about by Sultan Selīm I's compulsory conquest of the Empire of the Egyptian Mamlūks. It is this composite Ottoman Society— part Iranic and part Arabic—that is uppermost in our minds when we think of 'the Islamic World' as a unity to-day; and we are rather apt to leave the obstinate dissidence of Shīʿī Iran out of the picture as an anomalous feature. Actually, the feud between this Shīʿī Iran and the rest of the modern Islamic World has had a disastrous effect upon the fortunes of both parties to it; and it has proved exceedingly intractable to any attempts at reconciliation.

In the first place, this feud was probably the most important single factor in the *débâcles* of the three Islamic Great Powers—the Ottoman Empire in Orthodox Christendom and the Arabic World, the Safawī Empire in Iran, and the Timurid Empire which had been established by Bābur's grandson Akbar in India—which all went to pieces simultaneously, at the turn of the seventeenth and eighteenth centuries of the Christian Era, some two centuries after the time of Bābur and Ismāʿīl and Selīm. Thereafter, the tyrant Nādir Shāh (*dominabatur* A.D. 1730–47), who arose in the vacuum which the downfall of the Safawis had left, made an abortive attempt to bring the feud to an end by reconverting Iran from the Shīʿah to the Sunnah; but his failure demonstrated that, with the lapse of two centuries, a minoritarian religion which had originally been imposed by sheer force upon the majority of the people of Iran by Ismāʿīl Shāh Safawī had entrenched itself in the hearts of the Persians as their national religion. After Nādir Shāh's fiasco, there was no further serious attempt to heal the feud till the last decade of the nineteenth century of the Christian Era, when the rising pressure of the Western World upon all Islamic countries alike evoked the Pan-Islamic Movement.

The programme of Pan-Islamism has been to compose even the most serious internal differences in the bosom of the Islamic Society in order to close the ranks of Islam in face of the overwhelming common danger which now confronts the whole Islamic

World. But this movement has had no time to gather momentum before it has been overtaken, and overruled, by an alternative programme for dealing with 'the Western Question' on diametrically opposite lines. This rival scheme of salvation proposes to exorcize the menace of the West by an 'offensive defensive'. The Islamic peoples are to make sure of their footing in a Westernized World by adopting the aggressive Western Civilization themselves and adopting it *in toto*. This policy of radical Westernization involves, of course, among other things, the adoption of the Western theory and practice of Nationalism; and it now looks as though it were the destiny of the Islamic World to be incorporated piecemeal into our Western World as one Islamic people after another 'goes nationalist'. The Ottoman Turks have already taken the plunge; the Egyptians are following in their wake at a less revolutionary pace; and the Persians, for their part, are finding it peculiarly easy to fall into line, because, as we have seen, the Shi'ism which was imposed by Shāh Ismā'īl upon modern Iran has already produced in Persian minds a political consciousness which is closely analogous to the Nationalism which has been the product of Protestantism in our Western World.

On this showing, it seems possible that the wreckage left by the great Islamic catastrophe of the sixteenth century of the Christian Era may be cleared up, in this twentieth century, at last through the incorporation of all the broken fragments of the former Iranic and Arabic societies into the wholly different structure of a Western World which has grown 'into an oecumenical 'Great Society'.

Note by Professor H. A. R. Gibb

The following valuable note on the first draft of this Annex (which has been amended accordingly) has been communicated to the writer by Professor H. A. R. Gibb:

'The chief point which I should question is the historical survey of the Shī'ah background, and especially the tendency to identify it with Persia as "the principal expression of an Iranian social consciousness" in opposition to the Arabs. Though this view had the powerful backing of Professor E. G. Browne, I do not think it can be sustained. The real history of Shi'ism is still uncertain, but there are several facts which are now more or less generally accepted.

'I. The historic centre of Shi'ism is Lower 'Irāq, where Arab, Aramaic, and Persian elements were most closely mingled. Its existence in all other centres—Bahrayn, the Jabal Summāq and Jabal 'Āmil districts of Syria, Qumm, N.W. Persia, Yaman, &c.—was due to propagation, directly or indirectly, from 'Irāq. Specially noteworthy is the very small extent of the areas of Persia in which the Shī'ah were in a majority—only Daylam and the neighbourhood, and one or two isolated towns, notably Qumm and Mashhad—and Qumm was an Arab colony from Kūfah.

'2. Elsewhere in Persia, Shi'ism appears to have been associated with a special element in the population of the great cities, provisionally identified with the artisan classes, as an expression of "class-consciousness" against the aristocracy, whether Arab or Iranian, or in later times Turkish. Thus the Shī'ah were opposed to the Iranian dynasty of the Sāmānids (which certainly embodied a reviving Iranian social consciousness) quite as much as to the 'Abbasids or the Turkish princes. Even in Daylam it may be regarded as a movement directed against the feudal aristocracy, who were (with rare exceptions) supporters of the Sunnī "Established Church".

'3. Shi'ism was thus in close relations with the trade guilds, and it is noteworthy that the Fātimids are credited with having done a great deal to foster the development of trade guilds in their dominions.

'4. The political failure of the Shi'ite movements under Buwayhids, Fātimids, and Carmathians probably played its part in producing a fresh orientation of this social movement in the form of religious brotherhoods under Sūfī auspices. While the specifically doctrinal variations of Shi'ism were rejected in the new organizations (at least for the most part), its programme of social reform and its historical theory, which was concentrated upon 'Alī, passed over into them; and it is significant that the ceremonies of initiation &c., were taken over with some modifications from those of the trade guilds.

'5. Thus, during the 6th (12th) and 7th (13th) centuries, by an act of unconscious statesmanship and the exercise of a wide toleration, the Sunnī community succeeded in absorbing, or at least reaching a kind of "Ausgleich" with, the greater part of moderate Shi'ism, and the extreme forms were practically rooted out.

'6. In the 8th (14th) century, it is evident from Ibn Battūtah that Lower 'Irāq was still (with al-Hasā and Bahrayn) the chief centre of Shi'ism. It would seem that relations between Shi'ites and Sunnīs were temporarily exacerbated by competition for the favour of the Mongol Il-Khans, but Baghdad, Shīrāz, and Isfahān are specifically mentioned as centres of resistance to the efforts of the Shi'ites.

'7. Ismā'īl Shāh Safawī's action seems to me in consequence a particularly wanton abuse of military power, which succeeded only because the people of Persia rallied round the Safawids in defence of their land (but hardly, as yet, their "nation") against the Ottoman and Uzbeg menaces. The price which they paid was religious conformity; and, by the double effect of political and religious particularism, the idea of a Persian nationality was in due course created.

'8. The final proof that Shi'ism was not a natural outcome or expression of the national Iranian genius is given by the intellectual deterioration which followed. Isolation and economic decay played their part in this; but, as Mirza Muhammad has remarked in the letter that you quote, the intellectual and literary genius of the Persians lay in the field of Mysticism. Shi'ism in power was bitterly hostile to Mysticism—perhaps partly because of the incongruity with the authoritarian doctrine of the Shī'ah, more (I think) because the Sūfī movement had been captured by the Sunnīs. Shi'ism thus killed the Persian "humanities" and left no outlet for intellectual activity except in scholasticism—for which the Persian genius seems totally unfitted. I should go further and hazard that it survived as a religion only because of the emotional outlet offered by the Muharram ceremonies. Apart from this, the average intelligent Persian, as de Gobineau remarked, seems to have sunk into a kind of sceptical religious lethargy.'

NAMES AND NATIONS OF THE LATE MINOAN AND THE EARLY HELLENIC AGE

1. *Minôs, the Mnôiâ, and the Minyae*

THE legendary name of Minōs, the sovereign of the seas, may preserve the historical name of an imperial people. For, in the Hellenic tradition, we seem to catch echoes of Μίνως in the plural number instead of the singular in the names Μνωῖται and Μινύαι.

The Μνωῖται (collectively called Μνοία, Μνωία, or Μνῴα) were the native serfs of the 'Dorian' conquerors of Crete; and in this term we may trace the degradation, in the latter-day Hellenic World, of a people who, in the *Odyssey*, are still remembered as the Ἐτεόκρητες μεγαλήτορες (*Odyssey*, Book XIX, l. 176).

The Minyae were a people of the pre-Hellenic Heroic Age who were located by Hellenic legend at three different points on the mainland of European Greece: along the southern part of the west coast of the Peloponnese at Pylos;[1] in the interior of Central Greece, midway between the Corinthian Gulf and the Euripus, at Orchomenos;[2] and on the fringe of Northern Greece, at the head of the Gulf of Volo, at Iolcòs.[3]

The bare name of Minyae is not the only common property of these three legendary Minyan settlements. The common worship of a god of healing seems to be indicated by a comparison of the name of the Minyan hero Ἰάσων (i.e. 'the Healer') of Iolcos with the name Ἀσκάλαφος—an obvious variant of Ἀσκληπιός—which is given to one of the two kings of Minyan Orchomenos in the Homeric Catalogue of Ships (*Iliad*, Book II, l. 512). Another link

---

[1] In the Homeric epic, Pylos is not called 'Minyan' as Orchomenos is, nor are the Pylians called 'Minyae' as are the Argonauts who sail from Iolcos. On the other hand, we hear casually of a ποταμὸς Μινυήϊος in the Pylian territory (*Iliad*, Book XI, l. 722); and in the fifth century B.C. the Greek inhabitants of one fragment of the *ci-devant* Pylian domain—the territory on the west coast of the Peloponnese, between Messenia and Elis, which is called first Paroreatis and afterwards Triphylia—are said to be Μινύαι by Herodotus (in Book IV, chap. 148). True, Herodotus brings his Minyae to the Paroreatis at a fairly recent date, as the last stage in a long migration which ultimately fetches them from Iolcos via Lemnos and Mount Taÿgetus. But this Herodotean saga (Book IV, chaps. 145–8) is a patchwork which is easily picked to pieces. The only solid fact which remains is that the Paroreatae who were conquered by the Eleans in the fifth century B.C. laid claim to the Minyan name; and the simplest explanation of this claim is to suppose that they had inherited the name from their predecessors on the spot in the Heroic Age: that is to say, from the time when the Paroreatis was a part of the Pre-Hellenic principality of Pylos, at a date anterior to the pre-Hellenic and post-Minoan Völkerwanderung.

[2] The standing epithet of this Orchomenos is Μινύειος or Μινυήϊος (e.g. in *Iliad*, Book II, l. 511).

[3] The heroes who sail from Iolcos under Jason's command on board the legendary ship Argo in quest of the Golden Fleece are called Μινύαι collectively.

is the name Ἀμυθάων which appears as a personal name in the genealogy of the Minyan rulers of Iolcos and as a place-name— Ἀμυθαονία[1]—in the Peloponnesian domain of the Minyans round Pylos. And if we take the name Amythaon and the cult of a healing god as clues to the presence of Minyan settlers, we can perhaps espy, in two passages of the Iliad, the traces of a fourth Minyan settlement of which the Hellenic tradition has not preserved a record. For the Ἀμυδών on the banks of the Axius, from which the Paeones came according to *Iliad*, Book XVI, l. 288, is simply the name Ἀμυθάων applied in Paeonia, as in the Peloponnese, to a place instead of a person and transliterated into its philologically correct equivalent in the Macedonian Greek dialect (in which the ordinary Greek θ is represented by δ).[2] And in another passage a Paeonian hero, Asteropaeus, whose grandsire is the River Axius himself, is given Ἀκεσσαμενός ('the Healer') for his great-grand-sire on his grandmother's side (*Iliad*, Book XXI, ll. 140–3). It would, indeed, be natural enough that a people which had picked out the head of the Gulf of Volo as one site for a settlement should plant a sister-settlement at the head of the Gulf of Salonica.

Where was the centre of dispersion from which the Minyae radiated to these four widely scattered points in Continental European Greece? Three out of the four points lie on the coast; two of these—namely Iolcos and the hypothetical Minyan settlement at the mouth of the Axius—are ideal sites for commercial *entrepôts* between the Aegean Archipelago and its Continental European hinterland; and the fourth Minyan settlement, Orchomenos, which is the only one of the four that lies inland, is at the same time situated at the key-point of one of the portages between the Aegean Sea and the Corinthian Gulf. (The spur of Mount Acontius, on which the city of Orchomenos stands, commands the passage across the River Cephisus for anybody travelling overland from the Aegean port of Larymna, on the Euripus, to the Corinthian Gulf port of Cyrrha, at the head of the Bay of Crisa.) We may therefore conjecture that the Minyae were a maritime commercial people who came by sea to the four points on the Continent at which we find their settlements.

From what base of operations overseas did the Minyae come? If we take the resemblance between the names Μινύαι and Μίνως as an indication that they came from Crete, we shall find independent legendary evidence of a Cretan origin for all four of the Minyan settlements. In the case of Iolcos, we may notice that the legendary

---

[1] Stephanus Byzantius, s.v., cited by Nilsson, M. P.: *The Mycenaean Origin of Greek Mythology* (Cambridge 1932, University Press), p. 141.

[2] Strabo (*Geographica*, p. 330) identifies the Homeric Ἀμυδών with an historic fortress called Ἀβυδών which overlooked the lower valley of the Axius.

name of Amythaon's father is Κρηθεύς. In the case of Orchomenos, we may notice that the route from Orchomenos to the head of the Crisaean Gulf passes, via the famous σχιστὴ ὁδός, through Delphi; and that, in the Homeric *Hymn to Apollo*, the historic Delphians are represented as being the descendants of a ship's company of Κρῆτες ἀπὸ Κνωσοῦ Μινωΐου (line 393), whose ship the God himself wafts to Crisa in order that these Cretans may settle at Delphi to preside over the Apollinean worship there. A connexion between Crete and Pylos is suggested in the point, incidentally mentioned in the Hymn (lines 397–9 and 469–70), that this Cretan ship was originally bound on a commercial venture from Crete to Pylos, and was only diverted to Crisa from its intended destination by the supernatural intervention of the God. The Cretan origin of our hypothetical Minyan settlement at the head of the Gulf of Salonica is suggested by the Hellenic tradition which ascribes a Cretan origin to the Βοττιαῖοι; for these Bottiaeans were the people who were found in possession of the lowlands at the head of the Gulf by the Chalcidian Greek colonists who settled in the neighbourhood at the turn of the eighth and seventh centuries B.C. and by the Macedonian Greek conquerors who descended upon this same coast from the continental hinterland at about the same date.[1]

On this showing, the Minyae may be regarded as Minoan pioneers who settled at these four points on the mainland of European Greece at the time when the waters and coastlands of the Aegean were subject to 'the thalassocracy of Minos'. But here a difficulty suggests itself. The results of our modern Western archaeological research would appear to show that Pylos, Orchomenos, Iolcos, and Amydôn were all alike situated on the outermost fringe of the Minoan World. The map of the distribution of the Minoan culture on the mainland, as it is revealed by the archaeological evidence up to date, seems now unlikely to be modified appreciably by future discoveries. We have thus to ask ourselves why the Minoan thalassocrats should have chosen to plant their colonies so far afield, instead of planting them on those coasts of Continental Greece that lay nearest to Crete.

Perhaps we may obtain an answer to this question by asking ourselves the corresponding question about the colonies which were planted upon Continental Greek coasts, in the course of Hellenic history, by the Hellenic thalassocrats of Chalcis and Corinth. Why did the Chalcidians sail right out of the northern end of the Euripus, and then on past the dangerous coast of Magnesia, in order to plant their overseas Chalcidicê, at last, ἐπὶ Θράκης? And

[1] For references to the original Hellenic authorities by whom the Bottiaeans are declared to be of Cretan origin, see Hogarth, D. G.: *Philip and Alexander of Macedon* (London 1897, Murray), p. 6.

why did the Corinthians sail right out of their own gulf in order to plant their colonies on the coasts of Acarnania and Epirus? In these cases, the answer is fairly clear. A colonizing Power can only plant its colonies on the territories of peoples who are so inferior to the intruders in culture that they are incapable of self-defence. But the immediate neighbours of the Chalcidians and the Corinthians were fellow Hellenes; and for one Hellenic community to attempt the subjugation of another was a superhumanly formidable undertaking for psychological as well as for material reasons. The inadvisability of making the attempt is illustrated by the history of the Spartan conquest of Messene and its sequel.[1] The Chalcidians and Corinthians showed their greater prudence by letting their Hellenic neighbours alone. In their voyages in search of new lands for Chalcidian and Corinthian ploughs, they did not put to shore till they had reached and passed the bounds of the Hellenic World as these bounds stood at the time. It is only at the outermost edge of the Hellenic World of the eighth century B.C. that the Chalcidian and Corinthian colonial areas begin.

On this analogy we may conjecture that the Cretan colonies at Pylos and Orchomenos and Iolcos and Amydôn were planted at the outer edge of the Minoan World of the day at a time when the regions of Continental European Greece that were less distant from Crete had already been 'Minoanized'—partly, perhaps, by Minoan cultural influences which had radiated out of Minoan Crete without any physical transfusion of blood from the island to the mainland, and perhaps also partly by earlier colonization which had proceeded not from Crete itself but from some of the other islands in the Aegean Archipelago which were likewise cradles of the Minoan Civilization. For example, Perseus, who is the mythical founder of Mycenae, is brought by the legend to Argos from Seriphos;[2] and Cadmus, the eponym of the Καδμεῖοι who are

---

[1] See I. B (ii), p. 24, above, and III. A, vol. iii, pp. 50–79, below. Our own Western history affords another illustration in the shape of the policy and fortunes of the Teutonic Knights. So long as the Teutonic Knights confined their enterprise to the subjugation of the heathen Prussians and Lithuanians and Letts and Ests, right beyond the north-eastern pale of Western Christendom, the Order prospered. The trouble which was to end in disaster can be traced to the moment when the Teutonic Knights turned their arms against their own fellow Western Christians nearer home, in Pomerania. They ventured upon this fratricidal warfare because the Poles in the thirteenth century, like the English two centuries earlier, at the time of the Norman Conquest, were still only in the penumbra of the Western Civilization. Yet, even so, the Poles were too little inferior in culture to the aggressive Teutonic Knights to submit tamely to a fate which was resisted desperately even by the heathen Prussians. The Poles fought for their existence with all the determination of the Messenians in their struggle against Sparta, and ultimately with a success which the Messenians never achieved. For the ultimate discomfiture of the Teutonic Knights by the Poles in alliance with the Lithuanians, see II. D (v), vol. ii, pp. 172–4, below.

[2] See Nilsson, M. P.: The Mycenaean Origin of Greek Mythology (Cambridge 1932, University Press), pp. 40–1. The legend, of course, makes Perseus come from Argos originally, so that he withdraws from Argos in infancy in order to return to his birthplace in his manhood (for the Perseus legend as a mythical illustration of the pheno-

the mythical occupants of Boeotian Thebes in the pre-Hellenic
Heroic Age, is brought by the legend to Thebes from Thera.[1] We
may therefore perhaps picture our Minoan colonists from Crete as
planting their colony of 'Minyan' Orchomenos just beyond the
radius of the 'Cadmean' colony which had been planted at Boeotian
Thebes by earlier settlers from a sister island. Moreover, there are
a number of correspondences between place-names and cult-
names that survived into Hellenic times in the 'Cadmean' part of
Boeotia on the one hand and on the other hand in a district along
the west coast of the Gulf of Volo which in Hellenic times was
called the Phthiotic Achaea.[2] These correspondences suggest that
'Cadmean' colonists from the Cyclades may have founded the
Phthiotic Thebes on the west coast of the Gulf of Volo at the same
time as the Boeotian Thebes in Central Greece, and that the
'Minyan' colonists from Crete, who followed in the Cadmeans'
wake, may have planted their Iolcos just beyond the Phthiotic
Thebes in the one direction as they planted their Orchomenos just
beyond the Boeotian Thebes in the other.

There is yet a third Thebes to be taken into account: the Asiatic
Θήβη Ὑποπλακίη which lies at the southern foot of Mount Ida
at the head of the Gulf of Edremid.[3] And, here again, we find a
Minyan settlement in the offing, on the Island of Lemnos. Between
the Asiatic and the Phthiotic Thebes there is no known connexion
beyond the bare identity of name. There seems to be no attempt
to bring the two places into any historical relation with each other
in the Hellenic tradition. On the other hand, the Minyae of
Lemnos are represented in the *Iliad* as an offshoot of the Minyae
of Iolcos. The King of Lemnos at the time of the Siege of Troy is

menon of 'Withdrawal-and-Return', see III. C (ii) (b), vol. iii, pp. 259–61, below).
For our present purpose, we may regard Perseus as the mythical representative of some
social movement which brought the Minoan culture to the Argolid from Seriphos. In
the Hellenic Age, the island of Seriphos was so unimportant and obscure that nobody
would have thought of making the founder of Mycenae come from Seriphos unless his
Seriphian origin was already an established feature of the legend. It was doubtless just
because of this obscurity of Seriphos that Perseus was now said merely to have been
brought up there and to have been born in Argos itself. In the Hellenic Age, it would
have seemed incredible that culture should ever have originated in Seriphos and spread
thence to Argos at second hand. To us, with the knowledge of early Aegean culture
which we have obtained through our archaeological research, a Seriphian origin of
Mycenaean culture is not incredible at all, since it is quite in harmony with the archaeological evidence.

[1] Herodotus, Book IV, chap. 147.

[2] In both Cadmean Boeotia and Phthiotic Achaea there were places called Θῆβαι and
Κορώνεια. In Cadmean Boeotia there was a cult of an Athena who was called Ἰτωνία after
a place named Ἴτων in Phthiotic Achaea; and, conversely, in Phthiotic Achaea, at Halos,
there was a cult of a Zeus who was called Λαφύστιος after a mountain named Λαφύστιον
in Cadmean Boeotia. These correspondences seem too numerous to be accidental. If
they do point to a Cadmean settlement in Thessaly, perhaps we may find an echo of this
in Herodotus's statement that the ancestors of the Dorians were driven by Cadmeans
from the Thessalian district of Histiaeotis (Herodotus, Book I, chap. 56).

[3] See Leaf, W.: *Troy: A Study in Homeric Geography* (London 1912, Macmillan),
pp. 213–16.

described as being a son of Jason, the Minyan hero from Iolcos who was the legendary leader of the Argonauts (*Iliad*, Book VII, ll. 468–9, and Book XXI, l. 41). Perhaps, in spite of the legendary voyage of the Argonauts from Iolcos to Colchis and back, 'Jason' never really sailed further from Iolcos than Lemnos, after all! Perhaps the Minyan principality on Lemnos and the Asiatic city of Thebes are the respective relics of two rival attempts, by the Minyan and the Cadmean settlers in the Gulf of Volo, to force their way up through the Dardanelles into the Black Sea—attempts which both alike failed because Troy was then still standing to bar the passage through the Straits against all interlopers.

2. *Minyae, Pelasgi, and* Τυρσηνοί.

Lying, as it does, at the focus of maritime communications in the North Aegean, the Island of Lemnos in Late Minoan and Early Hellenic times was the scene of successive interminglings of peoples; and these interminglings gave rise to a confusion of tongues and of names.

In the sixth century B.C., both Lemnos and the two neighbouring islands of Imbros and Samothrace[1] were inhabited by Πελασγοί; but before 500 B.C. the Lemnian and Imbrian Πελασγοί were conquered by the Achaemenian Empire (Herodotus, Book V, chaps. 26–7) and they were then not only conquered for the second time, but were this time also evicted, by the Athenian Miltiades, who was at that time the despot, under Achaemenian suzerainty, of the Gallipoli Peninsula (Herodotus, Book VI, chaps. 136–40).

Who were these Lemnian Pelasgi? To judge by their name, they were an offshoot of the Pelasgi of Continental Greece whose name was preserved in Hellenic times in the name of the Thessalian district of Pelasgiotis. And the original Pelasgi of the historical Pelasgiotis were presumably the same people as the historical Πελαγόνες or Πηλαγόνες of Macedonia and the legendary Φλεγύαι of Central Greece. (At least, if Πελασγοί stands for Πελαγ-σκοί, then the same root, PELAG-, can be discerned in all three names.) The Pelasgi of Lemnos and Imbros are not the only transmarine offshoot of this widespread Continental Greek people that has left a record of itself. On the Asiatic mainland, for example, the town of Antandros which was situated in the plain of 'Hypoplacian' Thebes on the shores of the Gulf of Edremid is called Πελασγίς by Herodotus (Book VII, chap. 42); and these historical Pelasgi in the Troad may reasonably be regarded as descendants of the Pelasgi

---

[1] For the presence of Pelasgi on the Island of Samothrace before the arrival of the Thracian population which occupied the island in Herodotus's day, see Herodotus, Book II, chap. 51.

who are mentioned among the allies of the Trojans in the *Iliad*
(Book II, ll. 840–3); for, in this passage of the *Iliad*, these Pelasgi
are located in a place called Larisa; and the existence of a Larisa in
the Troad, in the neighbourhood of Cape Lectum (Baba Burnu),
is attested, at the turn of the fifth and fourth centuries B.C., by
Thucydides (Book VIII, chap. 101) and Xenophon (*Hellenica*, III.
i. 16). Another overseas settlement of the Pelasgi—and this in
Crete—is mentioned in a famous passage of the Odyssey (Book XIX,
l. 177). In addition to the bare community of national or racial
name, the Pelasgi of Thessaly and the Troad and Crete have other
properties—place-names and genealogical names—in common not
only with each other, but also with the Pelagones of Paeonia and
with the Phlegyae of Central Greece.[1]

[1] The following correspondences between place-names and genealogical names may
be cited in support of the view that a real community of origin underlies the affinity of
name between the Pelasgi, Pelagones, and Phlegyae in the several regions in which these
national or racial names are found:

1. *Ληθαῖος* is the name of the river on which the town of Tricca stands in the Thessalian district of Histiaeotis (Strabo, p. 647) and likewise of the river on which the town
of Gortyna stands in the plain now called the Mesarà in South-Central Crete (Strabo,
p. 478). In the *Iliad* (Book II, l. 843) the two leaders of the Trojans' Pelasgian allies
from Larisa are described as υἷε δύω Ληθοιο Πελασγοῦ. Compare the name of the city
called *Λητή*, just east of the Lower Axius, in the district called Crestonia.

2. *Γυρτών* is the name of a town in the Thessalian district of Pelasgiotis (Strabo,
pp. 329 and 441–3). *Γορτυνία* is the name of a town in the Paeonian district of Amphaxitis
(Thucydides, Book II, chap. 100). *Γόρτυν* or *Γόρτυνα* is the name of a town in the
Mesarà of Crete, on the banks of the river *Ληθαῖος*.

3. *Εὐρωπός* is the name of a river which flows from the Perrhaebian district of Thessaly
into the Peneus close to Gyrton (Strabo, p. 329), and *Εὐρωπός* is the name of a town
in the Paeonian district of Amphaxitis, just below Gortynia (Thucydides, Book II,
chap. 100). Compare the name of the mythical heroine called *Εὐρώπη* whose adventures
are located in Crete.

4. *Εἰδομένη* is the name of a town in the Paeonian district of Amphaxitis, just above
Gortynia (Thucydides, Book II, chap. 100). Compare the name of the mythical hero
called *Ἰδομενεύς* who is represented in the Homeric epic as being the leader of the
Cretan contingent in Agamemnon's army at the siege of Troy.

5. *Ἀλαλκομεναί* is the name of a village in Boeotia between Haliartus and Coronea
(Pausanias, *Graeciae Descriptio*, Book IX, chap. 33) in the neighbourhood of the
traditional home of the legendary Phlegyae (op. cit. ix. 36). It is also the name of a
village in the canton of Deuriopus in what is now the plain of Monastir, which is drained
by a tributary of the River Axius; and Deuriopus, like the Amphaxitis, was a district
of Paeonia, since the Deuriopes were a subdivision of the Pelagones who, in their turn,
were a subdivision of the Paeones. For this Pelagonian Alalcomenae, see Strabo, p. 327.
It may also be noted that the Homeric hero. Asteropaeus, the leader of the Paeones, is a
son of *Πηλεγών* as well as a grandson of the River Axius (*Iliad*, Book XXI, ll. 140–2).

These correspondences are surely too numerous to be accidental.

We may equate the historical *Δευρίοπες* of *Δευρίοπος* in Paeonia with the *Δωριεῖς* of
Δωρίς in Central Greece, who are the only historical Dorians in the Hellenic World
apart from the inhabitants of the group of islands and peninsulas called *Δωρίς* off the
south-western corner of the Anatolian Peninsula. The links are supplied by the legendary
names of the father, *Λῆθος*, and the grandfather, *Τεύταμος*, of the twin leaders of the
Trojans' Pelasgian allies (*Iliad*, Book II, l. 843); for, according to Herodotus (Book I,
chap. 56), the Dorians of Doris in Central Greece had migrated to this Doris, via the
Pindus highlands, from the Thessalian district of Histiaeotis; and *Λῆθος* is the eponym
of the River *Ληθαῖος* in Histiaeotis, while *Τεύταμος* may be identified with the *Τέκταμος*
'son of *Δῶρος*' who is named by Diodorus of Agyrium (*A Library of Universal History*,
Book IV, chap. 60, and Book V, chap. 80) as a war-lord who led a war-band of 'Aeolians

What is the historical relation between the Pelasgi and the Minyae? The Pelasgi who are located by the *Odyssey* in Crete, and whose Cretan settlement is to be identified, on the evidence of place-names,[1] with the subsequent Hellenic city-state of Gortyna, in the Mesarà, must evidently have been deposited here by the last and greatest wave of the post-Minoan Völkerwanderung, which deposited Achaeans and 'Dorians' in Crete likewise, on the evidence of the same Homeric passage, besides depositing Ionians and Aeolians on the coast of Anatolia and Philistines on the coast of Syria.[2] In fact, the Pelasgi of Crete must have been one of the hordes of barbarian conquerors who reduced the Imperial people of Minos—the Ἐτεόκρητες μεγαλήτορες—to the status of a servile Μνωία. Were the Pelasgi who inhabited Lemnos in the sixth century B.C. in the same relation to the Minyae who are represented as being the masters of Lemnos in the Homeric epic? This is what is conjectured by Herodotus, who holds that the grandchildren of the Argonauts had been driven out of Lemnos by the ancestors of those Pelasgi whom the Athenians found in possession of the island (Herodotus, Book IV, chap. 145). But is it not also possible that the Lemnian Pelasgi and the Lemnian Minyae were really one and the same people? For the Lemnian Minyae derive, according to the legend, from the Minyae of Iolcos; and Iolcos lay on the narrow seaboard of the Thessalian district of Pelasgiotis. Any Pelasgian

and Pelasgi', or a war-band of Dorians, on a Völkerwanderung from Continental European Greece to Crete.

The upshot seems to be that the historical Dorians of Central Greece were Pelasgi, as the historical Deuriopes of Paeonia are known to have been Pelagones; and this would mean that the genuine Central Greek Dorians were originally 'Aeolians' and not 'Dorians' in the conventional generic sense in which the name Dorian was applied to a number of Hellenic communities in the Peloponnese and the Archipelago who spoke varieties of the North-Western dialect of the Greek language and who traced their descent to the barbarians that had come down upon the Aegean from the Continental Greek hinterland in the last convulsion of the post-Minoan and pre-Hellenic Völkerwanderung. This later Hellenic usage of the name 'Dorian', which was primarily a linguistic classification, was doubtless derived from the Doris off the south-west corner of Anatolia, where a settlement of 'Doric'-speaking Greeks had established themselves in juxtaposition to the 'Ionic'-speaking Greeks of Ionia and the 'Aeolic'-speaking Greeks of Aeolis. It must have been some time after this linguistic usage of the name 'Dorian' had been extended from the Anatolian Doris to the Peloponnese that the Peloponnesian 'Dorians' provided themselves with a fictitious descent from the genuine Central Greek Dorians in order to reconcile their acquired 'Dorian' name with their traditional North-Western origin, and at the same time to secure representation in the Central Greek Amphictyony, of which the Central Greek Dorians were old-established members.

Finally, we may take note of a kinship between the genuine Dorians of Central Greece and the Macedonians. It is recorded by Herodotus (loc. cit.) that the Central-Greek Dorians were called Μακεδνοί (an obvious variant of Μακεδόνες) during their sojourn in the Pindus highlands; while Diodorus (op. cit., Book IV, chap. 37) reports a legend that, during their previous sojourn in Histiaeotis, these Central-Greek Dorians came into collision with the Λαπίθαι of Pelasgiotis whose leader was Κόρωνος, son of Καινεύς (compare the *Iliad*, Book II, l. 746); and these Lapith heroes Κόρωνος and Καινεύς reappear in Macedonian legend as Κάρανος and Κοῖνος. (See Hoffmann, O.: *Die Makedonen* (Gottingen 1906, Vandenhoeck and Ruprecht), pp. 122-7.)

[1] See the preceding footnote.

[2] For this great upheaval *circa* 1200/1190 B.C., see I. C (i) (b), pp. 93 and 100-2, above.

adventurers from Pelasgiotis who were in search of new homes overseas would have to set sail from Iolcos or thereabouts. Is it not conceivable that the Minyan settlers at Iolcos coalesced with the Pelasgian natives of their Thessalian hinterland, and that the colonization of Lemnos was the joint work of a composite people which had an equal right to call itself by the Minyan and by the Pelasgian name?

Be that as it may, we have one more puzzle still to solve. Were the Pelasgi (and their congeners the Pelagones and the Phlegyae) a Greek-speaking or a non-Greek-speaking people? *A priori*, it would be somewhat strange if a non-Greek language had been the mother-tongue of this group of peoples; for the vast stretch of country (from Boeotia to Paeonia) which had once been occupied by peoples of this name was inhabited by Greek-speaking populations afterwards in Hellenic times. Nor can the *floruit* of these peoples in this region have been very remote; for, in Hellenic times, the name of the Pelasgi was still preserved in that of the Thessalian district of Pelasgiotis, while the Pelagones still survived as an independent people, so that it was only the Phlegyae that had passed altogether into the realm of legend. The Phlegyae or Pelasgi or Pelagones must have been the occupants of Central and North-Eastern Continental Greece immediately before the beginning of Hellenic history—that is to say, in the latter part of the second millennium B.C.; and it is hardly possible to imagine that the mass of the population of these regions was not already Greek-speaking by that date. As a matter of fact, the Pelasgian place-names and genealogical names which we have examined above[1] are all transparently Greek, with the possible exception of Gyrton or Gortyn. On this showing, it would be natural to suppose that the Pelasgi were a Greek-speaking people, and perhaps to equate them with the ancestors of those North-Eastern and Central Greek communities which were speakers, in Hellenic times, of the particular dialect of Greek which had come to be called 'Aeolic'.

At this point, however, we are pulled up short by the evidence of Herodotus and Thucydides, who both attest that, in their day, in the fifth century B.C., the scattered remnants of the Lemnian Pelasgi who survived as refugee communities in the regions round about were all speakers of a single specific language which was definitely non-Greek. Herodotus knew of Pelasgi who were to be found in his day at Placia and Scylacê on the south coast of the Marmara and of others who were to be found in a place called Κρηστών which was presumably the capital of the district called Crestonia, just to the east of the Lower Axius. And he testifies

---

[1] See the footnote on pp. 407–8, above.

that these two peoples still spoke, in his day, one identical non-Greek language which had no affinity with any of the languages of their respective neighbours in their new homes on the Asiatic and on the European Continent (Herodotus, Book I, chap. 57). Herodotus also states in the same passage, by implication, that the extant Pelasgi in the Marmara were of Lemnian Pelasgian origin.[1] The Crestonian Pelasgi he traces direct to Thessaly; but it seems much more probable that these also were the descendants of Lemnian refugees, since Thucydides (Book IV, chap. 109) positively attests that, in his day, Pelasgians of Lemnian origin constituted the majority of the mixed population of the Athos Peninsula. The most natural supposition is that Herodotus's Crestonian Pelasgi were a batch of these Lemnian Pelasgian refugees on the Athos Peninsula who had been given a new home in Crestonia by the Macedonian King Alexander I, when he annexed this district to his dominions after the ebb of the Achaemenian tide from Europe in 479–478 B.C.,[2] while Herodotus's Pelasgi on the Asiatic coast of the Marmara had presumably been planted there by the Achaemenian Government itself, to whom these victims of Miltiades and the Athenians would be *personae gratae*. Thucydides states that his Pelasgi on the Athos Peninsula were one of four non-Greek peoples who occupied the Peninsula between them and who were all bilingual. The inference is that Greek was their *lingua franca* and that their second language, whatever it might be in each case, was their mother-tongue. When this statement is taken together with Herodotus's statement that one and the same non-Greek language was spoken by the Pelasgi of Creston and of the Marmara, we can hardly avoid the conclusion that the Pelasgi who were evicted from Lemnos by Miltiades in the sixth century B.C. were a non-Greek-speaking people.

How are we to reconcile this conclusion with our previous conclusion that Greek was the mother-tongue of the original Pelasgians of Continental Greece from whom the Pelasgians of Lemnos were presumably descended? Herodotus—proceeding, scientifically enough, from the known to the unknown—takes the ascertainable and ascertained fact that the extant Pelasgi of his own day spoke a

---

[1] He says that they had once lived with the Athenians; and it was an Attic legend that the Lemnian Pelasgi had once sojourned for a time in Attica.

[2] For Alexander I's annexation of the country between the Lower Axius and the Lower Strymon to the Macedonian Kingdom, see Geyer, F.: *Makedonien bis zur Thronbesteigung Philips II* (Munich and Berlin 1930, Oldenbourg), pp. 46–7. It was the standing policy of the Kings of Macedon to extend their dominions eastwards by annexing successive strips of the barbarian hinterland; and if we may judge by the acts of King Alexander I's father, King Amyntas I, it was also their policy to secure and to civilize their new acquisitions in this quarter by planting them with cultivated refugees from the Aegean. On this principle, Amyntas I planted the evicted despot of Athens, Peisistratus, at Ῥαίκηλος (Aristotle: *The Constitution of Athens*, ch. 15) and afterwards offered Anthemus to Peisistratus's evicted son Hippias (Herodotus, Book V, ch. 94).

non-Greek language as evidence that the original Pelasgi were non-Greek-speaking likewise; and he seizes upon this hypothetical non-Greek and pre-Greek Pelasgian stratum of population in Greece to fill the perplexing void in the background of Hellenic history with which the Hellenic historian was confronted owing to his ignorance of the previous existence of the Minoan Society in the Aegean World. For us, with our archaeological knowledge of this ante-cedent Minoan Society, this historical void no longer exists; and at the same time our linguistic knowledge of the comparative philo-logy of the Indo-European languages informs us, by inference, that the Greek branch of the Indo-European *Ursprache* must already have been current in Greece before the middle of the second millennium B.C., when an Indo-European Centum-language is known, by direct evidence, to have been current in East Central Anatolia[1] and an Indo-European Satem-language in Palestine.[2] For us, therefore, the supposition that the original Pelasgi of North-Eastern Continental Greece were a non-Greek-speaking people is neither attractive nor plausible. Yet we shall be forced into accept-ing the Herodotean solution of the contradiction with which we are confronted unless we can find an alternative solution of the prob-lem on other lines. If the Pelasgi were originally a Greek-speaking people, can we explain how it could be that, by the sixth century B.C., the Pelasgian colonists of Lemnos should have lost their Greek mother-tongue? A possible explanation is offered by a further piece of information which Herodotus and Thucydides afford us between them.

Herodotus states (Book I, chap. 57) that the Pelasgi of Creston lived 'above' (i.e. inland of) the Τυρσηνοί; and Thucydides states (Book II, chap. 109) that the Pelasgi of the Athos Peninsula actually were Τυρσηνοί—a remnant of 'the Τυρσηνοί who had once inhabited Lemnos'. From these statements it is evident that the people who were evicted from Lemnos by Miltiades in the sixth century B.C. were called Τυρσηνοί as well as Pelasgi; and the double name may mean either one of two things. It may mean that the Pelasgian settlers on Lemnos happened to belong to a particular fraction, called Τυρσηνοί, of the Continental Pelasgian people; or else it may mean that the Pelasgian settlers on Lemnos had been overlaid subsequently by a fresh layer of settlers from elsewhere to whom the name Τυρσηνοί belonged. As between these two alterna-tive explanations of the application of both names to the same population on the Island of Lemnos, our judgement will be inclined in favour of the second explanation when we recall the other

[1] See I. C (i) (b), p. 113, footnote 3, above.
[2] See I. C (i) (b), pp. 104-5, above.

contexts, apart from Lemnos, in which the two names respectively occur. For while the name Pelasgi is connected, as we have seen, with North-Eastern Continental Greece, the connexions of the name Τυρσηνοί are not with Greece at all but with South-Eastern Anatolia;[1] and the monuments of the Etruscan language which have survived from the settlements of these Τυρσηνοί or Etruscans in Italy show that the language which they carried with them from Anatolia overseas was not only non-Greek but non-Indo-European. Two inscriptions in an unknown non-Greek language were actually discovered in A.D. 1885 on Lemnos, in the village of Kaminia; and these have been interpreted as Etruscan by a number of scholars; but our knowledge of Etruscan itself is still too slight to warrant our regarding this identification as assured.

Nevertheless, the clue provided by this non-Greek inscription and by the non-Lemnian context of the Tyrrhenian or Etruscan name does perhaps warrant us in reconstructing the history of Lemnos, tentatively and provisionally, as follows. In the latest age of Minoan history, the island was occupied by Minyae from Iolcos, in the Thessalian district of Pelasgiotis, who were either identical with the Pelasgi whom we subsequently find on Lemnos or else were evicted by these Pelasgi in the course of the post-Minoan and pre-Hellenic Völkerwanderung. Thereafter, these Pelasgian settlers on Lemnos were themselves not evicted but overlaid by a layer of Tyrrhenian or Etruscan settlers from South-Eastern Anatolia,[2] whose non-Greek language had ousted the Greek language of their Pelasgian predecessors by the time when the mixed Pelasgian-Tyrrhenian population of Lemnos was evicted from the island by Miltiades (before the year 493 B.C.). It was this Tyrrhenian or Etruscan language that was still spoken in the time of Herodotus and Thucydides by the descendants of the Lemnian refugees on the Athos Peninsula and at Creston and in Placia and Scylacê.[3] The people of these refugee communities were known as

[1] For the possible Hittite affinities of the Tyrrhenians or Etruscans, see I. C (i) (b), p. 114, footnote 2, above.

[2] For the probable date and purpose of the Etruscan settlement on Lemnos, see loc. cit., above.

[3] The testimony of Herodotus and Thucydides to the non-Greek character of the language that was spoken in their day by the various extant descendants of the Lemnian refugees is not our oldest testimony to the fact that Lemnos, before its colonization by the Athenians, was inhabited by a people who spoke a non-Greek language. There are two passages in the Homeric epic (*Iliad*, Book I, l. 594, and *Odyssey*, Book VIII, l. 294) in which Lemnos is described as being inhabited by a people called the Σίντιες; and in the second passage these Σίντιες are described as ἀγριόφωνοι, which implies that their language was not only non-Greek but that it sounded unmusical in Greek ears. In both passages, the Sinties are mentioned in connexion with the worship of Hephaestus. In the first passage they are said to have picked Hephaestus up when he fell on Lemnos after having been hurled out of Olympus by Zeus. In the second passage it is suggested that Hephaestus has gone on a visit to the Sinties on Lemnos from his Olympian home. It is hardly possible not to connect these legendary Σίντιες on Lemnos with the historical Σιντοί whose presence in the Strymon Valley is attested from the time of Thucydides

Pelasgi and *Τυρσηνοί* indifferently; and it was this local equivalence of the two names which gave rise to the mistaken belief that the Pelasgi and the *Τυρσηνοί* were one and the same people and that therefore the Pelasgi were not Greeks.

This disquisition on names will have served its purpose if it has helped to disperse some of the fog that still obscures our field of historical vision between the last glimmers of Minoan history and the first gleams of Hellenic.

(Book II, chap. 98) onwards. And since these Sinti are reputed to be Thracians in virtue of their habitat in Thrace, it is usual to write the Sinties down as Thracians too and to assume that they crossed over to Lemnos from the European mainland, in order to add to the confusion of peoples and tongues on the island, at some date unknown. It is conceivable, of course, that the Pelasgi of Lemnos, like those of Samothrace, were overlaid by a stratum of Thracian population from the European mainland before they were overlaid by the *Τυρσηνοί* from Anatolia. But no Thracian conquest of Lemnos is recorded by Herodotus, who is our authority for the Thracian conquest of the Pelasgi of Samothrace (Book II, chap. 51). The Lemnian picture would be simplified if it were permissible to identify the non-Greek-speaking Sinties on Lemnos with the non-Greek-speaking *Τυρσηνοί*, and to suppose that the Sinti in the Strymon Valley were an extreme outpost of Lemnian refugees which was planted here by King Alexander I of Macedon when he annexed the region between the Lower Axius and the Lower Strymon after 479–478 B.C. The domain of the Sinti in the Strymon Valley, as defined by the site of the town of Heraclea Sintice, lies next door to Crestonia, where the presence of a Pelasgian settlement, 'above the *Τυρσηνοί*', is attested in the fifth century B.C. by Herodotus (Book I, chap. 57).

THE RELATIONS OF 'THE INDUS CULTURE' WITH THE SUMERIC SOCIETY AND WITH THE INDIC SOCIETY

In the main body of this Study, on p. 108, the writer has raised, without attempting to answer, the question whether 'the Indus Culture' which has been brought to light by the Director-General of Archaeology in India, Sir John Marshall, at Mohenjo-Daro and Harappā is a 'colonial' offshoot or variation of the Sumeric culture of the Tigris-Euphrates Delta, or whether it is an independent culture of the same species as the Sumeric but without any closer connexion with the Sumeric than is displayed by any other representative of this class of societies. It may be convenient for the reader to have set before him, in the original, the views of Sir John Marshall himself, who is the first authority on the subject.

Sir John Marshall takes the view that 'the Indus Culture' is no more closely related to the Sumeric culture than it is to the cultures of the Egyptiac or the Minoan World. At the same time, he also takes the view that these four cultures have a special relation with one another which they do not share with the other representatives of the class: that they constitute, in fact, a sub-species within their species. Behind all four of them, he discerns a common parent—or, around all four, a common social environment—in the culture of the 'Chalcolithic' phase of material technique which was already diffused, at the simultaneous dawn of these four civilizations, over the whole region, extending from the south-eastern face of the Atlas to the south-western face of the Himalayas, which has since dried up (except for the valleys of four great rivers) into the Afrasian Steppe. In fact, Sir John Marshall almost goes so far as to regard this common Afrasian Chalcolithic culture as a unity of which 'the Indus Culture' and the Sumeric and the Egyptiac and the Minoan are mere articulations.

Sir John Marshall's exposition of these views needs to be quoted here, because the view which is expounded in this Study of History is not altogether the same. In the Second Part of this Study, which deals with the geneses of civilizations, the reader will find[1] that the cultures which have arisen in the several great river-valleys that cut across the face of Afrasia are grouped together, inasmuch as they have all alike arisen in response to one identical challenge: the challenge presented by the desiccation of the former Afrasian grasslands into the present Afrasian Steppe. When confronted by this

[1] See II. C (ii) (*b*) 2, pp. 302–18, above.

challenge, certain communities among the 'Chalcolithic' population of Afrasia plunged into the jungle-swamp of the lower valleys of the Nile and the Tigris and Euphrates—and possibly already, at this same epoch, into the jungle-swamp that likewise filled the lower valleys of the Indus and of its vanished sister-stream—and conjured out of these wildernesses the Egyptiac and the Sumeric worlds, and possibly the world of 'the Indus Culture' as well (if this was really an independent growth, and not a product of Sumeric 'colonial' expansion in a later age). In this Study, however, the common origin of the Egyptiac and the Sumeric cultures (and possibly also 'the Indus Valley Culture') in response to a common challenge is not regarded as making of these three cultures a kind of trinity in unity in contradistinction to all the other cultures of the same class. This sub-classification seems inapt, for one reason, because, in the writer's view, any special resemblances between the particular cultures are more convincingly explained as independent identic responses to a uniform challenge than as a common heritage from an age before this uniform challenge was presented. Another reason for refusing to make a special sub-class of these particular cultures is that the same challenge of the desiccation of Afrasia evoked not only the river-valley cultures, in which there is an obvious uniformity of physical environment, but also the maritime culture of the Minoan World,[1] as well as the Nomadic Culture which is common to the desiccated Steppes of Afrasia and Eurasia.[2] This Nomadic Culture is so distinctive that, if sub-classifications were to be made within the class, there would be more to be said for placing the Nomadic Culture in a sub-class by itself and including in a second sub-class all the sedentary civilizations of the Old World and the New, than for making a special sub-class out of the Afrasian river-valley cultures. On this showing, it has seemed better to eschew any attempt at sub-classifications and to leave each and all of these societies on an equal footing with one another as so many separate representatives of the species of societies called 'civilizations'. We have then to ask ourselves the question whether 'the Indus Valley Culture' is a civilization in its own right or whether it is a 'colonial' offshoot of the Sumeric Society.

Since this way of formulating the question is not quite the same as Sir John Marshall's, it may be convenient for the reader to acquaint himself with Sir John Marshall's view as it is set forth in the following passage:

'That this Indus Civilisation was part and parcel of that greater civilisation which during the Chalcolithic Age extended across the broad

[1] For the genesis of the Minoan Culture in the Aegean Archipelago, see II. C (ii) (b), 2, pp. 323–30, above.

[2] For the Nomadic Culture, see further Part III. A, vol. iii, pp. 7–22, below.

Afrasian belt, and that it was intimately related to other branches of that civilisation in Western Persia and Mesopotamia, became clear almost from the first moment of its discovery. And this, indeed, was only to be expected. . . . With the contributions to the common stock of this civilisation made by the other great rivers of Afrasia—by the Nile in Egypt, by the Euphrates and Tigris in Mesopotamia, by the Kārūn and Karkheh in Western Persia—we have long since been tolerably familiar, and we knew a little, too, of the part played by the Helmand. It can hardly surprise us, therefore, to find the river valleys of Sind and the Panjab—the broadest and richest of all the valleys of Southern Asia— taking their share in the evolution of this civilisation; nor will it surprise us if, as the field of exploration widens, we find that the valleys of the Jumna and the Ganges in India, of the Oxus and other rivers of Trans- caspia, prove to have been vital centres of human activity and progress in the Chalcolithic Age. . . .

'In the nature of things a civilisation as widely diffused as the Chalco- lithic, with ramifications extending as far west as Thessaly and Southern Italy, and as far east, perhaps, as the Chinese provinces of Honan and Chih-li, could not have been homogeneous throughout. The peoples who participated in it were of different races, spoke different languages, wrote different characters, worshipped different deities, and in other ways displayed different orders of mentality. It is too much, therefore, to expect that there should have been a close correspondence in their material cultures. Nevertheless, we must be careful not to exaggerate the differences between them or to regard them as entirely self-centred and self-sufficient communities. Each, no doubt, had its own particular type of civilisation, which was adapted to suit local conditions. But between them all was a fundamental unity of ideas which could hardly have been the result of mere commercial intercourse.

'Let me illustrate what I mean by taking one or two concrete examples. The signs which each country devised to record its speech differed materially from those of its neighbours—the hieroglyphs of Egypt from those of Crete, the Cretan from the Sumerian, the Sumerian from the Elamite, and so on. But, however much these scripts differed from one another, however much they demonstrated the independence of their authors, they were all based on one and the same idea—the idea of using pictured signs to represent not only objects or concepts but actual sounds. When, therefore, we attempt to estimate the degree of unity or diversity in the Chalcolithic Civilisation, we must admit that this wonderful invention, which is fundamental to each and every mode of writing, counts for far more than the diversity which distinguishes the various systems of pictured signs. Another typical illustration may be taken from spinning and weaving. On the Indus, cotton was used for the thinner textiles; on the Nile, flax. Each in its own way was an important discovery and a valuable contribution to the common stock of human knowledge. But more valuable than either was the discovery of how to spin, and how to weave, and this discovery was the universal possession of the then Civilised World—one of the many factors that justify us in regarding this culture as a more or less coherent whole. It is the same with the painted pottery. Each of the river valleys in which this civilisation was centred had its own ceramic wares, with shapes and designs adapted to local needs or ideas; but all alike shared the secret of the potter's wheel and of how to fix the colouring on the vessels by firing —secrets which are not likely to have been discovered independently.

'These examples—and many more might be cited—will suffice to make clear what I mean by the fundamental unity of this civilisation. The point is one that needs to be stressed, because it has been the fashion to emphasise the diversity of this civilisation, while ignoring its essential homogeneity; and, in the case of the particular branch with which we are now concerned, we should certainly misunderstand its evolution if we conceived of it as a wholly isolated and independent growth. It is just as individual, just as national, in character as other branches are— the Sumerian, for example, or the Egyptian; and it is no less typical of the region where it took shape than the former is of Southern Mesopotamia, or the latter of the Valley of the Nile. Thus, to mention but a few of its leading features, there are, first and foremost, the domestic houses, the unique character of which has already been emphasised; and with the private houses must be coupled also the great public baths, for which there is no parallel elsewhere until we come down to Roman times. A feature of another kind, but no less distinctive, is the remarkably naturalistic quality of the Indus art, which is wholly unlike the contemporary art of Elam, Sumer or Egypt; another is the decoration of its painted pottery, easily distinguishable from any other red-and-black wares known to us, still more easily from the paler wares of Persia and Mesopotamia; another, the use of cotton instead of flax for light textiles; another, the highly evolved type of the characters devised for writing. But behind these and manifold other traits that are peculiar to the Indus Civilisation and give it its national character, is a tissue of ideas, inventions, and discoveries which were the common property of the then Civilised World and cannot be traced to their respective sources. Some may have originated among the Indus people, but many must have been derived from elsewhere, borrowed, may be, from other regions, or in some cases inherited from earlier ages, when the races of Afrasia were perhaps less heterogeneous. Such are the domestication of animals; the cultivation of wheat, barley and other grains; the growing of fruits; the irrigation of land with the aid of artificial canals and embankments; the building of houses; the organisation of society in cities; spinning and the weaving of textiles and the dyeing of them in various colours; the use of the potter's wheel and the decoration of earthenware with encaustic designs; navigation by river and the use of wheeled vehicles on land; the working of gold and silver, of copper, and of tin; the recording of speech by means of picture signs; and the fashioning of ornaments from faience, ivory, bone, shell and semi-precious stones. Seeing that these and many other elements were basic to civilisation throughout the entire Afrasian belt and just as distinctive of it in other regions as they are in the Indus Valley, we should clearly be in danger of straying from the truth if we failed to recognise that the Indus Civilisation is an integral part of the whole. On the other hand, we should be equally far from the truth if we ignored those other and hardly less important features which are the special attributes of the Indus Civilisation and which give it its local and national complexion.'[1]

The general view of the relation between 'the Indus Culture' and the Sumeric culture which is put forward by Sir John Marshall in the foregoing passage is based, as will be seen, upon evidence taken from a number of different spheres of social life: for example, from the material arts and from the art of writing and from religion. The religion of 'the Indus Culture' with its dominant mother goddess, with its male god who performs the same function as the Minoan 'Master and Mistress of the Animals' besides being the prototype of Siva, with its tree-worship and personification of tree-spirits, and with its cult of phallic and baetylic stones, seems to have more points of contact with the Minoan Religion[2] and with latter-day Hinduism than with the Sumeric religion.[3] As for the Indus script, Sir John Marshall's collaborators, Messrs. C. J. Gadd and Sidney Smith, find no evidence of its having any direct connexion with the Sumeric script;[4] while another collaborator, Professor Langdon, pronounces that 'the Indus inscriptions resemble the Egyptian hieroglyphs far more than they do the Sumerian linear and cuneiform system'.[5] After a study, however, of some tablets inscribed with a prehistoric form of the Sumeric script which have been found at Jamdat Nasr in 'Irāq, Professor Langdon adds in a post-script[6] that he wishes 'to emphasise more definite connexion between the most archaic Sumerian script and the Indus Valley script than' he had been 'disposed to admit in' his 'preceding study'.

The question of the relation between 'the Indus Culture' and the Sumeric culture is also affected by the chronology of 'the Indus Culture', in so far as this can yet be ascertained.

The culture revealed in all the strata of human deposits that have been excavated at Mohenjo-Daro is uniform from bottom to top (except that the higher, i.e. the later, strata are the meaner).[7] Sir John Marshall estimates[8] that these strata correspond, from first to

---

[1] Marshall, Sir John: *Mohenjo-Daro and the Indus Civilisation* (London 1931, Probsthain, 3 vols.), vol. i, pp. 93–5.

[2] For the Minoan religion, see I. C (i) (b), pp. 95–100, above.

[3] See Marshall, op. cit., vol. i, chap. v. The points of special resemblance between the Sumeric religion and the religion of 'the Indus Culture' are the conception of the Tree of Life, the fantasy of mixed and semi-human monsters, and the portrayal of monsters and animals in the role of officient genii.

[4] Marshall, op. cit., vol. ii, chap. xxii, p. 411.

[5] Marshall, op. cit., vol. ii, ch. xxiii, p. 424. Cf. p. 427.

[6] In op. cit., loc. cit., p. 454.

[7] Marshall, op. cit., vol. i, p. 103. [8] In op. cit., loc. cit.

last, to a span of about 500 years; but he adds that this particular span, which happens to have left its material record in the debris of this one particular site, represents no more than a snippet out of the total life-span of 'the Indus Culture'. The state of the culture as it is revealed at Mohenjo-Daro presupposes many millennia of antecedent human endeavour;[1] and Sir John Marshall, believing 'the Indus Culture' to have arisen out of the Afrasian 'Chalcolithic Culture' independently, concludes that it is coeval with the early culture of Sumer and with the pre-diluvian culture of Egypt and Mesopotamia, and finds indications of a lively intercourse between the Indus Valley and both Sumer and Elam by the close of the fourth millennium B.C.

It remains to identify, if possible, the particular five centuries during which the city at Mohenjo-Daro was 'a going concern'; and some evidence has come to light in the shape of seals, recognizable by their style as products of 'the Indus Culture', which have been unearthed in deposits, left by the Sumeric culture in 'Irāq, of which we can approximately calculate the date. Five such seals are taken by Sir John Marshall[2] and by Professor Langdon[3] to prove, by the Sumeric context in which they have been found, that 'the Indus Culture', in the stage revealed at Mohenjo-Daro, was older than the Dynasty of Akkad (*in Sumeria imperabant circa* 2652–2456 B.C.); and Sir John Marshall infers[4] that Mohenjo-Daro itself flourished between 3250 and 2750 B.C. On the strength of another 'Indus Culture' seal found in 'Irāq, another scholar, Mr. H. Frankfort, the Field Director in 'Irāq of the Oriental Institute of the University of Chicago, concludes that 'the Indus Culture' of Mohenjo-Daro was contemporary with the Dynasty of Akkad rather than anterior to it.[5]

Even on this lower dating, it will be noticed that there is a chronological gap of at least 500 years between the terminal date of the history of 'the Indus Culture'—at least, at Mohenjo-Daro—and the arrival in the Indus Valley of the Aryan Nomads whose eruption out of the Eurasian Steppe into India and into South-Western Asia is to be dated, as we have seen,[6] between 1900 B.C. and 1700 B.C. This chronological discontinuity between 'the Indus Culture' and the advent of the Aryas, which is suggested by the chronological evidence, such as it is, is supported by the circumstantial evidence of Archaeology and of Literature.

---

[1] Marshall, op. cit., vol. i, p. viii.   [2] Marshall, op. cit., vol. i, p. 103.
[3] In Marshall, op. cit., vol. ii, p. 426.   [4] In op. cit., vol. i, p. 104.
[5] See a letter from Mr. Frankfort dated Baghdad, 5th March 1932, and published in *The Times* newspaper of London on the 26th March 1932. For the whole question of the chronological testimony of these seals, see Gadd, C. J.: 'Seals of Ancient Indian Style found at Ur'= offprint of *Proceedings of the British Academy*, vol. xviii (London 1932, Milford).   [6] On pp. 104–7, above.

'A comparison of the Indus and Vedic cultures shows incontestably that they are unrelated. Thus, the picture of Indo-Aryan Society portrayed in the Vedas is that of a partly pastoral, partly agricultural people who have not yet emerged from the village state, who have no knowledge of life in cities or of the complex economic organization which such life implies, and whose houses are nondescript affairs constructed largely of bamboo. At Mohenjo-Daro and Harappā, on the other hand, we have densely populated cities with solid, commodious houses of brick equipped with adequate sanitation, bathrooms, wells, and other amenities. The metals which the Indo-Aryans used in the time of the Rigveda are gold and copper or bronze; but a little later, in the time of the Yajurveda and Atharvaveda, these metals are supplemented by silver and iron. Among the Indus people silver is commoner than gold, and utensils and vessels are sometimes made of stone—a relic of the Neolithic Age—as well as of copper and bronze. Of iron there is no vestige. For offensive weapons the Vedic-Aryans have the bow and arrow, spear, dagger, and axe, and for defensive armour the helmet and coat of mail. The Indus people also have the bow and arrow, spear, dagger, and axe, but, like the Mesopotamians and Egyptians, they have the mace as well, sometimes of stone, sometimes of metal; while, on the other hand, defensive armour is quite unknown to them—a fact which must have told against them in any contests with mailed and helmeted foes. The Vedic-Aryans are a nation of meat-eaters, who appear to have had a general aversion to fish, since there is no direct mention of fishing in the Vedas. With the Indus people fish is a common article of diet, and so too are molluscs, turtles, and other aquatic creatures. In the lives of the Vedic-Aryans the horse plays an important part, as it did in the lives of many nations from the northern grasslands. To the people of Mohenjo-Daro and Harappā the horse seems to have been unknown; it has no place, at any rate, among the many animals figured at these places; and though some bones of a horse (*equus caballus*) were found on the surface at the former site, it is more than probable that they belong to a later, may be quite modern, period. By the Vedic-Aryans the cow is prized above all other animals and regarded with special veneration. Among the Indus people the cow is of no particular account, its place with them being taken by the bull, the popularity of whose cult is attested by the numerous figurines and other representations of this animal. Of the tiger there is no mention in the Vedas, and of the elephant but little, but both these animals are familiar to the Indus people. The Vedic religion is normally aniconic. At Mohenjo-Daro and Harappā iconism is everywhere apparent. In the Vedic pantheon the female element is almost wholly subordinate to the male, and neither the Mother Goddess nor Siva (with whom, however, the Vedic Rudra was afterwards to be identified) has any place among its members. Among the Indus cults those of the Mother Goddess and Siva are prominent, and the female elements appear to be co-equal with, if not to predominate over, the male. Fire (Agni) ranks among the foremost deities of the Veda, and the domestic hearth or fire-pit (*agni-kunda*) is a characteristic feature of every house. In the houses of

Mohenjo-Daro the fire-pit is conspicuously lacking. To the Indo-Aryan, phallic worship was abhorrent. Among the Indus people there is abundant evidence of its existence.'[1]

In another passage,[2] Sir John Marshall draws a comparison between the effacement of the memory of 'the Indus Culture' from the tradition of the subsequent Indic Society and the effacement of the memory of the Minoan culture from the tradition of Hellas.

How is this chronological gap and this cultural discontinuity to be explained? Without venturing to pronounce on the question whether the Indus Culture' was an independent culture or a 'colonial' offshoot of the Sumeric culture, we may perhaps point out that this hiatus in the evidence, so long as it remains unbridged in any other way, will permit us still to play with our conjecture[3] that, between the decay of Mohenjo-Daro and the arrival of the Aryans, the Indus Valley may have been temporarily relegated to an obscure and subordinate role on the stage of History as an outlying province of the Empire of Sumer and Akkad (*florebat circa* 2275–1875 B.C.) which was the universal state of the Sumeric Society of the Tigris and Euphrates Delta. If this conjecture proves to hit the mark, then it will follow that, in so far as the Indic Society can be regarded as being related to any antecedent society at all, its relations are with the Sumeric Society of the Tigris and Euphrates Delta, and not with 'the Indus Culture' which had once flourished in the plains upon which the Aryas descended when they made their way across the Hindu Kush from the Eurasian Steppe at some time in the first half of the second millennium B.C.

[1] Marshall, op. cit., vol. i, pp. 110–11.
[2] In op. cit., vol. i, p. viii.   [3] For this conjecture, see pp. 106–9, above.

THE UNIFORMITY THEORY AND THE DIFFUSION THEORY

In the relevant chapter, we have contradicted two of the principal dogmas of 'the Diffusionist School' of contemporary British anthropologists in two statements: the first being, 'We have found no evidence that any living civilization, either Western or non-Western, is in any way related to the Egyptiac'; the second, 'It is certain that none of them are related to any of the four extinct civilizations of the New World.'[1] These two negative statements, which we have made *en passant*, may appear, as they stand, to be as curtly dogmatic as the usual formulations of the two contrary dogmas of the 'Diffusionist' creed. It therefore seems desirable to look more closely into the issue between the Diffusion Theory and the Uniformity Theory of the acquisition of techniques and aptitudes and institutions and ideas—partly in order to make sure that we do not do less than justice to 'the Diffusionist School', but still more because this is an issue which will continue to arise in the course of this Study.

The British Diffusionists are believers in 'the Unity of Civilization' in a special sense: not as a fact of yesterday or to-morrow, which has just been accomplished, or is just about to be accomplished, by the world-wide diffusion of our own Western Civilization on the economic plane,[2] but as a fact which was accomplished several thousand years ago by the diffusion of an older civilization, the Egyptiac. In their belief, the Egyptiac Civilization is something unique; for they believe that the Egyptiac World is the one and only place in which such a thing as a civilization has ever yet been created independently, without assistance from outside. All other manifestations of the species of society called civilizations are regarded by these British Diffusionists as derivative. They seek to reduce the semblance of plurality to an original underlying unity by deriving all these other civilizations from the Egyptiac Civilization; and they apply this method of reduction to the pre-Columbian civilizations of the New World as well as to the non-Egyptiac civilizations of the Old World. Not content with explaining the origin of all the civilizations of the Old World by postulating the diffusion of the Egyptiac culture from the meeting-place of the three

---

[1] I. C (iii) (*b*), p. 164, above.
[2] At the same time, this latter-day diffusion of our own Western Civilization has manifestly had a profound effect upon our British Diffusionists' thinking. (On this point, see further pp. 427–8, below.)

continents of the Old World into the furthest extremities of Africa, Europe, and Asia, our Diffusionists waft the Egyptiac culture eastward through the Indonesian and Melanesian and Polynesian archipelagos and then carry it, in a flying leap, across the great gulf beyond Hawaii and Easter Island in order to land at last, triumphantly, on the western coasts of North and South America for the purpose of sowing there the seeds that have come to flower in the cultures of the Mayan and the Andean World.[1]

This bare summary of the British Diffusionist Doctrine in its canonical form is perhaps sufficient to indicate why, and to what extent, it is unacceptable. No one, of course, who was not an equally dogmatic doctrinaire of 'the Uniformitarian School' would seek to deny the validity of the Diffusion Theory *in toto*. The most cursory empirical survey of recorded history, from the history of Singer's sewing-machines *retrorsum* to the history of the Alphabet, makes it manifest that Diffusion has been one of the means by which the techniques and aptitudes and institutions and ideas of human societies have actually been acquired; and at a later stage of this Study we shall be tracing out some of the processes of Diffusion for ourselves when we examine the contacts between civilizations and barbarians in Part VIII and the contacts which civilizations have had with one another—in Space in Part IX and in Time in Part X. Moreover, it is no doubt theoretically possible that the diffusion of the achievements of one single original civilization might account for the existence of all the representatives of the species that are known up to date. But this is clearly the limit of the Diffusion Theory's legitimate application. For, *ex hypothesi*, the theory cannot be called upon to account for the original creation of the subsequently diffused hypothetical primary civilization, be it the Egyptiac or any other. And then, when once it is conceded that one civilization has been acquired by one human society through an original act of creation (instead of through an imitative act of adoption) at least once upon a time, it becomes sheer arbitrary caprice to deny that the same thing may have happened a second time already in some instance recorded or unrecorded, or at least that it is capable of happening at some unpredictable date in the future.

The simple fact is that, in every manifestation of Life, we find empirically, by observation, that a creative power is exhibited, and that acts of creation are performed, by some, but not by all,

---

[1] Two standard expositions of the British Diffusionist Doctrine by the two foremost authorities in this school of anthropology will be found in Professor G. Elliot Smith's *The Ancient Egyptians and the Origins of Civilisation* (2nd edition: London 1923, Harper), and in W. H. Perry's *The Children of the Sun: A Study in the Early History of Civilisation* (London 1923, Methuen). See also Professor G. Elliot Smith's *Human History* (London 1930, Cape).

representatives of any given species. And this fact in itself implies that there are two alternative independent means by which any given quality may have been acquired by any manifestation of Life in any given instance. One of these alternative means is original creation, since without creation the diffusion of the products of creation is impossible *ex hypothesi*. At the same time, it is not admissible to ascribe every acquisition of every quality by every representative of every species to a separate and original creative act, since our empirical observation shows us that, in any species, the creative individuals are in a minority, and that, in the life of any creative individual, his creative acts are rare events. Thus, in any objective study of the process of acquisition (or, in vital terms, the process of genesis and growth), we have to allow for the operation, side by side, of two different principles: the principle of the Uniformity of Nature and the principle of Diffusion through Radiation-and-Mimesis. The Uniformity of Nature guarantees that the germ or spark of creative power which is manifested in one or more representatives of a species is capable of reappearing in any other representative of the same species, though experience enables us to predict with confidence that, as a matter of fact, the creative gift will prove to be confined in practice to a rather small minority. Conversely, the same experience informs us that Diffusion is the means by which acquisitions are actually made in many cases, and perhaps in the majority. The proper task of the student of Life is not to magnify the potency of either principle tendenciously at the other principle's expense but to render to both principles their real due. Our attitude should be not fanatical but scientific, and our method not dogmatic but empirical. The right attitude of mind has been described, towards the close of a classical work of scholarship, by the greatest of living comparative anthropologists:

'If there is one general conclusion which seems to emerge from the mass of particulars, I venture to think that it is the essential similarity in the working of the less developed human mind among all the races, which corresponds to the essential similarity in their bodily frame revealed by comparative anatomy. But while this general mental similarity may, I believe, be taken as established, we must always be on our guard against tracing to it a multitude of particular resemblances which may be and often are due to simple diffusion, since nothing is more certain than that the various races of men have borrowed from each other many of their arts and crafts, their ideas, customs and institutions. To sift out the elements of culture which a race has independently evolved and to distinguish them accurately from those which it has derived from other races is a task of extreme difficulty and delicacy, which promises to occupy students of Man for a long time to come; indeed, so complex are the facts and so imperfect in most cases is the historical record that it may be doubted whether in regard to many of the lower races we shall ever arrive at more than probable conjectures.'[1]

This balanced judgement from the pen of a great scholar might dispose of the current controversy between the Diffusionists and the Uniformitarians, were it not for a fault of temper and a weakness of thought in the Diffusionist camp. The fault of temper is the curious vein of intolerance by which the British Diffusionists appear to be animated, as though they were conducting some kind of religious propaganda rather than collaborating with scholars of other schools in an attempt to discover the truth about a problem of common interest. The weakness of thought is the proneness of our contemporary British Diffusionists to allow their thinking about the phenomenon of Diffusion in general, in all times and places, to be dominated by the ephemeral fact of the contemporary world-wide diffusion of our Western Civilization—an instance of Diffusion which happens to loom large just here and just now. In the manifest—though mainly unconscious—distortion of our British Diffusionists' vision through this cause, we have a conspicuous illustration of that 'relativity of historical thought' which has been the first subject to engage our attention in this Study.[2] On these accounts, it seems advisable to carry our criticism of the British Diffusionist Doctrine rather further.

There are, in fact, two fallacies in the assumption that the geneses of civilizations can be accounted for by the fact that certain techniques and aptitudes and institutions and ideas can be proved historically to have been acquired, by the majority of those who have eventually acquired them, through the process of Diffusion.

Diffusion does, of course, account for the present ubiquity of such modern Western manufactures as Singer's sewing-machines, Mauser rifles, and Manchester cotton goods. More than that, it accounts for the present ability, on the part of a certain number of non-Western communities, to manufacture rifles and cotton goods for themselves by a mastery of the Western processes. Diffusion accounts likewise for the ubiquity of the Syriac Alphabet, which has now killed out and superseded every other known script that has ever been invented by any other society except the Sinic.[3]

---

[1] Frazer, Sir J. G.: *The Golden Bough*, 3rd edition, Part VIII: 'Balder the Beautiful' (London 1913, Macmillan), Preface, pp. vi–vii.

[2] In Part I. A, above.

[3] The diffusive power of the Alphabet, in virtue of its unrivalled technical merits, is impressively demonstrated by the fact that the scripts of the Mongols and the Manchus are of Syriac origin, notwithstanding the facts that these two peoples live at the opposite end of Asia from Syria; that they have been living for ages on the threshold of the Far Eastern World; and that the Manchus, at any rate, have been imitators of the Far Eastern culture in almost everything else. (As for the Mongols, they have taken their religion, in the form of Lamaistic or Tantric Mahayanian Buddhism, from the Indic Civilization, besides taking their script from the Syriac.) We may add that, nowadays, the currency

Diffusion accounts, again, for the ubiquity of the Far Eastern beverage tea, of the Arabic beverage coffee, of the Central American beverage cocoa, of the Amazonian material rubber,[1] of the Central American practice of tobacco-smoking, of the Sumeric practice of duodecimal reckoning, and of the so-called 'Arabic numerals', which are perhaps originally a Hindu system of mathematical notation.[2] But the fact that the rifle has attained its ubiquity through diffusion from a single place where it was once, and once only, invented is no proof that the bow-and-arrow attained its earlier ubiquity exclusively in this same manner. It remains equally possible, and indeed equally probable, that the bow-and-arrow has become ubiquitous not only through diffusion from one place but also through independent invention in others. Nor does it follow that, because the technique of spinning and weaving by power-driven machinery can be traced to a single point of origin, the technique of metallurgy must be traceable to a single point of origin likewise. This dogmatic line of argument from inference in circumstances in which the inference is manifestly inconclusive is our British Diffusionists' first major fallacy. Their second major fallacy lies in the tacit assumption that the essence of what we mean by a civilization is comprised either in those things that can be proved to have become ubiquitous through diffusion, or in those other things that may be inferred inconclusively to have attained their ubiquity through the same means on the strength of analogy.

As a matter of fact, it is instructive to take a glance at our foregoing list of the proved and acknowledged triumphs of Diffusion; for we have certainly hit upon the notorious examples which naturally come first to mind, and one glance is enough to show that they are all trivialities which do not touch the heart of what we

of the Sinic Script is no longer secure even in the Far Eastern World, where this script has been inherited directly from the antecedent Sinic Civilization. In Japan, and even in China, the substitution of the Latin form of the Alphabet for the Sinic script is now coming under consideration.

[1] Not merely the existence but the utility of rubber became known to our Western World through contact with the peoples of Amazonia. The peoples of Amazonia had already discovered for themselves how to make rubber bulbs and rubber balls in pre-Columbian times (see Nordenskiöld, E.: *Modifications in Indian Culture through Inventions and Loans* (Göteborg 1930, Elander), p. 13).

[2] One may perhaps add the military technique of infantry-fighting in phalanx formation, which may be regarded as a Sumeric invention, since the earliest evidence for its employment is the stele of the Sumeric militarist Eannatum of Lagash (*dominabatur* in Shinar some time between *circa* 3000 and *circa* 2800 B.C.). Thereafter we find the phalanx in use both in the Egyptiac World and in the Hellenic; and in the latter world it is diffused from the city-states round the Aegean into Macedonia (perhaps in the fifth century B.C.: see Geyer, F.: *Macedonien bis zur Thronbesteigung Philips II* (Munich and Berlin 1930, Oldenbourg), pp. 88–9) and later (by the beginning of the second century B.C.) up the Axius Valley, into Dardania (Livy, Book XXXI, chap. 43). Finally, in our own Western World, we find the phalanx turning up, from the twelfth century of the Christian Era onwards, in Flanders and Northern Italy, and thereafter in Switzerland, to become eventually the standard Western infantry-technique until it is gradually driven off the field by the diffusion of fire-arms. (See further vol. iii, p. 165, footnote 1.)

mean by a civilization in any respect. A civilization does not consist in machine-sewing or rifle-shooting or tea- and coffee- and
cocoa-drinking or tobacco-smoking. It does not even consist in
reading and writing or in metallurgy (assuming it to be proved that
metallurgy, like the Alphabet, has been invented once, and once
only, in a single place). To equate this kind of thing with Civilization' with a capital 'C' is an absurdity which would be inconceivable
to a cultivated mind that was either Hindu or Hellenic or Western
of an earlier generation;[1] and, if this palpable absurdity is plausible
to the minds of one school among our contemporary Western
scholars, this is presumably because they have been born and
brought up in an ultra-modern social environment in which the
material plane of human life looms large out of all proportion to
the spiritual.[2]

We are here confronted, once again, by the relativity of historical
thought. The ultra-modern Western scholar is apt to be betrayed
insidiously, by the mental atmosphere in which his mind is constrained to work, into persuading himself that, because Western
sewing-machines and Western rifles and Western cotton goods
have been diffused throughout the Orthodox Christian and Islamic
and Hindu and Far Eastern worlds in these latter days, this
diffusion of Western knick-knacks is tantamount to the conversion of
these four other living societies to our Western Civilization. For
those Westerners that have eyes to see, there is no obligation to
accept this preposterous hallucination; and in this Study we have
had occasion to see through it more than once already.[3] At this
day, when we have diffused all our Western knick-knacks with all the
'salesmanship' that we can command. the living non-Western
civilizations that have been flooded by the mass-produced spate of
our labour-saving machines and our lethal weapons and our textiles

---

[1] The point is well illustrated by the following anecdote of the Emperor Theodore of
Abyssinia (*imperabat* A.D. 1855–67). *Imperator ipse loquitur*:

'A man came to me riding on a donkey, and said that he was a servant of the great
Emperor of the French, and that he had come to my country for the sole purpose of
establishing friendship between me and his sovereign. I said: "I do not object to making
friends with great Christian kings; you are welcome." The next day he said he wished
to see me on business, and I assented; but to my astonishment he came to me with a
bundle of rags. I asked him what those were. He replied that the French had a large
town in their country where they make silks, and that the merchants of that place had
commissioned him to bring them to me for the sake of barter. I said to myself: "What
have I done that these people insult me thus by treating me like a shopkeeper?" I bore
the insult then and said nothing.'

This is part of a conversation between the Emperor and Mr. Hormuzd Rassam (a
special envoy to the Emperor from Queen Victoria), as recorded by Mr. Rassam himself.
The passage is quoted from Rassam's *Narrative of the British Mission to Theodore King
of Abyssinia* (London 1869, Murray, 2 vols.), vol. ii, pp. 60–1, by Woolf, L. S., in *Empire
and Commerce in Africa* (London 1920, Allen & Unwin), p. 142.

The offender was the French Consul, Monsieur Lejean; Monsieur Lejean's Imperial
Master was Napoleon III; the bundle of rags was a pattern-book of silks; the city from
which it came was Lyons.

[2] See I. C (iii) (b), p. 151, above.   [3] See I. B (iii), pp. 31 and 35, above.

can nevertheless lift up their heads and justly boast that, though they 'sink in deep mire, where there is no standing', and are 'come into deep waters, where the floods overflow' them, yet still 'the waters are' *not* 'come in unto' their 'soul'.[1] In spite of the overwhelming diffusion of our Western material technique, these non-Western civilizations can still call their souls their own. In their inner spiritual life, which is their real life, it is as true as ever, for them, that 'the Earth is the Lord's and the fulness thereof, the world and they that dwell therein';[2] and if ever they do open the 'everlasting doors' of their spiritual citadel, it will assuredly not be in order to grant admittance to the spirit that has been embodied in a Singer or a Ford.

It is no accident that the outstanding triumphs of Diffusion are mostly trivial and external and few of them intimate or profound; for, as we shall have occasion to observe at later points in this Study,[3] the process of Radiation-and-Mimesis, through which Diffusion works in human affairs, is vigorous and effective in inverse ratio to the value and importance of the social properties that are conveyed by it from the communicative party to the receptive party in this social commerce. The process operates with the greatest rapidity and the longest range on the economic plane; less quickly and penetratingly on the political plane; and least potently of all on the cultural or spiritual plane. It is the easiest thing in the world for a Western manufacturer to export a sewing-machine to Bombay or Shanghai. It is infinitely harder for a Western man of science or a Western poet or a Western saint to kindle in non-Western souls the spiritual flame that is alight in his own. Thus the importance of Diffusion in human history will be vastly over-estimated if it is accepted at its face value in quantitative terms; for the greater the volume of the social commerce, the lower, as a rule, is the spiritual value of the social goods that are exchanged.[4]

On this showing it seems both legitimate and desirable, here and now, to emphasize the part that has been played in human history by original creation, while being careful to give Diffusion no less than its due. And we may remind ourselves that the spark or germ of original creation may burst into flame or flower in any manifestation of Life in virtue of the principle of the Uniformity of Nature.

We may at least go so far as to place the *onus probandi* on the Diffusionists' shoulders in cases where it is an open question

----

[1] Psalm lxix. 2 and 1.   [2] Psalm xxiv. 1.

[3] See III. C (i) (*a*), vol. iii, pp. 151–2, and V. C (i) (*c*) 3, vol. v, pp. 196–203, below, as well as Parts VIII and IX.

[4] This proposition is discussed in Part IX, below.

whether Diffusion or Uniformity of Nature is entitled to claim the credit for some particular human achievement.

'There can be little doubt that many of the most essential inventions of civilized life have been invented over and over again in distant times and countries, as different nations have reached those particular points of social advancement when those inventions were first needed. Thus, printing has been independently invented in China and in medieval Europe;[1] and it is well known that a process essentially the same was in use for various purposes in Ancient Rome, though no one took the great step of applying to the reproduction of books the process which was familiarly used for various meaner purposes.[2] What happened with printing we may believe also to have happened with writing, and we may take another illustration from an art of quite another kind. There can be no doubt, from comparing the remains of the earliest buildings in Egypt, Greece, Italy, the British Islands, and the ruined cities of Central America, that the great inventions of the arch and the dome have been made more than once in the history of human art.[3] And moreover, much as in the case of printing, we can see in many places strivings after them, and near approaches made to them, which still never reached complete success. Nor need we doubt that many of the simplest and most essential arts of civilised life—the use of the mill, the use of the bow, the taming of the horse, the hollowing out of the canoe—have been found out over and over again in distant times and places. It is only when we find the unmistakeable witness of language, or some other sign of historical connexion, that we have any right to infer that the common possession of inventions of this kind is any sign of common derivation from one primitive source. So it is with political institutions also. The same institutions constantly appear very far from one another, simply because the circumstances which called for them have arisen in times and places very far from one another. The whole system of historical analogies rests on this doctrine. We see the same political phenomena repeating themselves over and over again in various times and places, not because of any borrowing or imitation, conscious or unconscious, but because the like circumstances have led to the like results. . . .'[4]

The judgement here recorded by a great Western historian some sixty years ago may be supported by a quotation from the work of a distinguished living Western anthropologist:

'The resemblances in Man's ideas and practices are chiefly traceable to the similarity in structure of the human brain everywhere, and in the consequent nature of his mind. As the physical organ is, at all known

[1] For a recent inquiry into this question, see Carter, T. F.: *The Invention of Printing in China and its Spread Westward*, revised edition (New York 1931, Columbia University Press).—A. J. T.

[2] Compare the history of the invention of the steam-engine in the Hellenic World.—A. J. T.

[3] the true arch and the true dome appear to have remained undiscovered by the Mayas.—A. J. T.

[4] Freeman, E. A.: *Comparative Politics* (London 1873, Macmillan), pp. 31–2. Compare pp. 16–17.

stages of Man's history, substantially the same in constitution and
nervous processes, so the mind has certain universal characteristics,
powers and methods of action.[1] . . . This similarity in the operation of
the brain is seen in the nineteenth-century intellects of Darwin and
Russell Wallace, which, working on the same data, arrived simultaneously
at the Theory of Evolution;[2] and it accounts for numerous claims in the
same age to priority with respect to the same invention or discovery.
The similar operations of the common mind of the Race—more fragmentary in their data, more rudimentary in their powers, and vaguer in
their results—explain the appearance of such beliefs and institutions as
Totemism, Exogamy, and the many purificatory rituals, in most widely
separated peoples and portions of the globe.[3]

'In particular, the data for the thoughts and inferences of Primitive
Man are very limited and are much the same everywhere. The nearer
we come to the earliest type of Man, the more the means to his ends
tend to coincide over the whole Race, as is shown by flint tools and
weapons scattered all over the World and in many strata of Time. Hence
the similarity of the means he takes in various peoples and ages to
express his early religious and social ideas, and to attain his crude moral
and spiritual ends.'[4]

In the two foregoing passages the potency of the principle of the
Uniformity of Nature in human affairs is effectively brought out;
but such representations as these are sometimes met with the
objection that certain inventions—e.g. the invention of the metallurgical art—are so complicated that they virtually must have been
unique. The test case of metallurgy is presented as follows by a
distinguished living archaeologist:

' "Where did the revolutionary discovery of metallurgy originate?"
It is, of course, theoretically possible that the properties of copper were
independently realised in Egypt and Hither Asia, or even in illiterate
Spain and Hungary, and that the barbarians of Cornwall and Bohemia
spontaneously hit upon the alloy, known before 3000 B.C. in Sumer and
India. Practically, in the case of the Old World where the first metal-
using civilisations had such wide foreign relations and were bound
together by so many common traits, no one, unprejudiced by the
passions evoked by a perverse Diffusionism, will suggest that all the
complex processes involved were elaborated separately at two or more

---

[1] 'Our reason is in its very essence more than individual; it is expressive of universality;
it is a part of that Order which regulates the Universe, and in a deep sense it is a creative
factor or co-creator of the Universal.'—Smuts, J. C.: *Holism and Evolution*, 2nd edition
(London 1927, Macmillan), p. 252.

[2] For this and other instances of one and the same invention being made independently but simultaneously by two or more inventors, see III. C (ii) (a), vol. iii, pp. 237–9,
below.—A. J. T.

[3] For the extreme complexity of some of the identic 'primordial images' which are
imprinted on the common mind of the Human Race and which reveal themselves in
individual human minds of every age and place and social environment, see Jung, C. G.:
Psychological Types (English translation: London 1923, Kegan Paul).

[4] Murphy, J.: *Primitive Man: His Essential Quest* (Oxford 1927, University Press),
pp. 8–9.

comparatively adjacent points in Eurasia.... The discoveries and inventions implicit in metal-working are so abstruse and complex that independent origin at several points—in the Old World at any rate—is excluded as fantastically improbable; knowledge of the essential techniques must, that is to say, have been diffused from some centre.'[1]

The reader of this passage will have noticed that the writer of it, with scholarly caution, explicitly confines his contention to the ambit of the Old World. And well he may! For, had he ventured to extend to the New World his claim that the art of metallurgy has become ubiquitous through diffusion from a single place of origin, he would have been challenged at once by another scholar who is at least his peer as an adept in the archaeology of the New World, and who is an anthropologist into the bargain. Nordenskiöld can testify that, in the original home of the Andean Civilization, the metallurgical art is coeval with the civilization itself. 'The people of the Proto-Chimu period ... were acquainted with gold, copper, and their alloys, and possibly also silver, and knew how to smelt and cast these metals.'[2] 'In all parts where at the time of the Discovery the Bronze Age prevailed, that cultural stage—which appears to have originated in the region surrounding Lake Titicaca—had been preceded by a copper age.'[3] In Colombia and Central America, moreover, at the same epoch, bronze was still unknown—in contrast to the knowledge of bronze as well as copper which was current, by then, in Mexico on the one side as well as in Peru on the other. These facts demonstrate, between them, that the unquestionably abstruse art of making and working bronze was not introduced into the New World all of a piece (as it must have been if it had been introduced by Diffusion from the Old World), but was invented out of the prior art of copper-working in the New World independently—however unlikely this independent invention might seem to be, *a priori*. 'The art of metallurgy, at any rate from the point when metal-casting became known, is in America an independent invention.'[4] More than that, the Incas had achieved, before the Discovery, 'an invention that we of the Old World only in recent times have succeeded in accomplishing—and then by a method quite different to that of the Indians—namely, the art of welding copper'.[5]

[1] Childe, V. G.: *The Bronze Age* (Cambridge 1930, University Press), pp. 23–4 and 10. See, again, the same author's *The Most Ancient East* (London 1928, Kegan Paul), pp. 224–7. In this latter work, Professor Childe also applies the Diffusion Theory to the invention of the wheel and the cart (p. 211) and to the device of artificial food-production by cultivation (pp. 228–31).

[2] Nordenskiöld, E.: *Origin of the Indian Civilisations in South America* (Göteborg 1931, Elander), p. 35.

[3] Nordenskiöld, op. cit., loc. cit. Compare the same author's *Modifications in Indian Culture through Inventions and Loans* (Göteborg 1930, Elander), p. 41, and his *The Copper and Bronze Ages in South America* (Göteborg 1921, Elander), *passim*.

[4] Nordenskiöld: *Origin of the Indian Civilisations in South America*, p. 75.

[5] Nordenskiöld: *Modifications in Indian Culture through Loans and Inventions*, p. 17.

The astronomical discoveries of the Mayas can be demonstrated, by similar proofs, to have been made independently of the identical discoveries in the Babylonic World; and in general the original creative capacity and achievement of the peoples who were in occupation of the New World, before its discovery by the Europeans, is summed up by Nordenskiöld in the following terms:

'I think we must admit that the Indians' contribution—as discoverers and inventors—to the cultural progress of Man is considerable. It may even surpass that of the Teutonic peoples during the era preceding the discovery of America. It is a proven fact that the Indians have achieved many discoveries and inventions that in pre-Columbian times were unknown in the Old World. They have invented many things that are adaptations to exceptional geophysical conditions. They have further made a number of inventions in connexion with culture-elements that in post-Columbian times have been introduced to them by Whites and Negroes. Many inventions have in America such an isolated area of distribution that they may properly be supposed to have been made there. Seeing that the Indians have discovered and invented a great deal that was unknown in the Old World at the time of the discovery of America, it does not seem unreasonable to wonder whether they may not also have invented something or other that also was known there. The actual fact of their having done so is proved by it being possible to trace several inventions of that class from their simplest to their most elaborate forms. In the case of certain very important inventions it can be shown that in America they in all probability were preceded by simpler devices founded on the same principles.'[1]

If this cumulative testimony from historians and archaeologists and anthropologists has failed to convince the reader that every human society is a potential vehicle of the creative spirit in virtue of the uniformity of a Human Nature which is instinct with this creative power, then we will win our case by calling next into the witness-box an eminent zoologist, to be followed by an eminent physiologist who is still more eminent as a philosopher. The zoologist shall speak first:

'I . . . have time', he says, 'to dwell on only a few of the many considerations suggested by the singular parallelisms or convergencies between the Termites and the Ants, such as the development in both of wingless worker and soldier castes, similar nesting and fungus-growing habits, trophallaxis, relations to guests, &c. The duplication of these phenomena in groups so wide asunder that they are placed by the systematists at the opposite poles of our classification of insects, may be

---

[1] Nordenskiöld, E.: *Modifications in Indian Culture through Inventions and Loans* (Göteborg 1930, Elander), pp. 89–90. See further the same author's résumé in seventeen points, on pp. 74–6 of his *Origin of the Indian Civilisations of South America*, in which he sums up the likenesses and differences and the contact and absence of contact between the primitive cultures and the civilizations of the New World among themselves, and also between the cultures of the New World, taken as a whole, and the cultures of the Old World and of Oceania.

of some interest to the anthropologist, because the study of human cultures reveals the same or very similar institutions and linguistic peculiarities in geographically widely separated peoples. Some anthropologists attribute such similarities to community of origin, while others insist that they are often inventions of independent origin and development. When we reflect that Ants and Termites have been able, through slow physiological and instinctive processes, independently to evolve such strikingly analogous peculiarities as those I have described, we can scarcely doubt that different human communities, belonging to the same species and endowed with some intelligence, may frequently have hit upon the same inventions.'[1]

As for our physiologist-philosopher, he is no less a scholar than Monsieur Henri Bergson; and the evidence that we are going to take from him is presented in the most famous of all his published works. In a characteristic passage of *L'Évolution Créatrice*,[2] a masterly physiological study, on comparative lines, of the eye of the Vertebrates and the eye of the Molluscs leads up to the following philosophical result:

'At every instant, before our eyes, Nature arrives at identical results, in species which are sometimes close to one another, by embryo-genical processes which are altogether diverse. . . . To take, as a case in point, . . . our comparison between the eye of the Vertebrates and the eye of the Molluscs, we shall observe that, in the Vertebrates, the retina is produced by an expansion that is emitted by the rudiment of the brain in the young embryo. It is a veritable nervous centre that has transferred itself to the periphery. On the other hand, in the Molluscs, the retina derives from the ectoderm directly, and not indirectly through the intermediary form of the embryonic *encephalus*. Here, again, we really have two different evolutionary processes which result, in Man and in the Scallop, in the development of an identical retina.'[3]

If the creative power which is instinct in all Life is able to invent independently the economic techniques of agriculture and stock-breeding and the social system of morphologically diversified castes in incarnations of Life which are so far removed from one another as the Termites and the Ants, and if it is also able to invent independently an identical structure for the eye in the Vertebrates and in the Molluscs, in a clam and in a human being, then it is assuredly not incredible that the economic technique of fusing copper and tin into bronze, or the social system of Totemism, should have been invented independently by different human societies—considering that, within the ambit of the Human Race, the Uniformity of Nature is, after all, so close that human beings

---

[1] Wheeler, W. M.: *Social Life among the Insects* (London, no date, Constable), pp. 280–1.
[2] Bergson, Henri: *L'Évolution Créatrice*, 24th edition (Paris 1921, Alcan), pp. 67–92.
[3] Bergson, Henri, op. cit., pp. 81–2.

of every physical variety are able to interbreed, while human beings of every cultural variety are able to master one another's languages and to exchange their ideas.

Perhaps we have now sufficiently reasserted the potency of original creation, and the role of the Uniformity of Nature, in human affairs; but, in our desire to restore a just balance between the Uniformity Theory and the Diffusion Theory, we must be on our guard against depreciating, as well as against over-estimating, the historical part which Diffusion has actually played. It may therefore be well to examine, briefly, the role of Diffusion, in contrast to original creation, in the geneses of civilizations both of the 'unrelated' and of the 'related' class.

The 'unrelated' civilizations, as we have found in another chapter,[1] have apparently emerged through the mutation, into civilizations, of primitive societies; and if we inquire into the role of Diffusion here we shall observe at least two instances in which more than one civilization has emerged from a single society of a transitional character: from a society, that is to say, which has not yet taken the shape of a civilization, though it has already differentiated itself from the primitive societies pure and simple.

One of these intermediate societies out of which several civilizations have sprung is that Afrasian culture in which Sir John Marshall discerns the common substratum of 'the Indus Culture' and the Sumeric culture and the Egyptiac and the Minoan.[2] The antecedent diffusion of this common intermediary culture from the Atlantic to the Indian Ocean over the vast Afrasian area within which—at four separate points—the four civilizations in question afterwards arose, is the cause to which Sir John Marshall ascribes the points of family likeness which these four civilizations display when they are compared with one another and are contrasted with the remaining representatives of the species. And this common substratum of culture, within these geographical limits, upon which the archaeologist strikes when he digs down below the foundations of the four Afrasian civilizations, is also encountered by the anthropologist when he makes his own researches for his own hidden treasure in the same area. Having once cited Sir James Frazer on behalf of the Uniformity of Nature, we are in duty bound to cite him on behalf of Diffusion as well.

'If there is any truth in the analysis of the Saturnalia and kindred festivals which I have now brought to a close, it seems to point to a remarkable homogeneity of civilisation throughout South-Eastern Europe and Western Asia in prehistoric times. . . . In the far east of

---

[1] In II. A, on p. 188, above.
[2] See the passage quoted from Sir John Marshall's *Mohenjo-Daro and the Indus Civilisation* in I. C (i) (b), Annex III, on pp. 417-20, above.

Asia we have met with temporary kings whose magical functions and intimate relation to agriculture stand out in the clearest light; while India furnishes examples of kings who have regularly been obliged to sacrifice themselves at the end of a term of years. All these things appear to hang together; all of them may, perhaps, be regarded as the shattered remnants of a uniform zone of religion and society which at a remote era belted the Old World from the Mediterranean to the Pacific.'[1]

This Afrasian intermediary culture has its analogue in the New World in the so-called 'Archaic Culture' which emerged above the primitive level, in the last millennium B.C., throughout the arid zone of Tropical America, over an area extending from what is now Southern Mexico, at one end, to what are now Colombia and Venezuela and Ecuador at the other. Over this area in this age, the fathers of 'the Archaic Culture' appear to have diffused an art of agriculture and an art of pottery and an art of weaving which were the common foundations of the corresponding arts, as these are found in a higher stage of development at a later date in both the Mayan World and the Andean.[2]

Thus the Mayan and Andean civilizations in the New World, as well as 'the Indus Culture' and the Sumeric, Egyptiac, and Minoan civilizations in the Old World, are found to possess certain characteristics in common which are traceable, in each of these two instances, to an antecedent process of Diffusion. In the light of this, are we to say that we really find ourselves in the presence, not of six separate and independent civilizations, but of two and two only—one in Afrasia and the other in Tropical America—which have each spread by Diffusion to such an extent that they have assumed a superficial appearance of multiplicity: an appearance which is contradicted, nevertheless, by the fundamental unity which persists below the surface all the time in either case? The answer to this question is in the negative; and this negative answer is formulated with admirable judgement and exemplary clarity by the Swedish scholar whom we have cited a number of times already.

'The connexion between the Central American and Peruvian Indians did not cause any fusion of cultures. The South American high civilization cannot be said to have been an off-shoot of the Central American or Mexican civilizations, or *vice versa*. On the other hand, I believe we are bound to assume that the civilizations of Western South America and

[1] Frazer, Sir J. G.: *The Golden Bough*, 3rd edition: 'The Scapegoat' (London 1913, Macmillan), p. 409.
[2] For this 'Archaic Culture' of the New World, see Spinden, H. J.: *Ancient Civilisations of Mexico and Central America* (New York 1922, American Museum of Natural History), pp. 49–60 (especially the maps on pp. 59 and 60); Thompson, J. E.: *The Civilisation of the Mayas* (Chicago 1927, Field Museum of Natural History), pp. 5–6; *Encyclopaedia Britannica*, edition xiii, new volume i, p. 193, *s.v.* 'Archaeology'.

Central America at some very remote period possessed a common origin. By this I do not mean that in some particular locality, say in Central America, at an earlier date than elsewhere, there existed some highly developed civilisation from which the South American higher civilisations took their rise, but that in America, in different regions, from a more primitive stage, and more or less independent of each other, the high cultures developed. Here development in the main proceeded on parallel lines, and in parts arrived at very divergent results.'[1]

The truth is that, although the two civilizations of the first generation in the New World and the four civilizations of the first generation in Afrasia may have emerged, in each case, from a common substratum which was intermediate in its cultural level between the relatively low level of the preceding and surrounding primitive cultures and the relatively high level of the subsequently super-imposed civilizations, these civilizations cannot be regarded simply as the automatic products of the diffusion of that 'archaic culture' which is the common platform upon which they severally stand. As we have seen at other points in this Study, every one of these civilizations has differentiated itself from the common archaic culture by a dynamic act;[2] and each of these separate and independent dynamic acts has taken the form of an individual response to a particular challenge. The Mayan Civilization arose out of the American 'Archaic Culture' in response to the challenge of the rain-soaked tropical forest,[3] in contrast to the Andean Civilization, which arose out of the same 'Archaic Culture' in response to the antithetical challenge of the waterless desert.[4] And in Afrasia, while it is true that the first impetus to the rise of the four Afrasian civilizations was given by a common challenge in the shape of the simultaneous desiccation of the grass-lands from one end of Afrasia to the other,[5] it is equally significant that a second and final impetus was given, in each case, by a peculiar local challenge which evoked an individual response. The Minoan Civilization was a response to the challenge of the sea,[6] the Egyptiac Civilization a response to the challenge of the Nile,[7] the Sumeric a response to the challenge of the Tigris and Euphrates,[8] while 'the Indus Culture' (on the assumption that it is to be reckoned as an independent civilization in its own right)[9] was a response to the challenge of the river after which it has been named.

[1] Nordenskiöld, E.: *Origin of the Indian Civilisations in South America* (Göteborg 1931, Elander), p. 70.   [2] See Part II. A, p. 188, above.
[3] See II. C (ii) (b) 2, p. 321, above.
[4] See II. C (ii) (b) 2, pp. 321-3, above.
[5] See II. C (ii) (b) 2, pp. 302-6, above.
[6] See II. C (ii) (b) 2, pp. 323-30, above.
[7] See II. C (ii) (b) 2, pp. 306-15, above.
[8] See II. C (ii) (b) 2, pp. 315-18, above.   [9] See I. C (i) (b), Annex III, above.

We can convey the situation in a simile by likening our two sets of civilizations—the set of four in Afrasia and the pair of civilizations in the New World—to two groups of pyramids which do not rise directly, in either case, out of the plain which they respectively dominate. The architects of each group have sought to enhance the imposing effect of their work by planting the pair of pyramids—or the foursome, as the case may be—not down upon the low-lying plain but up upon a ledge or shelf of natural rock that projects from the foot of the adjoining mountains, with the result that the plain is dominated by the very bases of the pyramids, not to speak of their summits. Here, then, in either case, we have a set of pyramids standing on a common platform which rises already in itself above the surrounding levels. And we are presented with the question: 'Ought the four pyramids in the one case, and the two pyramids in the other, to be regarded, in virtue of their common platforms, as four parts and as two parts respectively of one single building?' When this question is presented in these terms, we can see at once that the answer turns upon the question whether the common platform is an artificial structure of the same construction as the pyramids that rise from it, or whether it is a natural elevation of the same substance as the surrounding plains and the adjoining mountains. If the platform were artificial too, then the pyramids would certainly have to be regarded as parts of a single edifice in which the platform itself would be not only the connecting link but also, perhaps, the principal architectural member. When, however, we find, as we do find, that the platform is actually a natural elevation which has been singled out by the architect's eye but has not been constructed by the builder's hand, then, clearly, we have to pronounce that the building begins at the point where the builder has laid his foundations, and that, on this showing, each single pyramid is to be reckoned as a separate building, in spite of the common natural elevation on which the whole set of buildings has been planted.

Thus the individual independence of each of the six civilizations of the first generation which are here under consideration is not impaired by the palpable underlying diffusion of the Afrasian and the Tropical American intermediate cultures. And when we pass on from the 'unrelated' to the 'related' cultures, we shall find that, in their geneses too, Diffusion has played a role which is not to be ignored and yet is not of capital importance.

Ex hypothesi, every 'related' civilization has arisen in some kind of contact with an antecedent civilization either of the 'related' or of the 'unrelated' class; and this means that it is in some sense a product of Diffusion. Indeed, we have found grounds for the belief that genesis through relation to an antecedent civilization, or, in other words, through Diffusion in a certain sense of the term, is the only form of genesis by which civilizations have actually been brought to birth at any time since the first generation.[1] In order, however, to estimate this form of Diffusion at its true importance, we must remind ourselves of the way in which it works; and, as a matter of fact, it works by contraries.

A 'related' civilization is one which is created by the proletariat —either internal or external—of the antecedent civilization with which it is in relation; and we have already seen what the relation of a proletariat to a dominant minority is.[2] It is not a relation of Radiation-and-Mimesis but a relation of Challenge-and-Response. And the dynamic act in which the creation of a new civilization by a proletariat is accomplished is not an act of conversion but an act of secession—not a centripetal movement but a centrifugal one. The creative proletariat is not seeking to enter into an apostolic succession through a 'laying on of hands' on the part of a creative minority in the society to which it belongs; the proletariat is revolting against the domination of a minority which has ceased to be attractive because it has lost its creative power. Thus it will be seen that, in the geneses of the 'related', as in those of the 'unrelated', civilizations, Diffusion plays only a minor part. The Diffusion of the antecedent civilization may provide the stimulus to creation, but it cannot itself be identical with the creative force, since, *ex hypothesi*, it emanates from a source which has already become impotent. The creator, in this case, is a proletariat which resists the diffusion of the dead and deadening culture of the dominant minority; and this creative proletariat performs its act of creation by kicking against the pricks.

So much for the role of Diffusion in the geneses of civilizations.

[1] See Part II. A, pp. 185–7, above.
[2] See I. C (i) (a), pp. 54–6; and compare Part II. A, pp. 187–8 and 195–6, above.

METHODS OF APPREHENSION, SUBJECTS OF STUDY, AND QUANTITIES OF 'DATA'

In the relevant chapter, we have found that the comparability of the facts which are encountered in the study of social life in civilizations is vindicated by the practical operations of every-day business life in the contemporary Western World. Why is it, then, that this truth continues to be disputed in the teeth of our experience? This question cannot be answered without making a rather wider survey of the methods which we employ in our intellectual activities.

We have empirical knowledge of three different methods of viewing and presenting the objects of our thought, and, among them, the phenomena of human life. The first method is the ascertainment[1] and record of particular 'facts'; the second is the elucidation and formulation of general 'laws' through a process of comparative study; the third is the form of artistic creation and expression known as 'fiction'. We need not doubt that the clear distinction between the techniques of these three methods—a distinction of which we are empirically aware—corresponds to some equally clear distinction between the respective phenomena which are viewed and presented in these different ways. We are not bound, however, to accept without question either the names by which the three techniques are popularly known or the popular anatomy of their respective provinces.

According to the popular view, the ascertainment and record of particular 'facts' is the technique of 'History'; and the phenomena in the province of this technique are the social phenomena of civilizations. The elucidation and formulation of general 'laws' through a process of comparative study is the technique of 'Science'; and, in the study of human life, the science is Anthropology and the phenomena in the province of the scientific technique are the social phenomena of primitive societies. 'Fiction' is the technique of the Drama and the Novel; and the phenomena in the province of this technique are the personal relations of human beings. These popular equations have a respectable origin—they can be traced back to Aristotle[2]—but they break down under examination.

[1] Ascertainment or 'establishment' in the subjective sense of the French word *onstatation*.

[2] In the following passage of the *Poetics* (1451B) Aristotle draws the contrast between the first and the third equation as follows:

Τούτῳ διαφέρει [ὁ ἱστορικὸς τοῦ ποιητοῦ] τῷ τὸν μὲν τὰ γενόμενα λέγειν, τὸν δὲ οἷ᾽ ἂν γένοιτο· διὸ καὶ φιλοσοφώτερον καὶ σπουδαιότερον ποίησις ἱστορίας ἐστίν· ἡ μὲν γὰρ

In the first place, 'History', in the popular sense of the study of the social phenomena of civilizations, does not really present the facts, all the facts, and nothing but the facts in the lives of societies of this species. Besides presenting facts, it has recourse to fictions and it appeals to laws; and on the other hand there are certain facts which it leaves alone because they are not grist to its mill.

'History' grew out of Mythology, a primary intuitive form of apprehension and expression in which the Drama and the Novel likewise took their origin. In Mythology, the distinction between facts and fictions is left undrawn;[1] and while 'History' has differentiated itself from Mythology by making an effort to extract the facts, it has never succeeded in dispensing with fictitious elements altogether.

For instance, it is hardly possible to write two consecutive lines of historical narrative without introducing fictitious personifications of institutions[2] and ascribing to them anthropomorphically the desires, feelings, thoughts, actions, and in fact all the psychic activities of human beings. In so doing, we are succumbing to 'the pathetic fallacy' just as much as if we were personifying the objects and forces of inanimate Nature; for though institutions are manifestations of Life, and of human life, they are not human beings and do not become persons in virtue of being personified in a figure of speech. In making use of these mythological counters we are misrepresenting reality;[3] yet, however conscious we may be of their falsifying effect, we cannot do without them.

For example, if we are recording the history of our Western Society in our day, we cannot avoid using the mythological proper names of the states into which this society is at present articulated —Britain, France, Czechoslovakia, and their sixty or seventy

ποίησις μᾶλλον τὰ καθόλου, ἡ δ' ἱστορία τὰ καθ' ἕκαστον λέγει· ἔστι δὲ καθόλου μὲν τῷ ποίῳ τὰ ποῖ' ἄττα συμβαίνει λέγειν ἢ πράττειν κατὰ τὸ εἰκὸς ἢ τὸ ἀναγκαῖον—οὗ στοχάζεται ἡ ποίησις ὀνόματα ἐπιτιθεμένη· τὸ δὲ καθ' ἕκαστον τί 'Αλκιβιάδης ἔπραξεν ἢ τί ἔπαθεν.

'The historian differs from the poet in this, that the historian presents what did happen while the poet presents what might happen. For this reason Poetry is more philosophic and less trivial than History; for Poetry presents generalities, History merely particulars. Generalities mean the kind of thing that this or that person is apt or bound to say or do; and this is what Poetry aims at presenting under the mask of the proper names which it confers on its characters. Particulars mean what Alcibiades did or had done to him.'

In identifying the creations of 'Fiction' with generalities, Aristotle would appear to be confusing the technique of the Drama and the Novel with the technique of Science, in order to distinguish them both from the technique of 'History' (so called).

[1] How this is psychologically possible may be understood by observing how a child takes a fairy-story.

[2] For the nature of institutions, see pp. 453–5, below.

[3] 'We must avoid thinking of either the State or the Community as ends in themselves, as self-subsistent and individual realities similar to, or greater than, the persons who are members of them. We must never say that the State desires this or the Community wills that or the Church is aiming at so-and-so, without realizing clearly that the only wills that really exist are the wills of the individual human beings who have become members of these bodies. There is no such thing, strictly speaking, as the "will" of an association or institution; there are only the co-operating wills of its members.' (Cole, G. D. H.: *Social Theory* (London 1920, Methuen), p. 22.)

companions—and treating these fictitious persons as though they were human beings in personal relations with one another. The official-sounding and abstract-seeming name France is not nearer to reality than 'Marianne' or 'the Gallic Cock'; nor 'Britain' than 'Britannia' or 'John Bull' or 'the British Lion'; and we gain nothing by writing 'République Française' or 'His Majesty's Government'. We do not even solve the problem by making 'H.M.G.' govern a plural verb; for the decisions officially ascribed to 'His Majesty's Government' are not taken by the persons, all the persons, and none but the persons who happen at the moment to be holding office; and even if they were taken by just those persons and no others, we should still find ourselves confronting the age-long philosophical problem, never yet solved, of 'the common will'. The vice of fictitiousness inherent in 'H.M.G.' inheres equally in 'My Lords' of the Treasury or the Admiralty and in 'the Secretary of State' whose departmental letters are signed by the hand and his answers to parliamentary questions delivered through the mouth of men of flesh and blood who perpetuate his fictitious existence by impersonating him successively. No less fictitious is the simple 'secretary' to whom, in the printed letter-heads of all manner of private associations, it is stated that 'all communications should be addressed'. We can apply the same destructive analysis to the organs and officers and activities of 'the Church', 'the Bar', 'the Press', 'the Turf', and 'the Trade'. We can apply it to the twenty-one civilizations which we have identified and named in this Study, as Adam named the animals. We know with our minds that we have encountered these civilizations simply as objects of our thought—as intelligible fields of historical study—but we cannot express our notions of them in words without treating them to some extent anthropomorphically as 'men of like passions with ourselves'.

In fact, in viewing and presenting social institutions and recording their work, the use of fiction appears to be an indispensable artifice of thought; and the most blatant forms of the artifice are really the least objectionable, because they are the least likely to be mistaken for realities instead of being taken for what they are. This point is raised by the practice of the Hellenic Society, which had two alternative usages. One usage was to present the states of the Hellenic World under the guise of divinities—'Aθήνη Πολιοῦχος ('the keeper of the state') standing for Athens, 'Aθάνα Χαλκίοικος for Sparta, Τύχη 'Aντιοχέων for Antioch, Fortuna Praenestina for Praeneste, Dea Roma or Divus Caesar for Rome, and so on.[1] In the other usage, states, corporations, classes, and

---

[1] Some of these divinities had their animal counterparts, e.g. Athene's owl (the distinguishing mark of the Athenian coinage) and the Roman wolf and eagle. Compare

other associations of human beings were represented by the collective names of their members in the plural number[1]—οἱ Ἀθηναῖοι for Athens, οἱ Λακεδαιμόνιοι for Sparta, οἱ ἐν τέλει for the Government, οἱ θιασῶται for a church, οἱ φράτορες for a fraternity.[2] This second usage is realistic in appearance rather than genuinely expressive of reality as it is.[3] It does not answer the questions: 'Did all or only some of the Lacedaemonians do this or that? And, if only some of them, how did these arrive at their "common will" and how did they impose it on their fellow citizens?' In order to come to grips with reality we should have—*quod est absurdum*—to record the same transaction from the personal standpoint of every Lacedaemonian citizen in turn;[4] and even if we had the information and the industry to accomplish this labour, we should find ourselves hardly any nearer to our goal, for we should still have somehow to compose or abstract a single narrative from the several thousand different narratives which we should have accumulated. This is a feat which our minds, as they are, could only perform intuitively, and, in this last step, the leap in the dark would be just as great as the intuitional leap which we make when we take as our jumping-off-ground not the collective name οἱ Λακεδαιμόνιοι but the name of the tutelary Goddess of the Lacedaemonian state, Ἀθάνα Χαλκίοικος. It seems wiser to admit to ourselves that it is at present beyond our intellectual capacity to express the realities of institutions in direct terms; that we can only present institutions through the medium of fictions which misrepresent the realities for which they stand; that the best that we can hope to do is to make full allowance all the time for a distorting effect which we cannot avoid; and that we shall be least likely to

the British lion which is the counterpart of John Bull, the Gallic cock which is the counterpart of Marianne, and the Austrian, Prussian, Russian, Polish, and American eagles.

[1] There were, of course, variations on this usage. For instance, the constitutional monarchy of Macedonia was represented by coupling the community name with the name of the reigning king, as 'King Antigonus and the Macedonians' (see Tarn, W. W.: *Hellenistic Civilisation* (London 1927, Arnold), p. 44). On the other hand, the official designation of the Roman State, 'Senatus Populusque Romanus', which simply substitutes the names of two component institutions for the name of the institution which they together compose, is nearer to our modern Western usage than to the usual practice of the Hellenic World.

[2] These two Hellenic usages had their counterparts in our Western Society in the Dark and Middle Ages, when states were sometimes presented under the guise of Saints (e.g. St. Mark of Venice with his winged lion, St. Denis of France, St. George of England, St. Peter of the Holy See) and sometimes as incarnated in their reigning sovereigns under their territorial titles (e.g. 'France' meaning 'the King of France' in Shakspeare—a usage which still survives in England in the signatures of bishops, who substitute the territorial title of their bishopric for their personal surname, and of peers, when their personal surnames are replaced by place-names in their titles).

[3] It does not dispose of the problem of institutions, any more than Euhemerus's theory that the Olympian Gods were deified human beings disposes of the problem of Religion.

[4] This problem of the relation between a society and the individual human beings who are its 'members' is discussed further in III. C (ii), vol. iii, below.

forget to make this allowance when the fictions which we employ
are least realistic in form.[1]

Another sphere in which historians find themselves compelled
to have recourse to fiction is the presentation of the workings of
public feeling and opinion; and here again the franker they are
with themselves the better they fare. In this sphere, no school of
historians has been so successful as the Hellenic School, who were
not afraid to retain and turn to account the artifice of fictitious
speeches and dialogues—an artifice that had been brought to
perfection in the Homeric Epic, which was the literary vehicle of
the Hellenic Mythology and the common parent of Greek historical
and Greek dramatic literature. The passages in Thucydides' work
which purport to reproduce the debates at Sparta and Athens in
432 B.C. on the eve of the outbreak of the Peloponnesian War or the
debate at Athens in 427 B.C. over the punishment of the Mity-
lenaeans or the dialogue at Melos in 416 B.C. between the *parle-
mentaires* of the Athenian expeditionary force and the Melian
notables are not only literary masterpieces; they also present the
play of feeling and opinion in a more illuminating way, and with
greater psychological profundity, than has ever been achieved by any
other expedient. Our modern Western historians, who reject this
aesthetically and psychologically valuable method of presentation
with scorn, in the names of 'science' and 'reality', are deluding
themselves if they suppose that their own subterfuge of 'composite
photographs'—mechanically produced by the compression of ten
thousand newspaper cuttings—is any the less fictitious for being
aesthetically and psychologically jejune. It is idle for them to
protest that the state papers, parliamentary debates, leading
articles, letters to editors, private correspondence, diaries, and
other raw materials which they have worked into their syntheses
are the *ipsissima verba* of the people by whom, on each occasion,
public opinion was formed and public policy decided. The question
remains: 'How did the final resolution of these forces come about?'
And this question can neither be answered nor be evaded by
substituting a narrative presented in the historian's name for
speeches and dialogues put into his characters' mouths. His *oratio
obliqua* is not more objective than Thucydides' *oratio recta*. It is
merely more likely, by its specious appearance of objectivity, to
delude the reader as well as the writer himself.

[1] If this conclusion is right, it is a misfortune that our Western Society in modern
times has degraded the representative divinities of Hellenic usage and the representative
saints of medieval Western usage into caricatures. Our consciousness that John Bull,
Marianne, Uncle Sam, Uncle Jonathan, and the rest are not merely fictions but fictions
which we do not take seriously betrays us into assuming that the fictions which we do
take seriously—Britain, France, the United States, and so on—are not mere fictions but
realities.

Finally, we may take note of certain works of literature which are concerned with public affairs in the histories of civilizations and for this reason can only be classified as historical, although the technique of 'fiction' is employed throughout, so that these works are indistinguishable in form from other dramas and novels. Such works are Aeschylus's *Persae*, Thomas Hardy's *The Dynasts*, Feuchtwanger's *Jew Süss*, and Benet's *John Brown's Body*.[1]

So much for the recourse to fiction in 'History'. As for its appeal to scientific laws, we may remind our Western historians that they have latterly taken into their service a number of ancillary sciences which formulate general laws not about those primitive societies which are the province of Anthropology, but about civilizations. Such sciences are Political Economy,[2] Political Science, and Artistic and Literary Criticism.[3] Our historians are apt to pride themselves on the enrolment of these scientific auxiliaries as being the greatest advance which the study of history has made in recent times; and we may venture to agree with them in this without exposing ourselves to a charge of inconsistency; for while we have criticized them at the beginning of this Study[4] for trying to apply the technique of Science outside its province, we have never objected to their employing the sciences in a menial capacity as hewers of wood and drawers of water. The Israelites, who were forbidden to adopt the practices of the heathen, were permitted to enslave the Gibeonites and spoil the Egyptians; and so for us historians, in the intellectual arena, *fas est et ab hoste doceri*.[5]

The facts of human life which 'History' leaves alone because they are not grist to its mill are of two kinds. First, there are all

---

[1] Tolstoy's *War and Peace* does not, on the whole, come under this category. It does, of course, contain elements of historiography—for example the thesis, on which the author harps, that military commanders are passive instruments who register events without determining them, and again the rather wearisomely repeated comparison of the Grande Armée in retreat to a wounded beast. In essence, however, *War and Peace* is a true novel in the popular sense inasmuch as it is primarily concerned with the personal relations of human beings.

[2] The *Homo Economicus* of the 'classical' political economists, against whom Ruskin tilted, is a fictitious character employed as a mannequin for showing off 'economic laws' to advantage.

[3] There is also one ancillary science—Ethics—whose services have been found indispensable by historians always and everywhere.

[4] In Part I. A, above.

[5] Ovid: *Metamorphoses*, Book IV, l. 428. This position can be defended, if it needs defence, by appeal to another classical authority:

'THE APPALLING DIFFUSION OF TASTE

'Much as he hates a joke, Sir Pompey Bedell has a still greater loathing for Nature, Poetry, and Art, which he chooses to identify with Postlethwaite, Maudle and Co.; and Grigsby's lifelike imitations of these gentlemen—whom, by the bye, Sir Pompey has never seen—have so gratified him that he honours our funny friend with a call.

'*Sir Pompey* (aghast): "What, Mr. Grigsby, can this room really be *yours*? With a *Dado*!—and *Artistic Wall-Paper*!!—and a *Brass Fender*!!! and, gracious Heavens, a *Bunch of Lilies in a Blue Pot*!!!!"

'*Grigsby*: "They're not for *Luncheon*, Sir Pompey; they're only to smell and to look at, I assure you! Let me offer you one!"

'*Sir Pompey*: "Not for the world, Mr. Grigsby." ' *Punch*, 19th March 1881.

the facts relating to primitive societies, which are the province of Anthropology—for instance, the facts presented in Sir James Frazer's *The Golden Bough*. Second, there are all the facts relating to the private lives of human beings, whether these happen to be members of primitive societies or of societies in process of civilization[1]—for instance, the facts presented in the *Confessions* of Saint Augustine and Jean-Jacques Rousseau, in the *Meditations* of Marcus Aurelius Antoninus, in John Henry Newman's *Apologia*, in John Stuart Mill's *Autobiography*, in Paul Sabatier's *Life of Saint Francis of Assisi*, and in Lytton Strachey's *Life of Queen Victoria*.

The distinction between these biographical facts and the facts that come within the province of 'History' is apt to be obscured because persons whose private lives come to be recorded are apt to be persons who have lived public lives as well—persons, that is to say, who have impersonated institutions or movements or ideas and have served as vehicles for 'historical' events. Saint Augustine, Saint Francis, and Cardinal Newman all made their marks upon the history of the Christian Church; Marcus Aurelius and Queen Victoria were not only human beings but 'heads of states'; Rousseau's ideas were among the spiritual forces that carried our Western Society out of the so-called 'modern' age into the 'postmodern' age in which we are living to-day.[2] The lives of such persons are interesting to their fellow men by reason of their accidental 'historical' significance as well as in virtue of their intrinsic human significance. Hence the vast majority of biographies are literary hybrids in which the significant events of a private life are overlaid in the portrayal or are even crowded out of the picture by the mass of public affairs with which they happen to be mixed up. This is perhaps the reason why biographies are seldom good works of art; for private lives are not the pivots on which public affairs turn or the standpoints from which they can be seen in true proportion, however eminent the livers of these lives may be.[3]

To make biography a peg for history is as great a mistake in method as to make the record of historical transactions an occasion for illustrating the points of human interest in private lives. Both are false routes; but the lure of historical biography leads more writers astray than the lure of biographical history. Mr. Strachey's *Life of Queen Victoria* is a rare and noteworthy example of a work

[1] Of course, the great majority of private lives that come to be recorded are the lives of members of societies that belong to the latter class. Records of the lives of savages and barbarians are rare, and such as exist are mostly slight and superficial.

[2] For the transition between these two ages, see pp. 1 and 170–1, above.

[3] This point is brought out clearly by Eduard Meyer in his 'Zur Theorie und Methodik der Geschichte' (*Kleine Schriften* (Halle 1910, Niemeyer), p. 66).

of art in which this wrong turning has been avoided. The author disentangles the life of Victoria from the history of the Victorian Age and ignores public transactions except in so far as these throw light on the personality of the woman with whom he is concerned. This clarity of vision and sense of form are less rare in auto-biographies. The supreme example of the disentanglement of a private from a public life is the *Meditations* of the Emperor Marcus Aurelius—a book which provides no grist for the mill of historians of the Roman Empire,[1] but which has a human interest that is so deep and direct and permanent that the book is read to this day by innumerable people to whom the Roman Empire is no more than a name.

When we turn from 'History' to Anthropology, we find that, here too, the popular equation breaks down. Anthropology does not really present the laws, all the laws, and nothing but the laws, that govern the lives of primitive societies. Besides formulating laws, it ascertains facts and has recourse to fictions; and on the other hand there are certain laws which it leaves alone because they are not grist to its mill. As a matter of fact, Anthropology is only just beginning, in our generation, to emerge from the preliminary stage of fact-finding (a stage through which every science has to pass in its infancy) into the stage of using the 'data' which it has collected as a basis for elucidating and formulating those laws which anthropologists regard as their objective. Again, Anthropology shows off its laws by draping them round a mannequin called 'Primitive Man' who is a fictitious character of the same make as *Homo Economicus*. At the same time, it has no use for the laws of Political Economy and the other ancillary sciences of 'History', because these laws apply not to 'Primitive Man' but to Mankind in process of civilization.

Lastly, the Drama and the Novel do not present fictions, complete fictions, and nothing but fictions regarding the personal relations of human beings. Besides fictions, they present facts and laws, and there are some fictions that do not come within their province.

We have observed already that the Drama and the Novel grow out of Mythology, which is likewise the source of 'History', and that in Mythology the distinction between facts and fictions is left undrawn. We have also noted that the Hellenic Drama and Hellenic History had a common literary parent in the Homeric Epic, which

---

[1] This is perhaps too sweeping a statement; for, though the *Meditations* yield no single piece of information on the administration of the Roman Empire or on the policy of the Roman Government during Marcus Aurelius's reign, there is a historical signifi-cance in the bare fact that a 'philosopher-king' occupied the highest position in the Roman State at this time (see Part III. A, vol. iii, p. 99, below).

was the literary vehicle of the Hellenic Mythology; and when we examine the plots of the earliest known Greek plays, we find that they are taken from this or that incident or situation in the Epic Cycle.[1] Similarly, the 'Mystery Plays' in which our Western drama first emerged took their plots from the Gospels and from the legends of Christ and the Saints, which may be regarded as the epic cycle in the background of our Western history.[2] Thus, in Greek tragedies and in Western 'Mystery Plays' alike, the plots originally belonged to a realm in which the question 'Is this fact or fiction?' did not arise; and although our Western Drama made haste to step out of this Garden of Eden,[3] Greek Tragedy was content to stay within its borders to the end.[4]

Moreover, even in a mental atmosphere in which the distinction between facts and fictions is consciously felt, the Drama and the Novel can never dispense completely with facts or employ the technique of fiction exclusively. When we call a piece of literature a 'work of fiction', we mean no more than that the characters could not be identified with any persons who have lived in the flesh, nor the incidents and scenes with any events or situations that have actually occurred. In fact, we mean that this work has a fictitious personal foreground; and if we do not mention that the background is composed of authentic social facts, that is simply because this seems so self-evident that we take it for granted. Of course, if the background as well as the foreground were constructed of

---

[1] Aeschylus, in a famous epigram, describes his plays as 'slices from the mighty banquets of Homer'. (Τὰς αὑτοῦ τραγῳδίας τεμάχη εἶναι ἔλεγε τῶν Ὁμήρου μεγάλων δείπνων: Athenaeus, Book VIII, 347 E.)

[2] The germ of this epic cycle of Christian legend was transmitted to our Western Society by the internal proletariat of the 'apparented' society, whereas the germ of the Homeric Epic was transmitted to the Hellenic Society by the external proletariat of the earlier society to which the Hellenic Society was related. This difference in the origins of the two epic cycles is connected with the difference (investigated in I. C (i) (b), on pp. 95–100, above) in the origins of Western and Hellenic religion, which likewise differed in being derived from the earlier society's internal and external proletariat respectively. The Barbarians who overran those provinces of the Roman Empire which eventually became the home of our Western Society did, of course, produce an epic; but this epic is not the parent of our Western literature, for it met with a premature death and left no issue. The Christian epic tradition conquered Teutonic poetry when Teutonic paganism was conquered by the Church; and the literary as well as the religious victory was so complete that Christian legend actually took possession of the Barbarians' epic form before flinging it on the scrap-heap. In the English version of the Teutonic Epic, which happens to be the best preserved, the lay of Beowulf was followed, before the *genre* became extinct, by the lay of the *Heliand* (the Saviour). On this, see Ker, W. P.: *Epic and Romance* (London 1922, Macmillan), pp. 27–9 and 90, and Bridges, Robert: *The Testament of Beauty* (Oxford 1929, Clarendon Press), Book III, ll. 534–81. See further II. D (vii), vol. ii, p. 320, below.

[3] In the English version of the Western Drama, the plots had become differentiated, as early as the Elizabethan Age, into a fictitious and a historical class. The division between these two classes roughly corresponded to the division between Comedy and Tragedy.

[4] On the other hand, Greek Comedy reacted to the influence of the Athenian soil in which the Greek Drama had its roots. 'The Old Comedy' learnt to take its plots from contemporary history by playing upon public events and caricaturing public men. 'The New Comedy' became a comedy of manners which portrayed the personal relations of private life.

fictitious materials,[1] the work would make nonsense. It would convey no intelligible or sensible image of human life, and would therefore make no appeal either to the understanding or to the emotions of readers or spectators.[2]

The narrowness of the limits within which, in so-called 'works of fiction', the technique of fiction can be employed with success may be gauged by considering the *genre* which is represented by *Gulliver's Travels* or by the fantasias of Jules Verne or Edgar Allan Poe or H. G. Wells. These writers, who all possess a fine literary tact, are not attempting the folly of writing fiction through and through. The *tour de force* which they have set themselves to perform is to substitute fictions for facts in only one or two points in the backgrounds of their stories. Swift changes the size of human bodies while leaving human nature as it is in every other respect. Verne and Poe and Wells exaggerate—or in some cases merely anticipate by a few years—the performances of our modern Western Physical Science in its practical applications. In a numerical metaphor, one might put it that, whereas the fictitious element in ordinary 'works of fiction' is confined to the foreground and amounts, say, to ten per cent. of the whole, these daring writers, in their *tours de force*, have raised the percentage from ten to twelve by introducing a few grains of fiction into the background. Nor have they made this trifling departure from the ordinary percentages with ease. In order to make their few grains of fiction in the background plausible, they have had to exert all their literary power in giving additional touches of realism to that part of the background (and it is still the major part) which they construct out of real social facts in the ordinary way. This trick of the trade is never performed with success except by writers of uncommon ability. The difficulty of it gives a measure of the extent to which the employment of facts in 'works of fiction' is indispensable.

[1] Even a fictitious foreground must be plausible: that is, it must not be in flagrant contradiction with palpable facts in the real social environment of the fictitious plot. This point is made by Aristotle in the *Poetics* (1460A): Δεδίδαχε δὲ μάλιστα Ὅμηρος καὶ τοὺς ἄλλους ψεύδη λέγειν ὡς δεῖ. . . . προαιρεῖσθαί τε δεῖ ἀδύνατα εἰκότα μᾶλλον ἢ δυνατὰ ἀπίθανα, τούς τε λόγους μὴ συνίστασθαι ἐκ μερῶν ἀλόγων, ἀλλὰ μάλιστα μὲν μηδὲν ἔχειν ἄλογον, εἰ δὲ μή, ἔξω τοῦ μυθεύματος. 'Homer is the great master of the art of telling falsehoods right. . . . From him one learns to prefer what is impossible but plausible to what is possible but incredible, and not to construct works of literature out of irrational elements, but if possible to avoid irrationalities altogether and in any case to keep them out of the action of the piece.'

[2] This is why it is difficult to achieve success in writing 'historical' plays and novels, i.e. plays and novels in which the social background is not that of the writer or of the public for whom he is writing. The effort to resuscitate an alien social background seldom produces effects that do not seem either shoddy or laboured. The reason is that social facts, when presented as a setting for personal relations, must be sketched in with a touch which is at the same time light and sure; and this touch is difficult to achieve except when the artist is portraying social facts with which he is intimately acquainted at first hand.

Moreover, there are certain works of literature—biographies and autobiographies—which present pure records of facts without any fictitious elements at all but which are not 'History'. We can now see what the affinities of this biographical literature are. In spite of being entirely non-fictitious, it clearly comes under the same literary category as the Drama and the Novel because, like these, it is concerned with the personal relations of human beings. This is the converse of a fact of which we have already taken note, namely, the fact that certain other works of literature, such as *The Persae* or *The Dynasts* or *John Brown's Body* or *Jew Süss*, which in form are 'works of fiction', come under the category of 'History', because they are concerned, not with the personal relations of human beings, but with public affairs.

Finally, even if we do not go with Aristotle so far as to say that Poetry (meaning Dramatic Poetry) 'presents generalities' in contrast to 'History', which 'presents merely particulars',[1] we may declare without fear of contradiction, in this age of 'problem plays' and 'problem novels', that our dramatists and novelists are not indifferent to the 'laws' of the science of Ethics; and, if we are challenged, we can put Aeschylus and Sophocles and Euripides into the witness-box, to testify on our behalf side by side with Henrik Ibsen and Bernard Shaw. We have already come across Ethics among the ancillary sciences which historians have taken into their service; so that we find this versatile science serving two masters, neither of whom are men of science themselves.

As for the fictions which do not come within the province of the Drama and the Novel, these are, of course, the fictions which we have found in use among the historians and the anthropologists. Having examined them above, we need not recapitulate them here.

Our survey has perhaps sufficiently disproved the accuracy of the popular equations between the employment of certain literary techniques and the study of certain phenomena of human life. Each of the three techniques—the ascertainment and record of 'facts', the elucidation and formulation of 'laws', and the creation of 'fiction'—is employed on occasion in each of the three studies: in the study of social life in civilizations which is popularly called 'History', in the study of social life in primitive societies which is the province of Anthropology, and in the study of personal relations in the branch of literature which comprises plays, novels, and biographies. This shows that there can be nothing in the intrinsic nature either of the studies or of the techniques to equate any one study with any one technique *a priori*. Yet this negative result of our survey does not dispose of our problem; for although the

---

[1] Aristotle, *Poetics*, 1451B, cited in footnote 2 on p. 441, above.

popular equations do not hold good absolutely, they do hold good on the whole. Each study does tend to employ one of the three techniques either more frequently or more effectively or more characteristically than it employs either of the other two; and although in each case we can point out occasions on which it employs the other two as well, these occasions are still the exception and not the rule. Thus the popular equations, while not accurate, do nevertheless approximate to the truth; and indeed, if they did not justify themselves as a rule, the popular mistake of assuming that their validity is absolute could scarcely have arisen. Our problem remains unsolved until we have explained the equations as far as they go.

If, with this in mind, we now examine the three techniques again, we may observe a difference between them which we have not yet noticed: among other differences, they differ in their respective suitability for dealing with 'data' in different quantities. The ascertainment and record of particular facts is all that is either possible or necessary in a field of study where the 'data' happen to be few; the elucidation and formulation of general laws through a process of comparative study is both possible and necessary where the 'data' are too numerous to tabulate but not too numerous to survey. The form of artistic creation and expression known as 'fiction' is the only technique that either can be employed or is worth employing where the 'data' are innumerable.

Here, as between the three techniques, we have an intrinsic difference of a quantitative order. The techniques differ intrinsically from one another in their utility for handling different quantities of 'data'. Can we discern any corresponding difference in the quantities of the 'data' that actually present themselves in the respective fields of our three studies?

To begin with the study of personal relations which is the province of plays, novels, and biographies, we can see at once that students of human life in this province are confronted with innumerable instances of certain universally familiar experiences: for example, the experience of Marriage, which is the stock subject of Attic Comedy, and the experience of Death, which is the stock subject of Attic Tragedy.[1] In dealing with such experiences as these, an exhaustive record of the facts is utterly impossible; and a record of particular instances which have actually occurred is seldom worth while, because the chances are that any given single instance will contain nothing beyond what everybody feels and knows about the experience already from his or her own personal

[1] For this analysis of the two *genres* of Attic Drama, see Murray, Gilbert: *The Classical Tradition in Poetry* (London 1927, Milford), pp. 52–5.

life, and will therefore be without any special significance, either emotional or psychological. This is another way of saying that it will be so commonplace and dull that to single it out from the host of 'data' at command would seem arbitrary, and to place it on record would seem a misdirection of energy. It does, of course, occasionally happen that actual instances of such experiences have value and significance as they stand. The experiences recorded in the biographies and autobiographies which have been cited above are examples. Yet if we reflect how infinitesimal is the number of actual instances that have been found worthy of record compared with the number that are perpetually being allowed to pass into oblivion, we realize that the accident occurs so rarely as to be almost negligible. Again, any 'laws' that could conceivably be formulated about experiences so frequently re-experienced, and therefore so familiar, as these, would seem either intolerably platitudinous or intolerably crude. In such circumstances, the 'data' cannot as a rule be expressed significantly or even intelligibly except in some kind of notation which gives an intuition of the infinite in finite terms or (in the language of Hellenic philosophy) sets a πέρας to an ἄπειρον. And this is the virtue of those fictitious characters and fictitious situations and events which occupy the foreground of 'works of fiction' and give this category of literature its conventional name. They may be regarded, in one aspect, as notations for expressing intuitively certain phenomena of human life which happen to be so frequently repeated and so familiar that their significance is fined down to subtleties and niceties which, except in rare cases, can be seized by intuition alone.[1]

Having now found, in quantitative terms, at least a partial explanation of the empirical fact that, in the study of personal relations between human beings, the technique known as 'fiction' is usually, though not exclusively, employed, let us see if we can find similar, if only partial, quantitative explanations for the usual though not exclusive employment of the law-making technique in the study of primitive societies and of the fact-finding technique in the study of civilizations.

The first point to observe is that both these other studies are

[1] It will be seen that the fictitious names by which historians and anthropologists designate institutions, and the anthropomorphic language in which they describe the workings of institutions (see pp. 442–6 and 448, above), are notations of the same kind as the fictions in 'works of fiction', and that, in all three *genres*, this artifice is employed in similar circumstances. The working of any given institution means in reality the outcome of the individual behaviours of each of the hundreds or thousands of human beings whom this particular institution holds in an impersonal relation with one another. The outcome of these innumerable individual behaviours cannot be apprehended by human minds, as they are, except intuitively; and an intuition of either the infinitesimal or the infinite in finite terms can only be expressed by using the notation called 'fiction'. Hence, when the circumstances arise, recourse is had to this technique in all our three studies of human life.

likewise concerned with human relations, but not with relations of
the familiar personal kind which come within the direct experience
of every man, woman, and child almost from the moment of birth.[1]
The social relations of human beings extend beyond the furthest
possible range of personal contacts,[2] and these impersonal relations[3]

[1] Within a month of birth, a child distinguishes its mother or nurse from other people.

[2] This is true of social relations in primitive societies as well as in civilizations. The
truth is perhaps more readily apparent in the Time-dimension than in the Space-
dimension. In any society at almost any moment of its existence the majority of members are already dead (as is recognized in the formula of Roman funerary inscriptions:
'Migravit ad plures'). If we think of the Time-relation in generations, we realize that
effective personal relations in Time hardly ever exist between individuals further removed
from one another than grandparents and grandchildren, whereas institutional relations
may exist between individuals whose lifetimes are separated by intervals of centuries or
even millennia. In primitive societies 'the ancestors' whose prestige is the sanction of
social custom comprise many more past generations than the earliest with which the life-
span of any living member of the society at any given moment has overlapped. In
civilizations, the possible extension of institutional relations in the Time-dimension is far
longer. Millions of members of our Western Society who are alive in 1933 are in such
relations with Abraham Lincoln or John Wesley or St. Francis of Assisi or St. Paul. In
fact, social relations are distinguished from personal relations in being four-dimensional.
(Personal relations cannot arise exclusively in the Time-dimension, and indeed cannot
subsist in it exclusively except in so far as people are influenced by the memory of
contemporaries who have predeceased them.)'.

[3] To call institutional relations 'impersonal' is to state a matter of fact which carries no
implications. In particular, their impersonality does not imply that these relations are
less momentous than personal relations or less compelling. In the Western Society of our
generation, the number of people who have been called (and have responded to the call)
to sacrifice their lives for the sake of the institutions called states is vastly greater than the
number who have been called to make the same supreme sacrifice for their relatives or
friends. Again, the spiritual significance and emotional intensity of a man's relations to
his parents or wife or children may be far surpassed by his devotion to John Wesley if he
is a devout Methodist or to St. Francis if he is a devout Catholic or to George Washington if he is a patriotic citizen of the United States or to Johann Sebastian Bach if he is a
passionate musician. These examples show that, while institutional relations are truly
'impersonal', they are in no sense 'unreal'. Indeed, they are the element in human life
in virtue of which we have accepted the definition of Man as being 'a social animal'. (See
the quotation from Aristotle in footnote 3 on p. 173 above.)

At the same time, we must not let ourselves slip into the error of assuming that
institutional relations and personal relations cover, between them, the whole field of
human experience. There are certain human experiences that do not take the form of
relations of any kind with other human beings—for example, such experiences as those
of mystical religion or aesthetic perception (*Anschauung*) or mathematical apprehension
(which Plato considered to be the only perfect pleasure in life).

It may be noted, however, that mystics and artists and mathematicians are seldom so
divinely or so bestially unsocial as to be content to keep their experiences to themselves.
As a rule, they feel an impulse to communicate their individual experience, and this
impulse is apt to be strong in proportion to the intensity of the experience which is the
object of it. 'I am come to send fire on the Earth, and what will I if it be already kindled?
But I have a baptism to be baptized with; and how am I straitened until it be accomplished?' (The Gospel according to St. Luke, ch. xii, vv. 49–50.) When attempts to
communicate the individual experiences of religion take the form of the institutions
called churches, there is sometimes the Devil to pay; and yet, as we shall see at a later
point in this Study (in III. C (ii), vol. iii, below), it is in the nature of the mystical
experience to discharge itself in action—so much so that a mysticism which stops short
at ecstasy, without going on to tread the agonizing but creative path of return to the
World from which the mystic has previously withdrawn, is thereby virtually confessing
itself to be a mysticism *manqué*. Indeed, the very source and fountain-head of creation
in social affairs is this non-social experience of religious or aesthetic or intellectual
ecstacy which the psychological movement of 'Withdrawal-and-Return' enables rare
souls to attain. Thus, while it is true that there are certain human experiences which
do not take the form of relations with other human beings, it cannot be said that these
non-social experiences have nothing to do with social life. On the contrary, these non-
social experiences are socially creative just because they are individually intense; and it
is their potent social effect that gives them part—though, of course, only part—of the
importance which they are universally recognized as possessing.

are maintained through social mechanisms called institutions. Without institutions, societies could not exist. Indeed, societies themselves are simply institutions of the highest order—institutions, that is, which comprehend without being comprehended by others.[1] The study of societies and the study of institutional relations are one and the same thing.[2]

We can see at once that the quantity of 'data' confronting students of institutional relations is very much smaller than the quantity confronting students of personal relations. This follows directly from the two points in our definition of institutional relations: first, that they are relations with a wider range than personal contacts, and, second, that they are maintained through social mechanisms (unlike personal relations, which maintain themselves spontaneously). We can see further that the quantity of recorded institutional relations that are relevant to the study of primitive societies will be considerably greater than the quantity of those relevant to the study of civilizations, inasmuch as the number of extant primitive societies runs to more than 650,[3] whereas our survey of civilizations both extant and extinct has not so far enabled us to identify more than twenty-one of these, even when we include in our reckoning the ten representatives of the species whose claims to a distinct and separate existence may be challenged.[4] Now six or seven hundred instances of a phenomenon, while far from necessitating the employment of the technique known as 'fiction', are just enough to enable students to make a beginning in the elucidation and formulation of general laws; and this is, as we have seen, the stage which the infant science of Anthropology has reached to-day. On the other hand, students of a phenomenon of which only one dozen or two dozen instances are known can hardly do more than tabulate the facts; and this, as we have seen, is the stage in which 'History', in the sense of the study of social life in civilizations, has remained so far.

At first sight it may seem a paradox to assert that the quantity of 'data' which students of civilizations have at their command is inconveniently small, when our modern Western historians are complaining that they are being overwhelmed by the multitude and the mass of their materials. The paradox vanishes if we recall our observation—made at an earlier point in this Study[5]—that this complaint arises from a hallucination. Our historians cannot see the wood for the trees; and, being unable to distinguish parts from

[1] This is merely a statement in objective terms of the proposition that societies are the 'intelligible fields of study'. (See Part I. A, and p. 443, above.)
[2] For the nature of these institutional relations, see further III. C (ii) (a), vol. iii, below.
[3] See p. 148, above.
[4] See I. C (ii), above.   [5] See Part I. A, pp. 3-4 and 6, above.

wholes, they disintegrate the twenty-one 'intelligible fields of study' which are the only true integers on the board into an innumerable quantity of minute fractions and then complain of the chaos which they themselves have brought about. The legion of facts with which they believe themselves to be beset are phantoms conjured up by some pathological refraction of their mental vision. In reality, the integral 'facts' confronting students of civilizations are not overwhelmingly numerous, like the trees in a forest or the sands on the sea-shore or the integral 'facts' of personal relations. On the contrary, they are inconveniently few. In this study, the known number of 'facts' of the highest order—that is, the known number of the civilizations themselves—amounts up to date to twenty-one and no more.

Having thus cleared the ground, we may sum up the results of our present inquiry tentatively as follows. Our three techniques are intrinsically suited for dealing respectively with quantities of 'data' in different orders of magnitude; and their spheres of application are at least partially determined by this quantitative factor, whatever the nature of the 'data' may be. On the other hand, the techniques have no intrinsically and rigorously determined qualitative provinces; and the popular equations in which the three techniques are severally equated with the study of three different kinds of relations between human beings are found to be inaccurate. In each of these three studies, all the three techniques are actually employed. At the same time, the popular equations, though inaccurate, hold good as a rule; for in each study one particular technique is employed predominantly, while the other two play subordinate roles. This is perhaps largely because the quantities of 'data' at present confronting students of these different kinds of relations happen to differ in order of magnitude in degrees which render one or other technique at present particularly suitable for employment in one or other study on quantitative grounds.

At this point we can observe that the quantitative difference between the amounts of the 'data' which present themselves in the field of each of the three studies is not on a par with the qualitative differences between the natures of the relations which are the objects of study and between the natures of the techniques employed. The differences between the objects of study and between the techniques are intrinsic, invariable, and absolute; the difference in the quantities of 'data' is accidental, variable, and relative to the passage of Time. In the nature of things, the instances of any phenomenon or any experience tend to multiply so long as the phenomenon continues to appear or the experience to occur, and the representatives of a species tend to multiply so long

as the species continues to exist; and, if these instances and representatives are regarded as 'data' for study, it is evident that the
'data' for the study of any object whatsoever will tend, as they
multiply, to travel successively through the spheres of application
of our three techniques so far as Time allows. At the outset, the
'data' will always be so few that the establishment and record of
particular facts will be all that is either possible or necessary as a
rule; and if the phenomenon ceases to appear or the experience
ceases to be experienced or the species becomes extinct before this
quantity of 'data' has been exceeded, the occasion for employing
either of the other two techniques will seldom arise. If, however,
Time allows the 'data' to accumulate to a quantity too numerous
to tabulate but not too numerous to survey, then it will become
both possible and necessary to handle the same 'data'—which will
have changed in quantity merely and not in kind—by the elucidation and formulation of general laws through a process of comparative study (the ascertainment and record of particular facts
still retaining a value for certain purposes). Finally, if Time spares
the phenomenon or the experience or the species so long that the
quantity of the 'data' becomes innumerable, then students will
have to fall back upon the technique of 'fiction'; and the other two
techniques will become less and less possible to employ and at the
same time also less and less worth employing.

It is evident that the 'data' for some studies will accumulate
more rapidly than those for others. For instance, the 'data' for the
study of personal relations are so prolific that for practical purposes the periods during which they were travelling through the
two spheres of fact-finding and law-making may be ignored. In a
flash, both these periods had been left behind, before Man had
realized that he had become himself and long before he had
acquired the mental and material means of self-study. In fact, the
'data' for the study of personal relations had already entered the
sphere of application of the technique of 'fiction' before the study
was or could be initiated. On the other hand, the 'data' for the
study of the impersonal relations that are maintained through the
institutions of primitive societies are so much less prolific that in
our generation we can watch the 'data' for this study just passing
out of the sphere of fact-finding into the sphere of law-making.
Again, the 'data' for the study of that other set of impersonal relations that are maintained through the institutions of civilizations
are still so few in number that they have not yet passed the limits
within which the technique of fact-finding can be applied.[1]

[1] While the 'data' consisting of impersonal relations are not numerous up to date, we
have seen that any given impersonal relation, in its nature and in its working, involves—

We have now reached, by a second route, the answer to the question from which our present inquiry started. We set out, in the chapter to which this Annex attaches, to discover whether it was true, as our critics asserted, that every 'fact' encountered in the study of civilizations was intrinsically unique and therefore essentially incomparable with any other fact in the same field. We have now ascertained that the true facts in this field—that is, the facts which are integral and therefore intelligible—are at present not unmanageably numerous, as our critics suppose them to be, but inconveniently few. We have discerned that this smallness of the quantity of the integral 'data' that are to be found in this field up to date will account for the fact (which we freely admit) that in the study of civilizations hitherto the technique of fact-finding has been predominantly (though, as we have shown, by no means exclusively) employed. We now arrive at the conclusion that the facts encountered in the study of social life in civilizations are not unique intrinsically but only accidentally and provisionally, pending the multiplication of the data to a quantity suitable for the application of the technique in which laws are elucidated and formulated through a process of comparative study. In fine, the facts encountered in the study of social life in civilizations are not incomparable essentially or *a priori*.

Are they comparable in the quantity which is at our command here and now? Our critics may seize upon our observation that the study of institutional relations in primitive societies has not begun to employ the comparative, law-making technique until the number of integral facts of the highest order—that is, the number, known to students, of such societies themselves—has risen to a figure exceeding six hundred. In the study of institutional relations in civilizations, where the known number of integral facts of the highest order has not yet risen, on the most liberal reckoning, above the modest figure of twenty-one, can we seriously hope to apply the comparative method without having to allow for a margin of error relatively so wide that it will stultify our efforts by eliminating all certainty from our results? Notwithstanding the increase in the number of known civilizations which has been achieved by the recent discoveries of our Western archaeologists,[1] are we appreciably better equipped in our day for attempting a comparative study of civilizations than a Freeman and a de

in the multitude of human beings partaking in the relation—an innumerable factor which cannot be presented except intuitively by the technique of fiction. Thus, paradoxically, the fact-finding technique is applied in the study of social life in civilizations, and the law-making technique in the study of social life in primitive societies, to 'data' which are themselves presented in the form of fictions.

[1] For an appreciation of the value of these discoveries see, above, the note at the end of I. B (iv), Annex; footnote 1 on p. 129 in I. C (ii); and p. 157 in I. C (iii) (b).

Gobineau were in their day or a Gibbon and a Voltaire in theirs?
In the empirical spirit in which we propose to conduct this study
throughout, we may reply (as we have replied, on occasion,
already): 'Wait and see.' At our own peril, we intend to hazard the
attempt; and, through our failure or success, our critics' question
will answer itself.

There is one assertion, however, which we can make here and
now with confidence. If the quantity of 'data' available for the
study of civilizations grows beyond the present modest figure and
accumulates *ad infinitum*, it will not only become possible, without
question, to employ in this study the comparative, law-making
technique; it will eventually become patently impossible to employ
any technique except that of 'fiction'. The sole but indispensable
condition for the eventual supremacy of the technique of 'fiction'
in the domain of 'History' is the passage of Time without the
annihilation of the record.

This condition might be realized in either or both of two
possible ways: either through the rescue from oblivion of civilizations which have come and gone and been forgotten in the past, or
through the rise and fall and commemoration of fresh civilizations
in the future.

When human minds contemplate the passage of Time, they
often dwell upon the oblivion of human affairs which has followed
in the train of Time's passage in the past—whether or not they
believe, or play with the belief, that the record of the past is not
obliterated beyond all hope of decipherment. This attitude of
mind may be illustrated by two passages of Western poetry, one
inspired by the Syriac tradition and the other by the Hellenic:

> A thousand ages in thy sight
>   Are like an evening gone,
> Short as the watch that ends the night
>   Before the rising Sun.

> Time, like an ever rolling stream,
>   Bears all its sons away;
> They fly forgotten, as a dream
>   Dies at the opening day.

Isaac Watts is presenting, in Hebrew imagery, the same poetic
vision that Shelley beholds with Hellenic eyes:

> Worlds on worlds are rolling ever
>   From creation to decay
> Like the bubbles on a river
>   Sparkling, bursting, borne away.

The same idea is prosaically expressed by a Byzantine historian whose mind was formed through an education in the Hellenic humanities:

'Time, flowing unrestrainably and always on the move, carries away and carries off all things that come into being and engulfs them in the deep sea of oblivion, whether they be things not worth a song or things great and memorable. In the language of Tragedy, Time bringeth what was not to birth, and as for that which hath seen the Light, lo, Time shroudeth it and it is gone.'[1]

For an expression of the idea which is at once poetically imaginative and intellectually precise we may turn to the Hellenic philosopher who was Anna's and Shelley's master: Plato himself. The following passage occurs in the dialogue called *The Laws*:[2]

ATHENIAN STRANGER. . . . What is to be our theory of the origins of political life? I know the angle of vision which commends itself to me.

CLEINIAS OF CRETE. What angle?

ATH. The same angle that gives a perspective of the evolution of communities for better or for worse as the case may be.

CL. And what angle is that?

ATH. Why, the angle of the duration—the infinite duration—of Time and the changes proper to that medium.

CL. I don't understand.

ATH. Well, do you think that you could ever estimate the length of time that has elapsed since communities, and people living in them, first came into existence?

CL. Not at all an easy estimate to make!

ATH. You mean, it would be an enormous, overwhelming length of time?

CL. It would indeed.

ATH. Then must we not suppose that myriads upon myriads of communities have come into existence in this length of time and that, in the same ratio, as many myriads have been destroyed? And that in these communities, during their existence, every form of political life has been tried, many times over, in every part of the World? And that they have passed through all the permutations of increase and diminution in size and of improvement and deterioration in quality?

CL. One cannot suppose otherwise.

This intuition of the immense possibilities of oblivion through the passage of Time in the past has flashed upon Plato's inner vision without any ocular demonstration from the archaeologist's spade.[3] Had Plato lived in our generation in a world in which our

---

[1] Anna Comnena in her *Alexias, ad init.* Ῥέων ὁ χρόνος ἀκάθεκτα καὶ ἀεί τι κινούμενος παρασύρει καὶ παραφέρει πάντα τὰ ἐν γενέσει καὶ ἐς βαθὺ ἀφανείας καταποντοῖ ὅπου μὲν οὐκ ἄξια ⸆λιθιου⸆ πράγματα, ὅπου δὲ μεγάλα καὶ ἄξια μνήμης, καὶ τά τε ἄδηλα φύων κατὰ τὴν τραγῳδίαν καὶ τὰ φανέντα κρυπτόμενος. This is, of course, merely Anna's version of a Byzantine commonplace which has found its way into the prefaces of a number of Byzantine historians and which is perhaps originally a learned reminiscence of the famous exordium of Herodotus. [2] Plato: *Leges*, 676.

[3] In Plato's world in Plato's age, the Minoan palaces at Cnossos and Phaestus were buried out of sight, and the walls of Tiryns and Mycenae dominated the landscape of the

Western archaeologists have disinterred no less than seven buried and forgotten civilizations[1] during the century and a half that has passed since Volney wrote *Les Ruines*,[2] he would assuredly have presented his conjecture as a certainty. Would his judgement have been right? That is to say, is it probable that our archaeologists are to-day only at the beginning of their discoveries, and that, a few generations or a few centuries hence, the tale of forgotten civilizations that will have been rescued from oblivion since the end of the eighteenth century of the Christian Era[3] will have grown from seven to seventy or seven hundred? Such a prospect seems decidedly improbable to-day, though the present state of our archaeological knowledge would hardly warrant our denying the possibility dogmatically. On the whole, it seems more probable that in broad outline the picture of the history of civilizations which has been painted for us by the archaeological discoveries of the last century and a half is now substantially complete, and that future research, while greatly increasing our knowledge of detail, will not extend our range of historical vision in this domain more than perhaps one millennium farther back into the past, and will not add more than perhaps one or two still disinterred civilizations to the tale of its new discoveries. The fact that the picture, as we now have it, is incomparably vaster and fuller than the picture which we had before our archaeologists first set to work gives no ground for expecting that, after the archaeologists have remained at work for as long a period again, the picture will have been enlarged and articulated further to anything like the same degree.[4] It is more likely that the final effect of our archaeological research, when it eventually reaches the limits of what it can achieve, will be to refute Plato's brilliant conjecture by demonstrating conclusively that the age, up to date, of the species of human societies called civilizations

Argive plain without arousing sufficient curiosity among Plato's contemporaries to make them dig among the foundations. The record of Minoan history in the Hellenic tradition was reduced to a tenuous thread of legend: the Thalassocracy, the Labyrinth, the Minotaur. Still, it is at least a curious coincidence that Plato should have chosen Crete for the site of the imaginary commonwealth of *The Laws*, and it is an interesting suggestion that the legend of Atlantis which captivated Plato's imagination may have been an echo of the westward expansion of the Minoan Society in its latest age.

[1] These seven civilizations are the Egyptiac, Sumeric, Babylonic, Hittite, Minoan, Yucatec, and Mayan; and the number rises to eight if 'the Indus Culture' is entitled to take an independent place, side by side with the Sumeric, as a civilization in its own right. On the other hand, the Indic and the Sinic civilizations cannot be included in the list; for although the knowledge of their existence came as a new discovery to Western scholars, it had never been forgotten by scholars in the 'affiliated' Hindu and Far Eastern societies.

[2] Volney, C. F., Comte de: *Les Ruines, ou Méditation sur les Révolutions des Empires* (1st edition, Paris 1791).

[3] The rediscovery, by Western archaeologists, of civilizations of which no memory had survived in the living tradition of any extant society may be said to have been begun by the French savants who landed in Egypt with Napoleon in A.D. 1798.

[4] In venturing this opinion, we can support it by the authority of Eduard Meyer. See his *Geschichte des Altertums*, vol. i (i), 4th edition (Stuttgart and Berlin 1921, Cotta), p. 212.

is extremely young by comparison with the age of the species called primitive societies and with the age of the Human Race and with the age of life on the Planet and with the age of the Planet itself.[1]

We have still to consider the possibility that, in the future, as many myriads of civilizations may come into existence and pass out of existence again as Plato imagined to have come and gone in the past; and on this question, on which our archaeologists are necessarily silent, we may ask the opinion of our astronomers. Here is one opinion:

'Take a postage-stamp, and stick it on to a penny. Now climb Cleopatra's Needle and lay the penny flat, postage-stamp uppermost, on top of the obelisk. The height of the whole structure may be taken to represent the time that has elapsed since the Earth was born. On this scale, the thickness of the penny and postage-stamp together represents the time that Man has lived on Earth. The thickness of the postage-stamp represents the time he has been civilised, the thickness of the penny representing the time he lived in an uncivilised state. Now stick another postage-stamp on top of the first to represent the next 5,000 years of civilisation, and keep sticking on postage-stamps until you have a pile as high as Mont Blanc. Even now the pile forms an inadequate representation of the length of the future which, so far as Astronomy can see, probably stretches before Civilised Humanity. The first postage-stamp was the past of Civilisation; the column higher than Mont Blanc is its future. Or, to look at it in another way, the first postage-stamp represents what Man has already achieved; the pile which out-tops Mont Blanc represents what he may achieve if his future achievement is proportional to his time on Earth.'[2]

When the astronomer changes his medium of expression from imagery to figures, he tells us[3] that the Earth—which has existed up to date for about 2,000 million years altogether, and for about 300 million years as a habitat of Life, and for about 300,000 years as a habitat of Man, and for 5,000 or 6,000 as a habitat of civilizations—may remain habitable from now onwards for another 1,000,000 million years. In order to be on the safe side, let us halve this astronomical figure in applying it to the expectation of life of the species of human societies called civilizations.[4] On this 'conservative estimate', the species has at least 500,000 million years still ahead of it, as against the 5,000 or 6,000 years that are already

---

[1] On this point see I. C (iii) (c), above, especially p. 173, footnote 2.
[2] Jeans, Sir James: The Universe Around Us (Cambridge 1929, University Press), p. 342. [3] Jeans, op. cit., pp. 337–43.
[4] We must allow for the possibility that the figure itself may be excessive for any form of Life, and for the further possibility that the Earth may cease to be habitable for civilizations, or for human beings, or for mammalia, before it ceases to be habitable for any form of Life at all. This second possibility does not, on the whole, seem probable; for, in a struggle to survive under increasingly adverse physical conditions, the mental intelligence of Man will surely prove a more valuable asset, in the last resort, than the physical simplicity of the Amoeba.

behind it: that is to say, its present expectation of life is more than 83 million times as great as its present age. Let us assume, for the moment,[1] that, during these 83,000,000 × 6,000 years which are apparently to come, human affairs continue to be governed with as little wisdom as has been shown in their government during the 5,000 or 6,000 years that have actually passed since the first civilizations emerged;[2] or, in other words, let us assume that the expectation of life of any given specimen of the species remains as short as it has been hitherto. On this basis, a simple calculation shows that, if the species has thrown up 21 representatives of itself in 6,000 years, then, before the day of civilizations is done, the number of them that will have come and gone from first to last will be in the order of magnitude of $21 \times 83,000,000 = 1,743,000,000$!

Placing ourselves in the position of historians in those latter days, we have to imagine ourselves confronted by 1,743 million instances of the phenomena of civilizations; their geneses and growths and breakdowns and disintegrations, their universal states and universal churches and heroic ages, their contacts in Time and in Space. Imagine 1,743 million completed histories, each of which has been as long and as lively as the history of the Hellenic Society; 1,743 million reproductions of the Roman Empire and the Catholic Church and the Teutonic Völkerwanderung; 1,743 million repetitions of the relations between our Western Society and the Hellenic and between our Western Society and the other societies that are alive to-day! Our powers of imagination fail. By what technique should we handle historical 'data' that had accumulated in quantities so great as these? In this situation, the integral, intelligible facts in the histories of civilizations would really have become as unmanageably numerous as our present historians—mistaking fractions for integers and parts for wholes—erroneously suppose them to be now. In this historical landscape of the future,

[1] This assumption, while perhaps more reasonable than any other, is not, of course, beyond challenge. On this point, see further IV. C (i), vol. iv, pp. 9–10, as well as Parts XI and XII, below.

[2] The famous phrase was not coined until the species of societies called civilizations had been in existence for as long as 5,000 years. It was coined in the seventeenth century of the Christian Era, in the Western World, as a comment on the government of Western states during the so-called modern age of Western history. The new Western statecraft had been worked out experimentally on a miniature scale in Northern Italy towards the latter end of 'the Middle Ages' (see p. 19, above); since the close of the fifteenth century, it had been communicated to the Western World at large; and before the close of the seventeenth century it had brought forth its fruits in sufficient abundance to be known by them. This bitter knowledge was enshrined in an anonymous saying which can be found in the works of a famous seventeenth-century man of letters and will be searched for in vain among the writings of a famous seventeenth-century man of action to whom the coinage of the phrase has come to be ascribed. 'Thou little thinkest what a little foolerye governs the whole world' (Selden: Table Talk: ed. Pollock, p. 97; see also Note (a)); 'Quam, mi fili, parva sapientia mundus regitur' or 'Quantula sapientia nos regamur' (the variant forms in which the saying has been ascribed—though, at earliest, not until about fifty years after his death—to Axel Oxenstierna). For these references, the author of this Study is indebted to the kindness and the scholarship of Professor Harold J. Laski.

the features which loom largest in our present-day landscape—the Catholic Church, the Roman Empire—would be scarcely visible through the most powerful lens of the specialist's microscope. To require a specialist in universal states to identify our actual Roman Empire among the 1,743 million extant specimens of the institution would be to set him Psyche's task. To ask him to formulate the laws implicit in the workings of universal states would be to assume him capable of a synoptic vision beyond the capacity of human intelligence. Then by what technique could this hard-driven latter-day historian communicate the results of his studies to his contemporaries' minds? Only, perhaps, by the technique called 'fiction' which our dramatists and novelists employ in our time in order to communicate to their fellow men their thoughts and feelings about the personal relations of human beings—about those human loves and deaths, those personal successes and failures, those individual hopes and fears, which have repeated themselves, since Mankind became human, until their name is legion.

This distant prospect may daunt our minds, but it elates our hearts; for Hope steps in where Knowledge shrinks back abashed, and, flinging herself upon the abyss of Time, she flies forward invincibly to the farthest verge that Science reveals, irradiating the formidable void with the colour and warmth of Life. Here is the astronomer's vision translated into the language of a man of action:

'We have time in front of us. I do think that our political views are still to an immense degree coloured and over-coloured by the theological conceptions of the past. I am old enough to have been brought up to believe that the World was actually manufactured four thousand and four years before Christ, and also to believe that it might come to an end at any minute and almost certainly would come to an end in the next few generations. No doubt a decreasing number of people hold those views now; but they have been held so long in the Christian World that I honestly think they have coloured our political conceptions and have helped to bring about this feeling of a practical statesman that a man who is talking of results which can only be brought about generations ahead is not a practical person and you need not listen to him. If Science has taught us anything it is this, that in all human and reasonable probability we have more time in front of us than the anthropologists have shown that we have behind us; and I submit to you that it is not only practicable but wise to hold in front of our minds the goal to which we are travelling, . . . not to lose sight of the vision of the New Jerusalem descending on Earth itself as something which may be realised, and to hold in mind that memorable saying of the Book of Proverbs: "Where there is no vision, the people perish." '[1]

[1] Curtis, Lionel: Lecture delivered at the Institute of Politics, Williamstown, Mass., on the 28th July 1925.

THE HISTORICAL ANTECEDENTS OF THE VEIN OF RUTHLESSNESS IN THE MODERN ENGLISH METHOD OF OVERSEAS SETTLEMENT

THE wholesale extermination of the previously established population, which has distinguished our English method of overseas settlement from the method of overseas settlement practised by most other West-European peoples in modern times, is a trait which likewise distinguished the settlement of the English on the territories of the Roman Empire from the settlement of the other Barbarians during the interregnum which followed the break-up of the Empire and the dissolution of the Hellenic Society. In that Völkerwanderung, most of the Barbarian war-bands from beyond the former frontiers simply stepped into the shoes of the former Roman soldiers and officials—taking their places in ruling and exploiting the provincials, in the same fashion as in the New World, a dozen centuries later, the Spanish conquistadores took the place of the Aztecs and the Incas. The English war-bands alone more or less exterminated the local provincials in the provinces which they overran, and re-populated the country themselves,[1] instead of being content to rule and exploit the population which they found there, just as, a dozen centuries later, it was the English settlers alone who exterminated the population which they found in the New World. Thus, on two occasions, many centuries apart, the English have distinguished themselves from their fellows and contemporaries by a peculiar ruthlessness in their treatment of an alien population which they have conquered.

Is this repeated appearance in the same distinctive role no more than a coincidence, or were these two bouts of English ruthlessness historically connected, notwithstanding the long interval of time by which they are separated chronologically? Was there some tradition of ruthlessness towards 'Natives' which may have been driven under the surface or into a corner without ever quite dying out of English life? Conceivably there was; for we may observe that, at the time when the English began to settle in North America, their settlement of the British Isles was still incomplete. The movement which had turned the greater part of the *ci-devant* Roman island of Britain into English soil during the Völker-

---

[1] The results of recent research tend, on the whole, to diminish the blackness of the traditional picture; yet the replacement, in Britain, of the conquered people's language by that of the conquerors, in contrast to the survival of the Latin vernaculars on the Continent, is a hard fact which tells a tale.

wanderung in the post-Hellenic interregnum had slowed down before the previous population had been exterminated in every corner of the island; and the struggle for existence between invaders and invaded had become transformed into a border warfare which was conducted with all the old ferocity but without the old decisiveness in its results. Thus the tradition of the first English settlers in Roman Britain was kept alive in the English Marches on the fringe of Wales and along the line which divided the Lowlands from the Highlands of Scotland; and this ferocious frontier spirit afterwards asserted itself along the border between the Kingdoms of England and Scotland (though here the frontiersmen on both sides came of the same English stock) and also along the line of the Irish Pale.

In the seventeenth century of our era, the Governments of England and Scotland under all régimes—in the reign of James I and under the protectorate of Cromwell—were as active in 'planting' Ireland and the Hebrides with settlers from England and the Lowlands of Scotland as they were in 'planting' the Atlantic seaboard of North America; and on both frontiers the attitude towards the 'Natives'—whether 'Wild Highlanders' or 'Wild Irish' or 'Red Indians'—was the same. The 'Natives' were to be uprooted, in order that the settlers of English stock, from England and the Scottish Lowlands, might be planted in their stead. Thus, for a century or more, the border warfare which had never ceased in the British Isles since the time of the Völkerwanderung was going on in the British Isles and in North America contemporaneously. In the British Isles, this border warfare was brought to an end, during the half century between the Battle of the Boyne and the Battle of Culloden, by the complete union of the Kingdoms of England and Scotland and the complete subjugation of the Scottish Highlanders and the 'Wild Irish' to the authority of the United Kingdom. Therewith, the frontiersmen found their occupation gone, and their craft at a discount, on all the extinct frontiers—in Ulster and on the Border and along 'the Highland Line'—and many of them emigrated to the Indian frontier of the North American plantations, where, in following their habitual pursuits, they would still be looked upon as performing a public service rather than as leading a life of lawlessness and crime.

These were the ancestors of the 'Indian-fighters' who, in less than a century, carried the frontier of the United States from the Appalachian Mountains to the Pacific coast, exterminating the Indians as they advanced. It has been remarked that these English-speaking Protestant frontiersmen became assimilated to their Indian foes and victims—in dress, in habits, and above all in ferocity—

and that, as soon as they had completed the extermination of the Indians, they died out themselves (except in the fastnesses of the Appalachians, where their descendants are living the old life to this day). An assimilation between the Indian-fighters and the Indians certainly did take place, as usually happens on barbarian frontiers of this kind.[1] At the same time, it may not be fanciful to suggest that, in this instance, the assimilation was facilitated by the fact that the English-speaking Protestant frontiersmen in the New World had brought with them a ruthless tradition of their own which had been handed down unmitigated from an age when their forefathers had been no better than Red Indians themselves.

> When Severn down to Buildwas ran
> Coloured with the death of man,
> Couched upon her brother's grave
> The Saxon got me on the slave.
>
> The sound of fight is silent long
> That began the ancient wrong;
> Long the voice of tears is still
> That wept of old the endless ill.
>
> In my heart it has not died,
> The war that sleeps on Severn side;
> They cease not fighting, east and west,
> On the marches of my breast.[2]

[1] See II. D (vii), vol. ii, p. 312, and V. C (i) (*d*) 6 (α), vol. v, pp. 478–80, as well as Part VIII, below.

[2] Housman, A. E.: *A Shropshire Lad*. For the assimilation of Indian-fighters to Indians, see Turner, F. J.: *The Frontier in American History* (New York 1921, Holt), especially the eloquent passage on p. 4; for the historical connexion between the old English frontiers in the British Isles and the new English frontier in North America during the seventeenth century, see Macleod, W. C.: *The American Indian Frontier* (London 1928, Kegan Paul), ch. xiii: 'Celt and Indian: Britain's Old World Frontier in Relation to the New', especially the evidence, cited on pp. 153–4 and 168–9, which shows that some of the seventeenth-century 'Indian-fighters' on the American frontier had been first apprenticed in the British Isles by fighting the Scottish Highlanders and 'the Wild Irish', and the evidence, cited on p. 161, for James VI/I's policy of extermination in the Scottish Highlands. For the latter-day barbarism of the Appalachian 'Mountain People', see further II. D (vii), vol. ii, pp. 310–12, below.

DAVID HUME'S CONCEPTION OF THE FUNCTION OF ENVIRONMENT AS A FACTOR IN THE GENESES OF CIVILIZATIONS

OUR inquiry into the rival claims of Race and Environment to be regarded as possible positive factors in the geneses of civilizations will be manifestly incomplete unless we take some account of the views of a great eighteenth-century Western philosopher who was familiar with the Hellenic Environment-theory but who lived and died before the modern Western Race-theory had been distilled out of the theology of Protestantism by the genius of a de Gobineau.

As we have remarked, in passing, above,[1] the latter-day attempt of a certain school of Western thought to explain the empirically observed differences between one human society and another as the outward visible signs of an inward and innate diversity of Race is scarcely anticipated by Hume—apart from a footnote to his essay *Of National Characters* (published in A.D. 1748), in which he admits to a suspicion that 'the Negroes' are 'naturally inferior to the Whites',[2] and another passage in the same essay, in which he suggests that 'the manners of a people change very considerably from one age to another either by great alterations in their government, by the mixtures of new people, or by that inconstancy to which all human affairs are subject'. It will be seen that, in this passage, Hume mentions Race merely as one possible factor out of three; and while, in the illustrations with which he proceeds to support his proposition, he seems to regard a change of race as being responsible for the striking contrast in national character between the ancient and the modern inhabitants of Greece and of Britain, he apparently does not contemplate a racial explanation of the equally striking contrasts between the ancient and modern inhabitants of Rome and Spain and Holland.

Hume virtually ignores the Race-theory in order to concentrate his attention upon the Environment-theory which had once been paramount in the Hellenic World; but here, again, he considers

---

[1] In II. C (ii) (*a*) 1, on p. 216, footnote 2.

[2] Ibn Khaldūn concurs with Hume in tentatively admitting the possibility that the inhabitants of the extreme climates—that is, the First or Equatorial and the Seventh or Arctic Climate—may be racially inferior to the rest of Mankind. But, with this possible exception, he insists upon the racial equality of all members of the Human Race; and he explains the inferiority of the Magribī culture to the Eastern Islamic culture in his own time as the outcome of a historical difference in the respective social environments of the two regions in question, as against the vulgar view that this inferiority of culture reflected an innate inferiority of racial quality. (*Muqaddamāt*, translated by de Slane, Baron McG. (Paris 1863–8, Imprimerie Impériale, 3 vols.), vol. ii, pp. 445–8.)

the claims of the Physical Environment only to reject these claims outright.

'As to physical causes, I am inclined to doubt altogether of their operation in this particular; nor do I think that men owe anything of their temper or genius to the air, food or climate. . . . If we run over the globe or revolve the annals of history, we shall discover everywhere signs of a sympathy or contagion of manners,[1] none of the influence of air or climate.'

In support of this contention, which runs counter to the paramount Hellenic doctrine, Hume cites the authority of the Hellenic social geographer Strabo;[2] and he also presents some telling illustrations of his own under no less than nine heads: the uniformity of national character throughout China, in spite of the climatic diversity between one region and another of the Chinese Empire; the contrast in manners between ancient Athens and Thebes,[3] or between eighteenth-century Wapping and St. James's; the contrast in temperament between the contemporary populations on either side of the Pyrenees; the uniformity of the Jewish or the Armenian or the Jesuit *diasporà* with itself, however far it may be flung, and its constant difference from the various local majorities among which it is dispersed; the contrast between the Turks and Greeks who were geographically intermingled, in Hume's day, in the Ottoman Empire;[4] the diversity in manners between the Spanish, English, French, and Dutch colonies in the Tropics owing to their respective persistence in the diverse manners which had been imported by the colonists from their several mother-countries in the West-European section of the Northern Temperate Zone; the differences in manners between the successive inhabitants of certain countries in different ages; the almost Chinese social uniformity of 'the Franks' from Tromsö to Cadiz; with an exception, proving the rule, in the unparalleled social variety of the English.

'The only observation with regard to the difference of men in different climates on which we can rest any weight is the vulgar one that people in the northern regions have a greater inclination to strong liquors and those in the southern to love of women'—but here, too, Hume gives reasons for thinking that 'perhaps the matter may be accounted for by moral causes'.[5] Otherwise Hume

---

[1] The passage of this essay in which Hume points out the potency of Mimesis in human affairs has been quoted already in this Study in Part II. B, p. 191, footnote 2, above.

[2] The relevant passage of Strabo will be found in his *Geographica*, Book II, p. 103.

[3] For a discussion of this contrast between Athens and Thebes, see the present Study, II. D (ii), vol. ii, pp. 37–42, below.

[4] For the group-characteristics of διασποραί and other penalized minorities, see II. D (vi), vol. ii, below, *passim*.

[5] Hume, *Of National Characters, ad fin.*

comes—apparently quite independently—to the same conclusion as the Arabic philosopher Ibn Khaldūn. He rejects altogether the climatic explanation of the empirically observed differences between the various peoples of the Northern Temperate Zone—between those peoples, that is to say, among whom, alone, the societies of the species called civilizations have arisen in the Old World hitherto—and he is only prepared, and this rather dubiously, to recognize climate as a possible differentiating factor in regions where the climatic conditions are at their extremes. 'There is some reason to think that all the nations which live beyond the Polar Circles, or between the Tropics, are inferior to the rest of the species and are incapable of all the higher attainments of the human mind.' But he adds the suggestion that 'the poverty and misery of the northern inhabitants of the globe, and the indolence of the southern, from their few necessities, may perhaps account for this remarkable difference, without having recourse to physical causes'.[1]

Thus Hume not only ignores Race but, for practical purposes, rejects the Physical or Climatic Environment into the bargain as a possible cause of the actual difference in cultural achievement between one human society and another. The social environment is the differentiating factor to which Hume ascribes almost exclusive, and at the same time almost unlimited, potency.

In his essay *Of National Characters* he draws attention to the stock professional characters of priests and soldiers, which are to be ascribed to the standardizing influence that is exerted upon diverse individual characters by the respective social environments of these

---

[1] Ibn Khaldūn is likewise prepared to ascribe a differentiating effect to climatic influences in Climates I and II (i.e. the Tropics) and VI and VII (i.e. the Arctic Regions), but not in Climates III, IV, and V (the Northern Temperate Zone). He observes that both the Negro savages in the Tropics and the White savages (Slavs, Franks, Turks) in the Arctic Regions live almost like wild beasts. (Ibn Khaldūn: *Muqaddamāt*, French translation by de Slane, Baron (Paris 1863–8, Imprimerie Impériale, 3 vols.), vol. i, pp. 169–70.) Ibn Khaldūn also ascribes the gaiety of the Negro temperament to the physical effect of the tropical heat. He adds that a kindred tendency to take no thought for the morrow can be observed among the inhabitants of Egypt and of a district on the coast of Ifrīqīyah called the Jarīd—the climate of both the Jarīd and Egypt being exceptionally hot for their latitudes. As a contrast to the light-hearted êthos of the inhabitants of hot countries, he cites the êthos of the inhabitants of the Moroccan city of Fez. Fez is encompassed by cold uplands, and the people of Fez behave accordingly. When you see them as they walk through the streets, you would imagine that they were all plunged in gloom; and it is their practice to keep a reserve stock of food in their houses. Rather than break into this reserve, they will go to the trouble and expense of going out marketing (Ibn Khaldūn, op. cit., vol. i, pp. 174–5). Incidentally, Ibn Khaldūn avails himself of this concession which he makes to the Physical Environment theory of differentiation in the extreme cases in order to avoid being compelled to make any concession at all to the Race-theory. He maintains (in op. cit., vol. i, pp. 170–4) that the outstanding external differences in human physique—e.g. the difference between black and white skins—are not innate characteristics deriving from a racial inheritance but are the outcome of climatic influences. Like Professor Boas (see II. C (ii) (a) 1, p. 220, footnote 2, above), Ibn Khaldūn believes that physical characteristics change as a result of migration from one climatic environment to another. According to Ibn Khaldūn, Negroes who go north eventually turn White, while Whites who go to the Tropics eventually blacken into Negroes.

two professions. Again, in his essay *Of the Rise and Progress of the Arts and Sciences* (published in A.D. 1742), Hume ascribes the empirically observed differences of capacity and achievement in the cultural sphere to a particular difference in political institutions—the elementary difference between Republicanism and Monarchy —which had been taken by Hellenic thinkers in the fifth century B.C. as an explanation for the empirically observed differences in military valour.[1] 'It is impossible', Hume lays down in this essay, 'for the arts and sciences to arise at first among any people unless

[1] The popularity of this hypothetical correlation between military qualities and political institutions among Hellenic thinkers in the latter part of the fifth century B.C. is indicated by the fact that it is taken by Herodotus (in Book V, ch. 78) to explain the difference in the military prowess of the Athenians before and after the expulsion of the Peisistratidae, and by the author of the Hippocratean treatise on 'Influences of Atmosphere, Water, and Situation' (ch. 16) to explain the difference in military prowess between different communities of Asiatics in the author's own generation.

'The universal currency of the social value of civic equality (ἰσηγορίη) is demonstrated', says Herodotus, 'by the particular instance of the Athenians, who displayed no greater military prowess than their neighbours so long as they were under despotic government, but became far and away the first in the field as soon as they had thrown their despots off. This demonstrates that, so long as they were held down politically, the Athenians were deliberate shirkers on the field of battle because they felt that they were fighting for a master, whereas, when they had secured their freedom, each individual Athenian felt that he was fighting for himself and was therefore game to fight to a finish.'

The corresponding passage in the Hippocratean treatise runs as follows:

'The greater part of Asia is under monarchical government; and wherever men are not their own masters and not free agents, but are under despotic rule, they are not concerned to make themselves militarily efficient but, on the contrary, to avoid being regarded as good military material—the reason being that they are not playing for equal stakes. It is theirs, presumably, to serve and struggle and die under compulsion from their masters and far from the sight of their wives and children and friends. Whenever they acquit themselves like men, it is their masters who are exalted and aggrandized by their achievements, while their own share of the profits is the risking and the losing of their lives. And not only this but, in the case of people so circumstanced, it is also inevitable that the inactivity consequent upon the absence of War should have a taming effect upon the temperament, so that even a naturally courageous and spirited individual would be inhibited mentally by the prevailing institutions. A strong argument in favour of my contention is furnished by the fact that all the Hellenes and non-Hellenes in Asia who are not under despotic rule, but are free agents and struggle for their own benefit, are as warlike as any populations in the World—the reason being that they stake their lives in their own cause and reap the rewards of their own valour (and the penalties of their own cowardice, into the bargain).'

It will be seen that in this passage the author of the Hippocratean treatise finds an explanation, in the influence of the Social or Institutional Environment, not only (like Herodotus) for differences in military prowess, but also (like Hume) for differences in mental achievement. This tribute to the potency of the Social Environment is remarkable when it is remembered that it is made, as a parenthesis, in a treatise which is otherwise devoted to asserting the claims of the Physical or Climatic Environment—and this in an extreme form.

The climatic or regional explanation of differences in social ēthos is likewise rejected, in favour of an institutional explanation, by C. F. Volney, apropos of the Egyptian fallāhīn, in his *Voyage en Syrie et en Égypte pendant les Années 1783, 1784, et 1785* (Paris 1787, Desenne and Volland, 2 vols.), vol. i, pp. 177–86. In op. cit., vol. ii, pp. 422–51, the argument is taken up again by Volney in general terms and in explicit opposition to Montesquieu. On pp. 434–5 of this volume, Volney quotes the passage from the Hippocratean treatise which has been quoted in the present footnote, above. Turgot seems to refer to the same Hippocratean passage in the notes for his *Géographie Politique*. His comment is, 'Nécessité d'avoir épuisé les causes morales avant d'avoir droit d'assurer quelque chose de l'influence physique des climats' (*Œuvres de Turgot*, nouvelle édition (Paris 1844, Guillaumin, 2 vols.), vol. ii, p. 616). This topic is expanded by Turgot—this time, like Volney after him, in explicit opposition to Montesquieu—in his *Plan de Deux Discours sur l'Histoire Universelle* (op. cit., vol. ii, pp. 646–7).

that people enjoy the blessing of a free government'; and, after defending this thesis, he goes on to argue, in detail, 'that though the only proper nursery of these noble plants be a free state, yet may they be transplanted into any government; and that a republic is most favourable to the growth of the sciences, a civilized monarchy to that of the polite arts.'

In his exposition of the differentiating effect of social institutions upon the group-characters of the societies in which the different institutions respectively prevail, Hume shows the acumen that is to be expected of him. Yet, if his analysis ended here, it would carry us no farther than the point which we have reached in this Study as it is, without Hume's aid. For social institutions can only be regarded as a proximate, and never as an ultimate, cause of social conditions—and this for the simple reason that the institutions themselves are part and parcel of the conditions in question.

To take the cases in point, we may have succeeded in proving to our own satisfaction that a republican government is favourable, and a monarchical government inimical, to the display of military prowess or to the rise and progress of the arts and sciences. We may be able to point to an actual republican government which is patently producing the favourable effect in Attica, and to an actual monarchy which is patently failing to produce it in the Achaemenian Empire. But, when we have got thus far, we have still to discover how this momentous local diversity of political institutions itself has originated. Why, in the fifth century B.C., is the Syriac World united under a single universal monarchy, while the contemporary Hellenic Society is articulated into a multiplicity of tiny republics? Unless and until we can account for the antecedent differentiation of the differentiating institutions, we have accomplished no more than is accomplished by the people who seek to explain the diversity of êthos between fifth-century Athens and fifth-century Sparta by an antecedent diversity of Race.[1] Instead of having found a solution for our problem, we have merely pushed the unsolved problem backwards in Time from the present into the past.

Thus Hume's ascription of the differences in achievement between one society and another to corresponding differences in the several societies' respective institutions is inconclusive. As it happens, however, this is not Hume's last word on the problem under consideration; for we shall find, if we look closer, that Hume has not confined his inquiry to an examination of possible single differentiating factors: the Race-factor and the factors of Physical Environment and Social Environment and the like. He has also

[1] I. B (ii), pp. 25–6, and II. C (ii) (a) 1, pp. 244–5, above.

observed the play of the composite factor of Challenge-and-Response: a form of interaction or encounter which has come to our attention already in this Study, and will continue to occupy our attention throughout the second volume.

In his essay *Of the Rise and Progress of the Arts and Sciences*, Hume has put his finger on a significant historical fact to which we have frequently made reference here already: namely, the fact that, in the Hellenic World, the political field was occupied by a multiplicity of local states before these were all eventually superseded, in the last chapter of Hellenic history, by the single universal state which we call the Roman Empire. Hume has also noticed that, in common contrast to the universality of the Roman Empire, a multiplicity of local states is the political structure of the post-Roman modern Western World, as it was the political structure of pre-Roman Hellas; and in the relationship between a number of communities which are each and all independent politically without being economically or culturally isolated from one another, he has divined the presence of an abundant source of life and growth.

'Nothing is more favourable to the rise of politeness and learning than a number of neighbouring and independent states connected together by commerce and policy. The emulation which naturally arises among those neighbouring states is an obvious source of improvement; but what I would chiefly insist on is the stop which such limited territories give both to power and to authority. . . . Where a number of neighbouring states have a great intercourse of arts and commerce, their mutual jealousy keeps them from receiving too lightly the law from each other in matters of taste and reasoning, and makes them examine every work of art with the greatest care and accuracy. The contagion of popular opinion spreads not so easily from one place to another. It readily receives a check in some state or other, where it concurs not with the prevailing prejudices. And nothing but Nature and Reason, or at least what bears them a strong resemblance, can force its way through all obstacles and unite the most rival nations into an esteem and admiration of it.

'Greece was a cluster of little principalities which soon became republics; and, being united both by their near neighbourhood and by the ties of the same language and interest, they entered into the closest intercourse of commerce and learning. . . . Each city produced its several artists and philosophers, who refused to yield the preference to those of the neighbouring republics; their contention and debates sharpened the wits of men; a variety of objects was presented to the judgement, while each challenged the preference to the rest; and the sciences, not being dwarfed by the restraint of authority, were enabled to make such considerable shoots as are even at this time the objects of our admiration.

'After the Roman Christian or Catholic Church had spread itself over the Civilised World and had engrossed all the learning of the times—being really one large state within itself, and united under one head—this variety of sects immediately disappeared, and the Peripatetic Philosophy was alone admitted into all the schools, to the utter depravation of every kind of learning. But, Mankind having at length thrown off this yoke, affairs are now returned nearly to the same situation as before, and Europe is at present a copy at large of what Greece was formerly a pattern in miniature. . . .

'If we consider the face of the globe, Europe, of all the four parts of the World, is the most broken by seas, rivers and mountains; and Greece of all countries of Europe. Hence these regions were naturally divided into several distinct governments. And hence the sciences arose in Greece, and Europe has been hitherto the most constant habitation of them.'[1]

This diversity in unity and unity in diversity which, as Hume perceives, is characteristic both of Greece in the Hellenic World and of Europe in the Western World in a certain phase of their respective histories, is life-giving to the whole society because each part is constantly presenting challenges to the other parts and is thereby constantly provoking creative responses. And the converse of this truth is the relative deadness of societies that are consolidated into universal churches or universal states: a condition in which, *ex hypothesi*, the stimulus of multiplicity and variety and emulation is absent. Hume perceives that this is true not only of the Catholic Christian universal church but also of the universal state which was stifling the Far Eastern World in Hume's own day.

'In China there seems to be a pretty considerable stock of politeness and science, which in the course of so many centuries might naturally be expected to ripen into something more perfect and finished than what has yet arisen from them. But China is one vast empire, speaking one language, governed by one law, and sympathising in the same manners. The authority of any teacher, such as Confucius, was propagated easily from one corner of the Empire to the other. None had courage to resist the torrent of popular opinion; and posterity was not bold enough to dispute what had been universally received by their

[1] Hume: *Of the Rise and Progress of the Arts and Sciences*. The same idea appears, in a more nebulous form, in Turgot's *Second Discours sur les Progrès Successifs de l'Esprit Humain*, which was delivered at the Sorbonne on the 11th December 1750 (see *Œuvres de Turgot*, nouvelle édition (Paris 1844, Guillaumin, 2 vols.), vol. ii, pp. 602–3). Cf. Meyer, E.: *Geschichte des Altertums*, vol. i (i), 4th edition (Stuttgart and Berlin 1921, Cotta), p. 181. See also Headlam-Morley, J. W.: 'The Cultural Unity of Western Europe', in *The New Past*, ed. by Carter, E. H. (Oxford 1925, Blackwell). In this essay, Headlam-Morley points out (pp. 88–9) that the political pluralism of the Western World has made possible an immense variety of political experimentation; and (p. 93) that 'the political history of the Continent is marked . . . first by the absence of any kind of formal unity; secondly, by the presence of a real underlying unity, which belongs to the spirit and the intellect'. Apropos of the modern Western culture-languages, 'we may say that they were merely dialects, through which the common ideas and common thoughts found a varied expression' (p. 95).

ancestors. This seems to be one natural reason why the sciences have made so slow a progress in that mighty Empire.'[1]

If Hume had pursued his inquiry into Sinic and Far Eastern history, he would have found that the Continental Far Eastern Universal State which was embodied, in the eighteenth century of the Christian Era, in the Manchu Empire was the ghost of a previous Sinic Universal State—the Empire of Ts'in and Han[2]— a ghost which had been conjured up in the sixth century of the Christian Era and had continued to haunt the Far Eastern World ever since. And if he had then transported himself in imagination backwards through time into the age of the Han, and, from that age, had looked before and after over the course of Sinic and Far Eastern history, he would have found himself gazing, *mutatis mutandis*, at the historical landscape with which he was already familiar, nearer home, in ancient Hellas and in the modern West. In the Sinic, as in the Hellenic, World he would have watched the rise and progress of the arts and sciences being stimulated by the mutual emulation of 'a cluster of little principalities', to be checked at last when this variety was swallowed up in the uniformity of a single universal state. The history of Sinic philosophy ends at the moment when the Sinic universal state comes into existence, just as the history of Hellenic philosophy comes to an end upon the foundation of the Roman Empire. But it was also true in the Far East that, 'Mankind having thrown off this yoke, affairs ... returned nearly to the same situation as before'; for the interregnum which followed the fall of the Empire of the Han was succeeded by an outburst of fresh life—first in the field of Art and afterwards in the field of Philosophy—until this delicate flower of Far Eastern culture prematurely withered under the blighting influence of the Far Eastern *imperium redivivum* of the Suei and the T'ang and the Sung and the Ming and the Ts'ing.

Hume's study of Sinic and Hellenic history did enable him, however, to apprehend the social value of the impulse to sweep away the debris of dead or moribund civilizations: an impulse which we shall have occasion to examine, at a later stage of our own Study, under the name of Futurism.[3]

'I have sometimes been inclined to think that interruptions in the periods of learning, were they not attended with such a destruction of ancient books and the records of history, would be rather favourable to the arts and sciences by breaking the progress of authority and dethroning the tyrannical usurpers over human reason. In this particular, they

[1] Hume: *Of the Rise and Progress of the Arts and Sciences.*
[2] See I. C (i) (b), pp. 88–9, above.
[3] For the futurist state of mind, as one of the normal psychological phenomena of the disintegrations of civilizations, see V. C (i) (d) 9, vol. vi, pp. 97–132, below.

have the same influence as interruptions in political governments and societies. Consider the blind submission of the ancient philosophers to the several masters in each school and you will be convinced that little good could be expected from a hundred centuries of such a servile philosophy.'[1]

From these passages in Hume's essay *Of the Rise and Progress of the Arts and Sciences*, it is apparent that the penetrating mind of this eighteenth-century Western philosopher had gone far towards divining the fundamental as well as the superficial factors in the geneses and growths and breakdowns and disintegrations of civilizations.

––––––––––

The writer has received the following observations on II. C (ii) (a) 2 from Mr. Sydney Herbert of the University College of Wales:

'In your discussion of the Environment-theory in Vol. I you make a very striking comparison between human groups living in the steppes of different parts of the World. You contrast the Nomads of Eurasia and Afrasia with the peoples of "other areas in the World which offer environments for Nomad societies" (p. 255), and you argue that the theory breaks down because these peoples did not, in fact, produce "independent Nomadic societies of their own". I do not contest the general justice of your view, but I suggest that, so far as one of the human groups in question is concerned, the comparison fails because its environment differed markedly from those of the other groups. I refer to the Indians of the North American Prairies.

'These Indians, as you say, remained "on the primitive hunting and food-gathering level of economy to the end". I suggest that the reasons for their failure to develop Nomadism are to be found in their environment.

'(a) The Indians had at hand a source of food that was practically inexhaustible, viz., the buffalo. This not only gave them food but a great range of other necessary commodities. "The great, almost the sole, basis for Indian life lay in the immense, countless herds of buffalo . . . the buffalo herds meant sustenance of many kinds and products for trade.' (Brebner: *The Explorers of North America*, p. 332.) This source of subsistence was not seriously affected till the commercial exploitation of the buffalo was taken up by white men in the nineteenth century. The Indian, therefore, was not subjected to a challenge from his environment sufficient to induce him to change his hunting economy.

'(b) Had a sufficient reason, e.g. the disappearance of the buffalo, arisen to confront him with the need for change, he would not have been able to develop Nomadism because his environment did not include any animal capable of use for riding and pack-carrying. The Spaniards took the horse and the donkey to America, and the Indian could not have acquired either from them before the middle of the sixteenth century.

––––––––––
[1] Hume: *Of the Rise and Progress of the Arts and Sciences*.

According to Brebner (p. 345) the Indians wore out horses quickly and were for long unable to breed them; as late as the eighteenth century they seem to have relied largely on trade with the Spaniards to obtain them. But by that date the Indian's independent career was already coming to an end.

'I suggest, therefore, that the Indian could not, in any event, have developed Nomadism on the Eurasian or Afrasian models, because his environment did not provide him with the necessary instrument. Had the buffalo failed him, he would have had to fall back on agriculture, of which he had some knowledge. His development then would have been along the same lines as those of the Transcaspian people whom you describe in Vol. III, p. 8.'

Additional Note on the Annex to I. C (iii) (e)

Mr. E. F. Carritt, of University College, Oxford, has been kind enough to communicate to the writer a criticism on the thesis of this Annex, to the following effect:

'The difficulty I find in this arises fundamentally from the assumption that the methods correspond to (and I think, to be consistent, you ought to say: are in the end only distinguishable by) three different subject matters—just as I think Plato was wrong in trying to distinguish capacities not only (as he should) by ὁ ἀπεργάζεται but also by ἐφ' ᾧ τέτακται. If I have had three illnesses, may I not (i) write a diary of each, with temperature charts, &c.; (ii) by comparison and inductive methods endeavour to understand their causes and laws; (iii) write a lyric on each?

'I do not feel that your distinction of the methods by quantitative differences of the subject matter is convincing. We may record things that are very numerous: e.g. millions of criminal finger-prints. We may deal scientifically with very scarce things—e.g. comets—or very frequent things: e.g. embryos, excretion. We may deal artistically with very rare things—e.g. Robinson Crusoe's solitude or Keats' reading of Chapman —more easily than with very common ones: e.g. excretion.

'These attempts at discrediting your conclusion are all directed to urging that really we have three distinguishable activities, never, perhaps, separately exercised: (1) sense perception and memory, (2) thought, (3) "imagination". (1) has for its subjects real things or events in their individuality; (2) has the *same* things in their universal connexions; (3) uses the *same* things (objects seen, felt, tasted, smelt or heard—including words as names of them) to "express" or "embody" human feelings. Obviously, all "books" do all of these. A "history book" or portrait or historical novel will do most of (1), a "science book" most of (2), a "poetry book" or "romantic painting" or music-score most of (3).'

Civilization and Agriculture: An Additional Note on II. C (ii) (a) 2 and II. C (ii) (b) 2

The following criticisms, which mainly relate to these two

chapters, are taken from a letter which Dr. Ellsworth Huntington has been so kind as to send to the writer:

'My main criticisms deal with geographical interpretation. For example, the Jordan river is discussed as if it afforded unused possibilities for agriculture like those of the Nile or Euphrates. Such does not seem to me to be the case. To-day the Jordan river flows in a deep, narrow channel and has very little in the way of a flood plain. At none of the four points where I have crossed the river did I see any indication of the kind of floods which would favour a development like that of the Nile. Moreover, the soil is largely saline. The valley may, to be sure, have been different under the climatic conditions of earlier times, but even then it does not seem to me comparable to the Nile and Euphrates.

'A similar case occurs in the discussion of the Andean Civilization. As I understand it, the oldest civilization in the Andean region grew up on the low, desert coastal plain of Peru. There the floods on the alluvial fans and in the alluvial valleys at the base of the Andes appear to have afforded much the same challenge—and, I would add, much the same opportunity—as the Nile and Euphrates. Civilization appears to have grown up there in much the same way as in the Euphrates Valley. Then it spread to the highlands and there persisted, just as the Babylonian culture swept up into the highlands of Persia.

'Another query pertaining to rivers arises in regard to China. It seems to me somewhat misleading to compare a protected and relatively warm valley such as that of the Wei in latitude 35° with a far colder and vastly more rigorous valley 15° farther north, in the Amur region. The mean temperature at Si-an is about 32° in January and 78° in July, whereas on the Amur at Blagoveshchenk there are 46° of frost in January and a July temperature of about 70°. To a geographer this seems so great a difference that the two places are not comparable.

'I may be wrong, and I have not looked the matter up since reading your book, but my conception of the origin of agriculture in China does not make it a response to the floods of the Hwang-ho. I had supposed that those were too great a problem for men in the early stages of human culture. Were not the early Chinese agriculturists located on the flood plains of small streams coming out of the mountains and tributary to the Hwang-ho? In other words, the conditions appear to have been similar to those which fostered the development of the early Mexican and Peruvian cultures: namely, summer rain with floods from small streams spreading over alluvial plains.

'In this connection let me add something else. Are we justified in assuming that agriculture arose in the lowland areas occupied by the Mayas? In this respect I have had to change my own former opinion. Recent investigations seem to show abundant traces of a high culture in the relatively dry highlands in Guatemala as well as Mexico. There, as in each of the other places where agriculture developed very early, seasonal floods are accompanied or followed by a period of warmth during which crops can grow.

'In your discussion of the origins of Civilization have you not perhaps been fearful of attributing too much to a single cause? It looks to me as if the early development of agriculture occurred in every case under essentially the same conditions. The Nile, the Tigris and Euphrates, the Indus, the branches of the Hwang-ho, the piedmont Peruvian streams, and the small rivers of the North American highlands, from Guatemala to New Mexico, all seem to present the same general situation—that is, flood plains where agriculture was feasible for primitive people.

'I do not think that Crete should be brought into this same group. My own interpretation is that the riverine areas just mentioned form a distinct group. From each of these groups primitive civilization spread out into different habitats. Egypt, for instance, presumably gave agriculture to Crete, whereupon the presence of the sea and its challenge led to a new development. Similarly the Tigro-Euphrates Civilization penetrated the Persian highlands and was correspondingly modified. The Indus type spread to the wetter parts of India. In China the early valley type ultimately became strong enough and skilful enough to cope with the far more tremendous floods of the Hwang-ho. In South America, again, Peruvian agriculture spread from the lowlands into the comparatively cold highlands where life was more difficult. In North America, on the contrary, the highlands, being lower than in South America, were the regions where agriculture was feasible and yet difficult enough, so that the region offered a real challenge to Man, stimulating but not defeating him. Later, having acquired skill in the highlands, he was able to go down into the low, tropical forest and meet the far greater challenge of still another type of environment.'

In view of Dr. Huntington's great authority, and of the interest of the questions which he here raises, the writer may perhaps allow himself to make some comment on certain particular points and on one matter of general importance.

As regards the question of the comparability or incomparability of the Jordan Valley with the Nile Valley and the Tigris-Euphrates Valley, the writer accepts Dr. Huntington's judgement as against that of Professor Eduard Meyer, whose special knowledge and intuition did not lie in the climatological field and who did not, as far as the writer knows, ever make a first-hand study of the Jordan Valley on the spot. If the Jordan Valley has to be ruled out as a possible site for one of the 'fluvial' civilizations, and if the 'fluvial' civilization of the Indus Valley proves to have arisen independently of the 'fluvial' civilization of the Tigris-Euphrates Valley (see vol. i, pp. 107–8 and 257–8 and 416–23), and if the oasis civilization of Transcaspia proves to have arisen independently, in its turn, of the 'fluvial' civilization of the Indus Valley (see vol. iii, p. 9), then we may find ourselves left with no example in the Old World of a cultivable river-valley in a dry climate which did not become the seat of an agricultural civilization; yet even then we shall still be able to cite our examples from the New World—the valleys of the Rio Grande and the Colorado River in the South-Western United States (see vol. i, p. 258)—in support of our contention that a particular type of physical environment which happens to provide the cradle for a civilization in some instances will not necessarily be found to perform this role invariably.

As regards the original home of the Andean Civilization, Dr. Huntington has put his finger upon an inconsistency between certain passages in this Study. As far as the writer is competent to form any opinion on the archaeological and physiographical evidence, he agrees with Dr. Huntington in believing that the Andean Civilization arose on the coastal plain, and that, in its second home on the plateau, it was not an original creation but was an importation from its coastal place of origin. This view is stated in I. C (i) (b), vol. i, pp. 121–3, and again in II. D (ii), vol. ii, pp. 33–4. On the other hand, in II. C (ii) (a) 2, vol. i, pp. 258–9, the plateau is credited with being the original home of the Andean Civilization, and in II. C (ii) (b) 2, vol. i, pp. 321–3, it is assumed that the plateau and the coast were twin cradles of the Andean Civilization and that they were of approximately equal importance. These two last passages require correction; but perhaps such correction will not invalidate the particular argument that is presented in each of the passages in question. The purpose of the second passage (vol. i, pp. 321–3) was to show that the Andean Civilization arose in a harsh environment, and Dr. Huntington does not dispute the contention that the Andean Coastal Plain comes within this category as well as the Andean Plateau. The purpose of the former passage (vol. i, pp. 258–9) was to show that the type of physical environment which provided the cradle for a civilization in Equatorial America did not provide the cradle for a civilization in Equatorial Africa. Certainly, if the Andean Plateau was only a secondary seat of the Andean Civilization, the contrast which we have sought to draw between the social history of the Andean Plateau and that of the East African highlands turns out to be beside the point, since the East African highlands have, as we have pointed out, eventually been occupied, likewise, by civilizations that have originated elsewhere. The question then arises whether, in the African analogue of Equatorial America, there is any region which corresponds physiographically to the plain that lies between the Andean Plateau and the shore of the Pacific Ocean. Perhaps we may find an analogy in the lowlands that lie between the Abyssinian Plateau and the shores of the Indian Ocean and the Red Sea; for this, too, is a desert region across which the rivers that descend from the plateau make—or just fail to make—their way to the coast. If there is any validity in this comparison, then it duly illustrates our contention that a particular type of physical environment which provides the cradle for a civilization in some instances will not necessarily be found to perform this role invariably; for in the happy hunting grounds of the Somali and the Danakil we shall search in vain for the equivalent of a Chimu or a Nazca.

As regards the question whether the actual present state of the Ussuri Valley is comparable to the hypothetical primeval state of the original home of the Sinic Civilization (vol. i, pp. 320–1), the writer of this Study would point out that he was not, as Dr. Huntington assumes, proposing to compare the Ussuri Valley with the Wei Valley, since he has followed Maspéro (see the passage quoted in vol. i, pp. 318–20) in taking the view that the original home of the Sinic Civilization lay, not in the Wei and Fen valleys, but in the North China plain. The northern end of this plain, in the neighbourhood of Tientsin, to which Maspéro, in the passage quoted, is expressly referring, lies only about 5° south of Lake Khanka, and the winter on the Pei-ho, while not comparable in severity to that on the Ussuri (as the writer knows from having tasted both in quick succession at the turn of the years 1929 and 1930), is quite as severe as the winter on the North European plain, while on the other hand the summer on the Ussuri is surprisingly hot (see vol. i, p. 321). If we further take into account the probability that the neighbourhood of Tientsin, like the neighbourhood of Winnipeg, was considerably harsher in its climate before it was brought under cultivation than it is to-day, the difference in original climate between the two places that are compared in the passage in question may prove to be not so extreme as Dr. Huntington suggests. At the same time, the writer will readily admit that his comparison of the Yellow River Basin with the Amur Basin—and, for that matter, his comparison of Egypt with the Upper Nile Valley—is climatologically imperfect. In fact, he has made the admission, in principle, at the beginning of the second volume (vol. ii, pp. 2–3), and he has taken this as the starting-point for the inquiry in II. D (i)

In regard to the question whether the fathers of the Sinic Civilization served their apprenticeship in harnessing the Yellow River himself, or whether they practised first upon his less formidable tributaries, the writer is prepared to accept Dr. Huntington's view—which is presumably no less applicable to the history of the harnessing of the Nile and the Indus and the Tigris and Euphrates.

The writer also agrees with Dr. Huntington in feeling that the distinctive feature of the genesis of the Minoan Civilization is a response to the challenge of the Sea; and he is prepared to believe that the fathers of the Minoan Civilization brought with them to Crete a technique of agriculture which had previously been invented in Egypt. He has already followed Myres in the view that the first human inhabitants of Crete came from some part of the dying Afrasian grasslands that was in the vicinity of the Lower Nile Valley (see vol. i, p. 328).

Dr. Huntington's tidings of new archaeological discoveries in the home and hinterlands of the Mayan Civilization are tantalizing. Our archaeological knowledge in this field has hitherto been so fragmentary that any scholar who has attempted to make use of it must have been conscious that his hypothetical structures might be upset any day by a radical reconstruction of their foundations. It is manifestly possible that the lowlands of Northern Guatemala may prove, after all, not to have been the Mayan Civilization's original home; and if this civilization did prove to have originated either on the highlands overhanging the Pacific coast of Central America or else on the Mexican Plateau, then, no doubt, its origins might turn out to have a different bearing from that which the writer has believed them to have upon the problem of the geneses of civilizations.

Much turns upon the sense in which the culture that is coming to light in these hinterlands of the 'First Empire' of the Mayas is to be described as 'high'. Do these latest archaeological discoveries indicate that the spiritual and artistic and intellectual accomplishments of the Mayan Civilization, as we can infer these from the monuments of the 'First Empire', had already been anticipated by forerunners in these other regions? Or do they merely tell us that, before the Mayan Civilization, as we have known it hitherto, arose on the plains of Northern Guatemala, there were communities in these neighbouring, and less forbidding, regions who were conversant with the technique of agriculture? In the first of these two possible alternative cases, the new archaeological discoveries may throw new light upon the geneses of civilizations; in the second, the illumination might perhaps touch little or nothing beyond the origins of argiculture.

In regard to the origins of agriculture, Dr. Huntington has arrived at the most interesting conclusion that this wonderful piece of human technique has been invented 'in every case under essentially the same conditions'—the fundamental condition being the presence of 'flood plains where agriculture was feasible for primitive people'. A living instance of this kind of agriculture is the agriculture that is practised by the Hadendoa tribesmen in the

Taka country of Upper Nubia, to the north of the Atbara tributary of the Nile, as this is described by Burckhardt in a passage cited by Newberry (see vol. i, pp. 308–9). We may observe that the Hadendoa have remained almost as primitive down to the present day as they may be presumed to have been when they first took to this form of agriculture—some five or six thousand years ago—at the time when it was also taken to by the fathers of the Egyptiac Civilization; and this observation brings us to the matter of general importance which Dr. Huntington's letter raises: namely, the relation between agriculture and civilization. Surely the invention of agriculture, which is a piece of technique, is something quite distinct from the genesis of a civilization, which is a condition of the soul.

Of course the technical invention and the spiritual mutation might turn out, on an empirical survey, to go together in every known case; but, as a matter of fact, there is more to be said, on the evidence, for the view that the invention of agriculture is always prior to the genesis of a civilization; is not bound to lead on to it; is not an invariable or indispensable preliminary to it; and may actually be relegated to a subordinate role, or even abandoned altogether, as part of that response to a challenge through which a civilization is eventually brought to birth.

In another connexion (in I. C (iii) (b) Annex, vol. i, pp. 436–9, above), we have noticed that agriculture was an element both in 'the Archaic Culture' of the New World which was apparently the common ground of the Mayan and Andean civilizations and in the Afrasian intermediary culture which was apparently the common ground, in the same sense, of 'the Indus Culture' and the Sumeric, Egyptiac, and Minoan civilizations. On the other hand, the fathers of the Eskimo Civilization raised themselves above the primitive level without ever taking to agriculture or ceasing to gain their livelihood by hunting (see vol. iii, pp. 4–7). Conversely, there have been communities like the Hadendoa which have duly taken to agriculture—in this instance perhaps at an early date—without ever having entered upon the path of Civilization. Again, the fathers of the Minoan Civilization subordinated their old technique of agriculture to their new technique of seamanship when they created the Minoan Civilization by responding to the challenge of the Sea; and the fathers of the Nomadic Civilization actually abandoned an agriculture which they have previously practised, when they created the Nomadic Civilization by responding to the challenge of the Steppe (see vol. iii, pp. 11–14). Even in the cases of those civilizations in which agriculture was retained as the master-technique, the creation of the civilization and the invention of agriculture are separate events which are clearly distinguishable, as Dr. Huntington himself points out. This is clear, for example, in the case of the Sinic Civilization, if Maspéro is right in his view that the Sinic Civilization was created by Man's conquest of the Hwang-ho, and Huntington right in his view that in this region agriculture had been invented previously—not on the Yellow River himself, but on his tributaries. Similarly, we may still equate the creation of the Mayan Civilization with Man's conquest of the tropical forest of Northern Guatemala, and not with the previous invention of agriculture on the adjoining highlands—even if this previous invention be demonstrated by the progress of archaeological discovery.

On this showing, the writer is ready to agree with Dr. Huntington in believing that the technique of agriculture has been invented everywhere under more or less uniform conditions, but is at the same time inclined to retain his own belief (see vol. i, p. 438) in the essential diversity of the challenges and responses that have resulted in the geneses of civilizations.

GALAXY BOOKS

GALAXY BOOKS